Lecture Notes in Computer Science　　11803

More information about this series at http://www.springer.com/series/7411

Maria Rita Palattella · Stefano Scanzio ·
Sinem Coleri Ergen (Eds.)

Ad-Hoc, Mobile, and Wireless Networks

18th International Conference on Ad-Hoc Networks
and Wireless, ADHOC-NOW 2019
Luxembourg, Luxembourg, October 1–3, 2019
Proceedings

 Springer

Editors
Maria Rita Palattella ⓘ
Luxembourg Institute of Science
and Technology
Belvaux, Luxembourg

Stefano Scanzio ⓘ
CNR-IEIIT
Turin, Italy

Sinem Coleri Ergen ⓘ
Koc Üniversitesi Mühendislik
Istanbul, Turkey

ISSN 0302-9743   ISSN 1611-3349   (electronic)
Lecture Notes in Computer Science
ISBN 978-3-030-31830-7   ISBN 978-3-030-31831-4   (eBook)
https://doi.org/10.1007/978-3-030-31831-4

LNCS Sublibrary: SL5 – Computer Communication Networks and Telecommunications

This Springer imprint is published by the registered company Springer Nature Switzerland AG
The registered company address is: Gewerbestrasse 11, 6330 Cham, Switzerland

Preface

The International Conference on Ad-Hoc Networks and Wireless (AdHoc-Now) is one of the most popular series of events dedicated to research on ad-hoc, mobile and wireless sensor networks, and computing. Since its inception in 2002, the conference has been held 17 times in seven different countries and the 18th edition in 2019 was held in Luxembourg, during October 1–3.

We wish to thank all of the authors who submitted their work. This year, AdHoc-Now received 64 submissions and 37 papers were accepted for presentation as full contributions after a rigorous review process involving the Technical Program Committee (TPC) members, external reviewers, and the TPC chairs. Moreover, owing to the high quality of the received submissions, ten papers were accepted as short contributions.

The AdHoc-Now 2019 program was organized in eight sessions grouping the contributions into the following topics: IoT for Emergency Scenarios and Disaster Management, Scheduling and Synchronization in WSN, Routing Strategies for WSN, LPWANs and Their Integration with Satellite, Performance Improvement of Wireless and Sensor Networks, Optimization Schemes for Increasing Sensors Lifetime, Vehicular and UAV Networks, Body Area Networks, IoT Security and Standardization. In each of these sessions, new ideas and directions were discussed among attendees from both academia and industry, thus, providing an in-depth and stimulating view on the new frontiers in the field of mobile, ad hoc, and wireless computing.

The conference was also enriched by the following five distinguished keynote speakers that completed a high-level scientific program: Federico Clazzer, Stefano Cioni, Alexander Geurtz, Markus U. Mock, and Omar Qaise.

We would like to thank all of the people involved in AdHoc-Now 2019. First of all, we are grateful to the TPC members and the external reviewers for their help in providing detailed reviews of the submissions, to Albert Bel Pereira, our submission and proceedings chair, to Latif Ladid, our publicity chair, to Marylene Martin, our Web and registration chair. A special thanks goes to Marylene Martin for her valuable support in the local organization and the arrangements of the event. We also thank the team at Springer for their great support throughout the entire process, from the submission until the proceedings production.

Finally, the organization was made possible through the strong help of our supporters: Springer and Springer's *Lecture Notes in Computer Science* (LNCS), Wiley *Internet Technology Letters (ITL)*, IEEE COMSOC IoT Emerging Technologies Subcommittee. A special thank you to all of them.

October 2019

Maria Rita Palattella
Stefano Scanzio
Sinem Coleri Ergen

Organization

General Chair

Maria Rita Palattella   LIST, Luxembourg

Program Committee Chairs

Maria Rita Palattella   LIST, Luxembourg
Sinem Coleri Ergen   Koc University, Turkey
Stefano Scanzio   CNR-IEIIT, Italy

Publicity Arrangements Chair

Latif Ladid   University of Luxembourg, Luxembourg

Submission and Proceedings Chair

Albert Bel Pereira   Pompeu Fabra University, Spain

Registration Chair

Marylène Martin   LIST, Luxembourg

Local Arrangements Chair and Web Chair

Marylène Martin   LIST, Luxembourg

Steering Committee

Evangelos Kranakis   Carleton University, Canada
Violet R. Syrotiuk   Arizona State University, USA
Michel Barbeau   Carleton University, Canada
Ionise Nikolaidis   University of Alberta, Canada

Program Committee

Assis Flavio   Federal University of Bahia, Brazil
Barcelo-Ordinas Jose M.   UPC, Spain
Bel Pereira Albert   Pompeu Fabra University, Spain
Bramas Quentin   Université de Strasbourg, France
Bruneo Dario   University of Messina, Italy
Busnel Yann   IMT Atlantique, France

Calafate Carlos	Universitat Politècnica de València, Spain
Cena Gianluca	CNR-IEIIT, Italy
Cheminod Manuel	CNR-IEIIT, Italy
Cichon Jacek	Wroclaw University of Science and Technology, Poland
Colerie Ergen Sinem	Koc University, Turkey
De Paola Alessandra	University of Palermo, Italy
Di Maio Antonio	University of Luxembourg, Luxembourg
Dujovne Diego	Universidad Diego Portales, Chile
Durante Luca	CNR-IEIIT, Italy
El Jaouhari Saad	IMT Atlantique, France
Elsts Atis	University of Bristol, UK
Giacobbe Maurizio	University of Messina, Italy
Iova Oana	INSA Lyon, France
Karyotis Vasileios	National Technical University of Athens, Greece
Klasing Ralf	CNRS and University of Bordeaux, France
Leone Pierre	University of Geneva, Switzerland
Liang Weifa	Australian National University, Australia
Longo Francesco	University of Messina, Italy
Maillé Patrick	IMT Atlantique, France
Martinez Francisco J.	University of Zaragoza, Spain
Mitton Nathalie	Inria, France
Montavont Nicolas	IMT Atlantique, France
Montavont Julien	University of Strasbourg, France
Mosko Marc	Palo Alto Research Center, USA
Natalizio Enrico	Université de Lorraine Nancy, France
Palattella Maria Rita	LIST, Luxembourg
Papadopoulos Georgios Z.	IMT Atlantique, France
Pahl Marc-Olivier	Technical University of Munich, Germany
Papagianni Chrysa	Nokia Bell Labs, USA
Papavassiliou Symeon	Institute of Communications and Computer Systems, Greece
Postiglione Fabio	University of Salerno, Italy
Puliafito Carlo	University of Florence, Italy
Scanzio Stefano	CNR-IEIIT, Italy
Scarpa Marco	University of Messina, Italy
Soua Ridha	University of Luxemburg, Luxembourg
Syrotiuk Violet	Arizona State University, USA
Texier Geraldine	IMT Atlantique, France
Theoleyre Fabrice	CNRS, France
Tsiropoulou Eirini Eleni	University of New Mexico, USA
Turau Volker	Hamburg University of Technology, Germany
Valenzano Adriano	CNR-IEIIT, Italy
Vallati Carlo	University of Pisa, Italy
Weis Frédéric	University of Rennes 1, France
Wrona Konrad	NATO Communications and Information Agency, The Netherlands

Zhao Zhongliang	Beihang University, China
Zorbas Dimitrios	Tyndall National Institute, Ireland
Zunino Claudio	CNR-IEIIT, Italy

Additional Reviewers

Accettura Nicola	LAAS-CNRS, France
Braun Torsten	University of Bern, Switzerland
Dobre Octavia A.	Memorial University, Canada
López-Martínez Carlos	LIST, Luxembourg
Pradas David	Viveris, France

Contents

Optimisation Schemes for Increasing Sensors Lifetime

Vehicular and UAV Networks

Body Area Networks, IoT Security and Standardization

Posters and Demos

IoT for Emergency Scenarios and Disaster Management

Resilient Information Management for Information Sharing in Disaster-Affected Areas Lacking Internet Access

Toshiaki Miyazaki[1]([✉]), Kazuya Anazawa[2], Yasuyuki Maruyama[1],
Seiya Kobayashi[1], Toku Segawa[1], and Peng Li[1]

[1] The University of Aizu, Aizu-Wakamatsu, Fukushima 965-8580, Japan
{miyazaki,m5221147,m5231134,s1240191,
pengli}@u-aizu.ac.jp
[2] NTT Network Innovation Laboratories, Yokosuka 230-0847, Japan
kazuya.anazawa.xt@hco.ntt.co.jp

Abstract. We are developing a resilient information management (RIM) system that enables people to share critical information with each other to rescue victims just after disasters have happened. The RIM system works on a locally and quickly established WiFi network environment. Thus, using this system, people can manage and share various types of information including medical information, damaged area and map information, and supply/demand information even if the Internet and communication network infrastructures have collapsed. In this paper, we introduce the concept of the RIM system and its current status with some related-technologies.

Keywords: Disaster information management · WiFi network ·
Data synchronization · Localization

1 Introduction

Japan is one of the countries that are most vulnerable to natural calamities. In 2011, a catastrophic earthquake occurred in the northern part of Japan, which led to a tsunami that affected a huge area. At that time, lifeline and communication infrastructures were impaired or destroyed, leaving the physically damaged areas isolated. When a disaster occurs, people try to communicate with others to confirm their safety, seek help, and gather evacuation information. To support the public and understand the situation in the disaster-affected area, some systems have been proposed [1, 2]. In addition, the shared information platform for disaster management or SIP4D [3] system works today to realize information sharing among various governmental organizations in Japan. It is very useful for governmental organizations to formulate decision making to rescue victims. However, the above mentioned systems cannot operate without the Internet and communication infrastructure. To overcome this problem, Nippon Telegraph and Telephone (NTT) developed a movable and deployable information and communication technology resource unit, named MDRU [4]. A WiFi communication environment can be established quickly by deploying an MDRU in a disaster area. NTT also created

© Springer Nature Switzerland AG 2019
M. R. Palattella et al. (Eds.): ADHOC-NOW 2019, LNCS 11803, pp. 3–17, 2019.
https://doi.org/10.1007/978-3-030-31831-4_1

several applications using MDRU that are useful in disaster situations. A typical application is based on voice-over-internet protocol (VoIP). Using such an application, people can make phone calls to each other in a network isolated area using their own phone numbers. However, in the case of a disaster, a lot of information needs to be appropriately delivered to the public.

In this paper, we propose a resilient information management (RIM) system. The proposed RIM system consists of mobile terminals such as smartphones and/or tablets, and a RIM server. Using this system, people can manage and share important information including medical information for rescue plans and actions, damaged area and map information, and supply/demand information. The RIM system uses a locally established WiFi network environment established using an MDRU. Thus, a RIM system can be deployed even where the Internet or any other communication network infrastructure cannot be used. In addition, a mobile relay node, called a RIM extender, is introduced to expand the wireless communication range. It functions in a manner similar to a RIM server and automatically buffers information from mobile terminals and uploads the information to the RIM server if it comes within the communication range of the RIM server. Furthermore, it is critical to search for and discover any victims buried under collapsed buildings urgently after a natural disaster. In recent years, people have become accustomed to carrying smartphones. Based on this fact, we developed a smartphone finder to locate effectively a smartphone with its owner under a collapsed building.

The main contribution of this paper is to propose:

1. an integrated information management and sharing mechanism supporting rescuers and victims,
2. a map-based information sharing method not dependent on the Internet,
3. a RIM extender to expand a wireless communication area, and
4. a smartphone finder to find victims under collapsed buildings with their own smartphones.

The remainder of the paper is organized as follows. First, Sect. 2 provides an overview of the RIM system. Second, Sect. 3 explains implementation-related issues. Next, Sect. 4 discusses additional functions to expand the usage area of the RIM system. Then, Sect. 5 reports the current status of the RIM system and provides remarks. Finally, Sect. 6 presents the conclusions.

2 System Overview

Figure 1 is an overview of the RIM system depicting many mobile terminals such as smartphones and/or tablets, and a RIM server. The RIM server has a relational database management system (RDBMS) and a map information server to manage the information collected from mobile terminals. An application program called a RIM client runs on each mobile terminal. Users can view the information stored in the RIM server on their mobile terminals and share it with others. They can also input information through their own mobile terminals. To obtain the location of the information using maps, a map information server is installed locally since the RIM system is likely to be used in disaster situations where communication infrastructure and Internet-based map services such as Google Maps [5] would not be available.

Figure 2 displays the top view of the RIM client application. There are two view modes: normal mode and medical mode. The normal mode is for normal users, while the medical mode is for rescuers or doctors. The view modes can be switched depending on the user. As shown in Fig. 2(a) and (b), they have the same button menus from (1) to (8) except the HELP/TRIAGE button (7). The functions of some buttons are described below.

2.1 Medical Information Management

A triage support function is provided for rescuers/doctors. This function is activated by clicking the TRIAGE button (7) shown in Fig. 2(b). Triage is often performed using a standard triage flow called START [6]. Our triage function also follows the START flow and triaged colors (green, yellow, red, and black) which are automatically determined depending upon the button the user clicks or the information the user inputs. Even for well-trained rescuers, a quick triage scheme should be provided. To support both step-by-step and a quick triage, we introduced a unique menu set and menu transition path to help move from one menu to another. If the menu is swiped up, the four-color buttons are displayed and the user can decide the color immediately,

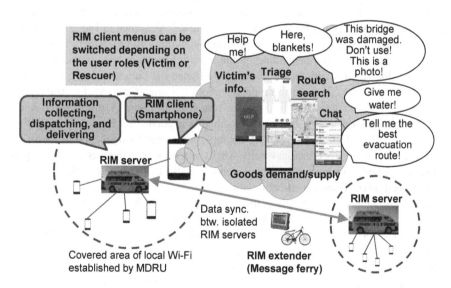

Fig. 1. An overview of RIM system

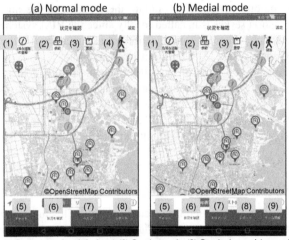

(1) Dangerous place info. input, (2) Goods supply, (3) Goods demand (request),
(4) Route search, (5) Chatfunction, (6) Display map, (7) Help/Triage,
(8) Display current terminal status &log, (9) Team info. (Medical mode only)

Fig. 2. Top views of RIM client application

which is intended to be convenient for well-trained rescuers. In addition to the color, some supplementary information for the injured person can be added. Figure 3 shows the unique graphical user interface (GUI) and menu structure for the triage function. By swiping right, the triage can be done step by step. Further, some detailed information, such as respiratory rate, can be input by swiping down. As shown in Fig. 3, the menus can be displayed to perform the triage process by swiping right/left, while an appropriate menu can be selected depending on the input information level or triage skill by swiping up/down. Furthermore, by clicking the upper-left button with the shape of a human body, the user can input more details about the injured person, i.e., the injured part of the body and its status such as fracture and bleeding. A photo taken using smartphone/tablets cameras can also be attached if needed (See Fig. 3). If the HELP button (7) shown in Fig. 2(a) is clicked, a simple menu will be displayed to report the injured person in need of medical help. There are only two buttons in the display representing whether or not the injured person can walk. This is based on the simplified triage method advised by a medical doctor.

Triage and help information is gathered at the RIM server, which helps in rescue team establishment and task assignment. The assigned task information should be delivered to the terminal of each rescuer. The assigned task information includes the first meeting place, locations and status of the injured persons, articles that the rescue team has to carry, and the best map route to reach injured persons. Figure 4 is GUI of the RIM server showing an established rescue team and the assigned task.

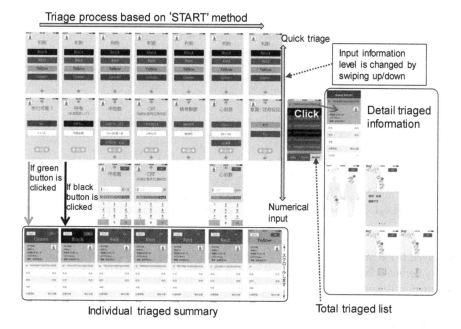

Fig. 3. Menu structure for triage

2.2 Damaged Area and Map Information Management

The RIM system also manages information on the damaged geographic area, including incidents, and their locations. The user can report damaged area information such as broken roads and bridges with photos and exact locations obtained using the GPS receiver in the mobile terminal. This type of information can be input using the menu button (1) shown in Fig. 2(a) or (b). All uploaded data to the RIM server, which include damaged areas and injured persons, are displayed on a map on each mobile terminal. The best transportation route to reach a destination while avoiding damaged areas is also suggested on the map. Here, as mentioned earlier, map servers such as Google Maps cannot be used, because in catastrophic situations the Internet and other commercial network services might collapse. Thus, we provide a map server function along with the RIM server.

2.3 Supply/Demand Information Management

The RIM system can also manage supply and demand (request) information for goods to be distributed among people in need. If the users register goods supply or demand information (e.g., goods names, and their quantity, time, and condition) via their mobile terminals, the RIM server stores this information and performs automatic supply/demand matching. If some matches are successfully established, the matching results will be delivered to the mobile terminal of the user who registered supply or demand information. Figures 5(a) and (b) show mobile terminal views on a map for the goods supply input, and the goods demand input, respectively. The view will be

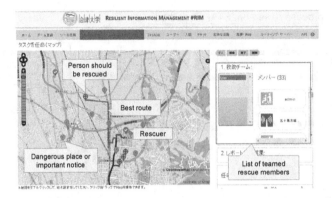

Fig. 4. Graphical user interface of RIM server to show established rescue team and assigned task

displayed if the menu button (2) or (3) shown in Fig. 2(a) or (b) is clicked. The goods supply/demand information is indicated on the map of each RIM client once the information is input as shown in Fig. 5(c).

2.4   Chat Function

A chat function is also provided to facilitate communication among people through short messages. Figure 6 shows a screenshot of the chat function on a mobile terminal. This function starts if the chat button (5) shown in Fig. 2(a) or (b) is clicked. By selecting chat groups or rooms, the user can join different chat groups if the join request is accepted by the group. The RIM server provides a chat broker function that saves all chat logs.

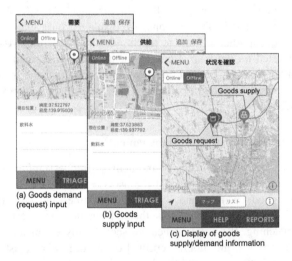

Fig. 5. Screen snapshots of goods demand (request) and goods supply information input menus and display to show matched supply/demand information

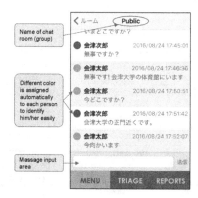

Fig. 6. Snapshot of the chat function

3 Implementation

Figure 7 shows the implementation architecture of the RIM system. The RM server can be realized in the server machine in the MDRU with an RDBMS and a map information server. We selected MySQL [7] for the first implementation of the RDBMS, but now we use SQLite [8] because of its lightness. The RIM server has an HTTP interface. Thus, we can access all RIM server functions using a web browser remotely under a security control. Figure 8 is the top view of the RIM server interface. Nine buttons are tiled and by clicking one of them, the corresponding function menu will be displayed.

3.1 Disaster Area Wireless Network

To build a disaster area wireless network as shown in Fig. 1, we use an MDRU [4] developed by NTT Network Innovation Laboratories. By setting up the MDRU, a WiFi access network with a radius of about 500 m is realized. The MDRU also has a server machine. The MDRU currently has three variations: a container-, minivan-, and attaché case-type MDRU, and they can be selected depending on the area to be covered with the MDRU. Figure 9 shows snapshots of the minivan-type and the attachécase-type MDRUs.

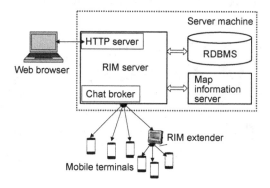

Fig. 7. Implementation architecture of RIM system

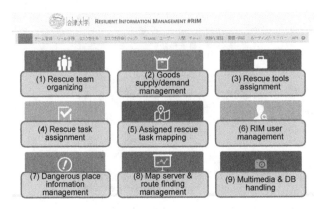

Fig. 8. Top view of RIM server

3.2 Map Information Server

A map information server is also provided to serve map information even if the Internet is not available. Currently, OpenStreetMap [9] is used to realize the map information server and all needed map information is downloaded to the local disk of the server machine beforehand. The interface of the map information service is generalized so as to permit switching easily to other map information servers. At this time, we have confirmed that the GEOSPACE map service [10] operated by NTT GEOSPACE Corp. and Google Maps are compatible with OpenStreetMap.

3.3 RIM Client Application

Currently, the RIM client application can be run on Android and iOS. An Android version of the RIM client application has been released via Google Play Store [11], and anyone can use it freely by downloading it into his/her smartphone. To handle the map information in the mobile terminal, Mapbox [12] is used. The mobile terminals can exchange data using the device-to-device (D2D) and delay tolerant network (DTN) techniques based on Bluetooth technology. However, it is difficult to transfer large amounts of data using the D2D and DTN techniques. Thus, we have implemented a mobile relay node called RIM extender, which is explained in the next section.

(a) Minivan-type MDRU   (b) Attaché case-type MDRU
                                          (Potable IP-PBX)

Fig. 9. Snapshots of minivan-type and attaché case-type MDRUs

4 Additional Functions

In addition to the RIM server and client, some additional functions shown in the following subsections were developed to expand the usage area and capabilities of the RIM system.

4.1 RIM Extender

The WiFi environment established by the MDRU is often unstable and it is sometimes difficult to transfer data from RIM terminals to the RIM server, especially if the geographical distance between them is relatively large. To resolve this situation, we provided a mobile relay node, called a RIM extender. The RIM extender has similar functions to the RIM server, except for the map information server. Thus, the mobile terminal can connect to the RIM extender and upload some data to it using the same functions and protocols as those of the RIM server. As shown in Fig. 10, the RIM extender can be carried using many carriers such as a person, a bicycle, and a drone, because it is a small device. Currently, a small laptop PC is used to realize the RIM extender. In addition, the RIM extender could be used as a message ferry [13] to carry data among isolated RIM servers. We have evaluated the effectiveness of the introduction of the RIM extender precisely [14], and confirmed that the data synchronization time among isolated RIM servers are tremendously improved by introducing several RIM extenders and moving around the disaster-affected area systematically.

4.2 Utilization of Free WiFi Spots

These days, free WiFi spots exist anywhere, especially in urban cities and sightseeing areas to enable people to connect to the Internet with their WiFi services. We are planning to use the WiFi spots to expand RIM service areas on the occasion of disasters. Even if the Internet is disconnected and daily services cannot be continued, we could use the WiFi spot itself as an alternative system of the MDRU. By connecting

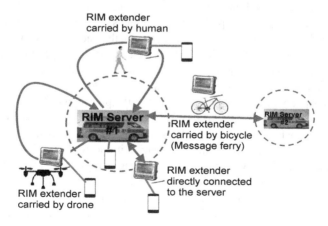

Fig. 10. Usage of RIM extender

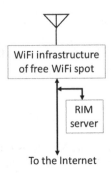

Fig. 11. Implementation mode for utilization of free WiFi spot. The RIM server is connected to the data line in parallel.

our RIM server to an isolated free WiFi spot, we can establish a RIM service area without the MDRU. Figure 11 shows an implementation model of this scheme. To detect directly whether or not the Internet traffic exists, we want to connect our RIM server to the data line of the free WiFi spot in series. However, free WiFi spot service providers never allow connections from external equipment, i.e., our RIM server, to protect their systems from unexpected interference. Thus, we will connect our RIM server to the line in parallel, and check if the Internet connection is alive or not by sending periodic "ping" packets to some well-known Internet service sites. Then, if the RIM server recognizes the fact that the Internet connection is closed, it will start the RIM services. We have already realized this mechanism using a small box-type PC in which the RIM server functions are installed.

4.3   Smartphone Finder

It is critical to discover the victims buried under collapsed buildings urgently after a natural disaster. In recent years, people have become accustomed to carrying smartphones with them. Based on this fact, we developed a smartphone finder to locate effectively a target smartphone with its owner under a collapsed building. The smartphone finder sends WiFi probe-request signals at regular time intervals. The smartphone finder captures WiFi probe-request signals, and estimates the location of the target smartphone using the RSSI (Received Signal Strength Indicator) of the signals. RSSI values are often reflected by obstacles and the environment. So, for the location estimation, we use a modified log-normal shadowing model, which uses a weighted least square method, in order to improve the precision of location estimation. Usually, we need three or more RSSI receivers to estimate a target smartphone location using the log-normal shadowing model. However, the location of our smartphone finder frequently changes, because the user carries it and walks around the collapsed buildings in the field. Thus, we can estimate the location of the target smartphone using RSSI values collected by a smartphone finder at the different locations. The detail estimation algorithms and evaluation results were reported in [15]. Figure 12 shows a screen snapshot of the smartphone finder. In this figure, the red marker indicates the current location of the smartphone finder, whereas the blue marker indicates the

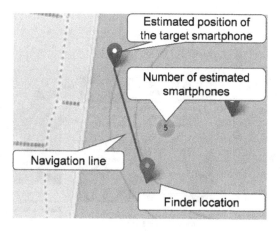

Fig. 12. A screen snapshot of the smartphone finder.

estimated position of the target smartphone. If the rescue worker selects the estimated position, the target smartphone is locked on, and a blue navigation line is displayed between the smartphone finder and the target. Subsequently, by following the navigation line, the worker can find the target smartphone together with the victim easily. In addition, the number "5" on the green circle in this snapshot indicates the number of estimated smartphones in that area. If the circle is clicked, detailed information would be displayed on the screen. This GUI is simple as it helps recognize the estimated position of the target smartphone easily by way of a simple online display of the relevant information.

5   Current Status and Remarks

A prototype of the RIM system has been developed and the feasibility of all functions has been confirmed. We have demonstrated the usability of the system to professional rescuers and inhabitants by using some events. Figure 13 shows snapshots displaying our promotion activities in anti-disaster drill events held last year.

5.1   Collaboration Works with a Local City Office

We are collaborating with Aizuwakamatsu City, Fukushima, Japan, where our university is located.

Integration of RIM and Daily-Use Application. We can provide a download server in the RIM server so that people can download the RIM client application. However, it is difficult to provide sufficient network performance to meet a lot of download requests following a disaster by using the locally established WiFi environment. Thus, it is important to encourage people to install the RIM client application in advance of potential disaster events. To disseminate RIM clients to citizens, we are trying to integrate the RIM client functions into a map-based daily-use SNS (Social Network

Fig. 13. Snapshots of demonstration and promotion activities in some events.

Service) application named "Pe.com.in" [16], which was developed by Aizuwakamatsu City office and released to citizens to encourage them to share local information. Pe.com.in has a map-based user interface, which is similar to that of the RIM client. If the citizens use the application daily, they could learn to use the RIM client functions smoothly in anticipation of a sudden major disaster.

Dedicated Functions for the City Office. As a result of discussions with the Aizuwakamatsu City office, additional functions relevant to the needs of city office staff were brought to our attention. We are implementing the following dedicated functions to the city office, based on their requirements.

1. Display the hazard map. Even after a disaster, the city office staff should check the hazard map frequently to identify possibilities of other dangerous situations. We have already realized this function. Figure 14 shows a screen snapshot displaying the hazard map.
2. Display designated evacuation shelters and the navigation route to the nearest one. People usually know the best route leading to the nearest shelter, but if the route is impassable, the RIM system should redirect them to a safe route.
3. Display care-requesting old/handicapped persons and their status.
4. Display examined houses and their damage levels. This is needed to quickly identify where support may be required by victims.
5. Control goods delivery to designated shelters. In addition to the volunteer-based goods sharing as shown in Fig. 5, contract-based goods handling is required for the city office to settle accounts later. The city has contracts with neighboring cities, convenience stores/shops, etc. in order to access food/goods on an emergency basis following disaster. Records must be kept to settle accounts afterwards.
6. Broad- or multi-cast message delivery from the city office to citizens/victims. A function to realize a bulletin board set up at a designated evacuation shelter is requested, in addition to the chat function shown in Fig. 6.

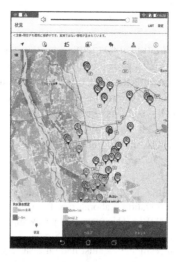

Fig. 14. A screen snapshot displaying the hazard map

7. Handle evacuated person information. Paper-based person information handling at a
   shelter is handled for the evacuated persons located there. The RIM system should
   handle this kind of information more effectively.

These functions should be released to the city office staff only. Therefore, a city
office operation mode is offered in addition to the normal and medical user modes
shown in Fig. 2. By setting the user attribute at the RIM server, only recognized RIM
clients can display the operation icons and information on its screen. Almost all
functions were developed last year, and we are scheduling a pre-release to the local city
office this year.

5.2   Integration of a Sensor Network System

We developed a sensor network system, named "die-hard sensor network" [17]. It is
dedicated to disaster monitoring. The sensor network system can automatically monitor
a disaster-affected area by scattering many sensor nodes in the area. The sensor node is
programmable, and its sensing and data sending behavior can be customized dynamically and remotely. It has some sensors like temperature, light, fire, acceleration,
motion (Infrared), and sound sensor, and new sensors can be easily attached. We are
planning to integrate the die-hard sensor network system to the RIM system, and
display the sensor information on the RIM client and/or server screen. The available
information could contribute to understanding the situation in the disaster-affected area
in detail, in addition to the information sent from people in the disaster-affected area
using the chat and other information provided by the reporting functions of the RIM
system.

6   Conclusions

This paper proposed an information management system called the RIM system. It is aimed at enabling the sharing of critical information in catastrophic situations even without the availability of the Internet and other commercial communication infrastructure. A prototype of the RIM system has been developed and the feasibility of all functions equipped in the RIM system has been confirmed. Some activities towards the practical use of the RIM system were also reported. In particular, it is the most important task for us to add new functions dedicated to the local city office by collaborating with them.

Acknowledgments. We would like to express our gratitude to Satoshi Kotabe and Atsushi Yamamoto of NTT Network Innovation Laboratories for their support and technical details provided by them regarding the MDRU. This work was partly supported by Council for Science, Technology and Innovation (CSTI), Cross-ministerial Strategic Innovation Promotion Program (SIP), "Enhancement of societal resiliency against natural disasters" (Funding agency: JST).

References

1. George, S.M., et al.: DistressNet: a wireless ad hoc and sensor network architecture for situation management in disaster response. IEEE Commun. Mag. **48**(3), 128–136 (2010)
2. Nelson, C.B., Steckler, B.D., Stamberger, J.A.: The evolution of hastily formed networks for disaster response technologies, case studies, and future trends. In: Proceedings of 2011 IEEE Global Humanitarian Technology Conference, Seattle, WA, USA, pp. 467–475, October 2011
3. Usuda, Y., Matsui, T., Deguchi, H., Hori, T., Suzuki, S.: the shared information platform for disaster management – the research and development regarding technologies for utilization of disaster information. J. Disaster Res. **14**(2), 279–291 (2019). https://doi.org/10.20965/jdr.2019.p0279
4. Sakano, T., et al.: Disaster-resilient networking: a new vision based on movable and deployable resource units. IEEE Netw. **27**(4), 40 (2013)
5. Google Maps. http://maps.google.com. Accessed 28 May 2019
6. Benson, M., Koenig, K.L., Schultz, C.H.: Disaster triage: START, then SAVE-a new method of dynamic triage for victims of a catastrophic earthquake. Prehospital Disaster Med. **27**(2), 117–124 (1996). https://doi.org/10.1017/s1049023x0004276x
7. MySQL. http://www.mysql.com/. Accessed 28 May 2019
8. SQLite. https://www.sqlite.org. Accessed 28 May 2019
9. OpenStreetMap. https://www.openstreetmap.org/. Accessed 28 May 2019
10. GEOSPACE (in Japanese). http://www.ntt-geospace.co.jp/. Accessed 28 May 2019
11. RIMCore. https://play.google.com/store/apps/details?id=com.aizulab.develop.rimcore. Accessed 28 May 2019
12. Mapbox. https://www.mapbox.com/. Accessed 28 May 2019
13. Bin Tariq, M. M., Ammar, M., Zegura, E.: Message ferry route design for sparse ad hoc networks with mobile nodes. In: 7th ACM International Symposium on Mobile Ad Hoc Networking and Computing (MobiHoc 2006), pp. 37–48, (2006), https://doi.org/10.1145/1132905.1132910

14. Anazawa, K., Miyazaki, T., Li, P.: Data synchronization method among isolated servers using mobile relays. IEICE Trans. Commun. **E101-B**(10), 2239–2249 (2018). https://doi.org/10.1587/transcom.2017ebp3468

15. Maruyama, Y., Miyazaki, T.: Smartphone finder: dedicated to seeking victims under collapsed buildings. In: Proceedings of the 13th International Conference on Ubiquitous Information Management and Communication (IMCOM), pp. 517–528 (2019). https://doi.org/10.1007/978-3-030-19063-7

16. Pe.com.in (Android version). https://play.google.com/store/apps/details?id=jp.lg.aizuwakamatsu.city.pecomin. Accessed 28 May 2019

17. Miyazaki, T., Shitara, D., Endo, Y., Tanno, Y., Igari, H., Kawano, R.: Die-hard sensor network: robust wireless sensor network dedicated to disaster monitoring. In: ACM 5th International Conference on Ubiquitous Information Management and Communication (ICUIMC 2011), Seoul, February 2011. https://doi.org/10.1145/1968613.1968678

Game Theoretic Optimal User Association in Emergency Networks

Christian Esposito[1]([✉]) [iD], Zhongliang Zhao[2] [iD], Ramón Alcarria[3] [iD],
and Gianluca Rizzo[4] [iD]

[1] Department of Electrical Engineering and Information Technology (DIETI),
University of Napoli "Federico II", 80125 Napoli, Italy
`christian.esposito@unina.it`
[2] Institute of Computer Science, University of Bern, Bern, Switzerland
`zhongliang.zhao@inf.unibe.ch`
[3] Universidad Politécnica de Madrid, Madrid, Spain
`ramon.alcarria@upm.es`
[4] University of Applied Sciences of Western Switzerland (HES-SO),
Sierre, Switzerland
`gianluca.rizzo@hevs.ch`

Abstract. The availability of effective communications in post-disaster scenarios is key to implement emergency networks that enable the sharing of critical information and support the coordination of the emergency response. To deliver those levels of QoS suitable to these applications, it is vital to exploit the multiple communication opportunities made available by the progressive deployment of the 5G and Smart City paradigms, ranging from ad-hoc networks among smartphones and surviving IoT devices, to cellular networks but also drone-based and vehicle-based wireless access networks. Therefore, the user device should be able to opportunistically select the most convenient among them to satisfy the demands for QoS imposed by the applications and also minimize the power consumption. The driving idea of this paper is to leverage non-cooperative game theory to design such an opportunistic user association strategy in a post-disaster scenario using UAV ad-hoc networks. The adaptive game-theoretic scheme allows increasing of the QoS of the communication means by lowering the loss rate and also keeps moderate the energy consumption.

Keywords: Game theory · Disaster resilient networking · Emergency networks · Vehicular crowdcell

1 Introduction

The current era is strongly characterized by the pervasiveness of ICT within our daily life and the ubiquitous accessibility of the Internet everywhere and every-time. Owing to one or more smartphones and using for almost everything is extremely normal in the current digital society so that human beings feel lost

M. R. Palattella et al. (Eds.): ADHOC-NOW 2019, LNCS 11803, pp. 18–31, 2019.
https://doi.org/10.1007/978-3-030-31831-4_2

without being able to access the web and its related services. However, large-scale natural and man-made disasters can negatively compromise the efficiency and effectiveness of the network, by causing failures of base stations composing cellular networks or truncating writes, causing permanent and/or temporary Internet inaccessibility or worsening. In post-disaster scenarios, being able to exchange data is particularly important for two main reasons. On the one hand, citizens need to inform their dear ones of their well-being, to know which of the possible escape routes is the best one to take, to ask for assistance/help or to receive updates on the current status of the neighboring environment and/or situation. On the other hand, the rescue teams need good networking to access satellite images or on-field assessment data to determine the entity of possible damages, the causalities or people in need, and to harmonize the recovery actions undertaken by the multiple teams involved in the damaged area. As a consequence, in the immediate aftermath of a disaster, the traffic demand may be overwhelming, with a high possibility of causing congestion phenomena. If we also consider that the network operational status is affected by failures, we can have a glimpse of how the perceived Quality-of-Service is much lower than the nominal levels and cannot keep with the high demands from the users reaching the point that the Internet becomes unavailable or offers degraded quality services [1,2]. This can harm the correct conduction of the rescue operations and increase the number of troubles caused by a disaster. As a concrete example, in the worst wildfire in Portugal in June 2017, a large number of users were cut off from using fixed-line or cellular communication services. This led to remarkable traffic congestion over the isolated areas, as well as affecting the emergency communications among rescue teams, which caused a large number of casualties.

We are witnessing a huge demand for resilient networking, as the occurrence of disasters is increasing, and their impacts are non-negligible [3]. Such a feature can be offered by properly rethinking the overall network by introducing redundant paths beforehand, or even by reacting to possible network saturation and service unavailability by deploying ad-hoc networking devices to substitute failed or overwhelming ones. This is the recent use of Unmanned aerial vehicles (UAVs) playing the role of a relay node to support cellular or ad hoc communications and strengthening the accessibility to the Internet offered to user devices. The work described in [4] proposed to use UAVs as aerial base stations (UABSs) to assist public safety communications during natural disasters, as soon as parts of the communication infrastructure is damaged and dysfunctional. This leads to the case that a user device can have multiple possible base stations towards the network: (1) the first exploits ad-hoc connections established with other user devices, acting as forwarders, (ii) the second leverage on base stations to access the Internet through cellular networks, (iii) the last one makes use of UAVs for communication purposes, and the contacted UAV can exploit an ad-hoc network with other UAVs or have direct Internet accessibility by means of long-range cellular or even satellite communication means. A user device can select one of these three communication opportunities, or even more than one to realize multi-path routing, based on the offered QoS and the required cost in terms of consumed energy. If fact, each of them can provide a certain degree of performance and success rate, but the required power consumption is not uniform as each of them leverages specific communication technologies. For example, ad-hoc networks among user devices are built based on low-range RF technologies such as Bluetooth and WiFi, which exhibits a lower energy cost than the cellular ones to connect to a base station. Reaching UAVs demands long-range RF technologies, where the energy cost can be higher. Such a selection depends on the actual network conditions and demands, and cannot be determined once but must be continuously conducted over time.

It is possible to model such an issue as an optimization problem; however, it is intractable in a centralized manner, even with heuristic approaches such as genetic algorithms and so on. In fact, on the one hand, it is a well known result in the theory of distributed systems that within the context of a fully asynchronous system (such as the one using the Internet as communication means) there is no global consensus and reaching a consistent view of certain pieces of data among asynchronous distributed processes despite of possible failures (in fact, this is theoretically unreachable due to the FLP impossibility proof [5]). This means that a single node cannot collect a consistent view of all the QoS levels experienced along with the links established by all user devices exploiting one or more of the three mentioned communication opportunities. On the other hand, even if this may be viable, the overhead to converge to a solution by resolving the optimization problem can be overwhelming due to a large number of nodes to be considered, and the consequent enormous solution space to be explored. Even the possibility of using optimized solutions to deal with large scale problems, such as s genetic algorithm with multiple populations, may not lead to a tractable problem. Such a problem can only be resolved in a distributed manner by leveraging on a game-theoretic approach, where each user device is considered as a player in the game, which picks up a given strategy (i.e., using one of the possible communication means or even more than one) by maximising the obtainable gain (in terms of meeting the demands of the applications and users in terms of performance and success rate) and minimising the consequent cost in terms of energy consumption. The driving idea of this work is to adopt a non-cooperative formulation of a resolution approach and this paper presents the design and challenges of the proposed system.

2   System Model

We consider a set of N cellular users, moving within a region in which several static cellular base station (BS) are deployed. We assume in such a scenario there is also a set of vehicles (such as UAV and ground vehicles) that carry cellular base stations, and which move according to a given mobility pattern. We consider the uplink channel of a cellular access network and the use of upcoming 5G technologies for next-generation mobile networks as in [28]. We assume BS in the considered scenario belong to three classes. The first is represented by a static cellular base station (BS). The second class is composed of a moving base station (MBS), installed on UAV or ground vehicles, and forwarding all traffic to a static BS via a wireless backhaul connection. Finally, we assume user devices can act as base stations too, relaying traffic originating from other user devices to a static BS. In this work, we assume that backhaul links are one-hop only, though our approach can be easily extended to multi-hop backhaul connections.

In such a scenario, we assume each user can associate to at most one BS for each class. This implies that each user can associate to at most three base stations at the same time. For instance, users may differentiate the access technology according to the QoS requirements of the traffic they exchange, sending delay-sensitive traffic to a nearby static BS under high load while forwarding delay-tolerant traffic to another, less loaded base station via multi-hop relaying. Note however that our approach can be easily extended to the case in which a user can associate to more than one BS for each class, as in the case of Heterogeneous Network (HetNet) [26], where in addition to selecting BS thee is also the problem of traffic splitting among the multiple BS.

We assume time to be divided into slots of equal duration and let $t \in \mathcal{N}$ be the index of the t-th slot. Each of the access modes is characterized by a loss pattern, i.e. by a mean rate of packet loss, which is a function of time. For every slot t, we assume to know the mean packet loss rate for each possible base station. Specifically, for each user n in the considered region, and for each static base station s, the coefficient $\pi_{n,s} \in [0,1]$, which indicates the mean packet loss experienced by the n-th user when associated to the s-th static BS in the given time slot. Analogously, for each vehicular BS v and each user-based BS u we introduce the coefficients $\pi_{n,v} \in [0,1]$ and $\pi_{n,u} \in [0,1]$. However, while packet losses for the static base stations coincide with packet losses experienced on the link between the user and the base station, the packet loss coefficient associated with moving base stations (either vehicle or user) are the resultant of the link between the user and the moving BS, and of the backhaul link between the moving BS and the static BS. We assume that at the beginning of each slot, such a coefficient is known through estimations based on the periodical exchange of CSI.

In each slot, we also introduce the variables $x_{n,s}$, $x_{n,v}$, $x_{n,u}$, which take values between 0 and 1. $x_{n,s}$ represents the fraction of the user traffic which is sent to BS s (resp. u, v). Therefore we have, $\forall n$,

$$\sum_s x_{n,s} + \sum_v x_{n,v} + \sum_u x_{n,u} = 1 \tag{1}$$

We assume that each class of base stations has a maximum number of users it can serve, denoted with M^S (resp. M^V, M^U). This implies that

$$\sum_n x_{n,s} \leq M^S \quad \forall s \tag{2}$$

$$\sum_n x_{n,v} \leq M^V \quad \forall v \tag{3}$$

$$\sum_n x_{n,u} \leq M^U \quad \forall u \tag{4}$$

The mean loss rate experienced by the n-th user in a given slot (which can be directly measured on the stability/QoS of running applications' performance or specific measuring tools such as in [29]) can therefore be expressed as

$$\Pi_n = \sum_u x_{n,u} \pi_{n,u} + \sum_v x_{n,v} \pi_{n,v} + \sum_s x_{n,s} \pi_{n,s} \tag{5}$$

Moreover, with $\epsilon_{n,u}$, $\epsilon_{n,v}$ and $\epsilon_{n,s}$ we indicate the mean amount of energy consumed by the device during the given slot when associated to the base station belonging to one of the three classes. Hence the mean amount of energy consumed by the device can be expressed as

$$E_i = \sum_u x_{n,u} \epsilon_{n,u} + \sum_v x_{n,v} \epsilon_{n,v} + \sum_s x_{n,s} \epsilon_{n,s} \tag{6}$$

While the experienced loss rate depends on the environmental conditions (such as network congestion, mutual RF technologies interference and so on) at run time and the possible failures caused by the disaster, the device energy consumption due to the specific communication technology mainly depends on the adopted technology. A concrete example is provided in the study presented in [6] and summarized in Fig. 1, where it is evident an ad-hoc communication technology, as Bluetooth in the figure, is more energy efficient that the WiFi, or other long-range communication means, which can be exploited to communicate with UAVs, while the highest energy consumption is exhibited by cellular technologies.

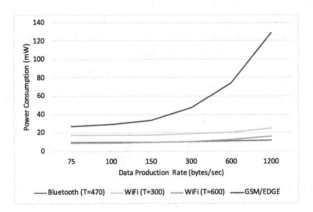

Fig. 1. Power consumption for a Bluetooth, WiFi and GSM/EDGE radio for different data production rates, and transmission intervals (T).

3   Formulation of the Optimization Problem

In this section, we formalize the problem of optimal user association in the considered scenario, to determine in each time slot the most energy-efficient user association strategy. We consider a single time slot, and we consider the problem of determining, $\forall n$, the variables $x_{n,s}$, $x_{n,v}$, $x_{n,u}$, that minimize the experienced loss rate and the cost function which accounts for the total energy consumed at the devices during the given time slot. Let $\mathbf{X}^{UAV}$, $\mathbf{X}^{BS}$ and $\mathbf{X}^U$ denote the arrays for the variables associated with the three classes of associations during the given time slot.

Problem 1 (Optimal user association in a time slot).

$$\min_{\mathbf{X}^{UAV},\mathbf{X}^{BS},\mathbf{X}^U} \left\{ \sum_n \Pi_n, E_n \right\} \tag{7}$$

Subject to:

$$Equation\ (1),\ (2),\ (3),\ (4),\ (5),\ (6)$$
$$\forall n, s, u, v$$
$$0 \leq x_{n,s}, x_{n,v}, x_{n,u}, \leq 1 \tag{8}$$
$$\tag{9}$$

In this problem we have not indicated the association with a single base station, as the user device when $x_{n,s} \neq 0$ automatically looks for the nearest base station and establishes a connection with it. This is a linear programming problem, and hence it can be solved optimally. However, a centralized approach in which a single coordination function collects the estimations of packet loss ratios for the whole network and computes the optimal user association does not scale, as it would require the collection and exchange of a substantial amount of delay-sensitive control traffic among the devices in the system. Moreover, such a centralized coordination function should dispose of substantial storage and computing resources, which are not always available in a disaster scenario.

Besides, given the mobility of users and part of the BS, the transmissive conditions (and hence the coefficients π) change over time. As a result, the duration of each time slot should be small enough to capture these variations and adapt accordingly to the user association. However, the solution of problem 1 may change drastically from a slot to the other due to fading. An ideal system that would configure user association according to the solutions of Problem 1 in each time slot would be forced to continuously adjust the selected strategy. As changes in user association bear costs in terms of control information and of time required to implement them, such a strategy would not be viable in realistic settings.

4   A Distributed Approach to Optimal User Association

Given the aforementioned issues, in this section, we propose a distributed heuristic to solving Problem 1, based on a game-theoretic approach. Our approach determines in each time slot the optimal user association configuration without the need for centralized coordination.

Distributed optimization using game theory consists of defining local decision strategies for the individual nodes, called players, based on their local knowledge acquired by neighbors, to ensure that the resulting global behavior satisfies a given global objective. In our case, we have a set of n players (*i.e.*, the user devices) that simultaneously select some of the three available communications means to which access to the network, at the cost of the lowest energy consumption possible. We consider a set of players $P := c_1, c_2, \cdots, c_n$ of finite size $n \geq 2$. Formally, the strategy set for each player $c \in P$ is defined as $S^c = Y$, such that a strategy of a player is the selection of a set of the possible connections towards some UAVs, base stations or neighboring nodes $\overline{s}^c \subset Y$. In what follows we assume that, for each class of BS, each user associates to the BS which delivers the strongest received signal. In our game, the strategy of a player is given by an integer number belonging to the interval $[1, 7]$, which are all the possible selection combinations (*i.e.*, 1 stands for base station only, 2 for UAVs only, 3 for neighboring nodes only, 4 to 6 only two modes of the three possible, while the last one encompasses all the three modes. Based on the adopted strategy, indicates as s_j, proper action is conducted by the j-th player, namely o_j, among the set of allowed actions $O_j(s_j)$. Specifically, these strategies are represented by the variable $x_{n,s}$, $x_{n,v}$, $x_{n,u}$ and their constraint expressed in Eq. 1. e.g., the strategy 1 is indicated by the following values: $x_{n,s} = 1$, $x_{n,v} = 0$, $x_{n,u} = 0$. While, the related actions when strategies are selected consists of establishing, or not, a connection to the nearest UAVs, base stations and nodes, usable by the communication means indicated by the strategy.

Combining the strategy sets of all the players, namely $S = S^{c_1} \times S^{c_2} \times \cdots \times S^{c_p}$, a strategy profile $s \in S$ implies a certain payoff to each player c, namely $\Phi^c(s)$, which are aggregated in the so-called profile of payoffs denoted as ϕ. The payoff is the gain achievable by a player to use a given communications means instead of the other possible ones, specifically, in our game, a player c receives a gain, namely α, for experiencing a good communication quality, *i.e.*, the reciprocal of the loss pattern reduced of the cost to send the messages by using such a communication means:

$$\Phi^c(s) = \alpha(o(s)) - E(o(s)) = 1 - \Pi(o(s)) - E(o(s)). \tag{10}$$

where $o(s)$ is the function that given a strategy properly returns the variable $x_{n,s}$, $x_{n,v}$, $x_{n,u}$ set according to the selected BS, UAV and user device, while the two functions for the loss pattern and the energy consumption are normalized by considering the highest value so that their return is within the interval $[0, 1]$. The scope of the game is to determine the best strategy profile that implies the maximum payoff for all the players.

$$s^* \in arg \max_{s \in S} \frac{1}{N} \sum_{i \in L} \Phi^c(s_i). \tag{11}$$

In our game, players are selfish, *i.e.*, there is no direct communication between the players, and each one only cares to maximize its profit or to minimize its costs without considering the state of the other players (with the eventuality of damaging them, even if it is not intentional). Then, the game is defined non-cooperative, and its normal form is given by $\Gamma = (P, S, \pi)$, to maximize the payoff for all the players. One of the most studied aspects of such class of games is the existence of Nash Equilibria (NE), *i.e.*, given a certain strategy $s \in S$, it is not profitable for a player to select a different node than the one in the current strategy profile since moving to a neighbor node will not change or even reduce the achievable payoff, so a player has no incentive to change strategy:

$$\exists s \in S : \forall c \in P, \forall x \in Y, \pi^c(s^c, s^{-c}) \geq \pi^c(x, s^{-c}) \quad \rightarrow s \text{ is a NE}. \tag{12}$$

The demonstration of the existence of such equilibria is a known NP-hard problem and is resolved using theorems by making proper assumptions of the characteristics of certain elements of the game. A well-known result of the research in non-cooperative games is that if the strategies are mixed, then the existence of at least one Nash Equilibrium is guaranteed. A pure strategic game consists in a player always picking the strategy of highest quality (i.e., the one with highest payoff), while a mixed strategic game encompasses players that have a probability associated to the selection of the strategy of highest quality (meaning that there may be cases where the player does not take that strategy but one with lower payoff).

In a typical application of game theory, the payoff functions of the players are assumed to be well known and externally given, and based on such a set of functions it is possible to drive each player's output and determine the existence of Nash Equilibria. Moreover, as the game is non-cooperative, a set of players may decide to exploit the same communication means, possibly causing congestion. To this aim, in Eq. 10, we add a contribution measuring the goodness of the selection concerning the other players, by inserting a form of cooperation. Such a contribution is not fixed a priori, but it is dynamically computed based on the feedback provided by the other players. Such feedback is -1 is the considered strategy is followed by the player returning the feedback, i otherwise. So at the time a player decides to pursue a strategy, it broadcast such a decision to its reachable peers, receiving back feedback to estimate the goodness of the decision in the next iteration of the game. This signaling among peers is not comparable to solving the linear program with a centralized solution, as loss statistics and feedback are not collected by a centralized node.

In this case, the resolution of our game is not possible through the typical means provided by the game theory to deal with non-cooperative games. In this work, we have drawn from the theory of distributed strategic learning [9], where each player can learn from the received feedback for their outputs to create a payoff value and to determine if a given strategy yields the best response. Specifically, the resolution of our game requires a Reinforcement Learning (RL) scheme [10], where the players interact with the other nodes and receive some feedback that represents the consequences of their actions and which depend on the state of the system and the actions of the other players. By using such feedback, each player learns to select or not a certain strategy based on its consequences. Strategies leading to high payoffs in a certain situation will be preferred whenever the same situation recurs, while those strategies leading to lower payoffs will be avoided.

To tackle this problem, in this paper we apply the COmbined fully DIstributed PAyoff and Strategy-RL (CODIPAS-RL) [9], a learning scheme derived from strategy and payoff (Q-learning) Reinforcement Learning. CODIPAS-RL is an exploration strategy characterized by high effectiveness in finding the best response dynamics in a game.

Let us denote with $y_{j,t}(s_j)$ the probabilities of the j-th player to choose s_j at time t, and $y_{j,t} = [y_{j,t}(s_j)]_{s_j \in A_j} \in Y_j$ be the mixed strategy of the j-th player. Moreover, we indicate with $r_{j,t}$ the perceived payoff at the time t, made of the two contributions of the loss rate and consumed energy aggregated with the estimation of the strategies based on the received feedbacks. CODIPAS works as follows:

- At time slot $t = 0$, each player chooses a strategy s and from it derives an action o. Then, it received a series of feedbacks for its action and builds a numerical value of its payoff. The payoff is properly initialized to $r_{j,0}$, given from the initial estimation of the loss rate and the energy consumption without the third contribution we envisioned to avoid congestion phenomenon.
- At time slot $t > 0$, each player has an estimation of its payoffs, namely $r_{j,t}$, chooses a strategy $x_{j,t+1}$ for the next time slot, which is a function only of the previous strategy $x_{j,t}$, the estimated payoff $r_{j,t}$ and the target value for the payoff function.
- The game moves to $t + 1$.

Such a scheme is combined with proper payoff and strategy learning, leading to CODIPAS-RL:

$$\begin{cases} y_{j,t+1} = f_j(\lambda_{j,t}, o_{j,t}, r_{j,t}, \hat{r}_{j,t}, x_{j,t}) \\ \hat{r}_{j,t+1} = g_j(\nu_{j,t}, o_{j,t}, r_{j,t}, y_{j,t}, \hat{r}_{j,t}), \end{cases} \quad j \in [1, N], t \geq 0, o_{j,t} \in O_j(s_j). \quad (13)$$

The function f_j determines the update of the strategy at the next time slot and defines the strategy learning pattern of the j-th player, where $\lambda_{j,t}$ is its strategy learning rate that may vary from player to player and/or during the learning process. The variable $r_{j,t}$ contains the feedbacks received by each contacted nodes, while $\hat{r}_{j,t}$ is the estimation of the payoff function. The function g_j updates the estimation of the payoff function for the j-th player, by specifying the payoff learning pattern and is characterized by a given speed named as $\nu_{j,t}$, which may be different than the speed of the strategy learning function. We assume that the learning rates are taken identical for all the players and equal to $\lambda_{j,t} = 0.1$ and $\nu_{j,t} = 0.6$, respectively. In this work we have adopted the Boltzmann-Gibbs based CODIPAS-RL, since it outperforms the standard RL algorithms, and has been proved the convergence of the algorithm toward a pure strategy Nash equilibrium with sufficiently small learning rates [9]. Specifically, let us define the Boltzmann-Gibbs distribution as a strategy mapping $\widetilde{\beta}_{j,\epsilon}$: $\mathbb{R}^{|S_i|} \to \mathbb{R}^{|S_i|}$ known as the soft-max function and formulated as follows:

$$\widetilde{\beta}_{j,\epsilon}(\hat{r}_{j,t})(s_j) = \frac{e^{\frac{1}{\epsilon_j}\hat{r}_{j,t}(s_j)}}{\sum\limits_{s'_j \in S^j} e^{\frac{1}{\epsilon_j}\hat{r}_{j,t}(s'_j)}}, \quad s_j \in S^j, j \in [1, N] \tag{14}$$

In such an equation, s'_j may be interpret as any possible strategy for the j-th player which is different to s_j, and the parameter ϵ_j for the j-th player may be identical to the one of the other players, or may be different, and its reciprocal can be interpreted as the rationality level of the player. When $\epsilon \to 0$, such a strategy mapping returns the strategy characterized by the maximum value for the estimated payoff $\hat{r}_{j,t+1}$; therefore we assume $\epsilon = 0.1$. Based on such a distribution, we can formulate the f and g functions of the learning pattern in Eq. 13 as follows:

$$\begin{cases} y_{j,t+1} = (1 - \lambda_{j,t})y_{j,t} + \lambda_{j,t}\widetilde{\beta}_{j,\epsilon}(\hat{r}_{j,t}) \\ \hat{r}_{j,t+1}(s_j) = \hat{r}_{j,t}(s_j) + \nu_{j,t}\mathbb{K}_{\{o_{j,t+1} \in O_j(s_j)\}} \quad j \in [1, N], t \geq 0, o_{j,t} \in O_j(s_j). \\ (r_{j,t+1} - \hat{r}_{j,t}(s_j)), \end{cases}$$

$$\tag{15}$$

The function $\mathbb{K}_{\{o_{j,t+1} \in O_j(s_j)\}}$ indicates the active strategy of the player and assumes 0 if the action $o_{j,t}$ has not been played by the j-th player at time t, 1 otherwise, so as to update only the component corresponding to the action that has been played. In Eq. 15, the learning of the payoff and the strategy are coupled and updated together: the feedback of an action at the time instance t is used to update the payoff estimation, and such an estimation is used to determine the strategy. The stable solution of such an equation can be assumed as an equilibrium for a modified game, where the payoff function of our game is perturbed with an extra entropy contribution indicating its dependency on the loss pattern applied by the network dynamics and the actions of other players.

5   Numerical Evaluation

We have implemented a Java application that randomly deploys BS, user devices and UAV within a Cartesian space, where each of them has a couple of coordinates. Initially, the application determines for each user device the closest BS and UAV based on the Euclidian distance among a user device to all the deployed BS and UAV and select those with the lowest distance. We have assigned as energy consumption three values 0.25, 0.5 and 0.75, respectively to the ad-hoc connection towards another user device, to UAV and BS. We assume that the communication between the user device and the UAV is not based on cellular technology, as with the BS, but by using WiFi, in an ad-hoc manner. As for the device-to-device communication, a low rate and efficient communication mean as Bluetooth can be exploited, with UAV this is not the optimal decision, so a more powerful RF technology as WiFi may be used. It is also true that a UAV can be equipped with a cellular antenna making it looks like a moving BS, so in that case, the cost value for the energy consumption is equal to the one of BS. Each element has a very low loss rate initially, equal to 0.1, as wireless communications always drop packets due to interference and other issues. So that at the beginning all the user devices only is associated with the nearest BS. At a time T_D, the disaster occurs and the loss rate of BS increases as a consequence of the occurred failure. We do not assume the destruction of a BS, but only its lossy behavior. The destruction of BS can be modeled by using a Poisson point process with a thinning operation [27]. With a given probability π_D each BS of N is tagged as compromised and the respective loss rate assumes a given value within a certain interval (*e.g.*, from 0.2 to 0.5). After running the game and computing the payoff for each possible strategy, we have fixed a starting probability equal to 0.9 (we want a slight variability in the winning strategy selection) that the player picks up the strategy with the highest gain.

Figure 2 shows the preliminary results obtained from our simulation (where the stability has been reached around the 6th iteration, i.e., after around 10 s from the start of the experiments, on average). Initially, the loss rate is low, equal to the initial value of 0.1. Later on, at iteration 3, the disaster occurs and the loss rate increases to a value that is stationary when the user is kept associated with its initial BS, such a value lower due to the adaptation of our approach to multiple associations. Such a reduction is valid until a point where the loss rate is almost stationary as the loss rate does not have any changes apart from the one caused by the disaster. The transitory is due to the learning scheme, which brings the system to an equilibrium point. Similar behavior can be seen in energy consumption, which starts with consumption due to the use of a BS. This is due to the case that most of the users try to select a neighbor device or a UAV, allowing the scheme to lower energy consumption.

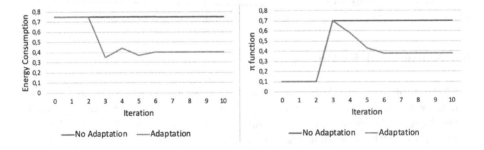

Fig. 2. Assessment results.

6   Related Work

Apart from centralized solutions, there are some distributed solutions providing mechanisms for user association. For example, in [20] the authors present a distributed algorithm considering previous paths of users in mobility and combines these data with wireless measurements to predict the upcoming connection quality of the network. Other works [21] consider an accurate model of two-dimensional and three-dimensional scenarios to determine user trajectories, when, for example, some vehicles (i.e. drones) are involved. However, these works assume that mobility patterns of users are known [21], or can be guessed by training [22]. Our solution does not require previous knowledge about users' behavior.

Regarding QoS-based network selection we can find different approaches considering QoS constraints [16,17] or Quality of Experience (QoE) [12]. Some of these works are focused on many factors including the mobility pattern of the mobile device, the load of the candidate access network, and the preference of the candidate access network to the call request [18]. Other works [19] consider also a trade-off between users and operator's preferences, such as quality of the connections or other network conditions. All these works, however, consider a single association between the user and an access point. Our approach considers, apart from the imposed QoS by executing applications, the possibility of connecting to multiple base stations.

Many of the previous works describe situations where the user terminal is associated with only one access point. The multi-RAT (Multiple Radio Access Technology) techniques have emerged for heterogeneous scenarios, considering that user equipment can transmit and receive data over multiple networks [23]. Apart from these multimode terminals, multi-RAT parallel transmission from more than one AP provides a new level of complexity, as some load-balancing capabilities [24] and other network congestion prevention methods [25] must be defined, and are also found in the literature. In this work, we incorporate the use of multi-RAT transmission to the scenario where BS load levels, energy and QoS requested by users are considered.

7   Conclusions

This paper presented a solution based on game theory for the resolution of the problem of selecting among multiple communication means to cope with network resiliency in a post-disaster scenario. As future work, we plan to implement the proposed solution and empirically assess the achievable quality against a centralized meta-heuristic approach based on genetic algorithms. The existence of a Nash Equilibrium in our game has been determined in [9], but the speed of convergence to an equilibrium point is still an open issue. In a potential scenario with a large volume of users, convergence speed can be an issue and needs to be properly investigated. This is further exacerbated by user mobility. In fact, in post-disaster scenarios is reasonable to have users moving around the damaged area, imposing novel challenging and issues to the mobile networking and the relative multiple associations. We plan to introduce the mobility pf users in our work and to study this augmented problem, starting from similar works as in [30,31]. The user-side of the presented approach is not complex and can be easily integrated within a user device. We plan to provide an implementation after a detailed analysis of the overall problem augmented with the mobility issues.

Acknowledgment. This work is supported by CAPES, CNPQ, the EU COST Action CA15127 RECODIS and the Hasler MOBNET project.

References

1. Mauthe, A., et al.: Disaster-resilient communication networks: principles and best practices. In: Proceedings of the 8th International Workshop on Resilient Networks Design and Modeling (RNDM 2016), pp. 1–10 (2016)
2. Furdek, M., et al.: An overview of security challenges in communication networks. In: Proceedings of the 8th International Workshop on Resilient Networks Design and Modeling (RNDM 2016), pp. 1–8 (2016)
3. Gomes, T., et al.: A survey of strategies for communication networks to protect against large-scale natural disasters. In: Proceedings of the 8th International Workshop on Resilient Networks Design and Modeling (RNDM 2016), pp. 1–12, September 2016
4. Merwaday, A., Guvenc, I.: UAV assisted heterogeneous networks for public safety communications. In: Proceedings of the IEEE Wireless Communications and Networking Conference Workshops (WCNCW), pp. 329–334, March 2015
5. Fischer, M., Lynch, N., Paterson, M.: Impossibility of distributed consensus with one faulty process. J. ACM **32**(2), 374–382 (1985)
6. Balani, R.: Energy consumption analysis for Bluetooth, WiFi and cellular networks. Technical report, Electrical Engineering University of California at Los Angeles (2007). http://www.nesl.ucla.edu/uploads/document/paperupload/254/PowerAnalysis.pdf
7. Mozaffari, M., Saad, W., Bennis, M., Debbah, M.: Efficient deployment of multiple unmanned aerial vehicles for optimal wireless coverage. IEEE Commun. Lett. **20**(8), 1647–1650 (2016)
8. Cochran, J.K., Horng, S.-M., Fowler, J.W.: A multi-population genetic algorithm to solve multi-objective scheduling problems for parallel machines. Comput. Oper. Res. **30**(7), 1087–1102 (2003)
9. Tembine, H.: Distributed Strategic Learning for Wireless Engineers. CRC Press, Boca Raton (2012)
10. Sutton, S.: Learning to predict by the method of temporal differences. Mach. Learn. **3**, 9–44 (1989)
11. Das, D., Das, D.: Efficient UE mobility in multi-RAT cellular networks using SDN. Wirel. Netw. **25**(1), 255–267 (2019)
12. Raschellá, A., Bouhafs, F., Deepak, G.C., Mackay, M.: QoS aware radio access technology selection framework in heterogeneous networks using SDN. J. Commun. Netw. **19**(6), 577–586 (2017)
13. Yang, W.: Conceptual verification of integrated heterogeneous network based on 5G millimeter wave use in gymnasium. Symmetry **11**(3), 376 (2019)
14. Giust, F., Bernardos, C.J., de la Oliva, A.: Analytic evaluation and experimental validation of a network-based IPv6 distributed mobility management solution. IEEE Trans. Mob. Comput. **13**(11), 2484–2497 (2014)

15. Zhang, H., Chu, X., Guo, W., Wang, S.: Coexistence of Wi-Fi and heterogeneous small cell networks sharing unlicensed spectrum. IEEE Commun. Mag. **53**(3), 158–164 (2015)
16. Kumar, A., Mallik, R.K., Schober, R.: A probabilistic approach to modeling users' network selection in the presence of heterogeneous wireless networks. IEEE Trans. Veh. Technol. **63**(7), 3331–3341 (2014)
17. Sui, N., Zhang, D., Zhong, W., Wang, C.: Network selection for heterogeneous wireless networks based on multiple attribute decision making and Evolutionary Game Theory. In: Proceedings of the 25th Wireless and Optical Communication Conference (WOCC), pp. 1–5, May 2016
18. Liou, Y.-S., Gau, R.-H., Chang, C.-J.: A bargaining game based access network selection scheme for HetNet. In: Proceedings of the 1st IEEE International Conference on Communications (ICC), pp. 4888–4893, June 2014
19. Nguyen-Vuong, Q.-T., Agoulmine, N., Cherkaoui, E.H., Toni, L.: Multicriteria optimization of access selection to improve the quality of experience in heterogeneous wireless access networks. IEEE Trans. Veh. Technol. **62**(4), 1785–1800 (2013)
20. Nicholson, A.J., Noble, B.D.: Breadcrumbs: forecasting mobile connectivity. In: Proceedings of the 14th ACM International Conference on Mobile Computing and Networking, pp. 46–57 (2008)
21. Robles, T., Bordel, B., Alcarria, R., Martín, D.: Mobile wireless sensor networks: modeling and analysis of three-dimensional scenarios and neighbor discovery in mobile data collection. Ad Hoc Sens. Wirel. Netw. **35**(1), 67–104 (2017)
22. Nguyen, D.D., Nguyen, H.X., White, L.B.: Evaluating performance of RAT selection algorithms for 5G Hetnets. IEEE Access **6**, 61212–61222 (2018)
23. Yu, G., Jiang, Y., Xu, L., Li, G.Y.: Multi-objective energy-efficient resource allocation for multi-RAT heterogeneous networks. IEEE J. Sel. Areas Commun. **33**(10), 2118–2127 (2015)
24. Ghatak, G., De Domenico, A., Coupechoux, M.: Coverage analysis and load balancing in hetnets with millimeter wave Multi-RAT small cells. IEEE Trans. Wirel. Commun. **17**(5), 3154–3169 (2018)
25. Iwasawa, H., Tokunaga, K., Takaya, N.: Available-bandwidth information based TCP congestion control algorithm on multi-RAT networks. In: Proceedings of the IEEE Global Communications Conference (GLOBECOM), pp. 1–6 (2017)
26. Shen, K., Liu, Y., Ding, D.Y., Yu, W.: Flexible multiple base station association and activation for downlink heterogeneous networks. IEEE Signal Process. Lett. **24**(10), 1498–1502 (2017)
27. Hayajneh, A.M., Zaidi, S.A.R., McLernon, D.C., Di Renzo, M., Ghogho, M.: Performance analysis of UAV enabled disaster recovery networks: a stochastic geometric framework based on cluster processes. IEEE Access **6**, 26215–26230 (2018)
28. Singhal, C., De, S.: Resource Allocation in Next-generation Broadband Wireless Access Networks. IGI Global, Pennsylvania (2017)
29. Baltrunas, D., Elmokashfi, A., Kvalbein, A.: Measuring the reliability of mobile broadband networks. In: Proceedings of the 2014 Conference on Internet Measurement (2014)
30. Tsiropoulou, E., Koukas, K., Papavassiliou, S.: A socio-physical and mobility-aware coalition formation mechanism in public safety networks. EAI Endorsed Trans. Future Internet **4**, 154176 (2018)
31. Liu, D., et al.: User association in 5G networks: a survey and an outlook. IEEE Commun. Surv. Tutor. **18**(2), 1018–1044 (2016)

A Validation Method for AdHoc Network Simulation Including MANETs, VANETs and Emergency Scenarios

J. R. E. Leite⓪, Paulo S. Martins⁽⊠⁾⓪, and Edson L. Ursini⓪

School of Technology, University of Campinas (UNICAMP),
R. Paschoal Marmo, 1888, Sao Paulo, Limeira 13484, Brazil
j750465@dac.unicamp.br, {paulo,ursini}@ft.unicamp.br

Abstract. This work presents a methodology for planning and validation of AdHoc and IoT network simulator, considering congested and uncongested nodes. The validated model is specialized to consider mobile and vehicular networks (MANET and VANET), and a disaster recovery scenario is introduced. The goal is to analyze the traffic of the destination node and estimate its capacity considering an AdHoc application. Specifically, we aim to use validation to further determine the processor utilization and message delay. The proposed model and simulation tool may be used not only to plan and dimension the network but also to guide the management of the network in critical situations that can be anticipated. In addition to the MANET validation, the results showed that a Monte Carlo routing optimization (VANET case) and availability/reliability (disaster recovery case) may be relevant to the effective resource usage of the network.

Keywords: AdHoc · IoT model validation · Simulation · Validation · Jackson networks

1 Introduction

Simulation and modeling are widely accepted techniques for analyzing real-world systems that are too complex to model analytically. Most communication networks fall into this category. They allow the examination of several scenarios for the dimensioning of a new system or the improvement and expansion of an existing one. Nevertheless, by virtue of the stringent deadlines imposed over simulation practitioners, substantial efforts are spent on the measurement of key properties of the system, the building of the system model, and actual simulation of the real system, thus leaving not enough time to reason about one of the most important steps of the simulation project, i.e. that of the validation and verification of the simulation model itself.

Conceptual model validation is defined as determining that the theories and assumptions underlying the conceptual model are correct and that the model

© Springer Nature Switzerland AG 2019
M. R. Palattella et al. (Eds.): ADHOC-NOW 2019, LNCS 11803, pp. 32–47, 2019.
https://doi.org/10.1007/978-3-030-31831-4_3

representation of the problem entity is reasonable for the intended purpose of the model. Validation, within the context of this work, is treated in a broad sense. It involves the verification, i.e. the simulator delivers correct processor utilizations and packet delays at every node in the system, which is the functionality that is required from the internal specification. From the end-user perspective, the main requirement for validation is a simulator that enhances both the correctness of simulation and the confidence placed in its results. One way of increasing the correctness of the model is by comparing the performance attribute values obtained from the simulation model with another implementation of the same model, be it real-word or analytical.

In this work, we present a methodology for the validation of simulated computer networks. It consists of a number of steps which are based on Jackson Networks Queueing model. In particular, a case study is shown for an AdHoc (MANET) Network consisting of a number of network clusters and two scenarios, one that includes a VANET and the other an emergency case where the links are disrupted. The proposed method provided satisfactory results and showed potential for further improvements and evolution.

The remainder of this paper is organized as follows: In Sect. 2 we review previous work. The network model is discussed in Sect. 3. The methodology for validation is presented in Sect. 4. A case study illustrating the application of the methodology is shown in Sect. 5. In Sect. 6, we address some key remarks mainly dealing with the applicability of the model. We summarize and present our conclusions in Sect. 7.

2   Related Work

Multivariate methods can be used to test the hypothesis of agreement between simulated predictions and empirical observations. The work by [1] proposes a statistical test for the validation of simulations. Their method uses a multivariate nonparametric rank sum test, with the aid of a computer-intensive randomization procedure, to assess the significance of the test statistic. Their goal was to strengthen the link between experimentation and simulation, which should be used in the evaluation of communications systems' performance measurements. The validation procedure was applied to networks for battlefield communication.

In [3], the authors address the validation of fully integrated multi train simulators. This type of validation can be complex as it includes the physical characteristics of the process, i.e. the train movements, the electrification system and rail potentials. The main goal of their validation was to show that the simulator behaves as expected, i.e. that the simulator provides the desired results. The authors point out that it is often challenging to achieve comprehensive validation of multi train simulation software without the co-operation of a railway authorities. Their work also reviews the technical necessities of validating multi train simulators.

Martens, Pauels and Put use neural networks for the validation of the simulation model of five variants of multi server queueing systems [9]. In particular, multi-layer perceptron and radial basis function networks techniques are used to learn the behavior of the simulation models. They found that classification using a multilayer perceptron (MLP) network produces better results than classification with a PN network, or using the k-nearest neighbor (KNN) method. One drawback of the method is that several replications are required with different calibrations of the simulation model to train the neural networks. In that respect, it does not allow to test individual simulation models. The method has the advantage that multiple statistics (means, variances, etc.) can be tested simultaneously.

In the work by Ursini et al. [10, 11] a virtual single-link IP network was simulated using the concept of incremental validation. The former consisted of only the elastic traffic whereas the latter considered the stream traffic. The work considered specific network parameters such as packet size and transmission rates. In the present work, we used more generic parameters (fixed packet size and transmission rates), a distinct type of traffic, adopted a new multi-link model with connectivity among nodes, and analyzed the performance of the IoT mediator.

In the paper by Leite et al. [6] the authors considered only an AdHoc network (i.e. without IoT) for traffic analysis. The work consisted of the analysis of mean queue delay and CPU utilization in each cluster and a small blocking value caused by loss of connectivity was included. In the present work, we added an IoT Network to the topology, and we varied the power transmission value to analyze the loss of node connectivity. Furthermore, the network included more IoT services, which correspondingly generated more traffic such as the one from RFID and network management services (Simple Network Management Protocol - SNMP).

Unlike previous work from other authors, which have used techniques such as hypothesis testing, simulation of physical (mechanical and electrical) processes, and artificial-intelligence based methods, our validation work relies on queueing theory and network of queues, specifically employing the Jackson network model and incremental validation. To our knowledge, we are not aware of similar work in the literature that attempts to validate an IoT/MANET network simulator using such approach.

Our previous work [10, 11] have validated simulation models using approximate traffic models for a single link. In [6], we have employed the Jackson Network validation, but the methodology was not exposed. Additionally, here we present additional scenarios, namely that of a VANET with routing optimization and a MANET for disaster recovery.

Through a search in the literature, we found no work that tackle the case of validation of IoT (MANET + RFID) by Jackson's network with the traffic aspects such as partial and global delays and CPU utilization. Jackson's networks are classical in computer networks but they are applied to a quite specific problem in this work. Furthermore, it is an intuitive approach, since the computer network topology is the same as the one for the Jackson network. Unlike work reviewed in this section, in this work we tackle the performance of the queues, CPUs and traffic in an IoT network, which includes clusters of sensors from an AdHoc network.

3   Network Model

The system comprises of a set of clusters, and each cluster has internally a number of internal nodes. In addition to motes, each cluster has cluster heads (i.e. output CPUs), which allow simultaneous transmission of traffic out of the cluster. Thus, each cluster may be modeled as a set of queues, where each queue is linked to an output link).

Inherent in each queue is the waiting delay before a TCP/IP packet can be processed by a server. Clearly, both queuing and processing times are subject to statistical distributions. The network components are the mediator, gateways, clusters and endpoints. The endpoints can be RFID and sensors for different applications. Figure 1 shows the network model with its inputs (packets) and outputs (packets) to each cluster. The upper part of the model includes the RFID network, which contains: (1) Two RFID clusters (CLR_1, CLR_2), which perform the acquisition/input of RFID tags; (2) Two RFID inputs, which receive data packets generated by IoT RFID tags (RFID reader), and (3) Internet, which models the traditional Internet.

A Mediator MD is shared by all subnets in the model, i.e. it performs the IoT mediation function and interconnects (physically and logically) with other network elements for the purpose of mediating data for applications. The model adds four representative applications that process and consume the information leaving the mediator: (1) RFID, (2) Sensor, (3) SNMP management, (4) Smart Cities. These applications receive information from application gateways (GAs) and store them in databases. The SNMP application offers two types of services: (1) Trap and (2) Command/Response. In typical IoT, the databases can be reached by mobile or cell phone applications through the secure HTTPS protocol.

The lower part of Fig. 1 is an AdHoc Network that generates data traffic which is aggregated by the IoT mediator. It consists of the following elements:

– Seven sensor clusters (CLT_1....CLT_7); these are non-mobile and homogeneous for the sake of simplicity. However, the model does not restrict the addition of heterogeneous clusters. Each cluster consists of n internal mobile nodes, where n is a configurable parameter. In our example, we used ten mobile motes (Fig. 1);
– Four gateways or Internet nodes (GW_1....GW_4); both GW_1 and GW_2 are output gateways; GW_3 is an emergency gateway, i.e. it is used as a backup gateway for GW_1, e.g. when the latter overflows its internal buffers; both GW_4 and GW_2 are protocol converters, i.e. they are used to integrate two subnets;
– Seven inputs: they model data packets generated by IoT sensors;
– Three Internet outputs: they model the flow of IP packets outbound;
– Mote mobility: for the sake of simplicity in the validation, node mobility was disabled in the model;

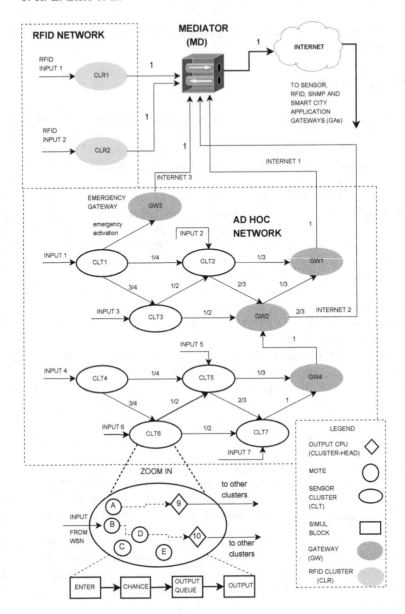

Fig. 1. IoT network model (Case 1).

- Input variables: data arrival and service time distributions in a node;
- Control variables: the probability of node connectivity in a cluster. This probability is provided by the Random Waypoint algorithm, which depends on a range of variables such as receiver threshold, area size, antenna type, height and gain, and system loss coefficient among others [6];

– Output variables: mean queue time and mean CPU utilization on each cluster for a given position of the motes in the cluster.

Each cluster is modeled as four simulation blocks connected in series:

1. *Enter block*: the enter block simulates the arrival of a packet in a cluster. It counts the number of packets entering the cluster;
2. *Chance* is a *decide block*, and it distributes the packets across a set of outgoing lines, where each line is associated with an outgoing queue; an important parameter in this block is the probability of packet loss, and its value was obtained from the case study (Sect. 5);
3. *Output queue* represents the queuing time in the outgoing line;
4. *Output cluster* simulates the output (i.e. forwarding) of packets from the cluster. It is also responsible for counting the number of packets leaving the cluster.

Each node receives packets at the input link and forwards them to one of the outbound links using UDP over IP (Datagram). If we assume that the arrival of requests for the RFID and AdHoc networks can be modeled as a Poisson process, the traffic volume of each individual mote can be extended to the traffic volume of a cluster by the simple sum of the rates of Poissonian arrivals. Thus, we sum the rates of each node to form a cluster of ten nodes. The configuration of clusters and CPU's is shown in Table 1.

4   Methodology for Validation

The methodology is based on the Jackson Network model. A Jackson network consists of a number of nodes, where each node represents a queue in which the service rate can be both node-dependent (different nodes have different service rates) and state-dependent (service rates change depending on queue lengths). Packets travel among the nodes following a fixed routing matrix. All packets at each node belong to a single "class" and packets follow the same service-time distribution and the same routing mechanism. Consequently, there is no notion of priority in serving the jobs: all packets at each node are served on a first-come, first-served basis.

4.1   Requirements for Validation

An AdHoc (or IoT) network of m interconnected clusters may be regarded as a Jackson network or Jacksonian network if it meets the following conditions:

1. If the network is open, any external arrivals to cluster i form a Poisson process;
2. All service times are exponentially distributed and the service discipline at all queues is a FIFO;
3. A packet completing service at queue i in a cluster head or gateway will either move to some new queue j in another cluster head or gateway with probability P_{ij} or leave the cluster or gateway with probability $1 - P_{ij}$, which, for an open network, is non-zero for some subset of the queues;
4. The utilization of all of the queues is less than one.

Table 1. Network configuration.

Function	Probabilities			Output CPUs		
GA_{12}	1			25		
GA_{34}	1			28		
GA_{57}	1			29,33		
GA_8	1			19,34		
AdHoc submodel	1,1,1,1			30,31,32,33		
CLR_1	1			21		
CLR_2	1			22		
MD	1/2, 1/2			24, discard		
GWI	1/3,1/3,1/3			23, 26, 27		
—	Vanet	Manet	Disaster	Manet	Vanet	Disaster
GW_1	1	1	0	5	5	0
GW_2	1/3, 2/3	1/3, 2/3	0	11,6	0	0
GW_3	1	1	1	14	14	14
GW_4	1	1	0	17	17	0
CLT_1	1	1/4, 3/4	0	1,2,20*	1, 20*	1,20*
CLT_2	1	1/3, 2/3	0	3,4	3	3
CLT_3	1	1/2, 1/2	0	7,8	8	8
CLT_4	1	1/4, 3/4	0	12,15	12	12
CLT_5	1	1/3, 2/3	0	16,13	13	13
CLT_6	1	1/2, 1/2	0	9,10	10	10
CLT_7	1	1	0	18	18	18

*output-CPU 20 to GW_3 is used only in an emergency

Once these conditions are met, the methodology for validation can be applied. It consists of a number of steps as outlined in the following sub-section.

4.2 Composition of the R Matrix

The R matrix, Table 2, is formed by the probability of transmission of each link between clusters in the network. It may be obtained by the simple inspection of Fig. 1, as in the example of Manet (Case 1). Specifically, we observe the probabilities of the outgoing links between the clusters in the system. The probabilities must be estimated in each real-world case, and in our model they are given input data. The R matrix has N × N dimension, where N is the number of nodes (i.e. GW, CLT, MD and CLR) in the network. Since in our example we have 14 nodes, the R matrix is a 14 × 14 matrix.

4.3   Composition of the γ Vector

γ is a vector where each element γ_i is a rate of packet generation at a cluster and destination node MD. It expresses the aggregated traffic generated in all elements (i.e. motes, vehicles, or smartphones) in the network. This is a 1×14 vector, since there are fourteen elements in the network. The γ vector for uncongested traffic is given by the vector $\gamma = [\gamma_1, \gamma_2, \gamma_3, ...0, 0, 0..\gamma_N]$. Note that the null elements are related to the devices (i.e. intermediate systems such as gateways), that do not generate traffic, i.e. they only relay packets from one input link to an output link.

4.4   Finding λ

The matrix equation that solves the Jackson network and allows us to find the arrival rate λ is given as follows:

$$\lambda = \gamma[I - R]^{-1}, \tag{1}$$

Once solved, it is given by the vector (2):

$$\lambda = [\lambda_1, \lambda_2, \lambda_3, ..., \lambda_N]. \tag{2}$$

where N is the number of nodes in the model (i.e. 14 in the sample network of Fig. 1).

4.5   Finding the Delays W_i at Each Node/Cluster

From the rates obtained from Eq. (2), it is possible to calculate the waiting time for each CPU (W_i, [i = 1....24]) by means of the Eq. (3), which gives the delay in an M/M/1 queue:

$$W_i = \frac{\lambda_i/\mu_i}{\mu_i - \lambda_i}, \qquad \mu_i = \frac{1}{\tau_i}, \tag{3}$$

where τ_i is duration of the transmission of a packet, and $1/\lambda_i$ is the packet arrival rate in a node (bps).

4.6   Running the Simulation Model

Clearly, the Jackson network is a collection of nodes connected by links that have the same exact topology of the simulation network model for the purpose of validation. The simulation model has to be run without channel/link losses for the sake of simplicity in the validation process. Once the model is validated, we may remove the assumption of perfect channel and introduce lossy channels due to e.g. node mobility.

The model may be deemed validated under the following conditions:

– First condition: $W_{i-calc} \approx W_{i-simul}$, i.e. the calculated delay equals the simulated delay for all nodes;

– Second condition: $\rho = \lambda_i/\mu_i$ and $\rho_{i-calc} \approx \rho_{i-simul}$, i.e. the calculated and the simulated utilization, i.e. within a certain confidence interval CI and significance value α (95%).

5   Case Study

In this section, we present three case studies using the model shown in Fig. 1. The first case is a full validation of the model using a MANET. It is a general case, whereas the two other cases approach more specific details (note that we omitted the full validation of cases 2 and 3 for the sake of space, and since it follows the same methodology). Once the model is validated in the first case, in the second case it is evolved (incremental validation) and applied to a VANET, and the Monte Carlo simulation is employed to the packet routing to minimize the delays in the network while maintaining the full communication amongst all nodes. In the third case, the main focus is to show the availability of the network in a disaster recovery scenario. It also consists of an evolution from case 1, but here all nodes are connected to a sink (emergency node).

5.1   Case 1 - MANET

The MANET is represented in the lower part of Fig. 1. This case under analysis is a network of low-capacity, low-cost and low-power devices (i.e. motes) which has the capability to sense a parameter of interest. The sensed parameter is relayed to a mediator through the network. Thus, the processing and transmission speeds are expected to be relatively low compared to the ones in traditional networks. Nevertheless, these features do not preclude the need for planning and dimensioning for the following reasons: (1) the number of devices can be quite large, which may amount to a correspondingly large traffic for a mediator; (2) an estimate of traffic allows the designer to determine the battery life of such system; (3) the capacity of the links must be determined to allow for an efficient use of the channel. Furthermore, the proposed model is general and scalable, i.e. it is not restricted to this class of networks, and thus higher-capacity networks with a larger number of devices may also be analyzed through this model. All connections are assumed to be wireless. However, the model does not restrict the use of wired connections. The probabilities of a packet being forwarded to an outgoing link are initially configured as shown in Fig. 1, assuming an estimation of this value (e.g. 1/4 from Cluster 1 to Cluster 2 and 3/4 from Cluster 1 to Cluster 3). Following the method proposed, we observed that all requirements for the application of the Jackson's Network model were met before we applied the Jackson model.

Composition of the R Matrix. The probabilities of the R-matrix were arbitrarily chosen (Table 2). In the real-world, these must be obtained from measurements or observations from the actual network.

Table 2. Case 1 - R matrix: probability of transmission per output link

——	CLT1	CLT2	CLT3	CLT4	CLT5	CLT6	CLT7	GW1	GW2	GW3	GW4	CLR1	CLR2	MD
CLT1	0	1/4	3/4	0	0	0	0	0	0	0	0	0	0	0
CLT2	0	0	0	0	0	0	0	1/3	2/3	0	0	0	0	0
CLT3	0	1/2	0	0	0	0	0	0	1/2	0	0	0	0	0
CLT4	0	0	0	0	1/4	3/4	0	0	0	0	0	0	0	0
CLT5	0	0	0	0	0	0	2/3	0	0	0	1/3	0	0	0
CLT6	0	0	0	0	1/2	0	1/2	0	0	0	0	0	0	0
CLT7	0	0	0	0	0	0	0	0	0	0	1	0	0	0
GW1	0	0	0	0	0	0	0	0	0	0	0	0	0	1
GW2	0	0	0	0	0	0	0	1/3	0	0	0	0	0	2/3
GW3	0	0	0	0	0	0	0	0	0	0	0	0	0	1
GW4	0	0	0	0	0	0	0	0	1	0	0	0	0	0
CLR1	0	0	0	0	0	0	0	0	0	0	0	0	0	1
CLR2	0	0	0	0	0	0	0	0	0	0	0	0	0	1
MD	0	0	0	0	0	0	0	0	0	0	0	0	0	0

CLT - cluster, GW - gateway, CLR - Cluster RFID, MD - mediator

Composition of the γ Vector and Finding λ. Two scenarios are considered, one for a uncongested network and the other for a congested network. The traffic generated in the congested network is shown in Table 3. For the congested network, we assumed a packet arrival each 0.4 s, which gives an arrival rate of $1/0.4 = 2.5$ packets/s. For the uncongested network, we assumed a packet arrival each 0.6 s, which gives an arrival rate of $1/0.6 = 1.67$ packets/s. This is a relatively low rate for conventional networks, it reflects a slow connection among battery operated motes in a sensor network. The mediator has a 5.0 packets/s generation rate (Table 3). This is 3×1.67 packets/s and it corresponds to the management traffic generated by the Simple Network Management Protocol (SNMP). Tables 3 and 4 show the rates calculated from Eq. 1 for both overload and uncongested traffic (i.e. decongested network).

Finding the Delays W_i at Each Node/Cluster and the Mean Global Delay. Equation 4 provides the total mean delay $\overline{W}$ for the network. For the simulation, the total mean delays was $\overline{W_s} = 247.3$ ms and the corresponding analytical value was $\overline{W_s} = 233.2$ ms, yielding a 5.7 % error. This error is a sufficient condition to allow the model to be deemed validated. Tables 5 and 6 show the analytical values of the mean traffic per CPU in the model.

$$\overline{W} = \sum \lambda_i \sum \gamma_i \cdot W_i \qquad (4)$$

$$W_i = \frac{\lambda_i/\mu_i}{\mu_i - \lambda_i}, \qquad \mu_i = \frac{1}{0.1} = 10 \qquad (5)$$

packets/s, where λ_i and μ_i are the rates for each CPU. Since all the delay values obtained from the simulation model matched the ones from the analytical model,

Table 3. Case 1 - calculated congested network traffic - arrival rates (γ and λ) in packets/sec

—	CLT1	CLT2	CLT3	CLT4	CLT5	CLT6	CLT7	GW1	GW2	GW3	GW4	CLR1	CLR2	MD
γ	2.5	2.5	2.5	2.5	2.5	2.5	2.5	0	0	0	0	1.67	1.67	5.0
λ	2.5	5.31	4.38	2.5	5.31	4.38	8.23	7.01	15.7	0	10.0	1.67	1.67	25.8

Table 4. Case 1 - calculated results for uncongested network traffic - arrival rates (γ and λ) in packets/sec

–	CLT1	CLT2	CLT3	CLT4	CLT5	CLT6	CLT7	GW1	GW2	GW3	GW4	CLR1	CLR2	MD
γ	1.67	1.67	1.67	1.67	1.67	1.67	1.67	0	0	0	0	1.67	1.67	5.0
λ	1.67	3.54	2.92	1.67	3.54	2.92	5.49	4.68	10.49	0	6.67	1.67	1.67	20

the simulation model may be deemed validated. This validation, is a crucial step since it allows further extensions to this model, i.e. the inclusion of other model features such as new types of distributions or new prioritization of services. Due to the high utilization of the mediator (output CPU 24), its service rate was increased 5 times (i.e. from 10 to 50 packets/s).

Running the Simulation Model. The initial distribution adopted for the arrival and service rate was the exponential. This distribution is suitable since (1) it allows the validation of the model by comparison with an analytical model; (2) it is the one that stresses the network (the worst case when there are no bursts). If the exponential distribution does not match the reality, it is possible to combine exponential distributions to form Erlang(k) distributions, which may better reflect and the actual traffic model in the network. Otherwise, if there are bursts in network, the Pareto or Hyper-exponential distributions may be employed, depending upon the application. Once the model is validated by incremental evolution other types of extensions may be studied.

Table 5. Case 1 - calculated results for congested traffic in each CPU (Erlang)

CPU	1	2	3	4	5	6	7	8	9	10	11	12
Traffic (Erl)	0.125	0.125	0.267	0.267	0.71	0.587	0.219	0.219	0.219	0.219	0.587	0.125
CPU	13	14	15	16	17	18	19	20	21	22	23	24
Traffic (Erl)	0.267	0	—	0.267	1.00	0.823	–	–	0.267	0.167	–	0.258

CPU 19 - application, CPU 20: Emergency, CPU 23, 25 to 34: Application, Total = 6.734 Erl

Regarding the 34 CPUs described in the general model, CPUs 1 through 24 (with the exception of 19 and 23) are part whose traffic was modeled as Jackson

Table 6. Case 1 - calculated uncogested traffic in each CPU (Erlang)

—	CPU ID											
CPU	1	2	3	4	5	6	7	8	9	10	11	12
Traffic	0.084	0.084	0.177	0.177	0.468	0.525	0.146	0.146	0.146	0.146	0.525	0.084
CPU	13	14	15	16	17	18	19	20	21	22	23	24
Traffic	0.177	0	0	0.177	0.667	0.549	0	–	0.167	0.167	–	0.20

CPU 19 - application, CPU 20: Emergency, CPU 23, 25 to 34: Application,
Total $= 4.896$ Erl

network. The other CPUs, from 25 to 34 (including 19 and 23) are part of the
applications proposed in the IoT network.

The traffic distribution for a MANET that consists of seven clusters, each
with 10 AdHoc users (Fig. 1), had the probabilities replaced by general values P_i
and $1 - P_i$ for each pair of outputs. Once the cluster utilization is known (or estimated), it is possible to dimension the network. After it is validated, it is possible
to move beyond the simple (e.g. exponential) and include new ones (i.e. not just
exponential), and other possible distributions. Table 7 shows the estimated traffic load for the uncongested network (in bps) (Table 6). By applying the equation
we obtain the values corresponding to λ in Table 2. The initial probabilities were
estimated as P12 $= 1/4$, P28 $= 1/3$, P32 $= 1/2$, P45 $= 1/4$, P57 $= 2/3$, P64 $= 1/2$,
and P77 $= 0$. The remaining probabilities for the GW's were unchanged.

Table 7. Results for the mediator (CPU 24)

—	CLT1	CLT2	CLT3	CLT4	CLT5	CLT6	CLT7	GW1	GW2	GW3	GW4	CLR1	CLR2	MD
γ	1.67	1.67	1.67	1.67	1.67	1.67	1.67	0	0	0	0	1.67	1.67	5
λ	1.67	3.54	2.92	1.67	3.54	2.92	5.49	4.68	10.49	0	6.67	1.67	1.67	20

Notice that GW3 does not forward traffic because it operates only during
disaster or emergency conditions. On the other hand, the clusters with 1.67 bps
do not relay traffic, they generate their only traffic (fresh traffic) CLT1, CLT4,
CLR1 and CLR2 only forward their own traffic (i.e. they are not used as relay
clusters). The assumption is that each cluster head has enough processing to turn
it stable, which is the case with $\mu_i = 10$ bps. The only exception is the mediator
(MD), considering $\mu_i = 50$ bps. The total rate resulted in 67.02 bps.

5.2   Case 2 - VANET

In this section, the network was configured as a VANET by changing the parameters of the Random Waypoint algorithm (e.g. speed, angle and range) and it
was submitted to the application of the Monte Carlo method for the minimization of the routing and consequently the total delay (thus reducing the number

of hops), which consequently resulted in the representation of each cluster with
a single cluster head.

Considering the dimensioning of a VANET in a freeway [2], we may optimize
the initial probabilities to obtain the least possible delay. We apply the Monte
Carlo method using Jackson Networks (implemented in Matlab), from an initial network condition. The Monte-Carlo optimization is based on the sorting of
the probabilities of connection between clusters (i.e. $P_{12}, P_{28}, P_{32}, P_{45}, P_{57}$, and
P_{64}), after which new arrival rates λ's were calculated using Eq. 1. The new values were compared with old ones and replaced for the next round (as the new
minimum) of execution if they resulted in a shorter delay (minimization function). An arbitrarily large number of runs was choses (320 million executions).
The communication between clusters contains now only one link (as opposed to
two link used in the initial MANET model).

Since P77 = 0, it was not incluced in the optimization. The results indicated
values near one (1) or near zero (0) and were approximated to one or zero,
i.e. P12 = 1, P28 = 1, P45 = 1, P32 = 0, P57 = 0, and P64 = 0. The sum of all
rates resulted in 66.22 bps (in this case). It is worth mentioning that there is an
analogy between the VANET optimization and the reduction in the road traffic.

5.3   Case 3 - Disaster Recovery (Worst-Case Scenario)

The fundamental issue in this case is network availability and reliability. All
probabilities P_{ij}'s are reset and all the traffic in the seven clusters is forwarded to
the GW3 gateway (emergency). Thus, the R-Matrix has all the elements related
to the CLT clusters (sensors) set to zero, except the ones from the GW3 column,
which are all 1's (one). The remaining rates were unaltered. The result indicated
that GW3 has to allow a flow of $7 \cdot 1.67 = 11.69$ bps. Thus, its processing capacity
has to be increased from 10 to 20 bps. Since the links are single links, they must
be duplicated for the sake of reliability. On the othe hand, within this context,
GW3 must also be duplicated. The rates are shown in Table 8.

Table 8. Case 3 - average arrival rates for each cluster

—	CLT1	CLT2	CLT3	CLT4	CLT5	CLT6	CLT7	GW1	GW2	GW3	GW4	CLR1	CLR2	MD
γ	1.67	1.67	1.67	1.67	1.67	1.67	1.67	0	0	0	0	1.67	1.67	5
λ	1.67	1.67	1.67	1.67	1.67	1.67	1.67	0	0	11.69	0	1.67	1.67	20.03

Another aspect to be taken into consideration is the loss of connectivity of
mobile devices. In [6], we have shown, through the Random Waypoint Algorithm,
that the loss of connectivity was around 5%. In order to absorb the loss of
connectivity, we suggest the insertion of a mobile macrocell that would cover
the whole area including the seven clusters, albeit incurring in increased costs.

6 Summary, Remarks and Discussion

In this section, we add a number of considerations and issues related to the validation of the proposed simulation model:

1. *Methodology assessment.* The focus of this work is the modeling at the IP layer in order to evaluate the traffic and the delays of the network from the IP layer and above. The goal of the work is to analyze the behavior of the network at the transport layers, to allow the proper dimensioning of the network capacity. Thus, the physical and data link layer are abstracted away. The behavior of the network at the IP layer captures the characteristics of the lower layers. For example, a noisy link channel would have a larger impact on the delays at the IP layer. The goal of the methodology is to validate the simulation model with an analytical model. The validated simulation model can then be run with measured data from a real-world network for network management. The performance parameters from the simulation model must approximate those of the analytical model in one first step. In a later step, the measured values should also approximate those from the simulation model in order to establish the correctness of the methodology. The methodology is based on well-established discrete event-simulation (using the Arena simulation tool). The full model is able to include behavior from the physical layer, e.g. mobility and packet losses and propagation model by the integration of the simulation tool with Matlab [7,8]. Once the model is validated, it is intended to be run with the actual features of the real-world input traffic (including packet size, input distributions or inter-arrival times). Priority messages and other real-world features are also easily incorporated in the simulation model according to the requirements.

2. *Network complexity.* The scope of this work is a simulation model (as opposed to a real-world network). Therefore, within this context, verification and validation of computer simulation models is conducted during the development of the simulation model with the ultimate goal of producing an accurate and credible model. The performance attributes that are under consideration are the delays in the queues (IP layer) and the processor utilization. For this purpose, the simulation model is compared with a network of queuing delays model (i.e. Jackson networks) which yields these same parameters under analysis. The goal of this paper is to validate a simulation model with an analytical one, which is one form of validation. However, one might be interested in modeling and validating features of the physical layer in isolation from the rest of the network. The modeling and simulation of the full features of the network is a challening task given the complexity of modern systems. However, in many cases, the designer is usually interested in designing, planning and dimensioning one or a few layers of the model, and the capturing the whole behavior of the network is in most cases unnecessary. In any case, the idea of using Jackson's network does not exclude the need, in the real case, to perform monitoring and measurements in the network to adjust the probability distributions and the parameters to be considered in

the simulation. There must be a feedback between the simulation model and the real world and vice-versa.

3. *Jackson network model.* The Jackson networks [4] used in the methodology belong to the field of queueing theory. The typical IoT network that was proposed has 14 global nodes. This type of configuration allows the adjustment of a Jackson network of size 14 X 14 nodes. For the purpose of validation, a Jackson network is a collection of queues (nodes) connected by links that have the same topology of the simulation network model (Fig. 1). The mapping of the physical topology of the network is captured by the analytical model through the R matrix (Table 2). From there, the correct application of the equations defined by the Jackson model [4] leads to the desired delays and processor utilizations. It is also possible through the model to calculate the mean global delays.

4. *Structure of case studies.* In Case 1 we have simulated the whole network in order to find out the network delays and processor utilization. In Case 2 we have not simulated the network, but instead we used the Jackson queueing model to minimize the network delays using the Monte Carlo method and the probabilites as the input parameter (to be randomly selected). On the other hand, in Case 3 (not a simulation case), we used the Jackson network to run a worst-case where all nodes have collapsed and all the traffic flows to the mediator through Gateway 3 (which has redundance and spare capacity). The topology used is the same in all cases (i.e. Fig. 1). One basic assumption is that the simulation model is to be fed with measurements from a real-world network, and these observations do capture the behavior of the protocols and their implementations. Therefore, the specifics about the protocols, the underlying technology and the implementation in use can be abstracted away without sacrificing the quality of results (delays and processor utilizations).

5. In particular, the use Jackson networks for the analytical model is relatively straightfoward, since the Jackson network has the same topology as the simulated network, and the analytical model is quite simple. The simulation model and the simulation results and confidence intervals were presented in [2, 5–8] and were not repeated in this work.

7 Conclusion

In this work, we have shown the steps towards validation of a simulation model with an analytical model based on Jackson networks. We have considered the mean delay for the total traffic in the network (flowing to the mediator MD or destination node) as the parameter for comparison. A basic model was validated and then two variants were added, one for a VANET and the second for an emergency scenario. The latter cases were validate through incremental validation, i.e. the models were slightly changed (their probabilities), thus resulting in validated increments.

In future work, we envisage the validation of the models considering the traffic for each CPU in the model individually. This would be carried out from a simple network and moving on to a more complex system. Another possible avenue would be the comparison of alternative approaches to validation, especially those stemming for the artificial intelligence domain.

References

1. Brodeen, A.E.M., Taylor, M.S.: A multivariate rank sum test for network simulation validation. In: Proceedings of TCC 1994 - Tactical Communications Conference, pp. 475–482, May 1994. https://doi.org/10.1109/TCC.1994.472085
2. Emiliano, J., Martins, P.S., Ursini, E.L.: Analysis of an AdHoc network in an intelligent transportation system. In: IEEE IEMCON 2018, pp. 1–7 (2018). https://doi.org/10.1109/IEMCON.2018.8615061
3. Fella, T., Goodman, C., Weston, P.: Validation of multi train simulation software. In: IET Conference on Railway Traction Systems (RTS 2010), pp. 1–4, April 2010. https://doi.org/10.1049/ic.2010.0033
4. Jackson, J.R.: Networks of waiting lines. Oper. Res. **5**(4), 518–521 (1957). https://doi.org/10.1287/opre.5.4.518
5. Leite, J.R.E., Ursini, E.L., Martins, P.S.: Integration of IoT with RFID and sensor networks: a literature review (in portuguese). In: Brazilian Technology Symposium (BTSym 2016), December 2017
6. Leite, J.R.E., Ursini, E.L., Martins, P.S.: Simulation of AdHoc networks including clustering and mobility. In: 16th International Conference on Ad Hoc Networks and Wireless (AdHocNow-2017), pp. 199–209, September 2017
7. Leite, J.R.E., Ursini, E.L., Martins, P.S.: Performance analysis of a multi-mode AdHoc wireless network via hybrid simulation. In: Brazilian Telecommunication Symposium (SBrT 2017) (2017)
8. Leite, J., Ursini, E.L., Martins, P.S.: Performance analysis of IoT networks with mobility via modeling and simulation. In: The International Symposium on Performance Evaluation of Computer and Telecommunication Systems (Summer Simulation 2018), July 2018
9. Martens, J., Pauwels, K., Put, F.: A neural network approach to the validation of simulation models. In: Proceedings of the 2006 Winter Simulation Conference, pp. 905–910, December 2006. https://doi.org/10.1109/WSC.2006.323174
10. Ursini, E.L., Martins, P.S., Timóteo, V.S., Massaro, F.R.: Modeling and simulation applied to link dimensioning of stream ip traffic with incremental validation. In: 2015 Winter Simulation Conference (WSC), pp. 3049–3060, December 2015. https://doi.org/10.1109/WSC.2015.7408408
11. Ursini, E.L., Timóteo, V.S., Santos, V.F., Martins, P.S.: An IP VPN network design and dimensioning approach using analytical-simulation models with incremental validation. In: Proceedings of the Winter Simulation Conference (WSC 2014), pp. 4095–4096, December 2014

Tracking of Rescue Workers in Harsh Indoor and Outdoor Environments

Rihab Lahouli$^{(\boxtimes)}$, Muhammad Hafeez Chaudhary, Sanjoy Basak,
and Bart Scheers$^{(\boxtimes)}$

Royal Military Academy, Brussels, Belgium
{Rihab.Lahouli,mh.chaudhary,Sanjoy.BASAK,bart.scheers}@rma.ac.be

Abstract. Making use of reliable and precise location and tracking systems is essential to save firefighters lives during fire operations and to speed up the rescue intervention. The issue is that Global Navigation Satellite System (GNSS) (e.g., GPS and Galileo) is not always available especially in harsh wireless environments such as inside buildings and in dense forests. This is why GNSS technology needs to be combined with auxiliary sensors like inertial measurement units (IMU) and ultra-wideband (UWB) radios for ranging to enhance the availability and the accuracy of the positioning system. In this paper, we report our work in the scope of the AIOSAT (Autonomous Indoor/Outdoor Safety Tracking System) project, funded under the EU H2020 framework. In this project, the Royal Military Academy (RMA) is responsible for developing a solution to measure inter-distances between firefighters, based on IEEE Std 802.15.4 compliant UWB radios. For these inter-distance measurements, accuracy better than 50 cm is obtained with high availability and robustness. Medium access control based on time division multiple access (TDMA) mechanism is also implemented to solve the conflict to access the UWB channel. As a result, each node in a network can perform range measurements to its neighbors in less than 84 ms. In addition, in this project, we are in charge of developing a long-range narrow-band communication solution based on LoRa and Nb-IoT to report updated positions to the brigade leader and the command center.

Keywords: Location · Tracking · Firefighters · UWB RF-ranging · LoRa · NB-IoT

1 Introduction

Real time localization and tracking of fire responders is an important feature in rescue services management, in order to ensure the safety of the rescue workers

Results incorporated in this paper received funding from the European GNSS Agency under the European Union's Horizon 2020 research and innovation program under grant agreement No 776425 Consortium: Ceit-IK4, ERM-KMS, SAXION, FRS Centrum, TSC.

© Springer Nature Switzerland AG 2019
M. R. Palattella et al. (Eds.): ADHOC-NOW 2019, LNCS 11803, pp. 48–61, 2019.
https://doi.org/10.1007/978-3-030-31831-4_4

and to accelerate the search and rescue process [1]. The satellite-based positioning technology, generally known as the global navigation satellite system (GNSS), allows rescue workers to operate efficiently, however, the reliability and accuracy of such a system are often poor or absent during fire operations, at places like dense forests, underground parking, and inside buildings.

In this context, our work fits in the framework of an EU H2020 project named AIOSAT (Autonomous Indoor/Outdoor Safety Tracking System). The main objective of the project is to develop an integrated positioning and alerting system that aims to overcome aforementioned limitations of GNSS usage in rescue interventions in harsh signal propagation environments, and to improve the safety of first responders [2].

For this purpose, GNSS absolute position estimate is improved by the satellite-based augmentation system provided by the European Geostationary Navigation Overlay System (EGNOS). Furthermore, support of inertial measurement units (IMU) and radio frequency (RF) UWB ranging transceivers will be used to face GNSS-disadvantaged environments. Accordingly, GNSS positions are enhanced with EGNOS and fused with position information inferred from IMU sensors and range measurements from UWB radios, to provide high availability and high integrity positioning and tracking information of all members in a rescue team. A robust wireless communication system based on three technologies: LoRa standard, narrowband IoT (NB-IoT) and Bluetooth 5 (BT5) will be used to report calculated positions of the individual team members to the brigade leaders and to the coordination center.

The task of the Royal Military Academy (RMA) in this project is to develop an RF system based on IEEE Std 802.15.4 compliant UWB transceivers to measure inter-distances between the firefighters [3]. In addition, our task consists also in the development of the long-range communication system of the AIOSAT project, to allow sending position data to the intervention supervisors using LoRa and NB-IoT links. BT5 communication sub-system is implemented by another partner in the project. Each firefighter will be equipped with a portable AIOSAT module, including a GNSS receiver, an IMU sensor, and an UWB radio. These modules are controlled by a main processor, typically a Raspberry Pi that performs mainly the fusion algorithm and controls communication flows.

Nowadays, many real-time indoor localization systems (RTLS), based on UWB transceivers are commercially available, from companies like: Decawave, Ubisense, Time Domain, Zebra and Nanotran. Traditionally, the RTLS system consists of multiple fixed reference points, called anchor nodes, with known positions and mobile tags with unknown positions [4]. The tags try to estimate their positions relative to the anchors [5]. In the AIOSAT project, it would be impractical to set out anchor nodes. Therefore, we propose to implement, on the integrated UWB transceivers, a ranging scheme to measure inter-distances between freely moving UWB nodes, without a need for fixed reference nodes. This inter-distance information can then be used to enhance the estimated positions of the portable AIOSAT modules. A time division multiple access (TDMA) mechanism is also implemented to control the UWB medium access. This medium access mechanism is important to schedule the time slots relative to the different devices in the network to perform their ranges estimate.

In this project, we used DW1001 miniaturized UWB transceivers from Decawave on which we implemented our ranging scheme. This device has an IEEE Std 802.15.4-2011 compliant radio (DW1000), and a microcontroller from Nordic Semiconductor (nRF52832) [5,6]. Tests results of range measurements between first responders developed using these devices are discussed in this paper.

The paper is organized as follows: Sect. 2 describes the architecture of the distributed AIOSAT system, Sect. 3 describes the RF-UWB ranging principle, the implemented scheme, and the scheduling mechanism. In Section 4, the experimental results of the UWB ranging system are presented and discussed. And finally, Sect. 5 describes the IoT communication solution and gives some field tests results and concluding remarks.

2   Architecture

2.1   Distributed System Architecture

On the next page, Fig. 1 represents the system level architecture of the AIOSAT system, which is designed in order to meet the user requirements. The rescue intervention is composed of few fire trucks staffed with 4 firemen, one fireman driver, and one brigade leader. They are supervised by a mobile coordination center (MCC). Each firefighter is equipped with an integrated AIOSAT module, composed of a GNSS receiver, an IMU and an UWB transceiver. The gathered data, from the three sensor systems, is locally processed at the level of the firefighters to give enhanced position estimates. The estimated positions are reported to the brigade leader and the MCC that are in charge of the coordination and control of the rescue operation. They are equipped with a visualization tool for the real-time tracking of moving resources. Estimated positions are sent using one of the two communication links (LoRa, NB-IoT) [2]. Downlink alert messages sent from higher levels to firefighters are also supported by this architecture.

2.2   Portable AIOSAT Module Architecture

In order to enhance the accuracy and availability of firefighters positions, their locations are measured from three types of sensors: GNSS, IMU, and UWB transceivers. The data of each sensor is locally published to a broker using the MQTT publish-subscribe based messaging protocol, then a fusion algorithm process those inputs to provide enhanced estimated positions that are sent over communication links to the team leaders and the MCC. This process is presented in Fig. 2 [2]. Our contribution in this project are following:

- Inter-distance ranging between firefighters in indoor environments measured using RF UWB technology. Firefighters are equipped with UWB transceivers

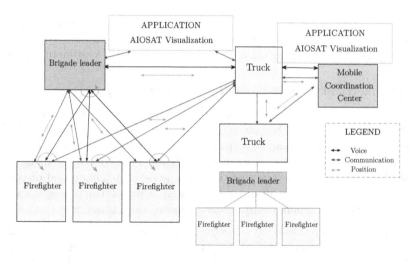

Fig. 1. Distributed AIOSAT system architecture.

that compute the range between them based on the time of flight (ToF) of exchanged packets.

- The transfer of enhanced positions from the firefighters to the brigade leader and to the MCC is ensured using either LoRa technology or NB-IoT if coverage is available [7].

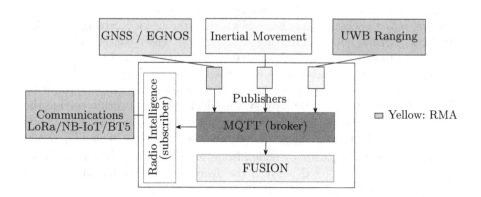

Fig. 2. AIOSAT portable module architecture.

3   RF-Ranging Principle

A promising positioning solution for areas with poor or no GNSS coverage, typically indoor environments, is to make use of RF-based UWB technology

[3]. The principle is to estimate the ToF of exchanged RF signals between UWB transceivers from which we can derive ranging information. A symmetrical double-sided two-way ranging (SDS-TWR) scheme is used to estimate this ToF.

3.1 Symmetrical Double-Sided Two-Way Ranging

The mechanism relies on time-stamping the instances when a packet leaves the transmitter and arrives at the receiver measured according to their own clocks. Figure 3 describes the messaging sequence that we applied for range measurement initiated by node i to all its 1-hop neighbors based on the SDS-TWR scheme. This ranging process is preceded by a phase of neighborhood discovery using so-called *hello* packets in order to draw up a list of 1-hop neighbors of a node. The SDS-TWR scheme relating two or more nodes is organized as follows:

- Node i starts by broadcasting a ranging request packet called *probe* to all its neighbors. This packet includes the beforehand carried out neighbors list.
- When receiving this *probe* packet, each UWB node that finds itself in the neighbors list sends a *response* packet after waiting a certain delay relative to its position on the list, that is to make the neighbors respond in a certain order. Although, those delays are dictated by the node i in its communicated neighbors list, they are measured independently according to each neighbors own clock.
- After sending *probe* packet, node i waits a predetermined time (c) relative to an estimation of the required waiting time to receive *response* packets from the last neighbor in the list, then it broadcasts the second packet called *feedback*.
- Upon receiving the *feedback* packet by the 1-hop neighbors, they reply by sending *report* packets where they include timestamps for receiving *probe* and *feedback* packets, and transmitting *response* and *report* packets. this allows the node i to estimate the ToF of the exchanged packets and thus to deduce the distances that separate it to each neighbor. The neighbors send *report* packets in an inverse order to the one used for sending *response* packets. With this order reversal, we have symmetrical delays between receiving the *feedback* ($T_{rx,j}^{f}$) and sending the *response* packet ($T_{tx,j}^{rs}$) by a neighbor node 'j' from one side and receiving the *report* packet from that node ($T_{rx,j}^{rp}$) and sending the *feedback* packet by node i from the other side ($T_{tx,i}^{f}$). In this way, a symmetry is also applied between the delay between sending the *feedback* packet ($T_{tx,i}^{f}$) and receiving the *response* ($T_{rx,j}^{rs}$) from neighbor 'j' in one side, and the delay between sending the *report* ($T_{tx,j}^{rp}$) and receiving the *feedback* packet ($T_{rx,j}^{f}$) from that neighbor, in the other side. Therefore, a precise estimation of the ToF and thereby of the range is guaranteed.
- Node i estimates the ToF to a neighbor node j, after receiving the corresponding *report* packet, as given by (1) [15].

$$t_{ToF} = \frac{(T_{rx,j}^{f} - T_{tx,j}^{rs}) - (T_{tx,i}^{f} - T_{rx,j}^{rs})}{4} + \frac{(T_{rx,j}^{rp} - T_{tx,i}^{f}) - (T_{tx,j}^{rp} - T_{rx,j}^{f})}{4}$$

(1)

The main optimization that we introduced to the original SDS-TWR scheme results in a reduced number of exchanged packets compared to the typical or classical implementation of the SDS-TWR. When ranging with k neighbors, our scheme requires $2+2k$ packets whereas the classical SDS-TWR would require $3k$ packets to do the ranging with the same number of nodes. This reduction in the packets is achieved by broadcasting *probe* and *feedback* packets to k neighbors, compared to the classical implementation where range measurement is done pairwise—in which case one *probe* packet and one *feedback* packet are required per node-pair. In addition, we reduce the error in the ToF estimation by reversing the order of sending *report* packets by the neighbors compared to the order of sending *response* packets. This ensures an accurate range estimate. With the ToF estimate and knowing the propagation speed of the RF signal, node i can estimate the range to all its 1-hop neighbors.

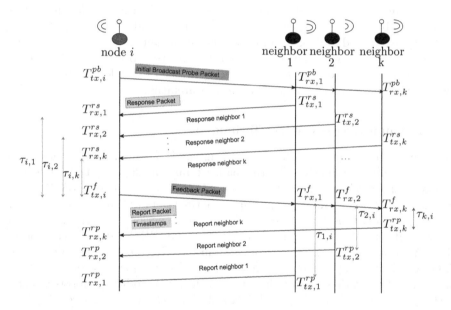

Fig. 3. Packet sequence exchange in SDS-TWR with 1-hop neighbors.

3.2   Performances

We need to minimize the ToF estimation error in order to enhance the accuracy of the calculated range between UWB radio nodes. The error in ToF estimate, and thereby in the range estimate, depends on the precision of the crystal oscillators driving the clocks of the nodes, and the waiting time between receiving a packet and transmitting the corresponding reply, as in (2) [3].

$$e \approx \frac{1}{4}(\tau_{j,i} - \tau_{i,j})(\epsilon_i - \epsilon_j). \tag{2}$$

Where e denotes the estimation error in ToF for SDS-TWR, assuming both participating nodes remain static. The drifts on the clocks of the two ranging nodes are denoted by ϵ_i and ϵ_j. We can see that the error in ToF estimate for SDS-TWR, is proportional to the difference in $\tau_{i,j}$ and $\tau_{j,i}$, which denotes the waiting times between receiving a packet and sending the corresponding *response* packet for given node i and its neighbor j, respectively (c.f., Fig. 3). The delay depends on the packet airtime, radio turnaround time, and required time to process the ranging packet. Note that, these waiting times are on the order of a few milliseconds, while their difference $\tau_j - \tau_i$ can be easily controlled to the order of a few tens of microseconds using low stability commodity clocks. It is important to notify that the timestamps are captured close to the physical layer, consequently, the jitter is minimal. For example, for a difference of waiting times between two ranging UWB nodes of $100\,\mu s$, with clocks drift of 8 parts per million (ppm), we have an error on the ToF estimate of about 0.2 ns. Knowing that, for a target ranging accuracy of 33 cm, the estimated ToF needs to lie within 1 ns of the true ToF given the speed of light. We can conclude, that the SDS-TWR can provide required ranging accuracy despite significant clock errors. Note that each 1-hop neighbor will include also, its own estimated position, in the *response* packet that it sends to node i, as this will be needed by node i to estimate its own position based on the inter-distance measurements.

3.3 Medium Access Control Technique

To support conflict-free measurements using the UWB link, it is important to use a scheduling mechanism. To this end, we implemented a TDMA medium access control mechanism, where the transmissions of the different UWB nodes in a neighborhood, are arranged in respective time slots within a periodic frame. In each allocated time slot, the corresponding node performs ranges estimate to all its neighbors. We chose to use 1 pulse per second (PPS) signal to synchronize the UWB frames. We get the PPS signal from the GNSS receiver included in the AIOSAT module as presented in Fig. 2. The results of implementation and tests of this synchronization scheme show that each UWB module performs ranging with up to 11 neighbors within a TDMA slot of 83.33 ms. Therefore, 12 UWB nodes can perform range estimate to each other in their corresponding time slots in a frame of 1 s.

4   Experimental Results of the RF-Ranging System

We want to reduce the duration of the ranging sequence presented in Fig. 3. To this end, we need to reduce the size of the exchanged packets. The packet airtime can be reduced by decreasing the preamble length (number of symbols) and increasing the data rate. Tests are required to assess the influence of these two parameters on the ranging performance in terms of success rate of ranging sessions, and accuracy and precision of range measurements. We assume that a ranging session has succeeded when all packets needed to be exchanged are properly received, see Fig. 3, and we are able to calculate the distance. For each of the tests that we will discuss in this section, we conducted a set of 1000 measurements and out of that we counted the number of the succeeded ranging sessions. This number out of the total attempted sessions gives us the ranging sessions success rate.

To this end, we have used Decawave DWM1001 UWB transceivers to implement our modified SDS-TWR algorithm that provides range measurements between an initiating UWB node and its dynamically discovered neighbors. These devices support 7 frequency channels among 16 channels provided by the IEEE 802.15.4 standard and 4 different bandwidths [3,5]. For the tests, we configure the transceivers to operate on channel 5 [6240–6739.2 MHz] for which the integrated antenna on the DW1001 module is tuned [5]. Decawave gives the possibility to configure its devices on three different data rates (110 kb/s, 850 kb/s and 6.8 Mb/s), and 7 different preamble lengths (64, 128, 256, 512, 1024, 2048, 4096) [6]. In fact, the sensitivity of the DW1000 radio improves as we go from the highest data rate to the lowest available one [14]. Moreover, the choice of the preamble length affects the ability of the receiver to detect the incoming signal in the noise [14].

We conducted a series of tests for different radio parameters (e.g., data rate and preamble), and in different locations (e.g., outdoor, indoor). For each test setup, we collected 1000 range measurements which enable us to compute descriptive statistics of the results (e.g., ranging session success rate, average range, and standard deviation of the measured range). With these descriptive statistics we characterize the performances of the implemented ranging algorithm. By decreasing the data rate and increasing the preamble length, it is expected that the UWB communication reliability and operational range will improve in free space line-of-sight (LoS) scenario [6]. Nevertheless, this leads to an increase in the packet airtime, with corresponding increase in the required time to conclude a range session, and consequently increases error in range estimation. Based on the test results we find that we need to make a trade-off between the availability and the precision of the ranging on one side and the range session duration on the other side.

We conducted the first set of tests in an outdoor environment with LoS. The main objective of these tests is to identify the maximum operational range that can be achieved for different configurations of data rates and preamble lengths as resumed by Table 1. In order to look for the maximum achievable range, we increase progressively the separating distance between the UWB transceivers and we stop at a threshold of ranging sessions success rate that we fixed at 80%. Success rate, mean range and standard deviation have been depicted in Fig. 4. From the figure we can find that the range sessions success rates is always better than 80% for all the tests. The mean range is calculated as the average value over all the range measurements. We also measured the systematic error for these sets of tests as given in Table 1. The systematic error represents the error between the measured distance and the actual distance measured manually using a laser range finder. The systematic errors are mainly caused by antenna delays [15,16]. Therefore, transceiver calibration is required to eliminate this error. Consequently, further better accuracy are expected on the range estimate [15].

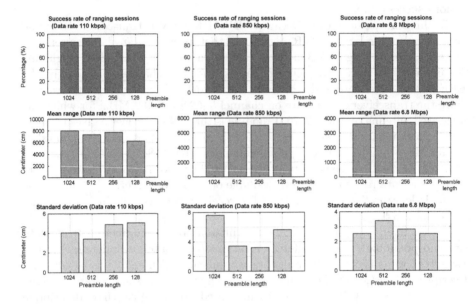

Fig. 4. Success rate, mean range and standard deviation of measurements in outdoor tests for various data rates and preamble lengths.

It is important to note that in outdoor open spaces, the most common form of multipath is caused by RF reflections from the ground that can interfere constructively or destructively (causing fading) with the direct path signal at the receiver [14]. For this reason, we need to take this fading effect into consideration before we start recording the measurements. We can see from Fig. 4 that the standard deviation remains less than 8 cm. We can also notice that the highest maximum range, which is 80 m, is reached as we operate with the lowest data rate (110 kb/s) combined with the highest preamble lenfth (1024). The maximum operational range achieved for a data rate of 850 kb/s is also important (between 70 and 73 m) which is sufficient for AIOSAT system requirements. What is also interesting in this data rate is that the maximum range does not vary more than 3 cm for the 4 different preamble lengths, moreover, the standard deviation is limited to 3.2 cm for a preamble length of 256.

Using this combination of data rate and preamble length (850 kb/s and 256) can provide us a good operational range and accuracy for AIOSAT ranging sub-system. We can see in Table 2 that the systematic error for this configuration is lowest (23 cm) compared to the other data rates and preamble lengths combinations. This configuration is preferred to the first one (a data rate of 110 kb/s and a preamble length of 1024) because the airtime of the frame is lower and so is the

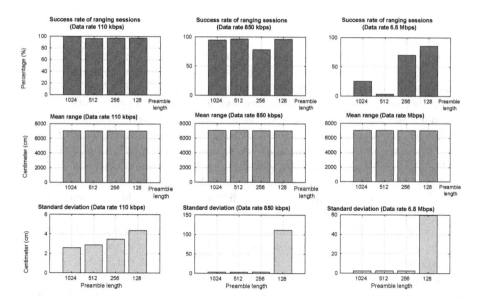

Fig. 5. Success rate, mean range and standard deviation of measurements in indoor tests with a fixed distance of 70 m and for various data rates and preamble lengths.

Table 1. Summary of outdoor tests for different data rates and various preamble lengths.

Data rate	110 kb/s			
Preamble length	1024	512	256	128
Average range (m)	80	73	77	62
Average systematic error (cm)	42	38	36	37
Data rate	**850 kb/s**			
Preamble length	1024	512	256	128
Average range (m)	70	73	70	72
Average systematic error (cm)	27	38	3	25
Data rate	**6.8 Mb/s**			
Preamble length	1024	512	256	128
Average range (m)	36	35	37	37
Average systematic error (cm)	41	5	43	42

range session duration. For example for the *report* packet which is the longest one with 44 bytes payload, the airtime is estimated at 0.65 ms for 850 kb/s and 256, compared to 4.13 ms for 110 kb/s of data rate and 1024 of preamble length. We can assume from Fig. 4 and Table 1 that we need to give up the option of operating at 6.8 Mb/s for the AIOSAT project, due to its lowest maximum range (less than 37 m) and its high systematic error (more than 41 cm).

In addition to these outdoor experiments, we also conducted tests inside a building where we positioned the two UWB nodes in a corridor of more than 80 m long with a LoS. In this typical indoor environment maximum range that can be achieved is expected to be larger to the quoted for outside free space, because on top of the ground reflection we have additional multi-path reflections from walls that give extra usable receive signal [6]. Figure 5 presents the results of indoor tests for different configurations of data rates and preamble lengths. In this case, the separation between the two nodes is fixed at a distance of 70 m. Success rate, mean range and standard deviation are presented in Fig. 5. We can see that the range sessions success rate remains higher than 77 % for data rates of 110 and 850 kb/s for the different preamble lengths. The standard deviation stays less than 5 cm for all cases in the figure except for the configuration of 850 kb/s data rate and 128 preamble length where the standard deviation reaches as much as 1.1 m. This latter combination is excluded from use in the AIOSAT project. The ranging success rate is very low (less than 25 %) for a data rate of 6.8 Mb/s with preamble lengths of 1024 and 512. For this data rate combined with a preamble length of 128, the standard deviation is very high (about 60 cm), so we exclude these last combination too. We can use a data rate of 6.8 Mb/s combined with a preamble length of 256 where the success rate is about 70 %. To conclude, considering the tests results performed in outdoor environment for maximum operational ranges, and the experiments results conducted in indoor with fixed distance, and with a concern to minimize the UWB frame airtime and consequently the range session duration, we assume that the combination that fits more to this compromise is the one with 850 kb/s data rate and 256 preamble length.

5   Communication System

The transfer of firefighters computed positions is ensured using long range communication links (LoRa and NB-IoT). We have established on computer a private LoRa network based on an open-source implementation of LoRaWAN network server [8].

The firefighters are equipped with LoRa end-devices from Pycom (FiPy) [9]. For NB-IoT connectivity, FiPy module can be used with a SIM card that provides access to the NB-IoT network. Bidirectional LoRa communication is implemented on Pycom class-A end devices. LoRa uplink communication serves to send updated firefighters positions to the brigade leader and the MCC. Over-the-air authentication is used by the end devices to join the LoRa network. We also implemented the Listen Before Talk Adaptive Frequency Agility (LBT AFA) protocol to access LoRa frequency channels; in order to avoid the end device transmit duty cycle limitation of 1% imposed by the ETSI regulations [10], and to lower the risk of collisions. LoRa downlink communication has also been implemented in order to send alert messages from LoRa network to Pycom devices. A MultiConnect Conduit IP67 gateway is used to relay messages between end devices and the central LoRa local Network at the backend [11]. It is attached to the light pole of the firefighters truck and connected via Ethernet to the local network as presented in Fig. 6. It forwards the received messages from the end-devices to the LoRa server. This gateway is dedicated for outdoor environments and it supports LTE back haul capabilities [11]. In some scenarios, we can use more than one gateway in a rescue intervention, all forwarding packets to the same local network server. Transmitted messages in this case can be received by all gateways, where duplicated packets are removed by the LoRa server.

Fig. 6. Field test setup of LoRa communication.

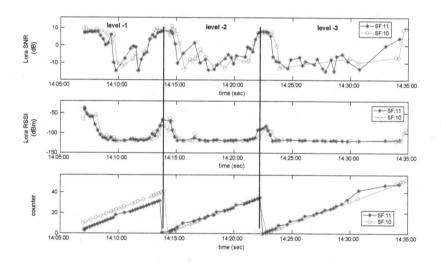

Fig. 7. LoRa tests in a parking scenario.

When NB-IoT coverage exists, FiPy devices are configured to send data using NB-IoT uplink to the operator server. In rescue interventions in Belgium, we use orange network [13]. Field tests of LoRa and NB-IoT communications have been performed in an underground parking in Ghent, Belgium, in collaboration with the fire station center of Ghent (FRS Centrum). The goal is to test the communication system in a critical underground fire scenario. This parking is situated in the center of Ghent, which is an old construction composed of 3 levels in the underground. Figure 7 presents the tests results in terms of SNR and RSSI of LoRa communication using FiPy devices with spreading factors of 10 and 11. We chose these high spreading factors to make the demodulation of received packets possible even with very low SNR [12]. For the tests we sent packets using sequence numbers as a useful data with an interval of 12 s. This sequence number is used to track the successfully transmitted packets and the lost ones. The success rate of transmitted packets from the −3 level to the gateway placed on a firefighter truck at the entrance of the parking is of 50% with a spreading factor of 11. NB-IoT communication have also been tested in this parking but the communication was bad. We could not transmit packets successfully from −3 level. So for this critical scenario, we prefer to use LoRa communication solution for sending estimated positions of the rescue workers to the command center.

6   Conclusion

The aim of the AIOSAT tracking and alerting project is to exploit the positioning, ranging and communication subsystems to develop an application that provides mobile situational awareness. Members positions, inter-distances, and other sensor information are fused to give enhanced position estimates and alerting functionality supporting the decision-making and safety operations of the mission members. In this paper, we reported our work on developing the RF-UWB ranging sub-system to measure the inter-distances between firefighters. Experiments in outdoor and indoor scenarios have been conducted and discussed in order to characterize the influence of relevant parameters such as the data rate and the preamble length, on the ranging performances in terms of availability, accuracy, and precision. Furthermore, a long-range communication system based on LoRa and NB-IoT has been implemented and results from field tests in a critical underground fire scenario have been presented in this paper.

References

1. Ferreira, A.G., Fernandes, D.M., Catarino, A.P., Monteiro, J.L.: Localization and positioning systems for emergency responders: a survey. IEEE Commun. Surv. Tutor. **19**, 2836–2870 (2017). https://doi.org/10.1109/COMST.2017.2703620
2. AIOSAT: Autonomous Indoor/Outdoor Safety Tracking System. http://www.aiosat.eu/
3. IEEE Std. 802.15.4-2011: IEEE Standard for Local and Metropolitan Area Networks Part 15.4: Low-Rate Wireless Personal Area Networks (LR-WPANs) (2011)
4. Dardari, D., Closas, P., Djuric, P.M.: Indoor tracking: theory, methods, and technologies. IEEE Trans. Veh. Technol. **64**, 1263–1278 (2015). https://doi.org/10.1109/TVT.2015.2403868
5. Decawave: DWM1001 System Overview And Performance. http://www.decawave.com/products/dwm1001-module
6. Decawave: DWM1000 user manual. http://www.decawave.com/products/dwm1000-module

7. Martinez, B., Adelantado, F., Bartoli, A., Vilajosana, X.: Exploring the performance boundaries of NB-IoT. IEEE Early Access Artic. IEEE Internet Things J. 1–1 (2019). https://doi.org/10.1109/JIOT.2019.2904799
8. LoRa Server, open-source LoRaWAN network-server. https://www.loraserver.io/
9. Pycom, support-community. https://docs.pycom.io/
10. LoRa Alliance Technical Committee: LoRaWAN 1.0.2 Regional Parameters, Revision B, February 2017
11. MultiConnect® Conduit® IP67 Base Station: IP67 Conduit for Outdoor LoRa® Deployments (MTCDTIP Series). https://www.multitech.com/brands/multiconnect-conduit-ip67
12. Mekki, K., Bajic, E., Chaxel, F., Meyer, F.: A comparative study of LPWAN technologies for large-scale IoT deployment. ScienceDirect ICT Express (2018). https://doi.org/10.1016/j.icte.2017.12.005
13. AllThingsTalk, Innovate your business with the Internet of Things. https://docs.allthingstalk.com/
14. Decawave: APS017 Appplication Note: Maximizing Range IN DW1000 Based Systems. http://www.decawave.com/products/dwm1000-module
15. Chaudhary, M. H., Scheers, B.: Software-defined wireless communications and positioning device for iot development. In: IEEE Xplore, 2016 International Conference on Military Communications and Information Systems, ICMCIS, ICMCIS, Brussels (2016). https://doi.org/10.1109/ICMCIS.2016.7496555
16. Decawave: APS014 Appplication Note: Antenna Delay Calibration of DW1000-Based Products and Systems. https://www.decawave.com/application-notes/

Topology Discovery Delay Evaluation in Star Topology Network with Switched-Beam Antenna Sink

Guéréguin Der Sylvestre Sidibé[✉], Hamadoun Tall, Raphael Bidaud,
Marie-Françoise Servajean, and Michel Misson

Clermont Auvergne University/LIMOS CNRS, Aubière, France
guereguin_der_s.sidibe@uca.fr,
{hamadoun.tall,raphael.bidaud,marie-francoise.servajean,
michel.misson}@uca.fr

Abstract. Wireless Sensor Networks (WSNs) are useful in several application domains. They are often used for data gathering in an interested area. The popularity of WSNs is due to their ease of deployment and auto-configuration capabilities. A WSN network is composed by several sensor nodes that must cooperate and build the network where each node is in range of at least one other node. In star network topology, the sink node is in range of the all others and the communication from each node to the sink is assumed to be a single hop. So, the sink node can discover all the others nodes around it belonging to the star topology.

In most cases, the network set-up phase begins with a topology discovery. One usual way for the discovery process is to allow each node to broadcast hello messages during a given period of time. When the sink located at the center of the star topology is equipped with a directional antenna, this discovery process has to be done for each beam direction of the sink antenna. In this work we are dealing with a star topology having a sink with a directional switched-beam antenna. In such case, the connectivity between the sink and other nodes is intermittent.

In this paper, we present an optimized approach called WAYE that helps to reduce the network discovery time using a sink with a switched-beam antenna. The performance evaluation using Contiki Os Cooja simulator shows that the proposed approach outperforms the IEEE 802.15.4 CSMA/CA algorithm with directional and omni-directional antenna.

Keywords: Switched topology · Directional antenna · Network discovery delay · Star topology · Wireless Sensor Network · Medium access protocol

1 Introduction

Thanks to their ease of deployment and auto-configuration capabilities, Wireless Sensor Networks (WSNs) are useful and applied in many aspects of our daily

© Springer Nature Switzerland AG 2019
M. R. Palattella et al. (Eds.): ADHOC-NOW 2019, LNCS 11803, pp. 62–73, 2019.
https://doi.org/10.1007/978-3-030-31831-4_5

life such as home monitoring [1], heath care monitoring [2], industrial plan monitoring [3], or volcanic earthquake monitoring [4]. In most cases, WSNs are used for data collection where all nodes that collect data need to transmit them to a central node usually called the sink in the literature. In star topology, data collecting nodes are in the communication range of the sink and multi-hop data transmission is not necessary.

Several works in the literature show that directional antennas are benefit for wireless networks, such as increasing network capacity [5], extending transmission range [6] and reducing energy consumption [7]. However, when directional antennas are used, many trivial mechanisms, such as medium access protocol, routing protocols and neighbor discovery, become more challenging and need to be redesigned.

In this work, we propose a directional antenna based network discovery approach to help the sink node to discover the whole network topology at the network start-up phase. The proposed mechanism is applied in a star network topology where the sink is equipped with a directional antenna and an omni-directional antenna for the other nodes.

The efficiency of the approach is evaluated and compared to the well-known CSMA/CA protocol with and without directional antenna at the sink node. The obtained results using the Contiki OS Cooja simulator show that the proposed mechanism is efficient compared to CSMA/CA protocol.

The rest of the paper is organized as follows. In Sect. 2, we present an overview of the related works dealing with neighbor discovery with directional antennas. The different assumptions used in this work and our proposed neighbor discovery mechanism called WAYE (Who Are You Enquiry) are described in Sect. 3. In Sect. 4, we present the simulation environmental, the simulation parameters and the obtained results. Section 5 conclude the paper and state future work.

2   Related Work

In wireless network with directional antennas, many early works such as [5,7,8] have been done showing the advantages of directional antennas over omni-directional antennas. The benefit of the directional antennas are several kinds such as extending transmission range [5,8], increasing network capacity and reducing energy consumption [7]. In [5], two neighbor discovery schemes were compared: (i) in the first scheme, omni-directional antennas are used and all neighbors discovery *Hellos* message are sent omni-directionally; (ii) in the second scheme directional antennas are used and *Hellos* messages are sent directionally. Nodes in the both mechanisms use CSMA/CA to access to medium. Authors argue that the generated topology with neighbor discovery exploiting directional antennas is better because Hellos messages can travel farther; they also found that when beam forming antennas are used, the CSMA is unsuitable due to collisions.

Probabilistic neighbor discovery algorithms with directional antennas were proposed in [9]. The authors discussed the choice of antenna beamwidth, they showed that the choice depends on the time Δt allocated for the neighbor discovery process. When Δt is small, it is shown that large beamwith is preferable because it results in a greater number of discovered neighbors. However, in case Δt is large, narrower beamwidths are a good choice. A large beamwidth covers a more large transmission area that can cause greater collision than a small beamwidth. But it has the advantage to allow many nodes to receive transmissions simultaneously.

The authors in [10] also proposed two kind of neighbor discovery algorithms: scan based algorithms exploiting directional antennas and random based algorithms using omni-directional antennas. They showed that algorithms exploiting directional antennas outperformed those using omni-directional antennas in terms of data discovery delay.

In [11], authors compared the performance of CSMA based protocol with MDMAC (Memory guided Directional MAC) protocol in which they added a randomized neighbor discovery. MDMAC is directional MAC protocol for millimeter wave networks. The authors shown through simulations results that the MDMAC protocol outperforms the CSMA based protocol in term of throughput. They also shown that the MDMAC throughput is improved when the antenna beamwith is small.

Through the existing works, we notice that directional antennas have several advantage in wireless communication. Such as extending the communication range [6], increasing the network capacity [5] and reducing the energy consumption. However, due to the particularity of the directional antennas and its difference to the omni-directional ones, most of the medium access schema and network discovery mechanisms must be adapted or redesigned to feet directional antennas. In this work we propose a new mechanism used for neighbors discovery by a sink equipped with directional antennas.

3   System Description

3.1   Directional Antenna Model

The directional antenna model considered and used at the sink node in this paper, is composed of 12 overlapped sectors or beams that cover the entire omni-directional 360° plane as shown in Fig. 1. Each beam width is about 30° and has one main lobe, two side lobes and one back lobe as depicted in Fig. 2. The antenna sectors can be activated independently but two or more can not be activated at the same time. The antenna model is proposed in [12].

3.2   The System Model and the Network Topology

A star wireless network as shown in Fig. 3 is considered in this work, where the central node (sink) is equipped with a switched beam directional antenna and sensor nodes randomly deployed around the sink are using omni-directional antenna. Furthermore, the following assumptions are made for this work:

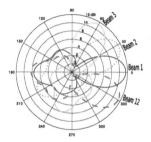

Fig. 1. Directional antenna beams

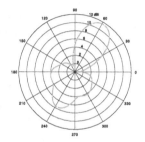

Fig. 2. Single beam orientation

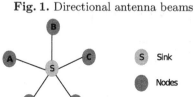

Fig. 3. Star topology

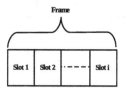

Fig. 4. The structure of the frame

1. Each node has an unique identifier (ID).
2. The discovery process is started by a request of the sink node.
3. Sink node can detect collisions.
4. Time is divided into several time slots called a frame as shown in Fig. 4.
5. The network topology is assumed to be stable during the discovery process.

In Table 1, we presents the different parameters and terms used in this paper.

Table 1. Parameters and terms

Parameters	Definition
S_0	Number of idle slots (a slot in which no node responds)
S_1	Number of successful slots (a slot in which the sink receives correctly a response)
S_2^*	Number of collided slots (a slot in which a collision occurs due to simultaneous transmissions of two or more nodes.)
N	The number of sensor nodes in the network
K	Switched beam antenna sectors or beams number. $K = 12$
NS	Allocated time slots number by the sink node

3.3 WAYE: The Proposed Neighbor Discovery Protocol

In this section we present WAYE (Who Are You Enquiry), our proposed mechanism. It helps the sink node to discover its neighboring nodes, and is based on dynamic time slotting. The discovery process is divided into cycles and triggered by the sink. Each cycle begins with a sink discovery request message (as shown in Fig. 5) called WAYE.

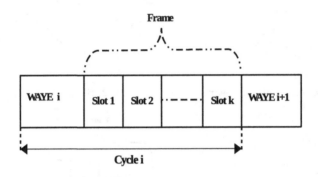

Fig. 5. Cycle in WAYE protocol

3.4   The Description of the WAYE Algorithm

At the beginning of the discovery process, the sink selects its antenna sector (Sector 0 in Fig. 1) and initializes the first cycle by sending WAYE toward its neighbor nodes that are located in the sector coverage area. The WAYE contains the current sector number (Sector ID), the initial number of allocated time slot (NS) that will be used by neighbor nodes to send their reply message, and the list of discovered nodes ID. It stays in the selected sector sending discovery request cycle after cycle until all neighboring nodes located in that sector are found, then it goes to the next sector, put the number of allocated time slot to the initial value and set the list of discovered nodes ID to empty. In each cycle, the sink checks the outcome of each allocated time slot. The sink uses these outcomes to estimate the number of its potential neighbors and decides whether more cycles are needed or not. A time slot has three possible outcomes as presented in Fig. 6:

1. Slot with collision which occurs when two or more nodes try to reply in the same slot.
2. Slot with success when only one node selects and replies in that slot
3. Idle slot, which indicates that no neighbor node has selected the slot.

When a node hears the sink WAYE, it reads the current sector ID and the number of allocated time slots (NS), and checks if its ID is in the sink discovered list. If it finds that it is among the sink discovered nodes, it remains silent for next cycles related to the current sector. Otherwise, it selects randomly a slot in [1, NS] in which it will send its reply message named "Hello" to the sink. After a node sends its Hello, it waits for the next cycle.

Whenever the sink receives correctly a reply message from a neighboring node, it adds that node ID to its list of discovered node.

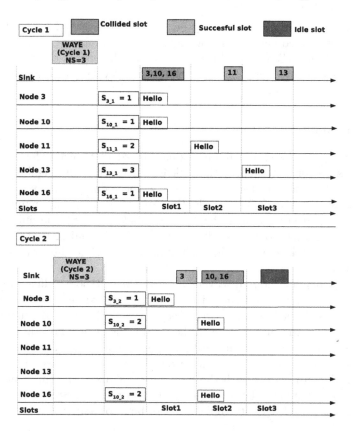

Fig. 6. Possible outcomes for a time slot. In this figures S_{x_y} means selected slot for node x at the cycle y

3.5 Estimation of the Number of Sink Neighbors

In each cycle, the sink checks each time slot status. For a given time slot, if the sink receives correctly a Hello from a neighbor, it increments the counter of successful slots (S_1). If a collision is detected, it increments the counter of collided slots (S_2^*). Otherwise, the sink consider the slot as idle slot and increments the counter of idle slots (S_0). At the end of the cycle, the sink uses the value of S_0, S_1 and S_2^* to estimate the number of its neighboring nodes according to the following relation: $S_1 + (1.5 - \frac{S_0}{NS}) \times 2 \times S_2^*$. At the beginning of each cycle, S_0, S_1 and S_2^* are set to zero.

3.6 Time Slots Adjustment

The allocated time slots number (NS) is different from one cycle to another as it is dynamically adjusted by the sink. At the end of a cycle, the sink estimates the number of its neighbors and the remaining nodes to be discovered in the next cycle. The number of remaining nodes to be discovered is the difference between the estimated number of neighbors and the number of discovered nodes in the current cycle. Based on this estimation at the end of current cycle, the sink allocates a number of time slots for the next cycle which is closer to the number of remaining nodes.

3.7   Time Slots Adjustment

The discovery process ends when the sink has visited all its sectors for discovering neighbors. A sector is visited, if the sink has discovered all neighbor nodes in that sector. The neighbor discovery in each sector is done cycle by cycle by the sink. For a given sector, if after a cycle, the sink observes that the number of idle slots (S_0) is equal to the number of allocated slots $(S_0 = NS)$, the sink initializes a new cycle containing only one allocated slot. At the end of that cycle, if no node replies, the sink considers that it has discovered all neighbors and switches to the next sector.

During the neighborhood discovery process, the sink node fulfils a table that contains the ID of discovered nodes in each sector. An example of the number of nodes discovered in each sector is presented by the Table 2 with the network scenario of 24 nodes. An other table with the RSSI value of each node in each sector is also fulfilled as we can see on the Fig. 3 presenting the results of nodes with ID 7. This Table 3 can be useful during data transmission phase. For example to transmit data to node 7 with the best observed RSSI, the sink can activate the sector 150°. We gave the example of Fig. 3 based on RSSI value but other metrics like LQI (Link Quality Indicator) can be also used.

Table 2. Nodes discovered in each beam.

Number of sector	Discovered nodes ID	Number of discovered nodes
1(0°)	14, 22, 19, 11, 13, 6	6
2(30°)	22, 19, 9, 16, 14, 11, 13, 5, 6	9
3(60°)	19, 21, 9, 16, 14, 11, 2, 13, 5, 6	10
4(90°)	19, 16, 2, 13, 25	5
5(120°)	25, 23, 19, 11, 13, 24	6
6(150°)	4, 14, 23, 7, 19, 11, 13, 18	8
7(180°)	22, 6, 16, 14, 7, 19, 12, 11, 13, 18	10
8(210°)	6, 16, 19, 20, 12	5
9(240°)	17, 21, 16, 15, 19, 5, 11, 2, 13	9
10(270°)	8, 17, 21, 3, 14, 13, 19, 11	8
11(300°)	11, 19, 3, 13, 24, 10, 14	7
12(330°)	7, 10, 14, 24, 19, 11	6

Table 3. Discovering node 7 in different sector with different RSSI values

Node ID	Sector	RSSI value
7	150°	−81
7	180°	−82
7	330°	−84

4   Simulations Environment and Performance Evaluation

We used Cooja simulator [13] to evaluate the performance of our proposed WAYE protocol. Cooja is a java-based simulator designed to simulate sensor networks running the Contiki operating system. WAYE is compared to the CSMA/CA algorithm in both directional (CSMA-D) and omni-directional (CSMA-O) antennas on the sink node. We used the standard version of the unslotted CSMA/CA protocol of IEEE 802.15.4 [14].

Some rules are used to generate topologies for simulations. Nodes are spread on a square generic deployment area which is divided in four quadrants. The random positioning of nodes is used to remain close to a realistic positioning. However, to avoid having less covered places than others, overlays and nodes which are too distant each from others, we impose some constraints: (i) a new node is deployed at a minimal distance from the nodes already positioned (ii) the distribution of the nodes in the four quadrants has to be balanced.

An example of application of these two filtering rules is given in Fig. 7 for 40 deployed nodes on an area of $300 \times 300 \, \text{m}^2$, spaced at least two meters apart.

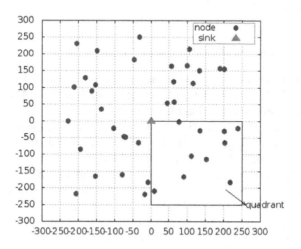

Fig. 7. Topology generation

For each topology, all node are in communication range of the sink (star topology) and we ensure that the network is connected (no isolated nodes) before starting the evaluation process. We used 3 network sizes with 24, 34 and 44 nodes. For each iteration, the same topology is used to evaluate each mechanism. We used the Multipath Ray tracer radio Medium (MRM) provided in Cooja simulator and we added a path loss random component with a standard deviation of 5 dBs in order to emulate the instability of radio links. We also introduce an outage probability of 5%, that means in 5% of attempts, node are out of range of the sink. Doing so, helps to emulate slight unreliable link with 95% of transmission success.

In the presented results, each value is an average of ten different simulations for each scenario. We evaluated the performance of our contribution according to the time needed by the sink to discover all nodes in the network. The simulations parameters are presented in Table 4.

Table 4. Simulation parameters.

Deployment area	$300\,\text{m} \times 300\,\text{m}$
Radio frequency	$2.4\,\text{GHz}$
Transceiver	CC2420
Receiver sensitivity	$-85\,\text{dBm}$
Propagation model	Shadowing with outage probability
Antenna type	- Switched beam antenna at the sink
	- Omni-directional for other nodes
Slot length	8 ms

4.1 Sink Neighbor Nodes Discovery Delay

We evaluate the time necessary to the sink node to discover all its neighbors in our approach WAYE with directional antenna sink and CSMA/CA with both directional and omni-directional antenna sink.

Figures 8, 9 and 10 present the delay needed for sink neighbors discovery according to the number of node in the network. In Fig. 8, the obtained delay with WAYE is compared to the delay of CSMA/CA with an omni-directional antenna. The observed results show that the sink running WAYE with a directional antenna takes less time to discover its neighbors. For example with 44 nodes to discover by the sink, WAYE needs less than 1.5 s to discover all the nodes while CSMA/CA needs more than 4 s.

In Fig. 9, the neighors discovery delay for the sink using WAYE and CSMA/CA with directional antenna is presented. These results show that WAYE also outperforms CSMA/CA with directional antenna on the sink. The results for WAYE, CSMA/CA with directional and omni-directional antennas are depicted in Fig. 10.

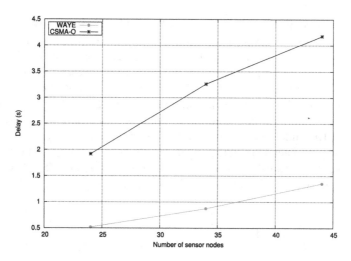

Fig. 8. Network discovery delay with omni-directional (CSMA-O) antenna sink in CSMA/CA vs directional (WAYE) antenna sink in WAYE

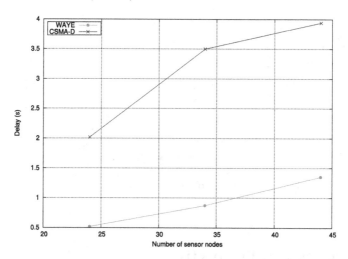

Fig. 9. Network discovery time for WAYE mechanism vs CSMA/CA algorithm with directional antenna sink.

The good performance of WAYE is due to on the one hand the reduction of the interference and collisions between nodes surrounding the sink thanks to the fact that beams covered around 1/12 of the collision area for each orientation. On the other hand, thanks to the optimized number of time slots allocated at each orientation of the beam. The allocated slots are closer to the number of nodes to discovery for each beam orientation, that helps to avoid wasting some time slots.

We also notice in Fig. 10 that the CSMA/CA with directional antenna has lower neighbors discovery delay than CSMA/CA with the omni-directional antenna once the number of nodes to discover is greater than 38. With omni-directional antenna at the sink node, we notice that the contention and collisions increase with the number of nodes to discover. That is not the case with the directional antenna. CSMA/CA with directional antenna outperforms the omni-directional one thanks to the reduction of the contention and collisions between nodes around the sink using beams. With the directional antenna, the collision zone is reduced for each orientation of the beam that explains its performance. The Fig. 10 confirms that WAYE outperforms both version of CSMA/CA in the three evaluated network scenarios (24, 34 and 44 nodes).

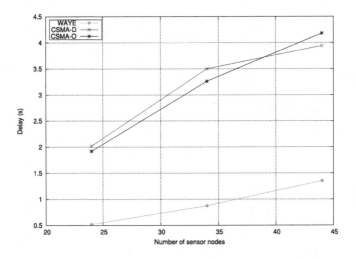

Fig. 10. Comparison of the three approaches.

5 Conclusion and Perspectives

Directional antennas have several advantages when applied in WSNs. They help to improve the connectivity between nodes in the network. In this paper, we presented our new mechanism WAYE that helps to shorten the time needed by a sink equipped with a directional antenna to discover its neihgors nodes. This mechanism is compared to the standard version of the CSMA/CA algorithm running on the sink equipped in the one hand with omni-directional antenna and in the second hand with a directional antenna. This performance of WAYE is mainly due to (i) the reduction of interference and collisions between nodes transmitting to the sink thanks to using beams of the antenna. And (ii) thanks to providing an optimized number of time slots in each orientation of the beam which is closer to the number of nodes covered by each beam orientation.

The number of collisions during the discovery process is shown to have an impact on the delay, in the future work, we would like to reduce as much as possible the number of collisions by reducing the number of contenders in each cylce with persistence based approach.

References

1. Yang, L., Ji, M., Gao, Z., Zhang, W., Guo, T.: Design of home automation system based on ZigBee wireless sensor network. In: International Conference of ISE, Nanjing, China, pp. 2610–2613 (2009)
2. Nourizadeh, S., Deroussent, C., Song, Y.Q., Thomesse, J.P.: Medical and home automation sensor networks for senior citizens telehomecare. In: IEEE International Conference of Communications Workshops, Dresden, Germany, pp. 1–5 (2009)
3. Sikka, P., Corke, P., Valencia, P.: Wireless AdHoc sensor and actuator networks on the farm. In: ACM SenSys 2006, Boulder, CO, USA, pp. 492–499, November 2006
4. Werner, G., Swieskowski, P., Welsh, M.: Demonstration: real-time volcanic earthquake localization. In: ACM SenSys 2006, Boulder, CO, USA, pp. 357–358, November 2006
5. Choudhury, R.R., et al.: Using directional antennas for medium access control in Ad Hoc networks. In: Proceedings of the 8th ACM MCN Conference (2002)
6. Ramanathan, R.: On the performance of Ad Hoc networks with beamforming antennas. In: Proceedings of the 2nd ACM International Symposium on Mobile Ad Hoc Networking & Computing. ACM (2001)
7. Cho, J., et al.: Directional antenna at sink (DAaS) to prolong network lifetime in wireless sensor networks. In: 12th European Wireless Conference 2006-Enabling Technologies for Wireless Multimedia Communications. VDE (2006)
8. Ramanathan, R.: On the performance of ad hoc networks with beamforming antennas. In: Proceedings of the 2nd ACM International Symposium on Mobile Ad Hoc Networking & Computing (2001)
9. Vasudevan, S., Kurose, J., Towsley, D.: On neighbor discovery in wireless networks with directional antennas. In: Proceedings 24th Annual Joint Conference of the IEEE CCS, vol. 4 (2005)
10. Zhang, Z.: Performance of neighbor discovery algorithms in mobile ad hoc self-configuring networks with directional antennas. In: MILCOM 2005–2005 IEEE Military Communications Conference. IEEE (2005)
11. Mudliar, S., Pillutla, L.S.: Performance evaluation of memory guided directional MAC protocol in the presence of relays. In: The proceedings of IEEE ANTS (2017)
12. Leingthone, M.M., Hakem, N.: A reconfigurable beam swhitching antenna using active cylindrical FSS structure. In: Proceedings of IEEE International Symposium on Antennas and Propagation & USNC/URSI National Radio Science Meeting (2017)
13. Osterlind, F., Dunkels, A., Eriksson, J., Finne, N., Voigt, T.: Cross-level sensor network simulation with COOJA. In: The 31st IEEE LCN, pp. 641–648 (2006)
14. Tall, H., Chalhoub, G., Misson, M.: Implementation and performance evaluation of IEEE 802.15. 4 unslotted CSMA/CA protocol on Contiki OS. Ann. Telecommun. **71**(9–10), 517–526 (2016)

Scheduling and Synchronization in WSN

Convergecast in a TSCH Network Under a Physical Interference Model

José Carlos da Silva[1,2] and Flávio Assis[2(✉)]

[1] Department of Information Systems,
UFS - Federal University of Sergipe,
Itabaiana, Brazil
`jose.carlos@ufs.br`
[2] LaSiD - Distributed Systems Laboratory
Graduate Program on Mechatronics,
UFBA - Federal University of Bahia,
Salvador, Brazil
`fassis@ufba.br`

Abstract. We describe a distributed algorithm to build a convergecast tree and a corresponding schedule for a given wireless network executing under Time Slotted Channel Hopping (TSCH). TSCH is one of the modes of operation defined in IEEE 802.15.4e and is the communication basis of current industrial wireless networks standards and the Internet of Things. In particular, the algorithm we describe is efficient, scalable, provides *deterministic* communication (no collisions) and is based on the Signal-to-Interference-plus-Noise-Ratio (SINR) model, currently considered the most appropriate to develop and analyze algorithms for wireless networks when interference is taken into consideration.

1 Introduction

IEEE 802.15.4 [10] specifies the physical layer and the medium access control (MAC) sublayer for low-rate wireless sensor networks. In order to accommodate requirements of fabric and process automation applications, this specification was amended by IEEE 802.15.4e [9], which introduced a set of new modes of operation. In this paper we focus on one of these modes, called *Time Slotted Channel Hopping* (TSCH). TSCH is the basis of operation of important industrial wireless sensor network standards (WirelessHART and ISA 100.11a) and has become an important part of the Internet of Things (IoT).

In TSCH, transmissions occur in specific combinations of time slots and physical channels. Managing communication in a TSCH network thus requires the definition of *schedules*, i.e., assignment of pairs of time slots and channels to communication links between nodes so as to minimize interference. Scheduling problems in TSCH networks have attracted much attention recently.

In [15,16] we presented a (localized) distributed algorithm to compute a schedule *given a communication topology*, which is an arbitrary graph representing which nodes need to send messages to each other nodes. In this paper we

© Springer Nature Switzerland AG 2019
M. R. Palattella et al. (Eds.): ADHOC-NOW 2019, LNCS 11803, pp. 77–89, 2019.
https://doi.org/10.1007/978-3-030-31831-4_6

present a related but different problem. We describe a *distributed* algorithm to build a *convergecast tree* and a *corresponding schedule* for transmissions over this tree on a TSCH network. A convergecast tree is a spanning tree that can be used by nodes to send data to a specific destination node (a base station, for example). A schedule is an assignment of a time slot and a channel to each edge of the tree. We build schedules such that transmissions can occur *without collision (deterministically)*. In particular, we want to *minimize the schedule size*, i.e. the number of time slots needed to schedule all edges of the tree. We assume a *Signal-to-Interference-plus-Noise-Ratio* (SINR) model [6]. SINR is currently the most appropriate model for the analysis and development of algorithms for wireless networks when interference is taken into consideration. Previous works on this problem either do not provide deterministic communication or are based on a simpler (graph-based) interference model. Although we describe an algorithm for a (theoretical) model, we contrast our results with figures of a real deployment to argue on the potential of our approach to improve scheduling in real settings.

After introducing TSCH in Sect. 2, we discuss related work in Sect. 3. In Sect. 4 we describe the assumed system model. In Sect. 5 we describe dilution, the most fundamental concept upon which our algorithm is based. In Sects. 6, 7 and 8 we describe our algorithm, present its complexity and a performance evaluation, respectively. Section 9 concludes the paper.

2   TSCH

In TSCH [9], communication is structured in *slotframes*. A slotframe is a set of time slots that repeats continuously in time. Each slot is long enough to allow a node to send a maximum length frame to another node and receive an acknowledgement. The number of slots in a slotframe defines its *size*.

Direct communication between nodes happens in a given time slot and using a specific *channel offset*. A channel offset is a number that identifies one out of a set of channels available for communication. Each channel represents a specific *frequency hopping sequence*, i.e. a predetermined sequence of frequencies that will be used during transmissions (one frequency per time slot). A network operates with a fixed number of possible channel offsets (typically 16). Time slotted access and multichannel functionality provides robustness and deterministic latency needed in critical applications.

The pairwise assignment of a directed communication between devices in a time slot and a channel offset is called a *link*. Two types of links are defined: *dedicated* and *shared links*. A dedicated link is associated with a single transmitting node and one or more receiving nodes. A shared link is assigned to more than one device for transmission.

In this paper, we only consider networks operating with dedicated links, each with a single receiver. Additionally, although a network might operate with multiple slotframes, we assume the use of a single one.

3 Related Work

The development of distributed scheduling algorithms for TSCH has recently attracted much attention (e.g., [1,5,7,8,13,17]).

In [1,8,17] the authors describe scheduling algorithms for convergecast trees in TSCH. However, the algorithms are based on simple graph-based conflict models. For example, only transmissions through edges involving a common node interfere with each other. Conflicts in wireless networks are much more involved, depending on the relationship between signal power of concurrent transmissions. The inefficiency of graph-based models has already been documented, theoretically, by simulation and experimentally (e.g. [12]). SINR is currently considered the best model to analyze and design algorithms for wireless networks.

A different approach to distributively build schedules is described in [5]. The authors describe Orchestra, a protocol for nodes to autonomously build local schedules without signalling overhead. Orchestra is based on a routing tree and has been the basis for other scheduling strategies, e.g. [13] where it is extended to address different traffic loads in the tree. Algorithms based on Orchestra, however, do not guarantee collision-free communication as in our algorithm, except for slotframes with sizes greater than the number of nodes. As discussed later, our algorithm achieves collision free schedules with much shorter schedules.

We have addressed scheduling under SINR in [15,16] for a related but different problem. We have described an algorithm to find a schedule *given a set of edges* representing a communication topology. In this paper we describe an algorithm to build a specific communication topology (convergecast tree) and a suitable corresponding schedule. The algorithm to build the tree is based on our algorithm in [2], but modified in such a way to minimize the schedule size (we discuss it further in Sect. 6).

Scheduling has been considered under SINR for additional different problems (e.g. in [3,14]). In [3] the authors address the question of how many colours are needed to create a schedule that guarantees strong connectivity. In particular, the problem for arbitrary graphs is left open. In [14] the authors address the problem of disseminating k messages stored in k arbitrary nodes to the entire network with the fewest time slots in a complete graph (single-hop network).

A (partial) survey of scheduling strategies for TSCH networks can be found in [7].

4 System Model and Notation

Network Model. We assume a network composed of n static nodes spread on an Euclidean plane and communicating by wireless medium. Each node v has a unique id, denoted $id(v)$, and a unique pair of x, y-coordinates. Each node is equipped with an omni-directional antenna and all nodes transmit with the same (maximum) power. We denote by r the *maximum transmission range*, i.e. the maximum distance from a transmitting node at which another node can still receive the message when maximum transmission power is used. Without loss of generality, we normalize the maximum transmission range to 1. Each node knows: its id, its x, y-coordinates, the number n of nodes in the network and the number of communication channels available.

Granularity. The granularity of the network, denoted by g, is defined as the maximum transmission range divided by the minimum Euclidean distance between any two nodes, i.e., $g = r/d_{min} = 1/d_{min}$, where d_{min} denotes the minimum distance between any two nodes.

Communication. Each node might transmit in one out of a set $\mathcal{C}$ of *channel offsets*, or simply *channels*. Communication is structured in a *slotframe*, composed of a sequence of *time slots*. During network operation (after the schedule is built) a message and its acknowledgment (if sent) can be both transmitted during the same time slot. A slotframe repeats continuously in time.

Interference. Transmissions on different channels are assumed not to collide. Communication between nodes *on the same channel* is defined by the SINR model. This model has three fixed parameters: path loss $\alpha > 2$, receiver sensibility $\beta \geq 1$ and ambient noise $\mathcal{N} \geq 1$. Let P_v be the transmission power used by a node v. The $SINR(u, v, \mathcal{T})$ ratio for nodes u, v and a set $\mathcal{T}$ of nodes transmitting on a channel c is defined as follows:

$$SINR(u, v, \mathcal{T}) = \frac{P_u \cdot dist(u, v)^{-\alpha}}{\mathcal{N} + \sum_{w \in \mathcal{T} \setminus \{u\}} P_w \cdot dist(w, v)^{-\alpha}} \qquad (1)$$

A node v successfully receives a message from a node u if $u \in \mathcal{T}$, v is not transmitting, v is listening to messages in c, and:

$$SINR(u, v, \mathcal{T}) \geq \beta$$

Communication Graph. According to SINR, a node v located at distance r from a node u can only receive successfully a message from u on a channel if u is the only node transmitting in the whole network on that channel. Thus we assume here (as it has become usual) a *communication graph* $G(V, E)$ of a network as consisting of all nodes and edges (u, v) such that $dist(u, v) \leq (1 - \epsilon)r = 1 - \epsilon$, where $0 < \epsilon < 1$ is a fixed model parameter. The communication graph is assumed to be connected.

Grids. The algorithm described in this paper is based on divisions of the plane into grids. A grid of square boxes of size $c \times c$ is denoted G_c. In a grid: all boxes are aligned with the coordinate axes; point $(0, 0)$ is a grid point; each box includes its left side without the top endpoint and its bottom side without the right endpoint and does not include its right and top sides. In a grid G_c, we will call a k-*superbox* (for example, a 4-superbox, for $k = 4$) a set of k adjacent boxes of the grid forming a square.

5   Basic Procedure: Dilution

Our algorithm is based on *dilution*. Dilution is a procedure that guarantees that nodes far away enough from each other can transmit successfully within a certain

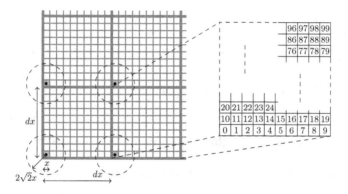

Fig. 1. Dilution

range on a given communication channel [11]. The basic idea of dilution is that given a grid G_x where a single node might transmit per grid box at a time, there is a *constant* distance d (in numbers of grid boxes) such that if nodes that are in boxes at distance d from each other transmit simultaneously, their transmissions will be successfully received within the $(2\sqrt{2})x$ distance from each of them.

Figure 1 illustrates dilution. It shows a grid G_x and a distance d ($d = 10$ in the figure). Observe that d defines d^2-superboxes, i.e., squares of $d \times d$ grid boxes. If at most a single node transmits per box of the grid, dilution guarantees that nodes in boxes in the same relative position within the d^2-superboxes can transmit simultaneously and successfully within the $(2\sqrt{2})x$ range. Figure 1 shows nodes (little black dots) in boxes index 0 of each d^2-superbox. If they transmit simultaneously their transmissions will be successfully received in the indicated range (dashed circles). Dilution consists of first scheduling nodes in boxes index 0 to transmit, then those in boxes index 1, then index 2, and so on, until boxes index $d^2 - 1$. Details about how d is computed are found in [11,16].

6   Building a Convergecast Tree

6.1   Overview

The algorithm to build a convergecast tree has two phases: a first phase, when *ranks* are assigned to nodes; and a second phase, when the tree is built. It is illustrated in Fig. 2.

Ranks are assigned to nodes using a simple variation of the broadcast algorithm described in [11]. A broadcast algorithm disseminates the *same* message from a source node to all other nodes. In our case, each node behaves as defined by the algorithm in [11], but, instead of forwarding the message from the source node, it transmits a new message with its own id, rank, position and additional information needed to guarantee that the broadcast tree will only contain edges of length at most $1 - \epsilon$. Each node defines its own rank when it receives a message for the first time. An example broadcast tree is illustrated in Fig. 2(a).

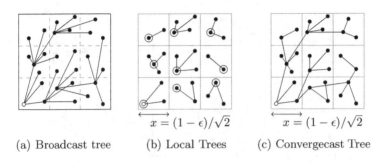

(a) Broadcast tree   (b) Local Trees   (c) Convergecast Tree

$$x = (1 - \epsilon)/\sqrt{2} \qquad x = (1 - \epsilon)/\sqrt{2}$$

Fig. 2. Phases of the algorithm to build a convergecast tree

In the second phase, the plane is divided into a grid G_x, for $x = (1 - \epsilon)/\sqrt{2}$ (see Fig. 2(b)), such that the maximum distance in a box (diagonal) is the maximum transmission range in the communication graph $(1 - \epsilon)$. The nodes in each nonempty box will elect a leader (marked with a circle in Fig. 2(b)). The leader will be the node with the highest rank in the box. The leader election procedure defines a *local tree* inside the box (see Fig. 2(b)). Along this procedure, the nodes exchange information such that at the end the leader will know the structure of the local tree. The local tree will be used by nodes to convergecast data locally to the box leader.

The global convergecast tree will be built by connecting each leader of a box to the node from which it received the first message in the rank assignment phase (see Fig. 2(c)).

The global schedule is defined based on the existence of two types of edges in the convergecast tree: edges inside boxes of grid G_x (*internal edges*) and edges whose adjacent nodes are in different boxes of this grid (*external edges*).

The details of each part of the algorithm are described in the next subsections. Due to lack of space, we will not provide formal proof of correctness of the algorithm.

6.2   Assigning Ranks

A rank of a node is an ordered pair containing an integer number and the node's id. Initially the source node builds its rank using any integer number and its id. When any other node v receives a rank from a node w for the first time, v builds its own rank using its own id and 1 less than the integer number in w's rank. Ranks are thus totally ordered, as ranks with the same integer will have different node ids (which can be totally ordered).

We assume the use of a modified version of the broadcast algorithm for known granularity described in [11]. This algorithm works as follows. A node can be either active or inactive during any instant. Initially only the source node is active. The source node broadcasts the message and becomes inactive. The nodes that have received the message become active. The plane is then divided into a grid G_z, for $z = \epsilon/(2\sqrt{2})$. The nodes in each nonempty box elect a leader for the

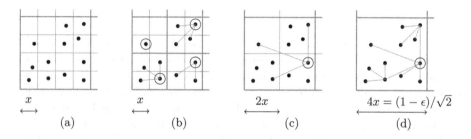

Fig. 3. Local tree

box. The leaders then broadcast the message again and the process continues. This procedure builds a broadcast tree, where the parent of a node is the node from which it has received the message for the first time.

We assume two modifications in this algorithm: (a) when the leaders transmit the message, they transmit the ids, ranks and coordinates of all nodes inside its box - these data are collected during leader election; (b) when an inactive node receives a message, it checks the ids and coordinates of nodes in the message and chooses as its parent a node whose distance to it is less than or equal to $(1 - \epsilon)$.

This algorithm will generate a tree spanning all nodes in the graph, every node will have a rank (less than its parent's rank) and all edges of the tree will have length that is equal or less than $(1 - \epsilon)$. This is a consequence of the fact that the communication graph is connected and the properties of the broadcast algorithm from [11].

6.3   Local Trees

Local trees are built in each nonempty box of grid G_x, for $x = (1 - \epsilon)/\sqrt{2}$ (see Fig. 2(b)). As previously said, this box size is such that the maximum distance inside a box is the maximum transmission range in the communication graph $(1 - \epsilon)$.

To build the tree, we use a variation of the leader election with known granularity described in [11]. This algorithm builds a tree rooted at the leader node. Based on the granularity of the network, we define a grid G_x, such that there is at most a single node in each grid cell: $\sqrt{2}x$ must be less than or equal to the minimum distance between any two nodes (Fig. 3(a)). Then nodes in each 4-superboxes elect a leader among themselves and become children of this leader in the local tree (Fig. 3(b) - the leaders are identified by circles). The value of x is then doubled, defining a new grid G_{2x}. Then the leaders in each 4-superbox in this grid elect a leader among themselves (Fig. 3(c)) and become children of this new leader in the local tree. This process is repeated until $x = (1 - \epsilon)/\sqrt{2}$ (Fig. 3(d)), when the local tree is finished. This is a variation of the leader election algorithm from [11] as along the leader election procedure the nodes transmit to their parent in the tree the structure of its subtree. Thus, at the end of the algorithm, the leader in each box will know the ids and the structure of the whole local tree in its box.

6.4 Global Tree

After a local tree is built in each nonempty box of the grid, the global converge-cast tree spanning all nodes in the graph is built by connecting the leaders in each box to their parent in the broadcast tree (see Fig. 2(c)). Convergecast will be performed locally in the boxes to the leaders using the local trees, from the leader to some node outside the box and then again up to the global tree root.

An important property of the global convergecast tree is that there will be a *single* edge in each nonempty box used to flow data from the box to some other box (except for the box containing the source node, that will have no such edge).

6.5 Global Schedule

The scheduling will be made differently for *internal* and *external edges*. An internal edge in a grid is one that has both endpoints inside the same box. An external edge connects a node in a box to a node in some other box of the grid. In the global tree, internal edges are the edges of local trees (see Fig. 2(b)). External edges are those that connect a leader of a local tree to some node outside its box (see Fig. 2(c)).

Scheduling Internal Edges. Scheduling of internal edges is made based on dividing the grid G_x for $x = (1 - \epsilon)/\sqrt{2}$ in superboxes in such a way that we can assign one different channel to each of the boxes in these superboxes. We will explain the process with an example. Suppose that we have 16 channels, i.e. $|\mathcal{C}| = 16$. So we can divide G_x into 16-superboxes. These superboxes are represented as $B_1, B_2, ...B_{16}$ in Fig. 4. Consider now superboxes whose inner boxes in the same relative position satisfy the distance d in boxes, where d is the dilution distance[1]. Assuming that $d = 8$, we would have the following sets of superboxes: B_1, B_5, B_9, B_{13}; B_2, B_6, B_{10}, B_{14}; B_3, B_7, B_{11}, B_{15}; and B_4, B_8, B_{12}, B_{16}.

Scheduling internal edges is now done by scheduling these superbox sets. Consider, for example, when set B_1, B_5, B_9, B_{13} is scheduled. We will have that nodes in boxes in the same relative position inside each of these superboxes satisfy the dilution distance d (in boxes). Consider, for example, nodes in boxes B_1^0, B_5^0, B_9^0 and B_{13}^0. They will be able to transmit simultaneously and each transmission will be guaranteed to be received in their local range, as they satisfy the dilution distance. Observe that the same will happen for nodes in boxes B_1^1, B_5^1, B_9^1, B_{13}^1, as well as in boxes B_1^2, B_5^2, B_9^2, B_{13}^2, etc. Additionally, as transmissions in each box inside these superboxes will happen in a different channel, one transmission per each of these boxes can be done concurrently.

Thus we first schedule the set B_1, B_5, B_9 and B_{13}. A simultaneous transmission can occur in each non-empty box of these superboxes. Transmissions in boxes in the same relative position in superboxes use the same channel and

---

[1] This distance is a bit longer than the dilution distance computed in [11], as done in [16], since dilution is originally defined for box sizes at most $(1 - \epsilon)/(2\sqrt{2})$ and we have boxes of size $x = (1 - \epsilon)/\sqrt{2}$.

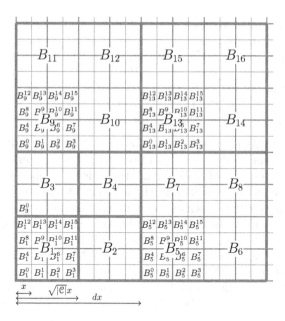

Fig. 4. Boxes and superboxes

transmissions in different boxes in the same superbox use different channels. For example, $B_1^0, B_5^0, B_9^0, B_{13}^0$ use channel 0, $B_1^1, B_5^1, B_9^1, B_{13}^1$ use channel 1, and so on. Then we schedule the set B_2, B_6, B_{10}, B_{14}, then B_3, B_7, B_{11}, B_{15}; and finally B_4, B_8, B_{12} and B_{16}. Each time one of these sets is scheduled an internal edge in each constituent box is chosen.

Scheduling External Edges. We will illustrate the procedure using again Fig. 4. As previously described, there will be at most a single external edge in each grid box: the edge from the leader of the box to a node outside the box.

Local trees are built for boxes in grid G_x, for $x = (1 - \epsilon)/\sqrt{2}$. A transmitting node in a box of G_x can only reach another node at a maximum distance which is less than $1.5x$, as the maximum range in the communication graph is $1 - \epsilon$. A node, for example, in box B_1^0 and a node in B_3^0 cannot have intersecting communication ranges. Thus leaders in boxes in the same relative position in superboxes B_1, B_2, B_3 and B_4 can transmit simultaneously. However, the distance between these leaders do not satisfy the dilution distance d (see Fig. 4). Thus these leaders might transmit at the same time *as long as they use different channels*.

We schedule external edges as follows. We divide the grid into d^2-superboxes and then subdivide them in 16-superboxes (B_1, B_2, B_3 and B_4 in Fig. 4). We then assign a different channel to each of these 16-superboxes. Each of the boxes in these 16-superboxes is scheduled a time. First box index 0, then box index 1, and so on, until all 16 boxes have been scheduled. Transmissions in boxes in the same relative position inside the 16-superboxes can occur simultaneously, as they occur on different channels and cannot have receivers in common. When a box is scheduled the transmission corresponding to its external edge is done.

In the example shown in Fig. 4, 16 time slots (one for each box inside 16-superboxes) and 4 channels (one for each 16-superbox inside d^2-superboxes) are enough to schedule all external edges *of the whole network*. If there are not enough channels to each of the 16-superboxes, the procedure can be done using bigger superboxes, however resulting in longer schedules.

Global Schedule. As the schedule in a box is not known by other boxes, the network operates repeatedly in periods of transmissions of internal and external edges, for a fixed number of slots for internal edges. A node knows when to transmit based on data received from the leader in its box, on its coordinates and on network parameters, such as the number of available channels.

Important to notice is that due to dilution the algorithm to build the schedule as well as the schedule itself are *collision-free* (there is no collision during these procedures). Additionally, although similar to the algorithm in [2], the algorithm in this paper differs from that one during the ranking assignment phase (transmitting coordinates of nodes to avoid edges longer that $(1 - \epsilon)$) and limits external edges to one per box. These variations are important to generate shorter schedules.

7   Runtime Complexity

The scheduling algorithm involves: (a) the execution of a deterministic broadcast algorithm to assign ranks to nodes (Sect. 6.2); (b) electing a leader and sending to it data about all nodes in boxes (Sect. 6.3); (c) local computation by box leaders to define the schedule for local trees; and (d) transmission of schedules to all nodes in the boxes.

Step (a) is done in $O(D \log g)$ rounds and step (b) is done in $O(\log g)$ rounds, where D is the diameter of the network and g is its granularity, as these algorithms are variations of the deterministic broadcast and leader election algorithms with known granularity, respectively, described in [11]. The variations in these algorithms that we described do not change their time complexity. Step (c) does not involve distributed computation. Step (d) is done in constant time, as it is done by dilution [11]. Thus the total computation time is $O(D \log g)$.

8   Performance Evaluation

The algorithm was evaluated by simulation, using Sinalgo [4]. Due to lack of space, we only present here results related to the size of the computed schedules. As we are not aware of any other distributed convergecast algorithm for TSCH based on SINR, we do not compare the performance of our algorithm with others.

Figure 5 shows graphics with the results of simulations. Each point in the graphic corresponds to an average value from 50 topologies. Each topology was generated spreading the nodes randomly in a 500×500 area. Additional fixed

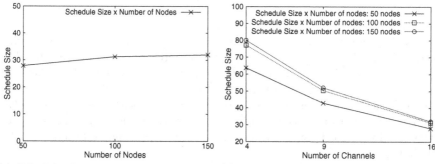

(a) Schedule Size vs. Number of Nodes (b) Schedule Size vs. Number of Channels
($|\mathcal{C}| = 16$)

Fig. 5. Number of rounds and size of schedules

parameters of the simulations are: $range = 100$, $\alpha = 3$, $\epsilon = 20$, $\beta = 1$ and noise equal to 1. All simulations have yielded narrow 95% confidence intervals. For the graphic presented in Fig. 5(a), we have $|\mathcal{C}| = 16$. In Fig. 5(b) the value of $|\mathcal{C}|$ varies as indicated in the figure.

Figure 5(a) shows the schedule sizes for networks with increasing number of nodes: 50, 100 and 150. The figure shows that: (a) the sizes of the schedules are very small; and (b) the increase rate of the size of the schedules was lower than that of the number of nodes. The size of the schedule has been thus scalable in the number of nodes. Recall that the algorithm is *deterministic* and the size of a schedule means the number of time slots that is enough for *all* nodes to send a message successfully to its parent.

Figure 5(b) shows the impact of the number of channels in the size of the schedules. It shows the average size of schedules for networks with 50, 100 and 150 nodes when 4, 9 and 16 channels are available. A higher number of channels had a reasonable impact on the size of schedules. As stated before, 16 channels are typically found in currently available transceivers of wireless sensor nodes.

Although we present our figures based on a (theoretical) model, it is interesting to contrast them to figures of real deployments. In [5], although the scheduling approach (Orchestra) achieves a low contention rate (below 3%) for 98 nodes and slotframes of sizes 3 to 47, contention-free schedules are only achieved with a number of slots (schedule sizes) which is greater than the number of nodes. Observe that our approach achieves collision-free schedule for networks with 150 nodes with around 80 and 30 slots, respectively, using 4 and 16 channels (Fig. 5(b)). Additionally our approach does not depend directly on the number of nodes (Fig. 5(a)), being highly scalable. Although these two approaches are not comparable as they are based on very different assumptions and conditions, this contrast illustrates the potential to improve scheduling that implementations based on our algorithm might have.

9 Conclusion

We described an algorithm to build a convergecast tree and a corresponding schedule for a TSCH network under a physical interference model (SINR). The algorithm *deterministically* builds the tree *and* provides a schedule that allows *all* nodes to send messages to their parents in the tree. The algorithm yielded a very good performance in terms of the sizes of the generated schedules. The algorithm is also very efficient in terms of runtime complexity. This is a direct consequence of the use of the broadcast and leader election algorithms and dilution from [11] as building blocks.

Acknowledgement. This work is based on previous related work developed in cooperation with Prof. Dariusz Kowalski from the University of Liverpool, UK. This work was partially supported by the UFBA CAPES Print Program (Edital 002 2019 Print UFBA).

References

1. Accettura, N., Palattella, M.R., Boggia, G., Grieco, L.A., Dohler, M.: Decentralized traffic aware scheduling for multi-hop low power lossy networks in the Internet of Things. In: WoWMoM (2013)
2. Assis, F.: A deterministic and a randomized algorithm for approximating minimum spanning tree under the SINR model. In: WMNC (2015)
3. Avin, C., Lotker, Z., Pasquale, F., Pignolet, Y.-A.: A note on uniform power connectivity in the SINR model. In: Dolev, S. (ed.) ALGOSENSORS 2009. LNCS, vol. 5804, pp. 116–127. Springer, Heidelberg (2009). https://doi.org/10.1007/978-3-642-05434-1_12
4. Distributed Computing Group - ETH: Sinalgo - simulator for network algorithms. http://disco.ethz.ch/projects/sinalgo/
5. Duquennoy, S., Al Nahas, B., Landsiedel, O., Watteyne, T.: Orchestra: robust mesh networks through autonomously scheduled TSCH. In: SenSys (2015)
6. Gupta, P., Kumar, P.R.: The capacity of wireless networks. IEEE Trans. Inf. Theory **46**(2), 388–404 (2000)
7. Hermeto, R.T., Gallais, A., Theoleyre, F.: Scheduling for IEEE802.15.4-TSCH and slow channel hopping MAC in low power industrial wireless networks: a survey. Comput. Commun. **114**(C), 84–105 (2017)
8. Hwang, R.-H., Wang, C.-C., Wang, W.-B.: A distributed scheduling algorithm for IEEE 802.15.4e wireless sensor networks. Comput. Stand. Interfaces **52**, 63–70 (2017)
9. IEEE: IEEE standard for local and metropolitan area networks - part 15.4: low-rate wireless personal area networks (LR-WPANs) amendment 1: MAC sublayer - IEEE std 802.15.4e-2012 (amendment to IEEE std 802.15.4-2011) (2015)
10. IEEE: IEEE standard for low-rate wireless networks - IEEE std 802.15.4-2015 - revision of IEEE std 802.15.4-2011) (2015)
11. Jurdzinski, T., Kowalski, D.R., Stachowiak, G.: Distributed deterministic broadcasting in uniform-power ad hoc wireless networks. In: Gąsieniec, L., Wolter, F. (eds.) FCT 2013. LNCS, vol. 8070, pp. 195–209. Springer, Heidelberg (2013). https://doi.org/10.1007/978-3-642-40164-0_20

12. Moscibroda, T., Wattenhofer, R., Weber, Y.: Protocol design beyond graph-based models. In: HotNets, November 2006
13. Rekik, S., Baccour, N., Jmaiel, M., Drira, K., Grieco, L.A.: Autonomous and traffic-aware scheduling for TSCH networks. Comput. Netw. **135**, 201–212 (2018)
14. Shi, W., Hua, Q.-S., Yu, D., Wang, Y., Lau, F.C.M.: Efficient information exchange in single-hop multi-channel radio networks. In: Wang, X., Zheng, R., Jing, T., Xing, K. (eds.) WASA 2012. LNCS, vol. 7405, pp. 438–449. Springer, Heidelberg (2012). https://doi.org/10.1007/978-3-642-31869-6_38
15. Silva, J.C., Assis, F.: A distributed algorithm to schedule TSCH links under the SINR interference model. In: SBESC (2017)
16. Silva, J.C., Assis, F.: A distributed algorithm to schedule TSCH links under the SINR model. Des. Autom. Embed. Syst. **23**(1–2), 21–39 (2019)
17. Soua, R., Minet, P., Livolant, E.: Wave: a Distributed Scheduling Algorithm for Convergecast in IEEE 802.15.4e Networks (Extended Version). Research Report RR-8661, INRIA, January 2015

Analysis of the Network Attachment Delay of Mobile Devices in the Industrial Internet of Things

Rodrigo Teles Hermeto[1]([✉]), Quentin Bramas[1], Antoine Gallais[1,2], and Fabrice Théoleyre[1]

[1] ICube Laboratory, CNRS, University of Strasbourg, Strasbourg, France
{teleshermeto,bramas,gallais,theoleyre}@unistra.fr
[2] FUN (Self-organizing Future Ubiquitous Network) Inria Lille - Nord Europe, Lille, France

Abstract. Industrial networks are typically used to monitor safety-related processes where high reliability and an upper bounded latency are crucial. Because of its flexibility, wireless is more and more popular, even for real-time applications. Because radio transmissions are known to be lossy, deterministic protocols have been proposed, to schedule carefully the transmissions to avoid collisions. In parallel, industrial environments now integrate mobile industrial robots to enable the Industry 4.0. Thus, the challenge consists in handling a set of mobile devices inside a static wireless network infrastructure. A mobile robot has to join the network before being able to communicate. Here, we analyze this attachment delay, comprising both the synchronization and the negotiation of dedicated cells. In particular, since the control frames (EB and 6P) have a strong impact on the convergence, our proposed model carefully integrates the collision probability of these packets. We validate the accuracy of our model, and we analyze the impact of the different EB transmission policies on the discovery delay. Our performance evaluation demonstrates the interest of using efficiently the radio resources for beacons to handle these mobiles devices.

1 Introduction

Industrial networks are now widely used for many industrial applications, where high reliability and an upper bounded latency are critical. They typically rely on a costly and inflexible wired infrastructures to attend these strict requirements. In order to reduce deployment and maintenance costs, industrial networks have started to replace this legacy infrastructure with wireless sensor networks.

Due to its low-power nature, a sensor network is known to be lossy with no delivery guarantees. Thus, standards such as IEEE 802.15.4-TSCH have been released, proposing reliable mechanisms to the MAC layer in order to implement deterministic protocols. Combining the schedule of transmissions and a slow-channel hopping mechanism, a network can achieve 99.99% of end-to-end

© Springer Nature Switzerland AG 2019
M. R. Palattella et al. (Eds.): ADHOC-NOW 2019, LNCS 11803, pp. 90–101, 2019.
https://doi.org/10.1007/978-3-030-31831-4_7

delivery rate, while upper bounding the end-to-end latency [1]. Specifically, the transmissions are carefully scheduled to avoid collisions, either in a distributed or a centralized manner [2].

Although mobility plays an increasingly important role for many industrial deployments [3], the IEEE 802.15.4-TSCH standard does not propose a clear approach to handle a high rate of topology changes due to the association/dissociation of mobile devices. Additionally, the slow-channel hopping mechanism introduces a new layer of complexity: a joining node has to wait for receiving the synchronization beacon on its active listening channel, delaying its association to the network. A fast association is a key factor to enable mobility over low-power wireless networks [4].

The use of mobile devices in wireless industrial networks has already been investigated in the past [3,5,6]. They mainly focus on proposing mechanisms to reduce the attachment delay. Indeed, discovering the network is particularly challenging in multichannel environments, since the discovering node has to find the right channel to listen to [7]. Besides, the novel device has to reserve some transmission opportunities, using control packets. Unfortunately, these control packets are prone to collisions since they are transmitted through contention-based cells [8]. Mechanically, these collisions increase the attachment delay.

The contributions presented in this paper are as follows:

1. we propose here an analytical Markov chain to model the first association of a mobile node in a multi-hop network. We consider both the discovery of a neighboring device, and the negotiation of cells.
2. we evaluate the gain of transmitting Enhanced Beacons (EB) on multiple channels in order to reduce the synchronization delay. Using multiple channels allows to spread the load on shared cells, reducing the collision probability;
3. we quantify the impact of the network density on the discovery and negotiation time. More neighbors mean also more collisions, very prejudicial to the synchronization.

2   Background and Related Work

We present here the most important mechanisms of IEEE 802.15.4-TSCH and 6TiSCH, since we rely on these two standards for modeling the attachment delay of mobile nodes in networks with real-time performance.

2.1   6TiSCH Stack

The IEEE 802.15.4-TSCH standard has defined the TSCH mode [9], where nodes schedule the transmissions such that each application has enough transmission opportunities while avoiding collisions. The network is globally synchronized, each node maintaining the number of timeslots since the network has been created, aka. the Absolute Slot Number (ASN). A slotframe in TSCH consists in a matrix of *cells* of equal length, each cell being defined by a pair of *timeslot* and *channel* offsets. The schedule comprises two types of cells:

shared cells implement a slotted-Aloha approach. For unicast packets, the absence of acknowledgment is interpreted as a collision. In that case, the transmitter triggers a random backoff value and skips the corresponding number of shared cells;

dedicated cells are allocated to interference-free transmitters to avoid any collision. This allocation may be centralized or distributed [2]. The transmitter may trigger a Clear Channel Assessment (CCA), but only to combat external interference.

6TiSCH has defined the 6top Protocol (6P) to allocate/deallocate cells with a neighbor node [10]. By default, each schedule modification is based on a two-way handshake. The inquirer sends a request to a neighbor (e.g. preferred parent), piggybacking a list of possible cells. Then, the neighbor will acknowledge the request, selecting the cells present in the list which are also available in its schedule. When a node joins the network, it relies on shared cells to bootstrap a negotiation with its next-hop neighbor [11], since the two nodes have no common preallocated dedicated cells.

2.2   Mobility in Industrial Scenarios

Tinka *et al.* [12] detail a scheduling algorithm to handle a network infrastructure where all the devices are mobile. A gossip mechanism makes the schedule dissemination robust. Similarly, Vahabi *et al.* [13] address a mobile sink scenario. However, fully-mobile topologies make high-reliability very challenging, which jeopardizes the correct operation of many industrial applications.

A mobile node has first to discover the network, i.e. to receive an Enhanced Beacon (EB) which contains all the information for the synchronization (e.g. slotframe length, ASN, hopping sequence, etc.). However, IEEE 802.15.4-TSCH lets the schedule policy of EB unspecified, while it has a strong impact on the discovery time.

Nidawi *et al.* [5] propose to modify the acknowledgment packets to accelerate the discovery. Acks are grouped at the end of the slotframe, and piggyback the time that the node will keep its radio on to receive possibly new association requests. However, it requires to modify the standard.

Vogli *et al.* [14] consider to broadcast EB on multiple channels at once. For that purpose, they allocate exclusive timeslots for EB transmissions, with a Random Filling scheduling, where the channel offsets are selected randomly among the available ones.

Zhou *et al.* [15] propose rather to schedule the Enhanced Beacons to reduce the collisions, and thus, the attachment delay. However, the proposition targets more the co-existence of multiple TSCH star networks, where EBs are scheduled independently. De Guglielmo *et al.* [16] present a Model-based Beacon Scheduling (MBS) algorithm that minimizes the average joining time. Karalis *et al.* [17] propose to assign one dedicated cell for each EB, using multiple channels to avoid collisions. However, these last two approaches rely on a perfect, centralized, collision-free schedule, which makes the scheme less scalable.

Dezfouli *et al.* [6] also consider the time required to negotiate dedicated cells. Indeed, being synchronized is not sufficient, the mobile device has to know when it can transmit safely its packets. For this purpose, the scheduler computes a path for each mobile device for each of its possible locations. Then, it allocates statically a collection of cells along each of these paths. However, the trajectory has to be known a priori, and it consumes much radio resource, since one single path is used at a time.

Haxhibeqiri *et al.* [18] focus on the handover process by employing a single-hop network with multiple gateway nodes and a centralized manager. Once a mobile node reserves dedicated cells to one gateway, the network manager instructs the others gateways to install the same cell for that node. This way, gateways have pre-allocated dedicated cells for each mobile node, reducing the handover latency. However, the proposed architecture cannot be easily extended due to deployment costs. In particular, the infrastructure requires devices with higher computational power connected through wires for the control plane.

3   Joining Time Model

We analyze here the joining time, i.e. time interval between a mobile device wakes-up, and it can start transmitting data packets through dedicated cells.

3.1   Scenario and Assumptions

We focus here on a network topology where the sink and a collection of relay nodes are static. Only a few devices (e.g. robots) are mobile and represent the *leaves* of the network infrastructure. Thus, a mobile device sends its packet to a neighboring relay node, which forwards them through a path of relays to the sink. Each static node has a collection of dedicated cells in its schedule, maintained by a scheduling function such as SF0 [11]. Thus, each relay node can forward the packets from mobile devices without any collision.

Mobile devices constitute the leaves and have to identify a single neighboring relay node to send their packets. They need to capture its Enhanced Beacons, to adjust their clock and know when are the next shared cells, to be able to transmit their first messages. After selecting a next hop, a mobile node engages a 6P two-way handshake [10] to reserve dedicated cells for its transmissions.

We focus on the discovery that a node has to trigger when it is unsynchronized. This procedure comprises:

synchronization: the joining node has to receive an Enhanced Beacon (EB) to synchronize itself with the network. Then, it gets the frequency hopping sequence and the shared cells for broadcast packets;

negotiation: the node has selected the source of the EB as parent, and then negotiates a set of dedicated cells to use to transmit its data packets.

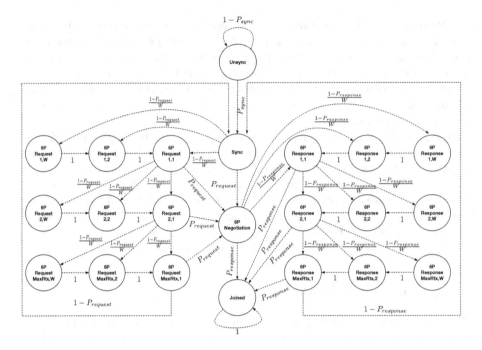

Fig. 1. Model for the association time of a joining node.

3.2 Markov Chain

We define here a discrete time Markov chain (Fig. 1) to represent the joining process of a new (mobile) node, hereafter denoted as *joining node*, when it joins the network for the first time. We will detail here the different parts of our model.

3.3 Synchronization

The joining node is initially in the unsynchronized state, listening for EB sent by neighboring fixed nodes. In IEEE 802.15.4-TSCH, all synchronized nodes broadcast EB periodically to announce the existence of the network. We make here a distinction between the two factors that impact directly the synchronization time of the joining node: EB collision and the channel hopping mechanism.

Since IEEE 802.15.4-TSCH adopts a slotted Aloha mechanism for shared cells, the collision probability may be quite high. Indeed, an EB packet is enqueued until the next shared cell. Thus, when multiple nodes enqueue EB packets simultaneously between consecutive shared cells, their transmissions collide. In addition, because of the channel hopping characteristic, the EB is successfully received by the joining node only if the latter is listening to the right channel.

All nodes in a IEEE 802.15.4-TSCH network enqueue EB at the same frequency after they synchronize. To reduce the amount of collisions among EB,

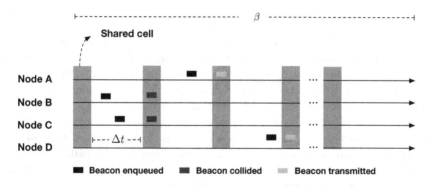

Fig. 2. Beacon queuing over the time. A collision occurs when two or more nodes enqueue simultaneously between consecutive shared cells (nodes B and C).

we consider adding jitters before EB transmissions, which represents the default behavior of OpenWSN [19]. The jitter increases the time window in which a node enqueues Enhanced Beacons. For instance, for a beacon period β and jitter γ, the generation time of the next Enhanced Beacon will be randomly selected within the interval $[\beta - \gamma, \beta + \gamma]$.

Let us model the EB generation as a Poisson Process. Let us consider λ as the expected number of EB queued by all nodes during a given time interval of length L. Let Δt be the time between consecutive shared cells, in a such way that $L \geq \Delta t$. During the period L, the nodes have $\lfloor \frac{L}{\Delta t} \rfloor$ possibilities to enqueue their respective EB packets between consecutive shared cells. Since we assume that the rate λ is constant over the time, we can compute the rate of beacons to be enqueued during any Δt interval as:

$$\mu = \lambda * \left\lfloor \frac{L}{\Delta t} \right\rfloor^{-1} \tag{1}$$

The transmission is only successful when a single device enqueues an EB during a given Δt interval. For instance, Fig. 2 depicts two colliding transmissions (from nodes B and C). It also shows that those from A and D are successful since enqueued during different Δt periods. From the Poisson distribution, the probability of having a single node generating an EB for any Δt interval is:

$$P_{beacon} = P(X = 1) = \mu e^{-\mu} \tag{2}$$

Additionally, we need to account the probability that the joining node is listening to the right channel. Since the frequency hopping sequence uses all the channels uniformly, the joining node has a uniform probability of matching the channel of the EB transmission. Thus, the probability of reception is finally:

$$P_{sync} = P_{beacon} * \left(\frac{1}{N_{ch}} \right) \tag{3}$$

where N_{ch} is the number of channels.

3.4 Negotiation

After having received an EB, the joining node is able to synchronize itself with its parent, and to identify the shared cells to listen to. However, no bandwidth is yet available: it has to send 6P request packets and to wait for a confirmation before starting using dedicated cells for communication. Unfortunately, collisions are frequent in shared cells, since EB, routing control packets (i.e. DIO used by IETF RPL) and 6P control packets compete for the same resource.

6P uses a two-way handshake mechanism: both the request and the response are subject to transmission failures. The negotiation is successful if both the request and response are transmitted without collision. Thus, we can employ here Eq. 2 with $X = 0$ to compute the probability of success.

$$P_{request} = P_{response} = e^{-\mu} \tag{4}$$

In case of collision, the transmitter selects a random backoff value and skips the corresponding number of shared cells. We represent the backoff state as a 2-tuple (r, w), where r is the current transmission attempt and w is the backoff counter. The probability of reaching any subsequent backoff state after a collision is equally likely. For all states (i, w), where $w > 1$, the transmitter does not try to retransmit and it transits to state $(i, w - 1)$ with probability 1. After reaching a maximum number of attempts (MaxRtx), the node discards the current packet and starts over the negotiation, i.e. go back to the *sync* state.

3.5 Handover

Since mobile devices are constantly moving around the environment, the link between the device and its point of attachment may eventually start to provide a low reliability due to the long distance between them. In that case, the mobile device has to select a more reliable relay node to forward its packets, i.e. to perform a handover. Specifically, the mobile device deallocates the cells toward its previous next hop, and negotiates novel cells with its novel relay node.

We can neglect the deallocation time, as the 6P packets will be transmitted without contention, i.e. dedicated cells already exist in their schedule. On the other hand, novel cells have to be negotiated with the novel relay node. Since the mobile node is already synchronized (*Sync* state), it can immediately engage a negotiation. Thus, we can employ Eq. 4 to compute the probability that the negotiation will succeed.

3.6 Estimating the Joining Time

Since we rely on an absorbing Markov chain, we can estimate the joining time by computing the average number of steps to reach the absorbing state from the initial state *Unsync*. In our DTMC depicted in Fig. 1, the *Joined* state is the absorbing state. Every step in our model represents the interval between two consecutive shared cells (i.e. Δt). We rely on the Fundamental Matrix to compute the average absorbing time: i.e. number of transitions from the initial state (*Unsync*) to the absorbing state (*Joined*).

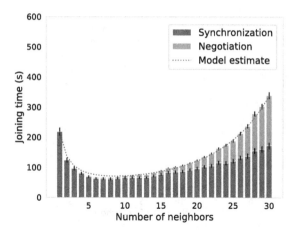

Fig. 3. Comparison of the average joining time given by the model and simulations with an EB period of 15 s, and a jitter of 200 ms

4   Numerical Analysis

We propose first to verify the accuracy of our DTMC model when estimating the joining time in 6TiSCH networks. Then, we will analyze the joining time for a joining node, as well as assessing the gain of using multiple channels for EB transmissions.

4.1   Model Validation

We rely on simulations to validate our DTMC model. We implement a lightweight 6TiSCH simulator written in Python focusing exclusively on the joining procedure of a mobile node. Our simulator is freely available on GitHub[1]

In our scenarios, we consider an existing network composed of fixed nodes (i.e. the infrastructure) and one joining node. The fixed nodes broadcast EB and DIO regularly during shared cells. For sake of simplicity, we assume that the infrastructure has enough bandwidth to accommodate the novel flows. Thus, only the joining node and its point of attachment have to negotiate dedicated cells. Additionally, we assume perfect links conditions. Thus, collisions are the only causes of packet drops.

We employ a slotframe composed of 101 timeslots, and 26 channel offsets, with two shared cells placed uniformly in the slotframe. The joining node selects randomly one channel to listen for EB. All nodes in the infrastructure enqueue EB and DIO every 15 s in average, considering a jitter of 200 ms. We plot systematically the 95% confidence intervals.

The comparison between our analytical model and simulation results are depicted in Fig. 3. We perform 1,000 repetitions for each number of neighbors to

---

[1] https://github.com/rodrigoth/Simulator/tree/optimized.

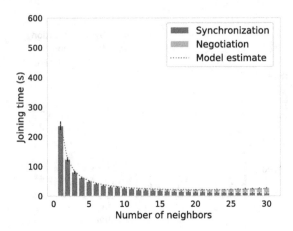

Fig. 4. Impact of the multi-channel EB broadcasting on the joining time.

make our results more representative. We observe that the analytical values fit very well the simulation results. As expected, with few nodes, the synchronization takes longer, since the joining node has a smaller probability to receive a valid EB. On the other hand, the negotiation is fast, since there are less competition in the shared cells. Increasing the number of neighbors improves the joining time to a certain extent (i.e. 9 neighbors in our scenario). For higher values, the probability of collision increases impacting both the synchronization and negotiation times. Thus, the joining time presents an exponential growth.

4.2   Multi-channel EB to Reduce the Attachment Delay

By definition, all transmissions in shared cells occur exclusively in a single channel offset. Therefore, the probability of collision increases, since only one cell is used for transmissions. We propose to assess the gain of the Random Filling approach [14] to transmit EB on multiple channels, and thus, to reduce the synchronization time.

We redefine Eq. 3 to account simultaneous transmissions on different channels. Now, on each channel, EB arrival follows a Poisson Process of parameter μ/N_{ch}, since the EB are uniformly distributed on all N_{ch} channels. Hence, the probability that only one EB is transmitted on the channel that the joining node is listening to is:

$$P_{sync} = \left(\frac{\mu}{N_{ch}} \right) e^{\left(-\frac{\mu}{N_{ch}} \right)} \tag{5}$$

Figure 4 highlights the gain of broadcasting EB on multiple channels. The synchronization time decreases heavily compared to the single channel case depicted in Fig. 3. In a general way, we can expect less EB arrivals, but the EB are now transmitted on multiple channels simultaneously. Thus, the probability that the joining node is listening to any of the transmitted channels increases.

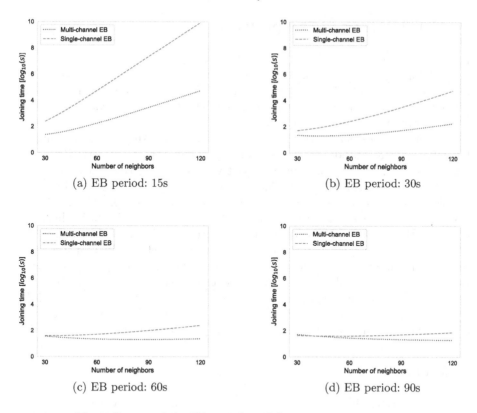

Fig. 5. Impact of the EB period on different network densities.

In addition, spreading EB on multiple channel impacts directly the negotiation time, since the EB and the 6P packets are transmitted mostly on different channels. We can now accommodate much larger densities with a very reasonable attachment delay.

4.3   Large Scale Performance

Finally, we analyze the impact of the EB period on the joining time with different densities. For the sack of simplicity, we consider that the EB and DIO are transmitted at the same frequency.

Figure 5 compares the joining time when EB are transmitted on single vs. multiple channels. As expected the EB frequency has a crucial importance on the joining time on large scale deployments. However, shorter EB periods increase the probability of collisions when using a single channel. Using multiple channels allows to spread the load, and thus reduces significantly the collision probability.

We can note that the optimal EB period, minimizing the joining time, depends on the density. More nodes mean a larger number of EB transmissions, and thus a larger optimal EB period.

5   Conclusions and Perspectives

In this work, we focused on the joining time of a mobile node when it joins the network for the first time. Mobile devices have to fast attach to the network, and reserve some resources for their critical flows. We modeled the joining process using a Discrete Time Markov Chain. Our model takes into account both the synchronization and negotiation times in 6TiSCH networks.

Our simulations demonstrate the accuracy of our DTMC model to estimate finely the synchronization and negotiation time. Obviously, dense networks mean a larger number of collisions, which impact very negatively the synchronization time. Even worse, negotiating dedicated cells is also very expensive, since the collision rate for control packets is very high. We also use our DTMC model to assess the gain of using multiple channels. By spreading the EB on the different channels, the collision rate is significantly reduced, improving the scalability.

As a future work, we plan to propose an handover scheme, so that a mobile device can maintain several next hops, to avoid dropping data packets. In particular, we have to reduce the negotiation time, when a novel relay node is identified. Recent approaches based on autonomous scheduling, such as MSF [20], seem promising to reduce the contention, particularly when a large number of mobile devices has to attach to the network simultaneously.

References

1. Duquennoy, S., Al Nahas, B., Landsiedel, O., Watteyne, T.: Orchestra: robust mesh networks through autonomously scheduled TSCH. In: SenSys, pp. 337–350. ACM (2015)
2. Hermeto, R.T., Gallais, A., Theoleyre, F.: Scheduling for IEEE 802.15.4-TSCH and slow channel hopping MAC in low power industrial wireless networks: a survey. Comput. Commun. **114**, 84–105 (2017)
3. Silva, R., Silva, J.S., Boavida, F.: Infrastructure-supported mobility in wireless sensor networks – a case study. In: IEEE International Conference on Industrial Technology (ICIT), pp. 1895–1900, March 2015
4. Sthapit, P., Choi, Y.-S., Kwon, G.-R., Hwang, S.S., Pyun, J.Y.: A fast association scheme over IEEE 802.15. 4 based mobile sensor network. In: Proceedings of ICWMC (2013)
5. Al-Nidawi, Y., Kemp, A.H.: Mobility aware framework for timeslotted channel hopping IEEE 802.15.4e sensor networks. IEEE Sens. J. **15**(12), 7112–7125 (2015)
6. Dezfouli, B., Radi, M., Chipara, O.: Real-time communication in low-power mobile wireless networks. In: 13th IEEE Annual Consumer Communications Networking Conference (CCNC), pp. 680–686, January 2016
7. Karowski, N., Viana, A.C., Wolisz, A.: Optimized asynchronous multichannel discovery of IEEE 802.15.4-based wireless personal area networks. IEEE Trans. Mob. Comput. **12**(10), 1972–1985 (2013)
8. Theoleyre, F., Papadopoulos, G.Z.: Experimental validation of a distributed self-configured 6TiSCH with traffic isolation in low power lossy networks. In: International Conference on Modeling, Analysis and Simulation of Wireless and Mobile Systems (MSWiM), pp. 102–110. ACM (2016)

9. IEEE Standard for Low-Rate Wireless Networks. IEEE Std 802.15.4-2015 (Revision of IEEE Std 802.15.4-2011), April 2016

10. Wang, Q., Vilajosana, X., Watteyne, T.: 6top Protocol (6P). draft, IETF, October 2017. draft-ietf-6tisch-6top-protocol-09

11. Dujovne, D., Grieco, L.A., Palattella, M.R., Accettura, N.: 6TiSCH 6top Scheduling Function Zero (SF0). Internet-draft, IETF, 2016. draft-ietf-6tisch-6top-sf0-00

12. Tinka, A., Watteyne, T., Pister, K.S.J., Bayen, A.M.: A decentralized scheduling algorithm for time synchronized channel hopping. EAI Endorsed Trans. Mob. Commun. Appl. 1(1), 201–216 (2011)

13. Vahabi, M., Faragardi, H.R., Fotouhi, H.: An analytical model for deploying mobile sinks in industrial Internet of Things. In: IEEE Wireless Communications and Networking Conference Workshops (WCNCW), pp. 155–160, April 2018

14. Vogli, E., Ribezzo, G., Grieco, L.A., Boggia, G. Fast network joining algorithms in industrial IEEE 802.15.4 deployments. Ad Hoc Netw. **69**, 65–75 (2018)

15. Zou, M., Lu, J.-L., Yang, F., Malaspina, M., Theoleyre, F., Wu, M.-Y.: Distributed scheduling of enhanced beacons for IEEE802.15.4-TSCH body area networks. In: Mitton, N., Loscri, V., Mouradian, A. (eds.) ADHOC-NOW 2016. LNCS, vol. 9724, pp. 3–16. Springer, Cham (2016). https://doi.org/10.1007/978-3-319-40509-4_1

16. De Guglielmo, D., Brienza, S., Anastasi, G.: A model-based Beacon Scheduling algorithm for IEEE 802.15.4e TSCH networks. In: International Symposium on A World of Wireless, Mobile and Multimedia Networks (WoWMoM), pp. 1–9. IEEE, June 2016

17. Karalis, A., Zorbas, D., Douligeris, C.: Collision-free broadcast methods for IEEE 802.15.4-TSCH networks formation. In: International Conference on Modeling, Analysis and Simulation of Wireless and Mobile Systems (MSWiM), pp. 91–98. ACM (2018)

18. Haxhibeqiri, J., Karaağaç, A., Moerman, I. and Hoebeke, J.: Seamless roaming and guaranteed communication using a synchronized single-hop multi-gateway 802.15.4e TSCH network. Ad Hoc Netw. **86**, 1–14 (2019)

19. Watteyne, T., et al.: OpenWSN: a standards-based low-power wireless development environment. Trans. Emerg. Telecommun. Technol. **23**(5), 480–493 (2012)

20. Chang, T., Vucinic, M., Vilajosana, X., Duquennoy, S., Dujovne, D.: 6TiSCH Minimal Scheduling Function (MSF). Internet-draft, IETF, April 2019. draft-chang-6tisch-msf-03

Performance Analysis of the Slot Allocation Handshake in IEEE 802.15.4 DSME

Florian Meyer, Ivonne Mantilla-González, Florian Kauer, and Volker Turau[✉]

Institute of Telematics Hamburg University of Technology, Hamburg, Germany
turau@tuhh.de

Abstract. Wireless mesh networks using IEEE 802.15.4 are getting increasingly popular for industrial applications because of low energy consumption and low maintenance costs. The IEEE 802.15.4 standard introduces DSME (Deterministic and Synchronous Multi-channel Extension). DSME uses time-slotted channel access to guarantee timely data delivery, multi-channel communication, and frequency hopping to mitigate the effects of external interferences. A distinguishing feature of DSME is its flexibility and adaptability to time-varying network traffic and to changes in the network topology. In this paper we evaluate the ability of DSME to adapt to time-varying network traffic. We examine the limits for slot allocation rates for different topologies. The evaluation is performed with openDSME, an open-source implementation of DSME.

1 Introduction

Since a few years wireless technologies penetrate industrial applications. To satisfy the stringent requirements in terms of timeliness and reliability found in this application context industrial wireless standards are emerging: ZigBee, WirelessHART, ISA100.11a, and WIA-PA. In 2015 the IEEE 802.15.4 standard was extended for this new application segment by new MAC-layer protocols addressing robustness and reliability: Deterministic and Synchronous Multi-Channel Extension (DSME) and Time-Slotted Channel Hopping (TSCH). Both protocols schedule time and frequency slots to one or multiple communication partners, thus eliminating packet collisions due to interferences within the network. In DSME time frames are split into a contention access period (CAP) and a contention free period (CFP). While the CFP is used for regular traffic, the CAP is mainly used for management messages. The CFP is divided into time slots. Nodes only transmit data in allocated slots of the CFP. This allows nodes to completely turn off transceivers when outside transmitting or receiving slots. In addition, TSCH and DSME utilize channel diversity allowing temporal overlapping transmissions at nodes in interference range. Especially in large networks with a high traffic load, TSCH and DSME outperform traditional protocols like CSMA/CA [9].

© Springer Nature Switzerland AG 2019
M. R. Palattella et al. (Eds.): ADHOC-NOW 2019, LNCS 11803, pp. 102–117, 2019.
https://doi.org/10.1007/978-3-030-31831-4_8

A distinguishing feature of DSME is its flexibility and adaptability to time-varying network traffic and to changes in the network topology by purely local actions with low overhead. In particular DSME allows to dynamically establish dedicated links between any two neighboring nodes. This enables the operation of multi-hop mesh networks with deterministic latency. Slot allocations and deallocations are performed in a distributed manner, i.e., each pair of nodes can autonomously allocate or deallocate slots according to their needs.

The allocation of a slot in the CFP is based on a three-step handshake that takes place in the CAP phases. Deallocations and duplicate allocation notifications also follow a similar handshake. In order to autonomously perform slot allocations, each node stores a table containing information about the slots assigned to the node and the channel/timeslot pairs allocated to neighboring nodes. While allocating new slots these data structures can become inconsistent. This can lead to the abandonment of an allocation process and a rollback of the changes to the data structures to regain consistency. Furthermore, the slot allocation itself is executed via CSMA/CA, so it is subject to message collisions (hidden terminal) and race-conditions. Naturally this also holds for the mentioned rollback operation. All this makes the allocation process a complex undertaking and estimating the required times is challenging.

This paper analyzes the performance of the slot allocation/deallocation process of DSME and evaluates the ability of DSME to adapt to time-varying network traffic. We show that the performance is tightly correlated with the chosen frame structure and accordingly with the values of the configuration parameters. We examine the limits for slot allocation rates for different topologies. The evaluation is done with openDSME, an open-source implementation of DSME [10]. We also provide theoretical insights into the DSME handshake and make recommendations for the various configuration parameters. With the proposed optimizations, the performance of DSME networks can be considerably improved. This makes the usage of DSME for a broad range of demanding applications in the industrial IoT a competitive option.

2   Description of DSME

As depicted in Fig. 1, DSME divides time into *superframes* (SF), each consisting of 16 time slots. The first of these is used to transmit beacons containing network and time information while the remaining time slots are split into a CAP with 8 time slots and a CFP with 7 time slots. The CFP is further subdivided into *guaranteed time slots* (GTS) which are spread over time and frequency and grant exclusive access to the shared medium. In the 2.4 GHz band, 16 channels with 5 MHz channel spacing can be used. During the CAP, network participants can exchange messages via CSMA/CA and allocate or deallocate GTS. The communication during the CAP usually occurs on a single predefined channel. One or more superframes form a multi-superframe (MSF) to extend the number of allocatable GTS [7].

The structure of a MSF is defined by the *superframe order* (SO) and the *multisuperframe order* (MO). Here, SO determines the duration of a slot and

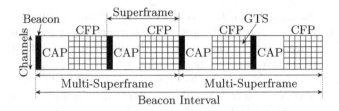

Fig. 1. Structure of an IEEE 802.15.4 DSME superframe.

thus the duration of a superframe D_F. The duration D_{MF} of a MSF is specified by the MO. Both durations can be calculated as multiples of 15.36 ms: $D_F = 15.36 * 2^{SO}$ and $D_{MF} = D_F * 2^{MO-SO}$. Therefore, the number of superframes per MSF is equal to 2^{MO-SO}. A schedule of allocated GTS is repeated after every MSF. In order to transmit a packet with the maximum payload length of 116 bytes, $SO \geq 3$ is required. With $SO = 2$ and $SO = 1$, 66 bytes and 18 bytes of payload can be transmitted respectively. Hence, MO and SO are a natural choice as parameters for the analysis of the slot allocation handshake in DSME, as they determine the frequency and the length of the CAPs.

2.1 GTS Allocation and Management

In contrast to the original IEEE 802.15.4 standard, DSME features a 3-way handshake for the distributed allocation and deallocation of GTS between a neighboring pair of nodes [7]. Consequently, a GTS must be allocated on a per-hop basis. The handshake, as show in Fig. 2, is performed in the CAP using CSMA/CA and is therefore prone to contention. Two main structures are used for the management of GTS: The *allocation counter table* (ACT), which contains information about the locally allocated GTS, and the *slot allocation bitmap* (SAB), which marks the GTS used by a node's neighbors.

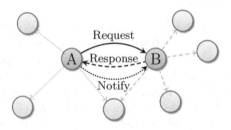

Fig. 2. Distributed slot allocation handshake in IEEE 802.15.4 DSME.

As exemplified in Fig. 2, the GTS allocation between two nodes A and B is triggered by A sending a *GTS Request* to B as an acknowledged unicast message.

The request contains a preferred GTS and a sub-block of A's SAB. After receiving the request, B selects a GTS for allocation, considering A's preference or the received sub-block and its own SAB if the preferred slot is unavailable. Then, B broadcasts a *GTS Response* with the selected GTS to its neighbors, including A. If A does not receive the response within a certain time, the allocation fails. If A receives the response, it broadcasts a *GTS Notify* to its neighbors, including B, and marks the selected GTS as allocated in its ACT. At last, B also marks the GTS as allocated in its ACT after receiving the *GTS Notify*.

Since the *GTS Response* and *GTS Notify* messages are sent as broadcasts, the neighbors of A and B have the chance to check if the selected GTS is already used by them by checking their own ACT. If this is the case, they send a *Duplicate Allocation Notification* to B or A, respectively, and the allocation is rolled back. The deallocation of GTS is performed analogously.

2.2   Specifics of OpenDSME

openDSME is an open source implementation of the IEEE 802.15.4 DSME data link layer [10]. It provides not only functionalities defined in the standard, but also additional features to cover the missing gaps and provide a fully functional data link layer. Three of these features are of interest to this work.

Scheduling Module: DSME defines a distributed mechanism for slot negotiations. Additional features, such as how many slots are to be allocated at what time are out of the scope of the standard. openDSME provides a scheduling algorithm (*Traffic-Aware and Predictive Scheduling*, TPS). It is based on an exponentially weighted moving average filter using a smoothing parameter α to estimate the required GTSs to meet the traffic demand per link. Moreover, a hysteresis is included to reduce the amount of management traffic [9].

Invalid Slot Extension: Inconsistent slot allocation situations, as evidenced in [8], are handled in openDSME through a slot management mechanism, introducing an additional flag in the allocation counter table that allows an early detection of invalid slots due to lost of packets during the GTS handshake.

Active Backoff Mechanism: openDSME allows a node to receive messages during backoff periods (i.e. set the radio in reception mode during backoff time). Four parallel transactions can be handled by a node, using a finite multistate machine that manages transactions in a CAP. This feature virtually increases the capability of the network to speed up processes in the contention period.

3   Related Work

There is a variety of works dealing with IEEE 802.15.4 and its recent extensions. Duquennoy et al. propose Orchestra, a scheduler for TSCH which computes local schedules at every node and avoids the distributed slot negotiation [4] altogether. Similarly, a distributed scheduling algorithm for on-the-fly bandwidth reservation in 6TiSCH, an IPv6 layer over TSCH, is proposed in [13]. Fewer works exist regarding the slot allocation in DSME, still there are some works analyzing the CSMA/CA medium access mechanism [5,18]. The impact of CSMA parameters and collision probability on delay in such networks for unsaturated traffic is analyzed in [14]. In the same direction, Koubaa et al. show the influence of the parameter *macMinBE* on slotted CSMA/CA for broadcast transmissions in small and large scale networks [11]. To properly dimension IEEE 802.15.4 networks, adaptive protocols for estimating CSMA parameters have been proposed. There are some centralized approaches [1], in which the coordinator adjusts the backoff exponent (BE) for nodes depending on the traffic patterns, and some distributed approaches [3], in which nodes locally compute the CSMA parameters to meet a predefined packet delivery ratio.

In IEEE 802.15.4 TSCH networks nodes communicate using shared and dedicated links. [19] formulates the collision probability to access a shared link for non-periodic traffic patterns to determine the number of nodes to allocate per link. In [2], measurements (e.g. delivery probability, packet latency, energy consumption) are obtained from an analytical model of the TSCH CSMA/CA algorithm, to determine the performance per node in transmissions over shared links. Different works have been focused on analysis and improvements in IEEE 802.15.4 DSME networks [6,12]. [15] shows that modifying the Clear Channel Assessment (CCA) scheme, the channel busy condition due to acknowledge can be avoided. Additionally, a restrictive contention access scheme is proposed to reduce probability of collisions and busy channel condition.

An analysis of the GTS allocation process [16] leads to an analytical method to select CSMA/CA parameters that minimize the number of contention access periods demanded to complete this procedure. They consider different multihop topologies and and simulate the networks using network simulator Cooja. Finally, [8] presents a formal analysis of the distributed slot allocation procedure in DSME, identifying some weaknesses related to packet loss, which eventually leads to inconsistent slot allocations. Despite the fact that the DSME allocation process allows reliable data transmissions, vulnerabilities of CSMA/CA affect the slot management.

4   Scenario Description

In order to evaluate the influence of frame structure parameters such as *MO* and *SO* on the allocation process, we define the *setup time* as the total time required by nodes to successful allocate a GTS. Hence, the setup time is measured from the time a node issues a *GTS Request* until the last *GTS Notify* has been successfully sent. We evaluate contention-free and contention-based scenarios for line and grid topologies. To this end, for all experiments, a number of packets δ is generated at fixed intervals equivalent to the duration of a multisuperframe of order $MO = 9$. By varying the value of δ we analyze the behavior of these networks under non-saturated and saturated conditions. We also scrutinize the reasons for failures during the setup time. To estimate the minimum setup time we set the TPS smoothing parameter α to aggressively perform allocations.

Since this would also induce more deallocations and thus might destabilize the network, a second filter is introduced that is used for deallocations.

In the considered scenarios, the evaluation begins after the association phase is completed. Table 1 summarizes the values of CSMA parameters and network configurations used for evaluating various scenarios. The *macMinBE* and *macMaxBE* parameters determine the minimum and the maximum backoff exponent of the CSMA algorithm and *macMaxCSMABackoffs* is the maximum number of backoffs for every transmission of a packet, until it is considered lost after *macMaxFrameRetries* retransmissions [7]. The simulations are conducted using openDSME and OMNeT++, a discrete event simulator [17]. The results are shown with a 95% confidence level.

Table 1. Setup of CSMA and DSME network parameters used in the evaluation.

Parameter	Set of values	Parameter	Set of values
macMinBE	$\{1, \ldots, 5\}$	*BO*	9
macMaxBE	$\{3, \ldots, 7\}$	*MO*	$\{7, \ldots, 9\}$
macMaxCSMABackoffs	4	*SO*	$\{3, \ldots, 7\}$
macMaxFrameRetries	3	δ	$\{1, 2, 4, 6, 8\}$

5   The 3-Way Handshake in DSME

This chapter provides insights into the influence of some parameters on the *setup time* for different network topologies. Sect. 5.1 theoretically analyzes the duration of a single 3-way handshake in an ideal scenario. This allows to determine the maximum number of handshakes per CAP for different configuration parameters. Sect. 5.2 presents simulation results for a minimal scenario with two nodes and no contention. This allows to give an upper bound for the number of allocations per CAP. Sect. 5.3 considers a scenario with increasing contention for a line topology.

5.1   Theoretical Evaluation

First we present a theoretical estimation of the *GTS setup* time between two nodes. This time corresponds to the elapsed time from the moment the first message *GTS Request* is ready to be sent, until the third exchanged message *GTS Notify* is sent. Some approaches disregard the *GTS Notify* message when estimating the *GTS setup* time [16], under the assumption that this message has no effect on the GTS negotiation process once the *GTS Response* message is received. However, *GTS Notify* is a broadcast message that must be sent to update neighbor's SAB, before the GTS can be effectively used. Therefore, the *GTS setup time* can be expressed as:

$$t_{GTS\_setup} = t_{GTS\_req} + t_{GTS\_resp} + t_{GTS\_notf} \tag{1}$$

We consider a DSME network in which a node A wants to negotiate a GTS to transmit data to node B. In order to estimate the *GTS setup* time, we make the following three assumptions. Firstly, there is no busy channel condition when a node verifies the channel state. The channel is assumed to be always idle and available. Hence, the CSMA/CA algorithm performed to determine the channel condition, executes only one backoff period. Secondly, there is no interference and no fading effect. That is, the communicating nodes A and B are always able to detect the incoming signals from each other, and there are no missing or corrupted packets. And finally, the link is active and channel conditions allow for an error-free message delivery. The different times relevant for the slot negotiation handshake are defined in the following and summarized in Table 2. Figure 3 shows the times in a sequence diagram.

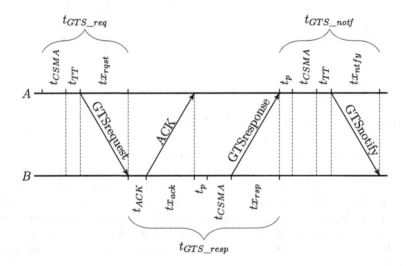

Fig. 3. Message sequence of GTS negotiation.

$t_{Backoff}$: The backoff time a node must wait until verifying the channel state. This time is ruled by the unslotted CSMA/CA algorithm and calculated as

$$t_{Backoff} = \text{random}(2^{BE} - 1) \times aUnitBackoffPeriod$$

where $aUnitBackoffPeriod = 20$ symbols. The random selection is uniform in the interval $[0, 2^{BE} - 1]$ and, for our calculations, we use the default value $BE = 3$. Therefore, the expected value of the backoff time is

$$Ex[t_{t_{Backoff}}] = 0.5 \times (2^{BE} - 1) \times aUnitBackoffPeriod = 70 \text{ symbols}.$$

t_{CCA}: The time in which a node determines whether the channel is idle. By default, this is equal to 8 symbols.

t_{CSMA}: The total time to perform the CSMA/CA algorithm. Its expected value is obtained as

$$Ex[t_{CSMA}] = Ex[t_{Backoff}] + t_{CCA}.$$

t_{TT}: The time for a node to toggle the transceiver from transmission to reception mode. It is equal to $aTurnaroundTime$.

$t_{tx_{rqst}}$, $t_{tx_{ack}}$, $t_{tx_{rsp}}$ and $t_{tx_{ntfy}}$: The transmission times of messages *GTS Request*, *GTS Response*, *ACK* and *GTS Notify* based on a data rate of 250 kbps. The transmission time is calculated as a function of the packet size. A general expression for this value is:

$$phySHRDuration + \lceil o \cdot phySymbolsPerOctet \rceil \text{(symbols)},$$

where o is the number of PHY header octets plus the number of PSDU octets in a frame (e.g. $o = 6$, for *ACK*).

t_p: An estimation of the average time in which a node processes an incoming message. Experiments using an Atmel ATmega256 RFA2 node with an adapted DSME layer for the physical layer lead to $t_p = 300$ μs.

t_{ACK}: The time in which an acknowledgement for a *GTS Request* is issued. This is calculated as: $t_{ACK} = aUnitBackoffPeriod + aTurnaroundTime$.

Table 2. Timing values for DSME-GTS negotiation

Time	Symbols	ms	Time	Symbols	ms	Time	Symbols	ms
t_{CSMA}	78	1.248	$t_{tx_{rsp}}$	67	1.072	$t_{tx_{ack}}$	6	0.096
t_{TT}	12	0.192	$t_{tx_{ntfy}}$	40	0.640	t_{ACK}	32	0.512
$t_{tx_{rqst}}$	51	0.816						

The message sequence of a GTS negotiation is depicted in Fig. 3. Times to exchange those messages are defined and calculated as:

1. Time to send a GTS Request from node A to node B:

$$t_{GTS\_req} = t_{CSMA} + t_{TT} + t_{tx_{rqst}} = 2.256 \text{ ms} \qquad (2)$$

2. Time elapsed from the moment that node B receives the *GTS Request* command, acknowledges it and sends back a *GTS Response*:

$$t_{GTS\_resp} = t_{ACK} + t_{tx_{ack}} + t_p + t_{CSMA} + t_{tx_{rsp}} = 3.228 \text{ ms} \qquad (3)$$

3. Time to process a *GTS Response* message at node A and to issue a *GTS Notify*:

$$t_{GTS\_notf} = t_p + t_{CSMA} + t_{TT} + t_{tx_{ntfy}} = 2.38 \text{ ms} \qquad (4)$$

From (2), (3) and (4) in (1), the *GTS setup* time can be estimated as

$$t_{GTS\_setup} = 7.864 \text{ ms} \tag{5}$$

In summary, the *GTS negotiation time* for one slot between two nodes in an ideal scenario is independent on the parameters *MO* and *SO*. The dominant value of this term is given by the minimum backoff exponent (*macMinBE*), which determines the final set up time.

In case of multiple consecutive negotiations, there is a limit on the number of possible negotiations per CAP given by the parameter *SO*. The effective time to perform a GTS negotiation is determined by *CAP length - IFS* [7], where *CAP length* is the duration of a contention access period and *IFS* is the interframe space. Therefore, allocation processes that take longer than this effective time are deferred to subsequent CAPs.

5.2   Contention-Free Scenario

In this section the setup time of a network without any contention is analyzed, i.e., under optimal conditions. The evaluation is simulation-based. For this, we consider a network with two nodes, a sink and a source, where the source periodically transmits packets to the sink as described in Sect. 4. Additionally, packets are generated at a high rate to evaluate the behavior of a saturated network.

Figure 4 shows the setup time of the network for various values of *MO* and *SO* and an increasing number of generated packets. As expected, there is no significant difference in the setup time for 1 packet, since it is simply transmitted at the start of the CAP following the generation. For 8 packets, however, the setup time for $SO = 3$ increases drastically in relation to the other *SO* s. The reason for this is that in a CAP with $SO = 3$, a maximum of 7 handshakes can be realized. The 8th handshake does not fit into the same CAP and the node has to wait a full CFP until the next handshake can be performed. For larger *SO* s, the CAP is longer and all GTS can be allocated in one CAP.

For 8 packets and $MO = SO = 7$, the setup time is slightly lower than for the other configurations because it only allows for a single superframe. In other words: The network is saturated when 7 GTS are allocated and DSME does not try to allocate more slots afterwards because all allocated slots are marked in the ACT, resulting in a lower setup time but an increased transmission time for data packets. This also holds true for the scenarios with 16 and 32 packets where $7 * 2^{MO-SO} < 16$ and $7 * 2^{MO-SO} < 32$, respectively.

Looking at Fig. 4, it may seem counter intuitive at first that the setup time for $MO = 9$, $SO = 3,4,5$ and 32 packets is the same because less packets can be sent with a smaller *SO* as shown in the 8 packet scenario. However, by reducing the *SO* by one, the length of a CAP halves but the number of CAPs per MSF doubles. Therefore, the accumulated duration of all CAPs of a MSF stays the same, resulting in the same setup time for a scenario without contention. The influence of minBE and maxBE is not explicitly shown here, since a larger minBE simply results in a larger setup time.

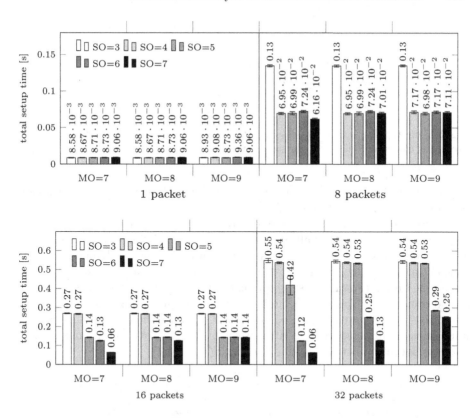

Fig. 4. Setup time for two nodes with a varying number of generated packets.

The theoretical estimation obtained in Sect. 5.1 for the network setup time can be compared with the simulation results depicted in Fig. 4, for one generated packet (i.e. one GTS negotiation). To this end, it must be considered that simulations do not make allowance for the processing time t_p included in (3–4). Additionally, the backoff time in the openDSME is obtained by biasing the random($2^{BE} - 1$) in one, to avoid getting $t_{Backoff} = 0$ when $BE = 0$, because it is unfeasible to trigger a waiting event instantaneously in a real implementation. This situation would produce a so-called scheduling in the past event. Therefore, in openDSME $Ex[t_{Backoff}]$ is 1 $aUnitBackoffPeriod$ larger than in the theoretical case. Bearing this in mind, we obtain that the experimental results agree with theoretical estimation within a margin of error of 8.2%

5.3   Contention-Based Scenario

This section considers scenarios with increasing contention. For this, the line topology depicted in Fig. 5 is utilized, where every node $v_{i \neq 0}$ sends its self-generated packets towards its parent v_{i-1}. Packets received from its child v_{i+1}

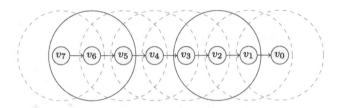

Fig. 5. Line topology with 8 nodes and the respective communication ranges. Only two nodes can communicate at the same time.

are not forwarded. The communication range of v_i is chosen in a way that it can only reach its parent and its child.

Figure 6 shows the setup times for different line topologies. It can be seen that the setup time increases for all *SOs* for up to 6 nodes. Afterwards, it stagnates. This is due to the fact that in a network with up to 5 nodes only one node can transmit at same time. From 6 to 8 nodes, 2 nodes can transmit packets at the same time through spatial reuse, speeding up the setup process when the number of nodes increases. The setup time increases for an increasing *SO* because slot allocations are triggered at the start of every CAP and when the last handshake finishes successfully (see Sect. 4). Because of this, nodes have to wait longer until the next allocation is triggered for a higher *SO*.

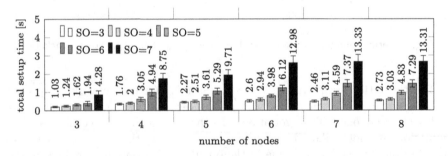

Fig. 6. Setup time for a line topology with an increasing number of nodes, $\delta = 8$, $MO = 9$ and $SO = 3$.

There can be several reasons for a failing 3-way handshake. For the line topology, these are presented in Fig. 7. It can be seen that increasing *SO* does not increase the number of initiated handshakes. In fact, the number of failed handshakes was slightly lower. The main reason for a failing handshake is that the *GTS-Response* or *GTS-Notify* message did not arrive in time. The latter case cannot be detected by DSME, as given by the standard [7]. By slightly adapting the handshake, openDSME guarantees the detection of this case and the timely deallocation of the involved slots. This is denoted by *Deallocated* in Fig. 7.

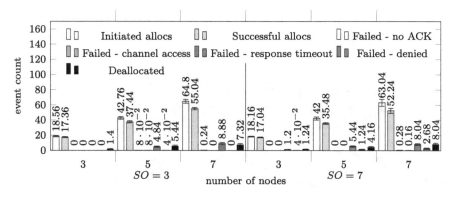

Fig. 7. Number of initiated, successful and failed handshakes for $MO = 9$ and $\delta = 8$.

5.4 CSMA Parameters

Apart from the slot length (SO), the minimum backoff exponent (minBE) and the maximum backoff exponent (maxBE) are the most relevant parameters influencing the total network setup time. They determine the backoff durations of the CSMA/CA algorithm. Figure 8 shows the impact of different combinations of minBE and maxBE on the setup time of a line topology with 6 nodes, 5 generated packets, $MO = 9$ and different SOs. The default parameters for DSME, as specified in [7], are minBE = 3 and maxBE = 5. The color gradient gives the setup time in seconds from 20 s (red) to about 1 s (blue).

It can be seen that the network setup time strongly depends on the combination of minBE/maxBE. For the given scenario, higher values for both parameters lowers the setup time. E.g., the setup time for $SO = 6$ decreases from 8.73 to 4.65 s for the minimum and maximum exponents, respectively. The determining factor here is minBE, since the CSMA/CA algorithm calculates a random backoff exponent smaller than $\min\{macMinBE + NB, macMaxBE\}$, where NB is the number of already executed backoffs of a specific packet. Therefore, large values for $macMinBE$ and $macMaxBE$ increase the chance that two nodes choose a different backoff exponent. Thus, less collisions occur and packets are transmitted faster. As explained in Sect. 5.3, a smaller SO results in a shorter setup time.

6 Triggering GTS Allocations

At last, we evaluate the influence of the time at which a GTS allocation is triggered. For this, we choose a grid topology with $m \times m$ nodes, where $2 \leq m \leq 7$. A node's communication range is configured such that it can communicate with its 9 surrounding nodes. Therefore, the contention is higher than in the scenario from Sect. 5.3. Every node generates one packet per 7.864 s and transmits it to a predefined, randomly chosen communications partner that changes every run. A total of 20 runs is conducted. A node is the sink for exactly one other node. We test three different approaches: Performing multiple GTS allocations per CAP

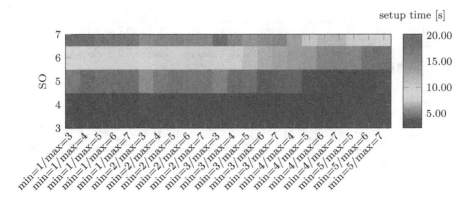

Fig. 8. Setup time for *SO* vs combinations of *macMinBE*/maxBE and *MO* = 9. (Color figure online)

if the last allocation was successful (M_1), performing exactly one allocation per CAP (M_2) and performing one allocation per MSF on average (M_3). The superframe within the multisuperframe is chosen randomly for the last method.

Figure 9 shows the setup time for the three methods. It can be seen that M_1 performs better than the other two methods for small networks with 4 and 9 nodes because the contention is not that high and packets do not collide that often. Therefore, it is possible for a node to transmit multiple packets in a single CAP, speeding up the allocation process. From 16 nodes on, however, the other two methods perform better. M_3 performs strictly better than M_2, because less traffic and therefore less congestion is created. This is also illustrated by Fig. 10. Here, it can be seen that M_3 initializes significantly less allocations than the other methods, increasing the energy-efficiency of the network. The main reasons for a failed allocation are unacknowledged requests, most likely due to hidden nodes.

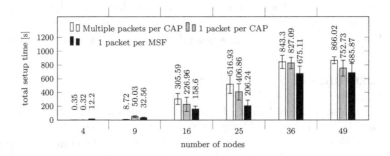

Fig. 9. Setup time with different GTS allocation triggering intervals for $MO = 9$, $SO = 3$, $\delta = 1$ and an increasing number of nodes.

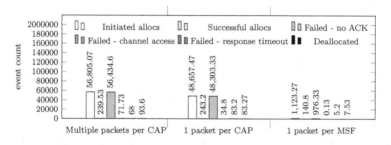

Fig. 10. Initialized, successful and failed GTS allocations with different triggering intervals for $MO = 9$, $SO = 3$, $\delta = 1$ and 49 nodes.

The results indicate that a high level backoff for the allocation procedure can significantly decrease the setup time and energy-consumption of a network. In comparison to dynamically adjusting the minimum backoff exponent and maximum backoff exponent of the CSMA/CA algorithm, as discussed in Sect. 3, this method has the advantage that the CAP queue is kept small because less allocations are initialized in comparison to just delaying the transmission of the respective packets.

7 Conclusion

This paper analyzes the slot allocation handshake in DSME and evaluates its ability to adapt to time-varying network traffic and to changes in the network topology. The parameters that most influence the slot negotiation process were determined, considering different traffic conditions, network configurations and topologies. The experimental results are obtained with openDSME, an opensource implementation of DSME.

A theoretical evaluation of the slot allocation handshake in a contention free scenario is made to estimate the setup time. This evidences that the setup time depends on the parameters $macMinBE$ and SO. This is, the smaller the parameter $macMinBE$, the smaller the waiting time to access the medium. In the same way, the parameter SO determines the maximum number of slot negotiations per CAP. Therefore, the smaller the $macMinBE$ and the larger the SO, the smaller setup time obtained. Theoretical and experimental results agree within a margin of error of 8.2%. The source of this error is still an issue to be explored.

We show how SO affects the setup time of a contention-based scenario with a line topology. For small networks with less than 6 nodes, the setup time increases almost exponentially as SO increases. Although the slot allocation process speed up as the number of nodes increases, due to spatial reuse, the setup time keep increasing with SO, essentially because of the increase of the CAP length. Additionally, it is verified that the larger the $macMinBE$ and $macMaxBE$, the smaller the probability of collisions due to nodes selecting the same backoff period.

Furthermore, grid topology networks were examined as case study of limits of slot allocation rates. To this end, three different allocation rates were considered:

single and multiple allocations per CAP and single allocation per MSF. Results from a comparative analysis of these approaches show that, triggering multiple allocations per CAP in small networks performs better in terms of the setup time. However, as the size of the network increases this performance is degraded given the increasing congestion. Therefore, disseminating slot allocations (i.e. single allocations per CAP and single allocations per MSF) is desirable for medium and large scale networks.

Finally, these results provide a basis for developing future work focused on the slot negotiation management. Developing adaptive algorithms that take into consideration relevant protocol and network configuration parameters would exploit DSME adaptability to achieve an optimal performance regarding slot allocation time and energy consumption.

Acknowledgement. This research was supported by the German Academic Exchange Service (DAAD) through financial benefits for foreign scholarship holders.

References

1. Abdeddaim, N., Theoleyre, F., Heusse, M., Duda, A.: Adaptive IEEE 802.15.4 MAC for throughput and energy optimization. In: 2013 IEEE International Conference on Distributed Computing in Sensor Systems, pp. 223–230. IEEE (2013)
2. De Guglielmo, D., Al Nahas, B., Duquennoy, S., Voigt, T., Anastasi, G.: Analysis and experimental evaluation of IEEE 802.15.4e TSCH CSMA-CA algorithm. IEEE Trans. Veh. Technol. **66**, 1–1 (01 2016)
3. Di Francesco, M., Anastasi, G., Conti, M., Das, S.K., Neri, V.: Reliability and energy-efficiency in IEEE 802.15.4/ZigBee sensor networks: an adaptive and cross-layer approach. IEEE J. Sel. Areas Commun. **29**(8), 1508–1524 (2011)
4. Duquennoy, S., Al Nahas, B., Landsiedel, O., Watteyne, T.: Orchestra: robust mesh networks through autonomously scheduled TSCH. In: Proceedings of the 13th ACM Conference on Embedded Networked Sensor Systems, pp. 337–350. ACM (2015)
5. Hussein, O., Sadek, N., Elnoubi, S., Rizk, M.: Analytical model of multi-hop IEEE 802.15.4 with unslotted CA/CSMA. Int. J. Comp. Com. Eng **3**, 226–230 (2014)
6. Hwang, K., Nam, S.: Analysis and enhancement of IEEE 802.15.4e DSME Beacon Scheduling Model. J. Appl. Math. **2014** (2014)
7. IEEE Computer Society: IEEE 802.15.4-2015 - IEEE Standard for Local and metropolitan area networks-Part 15.4: Low-Rate Wireless Personal Area Networks (WPANs) (2016)
8. Kauer, F., Köstler, M., Lübkert, T., Turau, V.: Formal analysis and verification of the IEEE 802.15.4 DSME slot allocation. In: Proceedings of 19th ACM International Conference on Modeling, Analysis and Simulation of Wireless and Mobile Systems, pp. 140–147. ACM (2016)
9. Kauer, F., Köstler, M., Turau, V.: Reliable wireless multi-hop networks with decentralized slot management: an analysis of IEEE 802.15.4 DSME. arXiv:1806.10521 (2018)
10. Kauer, F., Köstler, M., Turau, V.: openDSME: reliable time-slotted multi-hop communication for IEEE 802.15.4. In: Virdis, A., Kirsche, M. (eds.) Recent Advances in Network Simulation. EICC, pp. 451–467. Springer, Cham (2019). https://doi.org/10.1007/978-3-030-12842-5_15

11. Koubaa, A., Alves, M., Tovar, E.: A comprehensive simulation study of slotted CSMA/CA for IEEE 802.15.4 wireless sensor networks. In: IEEE Workshop on Factory Communication Systems, pp. 183–192. IEEE (2006)
12. Liu, X., Li, X., Su, S., Fan, Z., Wang, G.: Enhanced fast association for 802.15.4e DSME Mac protocol. In: Proceedings of 2nd International Conference on Computer Science & Electronics Engineering (2013)
13. Palattella, M.R., et al.: On-the-fly bandwidth reservation for 6TiSCH wireless industrial networks. IEEE Sens. J. **16**(2), 550–560 (2015)
14. Park, P., Di Marco, P., Soldati, P., Fischione, C., Johansson, K.H.: A generalized Markov chain model for effective analysis of slotted IEEE 802.15.4. In: 6th International Conference on Mobile Adhoc and Sensor Systems, pp. 130–139 (2009)
15. Sahoo, P., Pattanaik, S., Wu, S.L.: A novel IEEE 802.15.4e DSME MAC for wireless sensor networks. Sensors **17**, 168 (2017)
16. Vallati, C., Brienza, S., Palmieri, M., Anastasi, G.: Improving network formation in IEEE 802.15.4e DSME. Comput. Commun. **114**, 1–9 (2017)
17. Varga, A., Hornig, R.: An overview of the OMNeT++ simulation environment. In: Proceedings of the 1st International Conference on Simulation Tools and Techniques for Communications, Networks and Systems & Workshops, p. 60. ICST (2008)
18. Xiao, Z., Zhou, J., Yan, J., He, C., Jiang, L., Trigoni, N.: Performance evaluation of IEEE 802.15.4 with real time queueing analysis. Ad Hoc Netw. **73**, 80–94 (2018)
19. Yaala, S.B., Théoleyre, F., Bouallegue, R.: Performance modeling of IEEE 802.15.4-TSCH with shared access and ON-OFF traffic. In: 14th International Wireless Communication & Mobile Computing Conference, pp. 352–357 (2018)

Comparison of Mixed Diversity Schemes to Enhance Reliability of Wireless Networks

Gianluca Cena(ID), Stefano Scanzio(✉)(ID), Lucia Seno(ID),
and Adriano Valenzano(ID)

National Research Council of Italy (CNR-IEIIT),
Corso Duca degli Abruzzi 24, 10129 Torino, Italy
{gianluca.cena,stefano.scanzio,lucia.seno,
adriano.valenzano}@ieiit.cnr.it

Abstract. Erraticness of the radio spectrum makes communication on wireless networks scarcely deterministic, which renders them hardly suitable for the use in application scenarios that demand high reliability, e.g., industrial wireless control systems. To counteract unpredictable phenomena like electromagnetic noise, moving obstacles, and collisions with interfering traffic, diversity in time, frequency, and space is customarily exploited.

Recently, a number of solutions have appeared, possibly relying on redundant communication hardware, that combine more than one diversity scheme. In this paper, such strategies are analyzed using a simple, yet significant, mathematical model, and their performance compared to determine trade-offs between implementation complexity and the achieved level of dependability.

Keywords: Ultra-reliable wireless networks · Real-time communications · Diversity · Redundancy · TSCH · Wi-Red

1 Introduction

Transmission of signals on radio channels is known to be much less reliable than on wires. This is due to both interference and disturbance. Interference originates from the shared transmission support, and can be effectively dealt with by means of deterministic Medium Access Control (MAC) mechanisms. Conversely, disturbance is mostly caused by unpredictable phenomena, like electromagnetic noise, whose effects can not be counteracted by simply resorting to a better coordination scheme among nodes to access the wireless medium.

This work was partially supported by Regione Piemonte and the Ministry of Education, University, and Research of Italy in the POR FESR 2014/2020 framework, Call "Piattaforma tecnologica Fabbrica Intelligente", Project "Human centered Manufacturing Systems" (application number 312-36).

M. R. Palattella et al. (Eds.): ADHOC-NOW 2019, LNCS 11803, pp. 118–135, 2019.
https://doi.org/10.1007/978-3-030-31831-4_9

It is worth noting that the distinction between interference and disturbance is actually not sharp. Think, e.g., to the case when there are nearby wireless nodes that operate on the same frequency range (or on overlapping ranges) but rely on different kinds of MAC. This is the case, e.g., of co-located Wi-Fi Basic Service Sets (BSSs) and Wireless Sensor Networks (WSNs). In such conditions, the only mechanism that could bring some benefit is the Clear Channel Assessment (CCA) function, which permits to determine if the channel is currently idle. Thanks to CCA, unless two or more nodes start transmitting at the same time (and neglecting the hidden node problem), no collisions may happen. In the following, we will assume that the MAC mechanism is able to coordinate access of compliant nodes, so that interference internal to the network is prevented (or, at least, kept to a minimum). Therefore, we will only focus on disturbance and collisions with non-compliant nodes, both of which can be assumed to occur according to completely random patterns.

In order to ensure that the information received by recipients corresponds exactly to what has been sent by the originator (data integrity), a suitable checksum, based, e.g., on a Cyclic Redundancy Check (CRC), is customarily appended to the transmitted frames by the MAC layer in the originating node. By recalculating the CRC, every recipient is enabled to verify, with high likelihood, the integrity of the received frames, discarding those which are corrupted for sure. Clearly, there is a chance that a corrupted frame is taken for good by some receiver (errors can be either global or local, depending on whether they affect all the intended recipients or only part of them). However, the probability of this event happening can be made small enough by proper CRC selection. In those cases where this is not acceptable, as for protocols related to functional safety, a black channel can be set up above the MAC layer.

To achieve a reasonably low packet loss ratio, in spite of the presence of unpredictable errors affecting frame transmissions, almost every existing wireless communication technology relies on some kind of *diversity*, which is typically incorporated in the MAC layer to enhance performance. By far, the most popular solution is *time* diversity, which simply consists in sending the same packet multiple times. When packets are delivered to individual destinations, time diversity is customarily exploited through Automatic Repeat reQuest (ARQ) techniques. In practice, every time the recipient receives a correct data frame (better, one that passes the integrity check), it immediately replies by sending an acknowledgment (ACK) frame back to the originator. If the originator does not receive the ACK frame within a given timeout ($ACKtimeout$), it sends the data frame again (retransmission). In typical operating conditions, ARQ permits tangible savings (in terms of spectrum consumption) with respect to a mere repetition of the same frame for a fixed number of times. Although ARQ may be used, in theory, also with multicast addresses, efficiently managing ACK frames returned by a plurality of nodes is not easy. For this reason, support for confirmed multicast transmissions is seldom included in real-world solutions. It is worth pointing out that plain repetition, which does not require any feedback from the recipient, can be profitably used to provide time diversity to unconfirmed multicast transmissions.

ARQ techniques offer satisfactory behavior in most application scenarios, like personal mobility, home/office automation, building automation, precision agriculture, and environmental monitoring, to cite a few. Therefore, currently available protocols for wireless networks almost always include ARQ right in the MAC layer. However, other contexts exist that demand noticeably higher reliability. This is the case, for instance, of industrial plants, and in particular of distributed real-time control applications in factory and process automation, as well as of ad-hoc networks set up on demand for disaster management or mission-critical purposes. In these cases, a possible solution is to exploit more than one kind of diversity at the same time. In practice, this means adopting (at least) one additional diversity scheme (e.g., *spatial* or *frequency*) besides time diversity. See, e.g., in [7], where a redundant Ultra Wide Band (UWB) network is considered to set up a wireless backup for wired avionic networks.

In this paper, a review of these mixed diversity schemes is performed, and a comparison is carried out considering their performance and resource requirements. Unlike [10], which focuses on reliability in multi-hop networks, the behavior of a single hop between a pair of adjacent nodes is taken into account here. The paper is organized as follows: in Sect. 2 some definitions are given and a taxonomy is sketched to classify approaches based on more than one kind of diversity, after which a number of existing solutions are described. Section 3 presents some theoretical results, evaluated for a very simple channel error model, about key performance indices relevant to applications that demand high reliability, and a brief discussion on advantages and drawbacks of each solution is included in Sect. 4. Finally, in Sect. 5 some conclusions are drawn.

2   Diversity and Redundancy

Diversity and redundancy can be profitably exploited, at the lower protocols layers (MAC and PHY) of wireless communication networks, in order to improve reliability of data exchanges. While not the same, they are closely related.

In the following, *diversity* refers to techniques where multiple transmission attempts can be performed for the same packet by varying some boundary condition. In the simplest case, the attempt is repeated automatically by the same hardware component, without varying any operational parameters, after some time has elapsed (time diversity). A slightly more complex case is when some parameters are changed attempt by attempt, e.g., a new Modulation and Coding Scheme (MCS) or a new channel is selected on every retry. Finally, if multiple hardware components are available at either the MAC or PHY (radio) levels, attempts can be carried out in parallel using different MAC/radio blocks.

The concept of *redundancy* focuses instead on the availability (or, in our case, on the concurrent use) of more resources than strictly required to perform a packet exchange. In some cases, redundancy refers to *physical resources*. For example, it is possible to foresee multiple antennas with different orientation/polarization, multiple radio blocks tuned on different frequencies, or multiple MAC blocks able to operate independently (enabling concurrent frame transmissions/receptions). In other cases, redundancy refers to *time*. Repetition mechanisms perform packet transmission multiple times in sequence, whereas Forward Error Correction (FEC) codes allocate additional bits in each frame to enable suitable encoding. While no additional hardware is in theory required, transmission times (and spectrum consumption) obviously increase.

As an aside, time diversity implemented by ARQ mechanisms does not imply, strictly speaking, true redundancy. In fact, ARQ is more like a protocol between originator and recipient and, unless ACK frames are lost, no useless (i.e., redundant) attempts may be performed when delivering a packet. The price to pay is the overhead for obtaining a feedback from the recipient (ACK frame duration). Likewise, redundancy provided by FEC encoding can hardly be classified as diversity, according to our previous definition.

2.1 Time vs. Frequency Diversity

Time and frequency diversity are not the same, and are not intended to counteract the same phenomena. Differences between them are provided below.

Repeating the same frame transmission after a while, as foreseen by time diversity, is only effective in the case of short noise pulses or when the amount of interfering traffic is low-to-medium. Prolonged disturbance or bursty interfering traffic may lead to many errors in a row. If the same packet incurs in more errors than the retry limit, it is definitely lost. Time diversity is quite inexpensive, as there is no need for redundant hardware. A possible way to lessen statistical correlation between the outcome of attempts is to enlarge inter-times. On the downside, doing so increases transmission latencies, which is hardly compatible with timing requirements of real-time control applications in industrial scenarios.

Frequency diversity is effective as long as not all the involved channels are affected by the same phenomena. It can be used against narrow-band disturbance, and also permits to cope with interfering traffic in the case a careful planning can not be done for frequency allocation. The price to pay is that a wider range of frequencies is required with respect to legacy solutions, even though the overall amount of consumed spectrum is in theory the same. We may distinguish among solutions based on how much the channels are spaced. For example, channels can be selected in the same band (TSCH) or from different bands (Wi-Red operating on the 2.4 and 5 GHz bands). Clearly, the second solution increases the likelihood that attempts are truly independent, hence improving the effectiveness of diversity, but it is also more expensive.

2.2 Mixed Diversity

In this paper, we will refer to approaches, where two or more kinds of diversity are exploited together for improving communication quality, as *mixed diversity*. Whenever conditions permit so (e.g., when unicast traffic is considered), one of such diversity schemes customarily consists in time diversity as per ARQ. This is due to two reasons: First, time diversity does not require any additional hardware components, which makes implementations simple and inexpensive; Second, but equally important, time diversity is the only diversity scheme that permits to conserve bandwidth, by allowing a packet transmission to be terminated as soon as one of the related frames is successfully exchanged (causal relationship). This is clearly impossible when attempts take place in parallel at the very same time, e.g., using different frequencies or propagation paths.

A first distinction among mixed diversity techniques depends on whether redundancy is required. Seamless link-level Wi-Fi redundancy, as implemented by the Wi-Red proposal [4], demands (at least) a pair of (almost) independent MAC/radio blocks, able to operate concurrently. Conversely, access mechanisms based on frequency hopping [13], like Time Slotted Channel Hopping (TSCH), whose specification is now included in the IEEE 802.15.4 standard document [2], only require a single MAC/radio block, and so they are intrinsically less expensive. All it is needed, in this case, is that the frequency on which the radio block is tuned can be quickly changed at runtime. A further distinction can be done based on the degree of coupling among wireless nodes, so that, e.g., the frequency on which recipients are tuned at any given time can be kept closely tied to the originator. This is only necessary when mixed diversity is implemented without resorting to redundancy, as in solutions based on channel hopping. Conversely, approaches based on seamless link-level redundancy do not require nodes to dynamically switch the transmission channel between attempts, and so synchronization is not needed.

As a rule of thumb, implementation complexity (and, consequently, cost), is related to the achievable performance. However, performance is not the only aspect to take into account. In some cases, backward compatibility has to be preserved. For example, Wi-Red relies on an asynchronous medium access (no time slotting), and provides almost the same behavior as legacy Wi-Fi, so that the same hardware components can be reused. Conversely, the TSCH protocol is implemented in software above IEEE 802.15.4 hardware, which means that noticeably higher flexibility was left to designers when defining the new protocol.

In the following, the specific case of *mixed time-frequency diversity* is taken into account. This does not mean that other techniques, like space diversity or code redundancy, are inadequate or useless: in fact, Wi-Fi [1] uses both. Space diversity, as implemented in Multiple-Input Multiple-Output (MIMO) systems, exploits a plurality of antennas. Besides achieving increased throughput (by supporting several concurrent data streams), MIMO can be also leveraged in Wi-Fi to improve the reliability of the wireless link. In this case, the same signal is sent by the originator on two or more propagation paths. Code redundancy, as implemented by FEC encoding, permits to overcome situations where a limited number of bits have been corrupted during transmission. For example, Wi-Fi relies on a Binary Convolution Code (BCC) since its early versions. Most of the considerations in the analysis below apply, with minimal changes, to mixed time-space diversity techniques, and even to time-frequency-space diversity. With limited effort, code redundancy as well can be thrown into the equation, by considering an enlarged duration for transmission attempts. A solution combining ARQ and

FEC, denoted Deadline Dependent Coding (DDC), is described in [14]. While very interesting, FEC techniques are not included in the following analysis for space reasons. A comprehensive survey on the topic can be found in [9].

2.3   Taxonomy of Mixed Diversity Schemes

A taxonomy of the strategies that combine multiple transmission attempts and mixed diversity is sketched in Table 1. From a general point of view, approaches can be classified as either *sequential*, when attempts are carried out one after another by the same MAC/radio block (possibly changing from time to time the channel or the propagation path), or *parallel*, when they are carried out by distinct blocks (using different channels or propagation paths). In the latter case, redundant hardware is necessarily required (see the fourth column in the table). We may further distinguish between *strictly-parallel* operations, where each MAC/radio block carries out exactly one attempt (usually at the same time), and *sequential-parallel* operations, where a number of attempts can be carried out in sequence by each block.

Legacy solutions, which do not employ any kind of diversity besides retransmissions (like the initial version of IEEE 802.15.4), are categorized as *strictly-sequential*. For the sake of completeness, we also included in the table the *one-shot* case, where a single attempt is carried out on a single-channel single-stream legacy network. Very often, broadcast transmissions fall under this category.

Table 1. Taxonomy of mixed diversity schemes.

Mixed time-frequency diversity scheme	Time diversity	Frequency diversity	Redundancy required	# of retries R_C	# of blocks C
Sequential	Yes	Maybe	No	>1	≥ 1
Parallel	Maybe	Yes	Yes	≥ 1	>1
One-shot (legacy)	No	No	No	1	1
Strictly-sequential (legacy)	Yes	No	No	>1	1
Sequential (chan. hopping)	Yes	Yes	No	>1	1
Sequential-parallel	Yes	Yes	Yes	>1	>1
Strictly-parallel	No	Yes	Yes	1	>1

2.4   Solutions Based on Mixed Diversity

Recently, an increasing interest has been devoted to mixed time-frequency diversity approaches for wireless networks, as witnessed by several existing standards and commercial solutions, as well as a number of proposals available in the literature. A raw performance comparison among such technologies is likely pointless, as they are intended for different application fields. As a consequence, their underlying radios have very different characteristics, and their bit rates may differ by many orders of magnitude (from a few hundreds of Kb/s to more than 1 Gb/s). In the following, some relevant solutions are described and classified according to the proposed taxonomy.

TSCH. Time Slotted Channel Hopping (TSCH) is a particular kind of deterministic MAC that is layered directly above the transmission services of IEEE 802.15.4 [2]. Nodes in the network are kept synchronized to a time master, which enables a scheduled access to the shared medium based on time slotting, where slots have a fixed duration. Unlike legacy Time Division Multiple Access (TDMA) solutions, the frequency on which a transmitter sends its frames is not fixed, but varies over time according to a known pattern. As a result, the transmission schedule (known as *slotframe*) is defined through a matrix, where the number of rows coincides with the available channels while the number of columns sets the periodicity of exchanges. Each cell in this matrix relates to a *link* between two specific nodes, and accommodates exactly one acknowledged frame exchange between a given source and a given destination (a broadcast destination is also allowed for unacknowledged frames).

TSCH is at the basis of new-generation Internet of Things (IoT) solutions like "IPv6 over the TSCH mode of IEEE 802.15.4e" (6TiSCH) [12]. Both the slot duration and the slotframe size can be configured depending on application requirements, but in 6TiSCH they are customarily set to 10 ms and 101 slots, respectively. This means that, in the case of a transmission failure, a new attempt can be performed after about 1 s. In the case of shared cells, a backoff procedure is defined to cope with collisions, which may enlarge this time. TSCH can be classified as a sequential mixed time-frequency diversity scheme, on which a synchronous access scheme is layered to prevent internal collisions.

Bluetooth. Besides being used for connecting wireless peripherals to mobile phones and PCs, Bluetooth [3] is sometimes adopted as the underlying transmission technology of wireless industrial networks because of its robustness. The MAC in Bluetooth [3] hops 1600 times per second over its 79 channels. This implies that every slot lasts 625 μs, much shorter than TSCH. However, the transmission frequency remains fixed for the whole duration of the packet. Bluetooth as well can be classified as a sequential time-frequency diversity scheme but, unlike TSCH, its access scheme is asynchronous and requires looser coordination among nodes.

Wi-Fi. IEEE 802.11 (also known as Wi-Fi) adopts a quite complex MAC. One of the main design goals of Wi-Fi is to ensure very high throughput, as required by applications in home/office environments (multimedia streaming, file transfer, and so on). Recent versions of Wi-Fi foresee a number of diversity/redundancy techniques that operate concurrently, e.g., space diversity (MIMO) and forward error correction (BCC). Most commercial chipsets also include the ability to automatically change the modulation and coding scheme on a per-attempt basis (TX_series). This is exploited, e.g., by the Minstrel algorithm [15].

In theory, a mixed time-frequency scheme, known as MCS32, is made directly available by IEEE 802.11, which relies on channel bonding. In MCS32, the same frame is concurrently sent on the two halves of a 40 MHz channel. In practice, this mechanism is hardly available in real chipsets, and hence, to the best of our knowledge, it is seldom used. This means that Wi-Fi does not actually exploit time-frequency diversity. However, Minstrel can be seen as a sequential mixed time-MCS diversity approach. Access in Wi-Fi is asynchronous, this meaning that time synchronization among stations (STA) is not required.

Wi-Red. The Wi-Red proposal [4] was defined as a proper extension of Wi-Fi that ensures backward compatibility. It relies on two distinct transmission channels, which are managed according to the seamless redundancy rules foreseen by the Parallel Redundancy Protocol (PRP) [8]. This implies that two MAC/radio blocks (sub-STAs) are required for each redundant station (RSTA). When more-than-duplex redundancy is needed, the number of such blocks consequently increases. Upon transmission request for a packet, identical copies are queued for transmission on the sub-STAs of the originator. On the recipient, duplicates are detected and removed. In order not to modify the original Wi-Fi protocol, the transmission processes on sub-STAs, once started, take place independently.

Bandwidth can be saved by relying on Reactive Duplication Avoidance (RDA), which terminates the transmission process on all the sub-STAs as soon as an ACK frame is received on any sub-STA. Suitably displacing the beginning of transmissions on the sub-STAs, as foreseen by Proactive Duplication Avoidance (PDA), may cut down dramatically spectrum consumption. Results about the packet loss ratio and transmission latencies, measured in a real-world experimental testbed, can be found in [5], whereas some hints about saving in spectrum consumption achieved by RDA/PDA techniques are reported in [6]. Wi-Red can be classified as a sequential-parallel mixed time-frequency diversity scheme. Importantly, the same asynchronous medium access as Wi-Fi is retained, in order to ensure full backward compatibility.

3   Quantitative Analysis

The basic point about the use of diversity to face unpredictable phenomena that may impair communication on air (e.g., disturbance and interference from non-compliant wireless nodes) is that, when the boundary conditions for transmission attempts are changed (e.g., if they take place at different times, on different channels, or over different propagation paths), the outcome likely is not the same. In the following, theoretical results are provided about some relevant performance indices for a very simple, yet no-nonsense, channel error model. In particular, we considered the packet delivery ratio (communication reliability), the spectrum consumption (protocol communication efficiency), and the transmission latency (communication timeliness).

3.1 Packet Delivery Ratio

Let m_j denote a packet to be exchanged over the network, by exploiting one or more diversity techniques, while $m_{j,\ell}$ refers to the ℓ-th transmission attempt related to m_j. Basically, the outcome of every transmission attempt can be modeled as a discrete random variable that can assume only two values, *success* or *failure*. Let $\epsilon_{j,\ell}$ be the probability that the transmission attempt $m_{j,\ell}$ fails (*failure probability*). If the transmission of every single packet is unconditionally repeated R times in a row, which means that exactly R distinct attempts are actually performed for it, the probability $P_{L,j}$ that packet m_j is lost (i.e., that it definitely fails to be delivered to destination), also denoted Packet Loss Ratio (PLR), equals the probability that all its attempts fail. In the simplest case, we may assume that the outcomes of transmission attempts related to the same packet are statistically independent. If so,

$$P_{L,j} = \prod_{\ell=1...R} \epsilon_{j,\ell}. \tag{1}$$

This is generally not true when frequency diversity is not exploited, as in strictly-sequential retransmission performed in legacy networks (Wi-Fi or WSNs), since disturbance phenomena may be characterized by a non-negligible duration, hence affecting many attempts in a row. However, it reasonably holds quite well for protocols based on channel hopping, like TSCH: it is unlikely that a transmission error taking place in a slot on a channel affects the probability that another error occurs, after a while, in a subsequent slot on a different channel.

In ARQ, the retransmission process for a packet is terminated as soon as the originator understands that one of its attempts succeeded, as determined by the feedback returned by the recipient (ACK frame). Performing further retries after a successful frame exchange is completely pointless and never done in practice. In this case, R coincides with the *retry limit* (possibly plus one, depending on the specific definition) and bounds the number of allowed attempts: exactly one initial attempt plus a variable number of retries. It is worth noting that Eq. (1) identically applies to ARQ as well.

By assuming that the wireless spectrum is time-invariant and channel-invariant, the packet loss ratio can be computed as $P_L^0 = \epsilon^R$, where ϵ represents the (constant) probability that a generic attempt fails, irrespective of the instant of transmission and the selected channel. In such conditions, the Packet Delivery Ratio (PDR) seen by applications can be defined as

$$\delta = 1 - P_L^0 = 1 - \epsilon^R, \tag{2}$$

and, under our hypotheses, it only depends on ϵ and R.

In Fig. 1, the packet delivery ratio δ is plotted versus the failure probability ϵ of single attempts in the cases when the maximum number R of allowed attempts is equal to 1 (i.e., diversity is not exploited), 3, and 9. Whatever the amount of disturbance affecting the channel, and as long as communication is

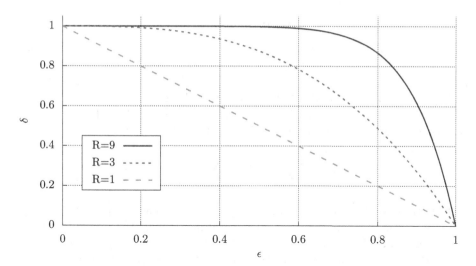

Fig. 1. Packet delivery ratio δ vs. failure probability ϵ under the hypothesis of ideal channel error model by varying the overall number R of allowed attempts.

not completely and permanently prevented, it is theoretically possible to obtain the desired reliability level δ^0 by simply increasing R:

$$R \geq \left\lceil \frac{\log(1 - \delta^0)}{\log(\epsilon)} \right\rceil \Rightarrow \delta(R, \epsilon) \geq \delta^0. \tag{3}$$

Clearly, there are some trade-offs in doing so, which will be discussed in the following sections.

Under the above simplistic assumption, δ does not depend on the kind of diversity exploited, but only on the overall number R of allowed attempts. As an example, let us consider, the case when $R = 9$. If sequential time-frequency diversity ("seq") is exploited, up to 9 transmission attempts are performed in a row (one after the other) by changing channel on every attempt. Alternatively, in a strictly-parallel frequency diversity ("par") implementation, $C = 9$ distinct MAC/radio transmission blocks, each one tuned on a different channel, perform a single *combined* transmission attempt at once.

More relevant to the sequential-parallel mixed time-frequency diversity ("msp") schemes we are considering here, we may also choose to rely, e.g., on $C = 3$ independent MAC/radio blocks tuned on different channels, and to separately schedule up to $R_C = 3$ transmission attempts on every channel (as happens in Wi-Red). Similarly (but behavior is not exactly the same), we may assume that $R_C = 3$ combined attempts are performed by the originator, each one involving all channels at exactly the same time. This leads to the same overall maximum number of transmission attempts as the above approaches, i.e., $R = C \cdot R_C = 9$. Whatever the case, if attempts are statistically independent and the probability they suffer from failures is the same, the same packet delivery ratio is achieved.

3.2   Overall Number of Attempts

One of the main downsides of diversity is that, spectrum consumption worsens because of the chance of multiple transmissions. In particular, it is directly related to the overall number of attempts that are performed, on average, for each packet. For sequential ARQ techniques in legacy wireless networks, the number ω_{seq} of transmission attempts per packet is bounded by the retry limit, that is, $\omega_{\text{seq}} \leq R$. The mean number $\overline{\omega}_{\text{seq}}$ of attempts per packet is equal to

$$\overline{\omega}_{\text{seq}} = 1 + \sum_{\ell=2...R} \epsilon^{\ell-1} = \sum_{\ell'=0...R-1} \epsilon^{\ell'} = \frac{1-\epsilon^R}{1-\epsilon}. \tag{4}$$

In fact, the initial attempt is always performed, whereas the probability that the ℓ-th attempt (where $2 \leq \ell \leq R$) is performed equals the probability that all the preceding $\ell - 1$ attempts have failed. It is worth noting that the same result identically applies to sequential mixed time-frequency diversity schemes (e.g., those based on channel hopping).

For strictly-parallel implementations, all attempts are carried out at once on the C physical channels, which implies that the overall number of attempts performed per packet, all channels considered, is $\omega_{\text{par}} = \overline{\omega}_{\text{par}} = C$.

The case of sequential-parallel mixed time-frequency diversity, where each node is provided with C MAC/radio blocks tuned on distinct channels and every block performs up to R_C attempts (as happens in Wi-Red), can be studied in approximate way by considering a sequential ARQ transmission performed on a redundant link that includes C physical channels. Every combined attempt on the redundant link consists in C distinct attempts, which are performed contextually on all physical channels. In this case, the *equivalent failure probability* ϵ_C on the redundant link coincides with the probability that all the C concurrent attempts fail, that is, under our simplified hypotheses, $\epsilon_C = \epsilon^C$.

The overall number ω_{msp} of transmission attempts per packet, all channels considered, is bounded by the retry limit on single channels, i.e., $\omega_{\text{msp}} \leq C \cdot R_C$, whereas the average overall number of attempts is equal to

$$\overline{\omega}_{\text{msp}} = C \cdot \left[1 + \sum_{\ell=2...R_C} \epsilon_C^{\ell-1} \right] = C \cdot \frac{1-\epsilon^{C \cdot R_C}}{1-\epsilon^C}. \tag{5}$$

Referring back to the example introduced in the previous section (where the overall number of attempts is $R = 9$ and the number C of MAC/radio blocks operating in parallel is 1, 3, or 9), the average overall number $\overline{\omega}$ of attempts, for sequential, strictly-parallel, and sequential-parallel mixed time-frequency diversity strategies, is plotted in Fig. 2. The overall number of attempts ω also provides some indication on energy consumption.

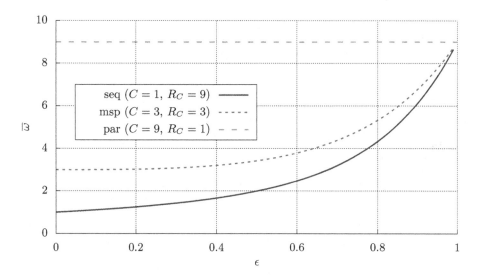

Fig. 2. Average overall number $\overline{\omega}$ of attempts per transmitted packet (all channels considered) vs. failure probability ϵ, for sequential (seq), strictly-parallel (par), and sequential-parallel (msp) diversity approaches.

3.3 Communication Efficiency

The communication efficiency η of protocols that foresee multiple transmissions attempts per packet can be conveniently defined as the inverse of $\overline{\omega}$, that is,

$$\eta = \frac{1}{\overline{\omega}}. \tag{6}$$

For the previously considered examples, it is plotted in Fig. 3. Concerning communication efficiency, sequential solutions like TSCH are always advantageous with respect to solutions that perform parallel transmissions using redundant communication hardware. This is because of ARQ, which terminates transmission as soon as there is evidence that the packet was correctly delivered. In this way, useless attempts are never performed. Differences among diversity schemes fade away as the failure probability grows. At worst, all the R envisaged attempts are carried out for the packet on very noisy channels, which means that the limit of η as ϵ approaches 1 from the left is

$$\lim_{\epsilon \to 1^-} \eta(\epsilon, R) = \frac{1}{R}. \tag{7}$$

3.4 Number of Attempts Before Success

This section analyzes how many attempts are carried out on average, at the level of the single MAC/radio block, to deliver a packet to the recipient. In the

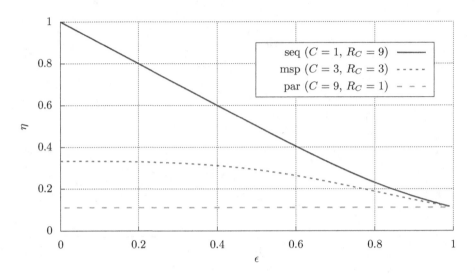

Fig. 3. Communication efficiency η vs. failure probability ϵ for sequential (seq), strictly-parallel (par), and sequential-parallel (msp) diversity approaches.

case of sequential mixed time-frequency diversity where at most R transmission attempts are allowed, the probability that a packet is sent exactly ℓ times by the originator (i.e., $\ell - 1$ failures followed by one success) is $\epsilon^{\ell-1}(1 - \epsilon)$. By considering only packets correctly delivered to the recipient, the above probability has to be divided by $1 - \epsilon^R$ (conditional probability). Thus, the average number of attempts performed for correctly delivered packets is

$$\overline{\alpha}_{\mathrm{seq}} = \sum_{\ell=1...R} \ell \cdot \frac{\epsilon^{\ell-1}(1-\epsilon)}{1-\epsilon^R} = \frac{1-\epsilon}{1-\epsilon^R} \sum_{\ell=1...R} \ell \cdot \epsilon^{\ell-1}, \tag{8}$$

which is a truncated geometric series that yields

$$\overline{\alpha}_{\mathrm{seq}} = \frac{1}{1-\epsilon^R} \left[\frac{1-\epsilon^{R+1}}{(1-\epsilon)} - (R+1)\epsilon^R \right]. \tag{9}$$

Quantity α can be used to estimate the transmission latency, unlike ω, which is related to the spectrum consumption. While $\overline{\alpha}_{\mathrm{seq}}$ is close to $\overline{\omega}_{\mathrm{seq}}$ in typical operating conditions, they are not the same. In particular, they may differ substantially when the failure probability ϵ is high. The limit of $\overline{\alpha}_{\mathrm{seq}}$ as ϵ approaches 1 from the left is

$$\lim_{\epsilon \to 1^-} \overline{\alpha}_{\mathrm{seq}}(\epsilon, R) = \frac{1+R}{2}. \tag{10}$$

In fact, if disturbance is very high, the probability that correct delivery occurs at the ℓ-th attempt only marginally depends on ℓ, and the related probability mass function is almost uniformly distributed between 1 and R.

When parallel frequency diversity schemes are taken into account, which foresee C redundant MAC/radio blocks, all attempts performed contextually

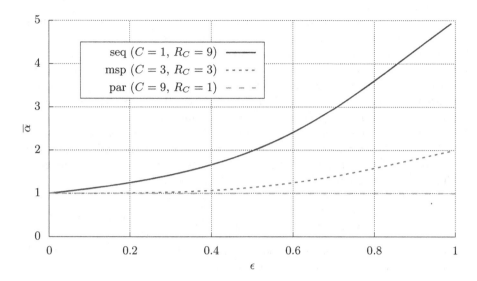

Fig. 4. Average number $\overline{\alpha}$ of (combined) attempts per correctly delivered packet vs. failure probability ϵ, for sequential (seq), strictly-parallel (par), and sequential-parallel (msp) diversity approaches.

count, from the point of view of α, as a single attempt (a combined attempt takes the same time as a single attempt). For example, let us consider combined attempts carried out on $C = 3$ channels at a time. Let us assume that the transmission of a packet initially fails on all channels, and that one (or more) attempts succeed at the second try. In this case, $\alpha = 2$, because the time taken for the packet to be delivered to destination corresponds to two attempts.

In the case of a strictly-parallel approach, every correctly delivered packet experienced exactly one combined attempt, and hence $\overline{\alpha}_{\mathrm{par}} = \alpha_{\mathrm{par}} = 1$.

For sequential-parallel mixed time-frequency diversity, we can consider again a sequential transmission performed on an redundant link with C physical channels and failure probability ϵ^C. This approximate analysis yields

$$\overline{\alpha}_{\mathrm{msp}} = \frac{1}{1 - \epsilon^{C \cdot R_C}} \left[\frac{1 - \epsilon^{C \cdot (R_C + 1)}}{(1 - \epsilon^C)} - (R_C + 1)\,\epsilon^{C \cdot R_C} \right]. \tag{11}$$

The mean number $\overline{\alpha}$ of combined attempts before success, for sequential, strictly-parallel, and sequential-parallel mixed diversity, is plotted in Fig. 4.

3.5   Transmission Latency

Transmission latency d_j measures the time between the transmission request for a packet m_j issued at the originator and its correct delivery to the recipient. This quantity is only defined for correctly delivered packets and, generally speaking, it depends on how many attempts are performed before the packet is received by the recipient with no errors and the time elapsing between subsequent attempts. Let $t_{j,0}$ be the time when the transmission request for packet m_j is issued, and $t_{j,\ell}$ the time when the j-th transmission attempt ends, either successfully or with a failure. The latency for m_j is equal to $d_j = t_{j,\alpha_j} - t_{j,0}$, where α_j denotes the attempt when the transmission of m_j succeeded. The contribution $\Delta d_{j,\ell}$ to the latency of m_j due to the ℓ-th attempt (where $1 \le \ell \le \alpha_j$) corresponds to $\Delta d_{j,\ell} = t_{j,\ell} - t_{j,\ell-1}$ (where $1 \le \ell \le \alpha_j$), and includes any initial access time, either due to random backoff or related to the position of the link in the slotframe, the times taken by the originator to send on air the DATA frame and by the recipient to return the ACK frame, as well as any fixed interframe gaps.

The mean transmission latency can be expressed as

$$\bar{d} = \frac{1}{N_{\text{pkt}}} \sum_{j=1...N_{\text{pkt}}} d_j = \frac{1}{N_{\text{pkt}}} \sum_{j=1...N_{\text{pkt}}} \sum_{\ell=1...\alpha_j} \Delta d_{j,\ell}, \qquad (12)$$

where N_{pkt} is the number of packets transmitted over a time interval wide enough. According to out simplifying hypothesis on channel error invariance,

$$\bar{d} = \sum_{\ell=1...R} \epsilon^{\ell-1} \frac{1-\epsilon}{1-\epsilon^R} \cdot \bar{d}_{(\ell)}, \qquad (13)$$

where $\bar{d}_{(\ell)}$ is the average latency experienced by packets that managed to be delivered to destination in exactly ℓ attempts.

Finding a closed-form expression for $\bar{d}_{(\ell)}$ is quite difficult, as it depends on the specific MAC of the underlying network technology. For instance, an exponential random backoff is performed in Wi-Fi on each failed attempt, which means that $\bar{d}_{(\ell)}$ grows more than linearly with ℓ, whereas transmission in TSCH has first to wait for a suitable cell (link) in the slotframe, with retries typically spaced by one slotframe. If shared cells are considered, an exponential backoff is carried out in TSCH as well, by which a random number of suitable cells are skipped in the case of a failed attempt.

For the sake of simplicity, we will hide MAC complexity by assuming that the contribution of attempts to the latency is fixed, that is, $\Delta d_{j,\ell} \simeq D$. This implies that $\bar{d}_{(\ell)} \simeq \ell \cdot D$, and the average transmission latency can be approximated as

$$\bar{d} \simeq \bar{\alpha} \cdot D. \qquad (14)$$

This is clearly a very rough approximation: since the inter-time between attempts related to any given packet usually increases as more attempts are carried out, the value of $\bar{d}$ provided by (14) is optimistic. For our purposes, this is acceptable, as we simply wish to compare retransmission strategies based on the same underlying MAC when the degree of parallelization (i.e., number of redundant MAC/radio blocks) is varied. Referring back to the previously introduced examples, the approximate shape of the average latency for the three considered strategies can be inferred from Fig. 4. As can be seen, when the failure probability for attempts is negligible, i.e., $\epsilon \ll 1$, the transmission latency is the same for all approaches. Conversely, when the failure probability increases, parallel schemes have a clear advantage over sequential solutions.

4   Discussion on Results

Validity of theoretical results derived in the previous section basically depends on the assumptions on the channel error model, either ideal or real.

Ideal Channel. Under the ideal channel error model we considered, communication reliability (as given by the packet delivery ratio δ) only depends on the limit R on the overall number of transmission attempts that are allowed per packet. Unfortunately, increasing R implies that a larger portion of the spectrum is used up, which makes this approach greedy, impairing coexistence with nearby wireless networks, and also worsens energy consumption.

When scenarios are considered where response times do definitely matter (e.g., in time-critical and safety-critical applications), there is however a second kind of drawback in increasing the number of attempts that can be performed in sequence. Repeating transmission of the same packet too many times worsens mean latency $\bar{d}$, which in turn may cause the deadline of time-critical data to be exceeded. In some contexts, a deadline miss can be as severe as a packet loss. For this reason, the Delivery Success Probability (DSP) is sometimes used to describe the fraction of packets arriving to destination correctly and timely [11]. In such cases, a suitable solution is to adopt a mechanism that parallelizes transmission attempts by means of redundant communication hardware. This is the case, e.g., of the Wi-Red proposal, which implements link-level seamless redundancy on Wi-Fi. Coupled with the high bit rate, this provides both good reliability and prompt data transfers at the same time. Clearly, such an approach is pointless for IoT solutions like TSCH, which demand inexpensive implementations and low energy consumption (and hence, no redundancy and lower bit rates).

Real Channels. Unfortunately, assuming that transmission attempts are statistically independent, with a time-invariant, channel invariant error probability, is only partially adequate in real scenarios, and sometimes it is just unacceptable. This is because, in spite of diversity, some dependence unavoidably exists between attempts. Usually, the nearer attempts are in time, frequency, or space, the more they are correlated, in such a way that the probability of multiple failures is higher than in the case of true independence, which implies that $P_L \geq P_L^0$ (and, sometimes, $P_L \gg P_L^0$).

Generally speaking, (2) provides the probability of correct packet delivery featured by a diversity scheme in optimal conditions, and is the target against which real solutions have to be checked. Referring to results in the previous sections, we can say that all of them are typically optimistic. A possible exception is given by sequential mixed time-frequency diversity schemes, like TSCH. In this case, assuming that attempts related to the same packet are mostly independent is typically possible, since both time and frequency are varied. A reasonable independence between attempts is achieved, to a lesser extent, in Wi-Fi (and Wi-Red), thanks to the coupling of time and MCS diversity (Minstrel), as well as to the possible adoption of space diversity (MIMO).

5   Conclusions

Coordination among nodes in wireless networks (as achieved when a deterministic MAC is adopted) permits to tangibly reduce internal interference and collisions. On the contrary, resilience against unpredictable phenomena that may severely impair communication, like noise pulses, relative movement between nodes and obstacles, multipath fading, and interfering traffic from nearby uncoordinated wireless nodes, can be only improved by resorting to approaches that employ one or more diversity schemes at a time. Recently, a number of solutions have appeared that combine retransmissions as per ARQ (i.e., time diversity) with other diversity/redundancy techniques, like channel hopping, antenna diversity, seamless channel redundancy, forward error correction codes, rate adaptation algorithms, and so on.

In this paper, these mixed diversity approaches have been classified according to a suitable taxonomy, and the improvements they are able to achieve evaluated using a simple yet no-nonsense channel error model. The most relevant performance indices when critical applications are taken into account are reliability, spectrum consumption, and transmission latencies, but implementation cost and energy consumption are also important. Clearly, a trade-off has to be found among them, depending on the specific scenario that is being considered.

Results confirm that tangible advantages over legacy solutions, based on plain ARQ, can be achieved by leveraging mixed diversity. In particular, higher levels of reliability and timeliness can be ensured at the same time. Sequential time-frequency diversity provided by channel hopping (TSCH) likely provides the best balance between implementation complexity and reliability. Seamless link-level redundancy (Wi-Red) is more expensive, but noticeably reduces transmission latencies. This aspect is certainly valuable when fast control loops have to be closed over the air. As part of our future activities, we plan to improve our analysis of mixed diversity, by considering more realistic channel error models.

References

1. IEEE Standard for Information Technology - Telecommunications and information exchange between systems Local and metropolitan area networks - Specific requirements - Part 11: Wireless LAN Medium Access Control (MAC) and Physical Layer (PHY) Specifications. IEEE Std 802.11-2016 (Revision of IEEE Std 802.11-2012), pp. 1–3534, December 2016. https://doi.org/10.1109/IEEESTD.2016.7786995
2. IEEE Standard for Low-Rate Wireless Networks: IEEE Std 802.15.4-2015 (Revision of IEEE Std 802.15.4-2011), pp. 1–709, April 2016. https://doi.org/10.1109/IEEESTD.2016.7460875
3. Bluetooth Core Specification v 5.1. Bluetooth SIG, pp. 1–2985, January 2019
4. Cena, G., Scanzio, S., Valenzano, A.: Seamless link-level redundancy to improve reliability of industrial Wi-Fi networks. IEEE Trans. Ind. Inform. **12**(2), 608–620 (2016). https://doi.org/10.1109/TII.2016.2522768
5. Cena, G., Scanzio, S., Valenzano, A.: Experimental evaluation of seamless redundancy applied to industrial Wi-Fi networks. IEEE Trans. Ind. Inform. **13**(2), 856–865 (2017). https://doi.org/10.1109/TII.2016.2641469

6. Cena, G., Scanzio, S., Valenzano, A.: Experimental evaluation of techniques to lower spectrum consumption in Wi-Red. IEEE Trans. Wirel. Commun. **18**(2), 824–837 (2019). https://doi.org/10.1109/TWC.2018.2884914

7. Dang, D., Mifdaoui, A.: Performance optimization of a UWB-based network for safety-critical avionics. In: IEEE Conference on Emerging Technology and Factory Automation (ETFA 2014), pp. 1–9, September 2014. https://doi.org/10.1109/ETFA.2014.7005191

8. IEC: Industrial communication networks - High availability automation networks - Part 3: Parallel Redundancy Protocol (PRP) and High-availability Seamless Redundancy (HSR). IEC Std 62439-3 ed 2.0, pp. 1–177 (2010)

9. Le Martret, C.J., Le Duc, A., Marcille, S., Ciblat, P.: Analytical performance derivation of hybrid ARQ schemes at IP layer. IEEE Trans. Commun. **60**(5), 1305–1314 (2012). https://doi.org/10.1109/TCOMM.2012.042712.110058A

10. Mahmood, M.A., Seah, W.K., Welch, I.: Reliability in wireless sensor networks: a survey and challenges ahead. Comput. Netw. **79**, 166–187 (2015). https://doi.org/10.1016/j.comnet.2014.12.016, http://www.sciencedirect.com/science/article/pii/S1389128614004708

11. Seno, L., Cena, G., Scanzio, S., Valenzano, A., Zunino, C.: Enhancing communication determinism in Wi-Fi networks for soft real-time industrial applications. IEEE Trans. Ind. Inform. **13**(2), 866–876 (2017). https://doi.org/10.1109/TII.2016.2641468

12. Thubert, P.: An Architecture for IPv6 over the TSCH mode of IEEE 802.15.4. IETF Std draft-ietf-6tisch-architecture-19, pp. 1–60, December 2018

13. Tinka, A., Watteyne, T., Pister, K.: A decentralized scheduling algorithm for time synchronized channel hopping. In: Zheng, J., Simplot-Ryl, D., Leung, V.C.M. (eds.) ADHOCNETS 2010. LNICST, vol. 49, pp. 201–216. Springer, Heidelberg (2010). https://doi.org/10.1007/978-3-642-17994-5_14

14. Uhlemann, E., Rasmussen, L.K.: Incremental redundancy deadline dependent coding for efficient wireless real-time communications. In: IEEE Conference on Emerging Technologies and Factory Automation (ETFA 2005), vol. 2, pp. 417–424, September 2005. https://doi.org/10.1109/ETFA.2005.1612708

15. Xia, D., Hart, J., Fu, Q.: Evaluation of the Minstrel rate adaptation algorithm in IEEE 802.11g WLANs. In: IEEE International Conference on Communications (ICC 2013), pp. 2223–2228, June 2013. https://doi.org/10.1109/ICC.2013.6654858

Asymptotic Load Balancing Algorithm for Many Task Scheduling

Anamaria-Raluca Oncioiu[1], Florin Pop[1,2(✉)], and Christian Esposito[3]

[1] University Politehnica of Bucharest, Bucharest, Romania
oncioiu.raluca@yahoo.com, florin.pop@cs.pub.ro
[2] National Institute of Research - Development in Informatics (ICI),
Bucharest, Romania
florin.pop@ici.ro
[3] Department of Electrical Engineering and Information Technology,
University of Napoli "Federico II", Napoli, Italy
christian.esposito@unina.it

Abstract. Cloud computing can enable the unraveling of new scientific breakthroughs. We will eventually arrive to compute overwhelmingly large sizes of information, larger than we ever thought about it. Better scheduling algorithms are the key to process Big Data. This paper presents a load balancing scheduling algorithm for Many Task Computing using the computational resources from Cloud, in order to process a huge number of tasks with a finite number of resources. As such, the algorithm can be also used for Big Data, because it scales easily for big applications if we put a load balancing algorithm on top of virtual machines. We impose an upper bound of one for the maximum nodes that can carry an arbitrary job without executing it and we show that this statement holds by simulating the algorithm in MTS2 (Many Task Scheduling Simulator). We also show that the algorithm's overlay performs even better when there are multiple nodes and we discuss about choosing the best local scheduling policy for the working nodes.

Keywords: Task Scheduling · Cloud computing · Load balancing · Scheduling policy

1 Introduction

Nowadays, distributed systems are more and more confronting with Many Task Computing (MTC) problems, because of the arrive of Big Data. Because in general, Clouds are processing loosely coupled tasks, it was necessary to introduce

The research presented in this paper is supported by the following projects: StorEdge (GNaC 2018 ARUT - AU11-18-07), ROBIN (PN-III-P1-1.2-PCCDI-2017-0734), NETIO ForestMon/Tel-MONAER (53/05.09.2016, SMIS2014+ 105976) and SPERO (PN-III-P2-2.1-SOL-2016-03-0046, 3Sol/2017). We would like to thank the reviewers for their time and expertise, constructive comments and valuable insight.

© Springer Nature Switzerland AG 2019
M. R. Palattella et al. (Eds.): ADHOC-NOW 2019, LNCS 11803, pp. 136–149, 2019.
https://doi.org/10.1007/978-3-030-31831-4_10

another type of programming model. MTC was first introduced by Ioan Raicu as an alternate programming model to High Performance Computing (HPC) and High Throughput Computing (HTC). It solves problems that can be structured as graphs of discrete tasks with edges formed by input and output. Tasks can be as large as possible and can use multiple cores. The set of tasks can be of any type: homogeneous or heterogeneous, static or dynamic, loosely coupled or tightly coupled [11].

We are addressing the following scheduling problem: we have a finite set of resources (a Hadoop cluster or a private Cloud dedicated to some specific types of operations), certain specific applications (like crawling on the Internet periodically) and the condition that every resource can be responsible for the execution of a large number of tasks, where a task is a set of operations and every operation needs a specific machine, this being the primary constraint. We have a group consisting in a limited number of heterogeneous machines, where a machine can process a specific number of tasks at a given time. The preemption of any task is not allowed and respecting the deadlines represents the second constraint. We must schedule and send to execution all the tasks with minimum penalties.

Our contribution is an algorithm that tries to reuse as much as possible the virtual machines (VMs) and balance the average work of each one, because when there are multiple idle VMs, more energy is consumed and more resources are wasted. This algorithm is not a resource management solution for VMs in Cloud, but a scheduling algorithm that does not require homogeneous nodes in order to work. We don't propose an algorithm that fits just one particular application, but one that fits all scheduling problems that confront with many tasks and asymptotic loads. The algorithm is designed to have an overlay for Cloud, which is the same with the overlay of a common network, except that nodes are composed of VMs. It has a generic load computation intended to show the availability of nodes for job execution, a dynamic switch of the central job distributor node with its first idle neighbour that requires $\mathcal{O}(1)$ and a forwarding scheme of jobs defined as Round Robin. The dynamic switch of distributor guarantees the overall load balancing in Cloud even for the distributor and also a fault tolerant mechanism when the distributor node has a load that is considerably larger than its neighbours. Jobs are treated as independent and having a short execution time. The algorithm has a linear complexity despite the context in which is being used, that is Big Data, because each job is not preempted and executed just by one node. Jobs can be passed from one node to another, but still they are executed on the first node that received the job or on the first neighbour of that node. In order to simulate the algorithm we choose MTS^2 (a simulator for Many Task Computing) because it has an MTC oriented architecture and it's faster than SimMatrix [12]: MTS^2 can simulate 10^6 nodes and 10^8 messages on 2 cores with just 700 MB of RAM in 340 s.

The paper is organized as follows. In Sect. 2, we highlight some existing scheduling algorithms for asymptotic loads in Cloud, focusing on their performance and requirements. In Sect. 3, we propose a load balancing algorithm for

Big Data using Cloud resources. Section 4 describes the design of MTS^2 and its usage in the context of proposed scheduling algorithm. Results from simulations with MTS^2 are shown in Sect. 5, along with the comparison with another existent scheduler in terms of performance. We also included in Sect. 6 conclusions derived from our work and future thoughts.

2   Background and Related Work

Exascale computing has multiple domains such as multimedia streaming, social-networks, medicine, weather, bioinformatics, astronomy, astrophysics, data analytics etc. All these domains have reached large amounts of data that need to be processed. As such, a new era has arrived, that is Big Data.

HPC systems are sharing the "multi-core" hardware resources among multiple applications. Some characteristics of HPC systems are cooling techniques, high speed of data processing, high processors and job management systems (JMS). Some of the most important technologies that were used for HPC systems are: Globus, Portable Batch System (PBS) Gridbus and Platform LSF (Platform Load Sharing Facility). These technologies improve the way that HPC systems are sharing, exchanging, selecting and aggregating the resources. The types of resources for a distributed system are computers, applications, data bases and tools for manipulating the data. These are geographically distributed and used by virtual organizations and enterprises.

Cloud computing started from the idea of grid computing and a pay-per-service business model. Few years ago, Grid computing was a distributed computing paradigm [14] that was mainly used in intensive scientific computations across a distributed network with hosts that use distributed resources. Every resource from the Cloud can be served from different services layers: IaaS or Infrastructure as a Service (virtual machines, servers, storage, network), PaaS or Platform as a Service (execution runtime, database, web server, development tools) and SaaS or Software as a Service (email, virtual desktop, communication, games, voice over IP etc.). The last layer can be seen as multiple layers of the same type, meaning that software can be categorized according to its complexity and facilities that is offering to clients.

High-performance computing is mainly focused on maximizing the computing power of a system, rather than dealing with large data sets. As such, we will use Cloud computing as a solution for Big Data Science in order to process a huge number of jobs with a finite set of resources. A resource can be responsible with the execution of a huge number of jobs, where huge means multiple execution times of the same job and multiple temporary jobs. However, a machine can process only one operation at a time and preemption is not allowed. An application is a specific set of jobs where each job needs a specific machine in order to run.

Some simulators for Big Data have been created, such as CloudSim [3], SimMatrix [11] and others. We will show later, in Sect. 4, the limitations of CloudSim in order to make dynamic simulations and present the design for another simulator: MTS^2 - Many Task Scheduling Simulator.

2.1 Specifications and Constraints for Scheduling Algorithms and Policies

Scheduling policies have multiple criteria such as: CPU, deadlines, preemption, fairness. The last criteria is known as having a single task or process that is running and all other processes being in starvation for operating system's resources.

There are multiple known scheduling policies: Processor Sharing (PS), First Come First Served (FCFS), Shortest Remaining Processing Time First (SRPT), Longest Remaining Processing Time First (LRPT), Least Attained Service (LAS) etc. For Cloud systems, a scheduling algorithm is crucial for processing large tasks. If a job was planned to be processed, it is ideal to wait until its completion and not to interrupt it for making anything else: processing another task, executing another operation mandatory for the operating system.

Different techniques and scheduling policies were developed until now for Big Data such as IBIS: Interposed Big-data I/O Scheduler [13]. But there is no such perfect algorithm that fits for all types of applications or types of Clouds (private, public or hybrid). Each algorithm is implemented taken into consideration the needs for a particular application. Some of the requirements can be met if part of the initial considerations of the application architecture are simplified. The types of requirements can be: dependencies between tasks (whether or not the tasks are independent, types of shared resources etc.), preemption, deadlines etc.

Some of the real problems that Big Data algorithms are confronting with are, according with [2]:

- **Streaming** includes multimedia streaming, rolling average of previous k items, the most frequent items seen so far. For example, the Bloom filter discovered in 1970 is used in market baskets in order to predict items that are more frequently purchased together.
- **Image extraction**. Software companies work at face image feature extractions for social networks, bioinformatics etc.
- **Content-based filtering**. Finding information about a person or a group of persons can result in targeted content for these people. This content may be suggested friends on social networks based on preferences, recommendations for movies, music or products on online stores etc.
- **Clustering**. This group of algorithms creates hierarchies of species, customers, scientific papers etc.
- **Classification** refers to computational models like neural networks and Bayesian decision trees.
- **Sorting**. This is very important when displaying websites according to relevance after a string query in web search engines.
- **Searching**. For example, this is important for finding the most relevant scientific paper according to some keywords that has the best quality of information.

2.2 Management of Resources in Cloud Systems

The resources in Cloud are memory, CPU, storage, applications, web services etc. Every resource is released whenever the demand is low. For every resource, clients must pay whenever they use it. Each task needs some specific types of resources. A single resource can be responsible for a huge number of tasks.

In Cloud, there are multiple virtual machines in every physical host. The idea is giving to the clients the exact resources and services that they need. Therefore, splitting storage and computational performance is done very easy with virtual machines. A virtual machine is seen as a process on the main operating system, without interfering with it in case of a failure. This type of virtualization is called full virtualization. There are another two types of virtualization called partial virtualization and para-virtualization, which consider that part of the hardware is simulated, or respectively, hardware must not be simulated and virtual machines are working in isolated domains [1,6,9].

Virtual machines can migrate from a specific machine to another without needing to shutdown them. Also, virtual machines can run multiple types of operating systems. Another feature of virtual machines is that resources are protected because there is a high level of isolation between virtual machines.

Managing the resources in Cloud also involves using advanced tools for monitoring the applications. Some of these advanced systems are Swift, Falkon and Karajan [15]. Swift is a parallel programming tool for management of engineering workflows. Falkon is a light-weight task execution service that can be integrated with Swift [7]. Karajan maps different computations to the system's resources.

There are some solutions for private Clouds in terms of resource management like VMware DRS and Microsoft PRO. However, these solutions don't scale for other types of Clouds [5].

Companies providing Cloud services have defined some levels of service agreements for their clients, in order to guarantee the quality of their services. However, each company tries to group their own metrics in four main metrics: availability, performance, reliability, scalability and cost. For example, Amazon EC2 (Amazon Elastic Compute Cloud) agrees in its SLA that the monthly uptime percentage is 99.95%, that is a considerable agreement made to its users.

3　The Asymptotic Load Balancing Scheduling Algorithm

3.1　Initial Scheduling Problem

We are addressing the following scheduling problem: we have a finite set of resources (a Hadoop cluster or a private Cloud dedicated to some specific types of operations), certain specific applications (like crawling on the Internet periodically) and the condition that every resource can be responsible with the execution of an infinite number of tasks, where a task is a set of operations and every operation needs a specific machine, this being the primary constraint.

We have a group consisting in a limited number of heterogeneous machines, where a machine can process a specific number of tasks at a given time. The preemption of any task is not allowed and respecting the deadlines represents the second constraint. We must schedule and send to execution all the tasks with minimum penalties.

The general context is Big Data Science, where the volume of data is very big, the speed of arriving data is also big, and there are multiple types of data. A concrete problem is represented by an application such as Flickr or Picasa, where the operations are defined such as writes and reads of data in distributed file sistems (HDFS, NFS etc.).

3.2 An Overlay that Solves Our Problem

Jobs for machines can be described as loosely coupled (meaning independent) or tight coupled. They can also run on a single core or multiple cores. Jobs can be running periodically or just for a few times. They need to store large amounts of data or they need CPU for a long time in order to finish the computations. Therefore, jobs can also be described as being CPU-intensive, IO-intensive or mixed [11].

We suppose that jobs are working independently and they are characterized by the above description. For example, this can work for the Internet search queries: some of them are running periodically and some of them only for a few times, but they are not influencing each other.

We introduce the definition of overlay for Cloud systems. The overlay is the same concept as the overlay for a common network: it defines the logical connections between the hosts in order to achieve great response times. Taking into consideration a large network, having a full mesh is not a good idea, because hosts are tightly coupled between them and they will not respond very well to technical failures.

Because we are dealing with a distributed network we must find an appropriate overlay in order to process jobs at high rates. Having only one node responsible for distributing the jobs for the other nodes in the network is not sufficient, because that node will be very soon high loaded. We must also take into consideration the fact that failures can happen at any time and a node with such responsibility of distributing jobs for other nodes can't be tolerable.

We chose an overlay similar to Chord, because it offers the following properties [8]:

- No overhead in communication, because paths between nodes are already known. Every node has a distributed hash table with node IDs as keys. Therefore retrieving a neighbour's ID is $\mathcal{O}(1)$.
- Fault tolerance if a node n crashes, because all the keys assigned to n will be sent to the first neighbour.
- Load balancing of information, because every node has the same number of neighbours in order to communicate.
- Scalability. When a node joins the system, just a few finger tables are modified in order to reflect the entrance of a new node.
- Distributivity. The overlay is supposed to work for a peer-to-peer decentralized network.

We chose the distributed hash table [10] for the overlay network, because it is suitable for the proposed scheduling model, that is a job is executed only one time by a single node, considering the time it enters in the system and the finish time and respecting the deadlines, while assuming a load balancing of the working nodes.

Every node will have a unique identifier in the network, along with a finger table with the neighbours' identifiers as keys and load information as values. These identifiers are arranged in a circle in clockwise direction. The loading information of a node will be periodically taken from the neighbours. Every node will have the finger table entries with keys ranging from 0 to $2^m - 1$, where an entry is of type $(p + 2^{k-1}) \mod 2^m$ (p is the node's identifier; k is ranging from 1 to m) and 2^m is the maximum number of nodes (m denotes the maximum number of entries in finger table or more precisely, the maximum number of neighbours that a node can have). As such, a node will communicate with nodes at distances increasingly higher. As far, we are not concerned about the physical distribution of the nodes, but the logical distances between them (Fig. 1).

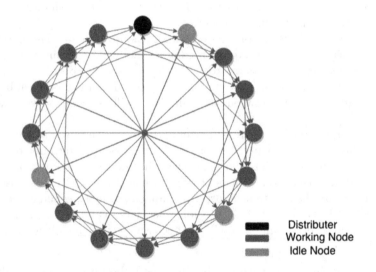

Distributer
Working Node
Idle Node

Fig. 1. The proposed overlay.

3.3   The Algorithm

Nodes are divided into three types: distributor node, working nodes and idle nodes. We consider the following aspects:

- The distributor node sends jobs to all the working nodes.
- Working nodes process jobs from their queue according to a local scheduling policy.
- Idle nodes have low identifiers and small loading values among the overlay ring and are possible candidates when the switching of roles is happening.

- The initial overlay will not be modified during the algorithm.
- The role of distributor can be passed to an idle neighbour.
- The queue of a working node can be passed to an idle neighbour if it's fully loaded. The maximum loading value must be carefully chosen at the initialization of the algorithm, because a small limit can cause multiple switches of roles, whereas a limit of 100% for loading makes the algorithm perform better.

Jobs are entering in the network (homogeneous or heterogeneous virtual machines in Cloud, Hadoop nodes or mobile devices in Cloud) from a well-known node called the distributor and are distributed to the other nodes from the network in accordance with a distribution algorithm. This algorithm is not supposed to replicate the jobs over the network, but to assure us that every job will always be computed only once. The distribution idea has the meaning that the distributor node will send a job to each node in clockwise direction, starting with the node that has the lowest identifier value and repeat this rule until it has no other job to distribute.

The well-known node can be any time high loaded because of the many tasks in the system that are entering. In order to avoid this situation, the distributor node will check the loading information of its first neighbour from the finger table that has the lowest identifier and also the lowest loading value. A small loading value means that the node is not performing so many jobs or it is idle. A signal from the distributor node will be sent to the second node. This time, it is the responsibility of the other node to distribute the tasks over the network. The first node will switch its purpose with its neighbour and it will start processing the jobs from its queue and also the new jobs that arrive.

The neighbours can be aware in any moment of the switching time if they know that they have the smallest loading value from their finger table. However, every node has different neighbours and it can happen that multiple nodes be idle. This is why a signal from the distributor node must be sent.

The newest distributor will start sending the remaining jobs from its queue if it did not process all of them and will also receive other jobs that will enter into the network. It is clear that a distributor must always pass the jobs to other nodes and is not responsible for anything else.

The loading information is periodically collected and updated for every node. This information is collected when a switch of the distributor is happening. The distributor will send its loading information to the neighbour and immediately switch its functionality. The neighbour will update the loading value in its finger table and continue to work as a distributor. The delegation of work is done because we are constantly aware that there is at least one node in the system that can be idle or is consuming its queue better that the other nodes, therefore its loading has the smallest value.

The queue of a working node will be passed to another neighbour when it is not possible to be processed, meaning that the latest responsible node for that queue has reached the maximum loading value. While sending the queue, it can happen that the neighbour could have been chosen as distributor. In this case, the remaining jobs will be send to the next idle neighbour, because we want jobs to be processed very quickly and not to be distributed among the overlay ring and possibly resent to another nodes if the first ones are too loaded. If a job is taking too long to be computed, we must be aware of not receiving it back to the initial node. We will demonstrate that every job that enters in the system will not be delayed while executing it and will be passed to another node at most once. It is better to let the working nodes process their queue if all the neighbours are approximately loaded, because the algorithm will behave better in terms of performance. Exchanging the queues while all the nodes are loaded can result in bottlenecks, therefore in delays of execution which we do not want. So an idle neighbour must have a small loading value or at least 30% less than the fully loaded node.

Switching the distributor too often can possibly cause overhead while processing jobs, because of the signalling and the load balancing information that must be periodically exchanged. As such, in the first part of the distributed replication algorithm every node from the network will know the loading information from its neighbours. The distributor will be decided with a distributed algorithm for choosing a leader (e.g. LeLann-Chang-Robert [4]). That node will run for a long period of time until it won't be able to distribute any other job over the network and then the switching time will occur.

This approach of dynamic roles will guarantee us that no overloading will happen for the distributor and that every working node will have the same loading approximately. The load balancing among the overlay ring will also be assured by the fact that the working nodes will exchange their queues whenever it needs. By choosing a distributed hash table, we don't have to compute any path between two arbitrary nodes in order to pass the jobs or exchange load information, meaning that no overhead is added to communication. The overlay is also tolerant to failures, because if a node is about to crash, just before the event will occur, it will send all its queue to its first idle neighbour.

4 MTS^2: Many Task Scheduling Simulator

We started simulating the algorithm with CloudSim, which is a simulation framework written in Java designed for Cloud concepts. The main constraint of this simulator was the fact that it did not allowed us to switch the distributor role during the simulation and only to switch the queues between the working nodes. This constraint is due to the concepts of deferred queue and future events queue in the simulator. We will talk a little bit about the main entities of every simulation in CloudSim [3] in order to explain the roles of those queues. The *DatacenterBroker* seen as the user's application is the class that assigns to each job a specific virtual machine (VM) before the simulation starts.

A *Datacenter* contains multiple hosts, a name, a VM scheduling policy and other characteristics: architecture, operating system, time zone, the cost of using memory, the cost of using storage and the cost of using bandwidth. The VM scheduling policy is responsible for provisioning of a host to a VM, VM creation,

VM destruction and VM migration. Every *Host* has specific characteristics like MIPS, ID, memory, storage, bandwidth, a list of cores (*Pe* elements), a *RamProvisioner*, a *BwProvisioner* and a VM scheduler that decides how multiple VMs are using the *Host*'s resources. A *Vm* has its specific characteristics along with a local scheduling policy. CloudSim supports by default space-shared and time-shared policies. A *Cloudlet* is the definition of a normal job in CloudSim and it must be assigned to a *Vm*.

4.1 MTS^2 Design

Our algorithm appreciates the loading information of every node in the overlay ring. It can't be possible to simulate a dynamic overlay into a static simulation. Therefore, we created our framework in Java. It borrows the main entities from CloudSim but with slight differences. Every entity excepting VMs is a Java process and not a thread, because we wanted to have as many VMs as possible.

There is a *Broker* that sends a limited number of jobs to the distributor *Vm*. The *Broker* receives as arguments the number of jobs, the distributor's ID and the type of job distribution. It communicates through sockets with the distributor whenever a switch occurs. The thread that does this is called *BrokerWorker*.

Cloudlets have a start time, a finish time, ID and length. A *Host* is a Java process that has a number of *Vms* working as threads. Each *Host* receives as arguments the ID value, the number of working *Vms* and the total number of *Vms* in a simulation. It waits until all the *Vms* are terminated and it's not involved in any communication.

A *Vm* is an abstract class that knows its ID and the total number of virtual machines. It also has a queue of *Cloudlets* and a thread called *QueueWorker* responsible for processing the queue.

For simulating our load balancing algorithm, we implemented *VMFIFO*. This class extends the abstract class and has more informations like: a specific role (distributor or working node), a list of its neighbours' IDs according with the ring. After a *VMFIFO* starts, it computes its neighbours' IDs. It waits for jobs from the distributor or the *Broker* (this depends on the source and its role) and adds them to the queue.

The *Vm* entities can receive the following types of requests:

– *MESSAGE*

  It will wait for receiving the informations about a *Cloudlet*. Depending on the role in the ring, it can start processing the *Cloudlet* or send it to a working node.
– *GET_LOADING*

  It will send its loading value because one of its neighbours is full loaded and wants to decide if it's an idle node. The distributor will send the largest loading value in order to not be taken into consideration as idle neighbour.
– *SWITCH_DISTRIBUTOR*

  It will switch its role as distributor and the *QueueWorker* will start distributing the jobs from the queue, rather than processing them.

- *FINISH_SIMULATION*
  The end message received from the *Broker* or distributor *Vm* according to the algorithm from Sect. 3.
- *FINISHED_SIMULATION*
  The end message from the *QueueWorker* meaning that the *Vm* can successfully shut down.

There is an interface called *DistributionFunction* that must be implemented in order to use another distribution type. There are already three distribution types: *IdenticalDistribution*, *NormalDistribution* and *ExponentialDistribution*. The type of distribution for a simulation is configured for the *Broker*, from the main script file that starts the simulation, *simulate.sh*.

5   Experimental Results

5.1   Overlay and Distribution Type Performances

We have tested MTS^2 on a virtual machine with *Ubuntu Server 14.04 LTS* and 3 GB of RAM. The number of processor cores was standard for VMware Player. We have simulated with MTS^2 for an overlay of 4, 8, 16, 32, 64 and 128 nodes and within a range of $[10, 10^5]$ jobs, in order to see how our algorithm is performing. We concluded that in simulations with a number of jobs less than or equal to 1000, all types of overlay finish all the jobs above 10 s. However, the simulator performed better with an overlay of 16 nodes, a total time of 2.898 s for 1000 jobs.

Starting with an overlay of 16 nodes, the simulator processed more quickly a larger number of jobs. In Fig. 2, we can see that if more nodes are used, then the algorithm performs better: a response time with 10^3 s less for an overlay with 128 nodes in comparison with an overlay of 4 nodes.

The simulator takes enough time until it has all the nodes up and running and because the communication through sockets between the nodes takes a reasonable time, the response times for simulations above 1000 nodes are greater for large overlays. However, what it is the most important is the fact that the algorithm and the simulator perform better when more nodes and more jobs are used. The average performance for a range of $[10, 10^5]$ jobs was made by an overlay of 16 nodes, with total execution times of: 0.573 s, 1.68 s, 2.898 s, 9.999 s, respectively 99.997 s for 10^5.

In order to see how the algorithm performs if jobs have different lengths, such as in a real environment, we simulated three types of distribution (identical, normal and exponential) for an overlay of 4 nodes. For the identical distribution, each job has a length of 100. So each job takes 0.1 s in order to be executed. For the normal distribution, we used the following formula: $100 \pm \sigma$ where σ has been chosen as 10. For the exponential distribution, we used the following formula: $-\frac{\ln(U)}{\lambda}$ where λ has been chosen as 10, and $U \in (0, 1)$. We ranged the number of jobs from 10 to 10^6. However, the algorithm performs in the same manner. No major differences were found even if the distribution type has changed.

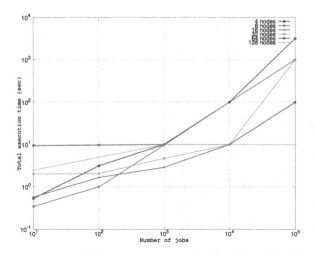

Fig. 2. Total execution time for jobs with the same length, for each type of overlay.

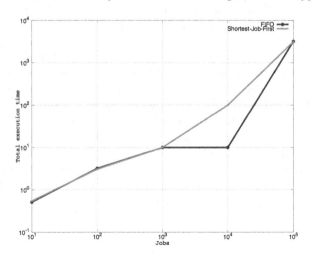

Fig. 3. Comparison between FIFO and SJF as local schedulers for a normal distribution.

5.2   Comparison with Shortest-Job-First

All the nodes from the overlay process the jobs in a FIFO manner. However, the working nodes can use any other scheduling policy for local processing according to our algorithm. We decided to implement the Shortest-Job-First policy for the working nodes in order to see if there are any improvements. We simulated with MTS^2 for an overlay of 4 nodes and with a range of $[10, 10^5]$ jobs. As we can see in Fig. 3, the differences are not so major between FIFO and Shortest-Job-First as local schedulers for the working nodes. We compared the results for a normal distribution of jobs.

This result is due to the fact that jobs are arriving with some delays in each queue. Therefore, all the nodes have the same response times for both schedulers, even if a normal distribution was used. However, it may happen for bigger overlays and more jobs that a local scheduler performs much better, but this result is left for future works and improvements.

6   Conclusions and Future Work

We have proposed and presented an algorithm for Big Data which makes the load balancing of resources in a Cloud system. We introduced the definition of overlay in Cloud as being the same with the overlay of a common network. We used the Chord overlay for the multiple properties that it offers and showed that the communication between two arbitrary nodes doesn't imply the cost of computing any path.

We simulated our algorithm with CloudSim, in order to have some theoretical results, but due to its limitations, we have created our own simulation framework called MTS^2: Many Task Scheduling Simulator. In this simulator we can develop any algorithm, because it's based on real messages sent between the nodes. The limitations imposed to this simulator are only due to the operating system.

We have presented the algorithm's performances and also prove that all the theoretical demonstrations made are holding. Starting from 10^5 jobs and with an overlay with 16 nodes, there have been switches of roles between the nodes. However, the load balancing across the overlay was still preserved and each job has been passed from one node to another at most once.

In our future work, we will add more functionalities to the simulator, such as job monitoring tools that will allow to view diagrams in real time. Also, we will redesign the simulator in order to let the user define more simulation entities.

With this algorithm, we tried to tackle the problem of Many Task Computing and hope to see future research in this field.

References

1. Bessis, N., Sotiriadis, S., Cristea, V., Pop, F.: Modelling requirements for enabling meta-scheduling in inter-clouds and inter-enterprises. In: 2011 Third International Conference on Intelligent Networking and Collaborative Systems, pp. 149–156. IEEE (2011)
2. Bonneau, J.: Algorithms for Big Data, 30 June 2014
3. Calheiros, R.N., Ranjan, R., Beloglazov, A., Rose, C.A.F.D., Buyya, R.: CloudSim: a toolkit for modeling and simulation of cloud computing environments and evaluation of resource provisioning algorithms. Softw.: Pract. Exp. **41**, 23–50 (2010)
4. Chang, E., Roberts, R.: An improved algorithm for decentralized extrema-finding in circular configurations of processes. Commun. ACM **22**(5), 281–283 (1979)
5. Gulati, A., Shanmuganathan, G., Ahmad, I., Holler, A.: Cloud scale resource management: challenges and techniques. In: HotCloud 2011 Proceedings of the 3rd USENIX Conference on Hot Topics in Cloud Computing, Berkeley, CA, USA, p. 3. USENIX Association (2011)

6. Iordache, G.V., Boboila, M.S., Pop, F., Stratan, C., Cristea, V.: A decentralized strategy for genetic scheduling in heterogeneous environments. Multiagent Grid Syst. **3**(4), 355–367 (2007)
7. Krieder, S.J., et al.: Design and evaluation of the GeMTC framework for GPU-enabled many-task computing. In: HPDC 2014. ACM (2014)
8. Lua, E.K., Crowcroft, J., Pias, M., Sharma, R., Lim, S.: A survey and comparison of peer-to-peer overlay network schemes. Commun. Surv. Tutor. **7**(2), 72–93 (2005)
9. Moise, D., Moise, E., Pop, F., Cristea, V.: Resource coallocation for scheduling tasks with dependencies, in grid. arXiv preprint arXiv:1106.5309 (2011)
10. Stoica, I., Morris, R., Karger, D., Kaashoek, M.F., Balakrishnan, H.: Chord: a scalable peer-to-peer lookup service for internet applications. SIGCOMM Comput. Commun. Rev. **31**(4), 149–160 (2001)
11. Wang, K., Brandstatter, K., Raicu, I.: SimMatrix: SIMulator for MAny-Task computing execution fabRIc at eXascale. In: HPC 2013. ACM (2013)
12. Wang, K., Brandstatter, K., Raicu, I.: SimMatrix: simulator for many-task computing execution fabric at exascale. In: Proceedings of the High Performance Computing Symposium, HPC 2013, San Diego, CA, USA, pp. 9:1–9:9. Society for Computer Simulation International (2013)
13. Xu, Y., Suarez, A., Zhao, M.: IBIS : Interposed big-data I/O scheduler. In: Proceedings of the 22nd International Symposium on High-performance Parallel and Distributed Computing, pp. 109–110. ACM, New York, June 2013
14. Zhang, Q., Cheng, L., Boutaba, R.: Cloud computing: state-of-the-art and research challenges. J. Internet Serv. Appl. **1**(1), 7–18 (2010)
15. Zhao, Y., Raicu, I., Foster, I., Hategan, M., Nefedova, V., Wilde, M.: Realizing fast, scalable and reliable scientific computations in grid environments. In: Grid Computing Research Progress. Nova Publisher (2008)

Routing Strategies for WSN

RETRACTED CHAPTER: Mobility Aided Context-Aware Forwarding Approach for Destination-Less OppNets

Vishnupriya Kuppusamy$^{(\boxtimes)}$ (iD), Asanga Udugama(iD), and Anna Förster(iD)

Sustainable Communication Networks, University of Bremen,
28359 Bremen, Germany
{vp,adu,anna.foerster}@comnets.uni-bremen.de

Abstract. Opportunistic networks enables the devices to communicate as and when the opportunity rises. This property of OppNets has been explored in routing approaches in a similar operating manner as the traditional infrastructure networks. Specifically, context aware routing approaches have been the major focus of OppNets in the recent literature. However, the potential of OppNets also extends to data dissemination in destination-less networks. Forwarding approaches in such a network need context such that the data dissemination is favored without the necessity to reach a particular set of users or a particular destination. Hence, the context-awareness need to be defined differently for destination-less OppNets as compared to OppNets in destination-oriented scenarios. In this paper, we propose a mobility aided context-aware mechanism for data dissemination in destination-less OppNets based on mobility based local information available at individual nodes. The results show that the proposed approach achieves high delivery ratios as epidemic routing while reducing the overhead by 70% as compared to epidemic routing.

Keywords: OppNets · Forwarding approach · Mobility-aware

1 Introduction

In Opportunistic Networks (OppNets), the devices communicate whenever they are in the range of each other [15]. They employ store and forward approach, where the messages are relayed between encountered nodes, until the destination is met. Mobility of the nodes is a major enabler for message delivery in this kind of data dissemination. Eventually, forwarding mechanisms to enhance delivery of messages with less delays were devised using predetermined or deductive knowledge about the network as a whole or about specific nodes. Such approaches for destination-oriented OppNets mainly involve storing some information about the encountered nodes [15]. For instance, this historic information could range from the list of encountered nodes [6], nodes with frequent neighbours, social

The original version of this chapter was retracted: The retraction note to this chapter is available at https://doi.org/10.1007/978-3-030-31831-4_48

© Springer Nature Switzerland AG 2019, corrected publication 2020
M. R. Palattella et al. (Eds.): ADHOC-NOW 2019, LNCS 11803, pp. 153–166, 2019.
https://doi.org/10.1007/978-3-030-31831-4_11

connections [1], utilizing nodes mobility predict contacts or meeting specific destinations, daily routines, correlating the schedules of destinations to the encountered nodes to storing the entire history of contacts [2]. However, many of these destination-oriented context is not directly suitable for destination-less OppNets.

In destination-less OppNets, information dissemination is not limited by destination aspects in any way. Though the most effective approach in these cases is flooding such as Epidemic Routing (ER) [19], it is not the most efficient approach owing to its heavy network overhead. Hence, there is a need for dissemination based context-aware approaches for destination-less OppNets rather than the destination-dependent context-aware approaches. However, the characteristics of the OppNets being the same regardless of destination-dependent or destination-less scenarios, context-aware approaches for destination-less OppNets encompasses a broad range of innovative solutions.

Mobility in OppNets [3] strongly influences the contact duration between nodes which is the effective time window for successful message exchanges between nodes. The length of contact durations directly impacts the number of message exchanges and therefore, translates to throughput of the network. Hence, prediction of contact times [14] and history of nodes with long contact times [1] are used to select forwarders in OppNets. While there is an additional overhead involved in calculating contact durations upon every new contact based on number of messages to be exchanged and buffer occupancy, utilizing contact durations is nevertheless, an intelligent context-aware approach for maximizing message deliveries. However, contact durations can also be predicted by using only the local information available at every node without any additional information exchange between nodes. Hence, we take an alternative path by considering the factors directly influencing the contact durations, namely the current speed of a node and waiting time of a node at any given location.

In this paper, we propose a novel mobility aided context-aware approach for destination-less OppNets. Thus, in our approach, we directly do not predict or capture the contact durations between encountered nodes nor store any historical information about contacts, contact patterns and contact times between nodes. Instead, we attempt to capture the effect of contact durations by using the speed at which a node is currently moving. Our main objective is to reduce the overhead while achieving message delivery ratios on par with ER, which is the most preferred reference protocol based on flooding.

We compare the performance of our proposed approach against ER [19] and Randomized Rumor Spreading (RRS) [10] based on the metrics of delivery ratio and overhead. The implementations of the protocols have been developed in OPS [18] based on OMNeT++ simulator. The evaluations have been performed with SWIM mobility model [11] considering three evaluation scenarios and analyzing the effect of network size for one of these evaluation scenarios. The results show that the proposed approach combines the best of ER and RRS, as it achieves high delivery ratios with less overhead without any additional information exchange.

The outline of the paper is as follows: Sect. 2 discusses the related work in this field. The proposed mobility aided context-aware forwarding approach for destination-less OppNets is discussed in Sect. 3. The experimental setup and simulation configuration is described in Sect. 4 and the results are presented in Sect. 5. Section 6 concludes the paper and discusses the future work.

2   Related Work

Several OppNets forwarding protocols have been proposed in the literature starting from the flooding approaches to the most recent approaches with machine learning algorithms [16]. In this section, we only focus on the forwarding approaches that is relevant or can be adapted for destination-less OppNets. ER [19] which is the simplest and most-straight forward approach for OppNets aims to spread all the messages in the network to all nodes in the network. This protocol was further modified by limiting the number of copies of each message in the network in order to reduce the overhead [17]. More efficient means of reducing the overhead was devised in the further protocols by analyzing various information about the nodes themselves. Such efforts seem to be mainly focused on gathering information about the profile of the nodes. This meta-data is exchange between encountered nodes prior to the actual message exchange. ProPhet [6] improved the message deliveries by keeping a list of encountered nodes and by selectively replicating or forwarding the messages to the most frequently encountered nodes. Mobility patterns between nodes were matched between nodes in Mobyspace [12] to improve the attempts on delivering messages with less delivery delays. More of these attempts have resulted in successful forwarding approaches like storing entire history of contacts in FiBop [2], identifying communities based on connectivity metrics in BubbleRap [9], utilizing daily routines and other profile attributes of the nodes in [13], predicting the strength of social ties by analyzing the similarity and friendship indexes between nodes in [5] etc., Though employing these kind of context aware approaches have enhances the delivery ratio and delivery delay of these proposed forwarding approaches, effective dissemination of messages is majorly determined by the length of contact durations in every encounter.

Considerable amount of forwarding approaches have identified that predicting realistic contact times can considerably improve the successful message deliveries and thus, predicting contact times has been a significant factor in analyzing the potential of a contact. If the nodes have sufficient contact times to complete a successful message exchange, those nodes are preferred as forwarders compared to the nodes expected to have short contact times. Expected encounter weights are predicted using per contact durations in EER [4] whereas social connections between nodes are identified based on the length of contact durations in SGBR [1]. This is a growing trend in OppNets and is also observed in protocols like 3R [20] and EIMCT [9]. Thus, the performance of OppNet forwarding approaches can be said to be based on the effective contact times between the nodes. However, all the above approaches entail additional meta-data information which could be a costly trade-off in OppNets especially in connections with short contact durations.

To overcome the above problem, friendly message sharing applications have been proposed [7] in a way that nodes can take action to wait based on the contact time left for a complete message transfer. Here, the forwarding mechanism uses ER, however the application running in a node notifies the user about the ongoing OppNet exchange and lets the user to wait or partial-wait until the full completion or partial completion of the ongoing OppNet session based on the expected contact duration.

While we advocate using contact times as a means of context-awareness in destination-less OppNets, we take an alternative approach without involving user's intervention and thus, we attempt to enable the forwarding protocol to make a decision about message exchange without actually predicting the contact times. For instance, contact times in VANETs are short depending on the speed of the vehicles and needs forwarding mechanisms which send data effectively in that short time. Therefore, the complete contact of nodes using ER like protocols is not effective in such cases as the nodes may not even be able to establish a successful contact. On the other hand, users in a library or coffee shop have long contact times and can very well use ER like behaviour for effective message exchanges.

Considering all the above said factors, we propose a novel mobility aided context-aware approach which, instead of using contact times to select forwarders, uses the knowledge about the length of contact times to select the communication mode of forwarding mechanism. Further, we deduce the length of contact time based on the current speed of the node without estimating the contact times directly.

3 Mobility Aided Context-Aware Approach

This section briefly outlines the motivation of our proposed approach and describes the approach in detail.

The main goal of our proposed approach is to achieve high delivery ratios while reducing the overhead significantly. We shortly describe ER and RRS here, as our proposed approach utilizes both these forwarding mechanisms.

In Epidemic routing (ER) [19], every node maintains a list of message identifiers of the messages in its cache in a Summary Vector (SV). Upon encountering a contact, the nodes establish a uni-cast connection and exchange their SVs. They compare their SVs and separately identify the list of messages missing from their own cache as compared to the encountered contact. Consequently, both the nodes send a data request to each other containing the list of the message-identifiers not currently in their respective cache, followed by the data exchange. When both nodes finish their contact, they have identical caches.

Randomized Rumour Spreading (RRS) [10] employs a randomized communication between nodes to ensure robust ness. As a result, no context is used, not even SVs. When it meets a contact, it randomly selects a message/data from its cache and transmits it. The main advantage of RRS is that the overhead can be reduced significantly while still maintaining achievable delivery ratios. The mechanism used can be broadcast or uni-cast.

We compare and contrast ER and RRS and further identify the scenarios where each of them is best suited as per their operation. ER is by far the Opp-Net protocol with the high delivery ratios. As ER uses uni-cast communication between nodes and it could involve the exchange of the entire list of messages from both nodes, the success of this scenario definitely excludes extremely short contact times. This can be well-suited for users with pedestrian speeds and also users with long waiting times at a location.

The downside of ER is the high overhead owing to the flooding approach, however it can be addressed with context-aware approaches as seen in Sect. 2. RRS [10] is also a flooding based protocol however with less overhead. In our implementation of RRS, the nodes select one message randomly from their cache at uniform time intervals and broadcast to their neighbours. It does not involve any intelligent selection of messages nor the prioritization of messages. Due to this process, the overhead is very less and the delivery ratios are mildly lesser compared to ER which also depends mainly on the mobility of the nodes. This forwarding mechanism suits the scenarios with short contact times where some message is exchanged without any other information exchanges. Hence, we identify this mechanism to be well-suited for vehicular users with high speeds.

In our proposed approach, we do not explicitly predict contact times and instead the nodes use the speed of their mobility as an indirect way of deducing the length of contact times. A node uses its speed to determine the length of its contact duration with its potential contacts. When nodes with vehicular speeds come in contact, they most likely have short contact times whereas the nodes in contact at walking speeds could have potentially long contact times. Furthermore, it is expected, the longer the waiting time of a node at a location, the longer the contact time between the node and its neighbours in that location. The waiting time is also reflected in the speed of the node. Thus, the number of messages exchanged is impacted by the contact times which in turn is affected by the speed of the nodes in contact. We use this speed based mobility context to switch the forwarding mechanism in each node depending on their speeds.

We call our proposed approach a hybrid approach in the rest of the paper, as we combine the best of ER and RRS, and establish a switching mechanism to identify the best suited forwarding approach at any given time instant. We achieve this by utilizing the current speed of the node as a decision factor in switching between the use of ER and RRS, which further use the modes of communication of uni-cast and broadcast, respectively. When the nodes move at pedestrian speeds, they connect to each neighbour in their vicinity individually and perform a uni-cast message exchange. Thus, the nodes use ER like behaviour where they initiate a summary vector exchange [19] and exchange their whole cache. When the nodes move in vehicular speeds, they use RRS as the short contact times may not facilitate the possibility of establishing a successful contact through uni-cast. Here, the nodes select one message randomly from their cache and broadcast to all the neighbours in their transmission range.

Algorithm 1 shows the proposed hybrid approach used when switching between ER and RRS. Since the velocity of devices may fluctuate unexpect-

Algorithm 1. Forwarder switching algorithm

1: **procedure** CHECKANDSWITCH(currFwd)
2:     $curr \leftarrow getCurr()$ ▷ current coordinates and time
3:     $last \leftarrow getLast()$ ▷ last coordinates and last time
4:     $lower, upper \leftarrow getThreshold()$ ▷ get lower and upper thresholds

5:     $dist \leftarrow computeEuclideanDistance(curr, last)$
6:     $speed \leftarrow computeSpeed(dist, curr, last)$

7:     **if** $(currFwd = RRS)$ and $(speed \leq lower)$ **then**
8:         **return** $Epidemic$

9:     **else if** $(currFwd = Epidemic)$ and $(speed \geq upper)$ **then**
10:        **return** RRS

11:    **else**
12:        **return** $currFwd$

---

edly, the switching algorithm uses thresholds to switch between the protocols. This helps in avoiding any adverse effects. Figure 1 shows an example of how the algorithm operates.

It is important to note that the nodes only know their own speeds and thus, utilize only this as the context in making a decision about their forwarding mechanisms. Further, the reception of the messages is not influenced by the forwarding mechanism of the nodes and hence, the receiving nodes can choose to accept both the broadcast and uni-cast data as much as they could without being restricted by the speeds.

4   Performance Evaluation

In this section, we present the evaluation of our proposed hybrid forwarding approach and compare it with ER and RRS. Then, we also describe the experimental scenarios and the simulation configurations used for the evaluation of our proposed approach.

4.1   Evaluation Scenarios

The efficiency of the hybrid forwarding approach depends on the mobility and speed of the users and therefore, our evaluation scenarios consists of pedestrian users and vehicles. We have designed three evaluation scenarios with three different compositions of pedestrians and vehicular users.

The first scenario is that of a mall in a city centre with many pedestrians and few vehicular users in the parking lot or in the road just outside the mall. We consider a 1000 m × 1000 m area with a total of 500 nodes of which 300 are

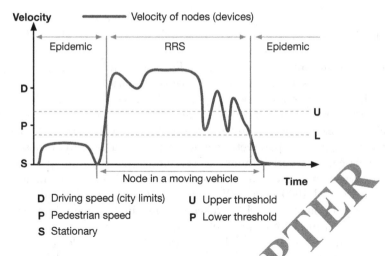

Fig. 1. Example of the switching operation

pedestrians and 200 are vehicles. The vehicles move at uniformly distributed speeds between 13 m/s and 17 m/s and the pedestrians move at uniformly distributed speeds between 1 m/s and 3 m/s. The pedestrians have a uniform wait time distribution of 15 min to 1 h and the vehicles have a uniform wait time distribution of 5 min to 15 min. The waiting time of pedestrians pertains to the idea that these users spend time in different shops in the mall and move to new locations in the mall after their respective wait time is completed. The vehicular users on the other hand spend rather short times, lesser than 15 min in parking spaces or in a traffic jam in the adjacent street.

The second scenario envisioned is that of a toll gate where users pay money, by cash or by cards. This scenario comprises of more vehicular users compared to the pedestrians. We consider a 1000 m × 1000 m area with a total of 500 nodes of which 100 are pedestrians and 400 are vehicles. The vehicles move at uniformly distributed speeds between 13 m/s and 17 m/s and, the pedestrians move at uniformly distributed speeds between 1 m/s and 3 m/s. The pedestrians have a uniform wait time distribution of 15 min to 1 h and the vehicles have a uniform wait time distribution of 5 min to 15 min.

The third scenario is that of a tourist centre in a city where tourists explore the area by foot. The tourist centre also involves some vehicular users passing by or using the nearby parking space. Thus, this scenario has a high number of pedestrians and a few vehicles. We consider a 1000 m × 1000 m area with a total of 500 nodes of which 400 are pedestrians and 100 are vehicles. The vehicles move at uniformly distributed speeds between 13 m/s and 17 m/s and, the pedestrians move at uniformly distributed speeds between 1 m/s and 3 m/s. The pedestrians have a uniform wait time distribution of 15 min to 1 h and the vehicles have a uniform wait time distribution of 5 min to 15 min.

Further, we also use a reference scenario where there are equal number of pedestrians and vehicles in the same configuration as the above three scenarios. For this purpose, we consider a $1000\,m \times 1000\,m$ area with 500 users where 250 are pedestrians and 250 are vehicles. The speed and wait time distributions are maintained the same as in the above three scenarios.

The main reason for essentially keeping the same area, speeds and wait time in all the three evaluation scenarios and also in the reference scenario is that, it facilitates the comparison and analysis of the protocols, though it may not always adhere to a realistic parameter configuration. Branching from these evaluations, one particular scenario, namely the second scenario pertaining to the toll gate area is taken and analyzed for network sizes of 100 nodes, 300 nodes, 500 nodes, 700 nodes and 1000 nodes. We have chosen this scenario mainly to show the advantage of our proposed approach in achieving comparable delivery ratios to epidemic routing with comparable overhead to RRS.

We have not considered the scenarios of all 500 nodes as pedestrians and all 500 nodes as vehicles, as our proposed hybrid approach tends to perform exactly in the same manner as ER and RRS in such configurations, respectively. Table 2 shows the node combinations of the evaluated scenarios. Table 1 shows the simulation configuration used in the simulation.

Further, in our evaluation, we have used these specific scenarios as our motivation was to check how the different ratios of pedestrians to vehicles affect the performance. However, other scenarios such as traces and different mobility models can also be considered for future evaluations.

Table 1. Summary of the node numbers in each scenario

Scenario	Pedestrians	Vehicles
Tourist area	400	100
Mall	300	200
Reference	250	250
Toll gate	100	400

Table 2. Simulation configuration

Parameter	Value
Wireless range	30 m
Area	1000 m × 1000 m
Upper threshold	3 mps
Lower threshold	5 mps

4.2   Experimental Setup

We have implemented the proposed hybrid approach, the epidemic routing and RRS forwarding protocols in the OPS simulator [18] based on OMNeT++. We have used the SWIM mobility model [11] implementation in OMNeT++ for all of our simulations. Every data point in the graph is the average of 10 runs with a 95% confidence interval.

We have considered the message size to be 1 KB and the cache size to be 5 MB throughout the simulation. The simulation time is 24 h without any warm-up phase. The traffic generator injects 1 message per 15 min for the whole network. The time-to-live of messages is equal to the simulation time and hence, all the messages are valid throughout the simulation.

The protocol specific parameters involved in all the three protocols are as follows: In the hybrid approach, every node checks its own speed every 5 s and makes an appropriate decision on selection of the best-suited forwarding mechanism. In ER, nodes maintain a visited neighbour list which gets refreshed every 300 s. This reconfiguration interval of 300 s is maintained as was given in [19]. In RRS, every node sends a message out from its cache, once in every minute. All the above parameters are configurable as input from the initialization file.

When switching between the protocols, the hybrid approach employs a threshold based mechanism to prevent a ping-pong effect of switching between ER and RRS due to sudden speed fluctuations (see Fig. 1).

5   Results and Discussions

The simulation results are presented in this section followed by the discussions and inferences based on the results obtained.

Figures 2a, b and c shows the results of simulations for the three application scenarios and the reference scenario. Figure 2a shows that the delivery ratios of ER, hybrid approach and RRS protocols are approximately above 98% for all the scenarios. It is also observed that as the number of vehicles increases, the delivery ratios of hybrid approach and RRS improve owing to the fact that mobility facilitates message dissemination.

In Fig. 2b, it is seen that the delivery delays of all the three protocols reduces as the number of vehicles increases. Also, the delivery delays for all the three protocols are higher for the tourist scenario with 400 pedestrians and 100 vehicles due to the decrease in mobility with decrease in vehicles and vice-versa. Approximately, there is a 40% increase in delivery delays from hybrid approach as compared to ER.

Figure 2c presents the total number of bytes sent in the network throughout the whole simulation. The total number of bytes comprises of the messages sent in bytes and also the summary vectors exchanged in bytes. RRS doesn't have summary vectors or any information exchange other than the messages sent as broadcast and hence, doesn't have any overhead at all. We can see that the total bytes sent in ER is highest among the three protocols and also, it increases with

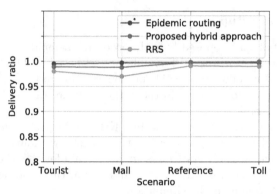

(a) Delivery ratios of ER, Hybrid and RRS for the evaluation scenarios

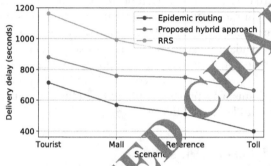

(b) Delivery delays of ER, Hybrid and RRS for the evaluation scenarios

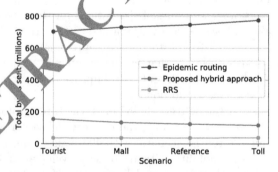

(c) Total bytes sent in the whole simulation for ER, Hybrid and RRS in the evaluation scenarios

Fig. 2. Performance of the hybrid approach compared to pure ER and RRS

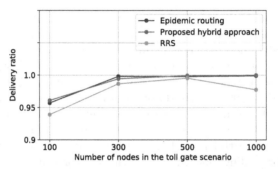

(a) Delivery ratios of ER, Hybrid and RRS for different
network sizes in the toll scenario

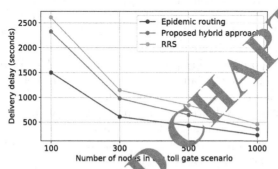

(b) Delivery delays of ER, Hybrid and RRS for different
network sizes in the toll scenario

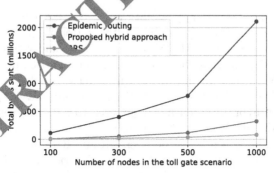

(c) Total bytes sent in the whole simulation for different
network size in the toll scenario

Fig. 3. Performance of the hybrid approach compared to pure ER and RRS when the
nodes vary

the increase in vehicles. This is because, the number of attempts to connect to neighbours increases when the number of vehicles increases. This also partly comes from the wait-times, as the wait-times for vehicles in locations are lesser compared to that of pedestrians. Hence, in general as the mobility increases, so are the contacts and the increase in bytes exchanged for ER. Approximately, the overhead is reduced by 70% in hybrid approach as compared to ER.

Further, Fig. 2c shows that the number of bytes exchanged in proposed hybrid approach decreases with the increase in vehicles as it directly impacts the number of connection attempts with ER. Instead in such scenarios, the hybrid approach switches to RRS forwarding mode. Hence, with the hybrid approach, we achieve the same delivery ratios with ER however, with less overhead and slightly higher delivery delays.

We wanted to analyze the behaviour of hybrid approach for different network sizes and different densities. Hence, we selected the toll gate scenario and varied the number of nodes to check the metrics of delivery ratio, delay and the total number of bytes exchanged in simulation. Figures 3a, b and c show these results. We see that the proposed hybrid approach combines the best of both ER and RRS in a scenario with pedestrians and vehicles. The thresholds of the hybrid approach can be adapted to enhance the performance in multi-speed scenarios.

For the performance evaluation in this paper, we have taken two extreme protocols in terms of overhead; 2 ER, that has a very high overhead and RRS, that does not. Optimized protocols can also be used, but their performance will be in between. These evaluations are not focussed

6   Conclusion and Future Work

In this paper, we have proposed a mobility aided context-aware approach for destination-less OppNets. We have evaluated the performance of the proposed approach in OPS [18] using SWIM [11] mobility model under three evaluation scenarios. The results show that the proposed hybrid approach performs better than ER in terms of overhead with trade-offs in increase in delivery delays while maintaining the delivery delays on par with ER. There is a 40% increase in delivery delay from hybrid approach as compared to ER, however, the hybrid approach reduces the overhead by 70% as compared to ER. Thus, the performance of the hybrid approach lies in between ER and RRS in terms of delivery delays and reduces the overhead considerably in scenarios with higher number of vehicular users.

Our future work will focus on two main goals; first, intensive evaluations of hybrid approach and second, the optimizations for the hybrid approach. For the evaluations, we will evaluate the hybrid approach with different mobility models and also explore the parametrizations. Analyzing the number of contacts and contact durations will certainly enable us to present a clear picture in the differences of ER, hybrid approach and RRS. For the optimizations, we will extend this work to develop an adaptive threshold determination mechanism for switching the forwarding mechanism. This step further involves identifying other possible intelligent context-aware approaches for destination-less OppNets.

References

1. Abdelkader, T., Naik, K., Nayak, A., Goel, N., Srivastava, V.: SGBR: a routing protocol for delay tolerant networks using social grouping. IEEE Trans. Parallel Distrib. Syst. **24**(12), 2472–2481 (2012)
2. Boldrini, C., Conti, M., Jacopini, J., Passarella, A.: HiBOp: a history based routing protocol for opportunistic networks. In: 2007 IEEE International Symposium on a World of Wireless, Mobile and Multimedia Networks, pp. 1–12. IEEE (2007)
3. Chaintreau, A., Hui, P., Crowcroft, J., Diot, C., Gass, R., Scott, J.: Impact of human mobility on opportunistic forwarding algorithms. IEEE Trans. Mob. Comput. **6**, 606–620 (2007)
4. Chen, H., Lou, W.: Contact expectation based routing for delay tolerant networks. Ad Hoc Netw. **36**, 244–257 (2016)
5. Daly, E.M., Haahr, M.: Social network analysis for information flow in disconnected delay-tolerant manets. IEEE Trans. Mob. Comput. **8**(5), 606–621 (2008)
6. Grasic, S., Davies, E., Lindgren, A., Doria, A.: The evolution of a DTN routing protocol-PRoPHETv2. In: Proceedings of the 6th ACM Workshop on Challenged Networks, pp. 27–30. ACM (2011)
7. Herrera-Tapia, J., Hernández-Orallo, E., Tomás, A., Manzoni, P., Tavares Calafate, C., Cano, J.C.: Friendly-sharing: improving the performance of city sensing through contact-based messaging applications. Sensors **16**(9), 1523 (2016)
8. Hui, P., Crowcroft, J., Yoneki, E.: BUBBLE rap: social-based forwarding in delay-tolerant networks. IEEE Trans. Mob. Comput. **10**(11), 1576–1589 (2010)
9. Jia, W., Chen, Z., Zhao, M.: Effective information transmission based on social-ization nodes in opportunistic network. Comput. Netw. **129**, 297–305 (2017)
10. Karp, R., Schindelhauer, C., Shenker, S., Vocking, B.: Randomized rumor spread-ing. In: Proceedings 41st Annual Symposium on Foundations of Computer Science, pp. 565–574. IEEE (2000)
11. Kosta, S., Mei, A., Stefa, J.: Small world in motion (SWIM): modeling communities in ad-hoc mobile networking. In: 2010 7th Annual IEEE Communications Society Conference on Sensor Mesh and Ad Hoc Communications and Networks (SECON), pp. 1–9. IEEE (2010)
12. Leguay, J., Friedman, T., Conan, V.: MobySpace: mobility pattern space routing for DTNs. In: ACM SIGCOMM Conference (2005)
13. Moreira, W., Mendes, P., Sargento, S.: Opportunistic routing based on daily rou-tines. In: 2012 IEEE International Symposium on a World of Wireless, Mobile and Multimedia Networks (WoWMoM), pp. 1–6. IEEE (2012)
14. Moreira, W., Mendes, P., Sargento, S.: Social-aware opportunistic routing protocol based on user's interactions and interests. In: Mellouk, A., Sherif, M.H., Li, J., Bellavista, P. (eds.) ADHOCNETS 2013. LNICST, vol. 129, pp. 100–115. Springer, Cham (2014). https://doi.org/10.1007/978-3-319-04105-6_7
15. Pelusi, L., Passarella, A., Conti, M.: Opportunistic networking: data forwarding in disconnected mobile Ad Hoc networks. IEEE Commun. Mag. **44**(11), 134–141 (2006)
16. Sobin, C., Raychoudhury, V., Marfia, G., Singla, A.: A survey of routing and data dissemination in delay tolerant networks. J. Netw. Comput. Appl. **67**, 128–146 (2016)
17. Spyropoulos, T., Psounis, K., Raghavendra, C.S.: Spray and wait: an efficient rout-ing scheme for intermittently connected mobile networks. In: Proceedings of the 2005 ACM SIGCOMM Workshop on Delay-Tolerant Networking, pp. 252–259. ACM (2005)

18. Udugama, A., Förster, A., Dede, J., Kuppusamy, V., Muslim, A.B.: Opportunistic networking protocol simulator for OMNeT++. In: Proceedings of 4th OMNeTT++ Community Summit (2017)
19. Vahdat, A., Becker, D., et al.: Epidemic routing for partially connected Ad Hoc networks (2000)
20. Vu, L., Do, Q., Nahrstedt, K.: 3R: fine-grained encounter-based routing in delay tolerant networks. In: 2011 IEEE International Symposium on a World of Wireless, Mobile and Multimedia Networks, pp. 1–6. IEEE (2011)

Multi-criteria Analysis to Select Relay Nodes in the ORST Technique

Suelen Laurindo[1]([✉]), Ricardo Moraes[1], Carlos Montez[1],
and Francisco Vasques[2]

[1] Federal University of Santa Catarina, Florianópolis, Brazil
suelen.m.l@posgrad.ufsc.br, {ricardo.moraes,carlos.montez}@ufsc.br
[2] Faculty of Engineering, University of Porto, Porto, Portugal
vasques@fe.up.pt

Abstract. Cooperative diversity techniques are being used to improve the communication reliability in Wireless Sensor Networks (WSN). Typically, these techniques use relay nodes to retransmit messages that otherwise would not be heard by their destination nodes. Thus, the relay selection techniques are fundamental to improve WSN's communication behavior. However, to perform the adequate relay selection, it is necessary to identify which are the most relevant parameters for the operation of the network and analyze their impact when used in the relay selection, that is, it is necessary to define which are the best parameters to use as selection criteria. In this context, this paper performs an analysis of the impact of each of the parameters used to perform the relay selection in the Optimized Relay Selection Technique (ORST). This analysis was assessed by simulation using the OMNeT++ tool and the WSN framework Castalia. It was considered a set of parameters, aiming to identify their relevance and possibly optimize the objective function used in this technique. Simulation results show that the objective function can be optimized considering a small number of parameters to perform the relay selection.

Keywords: Cooperative diversity · Relay selection ·
Wireless sensor network

1 Introduction

In wireless sensor networks (WSN), the wireless communication medium is inherently unreliable, where messages may be lost due to electromagnetic noise, other devices that operate in the same frequency range or obstacles between nodes. This problem may lead to a severe reduction of achievable throughput [6]. A possible solution to improve the reliability of WSNs is by providing multiple

This research was partially funded by CAPES Print Program (grant 698503P) and CNPq/Brasil (Project 870048/2007-4).

© Springer Nature Switzerland AG 2019
M. R. Palattella et al. (Eds.): ADHOC-NOW 2019, LNCS 11803, pp. 167–182, 2019.
https://doi.org/10.1007/978-3-030-31831-4_12

paths to transmit data from the source to the destination node; this type of communication is called cooperative diversity [14].

Cooperative diversity considers the existence of nodes that will cooperate with the transmitter-receiver pair, in order to increase the chances of the sent message being received in the destination [7]. Thus, nodes with a single antenna can share their antennas and produce a virtual multiple-antenna transmitter, as illustrated in Fig. 1, where there are two source nodes (N_1 and N_2) and one destination node. As the fading paths from two source nodes are statistically independent, the use of the cooperative diversity generates spatial diversity, improving the communication in the network. In the cooperative diversity technique, nodes that share their antennas retransmitting messages assume the role of relay nodes [11].

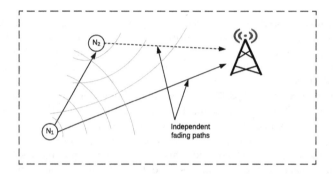

Fig. 1. Cooperative communication.

This behavior provided by cooperative diversity allows better use of the broadcast nature of wireless transmissions, in which nodes are usually able to hear messages transmitted by their neighborhood [9]. However, in a conventional communication in WSN, nodes discard listened messages that are not intentionally sent to them [7,11].

In the cooperative communication research area, the adequate relay selection is a key problem that must be addressed. The performance of cooperative retransmission techniques depends heavily on the efficiency of the process used to select one or more relay nodes [1,17,18].

An adequate relay selection will allow messages from a source node to reach the destination node even though the quality of the communication channel is degraded, as the source node will have a relay that will aid retransmitting the message to the destination.

In order to perform the relay selection, it is necessary to consider some important criteria for the operation of the network. However, there are few state-of-the-art works evaluating a different set of criteria when selecting the relay nodes. In a recent work [8], we proposed a relay selection technique to be used in WSN, named Optimized Relay Selection Technique (ORST). In this technique the selection of a set of relay nodes is based on multiple criteria, namely: the number of neighbors of the candidate node, their remaining battery energy, the quality of the communication link between the candidate node and its neighbor nodes (by using the RSSI) and the success rate's history in recent node transmissions. The ORST technique was formulated as an optimization problem, using a specifically selected objective function. When the technique was proposed, the aim was to consider all the criteria that are highly relevant for the operation of the network, but without analyzing the real impact of each criterion upon the network performance.

This paper performs an analysis considering each of the parameters individually and combining them, aiming to identify the importance of each one of them and possibly to optimize the objective function previously used [8].

This paper is structured as follows: Sect. 2 presents the state-of-the-art on relay selection techniques in WSNs. Section 3 briefly describes the ORST technique and the analysis of the criteria used to perform the relay selection, focusing on the improvements of the communication reliability in WSNs. Section 4 presents the simulation assessment and results. Finally, conclusions are presented in Sect. 5.

2   Related Work

In spite of the existence of multiple works related to relay selection techniques in the literature, many of these works do not give due relevance to the criteria used for the relay node selection. Nevertheless, the performance of the relay selection technique can be highly improved if the selected criteria are adequate.

In [23], the authors proposed a technique to select the best relay to cooperate in the transmission from the source node to the destination node. The relay that has the highest instantaneous SNR (Signal-to-Noise Ratio) of the combiner output at the destination is selected as the cooperative relay. The authors proposed in [22] a relay selection scheme to maximize the network lifetime. The authors considered the energy consumption rate in transmission and residual energy of each sensor node as criteria for the relay selection. The nodes that maximize the network lifetime are selected as relay nodes.

In [2], a relay selection technique using both AF (Amplify-Forward) and DF (Decode-Forward) protocols is proposed, which selects the AF or DF schemes to forward signals adaptively according to the CSI (Channel State Information) information. If the channel status of link $Source - Relay_i$ is good enough for the relay to decode the source information, the DF protocol is selected to forward signals in the relay. Otherwise, the AF protocol is selected. The relay selection occurs in the destination node based on the SNR value. The node that maximizes the SNR in the destination node is selected as relay and notified to forward the source information.

In [15], a relay selection based on the SNR is designed. The aim is to maximize the minimum received SNR for all users. The authors considered a multi-user multihop relay network where each hop is equipped with multiple relays that assist users to communicate with their designated destinations.

In [13], the authors presented a relay selection technique that aims to increase the network lifetime and to improve its packet delivery rate. The node with the highest residual energy level e_i^m and the lowest Energy-Per-Bit (EPB) value E_b will be the relay node. The authors proposed the calculation of a weight w for each cooperating node r, as: $w_r = \frac{e_i^m}{E_b}$, where, the relay with the highest weight value is selected.

In [4], a relay technique that selects the node that minimizes the energy consumption per bit in transmissions between source and relay nodes and between relay and destination nodes is presented. The nodes that listen to the RTS (Request to Send) and CTS (Clear to Send) messages (between source node and destination node) estimate the channel gain and the desired transmission power to reach the target BER (Bit Error Rate). Using an optimization strategy, the destination node selects the relay node, and signals through the beacon message which was the selected node.

In [20], it is proposed a technique that selects as relay the node that maximizes the number of packets successfully transmitted. It was considered that a transmission fails when the SNR signal arriving at the destination node is less than a predetermined threshold. This proposal considered that a data packet of size L is transmitted with an R rate and that each node can determine the number of packets successfully transmitted, called K. Thus, using an optimization technique, each node maximizes the K value, the node that presents the highest value should be selected as a relay.

In [19], the authors proposed a technique that considers the history of successful transmission rates and the LQI between each node and the coordinator. Nodes presenting the highest average between the history of successful transmissions and LQI will be selected as relays. The number of relay nodes is dynamically defined according to the percentage of message losses in the network.

Most of the works found in the state-of-the-art use as criteria of selection quality estimators based on hardware (LQI, RSSI,CSI, etc.) [2, 4, 15, 19, 23]. However, these metrics consider only the received frames. Thus, if a radio link presents excessive losses, the quality estimators may overestimate the quality of the link.

It is worth to mention that the different combination of relay selection criteria, how they were modeled and what parameters they use, directly impacts on the relay selection performance. However, analyzing the state-of-the-art approaches, it is possible to attest they generally do not justify their choices.

3   Relay Selection Technique

The Optimized Relay Selection Technique (ORST) is a centralized technique recently proposed in [8]. This technique considers an IEEE 802.15.4 network operating in time-slotted and beacon-enabled modes. It allows the adaptive selection of relay nodes in dynamic networks, where nodes may randomly leave/join the coverage area of the coordinator node. The time interval between two consecutive relay selections is dynamically determined, according to the message transfer success rate. If all messages successfully reach their destination, there is no need for a new relay selection. If the success rate decreases, it means that the current set of relay nodes is not meeting the communication requirements and a new relay selection procedure must be performed. This behavior may be a consequence of: relay nodes that left the coordinator coverage; new nodes that joined the network and there are no enough relay nodes; or an abrupt increase of the interference level in the network.

The ORST scheme aims to find a set of relay nodes $S^* = \{y_1, y_2, \ldots, y_m\}$ among a set of nodes $X = \{x_1, x_2, ..., x_n\}$ in WSNs, ensuring two conditions: (1) each node x_i $(1 \leq i \leq n)$ is covered by at least one relay node, (2) the sum of the weights (W_i) of the relays is minimized. In this scheme, x_i is used as node identifier, n is the total number of nodes in the network, m is the total number of relay nodes and $S^* \subseteq X$, i.e. relays are selected in the same set of nodes, transmitting not only their own data, but also cooperating by retransmitting data from other nodes. There is one node called coordinator in the WSN (C).

This technique was designed as an optimization problem using an objective function. The objective function (Eq. 1) takes into consideration the number of neighbors that each node can hear (v) (RSSI $\geq -87\,$dBm [16]), the available energy in the nodes (e), the quality of communication between the source node and the candidate relay node (s), as well as the history of successful transmission rates (H) of node x_i. These parameters were selected because they are highly relevant to the operation of the network. For instance, the residual energy of the nodes is an important parameter, considering that if a node has a low battery level it will stop being a promising candidate because soon it will exhaust its own energy resources. The number of neighbors that each node has is also a parameter that must be considered, since if a node does not have neighbors, it does not make sense to select it as a relay. The quality of the channel between the source and the relay nodes is another important parameter, because it allows knowing if there is a good communication link between these nodes, ensuring that the relay node correctly receives messages to be retransmitted. And finally the history of successful transmission rates is an indication that the selected node has a good communication link with the destination node, ensuring that messages sent by this node will correctly arrive at their destination. Combining these parameters as the selection criterion, the aim is to ensure that the appropriate nodes are selected as cooperating. Each node x_i will calculate its objective function value W_i and this information will be sent to the coordinator.

$$W_i \doteq \left(\frac{\beta^v}{v_i} + \frac{\beta^e}{e_i} + \frac{\beta^s}{s_i} + \frac{\beta^H}{H_i} \right) \tag{1}$$

where:

- W_i is the objective function value of the node x_i;
- v_i is the total number of neighbors of node x_i;
- $e_i = \frac{RE_i}{IE_i}$, where RE_i is the remaining energy and IE_i is the initial energy of node x_i, respectively. The e_i value is the normalized remaining energy of node x_i (a real value between 0 and 1);

- $s_i = \frac{1}{Limited\_RSSI} \sum_{j=1}^{n_i} RSSI_j$, where $RSSI_j$ is the Received Signal Strength Indicator (RSSI) among node x_i and its neighbors nodes x_j, and the constant $Limited\_RSSI$ is the minimum value of RSSI for an adequate communication (-87 dBm [16]);
- $H_i = (1 - \alpha) \times H_i + \alpha \times S_R$ is the history of successful transmission rates adjusted at each beacon interval. The value of variable α is adjusted according to each case, being defined between $0 < \alpha \leq 1$; variable S_R is equal to 1 in case of a successful transmission of node x_i or 0 otherwise;
- $\beta^v, \beta^e, \beta^s, \beta^H$ are the weights of each parameter for the objective function.

In order to select the minimum number of relay nodes, ensuring at the same time that every node has a reachable relay, an optimization problem is formulated as follows:

$$minimize \sum_{i=1}^{n} W_i y_i \tag{2a}$$

$$subject \quad to: \quad Ay \geq b \tag{2b}$$

$$Cy = d \tag{2c}$$

$$y_i \in \{0, 1\}$$

In the constraint presented in Eq. 2b, A is the adjacency matrix of order $n \times n$, where its element $a_{i,j} = 1$ if node x_i is a neighbor of node x_j and $a_{i,j} = 0$ otherwise. Matrix A is formed in the coordinator node based on the list of neighbors sent by each node of the network. Therefore, whenever the list of neighbors of a node x_j has not been received by the coordinator, all elements of row j of matrix A will be equal to zero; y is a vector of order $n \times 1$, where y_i will be equal to 1 when node x_i is selected as relay and 0 otherwise and; b is a vector whose b_i value has been defined as 1, representing the minimum number of relay nodes of each node x_i. As a consequence, based on the variables of the problem $y_i \in \{0, 1\}$, the ORST scheme can be considered as a Binary Integer Problem (BIP).

The constraint presented in Eq. 2c is determined by the coordinator node, where matrix C represents the set of nodes that do not have an adequate communication link with the coordinator node. Each row of matrix C represents a node x_i that does not communicate directly with the coordinator and each column represents a node that is able to hear this node. In this case, d will be equal to 1, in order to guarantee that at least one of these nodes will cooperate with node x_i.

3.1   Analysis of Criteria for the Relay Selection Technique

In this paper, the impact of each parameter to perform the relay selection, in the ORST scheme, will be analyzed. This technique considers a set of parameters that may have a significative impact upon an adequate relay selection (which are: e, v, s and H). This paper targets to identify the relative importance of each of them and possibly to optimize the used objective function, without reducing the quality of communication.

Table 1. Objective functions.

1	$W_i \doteq \left(\frac{\beta^H}{H_i} \right)$
2	$W_i \doteq \left(\frac{\beta^s}{s_i} \right)$
3	$W_i \doteq \left(\frac{\beta^e}{e_i} \right)$
4	$W_i \doteq \left(\frac{\beta^v}{v_i} \right)$
5	$W_i \doteq \left(\frac{\beta^v}{v_i} + \frac{\beta^e}{e_i} \right)$
6	$W_i \doteq \left(\frac{\beta^v}{v_i} + \frac{\beta^s}{s_i} \right)$
7	$W_i \doteq \left(\frac{\beta^v}{v_i} + \frac{\beta^H}{H_i} \right)$
8	$W_i \doteq \left(\frac{\beta^e}{e_i} + \frac{\beta^s}{s_i} \right)$
9	$W_i \doteq \left(\frac{\beta^e}{e_i} + \frac{\beta^H}{H_i} \right)$
10	$W_i \doteq \left(\frac{\beta^s}{s_i} + \frac{\beta^H}{H_i} \right)$
11	$W_i \doteq \left(\frac{\beta^v}{v_i} + \frac{\beta^e}{e_i} + \frac{\beta^s}{s_i} \right)$
12	$W_i \doteq \left(\frac{\beta^v}{v_i} + \frac{\beta^s}{s_i} + \frac{\beta^H}{H_i} \right)$
13	$W_i \doteq \left(\frac{\beta^v}{v_i} + \frac{\beta^e}{e_i} + \frac{\beta^H}{H_i} \right)$
14	$W_i \doteq \left(\frac{\beta^e}{e_i} + \frac{\beta^s}{s_i} + \frac{\beta^H}{H_i} \right)$

For this analysis, new objective functions were modeled considering each of the possible combinations of parameters, as presented in Table 1.

Table 1 shows fourteen possible objective functions, where functions $1, 2, 3$ and 4 consider the parameters individually, functions $5, 6, 7, 8, 9$ and 10 consider combinations two-by-two and functions $11, 12, 13$ and 14 consider combinations three-by-three. When performing the relay selection considering each of these functions, it will be possible to identify which parameters have the greatest influence upon the selection and thus it may be possible to simplify the problem of relay selection.

4   Simulation Assessment

A simulation assessment was performed using the network simulation tool OMNET++ [12] and the WSN framework Castalia [3]. The open source Solve Library *lp_solve* [10] was used to implement the relay selection in ORST, solving the resulting optimization problem.

4.1   Simulation Settings

Each function was performed in five scenarios defined with 21, 41, 61, 81 and 101 nodes, with one of the nodes being configured as the Personal Area Network (PAN) coordinator. Nodes were randomly deployed in an area of $50 \times 50\,\mathrm{m}^2$, with the PAN coordinator positioned in the center. The used channel model was the free space model without time-varying. Others simulation parameters are described in Table 2.

Table 2. Simulation setting.

Parameters	Values	Parameters	Values
Node distribution	Random with coordinator in center	BO	6
Radio	CC2420	SO	4
MAC layer	IEEE 802.15.4	β^n	0.5
Number of superframe slots	145 (5 are used by the CAP)	β^e	1.5
Data rate	250 kbps	β^s	1.0
Initial energy per node	18720 J	β^H	1.5
TxOutputPower	0 dBm	T_{IS}	4 (for PRS)

The simulation execution time was set to 450 s, during which the coordinator is able to send up to 50 *beacons*. The radio model used was CC2420, which is compliant with the IEEE 802.15.4 PHY standard. The β^n, β^e, β^s and β^H values were obtained through experiments performed in the simulator, where values were tested in a range of 0.5 to 5 for each of the parameters. To reduce the statistical bias, each simulation was performed 60 times with a confidence interval of 95%.

Simulations were performed considering a dynamic topology, where only 50% of nodes were associated to the network at time zero and the remainder were subsequently associated in groups of 5 by 5 nodes. The first group at time instant 50 s and then, all the other groups every 30 s. Considering the scenario with the highest number of nodes (100 nodes), after 320 s, all nodes were associated. Later, from the time instant 320 s of simulation, 20% of the nodes of the network randomly left the coverage of the coordinator node. This leaving operation was performed in groups of 4 nodes, every 10 s of simulation. Finally, all nodes again joined the network, in the same order (groups of 4 in 4), from the time instant 350 s of simulation, respecting an interval of 10 s for each group, except for the case of the network with 100 nodes, where only 10% of the outgoing nodes returned.

This topology was designed to force the list of neighbors to undergo multiple changes during the simulation time, in order to assess the reliability of the relay selection procedure.

4.2   Simulation Assessment

It was considered the following metrics in the evaluation scenarios: success rate, number of cooperations per node, energy consumption and the percentage of duplicate (useless) messages. The success rate represents the ratio between the number of sent messages and the number of messages that actually reach the coordinator. This metric considers messages transmitted in both the transmission attempt and the retransmission attempts performed by relayers. The number of cooperations represents the average number of cooperations performed per node, i.e., it is based on the number of retransmission messages sent by each relay node. Energy consumption represents the average amount of energy spent by each node, obtained through the resource management module available in Castalia framework. Finally, the percentage of duplicate (useless) messages represents the percentage of cooperation's messages that were not used, i.e., all messages that the relay node listened to and inserted in the cooperation message which had already arrived with success in the coordinator.

Simulations were performed evaluating the fourteen objective functions. However, only the most relevant results considering one, two, three or four parameters will be presented. When considering one parameter, the best results were obtained with Energy (e) one, as presented in Eq. 3 (Table 1). For two parameters, the best results were obtained with Energy (e) and History of Successful Transmission Rate (H), as presented in Eq. 9 (Table 1). And the combination of three parameters that presented the greatest impact was Energy (e), the RSSI among node x_i and its neighbors node x_j (s) and History of Successful Transmission Rate (H), as defined in Eq. 14 (Table 1).

Finally, these results will be compared with the results obtained with the ORST technique, where four parameters were considered together. Figure 2 presents the success rate results. It can be observed that the success rate can even be improved when the selection is performed, considering only the parameters of greatest impact. In this case, three new objective functions were advantageous when compared to the function that considers the four parameters. Among the three new modeled objective functions, we can highlight the function that considers only the energy resource as a parameter, because besides presenting a good performance in relation to the success rate is the function that best simplifies the optimization problem, due to the restricted number of variables involved in its formulation.

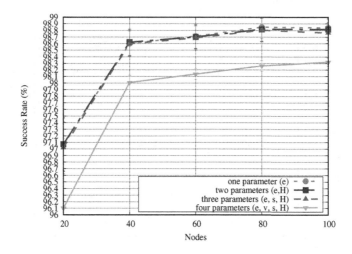

Fig. 2. Success rate.

Figure 3 illustrates the energy consumption of the overall network when considered different parameters for the relay selection. Again it is possible to observe that considering a smaller number of parameters can bring good results, considering that there was no increase in energy consumption.

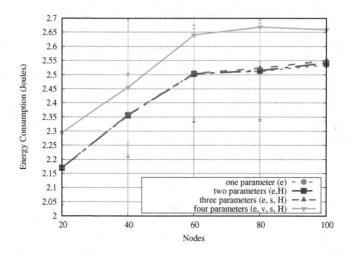

Fig. 3. Energy consumption.

Figure 4 presents the average number of cooperations per node. It is possible to verify that the average number of cooperations per node made by all the objective functions was very similar. This behavior is a direct consequence of the smaller number of selected relays, due to the optimization technique used for all the objective functions.

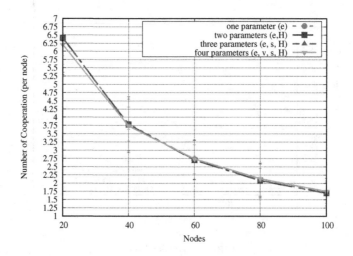

Fig. 4. Average number of cooperation exchanges.

Figure 5 presents the percentage of useless retransmission messages. The objective function that combines two parameters (e and H) presented the smaller value in the scenarios with 80 and 100 nodes when compared with the objective function that considered the four possible parameters. However, when compared to other objective functions, the percentage of useless retransmissions messages is very similar.

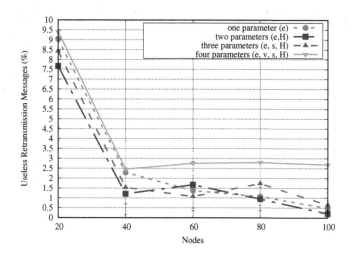

Fig. 5. Percentage of useless retransmission messages.

Considering that the purpose of this analysis is to identify the relevance of each of the parameters to simplify the objective function, it can be stated that the objective function that presented best results was the objective function that considers only the energy as a selection parameter.

The energy consumption parameter has great relevance to maximize the lifetime of the network, considering that if a node has a low battery level, it should not be selected as a relay. According to relays selection technique (Eq. 2), the nodes that have a higher energy load and comply the constraints will be selected as relays. In this way, the overall purpose of not contributing for the exhausting of the energy of a relay node is fulfilled.

According to the results obtained from the assessment, it was possible to optimize the ORST technique's objective function, reducing the number of considered criteria. The new objective function that will be considered for the ORST technique is the one that considers only the energy resource, as presented in Eq. 3:

$$W_i \doteq \left(\frac{\beta^e}{e_i} \right) \tag{3}$$

In [8], the ORST technique was compared with three state-of-the-art techniques: *Opportunistic* [19], which selects the cooperating nodes according to the network packet error rate, Random Around the Coordinator (*RAC*) [5], which performs a random selection of the nodes that have an adequate communication link with the destination node and Completely Random relay selection (*CR*) [21], which performs a random selection from all the nodes of the network. In this assessment, the ORST technique outperformed the other state-of-the-art techniques. We selected the state-of-the-art technique with the best performance in this evaluation (the *RAC* technique) to compare with the ORST technique using the new objective function and the ORST technique using the old objective function.

Figure 6 presents the success rate compared to RAC technique. It is possible to observe that the ORST technique with the new objective function achieve a high level of success rate, independently of the number of nodes.

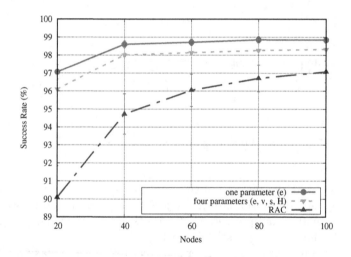

Fig. 6. Success rate compared to RAC technique.

Figure 7 illustrates the energy consumption compared to the RAC technique, again the ORST technique implementing the new objective function presented very promising results, having a lower energy consumption than the RAC technique.

Figure 8 presents the average number of cooperations per node compared to the RAC technique, this metric presents a great difference in results between the ORST (old and new) techniques and the RAC technique, being justified by the goal of the ORST technique, which is to select the lowest number of cooperating nodes, different from RAC, which randomly selects relay nodes.

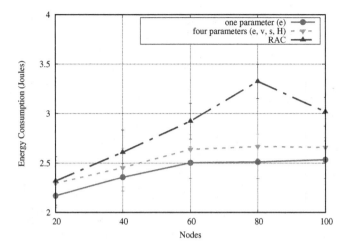

Fig. 7. Energy consumption compared to RAC technique.

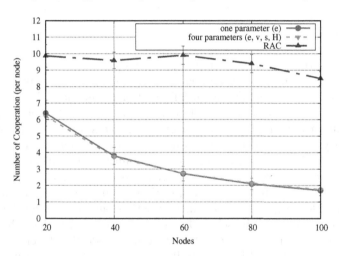

Fig. 8. Average number of cooperation exchanges compared to RAC technique.

Figure 9 presents the percentage of useless retransmission messages compared to RAC technique, it is possible to observe that the ORST technique with the new objective function presents the lowest percentage of useless retransmission messages, approaching zero in the scenario with 100 nodes. However, the RAC technique presents a high percentage of useless retransmission messages, being greater than 60% in the scenario with 100 nodes.

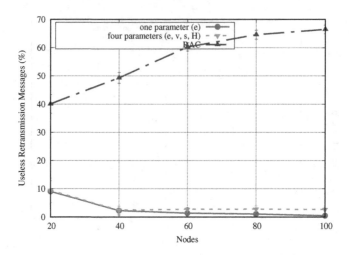

Fig. 9. Percentage of useless retransmission messages compared to RAC technique.

5   Conclusion

The relays selection is a decisive step to guarantee adequate cooperative communication. With the analysis performed in this paper, it was possible to simplify the objective function used by the ORST selection technique, reducing the number of parameters considered in this function and still properly selecting the set of relay nodes, promoting improvements in the success rate of the network.

Previously, we believed that it was necessary to consider all the parameters $(v, e, s$ and $H)$ in the objective function to obtain an adequate relay selection. However, what guarantees the adequate relay selection is the modeling of the problem of the ORST technique as an optimization problem (Eqs. 2a, 2b and 2c), that provides two guarantees. The first is that only a node that has at least one neighboring node will be selected as relay. The second is that when a node has no neighbors, it must necessarily have a relay node that listens to it. Both constraints are determined in the coordinator node, thus, the coordinator node knows the neighborhood of each node and also can define which nodes have good communication with it. In this way, considering only the energy resource in the objective function allows to complement the information that the coordinator already has, significantly improving the used relay selection technique.

References

1. Aziz, A.A., Ghani, H.A.: Energy efficiency in dynamic cluster selection for cooperative wireless sensor networks. In: Region Ten Symposium (Tensymp), pp. 155–159. IEEE (2019)
2. Bao, J., Wu, J., Liu, C., Jiang, B., Tang, X.: Optimized power allocation and relay location selection in cooperative relay networks. Wirel. Commun. Mob. Comput. **9**(3), 1–10 (2017)

3. Castalia: Framework castalia. https://github.com/boulis/Castalia. Accessed 03 Apr 2019
4. Cheikh, M.E., Simpson, O., Sun, Y.: Energy efficient relay selection method for clustered wireless sensor network. In: 23th European Wireless Conference in European Wireless 2017, Berlin, Offenbach, vol. 2017, pp. 92–97 (2017)
5. Etezadi, F., Zarifi, K., Ghrayeb, A., Affes, S.: Decentralized relay selection schemes in uniformly distributed wireless sensor networks. IEEE Trans. Wirel. Commun. 11(3), 938–951 (2012)
6. Iqbal, Z., Kim, K., Lee, H.N.: A cooperative wireless sensor network for indoor industrial monitoring. IEEE Trans. Ind. Inf. 13(2), 482–491 (2017)
7. Khan, R.A.M., Karl, H.: MAC protocols for cooperative diversity in wireless LANs and wireless sensor networks. IEEE Commun. Surv. Tutor. 16(1), 46–63 (2014)
8. Laurindo, S., Moraes, R., Nassiffe, R., Montez, C., Vasques, F.: An optimized relay selection technique to improve the communication reliability in wireless sensor networks. Sensors 18(10), 3263 (2018)
9. Liang, X., Balasingham, I., Leung, V.C.M.: Cooperative communications with relay selection for QoS provisioning in wireless sensor networks. In: Global Telecommunications Conference (GLOBECOM), pp. 1–8. IEEE, November 2009
10. LP Solve: LP solve library. http://lpsolve.sourceforge.net/. Accessed 05 Apr 2019
11. Nosratinia, A., Hunter, T.E., Hedayat, A.: Cooperative communication in wireless networks. IEEE Commun. Mag. 42(October), 74–80 (2004)
12. OMNeT++: OMNeT++. https://omnetpp.org/. Accessed 03 Apr 2019
13. Pham, T.L., Kim, D.S.: Efficient forwarding protocol for dual-hop relaying wireless networks. Wirel. Pers. Commun. 89(1), 165–180 (2016)
14. Phan, K.T., Nguyen, D.H., Le-Ngoc, T.: Joint power allocation and relay selection in cooperative networks. In: Global Telecommunications Conference (GLOBECOM), pp. 1–5. IEEE (2009)
15. Senanayake, R., Atapattu, S., Evans, J.S., Smith, P.J.: Decentralized relay selection in multi-user multihop decode-and-forward relay networks. IEEE Trans. Wirel. Commun. 17(5), 3313–3326 (2018)
16. Srinivasan, K., Levis, P.: RSSI is under appreciated. In: Third Workshop on Embedded Networked Sensors (EmNets), pp. 239–242, Cambridge, MA, USA (2006)
17. Valle, O.T., Budke, G., Montez, C., Moraes, R., Vasques, F.: Experimental assessment of LNC-based cooperative communication schemes using commercial off-the-shelf wireless sensor network nodes. Int. J. Commun Syst 31(7), e3508 (2018)
18. Valle, O.T., Milack, A.V., Montez, C., Portugal, P., Vasques, F.: Experimental evaluation of multiple retransmission schemes in IEEE 802.15. 4 wireless sensor networks. In: International Workshop on Factory Communication Systems (WFSC), pp. 201–210. IEEE (2012)
19. Valle, O.T., Montez, C., de Araujo, G., Vasques, F., Moraes, R.: NetCoDer: a retransmission mechanism for WSNs based on cooperative relays and network coding. Sensors 16(6), 799 (2016)
20. Wang, J., Wu, Q.: Relay selection for maximizing the number of successive transmission in cooperative networks. Int. J. Parallel Emerg. Distrib. Syst. 32(6), 632–646 (2017)

21. Willig, A., Uhlemann, E.: On relaying for wireless industrial communications: is careful placement of relayers strictly necessary? In: 9th IEEE International Workshop on Factory Communication Systems (WFCS), pp. 191–200 (2012)
22. Zhang, Y., Zhang, B., Zhang, S.: A lifetime maximization relay selection scheme in wireless body area networks. Sensors **17**(6), 1267 (2017)
23. Zhu, K., Wang, F., Li, S., Jiang, F., Cao, L.: Relay selection for cooperative relaying in wireless energy harvesting networks. In: IOP Conference Series: Earth and Environmental Science, vol. 108, no. c, p. 052059 (2018)

Opportunistic Data Collection and Routing in Segmented Wireless Sensor Networks

Juliette Garcia$^{(\boxtimes)}$, Alain Pirovano, and Mickaël Royer

ENAC/TELECOM/ReSCo, Toulouse, France
juliette.garcia@recherche.enac.fr,
{alain.pirovano,mickael.royer}@enac.fr

Abstract. In this paper we address routing in the context of segmented wireless sensor networks in which a mobile entity, known as MULE, may collect data from the different subnetworks and forward it to a sink for processing. The chosen settings are inspired by the potential application of wireless sensor networks for airport surface monitoring. In such an environment, the subnetworks could take advantage of airport service vehicles, buses or even taxiing aircraft to transfer information to the sink (e.g., control tower), without interfering with the regular functioning of the airport. Generally, this kind of communication problem is addressed in the literature considering a single subsink in each subnetwork. We consider in this paper the multiple subsinks case and propose two strategies to decide when and where (to which subsink) sensor nodes should transmit their sensing data. Through a dedicated simulation model we have developed, we assess and compare the performance of both strategies in terms of packet delivery ratio, power consumption and workload balance among subsinks. This paper is an intermediate step in the research of this problem, which evidences the benefit of storing the information on the subsinks and distributing it among them before the arrival of the MULE. Based on results, we provide some information on further works.

Keywords: Wireless Sensor Network · Segmented network · Routing

1 Introduction

A Wireless Sensor Network (WSN) is composed of a set of sensing devices, each able to collect information from the environment and transfer it to the others using wireless capabilities. The data gathered by the sensor nodes is sent to a node called sink for processing. These properties make WSNs deployment easier and quicker than for wired based solutions. Sensor nodes have the ability to determine paths to transfer information among them and to adapt in case a node is lost (e.g., due to failure or battery depletion). However, these have a limited communication range that only allows them to establish direct contact with nearby nodes. Due to this limitations, sometimes the network becomes

© Springer Nature Switzerland AG 2019
M. R. Palattella et al. (Eds.): ADHOC-NOW 2019, LNCS 11803, pp. 183–195, 2019.
https://doi.org/10.1007/978-3-030-31831-4_13

segmented (i.e., a network composed of multiple isolated subnetworks). This scenario often appears when the sensing field is too large to be exhaustively covered by a fully connected WSN or when there are physical constraints on the field (e.g., buildings, rivers, etc).

In this paper we consider the routing problem in the context of a segmented WSNs. To address this problem, an existing solution relies on mobile nodes that pick up data from the subnetworks along their path and forward it to the sink. This type of entities are known as Mobile Ubiquitous LAN Extensions (MULEs) [1]. The role of MULE can be played by vehicles or drones for instance. Those could be entities traversing the area with the sole purpose of data transfer (controlled data collection), or entities non-devoted to the operation of the communication network (opportunistic data collection). In this paper, we focus on opportunistic data collection. As it advances on its way, a MULE can successively get in contact with several nodes belonging to the same subnetwork. In this paper, those nodes are named subsinks. A strategy to assign a destination subsink to each sensor node has to be defined. In addition, a suitable routing protocol must be chosen to define the multi-hop path between each sensor and the selected subsink.

In this paper, we compare two strategies to decide when and where (to which subsink) sensor nodes should transmit their sensing data. Firstly, in the frame of a so-called *Reactive strategy*, gathered information is retained by each sensor node until the MULE visits the subnetwork. Then, each sensor node sends all gathered data only to the subsink in contact with the MULE. Results obtained with this strategy encourage to investigate an alternative method. Hence, we developed a second strategy called *Proactive strategy*. A relevant subsink for each node is proactively selected and the data sent progressively as collected, even if none of the subsinks has detected a MULE. In this way, the information will be stored only in the nodes that will have contact with MULE, that means, in the subsinks. We remark that the value of the paper is not in the routing strategies applied but in the results of computer simulations that evidence, through comparison of both strategies, the benefit of storing the information on the subsinks and distributing the information among them before the arrival of the MULE. Our results are based on a simple example case in which the subnetwork has a grid structure. However, this case is sufficient to conclude about the potential benefit of the two actions previously mentioned.

The remaining of this paper is organized as follows: Sect. 2 presents the application case that motivated this study and a description of our research problem. Section 3 discusses previous developments found in the literature related to our research. In Sect. 4 we present the Reactive strategy and then, in Sect. 5 we describe the Proactive strategy. The performance of both strategies is assessed in Sect. 6 through simulations. Finally, conclusions and further research directions are provided in Sect. 7.

2   Motivation Case and Problem Description

This work is inspired by the process of Airport Surface Area Surveillance (ASAS), which encompasses the set of strategies and techniques used to control operations in both, movement areas (taxiways and runways) and non-movement areas (aprons and aircraft parking spots) of an airport. ASAS procedures may involve both critical monitoring for short term decision making (e.g. detection and removal of foreign objects placed on a runway) and non-critical monitoring for long term decision making (e.g. control of pavement temperature and noise levels along and around runways). Nowadays, airports conduct ASAS procedures using regular visual inspections performed by ground personnel. This approach presents strong limitations. Notably, it requires stopping regular activities on the area under inspection and its effectiveness may be naturally affected by human factors. We propose an alternative and automated solution based on WSNs. This innovative approach is expected to be easy to deploy in a short delay and totally customized considering the environment, in addition to provide the ability to survey several types of events or parameters at a relatively affordable cost.

To transfer critical data we assume the use of long range radio communication technologies (e.g., LoRa [2]). This type of technology allows direct communication between any sensor node and the destination sink at a high energy cost for the sensor. Long range communication technologies are limited to relative low data transfer rates, so this solution should be suitable for the sending of critical data that are expected to be rare. Non-critical measurements are tolerant to delays in the order of minutes or even hours for some of them. Thus, the collection of information of this type from the different subnetworks by means of MULEs seems to be a reasonable approach. In the context of airports, the role of data MULE could be played by already operating airport service vehicles, buses or even by taxiing aircraft, all this in an opportunistic way.

We further assume that the system is aware of the nodes that will be potentially in contact with the MULE, but not of the time at which the contact will be effective. Thus, data transfer to the MULEs must be done in an opportunistic way (i.e., using the occasion each time a MULE gets in contact). As we assume that the set of subsinks is known and fixed, the MULE will always visit the same group of nodes for a given subnetwork at any time. In our airport application case, for instance, this setting may reflect a scheme where subsinks are located along or by the side of runways and taxiways. Each sensor node must send its data to the subsinks that will forward the packets to the MULEs later. Depending on the distance separating each sensor and the subsinks, such a transfer could be done via direct, or more often, multi-hop paths. The solution approaches proposed here decompose the problem for each subnetwork into: (a) selecting to which subsink and when a sensor node should send its data; and (b) building routes among resulting pairs.

Solution strategies will use a classic 5 layer WSN model as base. The application protocol is responsible for the decision about to which subsink and when a sensor must send data, while the routing protocol defines an appropriate path between sensor nodes and subsinks.

3   Related Work

The literature contains several approaches to address the routing problem in Segmented Wireless Sensor Networks (S-WSNs). Main differences lie on the degree of control that the communication system is assumed to have over the MULEs. Some studies assume that the communication system determines both, the routes and schedule of the MULES (see e.g., [3,4] and [5]). Some other studies consider the setting where the MULES are non-controlled by the communication system. In those cases the proposed methods are often based on opportunistic data collection (i.e., taking advantage of not known a priori visits of a MULE). In the remaining of this section we focus on this latter approach.

The type of path that MULEs follow under the opportunistic data collection scheme can be classified as random or fixed. If the path varies from one visit of the MULE to the other and thus, the set of nodes that get direct contact with the MULE at each visit vary too, we classify the trajectory as a random path. In contrast, if at each visit the MULE gets contact with the same set of nodes, the trajectory is considered as a fixed path. This type of trajectory is often subjected to the layout of traffic lanes present in the environment.

The fixed path scenario is addressed in [6] and [7] with the particular assumption that the network topology and MULE's path are such that only one sensor node is able to get direct contact with the MULE (i.e., there is only one subsink per subnetwork). As such an assumption is often limiting, we consider in our study several subsinks per subnetwork. In the frame of the current state of the art and in accordance with our airport use-case, we propose two solution strategies for this problem with predefined and multiple subsinks per subnetwork.

4   Reactive Strategy

In the reactive strategy, the system starts by building suitable paths from each sensor node to each subsink. Then, sensor nodes start collecting and storing data. Meanwhile, the MULEs travel in the surroundings of the network and periodically emit beacons to make subsinks aware of its presence. Once a subsink receives a beacon, it sends a message to the sensor nodes to inform them that it is in contact with the MULE. At this point, the sensor nodes start sending their data packets to the subsink using the previously defined paths. Finally, data is forwarded from the subsink to the MULE. If the MULE advances on its path and gets contact with another subsink, this last propagates a new message to update the destination subsink. Then, data transfer is redirected to the new destination subsink using the routes built at the beginning. During this updating process, if the former destination subsink retains data from other sensor nodes, it starts transferring it to the new destination subsink as all the other sensor nodes do.

This strategy is called *reactive* as the selection of the destination subsink for each sensor node and the subsequent transfer of gathered data are tasks triggered by an event: the reception of the message indicating that a subsink is in contact with the MULE. The core functions of this strategy are implemented in the network and application layers of the WSN node communication architecture. Those functions are listed below.

4.1 Network Layer Protocol

Routing Paths Establishment to Reach the Subsinks: when the system goes into operation each subsink builds a directed acyclic graph (referred to as tree hereon for concision) connecting itself to every other node in the subnetwork through the shortest path. In our study, the tree for each subsink is built using the IPv6 Routing Protocol for Low-Power and Lossy Networks (RPL [8]), a protocol standardized by the Internet Engineering Task Force (IETF). As most other shortest-path oriented methods, RPL works for a generalized cost that could be defined, for instance, in terms of time, distance, energy consumption, or number of hops. Here we assume that the cost is given by the number of hops.

4.2 Application Layer Protocol

We called this protocol Reactive Origin Destination Matching (R-ODM).

Notify Contact with the MULE: each MULE declares its presence to its nearby nodes by periodically broadcasting one-hop beacon messages. Once a subsink receives a beacon, it notifies all the nodes in the subnetwork that it is in contact with the MULE. It is done using short advertisement messages (ADVs) which cross the network through the minimum cost paths included in the RPL trees. To do that, we use a broadcast technique called Parent Flooding, proposed in [9]. This procedure starts from the root of the RPL tree (a subsink), which broadcasts the ADV packet. Nodes that receive the ADV packet only broadcast it if the node who sent it is its parent in the RPL tree. Otherwise the node does not broadcast the ADV. This way, the ADV packet is propagated through the network using efficient routes in the RPL tree avoiding loops.

Sending of Information: when a node receives an ADV, it starts sending its gathered information. To do so, the node sends the data to its parent on the RPL tree whose root is the subsink in contact with the MULE.

Notify Lost Contact with the MULE: when a subsink loses communication with the MULE, the former sends an ADV to all the network to indicate the other nodes its status has changed and the nodes stop sending packets to it. The procedure to notify lost contact uses the minimum cost paths provided by RPL.

Change of Subsink: when a new subsink receives a beacon from the MULE, it must notify the entire subnetwork its new status. This operation is also performed by means of ADVs that travel through RPL trees. Once all nodes get aware of the new destination, data transfer is redirected to it. If a subsink loses contact with the MULE but has still information stored, it forwards it to the new destination subsink. If the MULE has left the subnetwork, the subsink retains it for a future visit of a MULE.

5   Proactive Strategy

To overcome some deficiencies of the reactive strategy, we propose a new approach called proactive strategy. Its objective is to mitigate the packet storm that occurs when a MULE gets contact with the subnetwork and to improve the load balance between subsinks. To do so, we propose two main changes compared to the previous strategy. Firstly, each sensor node must choose in advance a destination subsink before the MULE gets contact with the subnetwork. In this paper, we use a simple heuristic rule for that end: each sensor node must select the closest subsink in terms of hops as destination. This information is given by RPL since a tree is built for each subsink based on the number of hops. Secondly, each time a sensor collects information, it does not store it locally but sends it to its chosen subsink.

As for the reactive strategy, the core functions of the proactive strategy are implemented in the network and application layers of a 5 layer WSN architecture.

5.1   Network Layer Protocol

Construction of Routes to Reach Any Subsink: each subsink builds a tree connecting to every node in the subnetwork using RPL as in the reactive strategy. This way, each node will be aware of the number of hops required to reach its destination subsink.

5.2   Application Layer Protocol

We called this protocol Proactive Origin Destination Matching (P-ODM).

Selection of the Subsink and Sending of Data: each node selects the subsink closest to it, that is, the subsink reachable in the lowest number of hops. Each time a node gathers new information, it forwards it immediately to its destination subsink.

6   Simulations and Results

6.1   MULE's Functioning

The way the MULE works does not have any impact on the reactive nature of the first solution strategy. In fact, the functioning of the MULE is exactly the same for both solution strategies. In both approaches, MULE's functioning requires a particular protocol in the application layer, responsible of: (i) the delivery of periodic beacons to alert the subnetworks about the presence of the MULE; and (ii) the storage of data received from the subsinks.

Application Layer Protocol

Sending of Beacons: each MULE broadcasts periodically beacon messages to warn nearby subsinks that it is close. When a subsink receives a beacon, the application layer protocol and network layer protocol for sensor nodes work together to transfer the data to the MULE.

Data Storage: this application allows the MULE to store information received from the subsinks in order to transfer it to the sink later.

6.2   Setup for Simulations

The performance of the reactive and proactive strategies was evaluated through computer simulations performed on the discrete event simulator OMNeT++ 5.2 [10]. The protocol stacks implemented for the sensor nodes and the MULE mainly differ at the application layer. Both architectures are based on the well-known IEEE 802.15.4 for the physical and the data link layers. Similarly, RPL is a control plane protocol specially designed for wireless networks with memory, power or processing constraints. It requires the use of IPv6 as data plane protocol. As data applications are tolerant to delay, UDP was chosen for the transport layer. Most of these protocols were already available in libraries of OMNeT++. However, RPL was not available, so we had to develop it. We also implemented the R-ODM and P-ODM protocols, required by the reactive and proactive strategy respectively, as well as the applications which simulate the collection of data for each sensor node. Those applications are detailed below.

Data Collection to be as representative as possible of the airport monitoring application, each sensor has to collect data using two strategies: in a periodic way or based on a threshold.

Periodic Data Collection: this function simulates the data collection in *almost* equally spaced periods of time (e.g. sense noise levels each ~10 min). Each time data is collected, it is passed to the R-ODM or P-ODM protocol (depending on the used strategy) to proceed with its transfer to the subsink.

Data Collection Based on Thresholds: as the previous approach, this function simulates data collection in almost equally spaced periods of time (e.g. collect pavement temperature levels each ~10 min). Each time data is collected, it is checked to determine if the sensed variable exceeded a predefined threshold assigned by the user (e.g., pavement temperature of 40 °C). If this is the case, the data packet is forwarded to the R-ODM or P-ODM protocol (again, depending on the used strategy). Otherwise, the data is discarded.

Simulation Parameters. We consider a scenario with a single MULE and a subnetwork composed of 50 sensor nodes. Among all the sensor nodes, 10 are subsinks while the other 40 remain out of the communication range of the MULE. We modeled a rectangular grid-like subnetwork with 5 rows and 10 columns, covering a rectangular area of dimensions 500×1000 m. This may correspond, for instance, to a section of a grass area between runways and taxiways in an airport (see Fig. 1).

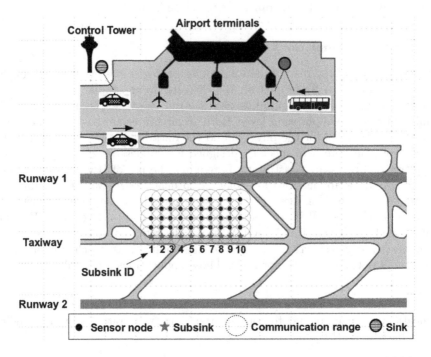

Fig. 1. Deployment of the subnetwork considered in the experiment for an ASAS case.

The speed of the MULE is fixed constant at 30 km h^{-1}. The MULE gets contact for the first time with a subsink after 30 min of simulation, along which the sensors are collecting information. After that first contact, the MULE keeps advancing at constant speed, parallel to the row of subsinks. Given the MULE's speed, there is a time-lapse of two minutes of continuous direct contact with at least one subsink and then the simulation stops (see Fig. 2). During the whole simulation, the MULE sends beacon messages at a constant rate of 1 message each 2 s. The transport of packets by the MULE and the sending of them to the sink are not considered in this paper since the MULE's route is not controlled by the communication system. On the other hand, we do not consider packet exchanges between sub-networks using the MULE since the final destination of the data is the sink. The Standard IEEE 802.15.4 protocol is setup with a bitrate of 250 kbps, a communication range of 100 m and a maximum queue length of

100 packets. Acknowledgement messages are activated and the maximum number of transfer attempts is fixed in 7. After that, a *loss due to collision* is registered and the message is dropped.

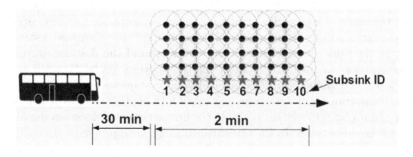

Fig. 2. Trajectory of the MULE in the experiment.

For the data collection, the periodic function and the one based on thresholds are assigned each, two variables to sense. In all cases, the first measurement at each node is performed at a random instant uniformly distributed in [1, 5] sec from the beginning of the simulation. From that moment and on, the time between measurements is uniformly distributed between 0.9 and 1.1 min. The function based on thresholds uses a random number uniformly distributed between 0 and 1 to determine if a given measurement should be sent to the MULE. The decision threshold is fixed in 0.8 so that in average, 20% of measurements performed by the function based on threshold are transferred.

The memory capacity for each node was set in 1 MB, taking as a reference a TelosB sensor [11]. This type of sensor is often used in WSN to simultaneously monitor multiple variables such as temperature, humidity and light intensity. This sensor works with AA rechargeable batteries, which could provide the sensor with up to 16,000 J of energy. As our main interest was to compare the performance of the reactive and proactive strategies, we chose large enough (but realistic) parameters that would not cause neither energy depletion nor memory overflow issues in our scenario.

Finally, in the R-ODM Protocol, ADVs and data packets are sent by each node with a delay uniformly distributed between 0.04 and 0.05 s and between 0.02 and 0.03 s respectively, to mitigate collisions. No aggregation approach (as those used in [12]) is considered in the proposed strategies to keep the comparison as simple as possible.

6.3   Results

The results of the reactive and proactive strategies are presented below. Because we used randomness in the selection of some parameters, we ran 30 simulations and calculated mean/standard deviation. We evaluated the proposed strategy in terms of three performance metrics:

Packet Delivery Ratio (PDR): percentage of data packets received by the MULE out of the total number of packets sent by all the sensor nodes. The PDR for the reactive strategy over the 30 runs was in average 45.73%, with a standard deviation of 8.58%. The main cause of packets loss was the queue overflow, accounting for 83.1% of the losses. The remaining losses were caused by data collisions. The reactive strategy is highly susceptible to queue overflow due to the fact that on this approach, all sensors node have the same destination subsink at the same time. This converts nodes around the destination subsink into bottlenecks, as they are included in the shortest paths between several sensor nodes and the subsink. Packet collisions and queue overflow took place during: (i) the transfer of data from one subsink to another, and (ii) the massive transfer of data from the sensor nodes to the first set of subsinks when the MULE arrived to the subnetwork. In the proactive strategy, both problems are mitigated as there is no communication among subsinks, data is sent at the subsinks as soon is collected before the arrival of the MULE and data is distributed among them. This way, localized congestion spots are avoided. Table 1 shows the positive impact on the PDR by using the proactive strategy. The standard deviation of the PDR shows that the proactive strategy is also considerably more stable in this performance measure than the reactive strategy.

Table 1. Comparison of reactive and proactive strategy in terms of PDR and PC.

	Performance metric	Mean	Standard deviation
Reactive Strategy	PDR (%)	45,73%	8%
	Energy (Joules)	203	1.02
Proactive Strategy	PDR (%)	98,10%	0.13%
	Energy (Joules)	198	0,36

Power Consumption (PC): total amount of energy used by all the sensor nodes. On the one hand, this measure is correlated with the length of the routes (number of hops) to reach the destination. Results in Table 1 show that the reactive strategy causes in average greater PC. In the reactive approach, the destination subsink is assigned without considering the distance separating it from the sensor nodes. In contrast, the proactive approach performs optimally in this aspect, as that strategy uses the nearest subsink as destination for each sensor node. On the other hand, the PC is related to congestion issues such as a high number of transfer attempts to avoid loss of packets due to collisions; problems that are mitigated in the proactive strategy. Similarly to the PDR, the standard deviation of the PC for the reactive strategy is bigger, which indicates less stable performance.

Subsink Load (SL): average over the 30 runs, of the percentage of packets received by each subsink out of the total number of packets received by all the subsinks. Figure 3 shows the SL for each of the 10 subsinks for each strategy. Results show a strong imbalance in the SL for the reactive strategy. Under this approach, there is a large amount of data stored at the sensor nodes when the MULE reaches the subnetwork. This data corresponds to 30 min of sensing. When the MULE gets in contact with the subnetwork, all that information is sent to the first subsink. This last sends as much data as it can to the MULE, but the contact time with the MULE is too short to transfer all stored data. Therefore, it had to redirect data to the second subsink and so on. In fact, it forwards 54.38% of the information it receives to the other subsinks. The remaining 45.61% is sent to the MULE. This indicates that the first subsink is overloaded. The large amount of data progressively shrinks as it moves forward in the subsinks line. The consequences of the first subsink being overloaded are: (i) this subsink consumes more energy than the other nodes in the network, since it often has to forward arriving packets to the subsink in contact with the MULE; and (ii) this subsink increases the probability of collision of a packet as some packets are forced to cover unnecessarily large paths to reach its location.

Unlike the results obtained with the reactive strategy, the proactive approach shows an almost perfect balance in the number of packets received by each subsink (see Fig. 3). This is the result of the even assignment of sensor nodes to subsinks, which helps to reduce the number of bottleneck nodes, and thus, the amount of dropped packets by queue overflow and collisions.

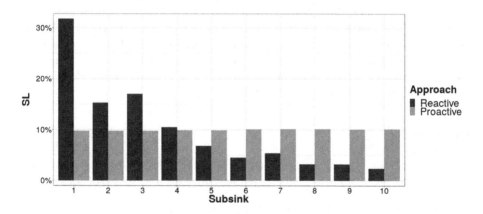

Fig. 3. Subsink load for each strategy.

We remark that our simple heuristic rule for proactive strategy offers good results in our case. This, due to the grid-like structure of the network considered and the fact that each sensor node generates the same amount of data. More sophisticated assignment rules should be applied in order to reach comparable results if the network presents other type of structure or if data collection is not homogeneous among sensor nodes.

7   Conclusions and Further Works

This paper aims to investigate routing and forwarding in segmented wireless sensors networks. Data collected in each subnetwork must be forwarded to the final destination, the sink, where they will be processed. Existing mobile nodes, such as vehicles, are involved in an opportunistic way to act as intermediate nodes between the subnetworks and the sink. These properties match with the considered use case of wireless sensor networks for airport surface monitoring. As the forwarder vehicles follow existing lanes, nodes that could be in contact with them in each subnetwork are fixed and considered as subsinks.

Firstly, we propose and assess the performance of a reactive approach. In this case, the sending of collected data from the sensor nodes to the relevant subsink is triggered by the fact that the subsink is in contact with a MULE. This approach offers poor results in terms of packet delivery ratio caused by many collisions around the subsink in contact with the MULE. Then, to mitigate this problem, we propose a simple proactive approach based on the assumptions of a regular grid topology with homogeneous nodes in terms of generated data traffic. Here, the relevant subsink selection for each sensor node and then the progressive sending of data packets to this subsink are anticipated. The obtained results show that the proactive approach avoids the congestion observed with the reactive approach, ensuring better results in terms of packet delivery ratio, subsink load and power consumption.

This study is a preliminary step whose results justify the development of a more complex methodology which uses strategies as storing and distribution of information among the subsinks, in networks with random structure. In this direction we are continuing this investigation. The new approach could be based on heuristic mechanisms (e.g., Ant Colony Optimization) taking into account multiple performance criteria and also the frequency of MULEs' visits to improve the routing strategy. To the best of our knowledge, this kind of methodology has never been considered in such a context.

References

1. Shah, R.C., Roy, S., Jain, S., Brunette, W.: Data MULEs: modeling and analysis of a three-tier architecture for sparse sensor networks. Ad Hoc Netw. **1**(2–3), 215–233 (2003)
2. Bertoldo, S., Carosso, L., Marchetta, E., Paredes, M., Allegretti, M.: Feasibility analysis of a LoRa-based WSN using public transport. Appl. Syst. Innov. **1**(4), 49 (2018)
3. Ma, M., Yang, Y.: Data gathering in wireless sensor networks with mobile collectors. In: 2008 IEEE International Symposium on Parallel and Distributed Processing, pp. 1–9. IEEE (2008)
4. Wu, F.-J., Huang, C.-F., Tseng, Y.-C.: Data gathering by mobile mules in a spatially separated wireless sensor network. In: 2009 Tenth International Conference on Mobile Data Management: Systems, Services and Middleware, pp. 293–298. IEEE (2009)

5. Singh, S.K., Kumar, P.: A mobile sinks based data collection scheme for isolated wireless sensor networks. In: Proceedings of 3rd International Conference on Internet of Things and Connected Technologies (ICIoTCT) (2018)
6. Tseng, Y.-C., Lai, W.-T., Huang, C.-F., Wu, F.-J.: Using mobile mules for collecting data from an isolated wireless sensor network. In: 2010 39th International Conference on Parallel Processing, pp. 673–679. IEEE (2010)
7. Tseng, Y.-C., Fang-Jing, W., Lai, W.-T.: Opportunistic data collection for disconnected wireless sensor networks by mobile mules. Ad Hoc Netw. **11**(3), 1150–1164 (2013)
8. Winter, T., et al.: RPL: IPv6 routing protocol for low-power and lossy networks. Technical report, Internet Engineering Task Force (2012)
9. Clausen, T., Herberg, U.: Comparative study of RPL-enabled optimized broadcast in wireless sensor networks. In: 2010 Sixth International Conference on Intelligent Sensors, Sensor Networks and Information Processing, pp. 7–12. IEEE (2010)
10. Varga, A.: OMNeT++. In: Wehrle, K., Güneş, M., Gross, J. (eds.) Modeling and Tools for Network Simulation, pp. 35–59. Springer, Heidelberg (2010). https://doi.org/10.1007/978-3-642-12331-3_3
11. Hof, H.-J.: Applications of sensor networks. In: Wagner, D., Wattenhofer, R. (eds.) Algorithms for Sensor and Ad Hoc Networks. LNCS, vol. 4621, pp. 1–20. Springer, Heidelberg (2007). https://doi.org/10.1007/978-3-540-74991-2_1
12. Ciciriello, P., Mottola, L., Picco, G.P.: Efficient routing from multiple sources to multiple sinks in wireless sensor networks. In: Langendoen, K., Voigt, T. (eds.) EWSN 2007. LNCS, vol. 4373, pp. 34–50. Springer, Heidelberg (2007). https://doi.org/10.1007/978-3-540-69830-2_3

DTN7: An Open-Source Disruption-Tolerant Networking Implementation of Bundle Protocol 7

Alvar Penning[1], Lars Baumgärtner[3], Jonas Höchst[1,2], Artur Sterz[1,2(✉)], Mira Mezini[3], and Bernd Freisleben[1,2]

[1] Department of Mathematics and Computer Science, Philipps-University, Marburg, Germany
{penning,hoechst,sterz,freisleb}@informatik.uni-marburg.de
[2] Department of Electrical Engineering and Information Technology, Technical University, Darmstadt, Germany
{jonas.hoechst,artur.sterz}@maki.tu-darmstadt.de
[3] Department of Computer Science, Technical University, Darmstadt, Germany
{baumgaertner,mezini}@cs.tu-darmstadt.de

Abstract. In disruption-tolerant networking (DTN), data is transmitted in a store-carry-forward fashion from network node to network node. In this paper, we present an open source DTN implementation, called DTN7, of the recently released Bundle Protocol Version 7 (draft version 13). DTN7 is written in Go and provides features like memory safety and concurrent execution. With its modular design and interchangeable components, DTN7 facilitates DTN research and application development. Furthermore, we present results of a comparative experimental evaluation of DTN7 and other DTN systems including Serval, IBR-DTN, and Forban. Our results indicate that DTN7 is a flexible and efficient open-source multi-platform implementation of the most recent Bundle Protocol Version 7.

Keywords: Delay-tolerant networking · Disruption-tolerant networking

1 Introduction

Delay- or disruption-tolerant networking (DTN) is useful in situations where a reliable connection to a communication infrastructure cannot be established, e.g., during environmental monitoring in remote areas, if telecommunication networks are destroyed as a result of natural or man-made disasters, or if access is blocked due to political censorship. In DTN, messages are transmitted hop-to-hop from network node to network node in a store-carry-forward manner. There might be larger time windows between two transmissions, and the next node to carry a message might be reached opportunistically or through scheduled contacts.

© Springer Nature Switzerland AG 2019
M. R. Palattella et al. (Eds.): ADHOC-NOW 2019, LNCS 11803, pp. 196–209, 2019.
https://doi.org/10.1007/978-3-030-31831-4_14

There are several mobile DTN applications, such as FireChat [13] and Serval [12], that rely on peer-to-peer networks of smartphones, where the pre-installed Wi-Fi or Bluetooth hardware of the mobile devices is used to create a large mesh network. µPCN [10] is a special purpose DTN application for planetary communication, and IBR-DTN [8] is a popular DTN platform, but does not implement the recently released Bundle Protocol (BP) Version 7 [5].

In this paper, we present DTN7, which (to the best of our knowledge) is the first and only freely available, open source implementation of the most recent draft of Bundle Protocol Version 7 (BP7) (draft version 13). DTN7 is designed to offer extensibility by allowing developers to easily replace or add individual components. DTN7 is a general purpose DTN software with support for several use cases, such as enabling communication in disaster scenarios or providing connectivity in rural areas. Our contributions are:

- We provide a memory-safe and concurrent open-source implementation of BP7 (draft version 13), written in the Go programming language.
- With its highly modular design and its focus on extensibility by providing interfaces to all important components, DTN7 is a flexible basis for DTN research and application development for a wide range of scenarios.
- We compare DTN7 with other well-known DTN systems including Serval, IBR-DTN, and Forban, using the CORE network emulation framework.
- Several experiments to mimic different DTN test cases, i.e., a chain of up to 64 nodes with different payload sizes, are conducted.
- The presented DTN7 software[1], the evaluation framework and its configurations[2], and the experimental fragments[3] are freely available.

The paper is structured as follows. Section 2 discusses related work. In Sect. 3, we briefly explain BP7. Section 4 discusses DTN7's design and implementation. Section 5 describes experimental results. Section 6 concludes the paper and outlines areas of future work.

2   Related Work

This section briefly reviews relevant publications in the area of DTN software.

2.1   DTN Software Implementations

IBR-DTN [8] is a lightweight, modular DTN software for terrestrial use. The Interplanetary Overlay Network (ION) focuses on the aspects of extreme distances in space [3]. DTN2 is the reference implementation of the BP, developed by the IETF DTN working group [7]. These three implementations are based on RFC 5050, i.e., BP Version 6 [19].

---

[1] https://github.com/dtn7/dtn7-go.
[2] https://github.com/dtn7/adhocnow2019-evaluation.
[3] https://ds.mathematik.uni-marburg.de/dtn7/adhoc-now_2019.tar.gz.

Designed for small satellites in low earth orbit, μPCN can be used to connect different regions of the world. It also implements BP Version 6, as well as an older draft of version 7 [10]. Furthermore, an older version of BP7 is implemented in Terra [15].

Serval focuses on node mobility by providing implementations that run on smartphones, as well as by incorporating different radio link technologies [12]. Forban is a peer-to-peer file sharing application that uses common Internet protocols like IP and HTTP to transmit files in a delay-tolerant manner [9]. With FireChat [13], it is possible to send messages via DTN without relying on Internet access or direct peer contacts.

Many of the mentioned DTN systems implement the BP as specified in RFC 5050 [19]. While some implement a draft of BP7, none of them implements the most recent draft. Serval, Forban, and FireChat have their own protocol definitions, which are not compatible with the BP. Furthermore, the mentioned implementations cannot be extended in a modular manner, are not written in developer-friendly high-level programming languages and are not intended as general purpose DTN platforms, but are designed for specific use cases. FireChat is not freely available, and thus cannot be extended.

2.2 DTN Software Evaluations

IBR-DTN, DTN2, and ION were evaluated by Pöttner et al. [14]. For a payload of 1 MB, DTN2 and IBR-DTN produced almost identical results. ION was slower in the conducted measurements. Furthermore, the interaction of the three DTN implementations was evaluated by transferring bundles between them, and the times measured varied significantly.

IBR-DTN was used to evaluate the connection between a stationary DTN node and a moving vehicle [8]. This vehicle passed the stationary node at an average speed of 20 km/h, and the transmission rate was measured in relation to the distance. Data could be transmitted within a range of about 200 m.

Serval was experimentally evaluated in our previous work [2], for scenarios with 48 nodes in a hub topology, 64 nodes in a chain topology, and 100 nodes in disjoint islands connected over time. The results indicate that Serval can achieve high network loads, while CPU usage remains relatively low.

3   Bundle Protocol Version 7

This section gives an overview of bundle protocols, referring to RFC 4838 [6] and the current version of the Bundle Protocol (BP) [5]. The latter has version number 7 and is currently still in active development. We discuss the status of the 13th draft from April 2019 below.

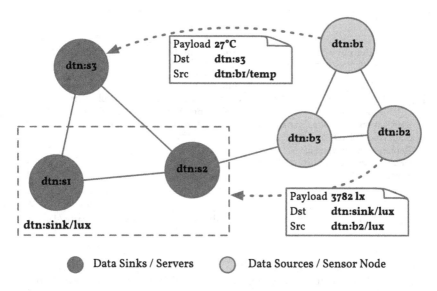

Fig. 1. Example sensor node scenario with multiple endpoints.

3.1   Basic Concepts

Endpoints. In DTN, there are nodes and endpoints. Nodes exchange bundles according to the store-carry-forward principle. Bundles are addressed at endpoints, or more precisely, their characterizing *Endpoint Identifier* (EID), which might not be a currently existing part of the network. Figure 1 shows an example of a scenario, where sensor nodes produce readings to be consumed by data sinks. The temperature bundle is addressed directly to `dtn:s3`, where the lux bundle is headed to `dtn:sink/lux`, an EID that is handled by two nodes, and thus a multicast. BP7 is endpoint scheme agnostic and supports the null endpoint for anonymous bundles. In BP version 6, only endpoints are defined, so it is not possible to address dedicated nodes.

Bundles and Blocks. Packets in a DTN consist of multiple *Blocks* to form logical units called *Bundles*. In Fig. 2, an example bundle containing the mandatory Primary Block, and two Canonical Blocks, namely a Hop Count Block and the actual Payload Block, is shown, following the example of Fig. 1.

Primary Block. Each bundle begins with a (since BP7 immutable) *Primary Block* (see Fig. 2), containing meta-information about the bundle with the following fields: Version; Bundle Processing Control Flags to provide information on the bundle, including fragmenting and reporting information; an optional CRC Checksum (added in BP7 and not available in BP version 6); Destination EID, Source Node ID and Report-To EID, as endpoints for administrative records regarding this bundle; Creation Timestamp, consisting of the actual timestamp

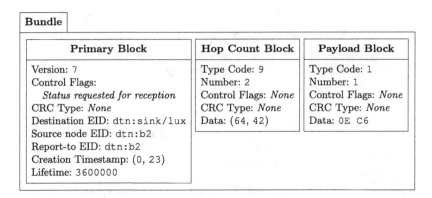

Fig. 2. A bundle transmitting a lux value from dtn:b2 to dtn:sink/lux.

and an incrementing sequence number; Maximum Lifetime of a bundle, expressed in microseconds after creation time; Fragment Offset and Total Data Length, if fragmented and indicated by the bundle process control flags.

Canonical Block. Payload and Extension Blocks in Fig. 2 are summarized as *Canonical Blocks.* These contain a payload in addition to a few block-specific characteristics. A Canonical Block consists of a Type Code to identify the kind of block, Number to address the specific block, Control Flags and Data.

The actual payload of the bundle is located in the Payload Block at the end of each bundle. In addition to sending user data from application programs, status information is also sent within bundles, called Administrative Records, automatically created and sent by DTN software as a response to a previous bundle. Extension Blocks are Canonical Blocks containing further information relevant for a DTN router depending on its configuration. In contrast to BP version 6, the BP7 specification defines the Previous Node Block, Bundle Age Block, and Hop Count Block, and allows user-defined blocks to be added.

3.2   Node Components

Bundle Protocol Agent. The *Bundle Protocol Agent* (BPA) offers BP and DTN specific services. It executes procedures of the BP. For example, communication between Application Agent and Convergence Layer Adapter (see below) is managed. The BPA also constructs bundles for the Application Agent.

Application Agent. The interface between the BPA and an application is defined as an *Application Agent* (AA). A generic AA needs the ability to receive incoming bundles and compose outbound bundles for user applications and services. Furthermore, an EID must be assigned for local bundle delivery.

Convergence Layers. Bundles are exchanged over connections between nodes of different types and characteristics, and connections are unidirectional or bidirectional, or vary in transmission speed and bandwidth. Depending on the connection technology used, more or less complex protocols are required for delivery, called *Convergence Layer (CL) Protocols* (CLP). A *Convergence Layer Adapter* (CLA) is an implementation of a CLP. There are two CLPs defined by the IETF DTN group to exchange bundles over a TCP connection, the bidirectional TCP Convergence Layer Protocol (TCPCL) [20] and the unidirectional Minimal TCP Convergence Layer Protocol (MTCP) [4]. In addition to transport layer CLs, there are approaches based on other technologies, e.g., DTN2 defining a Bluetooth and a serial CL, or IRB-DTN featuring an e-mail CL.

4 DTN7

In this section, we present the design and implementation of DTN7.

4.1 Requirements Analysis

There are several requirements that should be satisfied by DTN software. First, DTN software operating on a variety of laptops, smartphones, and routers should run on several hardware architectures (e.g., x86, ARM, and MIPS), based on the most popular operating systems (e.g., Linux, macOS, and Windows). Second, the individual components of the DTN software should be exchangeable. For example, there is the need to support different storage backends, CLAs, and DTN routing protocols. A suitable programming interface enabling concurrent execution is required for the interaction of components. Furthermore, a CLA implementation is required as well as a peer discovery mechanism to enable automatic establishment of connections between nodes. Finally, applications should to be independent of the DTN software, to allow easy creation of further applications and tools. Thus, a convenient interface between the DTN software and applications is required.

4.2 Implementation Decisions

As a result of these requirements, we selected the Go programming language[4] to develop DTN7. Go offers a large standard library and is rather developer-friendly. Its strengths are the simple creation and integration of programming libraries. Moreover, Go enforces good style guides and clean code plus provides memory-safety guarantees to increase security and stability of written programs. Thus, Go makes maintaining code and bringing in new developers very easy. The source code including all required dependencies are compiled into a single, static executable, removing the need for interpreters or further libraries. Furthermore, the Go compiler allows simple (cross-)compilation for many operating systems

---

[4] https://golang.org.

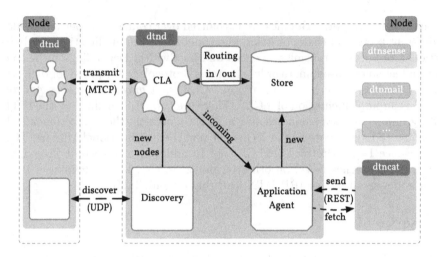

Fig. 3. Architecture and data flow in DTN7

and processor architectures. The concept of concurrency is implemented in Go through the interaction of Goroutines and Channels; concurrency was one of the design priorities of the language designers.

To support exchangeability of DTN7's components, we structured our implementation into *Bundles* and its corresponding *Store*, *Convergence Layer Adapters*, *Peer Discovery*, the *Application Agent*, *Routing*, and the *Core* package needed to connect the individual packages. The modules in the these packages are designed as generic interfaces and example implementations, e.g., there exists an interface for routing in general and an epidemic routing implementation. We decided to use MTCP for exchanging messages between two DTN7 nodes due to its simplicity. A third party application can also use parts of DTN7 as a library to, e.g., create and serialize bundles via the corresponding package. To make programming of applications against these interfaces simple and programming language independent, we decided to use a RESTful API.

4.3   DTN7 Architecture

Figure 3 shows the modules of DTN7 and their interaction. The arrows indicate the way a bundle is internally processed in DTN7. The links between two distinct DTN7 nodes are shown by both an active CLA and the Discovery on the figure's left hand side. Multiple client connections to the AA from within the node are delineated on the node's right hand side.

To store bundles locally, a serialized version as defined in BP7 is written to the file system. A central index of all known bundles manages their meta-data and links point to information of the specific file. This index supports a fast lookup of bundles. The module providing this functionality is called *Store*.

In DTN7, an AA is implemented as a RESTful Web API to support both dispatching and fetching of bundles. The API does not interact with entire bundles, but only with a subset of its fields. This allows a client to send a new bundle by only supplying the destination EID and a payload. Such a request can easily be created from the command line or possible third-party software. When fetched over the API, selected fields of those bundles are returned and the bundles will be removed from the store afterwards.

The concept of different CLs and their CLAs is also present in DTN7's architecture with an implementation of MTCP. Based on a specific CL's characteristics, bundles might be transferred in a uni- or bidirectional way. Thus, a CLA in DTN7 must supply one or multiple modules for inbound and outbound bundle processing. The unidirectional MTCP is designed using modules for sending and receiving bundles.

To support connections in dynamic networks, a *Peer Discovery* mechanism is provided. It announces a node's existence and listens for potential neighbors. This discovery mechanism broadcasts all of the node's CLAs continuously and notifies about received CLAs.

The previously defined components are linked together within DTN7's *Core* package. A central processing pipeline consumes both newly created and inbound bundles. Within this pipeline, a bundle will be marked to be delivered to a subset of known CLAs, to a local AA or to be discarded for later processing or even removed. The Core's internal links, visualized in Fig. 3, are related to the concept of a BPA, and serve as an interface between CLAs and the AA.

Every bundle that is not addressed to a particular node will be forwarded over one or multiple CLAs to neighboring nodes. The decision about which CLAs to select is made by a routing algorithm. To support the use of different routing algorithms, a generic interface needs to be informed about inbound bundles and, furthermore, a tight cohesiveness to the core is required. DTN7 implements an epidemic routing module, which is notified about received bundles, to memorize both sender and receiver. Before dispatching, the epidemic routing algorithm compiles a subset of known connections which have not received this bundle yet.

Finally, DTN7 is also intended to be used as a library and allows fast development of DTN applications. In particular, bundle package creation, serialization, and deserialization might be useful in other software.

4.4   Resulting Programs

DTN7 contains a DTN daemon, referred to as `dtnd` in Fig. 3, for storing and exchanging bundles and interfacing with applications. Currently, an example DTN application (`dtncat` in Fig. 3) for sending and receiving bundles, implemented as a command line tool, is included. `dtnd` initializes the previously defined modules according to the configuration provided by the user. `dtncat` processes user input, which is handed over to `dtnd`'s AA RESTful interface. The input is then encapsulated inside the Payload Block of a newly created bundle by `dtnd`. This bundle's Primary Block will be populated with basic defaults, like disabled CRC, and a delivery report request. As shown in Listing 1.1, `dtncat` is called by passing parameters on the command line. The first option selects between receiving or sending bundles. The local `dtnd`, running the RESTful API, is addressed by the second parameter. When sending new bundles, the content is read from the standard input.

```
# Sending a bundle
$ dtncat send http://localhost:8080 dtn:s2 <<< "3782 lx"

# Retrieving a received bundle
$ dtncat fetch http://localhost:8080
```

Listing 1.1. dtncat example

5   Experimental Evaluation

In this section, we experimentally evaluate DTN7 and compare it with other
DTN software.

5.1   Emulation Environment

To evaluate DTN7 in a realistic manner, we emulated up to 64 nodes in the
network emulation framework *Common Open Research Emulator* (CORE) [1].
CORE can emulate nodes using Linux namespaces to allow the execution of
native binary programs, which is not possible with purely simulation-based
approaches like NS-3 [16,18]. All experiments were performed on Intel Xeon E5-
2698 CPUs with 80 cores at 2.20 GHz and 256 GB RAM. To execute the total
number of 1,440 experiment runs, we used MACI, a framework for extensive and
reproducible experiments [11].

DTN Software. We compared DTN7 with three popular DTN software solutions. *Serval*[5] is a software suite centered around protocols designed for infrastructure independent communication [12]. To be able to transfer files in intermittently connected networks, Serval relies on Rhizome, a custom DTN bundle
protocol with epidemic routing. In our evaluation, we used the latest stable Serval release, which is from April 2016, since the recent development version has
stability issues. *IBR-DTN*[6] is an implementation of BP Version 6, aimed to be
lightweight and fast [8]. For comparability, we use the epidemic routing extension
instead of the default PRoPHET protocol used by IBR-DTN. We use the current
HEAD of the git repository to include the latest bug fixes. *Forban*[7] is mainly
used as a local peer-to-peer file sharing application using an epidemic routing
protocol based on HTTP. We used the latest HEAD of the git repository, but
had to introduce our own patches to make Forban usable.

Payload Sizes. DTN software is used in multiple applications and scenarios.
Serval, e.g., offers the SMS-like application MeshMS for short text messages.
IBR-DTN can be used in environmental monitoring, where transmission of short
audio recordings or images might be required. Therefore, we selected four different file sizes, representing a wide range of possible applications. All files were
generated randomly with the same seed for reproducibility in six sizes:

---

[5] https://github.com/servalproject/serval-dna/tree/batphone-release-0.93.

[6] https://github.com/ibrdtn/ibrdtn.

[7] https://github.com/adulau/Forban.

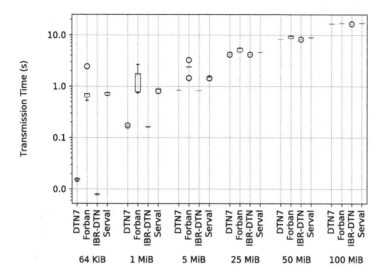

Fig. 4. Bundle transmission time for the 1-hop topology and different payload sizes

- 64 KiB for compressed images or map data;
- 1 MiB representing small images or short audio recordings;
- 5 MiB, e.g., smartphone images and audio recordings;
- 25 MiB representing longer audio recordings or short videos;
- 50 MiB for HD videos typically recorded by smartphones;
- 100 MiB, e.g., 4k smartphone videos [2, 17, 21].

Network Topologies. We used a chain topology of three different lengths, where nodes are connected pairwise, to benchmark the different DTN software systems. The first node is sending a bundle destinated to the last node in the chain. To get the baseline performance of the interacting components, a chain of two nodes was used. We measured the time it takes to read the data, serialize the bundle, send it over the network, deserialize it at the receiver and deliver it to the application. With 32 nodes, the forwarding capabilities were investigated. For an even larger scenario, we used 64 nodes, to evaluate how the DTN software systems behave when node numbers increase. We used a bandwidth of 54 MBit/s to match the speed of an IEEE 802.11g network.

Measurements. To measure CPU utilization for each process on every node, we used *pidstat*, which is part of the *sysstat* package[8]. Additionally, *bwm-ng*[9] was used for network statistics per node and network interface. Finally, every used DTN software logged both the timestamp of sending and receiving bundles, such that a detailed analysis of transmission time and network distribution can be performed.

---

[8] http://sebastien.godard.pagesperso-orange.fr/man_pidstat.html.
[9] https://github.com/vgropp/bwm-ng.

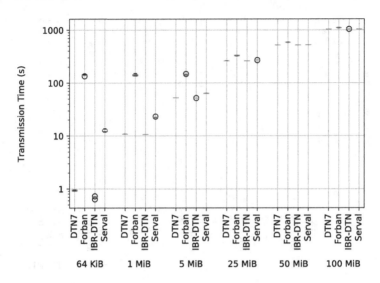

Fig. 5. Bundle transmission time for the 64-hops topology and different payload sizes.

5.2 Results

Transmission Times. Figures 4 and 5 show the bundle transmission times on the y-axes and payload sizes on the x-axes for the 1-hop and 64-hops topologies, respectively. Regardless of chain length and file size, DTN7 and IBR-DTN are always the fastest DTN software systems. The larger the files become, the transfer times of all DTN systems converge. This is due to the network configuration. All DTN systems manage to completely fill the 54 Mbit/s available, which is easier to achieve with larger files. As a result, the transfer times for large files hardly vary at all.

For a single hop, Forban and Serval take about the same time for transmitting files (e.g., about 0.6 s for 64 KiB files), but Forban shows a higher variance. For longer chains and files below 50 MiB, the differences between Forban and Serval are more noticeable. DTN7, however, is still up to 140 times (64 KiB over 1 hop) faster than Serval. Particularly in chat or text based applications, the speed advantage of DTN7 can be crucial if a message arrives below 0.01 s rather than after one second.

These results indicate that both BP6 and BP7 have a relatively small protocol overhead compared to the protocols used by Serval and Forban, which is especially noticeable for small files. The larger the files or the longer the chain, the less weight the low protocol overhead carries. Furthermore, it is also remarkable that DTN7, which is written in Go, does not take longer to transmit larger files from end to end in the chain, although IBR-DTN is implemented in C++ and optimized for speed. In terms of transmission speeds, Forban takes longer than the other DTN software systems, although differences get smaller the bigger the files are. One explanation is that Forban has a pull-based approach where

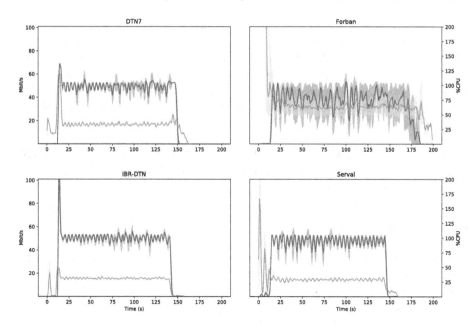

Fig. 6. CPU and network usage for transmitting 25 MiB over 32 hops.

it actively downloads new bundles after an announcement was received. Therefore, the announcement interval is a natural barrier. If quick data exchange is necessary, the other solutions provide better performance.

CPU Usage and Network Utilization. Figure 6 shows CPU usage and network utilization for transmitting 25 MiB over 32 hops. On the x-axes, the time for the entire experiment in seconds is shown, the left y-axes denote the network usage in Mbit/s and the right y-axes show the CPU usage in %, both of the entire network. The bold graphs denote the sum over all nodes, averaged over all experiment repetitions. The shaded areas denote the error band.

DTN7 requires about 34.3% of the available CPU (standard deviation of 16.7%). At the beginning of an experiment, DTN7 shows a short peak in CPU usage resulting from the first node, where the file is converted to base64, sent to the DTN7 AA, which decodes the file again, packs it into a bundle, and starts the transmission. Further nodes only have to retransmit the bundle and do not require the steps mentioned above. Forban uses about 163.1% CPU (646.3%). Forban shows a small peak at the start of the experiment, indicating the overhead when starting its daemons, where four Python interpreters have to be started. Additionally, the file has to be hashed at the beginning of the experiment. Serval consumes 29.3% (24.6%) CPU. Serval has an additional hashing step, which results in higher CPU load at the start of the experiment. With only 26.9% (13.1%), IBR-DTN is the most efficient tested DTN software in terms of CPU usage.

In terms of network usage, DTN7 reaches about 42.0 Mbit/s (19.7 Mbit/s) for transmitting bundles from node to node, while Forban achieves about 32.8 Mbit/s (22.8 Mbit/s). IBR-DTN and Serval achieve 42.3 Mbit/s (23.7 Mbit/s) and 39.5 Mbit/s (20.0 Mbit/s), respectively. Although the theoretical total network load for the entire network can be up to 1.674 Gbit/s, the tested DTN software systems used only the maximum bandwidth per link, which is 54 Mbit/s, in peak situations. This indicates that every DTN software needs to receive the entire bundle before transmitting it to the next node.

To summarize, DTN7 requires slightly more CPU utilization than IBR-DTN and Serval, but has the advantage of transmitting files faster than all other DTN systems in most cases, as shown in Sect. 5.2.

6   Conclusion

We presented an open source DTN implementation, called DTN7, of the recently released Bundle Protocol BP7 (draft version 13), written in the Go programming language. DTN7 is designed to offer extensibility and supports multiple use cases, such as enabling communication in emergency and disaster scenarios or providing connectivity for rural areas. Furthermore, we presented results of a comparative experimental evaluation of DTN7 and other DTN systems including Serval, IBR-DTN, and Forban. Our results indicated that DTN7 is a flexible and efficient open-source multi-platform implementation of the most recent version of BP7.

There are several areas for future work. For example, the BP does not define any kind of security or privacy mechanisms, although optional extension exist. This opens the field of DTN-related security and privacy research based on DTN7. Furthermore, for sensor networks or deployments in rural areas, DTN7's energy consumption should be evaluated. Due to DTN7's modular routing interface, new DTN routing algorithms for vehicular ad-hoc networks or UAV-based information dissemination should be investigated. Finally, new Convergence Layers based on emerging radio technologies, such as LoRa or mmWave communication, could be developed.

Acknowledgement. This work is funded by the HMWK (LOEWE Natur 4.0 and LOEWE emergenCITY) and the DFG (SFB 1053 - MAKI).

References

1. Ahrenholz, J.: Comparison of CORE network emulation platforms. In: 2010 Military Communications Conference (Milcom),pp. 166–171. IEEE (2010)
2. Baumgärtner, L., et al.: An experimental evaluation of delay-tolerant networking with serval. In: 2016 IEEE Global Humanitarian Technology Conference (GHTC), pp. 70–79. IEEE (2016)
3. Burleigh, S.: Interplanetary overlay network an implementation of the DTN bundle protocol. Technical report, JPL (2007)
4. Burleigh, S.: Minimal TCP convergence-layer protocol. Technical report, IETF (2019)

5. Burleigh, S., Fall, K., Birrane, E.J.: Bundle protocol version 7 (draft version 13). Technical report, IETF (2019)
6. Cerf, V.G., et al.: Delay-tolerant networking architecture. Technical report. RFC 4838, IETF (2007)
7. Demmer, M., Brewer, E., Fall, K., Jain, S., Ho, M., Patra, R.: Implementing delay tolerant networking. Technical report, Intel Research Berkeley and University of California, Berkeley (2003)
8. Doering, M., Lahde, S., Morgenroth, J., Wolf, L.: IBR-DTN: an efficient implementation for embedded systems. In: Third ACM Workshop on Challenged Networks, pp. 117–120. ACM (2008)
9. Dulaunoy, A.: Forban: a P2P application for link-local and local area networks (2016). https://github.com/adulau/Forban
10. Feldmann, M., Walter, F.: µPCN - a bundle protocol implementation for microcontrollers. In: 2015 International Conference on Wireless Communications & Signal Processing (WCSP). IEEE (2015)
11. Froemmgen, A., Stohr, D., Koldehofe, B., Rizk, A.: Don't repeat yourself: seamless execution and analysis of extensive network experiments. In: 14th International Conference on Emerging Networking Experiments and Technologies (CoNEXT'18) (2018)
12. Gardner-Stephen, P.: The serval project: practical wireless Ad-Hoc mobile telecommunications. Technical report, Flinders University, Adelaide, Australia (2011)
13. Open Garden: Firechat (2019). https://www.opengarden.com/firechat/
14. Pöttner, W.B., Morgenroth, J., Schildt, S., Wolf, L.: Performance comparison of DTN bundle protocol implementations. In: 6th ACM Workshop on Challenged Networks, pp. 61–64. ACM (2011)
15. RightMesh: Terra: Lightweight and Extensible DTN Library (2018). https://github.com/RightMesh/Terra
16. Riley, G.F., Henderson, T.R.: The NS-3 network simulator. In: Wehrle, K., Güneş, M., Gross, J. (eds.) Modeling and Tools for Network Simulation, pp. 15–34. Springer, Heidelberg (2010). https://doi.org/10.1007/978-3-642-12331-3_2
17. Schildt, S., Morgenroth, J., Pöttner, W.B., Wolf, L.: IBR-DTN: a lightweight, modular and highly portable bundle protocol implementation. Electron. Commun. EASST **37** (2011)
18. Schwerdel, D., Hock, D., Günther, D., Reuther, B., Müller, P., Tran-Gia, P.: ToMaTo - a network experimentation tool. In: Korakis, T., Li, H., Tran-Gia, P., Park, H.-S. (eds.) TridentCom 2011. LNICST, vol. 90, pp. 1–10. Springer, Heidelberg (2012). https://doi.org/10.1007/978-3-642-29273-6_1
19. Scott, K.L., Burleigh, S.: Bundle protocol specification. Technical report. RFC 5050, IETF (2007)
20. Sipos, B., Demmer, M., Ott, J., Perreault, S.: Delay-tolerant networking TCP convergence layer protocol version 4. Technical report, IETF (2019)
21. Trono, E.M., Arakawa, Y., Tamai, M., Yasumoto, K.: DTN MapEx: disaster area mapping through distributed computing over a delay-tolerant network. In: 2015 Eighth International Conference on Mobile Computing and Ubiquitous Networking (ICMU), pp. 179–184. IEEE (2015)

LPWANs and Their Integration with Satellite

LoRaWAN SCHC Fragmentation Demystified

Sergio Aguilar[1]([✉]), Alexandre Marquet[2], Laurent Toutain[2], Carles Gomez[1], Rafael Vidal[1], Nicolas Montavont[2], and Georgios Z. Papadopoulos[2]

[1] Universitat Politécnica de Catalunya, Barcelona, Spain
`sergio.aguilar.romero@upc.edu`, {`carlesgo,rafael.vidal`}`@entel.upc.edu`
[2] IMT Atlantique, IRISA, Rennes, France
{`alexandre.marquet,laurent.toutain,`
`nicolas.montavont,georgios.papadopoulos`}`@imt-atlantique.fr`

Abstract. Low Power Wide Area Networks (LPWANs) have emerged as new networks for Internet of Things (IoT). LPWANs are characterized by long-range communications and low energy consumption. Furthermore, LPWAN technologies have a small data unit and do not provide a fragmentation mechanism. To enable these technologies to support IPv6 and, thus, be compliant with the IPv6 Maximum Transmission Unit (MTU) of 1280 bytes, the LPWAN Working Group (WG) of the Internet Engineering Task Force (IETF) has defined a new framework called Static Context Header Compression (SCHC). SCHC includes Fragmentation/Reassembly (F/R) functionality for transmitting larger packet sizes than the layer 2 MTU that the underlying LPWAN technology offers and a header compression mechanism. Moreover, SCHC defines three operational modes to perform the F/R process: No-ACK, ACK-Always and ACK-on-Error. Each mode provides different reliability levels and mechanisms. In this paper, we provide an overview of the SCHC F/R modes and evaluate their trade-offs over LoRaWAN by simulations. The analyzed parameters are the total channel occupancy, goodput and total delay at the SCHC layer. The results of our analysis show that No-ACK mode is the method with lowest total channel occupancy, highest goodput and lower total delay, but lacks a reliability mechanism. ACK-Always and ACK-on-Error modes offer the same total delay, and similar total channel occupancy, whereas ACK-on-Error offers greater goodput.

Keywords: LPWAN · SCHC · Fragmentation · LoRAWAN · IoT · Duty-cycle · Reliability · Standardization · IETF · LoRa · IPv6

1 Introduction

The Internet of Things (IoT) refers to the interconnection of various objects (sensors, actuators, or goal-specific applications) to the global Internet. While

Supported by Spanish Ministry of Science, Innovation and Universities, the Spanish State Agency of Research and the European Social Fund (Project No. TEC2016-79988-P).

M. R. Palattella et al. (Eds.): ADHOC-NOW 2019, LNCS 11803, pp. 213–227, 2019.
https://doi.org/10.1007/978-3-030-31831-4_15

there are many different applications for IoT, with various constraints, many of them require to address a massive number of nodes, each of them having a limited amount of data to send (*e.g.*, one message per day). Another classical constraint is the low energy capacity of the nodes, as many IoT devices operate a on battery and should last for extended periods of time (months, years or even decades). These constraints led to the deployment of Low Power Wide Area Networks (LPWANs).

The huge number of heterogeneous devices brought by IoT networks stress the need for strong interoperability. The global Internet already provides this interoperability feature using a common set of protocols. However, these protocols were not designed with low bitrate and high latency networks. This is especially true for IPv6, even though its large address space would be a desirable feature to handle big amounts of IoT devices. As a result, using IPv6 on LPWAN implies numerous challenges, mainly due to its large header overhead (40 bytes). Indeed, having low bitrates means that it takes long time-on-air to send a large amount of data. This high Channel Occupancy (CO), in turn, reduces the probability of a node to access the radio channel in the case of frequency bands regulated by a duty cycle. For example, the 1% duty-cycle constraint of the European 868 MHz band requires devices to keep their radio quiet for 99% of the time.

Another issue with IPv6 is that it requires lower layers to support a Maximum Transmission Unit (MTU) of 1280 bytes. However, the maximum payload sizes supported by LPWAN technologies are typically much smaller. For instance LoRaWAN and Sigfox support MTUs of 242 bytes and 12 bytes, respectively.

To tackle these two problems, the LPWAN Working Group (WG) of the Internet Engineer Task Force (IETF) is defining a new framework called Static Context Header Compression (SCHC) [8]. This framework provides a header compression mechanism, as well as several Fragmentation/Reassembly (F/R) algorithms to satisfy both the large header and the large MTU size required by IPv6.

This article aims at describing and comparing the different fragmentation modes of SCHC in terms of channel occupancy, goodput, and total delay. To this extent, this article is organized as follows. In Sect. 2, we provide a comprehensive analysis of the state of the art regarding LPWAN, as well as fragmentation for LPWAN networks. In Sect. 3, we describe the three SCHC F/R modes of SCHC: No-ACK, ACK-Always, and ACK-on-Error. In Sect. 4, we develop and justify the performance metrics that will be used to evaluate the three SCHC F/R modes over LoRaWAN by means of simulation. Results are presented and discussed in Sect. 5. Section 6 concludes the paper with the main remarks from this work.

2   Related Work

The emergence and popularity of IoT is mainly due to the interoperability between heterogeneous systems, which avoids developing applications in silos. This interoperability is made possible with IPv6 as the glue between different wireless technologies on the one hand, and with different applications on the other hand. However, running IPv6 over low powered and lossy network is challenging, and adaptation layers are often required.

6LoWPAN was developed by the eponymous IETF working group to provide IPv6 support on top of IEEE 802.15.4 [7]. This adaptation layer mainly provides fragmentation and header compression to fit the maximum layer 2 MTU [9]. Papadopoulos et al. [12] highlighted problems when using fragmentation over a multi-hop network: in some route-over [6] implementations, each intermediate node reassembles the initial data packets, and there is inter-fragment interference on the forwarding path. Later on, the IETF 6Lo working group has defined specific adaptation layers for other short range wireless technologies (e.g. Bluetooth Low Energy, ITU-T G.9959, etc.) [5].

In the LPWAN realm (with technologies such as LoRaWAN, Sigfox or NB-IoT), there is also a need to provide adaptation layers to support IPv6, but the network characteristics are different. LPWANs are operated networks in which devices are usually organized in a star topology, around a radio gateway. The downlink is critical in these networks, and usually comes at a high cost in energy consumption and resources. This constrains the feedback that can be given to connected IoT devices (e.g. sensors or actuators) to its minimum. In practice, it prevents negotiations over the wireless medium, and greatly reduces the number of acknowledgments that can be sent. Furthermore, the maximum layer 2 MTU offered by most LPWAN technologies is significantly smaller than that of 6LoWPAN or 6Lo technologies. These are the main reasons why the IETF LPWAN working group is defining the SCHC protocol [8] in order to provide fragmentation [3,10,17], and header compression [1] over LPWAN technologies such as LoRAWAN.

Suciu et al. [17] analyzed the tradeoff between packet sizes, i.e., the optimal number of fragments, and goodput in LPWAN. While we are conducting a performance evaluation of the LoRaWAN adaptation layer to support IPv6 (i.e., data packets up to 1280 bytes), Suciu et al. evaluated whether sending several fragments is more efficient than sending large data packets (up to 250 bytes). They carried out Matlab simulations to study if fragmentation of a 250 bytes packet can show benefits in comparison to not using fragmentation. When considering a duty cycle of 1%, they actually showed that packet fragmentation increases reliability, with a higher impact in denser and slower networks (e.g., with a higher Spreading Factor – SF). The study highlights that there is a tradeoff between goodput performance, energy consumption and latency. However, in non-duty cycle restricted networks, they showed that throughput decreases when using thirty fragments per data packet or more.

Recently, Moons et al. [10] and Ayoub et al. [3] studied the benefits of using SCHC or 6LoWPAN for LoRaWAN networks. They performed the computation of the overhead in terms of headers and number of packets, and proposed an implementation for the OSS-7 operating system in [10]. They showed that the overhead is twenty times smaller with SCHC than with 6LoWPAN. In [3] they described an interesting implementation using the network simulator ns-3, but did not provide a performance analysis on the acknowledgment mechanisms.

While there are a number of LoRa performance studies in terms of data rate and coverage (*e.g.* [2,13,14,16,18]), as far as we know, only Suciu *et al.* [17], Moons *et al.* [10] and Ayoub *et al.* [3] discuss SCHC. In this paper, we study in-depth the performance of SCHC Fragmentation/Reassembly modes for data packets with a size up to 1280 bytes (IPv6 MTU), and we provide an overview of the acknowledgment mechanisms which have never been studied previously, to the best of our knowledge.

3   SCHC Fragmentation/Reassembly Modes Overview

This section provides a thorough description of the SCHC Framework F/R modes: No-ACK, ACK-Always and ACK-on-Error. These three modes share the same terminology, as explained below.

First, the F/R mechanism of SCHC operates on a *SCHC packet*, which corresponds to the output of the SCHC compressor (that is, basically, an IPv6 packet with compressed headers). This *SCHC packet* is segmented into several *tiles*, that are meant to be transmitted using *SCHC fragments*. When enabled, acknowledgements (ACKs) can provide information on the receiving status of individual tiles, and retransmissions can be done tile-wise. A *SCHC fragment* can carry one or more tiles, and is meant to be transmitted using exactly one layer-2 datagram. Finally, several tiles can be grouped to construct a *window*. Windows are used when ACKs are involved: one ACK message gives information about the receiving status of tiles belonging to one particular window. We denote $N_{\text{tiles/window}}$ the number of tiles per window (note that the last window may contain less than $N_{\text{tiles/window}}$ tiles, see Fig. 1).

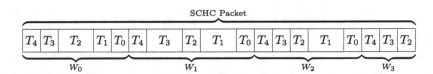

Fig. 1. Illustration of a *SCHC packet* fragmented into tiles, which are grouped into windows, with $N_{\text{tiles/window}} = 5$. Note that tiles size are not required to be uniform, depending on the chosen fragmentation mode. W_n denotes the n-th window and T_n is the n-th tile of the window.

A *SCHC fragment* carries one or more tiles, along with a header, whose fields carry information about the F/R process (see Fig. 2):

- Rule ID (L_r bits) carries an identifier for the SCHC rule associated with the *SCHC packet*. Such rule contains information on how F/R should be performed (see [8] for more details).

- DTag (T bits) stands for "Datagram Tag". It is used to associate *SCHC fragments* to the *SCHC packet* they belong to.
- W (M bits) stands for "Window". It is used to identify the window associated with the tile(s) carried by the fragment.
- FCN (N bits) stands for "Fragment Compressed Number". It is a counter that tells how many tiles have been transmitted in the window. It starts at $N_{\text{tiles/window}}$, and is decremented by one for each new transmitted tile.

Note that two values of FCN are reserved: *All-0*, and *All-1*. When the N bits of FCN are set to zero, then the associated fragment is the last fragment of the window, and is denoted as an *All-0 SCHC fragment*. When the N bits of FCN are set to one, then the associated fragment is the last fragment of the whole *SCHC packet*, and is denoted as the *All-1 SCHC fragment*. As it signals the end of the *SCHC packet*, this particular fragment also carries the Message Integrity Check (MIC) field (with size U bits). Note that, in order to accommodate for the size of the MIC, it is possible for the *All-1 SCHC fragment* not to carry any tile. These two reserved values help the receiver detect the end of transmission of a window (reception of an *All-0 SCHC fragment*), as well as the end of transmission of a packet (reception of an *All-1 SCHC fragment*). It can then initiate the appropriated actions associated such as issuing an ACK, or reassembling the whole *SCHC packet*.

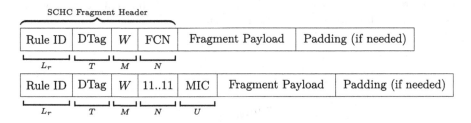

Fig. 2. Format of regular (up) and *All-1* (bottom) *SCHC fragments*. The length (in bits) of each header field is denoted below them.

Depending on the chosen SCHC F/R mode, the receiver may send *SCHC ACKs*, to inform the sender about the reception status (success or a failure) of tiles belonging to a given window. Fields of a *SCHC ACKs* are detailed below and in Fig. 3:

- Rule ID (L_r bits) has the same meaning as for a *SCHC fragment*.
- DTag (T bits) identifies the *SCHC packet* whose tiles are being acknowledged.
- W (M bits) identifies the window being acknowledged.
- C (1 bit) stands for "Check". Its value is one if every tiles of the window have been successfully received. Otherwise, its value is zero.
- Compressed Bitmap (size varies between 0 and $N_{\text{tiles/window}}$ bits) identifies which tiles, in a given window, need retransmission.

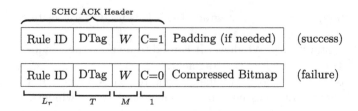

Fig. 3. Format of *SCHC ACK* messages. The length (in bits) of each header field is indicated below each field.

Note that any *SCHC message* (*e.g.*, *SCHC fragment* or *SCHC ACK*) may also contain padding bits to align the length with a multiple of 8 bits (more precisely, with the layer 2 default word length).

3.1 No-ACK Mode

The No-ACK mode is the most simple mode, where *SCHC packets* are simply fragmented and sent without any acknowledgment. Thus, if a fragment is lost, the sender will never know it and the *SCHC packets* will be lost without any retransmission (see Fig. 4).

In this mode, there must be only one tile per window ($M = 0$) and each *SCHC fragment* must carry exactly one tile. Tiles can be of different sizes, however this size should be chosen so that no fragments but the last (*All-1*) experience padding.

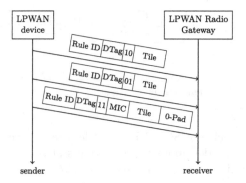

Fig. 4. No-ACK mode

3.2 ACK-Always Mode

The ACK-Always mode aims at providing high reliability. The receiver must send a *SCHC ACK* for each window, either positive (no lost tiles) or negative.

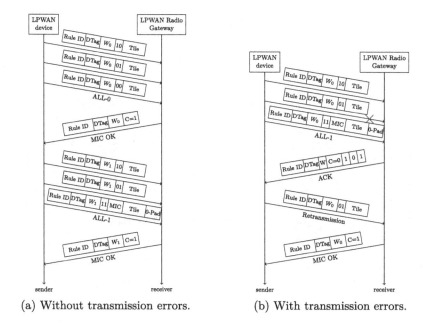

(a) Without transmission errors.   (b) With transmission errors.

Fig. 5. ACK-Always mode.

The acknowledgment embeds a field called *Compressed Bitmap* that indicates which tiles were received, and which ones were not (see Fig. 5).

Because the receiver only needs to discriminate between two consecutive windows, field W has a size of $M = 1$ bit. Tiles can be of different sizes, and each *SCHC fragment* must carry exactly one tile, just like in the No-ACK mode. Only the last fragment (*All-1*) can exhibit padding bits.

3.3 ACK-on-Error Mode

The ACK-on-Error mode can be seen as a compromise between No-ACK and ACK-Always. In this mode, only windows where the receiver experienced at least one missing or erroneous tile are acknowledged, with the exception of the *All-1 SCHC fragment* (which is always acknowledged). This mode supports variable layer-2 MTU. It also allows multiple tiles per window, and the window size can be up to $2^N - 1$ fragments. However, all tiles but the last one must be of equal size (Fig. 6).

4 Performance Metrics

In this section, we present the definition of a number of performance metrics that will allow evaluating the performance of the SCHC F/R modes presented in Sect. 3. The performance metrics are: total channel occupancy, goodput and

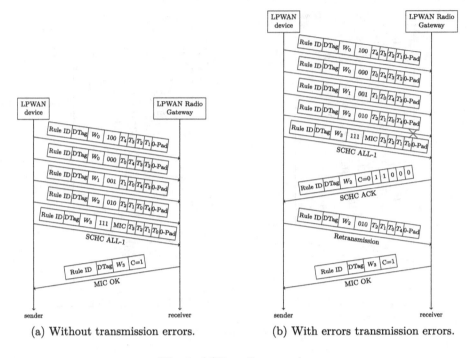

(a) Without transmission errors.   (b) With errors transmission errors.

Fig. 6. ACK-on-Error mode.

total delay at the SCHC layer. We take into consideration relevant aspects of LoRaWAN, which is the radio technology assumed in the evaluation provided in Sect. 5.

4.1 Total Channel Occupancy

The total Channel Occupancy (CO_T) is defined as the time during which the channel is busy during the transmission of a *SCHC packet*. That is, the time required by the sender to transmit all *SCHC fragments* plus, in the case of ACK-Always and ACK-on-Error, the time needed to transmit all *SCHC ACKs*. CO_T is calculated using the Channel Occupancy (CO) of each transmission and can be divided in two parts: the CO of the sender (CO_{tx}) and the CO of the receiver (CO_{rx}). The general formula of CO_T is given by:

$$CO_T[s] = CO_{tx}[s] + CO_{rx}[s], \tag{1}$$

where CO_{tx} (respectively, CO_{rx}) is the channel occupancy of all the fragments transmitted by the sender (respectively, the receiver).

Note that in LoRa/LoRaWAN networks, CO mainly depends on physical layer parameters, such as spreading factor (SF), channel bandwidth [15] and coding rate [4,17]. The larger the SF, the lower the LoRaWAN MTU size, and the higher the CO required for the transmission.

4.2   Goodput

We define the goodput as the ratio between the size of the original *SCHC packet* and the size of all fragments and acknowledgments transmitted. It takes into account the SCHC Headers, payload and padding bits:

$$\text{Goodput}[\%] = (\text{Packet size}/\text{Total data sent}) \times 100. \tag{2}$$

4.3   Total Delay

Total delay at the SCHC layer ($T_{d\ \text{SCHC}}$) is defined as the duration between the start of the transmission of the first *SCHC fragment*, and the end of the transmission (No-ACK), or the reception of the confirmation that the *SCHC packet* has been successfully transmitted (ACK-Always and ACK-on-Error).

In more details, for Ack-Always and Ack-on-Error, $T_{d\ \text{SCHC}}$ includes the CO of all the *SCHC fragments* and the corresponding T_{off} between transmission, except for the T_{off} after the transmission of the last *SCHC fragment*. This is measured until the sender receives the *SCHC ACK* signalling successful reception of the whole *SCHC Packet*. For No-ACK mode however, as there is no acknowledgment, $T_{d\ \text{SCHC}}$ is measured between the beginning and the end of the transmission.

In Europe, LoRaWAN is restricted in the frequency band by the duty-cycle (DC) [16] and the T_{off} can be calculated as:

$$T_{\text{off}}[s] = \text{CO}[s] \times \frac{100 - \text{DC}}{\text{DC}}. \tag{3}$$

5   Simulations

In this section we present the simulation results for the performance metrics presented in Sect. 4. We used the OpenSCHC simulator [11] to evaluate the performance of the three fragmentation methods, in an ideal scenario with no channel error nor collisions. OpenSCHC is an open source implementation of the SCHC Framework written in micropython. For this study, we created a program to obtain statistics of each *SCHC fragment* transmission, and adapted the simulator to support ACK-Always, which was previously not implemented in the simulator.

Rules are configured with $L_r = 6$ bits, $T = 2$ bits, $N = 3$ (which implies a maximum window size of $N_{\text{tiles/window}} = 7$), and $U = 32$ bits. This yields a SCHC header of 11 bits for No-ACK. For ACK-Always, M is supposed to be 1 (see Sect. 3.3). However, because of the way we implemented Ack-Always in OpenSCHC, the simulation were actually performed with $M = 3$ (that is, a penalty of 2 bits per fragment with respect to a correct implementation). Consequently, the total SCHC header length for Ack-Always is 14 bits. Finally, ACK-on-Error was configured with $M = 3$ bits, which means that there is at most 8 windows per *SCHC Packet*. This also gives a SCHC header length of 14 bits.

Regarding tile sizes, we selected 49 bytes when using a LoRa SF of 12 (SF12), and 240 bytes for when using a LoRa SF of 8 (SF8), in order to match LoRaWAN MTU for the EU 868-880 MHz ISM band. This last setting does not apply for No-ACK, as OpenSCHC does not require a tile size in this mode.

$N_{\text{tiles/window}}$ is set to 2 and 5 tiles for ACK-Always. A window size of 2 tiles requires more windows per packet than a window size of 5 tiles. Thus, we expect a larger overhead with smaller values of $N_{\text{tiles/window}}$, as *SCHC ACKs* are sent at the end of each window. In ACK-on-Error mode $N_{\text{tiles/window}}$ is set to 5 tiles, but the actual value has no impact in the absence of noise, as only one *SCHC ACK* is sent for the whole transmission (no negative ACK).

As the radio technology below SCHC, we considered a LoRaWAN network, working in the EU 863-880 MHz ISM band with one uplink channel (for data transmission) and one downlink channel. This configuration imposes a DC of 1%, by regulatory restrictions.

OpenSCHC provides a realistic simulation of a SCHC protocol implementation. However, it does not provide an implementation for Ack-Always. To simulate the ACK-Always mode, we considered that the *All-0 SCHC fragment* is carrying a MIC for the currently transmitted window. We also needed to set $M = 3$ instead of 1 (as required by the standard). This increases the overhead in the ACK-Always mode, but was necessary to perform simulations.

5.1   Total Channel Occupancy

The CO_T is directly related to the SF and the number of fragments exchanged. Figure 7a and b show the CO_T for SF8 and SF12, respectively. As expected, the only difference between ACK-on-Error and No-ACK over an ideal communication channel is the *SCHC ACK* at the end of the transmission. Comparing ACK-Always and ACK-on-Error, we notice no difference when the packet size is smaller than the window size (*i.e.*, only one window is required). Such a difference only appears when the packet size is larger than the window size (*i.e.*, more than one window is needed), as a result of the additional *SCHC ACKs* required for ACK-Always. The difference in the number of *SCHC ACKs* between ACK-on-Error and ACK-Always is proportional to the number of window required (*i.e.*, the number of additional *SCHC ACKs* in ACK-Always), and so is CO_{rx}. Moreover, we considered that ACK-Always must send a MIC in the *All-0 SCHC Fragment* (at the end of each window), implying a larger CO_{tx} when $N_{\text{tiles/window}}$ is smaller.

CO_T varies significantly with the SF because of the difference in MTU sizes. For instance, sending a 1280 bytes IPv6 packet with SF8 will require a CO_T approximately 20 times greater than with SF12.

No-ACK mode does not use windows nor *SCHC ACKs*. Thus, CO_T is only composed of the CO_{tx} component, which is related to the total number of fragments transmitted by the sender. For this reason, and as expected, No-ACK is the SCHC F/R mode with the lowest CO_T. The results in Fig. 7 confirm that ACK-Always is the method with the largest receiver overhead. Also, CO_T in ACK-Always depends directly on the windows size: as more windows are required to transmit a *SCHC packet*, the *SCHC ACK* overhead and the CO_T increase.

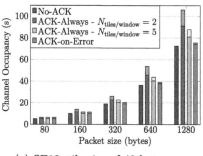
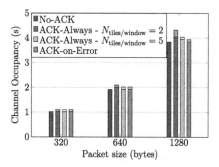

(a) SF12, tile size of 49 bytes. (b) SF8, tile size of 240 bytes.

Fig. 7. Channel Occupancy vs packet size. Darker colors correspond to CO_{tx}, and lighter colors correspond to CO_{rx}. (Color figure online)

Note that in terms of CO_T, considering the scenarios of Fig. 7, the extra price to pay for the extra reliability of ACK-Always over No-ACk ranges from 9% ($N_{tiles/window} = 5$, SF8, packet size of 320 bytes) to 46% ($N_{tiles/window} = 2$, SF12, packet size of 1280 bytes). This extra CO_T is however much more limited and stable between ACK-on-Error and No-ACK: ranging from 4% (SF12, packet size of 1280 bytes) to 9% (SF8, packet size of 320 bytes).

5.2 Goodput

Goodput results are presented in Fig. 8 for SF12 and SF8. As a trend, Goodput is negatively impacted by the overhead induced by the SCHC F/R mechanisms, and tends to an upper limit as the *SCHC Packet* size grows higher. In the details, though, all three modes show a sawtooth behaviour. This sawtooth profile is due to the extra overhead induced when the fragmentation process requires one more fragment to send the *SCHC Packet*. In ACK-Always, this sawtooth behaviour is amplified when more windows are needed, as more *All-0 Fragments* (including a MIC, in our implementation) are emitted.

As expected, No-ACK is the method with the lowest overhead, due to the lack of *SCHC ACKs*, therefore it is the method with the best goodput ratio. On the opposite side, ACK-Always yields the lowest goodput. However, as more fragments are sent in the same window, a better goodput is obtained, because more data is transferred and acknowledged for the same amount of *SCHC ACKs*. Finally, the results show that ACK-on-Error provide a trade-off between No-ACK and ACK-Always. Furthermore Fig. 8a confirm that, in the best case, ACK-Always reaches the same goodput as ACK-on-Error. This happens when only one window is needed for ACK-Always (thus only one *SCHC ACK* is sent).

Comparing Figs. 8a and b, one can observe that the lower the SF, the greater the goodput. This happens because higher SF implies smaller layer-2 MTU (hence, a smaller fragment sizes). In this case, more fragments are required for a given IPv6 packet size, which increases overhead.

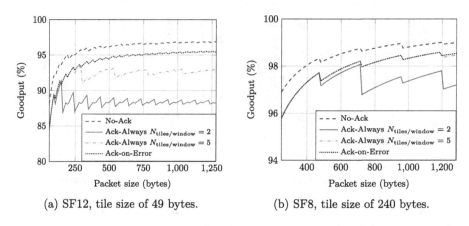

(a) SF12, tile size of 49 bytes.   (b) SF8, tile size of 240 bytes.

Fig. 8. Goodput vs packet size.

5.3   Total Delay

Total delay for the three SCHC F/R modes is presented in Fig. 9a and b for SF12 and SF8, respectively. In the simulated scenario, the three SCHC F/R modes perform more or less the same. Only No-ACK present a somewhat lower $T_{d\ SCHC}$ for high SF and *SCHC Packet* sizes, as a result of a lower CO_{tx} (hence, a lower T_{off}). In simulations of Fig. 9, we considered that *SCHC ACKs* generated between windows were received by the sender during its T_{off}. Under this assumption, there is a small difference between the $T_{d\ SCHC}$ of ACK-Always and that of ACK-on-Error.

The main teachings of Fig. 9 is that delays are high, even for moderate packet sizes and low spreading factors. Figure 9a shows that even if SCHC F/R mechanisms can provide support for the maximum IPv6 MTU, there are cases where such packet sizes are impracticable. For instance, $T_{d\ SCHC}$ for SF12 and a 1280 byte IPv6 packet is 2.0 h for the ACK-on-Error Mode. Using SF8, the time drops to 5.9 min (0.1 h, 20 times smaller than SF8). For smaller packet sizes, the $T_{d\ SCHC}$ difference is still considerable. For example, using a 320-byte IPv6 packet, the difference of $T_{d\ SCHC}$ between SF12 and SF8 is in the same order of magnitude: $T_{d\ SCHC}$ is 23 times higher with SF12, compared to SF8. In our scenario, these high values of $T_{d\ SCHC}$ are mainly due to DC restrictions. As an example, in a non-DC-restricted network, a 1280 byte packet would only require a $T_{d\ SCHC}$ of 72.65 s using the ACK-on-Error mode and SF12, instead of the 2 h of our 1% DC scenario.

Interestingly, while experimenting with SCHC parameters, we found out that a small variation in the SCHC header size can have large implications in terms of $T_{d\ SCHC}$. Not only because of the extra CO associated with the transmission of the additional bits in the SCHC Header, but also because of the corresponding T_{off} the sender must await after each transmission.

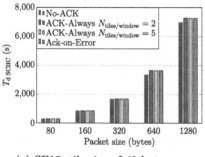

(a) SF12, tile size of 49 bytes.

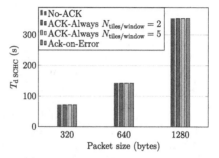

(b) SF8, tile size of 240 bytes.

Fig. 9. T_{d} SCHC vs packet size.

6   Conclusions

In this paper, we performed an analysis of the three F/R modes of the SCHC Framework and their trade-offs. Firstly, we provided an overview of the three SCHC F/R modes: No-ACK, ACK-Always and ACK-on-Error. Secondly, we explained the performance metrics used for the analysis. Lastly, we employed the OpenSCHC simulator (to which we added an implementation of the ACK-Always mode) to evaluate how the SCHC F/R modes perform under an error-free LoRaWAN communication channel. The three SCHC F/R modes have different characteristics and are focused on different use cases. Our evaluation shows that, in an ideal scenario with no errors, No-ACK mode can reduce the total delay and, due to its lower overhead, has a higher goodput, lower CO_T and does not consume receiver resources. In the considered scenarios, the differences in total delay and CO_T between ACK-Always and ACK-on-Error are directly proportional to the number of windows required to transmit a given packet. This yields lower values of goodput, while increasing total delay and CO_T. Even though ACK-on-Error outperforms ACK-Always, the latter may be preferred for downlink fragmentation as the LoRaWAN Gateway can be restricted to send a response right after the reception of a message.

The SF has a high impact on the performance achieved by the SCHC F/R modes. With higher SF, the differences observed between F/R modes increase. This is related to the fragment size, tile size and number of fragments required for a given IPv6 packet size. Moreover, this study shows that a 1280-byte IPv6 packet transmission, with SF12, can last up to 2 h over LoRaWAN in an ideal communication channel using SCHC F/R modes with 1% DC.

The reliability of No-ACK is very low, since the loss of any fragment will lead to the loss of the complete packet being carried and the associated resources involved (*i.e.*, channel bandwidth, energy, etc.). ACK-Always and ACK-on-Error, on the other hand, provide high reliability at the expense of more overhead and thus, more receiver resources. As future work, we plan to evaluate the impact of transmission errors and collisions in the performance of the SCHC F/R modes.

References

1. Abdelfadeel, K.Q., Cionca, V., Pesch, D.: LSCHC: layered static context header compression for LPWANs. In: Tarkoma, S., Wolf, L.C. (eds.) CHANTS Workshop at MOBICOM, pp. 13–18. ACM (2017). https://doi.org/10.1145/3124087.3124092
2. Angrisani, L., Arpaia, P., Bonavolontà, F., Conti, M., Liccardo, A.: LoRa protocol performance assessment in critical noise conditions. In: 2017 IEEE 3rd International Forum on Research and Technologies for Society and Industry (RTSI), pp. 1–5, September 2017. https://doi.org/10.1109/RTSI.2017.8065952
3. Ayoub, W., Nouvel, F., Hmede, S., Samhat, A.E., Mroue, M., Prévotet, J.C.: Implementation of SCHC in NS-3 simulator and comparison with 6LoWPAN. In: 26th International Conference on Telecommunications (ICT), HANOI, Vietnam, April 2019
4. Casals, L., Mir, B., Vidal, R., Gomez, C.: Modeling the energy performance of LoRaWAN. Sensors 17(10), 2364 (2017)
5. Gomez, C., Paradells, J., Bormann, C., Crowcroft, J.: From 6LoWPAN to 6Lo: expanding the universe of IPv6-supported technologies for the Internet of Things. IEEE Commun. Mag. 55(12), 148–155 (2017). https://doi.org/10.1109/MCOM.2017.1600534
6. Kim, E., Kaspar, D., Gomez, C., Bormann, C.: Problem statement and requirements for IPv6 over low-power wireless personal area network (6LoWPAN) routing. RFC 6606, RFC Editor, May 2012
7. Kushalnagar, N., Montenegro, G., Schumacher, C.: IPv6 over low-power wireless personal area networks (6LoWPANs): overview, assumptions, problem statement, and goals. IETF RFC 4919, August 2007
8. Minaburo, A., Toutain, L., Gomez, C., Barthel, D., Zuniga, J.: LPWAN static context header compression (SCHC) and fragmentation for IPv6 and UDP. Internet-Draft draft-ietf-lpwan-ipv6-static-context-hc-18, IETF Secretariat, December 2018
9. Montenegro, G., Kushalnagar, N., Culler, D.: Transmission of IPv6 packets over IEEE 802.15.4 networks. RFC 4944, September 2007
10. Moons, B., Karaağaç, A., Haxhibeqiri, J., De Poorter, E., Hoebeke, J.: Using SCHC for an optimized protocol stack in multimodal LPWAN solutions. In: WF-IoT2019, the IEEE World Forum on Internet of Things, pp. 1–6 (2019)
11. OpenSCHC: (2019). https://github.com/openschc/openschc
12. Papadopoulos, G., Thubert, P., Tsakalidis, S., Montavont, N.: RFC 4944: per-hop fragmentation and reassembly issues. In: IEEE CSCN. Paris, France, October 2018
13. Petrić, T., Goessens, M., Nuaymi, L., Toutain, L., Pelov, A.: Measurements, performance and analysis of LoRa FABIAN, a real-world implementation of LPWAN. In: 2016 IEEE 27th Annual International Symposium on Personal, Indoor, and Mobile Radio Communications (PIMRC), pp. 1–7, September 2016. https://doi.org/10.1109/PIMRC.2016.7794569
14. Rahman, A., Suryanegara, M.: The development of IoT LoRa: a performance evaluation on LoS and Non-LoS environment at 915 MHz ISM frequency. In: 2017 International Conference on Signals and Systems (ICSigSys), pp. 163–167, May 2017. https://doi.org/10.1109/ICSIGSYS.2017.7967033
15. Semtech: SX1272/3/6/7/8: LoRa Modem Designer's Guide AN1200.13, July 2013. https://www.semtech.com/uploads/documents/LoraDesignGuide_STD.pdf. Accessed 21 May 2019

16. Singh, D., Aliu, O.G., Kretschmer, M.: LoRa WanEvaluation for IoT communications. In: 2018 International Conference on Advances in Computing, Communications and Informatics (ICACCI), pp. 163–171, September 2018. https://doi.org/10.1109/ICACCI.2018.8554713
17. Suciu, I., Vilajosana, X., Adelantado, F.: An analysis of packet fragmentation impact in LPWAN. In: 2018 IEEE Wireless Communications and Networking Conference (WCNC), Barcelona, Spain (2018)
18. Zorbas, D., Papadopoulos, G.Z., Maille, P., Montavont, N., Douligeris, C.: Improving LoRa network capacity using multiple spreading factor configurations. In: Proceedings of the 25th International Conference on Telecommunication (ICT), pp. 516–520 (2018)

Revised Gateway Selection for LoRa Radio Networks

Przemysław Błaśkiewicz, Jacek Cichoń, Mirosław Kutyłowski,
and Marcin Zawada[✉]

Department of Computer Science, Faculty of Fundamental Problems of Technology,
Wrocław University of Science and Technology, Wrocław, Poland
{przemyslaw.blaskiewicz, jacek.cichon, miroslaw.kutylowski,
marcin.zawada}@pwr.edu.pl

Abstract. As many research papers show, one of the problems of a
LoRa network is its limit regarding the scalability. However, these papers
also indicate that it is possible to achieve the scalability for them by
dynamically selecting transmission parameters and/or by employing multiple gateways. In this paper, we build upon the latter solution and show
that although data extraction rate in such networks is quite good, it suffers hugely from data duplication on the communication path between
the gateways and network server. In remote areas, the gateways are usually connected to a network server by cellular networks, which yields
additional transmission costs. In LoRaWAN network topology, the gateways aren't connected to each other and therefore cannot actively filter
the traffic prior to sending it further downstream. Thus, we propose a
randomized algorithm allowing to reduce duplication of the packets sent
to the network server without communicating with other gateways.

1 Introduction

In recent years we have witnessed a fusion between Wireless Sensor Networks
(WSN) and the Internet of Things (IoT) concept. Within this paradigm, Long
Range (LoRa) communication has received a lot of attention [4,6]. LoRa is a
Low-Power Wide Area Network (LPWAN) radio technology that it is capable
of supporting long communication range and deploy autonomous, lightweight
radio-operated nodes powered from cell batteries for a span of even ten years.
This is all thanks to the physical layer technology of LoRa, that trades off range
with throughput.

LoRa itself is a physical layer technique and it is used together with the MAC
layer protocol LoRaWAN and operates in the license-free ISM-bands (Industry,
Scientific and Medical). The technology performance usually depends on the
channel access technique and the duty cycle regulations. The LoRa modulation
is based on CSS (Chrip Spread Spectrum) which spreads the communication
over a spectrum of frequencies and it is obtained by coding the information
using orthogonal codes, quantified by the Spread Factor (SF).

© Springer Nature Switzerland AG 2019
M. R. Palattella et al. (Eds.): ADHOC-NOW 2019, LNCS 11803, pp. 228–240, 2019.
https://doi.org/10.1007/978-3-030-31831-4_16

These technologies are generally used to form star-of-stars network topologies. This eliminates the need of developing and implementing certain complicated multihop network. The network server is connected to multiple gateways which in turn connect to multiple end-nodes. Thus, low power LoRaWAN end-node devices are connected to the Gateway, while the Gateway uses usually high-bandwidth networks like Wi-Fi, Ethernet or Cellular to connect to a network server. Next, the network server manages routing the data to adequate service servers, which finally process the information and, possibly, generate downlink payload. That is then sent back via the same route and sent to the node during a specified downlink slot.

In remote areas where there is no adequate infrastructure the gateway is usually connected to the network server by cellular networks and every byte sent to the network server incurs costs. This problem is aggravated even further by the fact that all gateways in the vicinity, regardless of which network provider they belong to (or which service server they have traffic for), will receive packets and forward them to the network server. The network server will remove duplicated messages and select the best gateway to forward any messages queued for downlink. A single gateway can serve thousands of end-nodes. Connection is bi-directional, although uplink communication is the expected predominant traffic type.

Gateways are running on a minimal firmware, making them low-cost and easy to use (e.g. The Things Gateway), executing only packet forwarding software. Therefore any attempt to remove duplicated messages on the gateways level is problematic. To achieve this, we would need for example to buffer messages (which can arrive at different times on different gateways) and have a connection to other gateways in the vicinity. This would complicate the gateway architecture considerably. Thus, we propose a simple (for implementation) randomized algorithm that enables us to largely reduce the number of redundant messages sent between the gateway and the network server in most cases by more than 50% with a small decrease in data extraction rate (DER).

In Sect. 1.1 we give a short presentation of LoRaWAN protocol. In Sect. 2 we show pseudocode of our algorithm and in the next Sect. 3, we carry out theoretical study of proposed algorithm. In Sect. 4, we perform simulations to assess our algorithm in practical scenarios. In Sect. 5, we conclude the paper.

1.1 LoRaWAN MAC Layer

LoRaWAN [5] is an open MAC protocol developed around LoRa. The LoRaWAN architecture consists of three important elements: end-nodes, gateways and the network server. Similar to cellular networks, gateways connect end-nodes within their coverage to network server. The difference is that gateways in LoRaWAN use non-licensed ISM bands and are targeted at extremely low power and long range communications. In LoRaWAN, nodes typically only have a few messages to transmit per day. The time a node can occupy (transmit) on a band is determined by *duty cycle* which, for LoRaWAN is typically set to 1% (also 0.1% and 10% are allowed, but only on specific band frequencies).

LoRaWAN end-nodes can be configured into three different types:

- Class A: Sensor nodes only send small number of data packets to the gateway and sleep for most of the time.
- Class B: Besides for the actions in Class A, end-nodes also can wake up at scheduled slots to receive downlink messages.
- Class C: Sensor nodes continuously listen to the channel.

Note that even though end-nodes, limited by their duty cycles and class can transmit only a few times per day, the gateways are always active and can be heavily loaded with traffic, since in larger networks there can be even thousands end-nodes, which may need to operate only per several gateways. In our algorithm we make use of RSSI – a signal strength indicator. In LoRaWAN this indicator is also used to govern the bitrate of downlink transmission. The general assumption is that nodes with stronger signals can employ faster, and therefore more error-prone bitrates, while nodes with weak signals should utilise lower bitrates to maintain the same BER.

1.2 Related Work

In paper [3] the authors study the problem of scalability of LoRa networks and show that one of the solutions is to multiply the gateways. However, we show that although it increases the data extraction rate considerably (as the paper showed) it also potentially increases the level of data duplication.

In paper [1] the authors optimize transmission for downlink in class A [5]. However, as we mention in Sect. 1 in specification LoRaWAN we have that the communication can be bi-directional, although uplink communication from end-device to the Network Server is expected to be predominant traffic. Consequently, the optimization of downlink traffic in most applications has little or no impact at all on the overall performance.

Although the researchers agree that the gateway selection is an important problem in LoRaWAN, they usually concentrate on downlink problem [1,2]. To the best of our knowledge there is no work that try to solve the issue of unique gateway selection for the uplink.

2   Algorithm for Gateway Selection

The basic idea of proposed algorithm is that it tries to favour packets received by a gateways that have the strongest signal thus it enables us to choose mostly just one gateway and, consequently avoiding duplication. Besides the analytical approach, we perform number of simulations that show that with the proposed simple modification on the gateway side, we can reduce the number of duplicated packets sent to network server more that by a half with small decrease of DER.

For described scenario, we introduce our proposed Algorithm 1 and analyse the process of gateway selection. We assume that each gateway executes the code from Algorithm 1, while the end-node starts the transmission at will.

Algorithm 1. GATEWAYSELECTION

Setup:
1: R - number of rounds
2: $g^r(x)$ - special function defined in the paper for r-round
Main algorithm:
1: **if** received message from the end-node **then**
2:     $x \leftarrow$ profit estimation   ▷ based on RSSI
3:     **for** $r = 0 \ldots R - 1$ **do**   ▷ loop for r-rounds
4:         **if** $\text{rand}(0, 1) < g^r(x)$ **then**
5:             send message to the network server
6:             **return**
7:         **end if**
8:     **end for**
9: **end if**

Once the RSSI from the transmitting end-node is obtained, the gateway uses it to determine if it should forward the message. This decision is made *locally* and independently by each gateway. When only a single gateway decides to forward the message then we say that the gateway was selected.

3 Probabilistic Analysis

In this section we calculate the probability for a particular gateway of becoming the selected gateway. We assume that we have a sending end-node with n gateways within its transmission range. To reflect a random profit of received message by the gateways, we use $X_1, \ldots, X_n$ e.g. the profit can be a signal strength RSSI from the sending end-node. For this theoretical analysis we assume that $X_i \sim \mathcal{U}(0, 1)$ are independent uniform random variables for $i = 1, \ldots, n$ that represent normalized random profit of gateways. Notably, for derived equations we can easily substitute different distributions. Let x_i denote the profit of gateway i from forwarding communication and let $g^r(x_i)$ denote the gateway i transmission probability for r-th round of the Algorithm 1. Let $S^R(x_1, \ldots, x_n)$ be a random variable denoting the selected gateway, then $P(S^R(x_1, \ldots, x_n) = i)$ denotes the probability that the particular i-th gateway becomes the selected gateway.

Consequently, the probability $P(S^R(x_1, \ldots, x_n) = i)$ for $R \geq 1$ rounds is:

$$\sum_{r=0}^{R-1} g^r(x_i) \prod_{j \neq i} (1 - g^r(x_j)) \cdot \left(1 - \sum_{k} g^r(x_k) \prod_{j \neq k} (1 - g^r(x_j))\right)^r. \quad (1)$$

If we choose the function $g^r(x)$ such that it does not depend on r i.e. for all r holds $g^r(x) = g(x)$ and $R \to \infty$. Then the infinite geometric series can be transformed into a more succinct form yielding:

$$P(S^\infty(x_1,\ldots,x_n) = i) = \frac{g(x_i)\prod_{j\neq i}(1 - g(x_j))}{\sum_{k=1}^{n} g(x_k)\prod_{j\neq k}(1 - g(x_j))}.$$

Moreover, we can calculate the expected profit of the selected gateway as

Theorem 1. $E[X_{S^R(X_1,\ldots,X_n)}]$ *is equal to*

$$\sum_{i=1}^{n} \int_0^L x_i P(S^R(X_1,\ldots,x_i,\ldots,X_n) = i) f_{X_i}(x_i) dx_i \,. \tag{2}$$

Proof. See Appendix A

Ideally, one should maximize Eq. (2) w.r.t all possible functions $g^r(x_i)$. However, at this point we perform calculations for carefully selected functions:

(i) Consider $g^r(x) = p$, meaning that all gateways who heard the message transmit with the same probability, regardless of their profit estimation. Then the probability $P(S^1(x_1,\ldots,x_n) = i) = p(1-p)^{n-1}$. Now we calculate the probability $P(S^\infty(x_1,\ldots,x_n) = i)$ as

$$\frac{p(1-p)^{n-1}}{\sum_{k=1}^{n} p(1-p)^{n-1}} = \frac{1}{n}.$$

Again, by setting a constant probability of transmission to all gateways we get a uniform probability of becoming the selected gateway. Then, assuming that $X_i \sim \mathcal{U}(0,1)$, we can calculate the expected profit as

$$E[X_{S^\infty(X_1,\ldots,X_n)}] = \frac{1}{2} \,.$$

(ii) Let us consider a function defined as

$$g^r(x) = \begin{cases} x^{n-1} & \text{for } r = 0 \\ p & \text{for } r \geq 1 \end{cases} . \tag{3}$$

It means that during the first round the gateways use function x^{n-1} and then they switch to constant distribution p. Then after the simplification of Eq. (1), we have that $P(S^\infty(x_1,\ldots,x_n) = i)$ is equal to

$$x_i^{n-1}\prod_{j\neq i}(1 - x_j^{n-1}) + \frac{1}{n}\left(1 - \sum_{k=1}^{n} x_k^{n-1}\prod_{j\neq k}(1 - x_j^{n-1})\right) .$$

Consequently, assuming that $X_i \sim \mathcal{U}(0,1)$, the expected profit is

$$E[X_{S^\infty(X_1,\ldots,X_n)}] = \frac{1}{2}\left(1 + \frac{n}{n+1}\left(1 - \frac{1}{n}\right)^n\right) .$$

Proof. See Appendix B

Asymptotically it improves the normalized profit from $1/2 = 0.5$ to $1/2 + 1/2e \approx 0.68$.

Notice that in the scenario (ii) we applied a hybrid function i.e. we combine two functions. This hybrid function has an important advantage which is supported by the following numerical solutions.

In this algorithm, apart from the profit another important characteristics is the expected number of rounds needed to select a gateway. Our goal is to repeat the main loop only a few times. For better performance, we assume that algorithm is executed on very weak devices. In other words, the number R of repeats until some gateway transmitted successfully in Algorithm 1 should be as small as possible. However, the advantage of function (3) is that it increases the profit without increasing the expected number of rounds needed to select a gateway. We investigated and compared both approaches. We performed calculations for the number of gateways usually found in practice, namely $n = 10, 100$ and even $n = 1000, 10000$. The results are given in table below.

Number of nodes	Scenario (i)		Scenario (ii)	
	Profit	Expected no. rounds	Profit	Expected no. rounds
10	0.50	2.58	0.65	2.57
100	0.50	2.71	0.67	2.70
1000	0.50	2.72	0.68	2.71
10000	0.50	2.72	0.68	2.71

As we can see, the expected number of rounds even slightly decreases in these scenarios and normalized profit increases from 0.5 to 0.68 for larger number of gateways. In other words, the proposed algorithms are capable of selecting a better gateway to forward the message than the approach without profit estimation. At the same time, choosing such gateway for message forwarding does not pose additional overhead in the number of rounds of the algorithm.

It is worth mentioning that numerical solutions also show that a partial function like (3) is a better choice than for example $g^r(x) = x^{n-1}$ for all r, which although increases profit further, but at the same time significantly increases the expected number of rounds needed for successful transmission.

From these calculations we conclude that by choosing the hybrid function from scenario (ii) and setting $R = 4$ in Algorithm 1 we can choose a single gateway that will forward the message to the network server. In the next section we will assess chosen functions and parameters by simulation in realistic environments and LoRa radio networks.

4   Simulations Results

In previous section we obtained some theoretical results, which assess our algorithm. However, in practice there are significant differences e.g. profit estimation couldn't be so uniformly distributed, messages can be transmitted at different times and so on. In this section we would like to analyse our algorithm in a more realistic scenario by performing simulation.

We define two metrics that will help in evaluation of the algorithm. First we define Date Extraction Rate (DER) as follows:

$$\text{DER} = \frac{\text{\#unique packets received by network server}}{\text{\#packets sent by end-nodes}}.$$

If the value of DER = 1 then all packets which sent by the end-nodes were received by gateways and forwarded to the network server. Notice that packets are usually duplicated since they can be received by all gateways in the vicinity of the end-node. However, if the value of DER < 1 then some packets were lost due to interference or collisions. For example DER = 0.5 means that we lost half of the packets sent by end-nodes. Thus, our goal is to have DER as close to one as possible.

Another metric we define is Packet Drop Rate (PDR). This value enables us to assess how many packets are dropped by our algorithm compared to all packets received by gateways from end-nodes (with possible duplication) and then sent to network server. Thus, we define PDR as follows:

$$\text{PDR} = \frac{\text{\#packets drop}}{\text{\#all packets received by gateways}}.$$

If the value PDR > 0 then it means that our algorithm running on the gateways sent less packets than was received. For example PDR = 0.5 means our algorithm reduced in half number of packets sent. Notice that for PDR = 0 we don't drop any packets; on the other hand for PDR = 1 we drop all packets. Ideally we should increase PDR to the point where all duplicated packets which can be potentially sent by other gateways are dropped, that is without changing DER. Because gateways cannot communicate, duplicate detection can be done only at the network server level, but by that time the transmission cost has already been paid. Therefore, we propose a randomized algorithm, namely Algorithm 1, that will be able to increase PDR at the cost of DER decrease. We designed simulations so as to determine the extent at which an increase in PDR will keep acceptable levels of DER.

To simulate LoRaWAN networks we used the LoRaSim [7], a simulator described by the authors in paper [3]. LoRaSim is a discrete-event simulator which allow to place N LoRa end-nodes in two-dimensional space and it is based on a mathematical model of LoRa communications, capable of monitoring the resulting number of collisions [8].

We modify the software to implement our gateway selection algorithm. We employ LoRaSim's native settings with the slowest data rate $SF = 12$, $BW = 125$ and $CR = 4/8$. The end-node chooses one of the three center frequencies (860 MHz, 864 MHz, and 868 MHz) uniformly at random for each frame and uses transmit power of 14 dBm. For comparison, we left the deployment of gateways as it is in the LoraSim, for more details see [3].

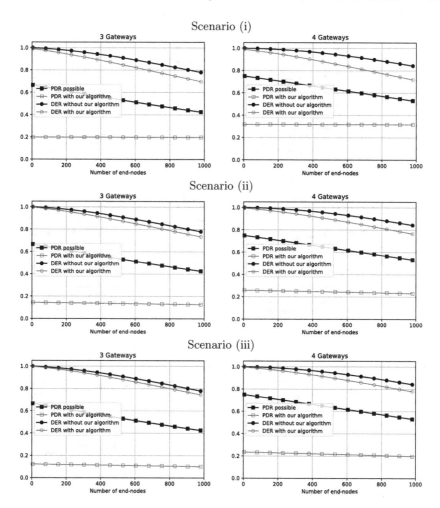

Fig. 1. DER and PDR for 3 and 4 Gateways with and without our algorithm for different scenario

The simulated time frame was for about 24 h. Each end-node sends packets towards gateways in the vicinity according to a Poisson process with intensity 16.6 min, so as to comply with the LoRaWAN specification duty cycle restrictions. The class A was selected since it is most often used in practice.

We consider three scenarios for simulations. In each scenario we used different selection function for our algorithm. For the scenario (i) and (ii) we chose the same function as in the previous section. For the scenario (iii) we modify the function from scenario (ii) such that the function x^{n-1} is selected for the first two rounds instead of only first round. Namely, for n number of gateways we are using the following functions for $r \in 1, 2, 3, 4$ $(R = 4)$:

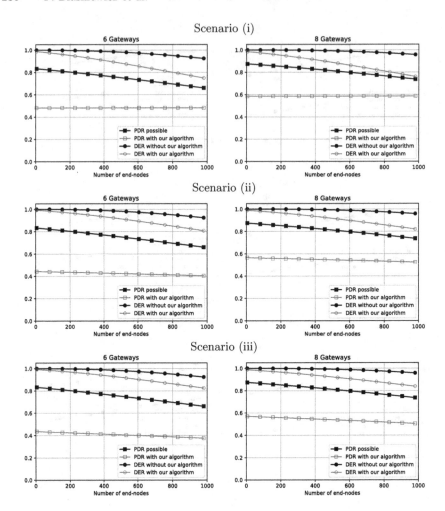

Fig. 2. DER and PDR for 6 and 8 Gateways with and without our algorithm for different scenario

| Scenario (i) | Scenario (ii) | Scenario (iii) |

$$g^r(x) = 1/n \qquad g^r(x) = \begin{cases} x^{n-1} & \text{for } r = 0 \\ 1/n & \text{for } r \geq 1 \end{cases} \qquad g^r(x) = \begin{cases} x^{n-1} & \text{for } r = 0,1 \\ 1/n & \text{for } r \geq 2 \end{cases}$$

In Fig. 1 we present the results of simulation obtained for 3 and 4 gateways. The plots show the possible PDR that is calculated as the ratio of a number of duplicated packets sent to network server to all packets sent, in other words, packets that can be dropped. It is worth noting that without our algorithm PDR $\equiv 0$, since gateways don't drop any packets (all traffic is forwarded to the network server). Also we show the PDR with our algorithm and DER with and without our algorithm. As we can see, the first results are very encouraging. For

Table 1. Numerical statistical results

8 Gateways					
		mean	std	max	min
	PDR possible	0.810	0.043	0.874	0.736
	DER without algorithm	0.987	0.013	0.999	0.957
Scenario (i)	PDR with algorithm	0.586	0.000	0.586	0.586
	DER with algorithm	0.882	0.071	0.985	0.760
Scenario (ii)	PDR with algorithm	0.545	0.012	0.566	0.524
	DER with algorithm	0.912	0.053	0.988	0.820
Scenario (iii)	PDR with algorithm	0.538	0.020	0.570	0.504
	DER with algorithm	0.919	0.047	0.987	0.838

Table 2. Simulation results summary for three analysed scenarios. Δ DER is a difference of DER relative to the case when our algorithm is not applied.

Gateways	Scenario (i)		Scenario (ii)		Scenario (iii)	
	PDR %	Δ DER %	PDR %	Δ DER %	PDR %	Δ DER %
3	19.7	8.1	12.6	4.5	10.1	3.4
4	31.6	12.3	23.0	7.7	19.8	6.3
6	48.2	17.4	40.3	11.5	37.5	9.8
8	58.6	19.7	52.4	13.7	50.4	11.9

example, for 4 gateways and scenario (iii), with our algorithm we drop almost 20% of packets with as little as 3% maximal decrease of DER. However, the results are much better if the number of gateways in the vicinity increases, which in reality (without our algorithm) would increase gateway-network server traffic. In Fig. 2 we present simulations for 6 and 8 gateways. For those simulations with 8 gateways in all three scenarios, we can drop almost 60% of packets with 10% decrease of DER. This is a lot of saving in transmission between gateways and network server. To be more precise we gather the numerical results in Table 1.

At the top of Table 1 we present numerical results showed in Fig. 2 for 8 gateways and three scenarios. We give precise statistical values from the function of PDR and DER. As we can observe a function of PDR for the first scenario it is constant and equal to 0.586 which mean that 58.6% of packets were dropped. However, DER obtained maximal value of 0.985 and decreases to minimal 0.76. So, we can deduce the maximal difference between DER with and without our algorithm as 0.197 (function are monotonically decreasing). Thus 19.7% decrease in DER. On the other hand, for third scenario we have minimal PDR as 0.504 which mean 50.4% of packets were dropped with DER decrease with and without our algorithm as 0.119. Which give 11.9% decrease in DER, this value we call ΔDER. The summary of such worst-cases are gather in Table 2.

5   Conclusions

We have presented a randomized algorithm that enables us to reduce the duplication of packets sent by gateways to network server. The algorithm can be easily executed on low-end devices and poses no additional computational or memory overhead and utilises traffic metrics already in use by the LoRaWAN MAC layer. Besides theoretical probabilistic analysis we implemented algorithm in LoRaSim simulator and performed a number of simulations. Our proposed algorithm proves the more effective, the more potential gateways are available, so the more duplicate traffic is generated. The simulations show that for 8 gateways and 1000 end-nodes we can drop more than 50% of packets thus cut the cost of transferring data between gateways and network server in half with small decrease of data extraction rate. As a result, we can reduce overall energy consumption of the whole network. In future work we would like address the problem of optimal selection of function g, which could enable us potentially to further reduce the cost.

A   Appendix

Proof of the Theorem 1

Proof. Notice that $E[X_{S^R(X_1,...,X_n)}]$ can be expressed as

$$\sum_{i=1}^{n} E[X_i|S^R(X_1,\ldots,X_n) = i]P(S^R(X_1,\ldots,X_n) = i).$$

Next, we can modify the above equation by expanding the conditional expected value and by assumption that X_i has density function f_{X_i}:

$$\sum_{i=1}^{n} \int_0^L x_i f_{X_i}(x_i|S^R(X_1,\ldots,X_n) = i)dx_i \cdot P(S^R(X_1,\ldots,X_n) = i).$$

Recall that $S^R(X_1,\ldots,X_n)$ is a discrete random variable. Hence, applying Bayes theorem, we further obtain

$$\sum_{i=1}^{n} \int_0^L x_i \frac{P(S^R(X_1,\ldots,X_n) = i|X_i = x_i)f_{X_i}(x_i)}{P(S^R(X_1,\ldots,X_n) = i)}dx_i \cdot P(S^R(X_1,\ldots,X_n) = i).$$

The desired formula is readily available after simplification of the above equation.

B   Appendix

We prove the equation from scenario (ii) in Sect. 3:

$$E[X_{S^\infty(X_1,...,X_n)}] = \frac{1}{2}\left(1 + \frac{n}{n+1}(1 - \frac{1}{n})^n\right).$$

Proof. Since $E[X_{S^\infty(X_1,\ldots,X_n)}]$ is given by

$$\sum_{i=1}^{n} \int_0^1 x_i P(S^\infty(X_1,\ldots,x_i,\ldots,X_n) = i) f_{X_i}(x_i) dx_i \ .$$

We need to calculate $P(S^\infty(X_1,\ldots,x_i,\ldots,X_n) = i)$ which can be done from the following equation:

$$\int_0^1 \cdots \int_0^1 P(S^\infty(x_1,\ldots,x_n) = i) \cdot f_{X_1}(x_1) \cdot \ldots \cdot f_{X_{i-1}}(x_{i-1}) \cdot$$
$$f_{X_{i+1}}(x_{i+1}) \cdot \ldots \cdot f_{X_n}(x_n) \, dx_1 \ldots d_{x_{i-1}} d_{x_{i+1}} \ldots d_{x_n} \ .$$

Since $P(S^\infty(x_1,\ldots,x_n) = i)$ is

$$x_i^{n-1} \prod_{j \neq i}(1 - x_j^{n-1}) + p(1-p)^{n-1} \cdot (1 - \sum_{k=1}^{n} x_k^{n-1} \prod_{j \neq k}(1 - x_j^{n-1})) \cdot$$
$$\cdot (1 + (1 - np(1-p)^{n-1}) + (1 - np(1-p)^{n-1})^2 + \ldots) \ .$$

then, after simplification we obtain

$$x_i^{n-1} \prod_{j \neq i}(1 - x_j^{n-1}) + \frac{1}{n}(1 - \sum_{k=1}^{n} x_k^{n-1} \prod_{j \neq k}(1 - x_j^{n-1})) \ .$$

The above equation can be integrated term-by-term:

(i) in the first term, we can integrate different variables separately:

$$\sum_{i=1}^{n} \int_0^1 \cdots \int_0^1 x_i \cdot x_i^{n-1} \prod_{j \neq i}(1 - x_j^{n-1}) f_{X_1}(x_1) \cdot \ldots \cdot f_{X_n}(x_n) dx_1 \ldots dx_n$$
$$= \frac{n}{n+1}(1 - \frac{1}{n})^{n-1}$$

(ii) the second term is constant $1/n$:

$$\sum_{i=1}^{n} \int_0^1 \cdots \int_0^1 x_i \cdot \frac{1}{n} \cdot f_{X_1}(x_1) \cdot \ldots \cdot f_{X_n}(x_n) dx_1 \ldots dx_n = \sum_{i=1}^{n} \frac{1}{n} \cdot \frac{1}{2} = \frac{1}{2}$$

(iii) for the third term, we integrate and add two cases separately, namely $i = k$ and $i \neq k$:

$$\sum_{i=1}^{n} \frac{1}{n} \sum_{k=1}^{n} \int_0^1 \cdots \int_0^1 x_i \cdot x_k^{n-1} \prod_{j \neq k}(1 - x_j^{n-1}) f_{X_1}(x_1) \cdot \ldots \cdot f_{X_n}(x_n) dx_1 \ldots dx_n =$$
$$\frac{1}{n+1}(1 - \frac{1}{n})^{n-1} + \frac{(n-1)^2}{2n(n+1)}(1 - \frac{1}{n})^{n-2}$$

Combining the above results and simplifying gives us the desired formula.

References

1. Abboud, S., Rachkidy, N.E., Guitton, A., Safa, H.: Gateway selection for down-link communication in LoRaWAN. In: 2019 IEEE Wireless Communications and Networking Conference, WCNC 2019, Marrakech, Morocco, April 2019 (2019)
2. Augustin, A., Yi, J., Clausen, T., Townsley, W.M.: A study of LoRa: long range & low power networks for the Internet of Things. Sensors 16(9), 1466 (2016)
3. Bor, M.C., Roedig, U., Voigt, T., Alonso, J.M.: Do LoRa low-power wide-area networks scale? In: Proceedings of the 19th ACM International Conference on Modeling, Analysis and Simulation of Wireless and Mobile Systems, MSWiM 2016, Malta, 13–17 November 2016, pp. 59–67 (2016)
4. Goursaud, C., Gorce, J.M.: Dedicated networks for IoT: PHY/MAC state of the art and challenges. EAI Endorsed Trans. Internet Things 1(1), e3 (2015)
5. LoraAlliance: Lorawan 1.1 specification. http://lora-alliance.org/lorawan-for-develo pers. 22 October 2017 (2017)
6. Nolan, K., Guibene, W., Kelly, M.: An evaluation of low power wide area network technologies for the Internet of Things, September 2016
7. Voigt, T., Bor, M.: Lorasim - a discrete-event simulator (2017). https://www.lancaster.ac.uk/scc/sites/lora/lorasim.html
8. Voigt, T., Bor, M.C., Roedig, U., Alonso, J.M.: Mitigating inter-network interference in LoRa networks. In: Proceedings of the 2017 International Conference on Embedded Wireless Systems and Networks, EWSN 2017, Uppsala, Sweden, 20–22 February 2017, pp. 323–328 (2017)

Direct-To-Satellite IoT - A Survey of the State of the Art and Future Research Perspectives
Backhauling the IoT Through LEO Satellites

Juan A. Fraire[1,2] (iD), Sandra Céspedes[3,4] (iD), and Nicola Accettura[5(✉)] (iD)

[1] CONICET-UNC, Córdoba, Argentina
juanfraire@unc.edu.ar
[2] Dipartimento di Elettronica, Politecnico di Torino, Torino, Italy
[3] Department of Electrical Engineering,
Universidad de Chile, Santiago, Chile
scespedes@ing.uchile.cl
[4] NIC Chile Research Labs, Santiago, Chile
[5] LAAS-CNRS, Université de Toulouse, CNRS, Toulouse, France
nicola.accettura@laas.fr

Abstract. The Internet of Things (IoT) has drawn an enormous attention into the scientific community thanks to unimaginable before applications newly available in everyday life. The technological landscape behind the implied surge of automated interactions among humans and machines has been shaped by plugging into the Internet very low power devices that can perform monitoring and actuation operations through very cheap circuitry. The most challenging IoT scenarios include deployments of low power devices dispersed over wide geographical areas. In such scenarios, satellites will play a key role in bridging the gap towards a pervasive IoT able to easily handle disaster recovery scenarios (earthquakes, tsunamis, and flash floods, etc.), where the presence of a resilient backhauling communications infrastructure is crucial. In these scenarios, Direct-to-Satellite IoT (DtS-IoT) connectivity is preferred as no intermediate ground gateway is required, facilitating and speeding up the deployment of wide coverage IoT infrastructure. In this work, an in-depth yet thorough survey on the state-of-the-art of DtS-IoT is presented. The available physical layer techniques specifically designed for the IoT satellite link are described, and the suitability of both the current Medium Access Control protocol and the upper layer protocols to communicate over space links will be argued. We also discuss the design of the overall satellite LEO constellation and topology to be considered in DtS-IoT networks.

Keywords: Internet of Things · Low-earth orbit satellite ·
Low Power Wide Area Networks (LPWAN) · Satellite networks

© Springer Nature Switzerland AG 2019
M. R. Palattella et al. (Eds.): ADHOC-NOW 2019, LNCS 11803, pp. 241–258, 2019.
https://doi.org/10.1007/978-3-030-31831-4_17

1   Introduction

By embedding computational capabilities into every-day objects, it is possible to easily interact with the environment and draw out complex monitoring and actuation operations in several challenging and critical application areas, such as disaster recovery, smart agriculture, and industrial processes, among others. The consequent tidal increase of communications among humans and objects has made actual the concept of pervasive computing through its natural accomplishment, the Internet of Things (IoT). Triggered by such a revolutionary networking paradigm, a huge number of concurrent technological solutions have been proposed. Some of them have been standardized [40], while others are getting momentum in recent years after some incubation time [51]. In general, each technology is tailored to provide a specific coverage, to support a target data-rate, and to transport specific message sizes.

Sensor-oriented technologies and protocols (e.g., ZigBee, 6TiSCH, and Z-Wave) have been designed to be used in small devices with low power consumption and with data rates in the order of hundreds of kbps. These protocols are only suitable for low traffic applications at both short range in *Wireless Personal Area Networks* (WPANs), and long range in multihop WPANs [40]. In contrast, *Cellular Networks* (e.g., UMTS and LTE) offer a rich variety of long-range, high-data rate, from tens of kbps up to several Mbps. Even though they can be used for IoT communications, traditional cellular networks were not designed for the transmission of small messages nor for low-consumption terminals. In this context, a new type of network is currently emerging: *Low-Power Wide-Area (LPWA)* Networks. Some representative LPWA technologies as LoRa [34] and SigFox [50] are specifically designed to share the properties of both WPANs and cellular networks: low-power and long-range (more than 10 km). From an architectural point of view, LPWA are featured by a hierarchical network organization: a network server coordinates several gateways through a reliable backhaul; in turn, gateways are in charge of interacting through wireless links with potentially billions of low power devices. LPWA protocols are tailored for low data rate applications, from hundreds of bps up to several hundreds of kbps, with messages no longer than 100 bytes, on average [48]. As a result, LPWA transceivers can offer several years of battery autonomy and provide very cheap service on cheap terminal devices.

The long-range, low-power, and low-data properties make the LPWA technology an appealing candidate for many IoT applications. Among them, developing countries with agriculture-based economies will benefit from keeping track and monitoring crops. Based on the sensing information, smart decisions can be taken to get better productivity, with a consequent positive impact on the national economy [55]. LPWA will play a key role in the development of smart agriculture solutions [5], as well as in many other applications, including Smart Grid, Environmental Monitoring, and Emergency Management, among others [17].

Although different in many aspects, the abovementioned terrestrial technologies have a common weakness: they fail to provide global connectivity. Terrestrial networks are also highly vulnerable in cases of natural disasters or terrorist attacks. Instead, satellite access networks, and, in particular, Large-scale Low-Earth Orbit (LEO) satellite constellations have shown their potential to extend terrestrial networks to address the above issues. In this context, satellites can be leveraged to support a world-wide expansion of the promising IoT market. Several long-range low-power satellite systems are already operational, while others are being prepared. Most of them make use of a LEO satellite constellation, such as Orbcomm, Iridium, Globalstar or Argos [46], each featured by a specific orbital formation. LEO satellites are characterized by an altitude between 160 km and 2000 km which renders a ground coverage of several hundreds of kilometers and a reasonable Round Trip Time (RTT) delay for most applications (i.e., less than 100 ms) [15, 36]. Contrariwise, Geostationary Earth Orbit (GEO) satellite links induce higher RTT in the order of 600 ms to 700 ms [38, 57]. Recently, the combination of satellite networks and LPWA technologies has been proposed as a promising hybrid networking architecture. Indeed, backhauling satellite networks interconnecting LPWA gateways provide both reachability in remote areas and redundancy in case of service disruption of the ground network. In the case of LEO deployments, even delay sensitive applications could be served by such a hybrid architecture; instead, in GEO deployments, backhauling with LPWA gateways will target applications that do not hold critical time constraints [41]. Hence, given that we target delay-sensitive applications, including disaster recovery scenarios, the focus of the present contribution is on the interconnection of LPWA gateways through LEO satellite networks.

We first note that, depending on the network configuration, data can be directly transmitted from LEO satellites to Internet via ground stations in range, or relayed to another satellite via inter-satellite links, or stored and carried until a suitable ground station is on sight. Indeed, users from the ground see a LEO satellite crossing the sky with a very high speed (several km/s), and within a time interval of no more than around 10 min on average. Further than the implied Doppler effects on communications, such a particular configuration impacts the overall network topology dynamics, that must seamlessly permit handover from one satellite to another. Nevertheless, satellite communications provide a more cost-effective solution with respect to other terrestrial technologies [22] and have the potential to play an important role for different reasons as listed in [17]: *(i)* smart objects are often remote or they are dispersed over a wide geographical area or they are inaccessible; *(ii)* satellites can naturally support broadcast transmissions (i.e., towards all nodes of the whole network), multicast transmissions (i.e., towards a portion of nodes of the whole network) or geocast transmissions (i.e., towards a portion of nodes placed in a given area of the network) [25]; *(iii)* satellites can provide an alternative redundant path for critical applications requiring high availability at reasonable cost; and *(iv)* existing LPWA applications generally target low data rate transmission indicating that current low bandwidth satellite infrastructures can be effectively reused

That being said, the most relevant scientific interest is focused on the network link between satellites and IoT devices on ground. As illustrated in Fig. 1, there

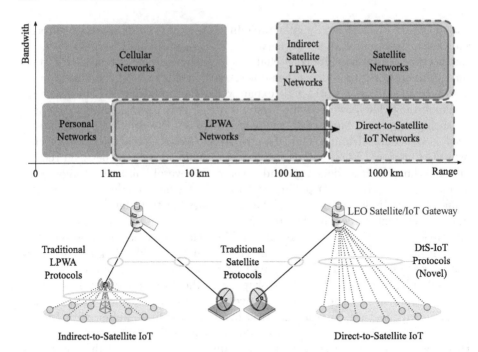

Fig. 1. Required bandwidth vs. range capacity for personal, cellular, LPWA and satellite networks. Direct Satellite LPWA domain is highlighted as an open research area requiring novel protocol design and/or adaptation of existing ones.

are two modes of interoperability envisioned for such a link: *direct* access and *indirect* access. The direct access mode allows devices to directly communicate with the satellite [29], while in the indirect access mode, each sensor and actuator in a network may communicate with the satellite through an intermediate sink node [11], i.e., the LPWA gateway in our scenario of study. Such a gateway is equipped with a traditional satellite terminal and a traditional LPWA radio interface to communicate with the sensor or actuator nodes in the area. On the one hand, the existing protocols can be leveraged in indirect mode, with the limitation that the area of a deployment is confined to the coverage of the gateway node on ground. On the other hand, a direct access from the sensor and actuator terminals to the satellite is a more appealing solution in challenging scenarios, for example: *(i)* in disaster areas where rapid and infrastructure-less deployments are required, *(ii)* in areas with very low device density where a gateway solution is not profitable, and *(iii)* in areas where devices will be present for a limited period of time and thus a gateway placement is discouraged.

However, existing LPWA protocols need to be revised as they were not designed to operate over several hundreds of kilometers in a ground-to-space link. Similarly, existing satellite protocols were thought to operate on highly directional point-to-point topologies and might not be fitted for LPWA applications. In this paper, we study the Direct-to-Satellite IoT (DtS-IoT) architecture as a novel networking domain in the intersection of traditional satellite networking and LPWA IoT networks, as illustrated in Fig. 1. We present a thorough overview of existing protocols and their limitations to serve DtS-IoT, to then survey existing research on the physical, link, and upper layers of this new networking area. We will specifically focus on LoRa technologies and argue that, despite a few relevant considerations, it can be adapted to fit the requirements of DtS-IoT.

To help the reading, we briefly sketch how this contribution is structured. In Sect. 2 we revise existing protocols in the satellite and LPWA areas and discuss their limitation to efficiently operate in DtS-IoT network. In Sect. 3 we provide a detailed survey of specific research of potential application in a DtS-IoT architecture. Section 4 discusses the challenges and considerations of DtS-IoT satellite constellations. Section 5 concludes and summarizes this survey and points towards future research directions to realize future DtS-IoT systems.

2   Existing Protocols

2.1   Satellite Network Protocols

Many of existent satellite protocols for scientific and Earth Observation missions are standardized by the Consultative Committee for Space Data Systems (CCSDS). However, these protocol set are not thought for networking hundreds of devices on sight. Commercial applications on this domain typically rely on proprietary protocols, while only a few support Internet protocols. The most representative protocols are discussed hereafter, and their applicability challenges are highlighting with respect to the DtS-IoT domain.

Multiple Channel Access. In the multiple channel access coordination, the standard DVB-RCS2 defines both contention-free and contention-based multiple access. Other commercial systems employ ALOHA-based protocols suitable for specific traffic patterns. A quantitative evaluation of traditional satellite Medium Access Control (MAC) protocols in DtS-IoT scenarios with LEO constellations is provided in [23].

DVB-RCS2: To support contention-based access, the standard provides two forms of random access methods: Slotted Aloha and Contention Resolution Diversity Slotted Aloha (CRDSA) [17]. The latter groups time-slots to form a frame and nodes send two or more copies of a packet, to later resolve the collisions using of a successive interference cancellation mechanism [13,18]. As for contention-free access, the standard defines the use of a Multi-Frequency Time Division Multiple Access (MF-TDMA) over the downlink channel, which in turn coordinates channel assignments by means of the Demand Assigned Multiple Access (DAMA) protocol [17]. Although high efficiency return channels can be adapted to the machine-to-machine communication services [18], they have been focused in hundreds of user terminals to provide remote Internet connectivity, but not for low power low datarate IoT terminals. Besides, time synchronization in LEO constellation-based IoT system is complex to achieve given the relative high motion between the satellites and ground devices [47].

Enhanced Aloha: This is a protocol operating in commercial telemetry satellite systems that exploits the periodicity of monitoring traffic sent by sensor nodes dedicated to Earth observation, scientific and environmental research. E-Aloha introduces a time window around the fixed sending times to reduce collisions among nodes attempting to transmit at the same time intervals. It is a simplified version of Aloha with no reliability features or additional control to avoid collisions [35]. Although part of the IoT traffic is well represented by periodic data transmission, there is also event-triggered transmissions with random generation patterns that will not be well-suited for the specific design of the E-Aloha protocol [29].

CubeSat Protocols: CubeSat deployments often employ frequencies in the range of the amateur frequency band, with very low data rates (i.e., in the order of 9.6 kbps to 100 kbps). Although other higher bands are also explored in recent developments, the CubeSat deployments are characterized by low data rates and restricted contact times [17]. Traditional satellite protocols tend to behave poorly or simply do not work on such constrained devices. As a result, specific CubeSat protocols to serve the specific characteristics of the IoT traffic has been studied in the literature. In [23], it has been identified that advanced techniques such dynamic channelling or precise channel estimation (employed for interference cancellation), require costly resources often not available in low-cost CubeSat deployments. Among the random access MAC protocols evaluated, only a few become near the region where DtS-IoT supported by CubeSats provides a scalable, energy-efficient, and non-complex channel access mechanism to the ground sensor nodes.

Upper-Layers Satellite Protocols. The support of IP is a requirement if network segments connected via satellite networks interact with the Internet. This is naturally well-supported in satellite systems providing Internet Broadband access; however, that is not necessarily the case for more isolated satellite sensor networks. One would expect that IP support is a must in satellite IoT networks. Currently, the DVB-RCS2 standard supports IPv6 with a generic stream encapsulation (GSE) [17]. In the case of transport layer protocols, a customization of TCP stack parameters has been defined back in the late 90's to improve the performance over satellite links [6]. With TCP support, it is possible to employ traditional application layer protocols such as HTTP and also MQTT. More recent IoT protocols such as CoAP, which relies on UDP, have been evaluated over disruptive satellite links, showing the need to adjust the protocol parameters to achieve reduced end-to-end delays and to increase the packet delivery rate [26].

2.2   LPWA Network Protocols

NB-IoT: it is an IoT technology set up by the 3GPP as a part of Release 13 [32]. Although it is integrated into the Long-Term Evolution (LTE) standard, it can be regarded as a new air interface that operates on licensed radio spectrum [16]. Licensed band spectrum auctions of the sub-GHz spectrum are typically over 500 million dollars per MHz [33]. NB-IoT may operate as a dedicated carrier, it may occupy bandwidth of a wide-band LTE carrier, or it may use the guard-bands of the LTE carrier [47]. Such a technology is also capable of guaranteeing higher datarates than common LPWA technologies, thus perfectly fitting disaster scenarios, where capturing videos/images would be needed for fine-grained control. If this capability perfectly match an emergency situation, it results as oversized (and expensive) for regular monitoring in normal situations. Eventually, although previous works has discussed the applicability of LTE over satellite links [42], they require complex coding and synchronous signaling protocol techniques which are not suitable for resource-constrained DtS-IoT devices [51].

LoRa: It is the LPWA technology getting the widest interest into the research community on IoT communications, for several reasons. LoRa works on unlicensed spectrum supporting an asynchronous bidirectional link layer protocol defined in the open LoRaWAN specification [3]. More interestingly, it implements roaming by allowing IoT devices to communicate to redundantly deliver information through all LoRa gateways in range. The LoRa physical layer uses the Chirp Spread Sprectrum (CSS) modulation to handle interference, and multipath fading, but it cannot offer the same Quality of Service that NB-IoT or LTE can provide over a licensed spectrum [51]. However, LoRa may have a wider network coverage than NB-IoT network. For example, in Belgium, a country with a total area of approximately 30500 km^2, the LoRa network deployment covers the entire country with only seven base stations [33]. However, LoRa physical layer is a proprietary technology, which might impose economical constraints if considered for DtS-IoT. At the link layer, LoRa defines a lightweight protocol, namely LoRaWAN, permitting different modes of operation [34]. In the most typical scenario, when the application running on a low power device intends to deliver some data through the Internet, it turns the radio on for the exact time needed to perform the frame transmission. As matter of facts, this mode of communication, namely Class-A, is an asynchronous Pure ALOHA-based protocol, and provides the maximum battery life-time for sensors and must be supported by all LoRaWAN devices. Bidirectional traffic is supported by a receive window which is opened two times exactly 1 s and 2 s after the end of the uplink transmission. Notably, downlink unicast transmissions are synchronous with the reception of an uplink frame by the intended recipient device. To allow asynchronous downlink communications, Class-B devices must first listen to beacons broadcasted by gateways. In such a way, they get synchronized to the network and can safely open receiving windows at regular times. Downlink frames can be received during such time windows. Interestingly, the use of slotted Aloha or collision-free protocols can be enabled through proper protocol enhancement

[3]. Finally, Class C devices are the main powered actuators that have sufficient power available to sustain a continuous receive window.

Given the few available applicability studies of LoRa technology over the satellite link, and the lack of performance evaluations of the LoRaWAN MAC protocols over DtS-IoT [23,41], it remains largely unknown if these protocols are suitable for the scenario of study. Moreover, the IoT standards did not consider any satellite segment in the overall architecture, nor satellite standards considered low-power devices on the ground segment. This derives in the emergence of a new area of research as illustrated in Fig. 1.

3   Direct-to-Satellite IoT

To successfully realize direct-to-satellite IoT, underlying protocol layers should be revised and adapted as necessary. In this context, we analyze *Physical*, *Link* and *Upper Layers* and they role in DtS-IoT. A cross-layer approach is not discarded as a means to achieve DtS-IoT.

Recent studies have shown the feasibility of using LPWA technologies over the satellite link for DtS-IoT architectures. In [47], Qu et al. explore the spectrum sharing of LEO satellite IoT constellation with terrestrial IoT systems such as LoRa and NB-IoT. Other experimental works defined LoRa performance over long distance links up to 250 km, which could be considered the distance for a LEO satellite deployment [19]. In [21], the authors established the Doppler effects over links lengths under and above 550 km, with a differentiated behavior that contradicts previous studies. The experiments were carried out in the laboratory and outdoors (with cars and line-of-sight conditions), using similar velocities and reproducing the Doppler effect over the link with software-defined-radios [21]. In all cases, the resulting data-rate at long distances is extremely low, enabling messages of a few bits, which indeed, are still valuable for many DtS-IoT applications.

In the following, we discuss the upcoming challenges at each layer to enable DtS-IoT with LPWA technologies.

3.1   Physical Layer

Frequency Spectrum: LoRa has been designed to be used while complying within the unlicensed 900 MHz Industrial, Scientific and Medical (ISM) frequency band in South America and within the unlicensed 868 Mhz ISM frequency band in Europe, while NB-IoT was designed to be used in licensed 3G/4G spectrum. Sharing the spectrum with terrestrial IoT systems will cause interference on both satellite and terrestrial segments, especially when large areas are covered by the satellite LEO system. Additional anti-interference measures are needed to enable the co-existence of these systems [47].

Multi-Beam Antennas: In order to deliver broadband data services, satellite systems have traditionally allowed to reuse the available bandwidth in beams with different frequencies, each serving one user. This scheme is known as frequency division multiplexing (FDM) [27]. Compared with a single global beam transmission, the use of a multi-beam architecture can bring several advantages, such as sending different symbols simultaneously to geographically separated areas. This indeed enabled an increment in the overall user bandwidth [28]; however, frequency reuse schemes cannot dramatically increase the channel capacity [54]. To further improve the spectral efficiency, full frequency reuse has been applied to modern multi-beam satellite systems, where interference mitigation techniques are implemented to mitigate interference between beams [56]. Multi-beams antennas will indeed become an appealing feature to provide enough channel diversity in DtS-IoT with thousands of devices at sight. However, technologies of hundreds of beams might be necessary to implement massive DtS-IoT.

Spread Spectrum Modulation: Signal transmissions for low-power devices have been studied on two fronts: spread-spectrum and narrow-band. Spread-spectrum techniques [44] consists in spreading the signal into a wider bandwidth, which render a good tolerance to interference. For example, LoRa leverages a unique chirp spread spectrum modulation (CSS), also defined as Direct-Sequence Spread Spectrum [10], to achieve exceptional link budget and low power performance within contested ISM channels. As shown in Fig. 2(a), symbols are represented as instantaneous changes in the frequency of a chirp. However, recent studies have demonstrated that LoRa modulation may introduce difficulties in decoding signals from multiple terminals when used over satellite links. The authors in [45] propose another modulation called symmetric CSS that addresses this problem. Moreover, the LoRa physical layer is closed source and proprietary, thus there is no official references or protocol specifications, which might hinder its effective and immediate application to the satellite domain. The interested reader is referred to the work in [30], which provides a blind analysis of the protocol.

Narrow Band Modulation: Other systems use the classical transmission scheme with a signal being transmitted on a carrier of very small bandwidth (less than 1 kHz), a.k.a. ultra-narrow-band transmission. With this scheme it is possible to use simpler transceiver than in the case of spread spectrum techniques [7]. It provides natural resistance to noise and interference, as well as long range communications, and the terminal can be implemented with very low cost electronic components with low power consumption [31]. However, small frequency variations over time may become relatively large compared to the signal bandwidth (up to several times the frequency bandwidth of the signal). This frequency drift is particularly present in the case of a LEO satellite. As illustrated in Fig. 2(b), for a satellite at an altitude of 720 km, the Doppler rate can be as high as -100 Hz/s for a carrier frequency of 400 MHz. Authors in [7] state that, to tolerate such frequency drifts, narrow-band access scheme should be considered a random access.

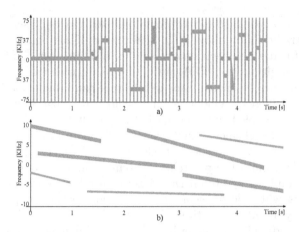

Fig. 2. Narrow-band and spread-spectrum illustration. (a) Chirp-based LoRa spread-spectrum signals occupying a channel of 125 KHz [30]. (b) Narrow-band signals of 100 Hz wide and 2.5 s long, with different frequency shifts [7].

3.2   Link Layer

Link layer duties such as error correction and detection in a DtS-IoT system are rather not modified with respect to what was discussed for general space-to-ground communications in Sect. 2.1. However, the main novelty in DtS-IoT is the need to control the channel access among thousands of devices to satellites over hundreds of kilometers. The challenges in designing link layer MAC protocols in satellite IoT contexts are surveyed in [17] and [23]. In general, when energy efficiency is very important, TDMA is the well suited multiple channel access scheme. On the other hand, in many IoT deployments featured by a very high numbers of devices, and a limited portion of them having data to send, a fixed-assignment multiple access scheme such as TDMA might be inefficient [17]. Nevertheless, contention-based protocols, when used in the DtS-IoT context, need to integrate mechanisms to manage the links power imbalances, the uneven link delays, and the lack of high quality channel estimations [23]. In the remaining part of this subsection, we review recent proposals of MAC layer protocols suitable for DtS-IoT architectures.

Contention-Free Direct Access. The algorithm proposed in [29] allows a satellite to collect data efficiently from sensor nodes through direct access. According to this scheme, the satellite allocates time slots on demand to sensor nodes which have data to send relying on a method consisting of a searching phase and an allocation phase. In the searching phase, the satellite finds the sensor nodes having data to send and divides the sensor nodes into two groups, and iterates until no more groups can be created. In the allocation phase, the satellite allocates time slots to all the sensor nodes of the remaining groups. Authors proved that this algorithm achieves higher efficiency in bandwidth utilization with respect to a TDMA-based fixed assignments scheme or a slotted ALOHA scheme discussed in Sect. 2.1.

Contended Direct Access: There are many random access techniques proposed in the literature [2,12,14,18,43,49]. Specifically, authors in [7] studied a version of Aloha extended for ultra-narrow-band signals, called Time/Frequency Aloha (TFA). In TFA, the frequency is chosen randomly within a specific bandwidth by the device. The analysis shows that the frequency drift in DtS-IoT narrow-band increases the probability of collision, drastically limiting MAC performance beyond a network load of 0.2. Other MAC protocol for sensor data collection satellite systems using LoRa technology over the satellite link is proposed in [20]. The authors propose to condense both the LoRa gateway and the network server on the satellite. They introduce a delay function to reduce collisions among terminal nodes, at the same time that define a power adaptation technique based on the location of sensor nodes. The protocol was evaluated in a simulated environment with several simplifications that require further improvements to verify the performance on more realistic satellite scenarios.

3.3   Upper Layers

Addresses: IPv6 has increased the number of addresses that can be used throughout Internet. Addressing huge numbers of nodes on the ground with IPv6 is then feasible within DtS-IoT systems, as analyzed in [17]. At the standardization level, there is an open issue about how to provide IP addressing capabilities to more and more constrained devices in more and more dense deployments. One major limitation of LPWA technologies (as well as DtS-IoT) is the reduced MTU, which creates the need to implement middle boxes (i.e., a gateway) to interface non-IP technologies with the IP world. If the backhaul of DtS-IoT architectures is implemented with LPWA technologies over the satellite link, standards for packet compression and packet fragmentation become relevant to enable IP support up to the end device [37]. Given the hub-and-spoke nature of LPWA networks, other IPv6-related standards such as Neighbor Discovery help in achieving a stateful compression of the IPv6 header [52]. Another aspect to consider is that LEO constellation are in facts mobile networks, with the infrastructure moving with respect to the ground nodes (that may be static). In such a case, the context of communications at the IP level may change. A study of dynamic contexts combined with IP packet compression is explored in [1]. Further research and experimentation of the IP support (and possibly the IP mobility management) over LPWA links in a satellite environment is required to understand the impact over the performance of both time-critical and delay tolerant IoT applications.

Broadcast and Anycast: Several applications for IoT will exploit DtS-IoT forward link for delivering commands and control information via satellite to the huge number of devices [4]. In emergency management systems, for example, the forward link communication could be used for providing group oriented services to support both remote sensors or actuators and human-type communications [24]. To efficiently exploit the large coverage provided by satellite systems, efficient broadcast and localized anycast will need to be supported. Moreover, geocast, or geographically localized distribution of messages are key features to motivate the deployment of future DtS-IoT systems.

Transport and Application layer protocols: Two of the most promising application layer protocols for small devices are MQTT and CoAP. Both are open standards better suited to constrained environments than HTTP, provide mechanisms for asynchronous communication, and run on IP, which facilitates their integration within Internet. On the one hand, MQTT was proposed by IBM implements a publish/subscribe paradigm and is TCP-based. MQTT gives flexibility in communication patterns and acts purely as a pipe for binary data. On the other hand, IETF has proposed the use of Constrained Application Protocol (CoAP) (RFC 7252), which relies on UDP and implements a request/response style. When used over satellite links, CoAP outperforms MQTT on random access channels [8,9]. Moreover, the authors of [39] proposed an integration of CoAP and MQTT over LoRaWAN, even though such application layer protocols cause extra overhead in terms of payload size, thus undermining the already limited performance of DtS-IoT links.

4   DtS-IoT Constellations

Depending on the satellite orbit and device latitude, a typical LEO satellite provides an average of 4 passes per day. Each pass, depending on the satellite altitude, offers data transfer opportunities in between 7 and 10 min duration when the satellite flies exactly over the spot on ground. When the satellite passes closer to the horizon from the device perspective, the contact duration is reduced and the channel conditions are worsened. This condition renders connectivity times in the order of 20 min per location per day, on which the channel resource will likely be shared among hundreds if not thousands of devices. Because of the limited data rate of a DtS-IoT link, the data transfer provided by a single satellite might result insufficient for a typical IoT application.

Satellites constellations are fleets of LEO satellites strategically distributed in orbit to provide continuous or quasi-continuous coverage of the whole planet's surface, or part of it. As a result, constellations enhance the overall data transfer and reduces the waiting time to access the network. For example, the constellation in Fig. 3(a) provides world coverage by leveraging polar orbits (i.e., orbits with 90 degree inclination that passes over the poles). Figure 3(b), on the other hand, provides better revisit of satellites over populated areas near the equator; but inclined orbits never flies on the poles rendering a partial planet coverage. There is not one-fits-all constellation topology configuration, a trade-off is always present between surface coverage and satellite revisit time.

In general, the application drives the constellation parameters. For example, voice and Internet data services constellation (i.e., Iridium) are configured to

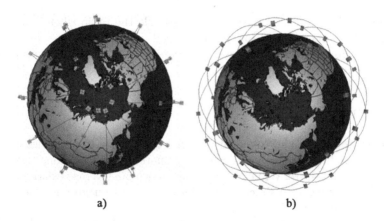

a)   b)

Fig. 3. LEO satellite constellation with a Walker Star formation on (a) and a Walker Delta (a.k.a. Ballard Rosette) on (b). Iridium constellation uses the former to provide world-wide connectivity including the poles, while Globalstar is based on the latter, which provides better coverage in populated areas. Images created with SaVi [53]

always have at least one satellite covering every telephone or Internet device on the Earth surface. A DtS-IoT application could indeed profit from a *full-coverage constellation* topology as devices could be permanently at sight of a passing satellite. However, continuous coverage is achieved at the expense of hundreds of LEO satellites, if not more. This can certainly make prohibitive the cost of the fleet for many IoT applications, which are designed to be predominantly low-cost.

Another possibility is to consider constellations with less satellites that provides partial and opportunistic connectivity. This is indeed an intermediate solution between a single LEO satellite and a full-coverage constellation. In this case, devices would need to store data until one of the constellation's satellite becomes reachable. These *sparse constellations* would provide a higher latency service, but at a reduced deployment and operation cost. This approach is likely to satisfy a large set of IoT applications requirements.

From an IoT protocol perspective, full-coverage constellations can provide continuous connectivity mimicking the permanent presence of an IoT gateway for all the serviced devices on ground. In the case of LoRa, a continuous gateway presence would facilitate a class A operation mode, the default mode for LoRa devices. However, a sparse constellation would require devices to sporadically operate in the so-called "beacon-less" mode in class B [34], when no satellite is on sight. In particular, devices are allowed to sustain a class B operation for two hours (120 min) after receiving the last beacon, in this case, from a DtS-IoT satellite. During this period, the device would need to rely on its local clock to keep timing.

As a result, a sparse DtS-IoT constellation design would need to consider such timing constraints not present in other types of satellite constellations. Furthermore, a discussion remains open on the feasibility of enabling DtS-IoT devices with simplified orbital information to only enable the radio when a satellite is on sight, a fundamental DtS-IoT battery saving feature. The effective DtS-IoT constellation topology design as well the implications on the specific protocol adaptations is left as an immediate future work.

5   Summary and Outlook

As we move towards an all-connected era, IoT networking technologies will need to embrace satellite as a means to connect remote devices over long-range, low-power and low data-rate. While indirect approaches can leverage existing satellite and LPWA protocols, a direct connection to devices on ground offers a real remote IoT experience.

In this paper, we have introduced and described Direct-to-Satellite-IoT as a promising research area where existing protocols need to be revised and adapted. A survey on relevant technologies showed that LoRa is an appealing approach towards DtS-IoT, but imposes severe challenges motivating future research efforts. Among them, we have highlighted the extremely low data-rate, the lack of knowledge on how the satellite channel affects the behavior of a proprietary technology, and the need of IP support for integration with Internet. We have also identified DtS-IoT constellations as a promising solution with pending challenges to tackle at a protocol level.

Future research is envisioned in developing a new LoRa-compatible interface including new MAC protocols designed for the low-power consumption but considering the satellite system, especially if deployed in constellations. Moreover, architectural decisions involving the satellites will need to be discussed. In particular, the LoRaWAN gateway and server roles might need to be distributed among satellites in order to get rid of the dependency of the network server for both data and control planes. To this end, the fact that gateways will be moving at high speeds will need to be studied and the role of routing via inter-satellite links will need to be analyzed in detail. Finally, upper layer transport and application protocols (CoAP and MQTT) will be evaluated over the DtS-IoT links.

References

1. Abdelfadeel, K.Q., Cionca, V., Pesch, D.: Dynamic context for static context header compression in LPWANs. In: Proceedings - 14th Annual International Conference on Distributed Computing in Sensor Systems, DCOSS 2018 (2018). https://doi.org/10.1109/DCOSS.2018.00013
2. Abramson, N.: The ALOHA system: another alternative for computer communications. In: Fall Joint Computer Conference, vol. 37, pp. 281–285, January 1977. https://doi.org/10.1145/1478462.1478502
3. Accettura, N., Alata, E., Berthou, P., Dragomirescu, D., Monteil, T.: Addressing scalable, optimal, and secure communications over LoRa networks: challenges and research directions. Internet Technol. Lett. 1(4), e54 (2018). https://doi.org/10.1002/itl2.54

4. Afolabi, R.O., Dadlani, A., Kim, K.: Multicast scheduling and resource allocation algorithms for OFDMA-based systems: a survey. IEEE Commun. Surv. Tutorials **15**(1), 240–254 (2013). https://doi.org/10.1109/SURV.2012.013012.00074

5. Agarwal, A., Gupta, S., Kumar, S., Singh, D.: An efficient use of IoT for satellite data in land cover monitoring to estimate LST and ET. In: 2016 11th International Conference on Industrial and Information Systems (ICIIS), pp. 905–909, December 2016. https://doi.org/10.1109/ICIINFS.2016.8263067

6. Allman, M., Glover, D., Sanchez, L.: Enhancing TCP over satellite channels using standard mechanisms. BCP 28, RFC Editor, January 1999

7. Anteur, M., Deslandes, V., Thomas, N., Beylot, A.: Ultra narrow band technique for low power wide area communications. In: 2015 IEEE Global Communications Conference (GLOBECOM), pp. 1–6, December 2015. https://doi.org/10.1109/GLOCOM.2015.7417420

8. Bacco, M., et al.: IoT applications and services in space information networks. IEEE Wirel. Commun. **26**(2), 31–37 (2019). https://doi.org/10.1109/MWC.2019.1800297

9. Bacco, M., Colucci, M., Gotta, A.: Application protocols enabling Internet of remote things via random access satellite channels. In: 2017 IEEE International Conference on Communications (ICC), pp. 1–6, May 2017. https://doi.org/10.1109/ICC.2017.7997292

10. Berni, A., Gregg, W.: On the utility of chirp modulation for digital signaling. IEEE Trans. Commun. **21**(6), 748–751 (1973). https://doi.org/10.1109/TCOM.1973.1091721

11. Bisio, I., Marchese, M.: Efficient satellite-based sensor networks for information retrieval. IEEE Syst. J. **2**, 464–475 (2008). https://doi.org/10.1109/JSYST.2008.2004850

12. Casini, E., De Gaudenzi, R., Del Rio Herrero, O.: Contention resolution diversity slotted ALOHA (CRDSA): An enhanced random access schemefor satellite access packet networks. IEEE Trans. Wireless Commun. **6**(4), 1408–1419 (2007). https://doi.org/10.1109/TWC.2007.348337

13. Casini, E., De Gaudenzi, R., Del Rio Herrero, O.: Contention resolution diversity slotted ALOHA (CRDSA): an enhanced random access scheme for satellite access packet networks. IEEE Trans. Wirel. Commun. **6**(4), 1408–1419 (2007). https://doi.org/10.1109/TWC.2007.348337

14. Choudhury, G., Rappaport, S.: Diversity ALOHA - a random access scheme for satellite communications. IEEE Trans. Commun. **31**(3), 450–457 (1983). https://doi.org/10.1109/TCOM.1983.1095828

15. Cocco, G., Ibars, C.: On the feasibility of satellite M2M systems. In: 30th AIAA International Communications Satellite System Conference (ICSSC), September 2012. https://doi.org/10.2514/6.2012-15074

16. Rohde, D., Schwarz, J.: Narrowband Internet of Things, August 2016. www.rohde-schwarz.com/us/applications/narrowband-internet-of-things-application-note56280--314242.html

17. De Sanctis, M., Cianca, E., Araniti, G., Bisio, I., Prasad, R.: Satellite communications supporting Internet of remote things. IEEE Internet Things J. **3**(1), 113–123 (2016). https://doi.org/10.1109/JIOT.2015.2487046

18. Del Rio Herrero, O., De Gaudenzi, R.: High efficiency satellite multiple access scheme for machine-to-machine communications. IEEE Trans. Aerosp. Electron. Syst. **48**(4), 2961–2989 (2012). https://doi.org/10.1109/TAES.2012.6324672

19. Demetri, S., Zúñiga, M., Picco, G.P., Kuipers, F., Bruzzone, L., Telkamp, T.: Automated estimation of link quality for LoRa : a remote sensing approach. In: Proceedings of the 18th International Conference on Information Processing in Sensor Networks, pp. 145–156. ACM, Montreal (2019). https://dl.acm.org/citation.cfm?doid=3302506.3310396

20. Deng, T., Zhu, J., Nie, Z.: An adaptive MAC protocol for SDCS system based on LoRa technology. In: 2017 2nd International Conference on Automation, Mechanical Control and Computational Engineering (AMCCE 2017). Atlantis Press, March 2017. https://doi.org/10.2991/amcce-17.2017.146

21. Doroshkin, A., Zadorozhny, A., Kus, O., Prokopyev, V.: Experimental study of LoRa modulation immunity to doppler effect in CubeSat radio communications. IEEE Access PP(c), 1 (2019). https://doi.org/10.1109/ACCESS.2019.2919274

22. Fairhurst, G., Caviglione, L., Collini-Nocker, B.: First: future Internet - a role for satellite technology. In: 2008 IEEE International Workshop on Satellite and Space Communications, pp. 160–164, October 2008. https://doi.org/10.1109/IWSSC.2008.4656774

23. Ferrer, T., Céspedes, S., Becerra, A.: Review and evaluation of MAC protocols for satellite IoT systems using nanosatellites. Sensors 19(8) (1947) (2019). https://doi.org/10.3390/s19081947

24. Franck, L., Suffritti, R.: Multiple alert message encapsulation over satellite. In: 2009 1st International Conference on Wireless Communication, Vehicular Technology, Information Theory and Aerospace Electronic Systems Technology, pp. 540–543, May 2009. https://doi.org/10.1109/WIRELESSVITAE.2009.5172503

25. Ghavimi, F., Chen, H.: M2M communications in 3GPP LTE/LTE-a networks: architectures, service requirements, challenges, and applications. IEEE Commun. Surv. Tutorials 17(2), 525–549 (2015). https://doi.org/10.1109/COMST.2014.2361626

26. Giotti, D., Lamorte, L., Soua, R., Palattella, M.R., Engel, T.: Performance analysis of CoAP under satellite link disruption. In: 2018 25th International Conference on Telecommunications (ICT), pp. 623–628. IEEE, St. Malo (2018). https://doi.org/10.1109/ICT.2018.8464881

27. Hu, D., He, L., Wu, J.: A novel forward-link multiplexed scheme in satellite-based Internet of Things. IEEE Internet of Things J. 5(2), 1265–1274 (2018). https://doi.org/10.1109/JIOT.2018.2799550

28. Joroughi, V., Vázquez, M.Á., Pérez-Neira, A.I.: Generalized multicast multibeam precoding for satellite communications. IEEE Trans. Wirel. Commun. 16(2), 952–966 (2017). https://doi.org/10.1109/TWC.2016.2635139

29. Kawamoto, Y., Nishiyama, H., Fadlullah, Z.M., Kato, N.: Effective data collection via satellite-routed sensor system (SRSS) to realize global-scaled Internet of Things. IEEE Sens. J. 13(10), 3645–3654 (2013). https://doi.org/10.1109/JSEN.2013.2262676

30. Knight, M., Seeber, B.: Decoding LoRa: realizing a modern LPWAN with SDR. In: Proceedings of the GNU Radio Conference, vol. 1, no. 1 (2016). https://pubs.gnuradio.org/index.php/grcon/article/view/8

31. Lassen, T.: Long-range RF communication: why narrowband is the de facto standard. Texas Instruments White Paper (2014)

32. Link Labs Inc.: A Comprehensive Look at Low Power, Wide Area Networks. http://cdn2.hubspot.net/hubfs/427771/LPWAN-Brochure-Interactive.pdf

33. LoRa Alliance: LoRaWAN What is it. Technical Marketing Workgroup 1.0, November 2015. https://www.lora-alliance.org/portals/0/documents/whitepapers/LoRaWAN101.pdf

34. LoRa Alliance Technical Committee: LoRaWAN^{TM} 1.1 Specification, v1.1, October 2017

35. Ma, H., Cai, L.: Performance analysis of randomized MAC for satellite telemetry systems. In: 2010 5th International ICST Conference on Communications and Networking in China, pp. 1–5, August 2010

36. Meloni, A., Atzori, L.: The role of satellite communications in the smart grid. Wirel. Commun. **24**(2), 50–56 (2017). https://doi.org/10.1109/MWC.2017.1600251

37. Minaburo, A., Toutain, L., Gomez, C., Barthel, D., Zuniga, J.: Lpwan static context header compression (SCHC) and fragmentation for IPv6 and UDP. Internet-Draft draft-ietf-lpwan-ipv6-static-context-hc-18, IETF Secretariat, December 2018. http://www.ietf.org/internet-drafts/draft-ietf-lpwan-ipv6-static-context-hc-18.txt

38. Minoli, D.: Building the Internet of Things with IPv6 and MIPv6: The Evolving World of M2M Communications, 1st edn. Wiley Publishing, Hoboken (2013)

39. Nguyen, T., Patonico, S., Bezunartea, M., Thielemans, S., Braeken, A., Steenhaut, K.: Horizontal integration of CoAP and MQTT on Internet protocol - based LoRaMotes. In: 2018 IEEE 29th Annual International Symposium on Personal, Indoor and Mobile Radio Communications (PIMRC), pp. 1–7, September 2018. https://doi.org/10.1109/PIMRC.2018.8580674

40. Palattella, M.R., et al.: Standardized protocol stack for the Internet of (important) Things. IEEE Commun. Surv. Tutorials **15**(3), 1389–1406 (2013). https://doi.org/10.1109/SURV.2012.111412.00158

41. Palattella, M.R., Accettura, N.: Enabling Internet of everything everywhere: LPWAN with satellite backhaul. In: 2018 Global Information Infrastructure and Networking Symposium (GIIS), pp. 1–5. IEEE, October 2018. https://doi.org/10.1109/GIIS.2018.8635663, https://ieeexplore.ieee.org/document/8635663/

42. Papaleo, M., Neri, M., Vanelli-Coralli, A., Corazza, G.E.: Using LTE in 4G satellite communications: increasing time diversity through forced retransmission. In: 2008 10th International Workshop on Signal Processing for Space Communications, pp. 1–4, October 2008. https://doi.org/10.1109/SPSC.2008.4686699

43. Pateros, C.: Novel direct sequence spread spectrum multiple access technique. In: MILCOM 2000 Proceedings. 21st Century Military Communications. Architectures and Technologies for Information Superiority (Cat. No.00CH37155), vol. 1, pp. 564–568, October 2000. https://doi.org/10.1109/MILCOM.2000.905024

44. Pursley, M.B.: Direct-sequence spread-spectrum communications for multipath channels. IEEE Trans. Microw. Theory Tech. **50**(3), 653–661 (2002). https://doi.org/10.1109/22.989950

45. Qian, Y., Ma, L., Liang, X.: Symmetry chirp spread spectrum modulation used in LEO satellite Internet of Things. IEEE Commun. Lett. **22**(11), 2230–2233 (2018). https://doi.org/10.1109/LCOMM.2018.2866820, https://ieeexplore.ieee.org/document/8444661/

46. Qu, Z., Zhang, G., Cao, H., Xie, J.: Leo satellite constellation for Internet of Things. IEEE Access **5**, 18391–18401 (2017). https://doi.org/10.1109/ACCESS.2017.2735988

47. Qu, Z., Zhang, G., Cao, H., Xie, J.: LEO satellite constellation for Internet of Things. IEEE Access **5**, 18391–18401 (2017). https://doi.org/10.1109/ACCESS.2017.2735988, http://ieeexplore.ieee.org/document/8002583/

48. Rebbeck, T., Mackenzie, M., Afonso, N.: Low-powered wireless solutions have the potential to increase the M2M market by over 3 billion connections. Analysys Mason, London, September 2014

49. Roberts, L.: ALOHA packet system with and without slots and capture. ACM SIGCOMM Comput. Commun. Rev. **5**, 28–42 (1975). https://doi.org/10.1145/1024916.1024920

50. Sigfox. https://www.sigfox.com

51. Sinha, R.S., Wei, Y., Hwang, S.H.: A survey on LPWA technology: LoRa and NB-IoT. ICT Express **3**(1), 14 – 21 (2017). https://doi.org/10.1016/j.icte.2017.03.004, http://www.sciencedirect.com/science/article/pii/S2405959517300061

52. Thubert, P.: IPv6 neighbor discovery on wireless networks. Internet-Draft draft-thubert-6man-ipv6-over-wireless-01, IETF Secretariat, April 2019. http://www.ietf.org/internet-drafts/draft-thubert-6man-ipv6-over-wireless-01.txt

53. Wood, L.: SaVi: satellite constellation visualization, June 2011. https://savi.sourceforge.io/

54. Yu, Q., Meng, W., Yang, M., Zheng, L., Zhang, Z.: Virtual multi-beamforming for distributed satellite clusters in space information networks. IEEE Wirel. Commun. **23**(1), 95–101 (2016). https://doi.org/10.1109/MWC.2016.7422411

55. Zhang, N., Wang, M., Wang, N.: Precision agriculture-a worldwide overview. Comput. Electron. Agric. **36**(2), 113 – 132 (2002). https://doi.org/10.1016/S0168-16990200096-0, http://www.sciencedirect.com/science/article/pii/S0168169902000960

56. Zheng, G., Chatzinotas, S., Ottersten, B.: Generic optimization of linear precoding in multibeam satellite systems. IEEE Trans. Wirel. Commun. **11**(6), 2308–2320 (2012). https://doi.org/10.1109/TWC.2012.040412.111629

57. Zhou, H.: The Internet of Things in the Cloud: A Middleware Perspective, 1st edn. CRC Press Inc., Boca Raton (2012)

Link Budget Analysis for Satellite-Based Narrowband IoT Systems

Oltjon Kodheli[1]([✉]), Nicola Maturo[1], Stefano Andrenacci[2],
Symeon Chatzinotas[1], and Frank Zimmer[2]

[1] Snt - Interdisciplinary Centre for Security, Reliability and Trust,
University of Luxembourg, 29 Avenue J.F. Kennedy,
1855 Luxembourg City, Luxembourg
`oltjon.kodheli@uni.lu`
[2] SES, Château de Betzdorf, Rue Pierre Werner, 6815 Betzdorf, Luxembourg

Abstract. Low-power wide-area networks (LPWAN) have been rapidly gaining ground in recent years, triggered by their capability to satisfy important market segments. Narrowband Internet of Things (NB-IoT) is one of the most appealing LPWAN technologies, foreseen to play an important role in the fifth generation mobile communication (5G) network. In order to guarantee a worldwide coverage to the low-cost devices distributed all over the globe, satellite connectivity is a key asset due to their large footprint on Earth, especially in remote areas where the investment towards a terrestrial infrastructure is not justified. However, such terrestrial networks aiming at deploying satellite systems either as an integrated part of it or a stand-alone solution, would require a careful and detailed analysis covering several aspects and all the layers of communication. In this paper, we demonstrate the link budgets of a satellite-based NB-IoT system under different parameters, providing some simulation results as a benchmark for further study. In addition, we analyze and discuss the impact that different power budgets would have in important features of the NB-IoT network, such as delay, capacity and device battery life.

Keywords: 5G · NB-IoT · Link budget analysis ·
Satellite communication · Spectral efficiency

1 Introduction

In the last years, the Internet of things (IoT) has drawn a great deal of research attention, both from academia and industry, due to the impact it is expected to have in the global economic processes and the quality of everyday life [9,18,22].

This work was supported by the Luxembourg National Research Fund (FNR) under Industrial Fellowship Scheme with industrial partner SES S.A., project title "Communication algorithms for end-to-end satellite-IoT (SATIOT)", grant FNR12526592.

© Springer Nature Switzerland AG 2019
M. R. Palattella et al. (Eds.): ADHOC-NOW 2019, LNCS 11803, pp. 259–271, 2019.
https://doi.org/10.1007/978-3-030-31831-4_18

The number of IoT devices generating and exchanging information with each-other is estimated to be three times as high as the global population by 2020 [12]. In order to satisfy this tremendous market demand, the 3rd Generation Partnership Project (3GPP) introduced the narrowband Internet of things (NB-IoT) standard [5], which is foreseen to play an important role in the fifth generation mobile communication (5G) network. A crucial key performance indicator (KPI) of this technology is to guarantee a worldwide connectivity to the low-cost IoT devices distributed all over the globe. However, in many cases the terrestrial infrastructure does not exist and it has a very high deployment cost. For this reason, the satellite connectivity is considered to be a very attractive solution in such areas in order to complement and extend the coverage of the terrestrial network. Several contributions have studied such systems, showing the fundamental features and the role of the satellites in the 5G IoT communications [10,11,21]. Moreover, in our previous works we studied an NB-IoT over a LEO satellite system, providing a solution to reduce the high differential Doppler shift [15,16].

Together with other technical challenges and considerations, link budget is an important aspect worth analyzing for satellite-based NB-IoT networks, motivated by the following reasons. On the one hand, even though the link budget is already well-studied for terrestrial NB-IoT through several contributions [17,19], a new analysis is needed since the constraints in a satellite system are different with respect to a terrestrial one. More specifically, because of the presence of the satellite, a power constraint will be present both in the downlink (forward link) and uplink (return link) case. Indeed, one of the main challenges in a satellite communication system is where to get the power from, which in a terrestrial system this is not an issue. Solar power is the most likely source of energy to be used in space, imposing a significant limitation in closing the communication link, due to the difficulty of generating large power quantities onboard the satellite. On the other hand, 3GPP recently completed a study item in 5G air interface to support non-terrestrial networks (NTN) [4], where the link budgets for different satellite altitudes and frequency bands were shown. However a specific analysis targeting only the NB-IoT is necessary, due to the particular technical peculiarities of this technology. In the literature, some research works already exist, studying the coverage extension of NB-IoT through LEO satellite [13,14]. Nevertheless, due to the recent development of the NB-IoT standard with improved capabilities and the new 3GPP agreements for the satellite link design in NTN 5G air interface, an updated and more detailed link budget analysis is of utmost importance.

As a result, in this paper, we analyze the link budget for a satellite-based NB-IoT network, having as a baseline the latest 3GPP specifications regarding the system level parameters. Additionally, we provide some simulation results as a benchmark for further study and discuss the impact that different power budget levels at the receiver would have in the overall system design.

The remainder of the paper is structured as follows. In the next section, we give a brief overview of the NB-IoT technology. Section 3 is devoted to the link budget analysis. Section 4 presents the impact of the link budget in the overall system design and the concluding remarks are given in Sect. 5.

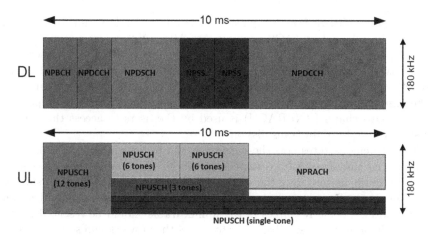

Fig. 1. NB-IoT Radio Frame Design [20]

2   NB-IoT Overview

The aim of this section is to recall only some important information related to the NB-IoT technology, which will be useful for a better understanding of the other sections of the paper.

2.1   General Features

The following features have been introduced in LTE Release 13 for NB-IoT [8]: (a) Support of massive number of low-throughput devices (around 52547) within a cell coverage; (b) Ultra-low complexity and low-cost devices; (c) Improved power consumption efficiency to allow battery life of more than ten years. The NB-IoT system requires a bandwidth of 180 kHz in order to operate. This also corresponds to a physical resource block (PRB) in LTE, since they are designed to co-exist. Based on where the NB-IoT carrier is placed within the LTE carrier there can be identified three operational modes: in-band, guard-band and stand-alone. The downlink transmission uses the conventional Orthogonal Frequency Division Multiple Access (OFDMA) with 15 kHz subcarrier spacing (SCS), whereas the uplink transmission uses the Single Carrier Frequency Division Multiple Access (SC-FDMA) with 3,75 SCS or 15 kHz SCS. For the uplink, both single-tone (ST) and multi-tone (MT) transmissions (i.e., 3, 6, and 12 subcarriers) are supported.

2.2   PHY Channels and Signals

There are three downlink physical channels in NB-IoT. The narrowband physical broadcast channel (NPBCH) sends the information related to the cell and network configuration. The narrowband physical downlink control channel (NPD-CCH) sends all the control signals regarding important procedures such as paging, random access, and data transmission. The narrowband physical downlink shared channel (NPDSCH) is responsible for sending the data and control information, acknowledgment (ACK) or negative ACK (NACK) of a Hybrid Automatic Repeat reQuest (HARQ) process, from the base station to the users.

Only two channels exist in the uplink. The narrowband physical uplink shared channel (NPUSCH) is used for sending user data transmission from the users to the base station or control information (ACK/NACK). Narrowband physical random access channel (NPRACH) is used by the users to access the network and synchronize for data transmission.

Figure 1 demonstrates how these channels can be scheduled in downlink and uplink in the time-frequency resources of the NB-IoT radio frame. It can be noted that in the uplink, since there exist different transmission modes, using less subcarriers in the frequency domain would result in a longer channel in the time domain. Besides, some resources in the uplink frame should be reserved for the NPRACH in order to allow other users to access the network and synchronize for uplink data transmission. Contrarily, in the downlink transmission, the channels are multiplexed in time, since one channel occupies all the available frequency resources of 180 kHz. An important aspect worth mentioning here is that the transmission can be configured with different modulation and coding schemes (MCS), causing this way different performance gain, device energy consumption, capacity and coverage levels. Last but not least, an important feature of NB-IoT is the use of the repetition code. This means that each channel can be repeated multiple times in time in order to improve the signal to noise ratio (SNR), thus extending the coverage. Together with the MCS selection, the number of repetition used would determine the overall system performance.

3 Satellite Link Budget Formula

In a telecommunication system, the link budget analysis is done to relate the power at the receiver with regard to the power at the transmitter, accounting for signal gains and losses in the propagation medium. By neglecting the interference, the link budget between a transmitter and a receiver in free space is given by the carrier power over noise density (C/N) as a function of other system and link parameters. The general formula of the link budget, accounting for all the gains and looses in the propagation medium from transmitter to receiver and neglecting the interference, is given as follows [3]:

$$\frac{C}{N}(dB) = EIRP(dBW) + \frac{G_r}{T}(dBi/K) - FSPL(dB) - A_{loss}(dB) - Ad_{loss}(dB)$$

$$- K\left(\frac{dBW/K}{Hz}\right) - 10 \cdot log_{10}(BW) \quad (1)$$

Let us now clarify each of the above parameters one by one.

– $EIRP$ is the effective isotopic radiated power of the transmitting antenna and can be calculated as:

$$EIRP = 10 \cdot log_{10}(G_T P_T) \quad (2)$$

where P_T is the transmitting antenna power and G_T is the gain.

– G_r/T is the figure of merit at the receiver having antenna gain G_r and equivalent system temperature T derived by the following:

$$\frac{G_r}{T} = G_r(dBi) - NF(dB) - 10 \cdot log_{10}(T_o + (T_a - T_o) \cdot 10^{-0.1 \cdot NF}) \quad (3)$$

where G_r is the gain of the receiving antenna, NF represents the noise figure, T_o is the ambient temperature and T_a is the antenna temperature.

– $FSPL$ is the free space path loss given by:

$$FSPL = 10 \cdot log_{10}(\frac{4\pi D}{c/f})^2 \quad (4)$$

with carrier frequency f, speed of light c and slant range D expressed as:

$$D = -R_E \cdot sin(\alpha) + \sqrt{R_E^2 \cdot sin(\alpha)^2 + h_s + 2 \cdot R_E \cdot h_s} \quad (5)$$

The slant range is the distance from the user device to the satellite and it can be noted from the formula that it is determined by the radius of Earth R_E, satellite elevation angle α and satellite altitude h_s.

– A_{loss} and Ad_{loss} represent the atmospheric looses due to gases, rain fades etc., and additional looses due to feeder link.

– BW is the communication bandwidth and K is the Boltzman constant.

3.1 Simulation Parameters and Results

The goal of radio link design is to guarantee a reliable communication between a transmitter and receiver. In the context of NB-IoT systems, link reliability is evaluated through the block error rate (BLER) associated with the specific MCS, which depends on the available SNR. By utilizing Eq. 1, it is possible to calculate the SNR (or written as C/N) at the receiver under specific system parameters, both in the downlink and uplink transmission. The user terminal parameters are the ones defined in the NB-IoT standard for 3GPP Class 3 devices [1], whereas the link parameters can be taken from the 3GPP specification for 5G over NTN [3], summarized in Table 1. Moreover, we leave on purpose undefined the satellite parameters (EIRP in downlink and G/T in uplink) because these are the ones that should be carefully designed before launching new satellites to support NB-IoT services or check whether the existing ones meet the power budget requirements. Changing these satellite parameters would directly affect the received SNR.

We use the link level performance results, shown in Appendix, to determine the required SNR values corresponding to a 10% BLER at the first HARQ transmission. Different MCS levels in NB-IoT can achieve different spectral efficiency as shown in Table 3. Therefore, combining these results with the link budget formula in Eq. 1, it is possible to obtain the spectral efficiency as a function of satellite EIRP for downlink case and G/T for uplink case, as illustrated in Fig. 2,

Table 1. Link budget parameters [3].

Link parameters	Downlink	Uplink
Carrier frequency (GHz)	2	2
Bandwidth (kHz)	180	3.75, 15, 45, 90, 180
Subcarrier spacing (kHz)	15	3.75, 15
Satellite altitude for LEO (km)	600	600
Satellite altitude for GEO (km)	35786	35786
Minimum elevation Angle (degree)	30	30
Atmospheric loss LEO and GEO (dB)	0.5	0.5
Additional loss LEO and GEO (dB)	1	1
Channel model	AWGN	AWGN
Terminal parameters		
Terminal type	3GPP Class 3	3GPP Class 3
Antenna type	Omnidirectional	Omnidirectional
Receiver antenna gain (dBi)	0	-
Terminal noise figure (dB)	9	-
Terminal ambient temperature (K)	290	-
Terminal antenna temperature (K)	290	-
Terminal transmit power (dBm)	-	23
Terminal transmit antenna gain (dBi)	-	0

3 and 4. We have taken into account only Low Earth Orbit (LEO) and Geostationary (GEO) satellite, with the corresponding altitudes given in the Table 1, because these are the ones considered in the latest 3GPP studies.

It can be noted that, in the downlink case, in order to enable an NB-IoT system capable of achieving the highest possible spectral efficiency, it is needed a minimum EIRP of 25 dBW for a LEO satellite at 600 km altitude and 57 dBW for a GEO satellite at 35786 km altitude. Having a higher EIRP at the satellite does not give any further gain since these are the NB-IoT system limitations. On the other hand, in case these EIRP values are not guaranteed, still it is possible to close the link, but with lower spectral efficiency.

In the uplink transmission, the analysis is a bit more complex due to the existence of several transmission modes. For a 12-carriers transmission mode it is required a minimum G/T of −2 dB/K for a LEO satellite and 28 dB/K for a GEO satellite. In case of lower values of G/T, the link can still be closed by reaching the peak spectral efficiency, but by using the other transmission modes (e.g. 1, 3 or 6 subcarriers) for the SC-FDMA signal. However, even though the peak spectral efficiency is guaranteed by means of different transmission modes, this will have an impact on the overall system design, as we will analyze in the following section.

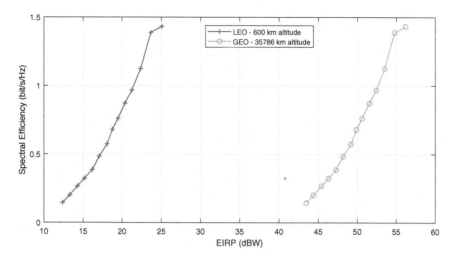

Fig. 2. Link budget result for downlink transmission.

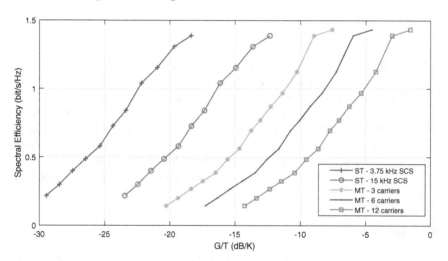

Fig. 3. Link budget result for uplink transmission, LEO satellite.

4 Link Budget Impact in System Design

Choosing one transmission mode or another, or sacrificing the spectral efficiency for the sake of closing the communication link, will directly impact the scheduling of the uplink and downlink channels. Consequently, the whole NB-IoT system will be affected, including important aspects such as delay, capacity and energy consumption. In this section, we will treat each of them separately, outlining some system design trade-offs that should be considered when designing a non-terrestrial NB-IoT network.

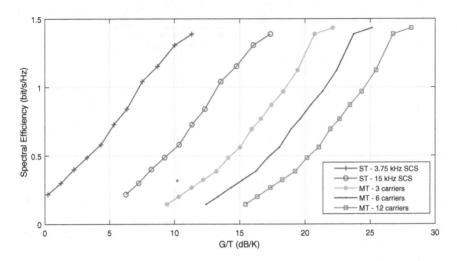

Fig. 4. Link budget result for uplink transmission, GEO satellite.

4.1 Delay

In the downlink case, a lower spectral efficiency means that less useful data can be sent through NPDCCH, which is responsible for user scheduling. As a consequence, since we can send less useful information through this channel, the users have to wait for a longer time until they get all the necessary information to schedule their uplink transmission. As a matter of fact, this would cause a delay in the overall system. In the uplink transmission, being constraint of using less tones due to a lower G/T, would result in longer channels in time. Thus, the base station is forced to wait more time to receive a certain data packet by the user device.

4.2 Capacity

The capacity of the NB-IoT system has to do with the number of user devices that can access the network and be satisfied with service. The more frequent the NPRACH is sent in the uplink frame, the larger the probability that more devices can access the network. However, if we are constraint to use less resources for transmission in the frequency domain (less subcarriers) because of a low satellite G/T, less frequent the NPRACH can be sent since the radio frame would be occupied by the long NPUSCH in time of other users. This would significantly limit the number of devices that can access the network.

4.3 Energy Consumption

As we already emphasized in the introduction, the extended battery life is a very important feature of the NB-IoT technology. For this reason, the more often the devices fall into deep sleep mode, the more battery can be saved. However, this would require very short transmissions in time, which in our NB-IoT over satellite scenario can be impossible due to satellite power limitations. Again like already emphasized, closing the link by using less frequency resources or a lower MCS (lower spectral efficiency) is possible in such situations. However, this would translate in a longer transmission time interval (TTI) and less frequent deep sleep modes by the user device, thus more battery will be consumed.

4.4   Other Considerations

It is worth reminding here that the above-shown link budget results are for the BLER target of 10%. By using the HARQ operation the link reliability would be improved because the same packed would be retransmitted if a NACK is received by the user or base station. Due to the presence of the satellite channel, the HARQ operation would cause a significant delay, which is much larger than the one experienced in a terrestrial network. Therefore, it has recently been discussed in the 3GPP the idea of deactivating the HARQ operation for NTN [2]. Doing this would require a BLER target adjustment (e.g. 1% BLER), thus more EIRP and G/T at the satellite for being able to close the communication link. Again, all the above-mentioned trade-offs should be considered in the system design.

5   Conclusions

In this paper, we studied the radio link budgets in order to support a reliable communication of IoT user devices with the corresponding base station in an NB-IoT over satellite system. The link and device parameters were chosen in accordance with the latest 3GPP specifications, while the satellite parameters were left open for design. The achievable spectral efficiency as a function of satellite antenna EIRP and G/T were shown through numerical simulations for both, LEO and GEO satellite, and under different transmission modes. It was shown that, in the downlink case, to enable an NB-IoT system capable of achieving the highest possible spectral efficiency, it is needed a minimum EIRP of 25 dBW for a LEO satellite at 600 km altitude and 57 dBW for a GEO satellite at 35786 km altitude. In the uplink, for a 12-carrier transmission mode it is required a minimum G/T of -2 dB/K for a LEO satellite and 28 dB/K for a GEO satellite. In case of lower values of G/T, the link can still be closed by using the other transmission modes (e.g. 1,3 or 6 subcarriers) for the SC-FDMA signal or sacrificing in spectral efficiency. Last but not least, the impact that different power budget would have in important features of NB-IoT technology, such as delay, capacity and power consumption, was discussed and analyzed.

Appendix: NB-IoT PHY Layer Simulation

To derive the required SNR value for each MCS level assuring BLER target of 10^{-1}, the NB-IoT PHY layer is implemented in Matlab and the performance in terms of BLER vs SNR is evaluated through numerical simulations. The baseband block diagram of the simulator is given in Fig. 5 and the simulation parameters are summarized in Table 2. Overall, the following steps are performed for the BLER, SNR and spectral efficiency (SE) calculations:

- The bits are transmitted in block according to the transmission block size (TBS) given in the standard [7]. Changing the TBS would change the transmission code rate, hence enabling different performance gains for different MCS levels.
- The OFDM/SC-FDM baseband waveform generation follow the steps determined in the standard [6]. Please note that the N-point DFT/IDFT is applied only for SC-FDM waveform.
- The channel used is an additive white Gaussian noise (AWGN) channel.
- The receiver operations are performed and the erroneous TBS are counted. We run the simulations in order to guarantee at least 100 erroneous TBS for each SNR value.
- Obtaining the BLER-SNR curves, we find the minimum value of SNR that guarantees the BLER target of 10^{-1} for each MCS level. We repeat the simulation for downlink and uplink under different transmission modes.
- To calculate the spectral efficiency for each MCS level and transmission mode, the following formula is used:

$$SE = \frac{TBS/TTI}{BW}(bit/s/Hz) \tag{6}$$

where TTI is the transmission time interval corresponding to a certain TBS in each MCS level. Please note that in each MCS level we choose the TBS that gives the maximum throughput.
- Please note that the performance of downlink and multi-tone uplink are almost the same (only different for some MCS). This is because table 16.5.1.2-1 and 16.5.1.2-1 from [7], containing the TBS value for each MCS, are almost identical.

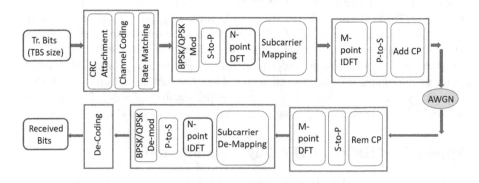

Fig. 5. Baseband Simulator Block Diagram

Table 2. Simulation parameters.

Parameter	Uplink MT	Uplink ST	Downlink
N FFT	128	128	128
Bandwidth	(45, 90, 180) kHz	(3.75, 15) kHz	180 kHz
SCS (kHz)	15 kHz	(3.75, 15) kHz	15 kHz
Modulation format	SC-FDM	SC-FDM	OFDM
Modulation order	QPSK	BPSK, QPSK	QPSK
MCS selection	Table 16.5.1.2-2 [7]	Table 16.5.1.2-2 [7]	Table 16.4.1.5.1-1 [7]
Coding scheme	Turbo Code	Turbo Code	Turbo Code
CRC bits	24	24	24
MCS range	0–13	0–10	0–13
Channel	AWGN	AWGN	AWGN

Table 3. Simulation results.

MCS	Uplink MT		Uplink ST		Downlink	
	SNR (dB)	SE (bit/s/Hz)	SNR (dB)	SE (bit/s/Hz)	SNR (dB)	SE (bit/s/Hz)
0	−5.8	0.1444	−4.2	0.2167	−5.8	0.1444
1	−4.9	0.2	−3.2	0.3	−4.9	0.2
2	−3.9	0.2667	−2.2	0.4	−3.9	0.2667
3	−3	0.324	−1.2	0.4867	−3	0.324
4	−2	0.3867	−0.1	0.58	−2	0.3867
5	−1.1	0.4844	0.9	0.7267	−1.1	0.4844
6	−0.2	0.5611	1.9	0.8417	−0.1	0.5733
7	0.7	0.6944	3.1	1.0417	0.6	0.68
8	1.4	0.7689	4.3	1.1533	1.3	0.7611
9	2.2	0.8722	5.6	1.3083	2.2	0.8722
10	3.1	0.9689	6.9	1.3887	3.1	0.9689
11	4.2	1.1244			4.2	1.1244
12	5.5	1.3889			5.5	1.3889
13	6.9	1.4333			6.9	1.4333

References

1. 3GPP: LTE, Evolved Universal Terrestrial Radio Access (E-UTRA), User Equipment (UE) radio transmission and reception (Release 14). Technical Specification (TS) 36.101, 3rd Generation Partnership Project (3GPP), April 2017
2. 3GPP: Discussion on HARQ for NTN, TSG RAN WG1 Meeting nr. 96bis, Xian, China, R1–1904859, 3rd Generation Partnership Project (3GPP), April 2019
3. 3GPP: Discussion on link budget for NTN, TSG RAN WG1 Meeting nr. 96bis, Xian, China, R1–1903998, 3rd Generation Partnership Project (3GPP), April 2019

4. 3GPP: Technical Specification Group Radio Access Network, Study on New Radio (NR) to support non terrestrial networks, (Release 15). Technical report (TR) 38.811, 3rd Generation Partnership Project (3GPP), version 15.0.0, June 2018
5. 3GPP: LTE, Evolved Universal Terrestrial Radio Access (E-UTRA), Radio Resource Control (RRC), Protocol Specification, (Release 13). Technical Specification (TS) 36.331, 3rd Generation Partnership Project (3GPP), version 13.2.0, August 2016
6. 3GPP: LTE, Evolved Universal Terrestrial Radio Access (E-UTRA), Multiplexing and channel coding, Version 15.3.0, (Release 15). Technical Specification (TS) 36.212, 3rd Generation Partnership Project (3GPP), version 15.3.0, October 2018
7. 3GPP: LTE, Evolved Universal Terrestrial Radio Access (E-UTRA), Physical layer procedures; (Release 14). Technical Specification (TS) 36.213, 3rd Generation Partnership Project (3GPP), version 14.7.0, August 2018
8. 3GPP: Cellular system support for ultra-low complexity and low throughput Internet of Things (CIoT) (Release 13). Technical report (TR) 45.820, 3rd Generation Partnership Project (3GPP), November 2015
9. Al-Fuqaha, A., Guizani, M., Mohammadi, M., Aledhari, M., Ayyash, M.: Internet of Things: a survey on enabling technologies, protocols, and applications. IEEE Commun. Surv. Tutorials 17(4), 2347–2376 (2015). https://doi.org/10.1109/COMST.2015.2444095
10. Alagha, N.: Satellite air interface evolutions in the 5G and IoT Era. SIGMETRICS Perform. Eval. Rev. 46(3), 93–95 (2019). https://doi.org/10.1145/3308897.3308941
11. Cioni, S., De Gaudenzi, R., Del Rio Herrero, O., Girault, N.: On the satellite role in the era of 5G massive machine type communications. IEEE Netw. 32(5), 54–61 (2018). https://doi.org/10.1109/MNET.2018.1800024
12. CISCO white paper: Cisco visual networking index: global mobile data traffic forecast update (2015–2020)
13. Cluzel, S., et al.: 3GPP NB-IoT coverage extension using LEO satellites. In: 2018 IEEE 87th Vehicular Technology Conference (VTC Spring), pp. 1–5, June 2018. https://doi.org/10.1109/VTCSpring.2018.8417723
14. Gineste, M., et al.: Narrowband IoT service provision to 5G user equipment via a satellite component. In: 2017 IEEE Globecom Workshops (GC Wkshps), pp. 1–4, December 2017. https://doi.org/10.1109/GLOCOMW.2017.8269209
15. Kodheli, O., Andrenacci, S., Maturo, N., Chatzinotas, S., Zimmer, F.: Resource allocation approach for differential doppler reduction in NB-IoT over LEO satellite. In: 2018 9th Advanced Satellite Multimedia Systems Conference and the 15th Signal Processing for Space Communications Workshop (ASMS/SPSC), pp. 1–8, September 2018. https://doi.org/10.1109/ASMS-SPSC.2018.8510724
16. Kodheli, O., Andrenacci, S., Maturo, N., Chatzinotas, S., Zimmer, F.: An uplink UE group-based scheduling technique for 5G mMTC systems over LEO satellite. IEEE Access 7, 67413–67427 (2019). https://doi.org/10.1109/ACCESS.2019.2918581
17. Kovács, I.Z., et al.: Lte IoT link budget and coverage performance in practical deployments. In: 2017 IEEE 28th Annual International Symposium on Personal, Indoor, and Mobile Radio Communications (PIMRC), pp. 1–6, October 2017. https://doi.org/10.1109/PIMRC.2017.8292260
18. Palattella, M.R., et al.: Internet of Things in the 5G era: enablers, architecture, and business models. IEEE J. Sel. Areas Commun. 34(3), 510–527 (2016). https://doi.org/10.1109/JSAC.2016.2525418

19. Ratasuk, R., Tan, J., Mangalvedhe, N., Ng, M.H., Ghosh, A.: Analysis of NB-IoT deployment in LTE guard-band. In: 2017 IEEE 85th Vehicular Technology Conference (VTC Spring), pp. 1–5, June 2017. https://doi.org/10.1109/VTCSpring.2017.8108184

20. Ratasuk, R., Vejlgaard, B., Mangalvedhe, N., Ghosh, A.: Nb-IoT system for M2M communication. In: 2016 IEEE Wireless Communications and Networking Conference Workshops (WCNCW), pp. 428–432, April 2016. https://doi.org/10.1109/WCNCW.2016.7552737

21. Scalise, S., Niebla, C.P., De Gaudenzi, R., Del Rio Herrero, O., Finocchiaro, D., Arcidiacono, A.: S-MIM: a novel radio interface for efficient messaging services over satellite. IEEE Commun. Mag. 51(3), 119–125 (2013). https://doi.org/10.1109/MCOM.2013.6476875

22. Xu, L.D., He, W., Li, S.: Internet of Things in Industries: a survey. IEEE Trans. Industr. Inf. 10(4), 2233–2243 (2014). https://doi.org/10.1109/TII.2014.2300753

Performance Improvement of Wireless and Sensor Networks

A Software-Defined Retransmission Mechanism to Manage Real-Time Traffic in Wi-Fi Networks

Gianluca Cena⬤, Stefano Scanzio(✉)⬤, Lucia Seno⬤, Adriano Valenzano⬤, and Claudio Zunino⬤

National Research Council of Italy (CNR-IEIIT), Corso Duca degli Abruzzi 24, 10129 Torino, Italy
{gianluca.cena,stefano.scanzio,lucia.seno,adriano.valenzano, claudio.zunino}@ieiit.cnr.it

Abstract. In several application contexts, keeping transmission latencies on a wireless network bounded is required. When high bandwidth is additionally demanded, IEEE 802.11 is certainly a reasonable choice. Reliable data delivery is customarily achieved through automatic retransmission upon errors. In Wi-Fi, retries are managed in hardware by adapters. Unfortunately, this constrains the possible sequences with which messages are sent on air, which increases latency and worsens communication determinism. Previous works showed that such limitations can be overcome by having frames retransmissions managed in software by conventional user-space applications. To do so, slight modifications are needed to device drivers to provide the required functions.

In this paper, a comprehensive performance analysis of software retransmission mechanisms is performed, which highlights that the related overhead is negligible when compared with the provided advantages and confirms that finely scheduling real-time traffic over Wi-Fi is actually possible. A pilot implementation showed that tangible improvements can be obtained by using a scheduling policy with packet granularity.

Keywords: Real-time communications · Software-Defined Retransmissions · SDRet · IEEE 802.11 · Traffic scheduling · SDMAC

1 Introduction

Many application contexts exist where a distributed system, made up of a plurality of nodes interconnected by means of a wireless network, demands determinism and bounded latency. A notable example is given by disaster management [1] but, to a lesser extent, also smart/precision agriculture [2] and building

This work was partially supported by Regione Piemonte and the Ministry of Education, University, and Research of Italy in the POR FESR 2014/2020 framework, Call "Piattaforma tecnologica Fabbrica Intelligente", Project "Human centered Manufacturing Systems" (application number 312-36).

© Springer Nature Switzerland AG 2019
M. R. Palattella et al. (Eds.): ADHOC-NOW 2019, LNCS 11803, pp. 275–289, 2019.
https://doi.org/10.1007/978-3-030-31831-4_19

automation [3] may benefit from a better communication quality. In particular, requirements about reliability and timings are quite common in industrial environments, and techniques for improving behavior of wireless networks in such scenarios are a thriving research topic. A remarkable example is represented by control/monitoring applications characterized by either hard or soft real-time constraints. In the former case deadlines cannot be exceeded, while in the latter deadline misses can be tolerated as long as they happen rarely.

Among the available wireless communication technologies operating in the unlicensed bands (without the need of a subscription) and featuring very-high·performance, IEEE 802.11 (Wi-Fi) [4] is probably the most popular one. An effective way to increase communication quality (in terms of reliable and timely data delivery) in such a kind of networks is to rely on a suitable scheduler (either centralized or distributed) that manages the packet transmission sequence on air in such a way to minimize the likelihood of deadline misses.

To increase reliability, Wi-Fi makes use of a conventional Automatic Repeat-reQuest (ARQ) mechanism based on acknowledgement (ACK) frames. Each time the ACK frame associated to a given data frame does not return back to the transmitter STA within a specified time, a new frame containing the same data is sent again. The number of transmissions (initial attempt plus retries) is bounded to a maximum value, known as *retry limit* (R).

In commercial Wi-Fi adapters, retransmissions are managed automatically by the hardware. This does not allow an adequate level of granularity in accessing the wireless communication support (i.e., a single frame transmission), as required by many scheduling algorithms and distributed applications demanding bounded latencies. As a consequence, the transmission of data packets with higher priority may be delayed due to the fact that the adapter is busy for the transmission of other, lower priority data. This way, the likelihood that these packets could miss their deadline increases. To overcome such limitation, specific modifications can be brought to the device driver of Wi-Fi adapters (a wide range of products compatible with this technique are available off-the-shelf) that allow to manage the retransmission process directly in software (SW). We name this technique Software-Defined Retransmissions (SDRet).

In this paper, the feasibility of SDRet, implemented by means of applications executed at the user-space level, was assessed, and its behavior compared with the existing retransmission mechanisms, which are automatically managed by the hardware (HW) of the Wi-Fi adapter. Then, as a possible example about the delivery of real-time deadline-constrained traffic, the performance achieved by the classic Earliest Deadline First (EDF) scheduling algorithm, with both SDRet and conventional HW retransmissions, was evaluated. It is worth noting that SDRet is orthogonal to other techniques aimed at improving the communication quality (e.g., those based on rate adaptation or network coding algorithms). In addition, SDRet eases research and prototyping for these and other techniques, because it allows to set with a fine frame-level granularity some Wi-Fi parameters.

With respect to the research literature, and in particular [5,6], which describe and test a prototype implementation of an enabling technology for SDRet called Software-Defined MAC (SDMAC), i.e., an Application Programming Interface (API) that permits to interact directly with the network adapter, this paper contains four new main contributions: (1) a new implementation is developed where frames retransmission is performed directly at the user-space level, exploiting new SDMAC features; (2) performance analysis also includes the code that manages a whole sequence of transmissions in user-space, and not only the part of software devoted to managing the exchange of a single frame; (3) experimental results are obtained for a real channel with concurrent interfering traffic (in [5,6] a channel was selected with no interfering load); and, (4) a real use case that practically demonstrates the advantages of managing transmissions at the user-space level is considered and performance is evaluated.

The next Sect. 2 introduces SDRet and provides details on how it was implemented and the benefits it achieves, while Sect. 3 describes the testbed we set up and the measurement system. In Sect. 4, performance of SDRet is compared with conventional Wi-Fi. Section 5 analyzes SDRet in a real application aimed at delivery deadline-constrained real-time traffic. Finally, Sect. 6 concludes this paper.

Table 1. Table of most important abbreviations.

Abbr	Description
ACK	Acknowledgement frame
CDF	Cumulative distrubution function
CW	Contention window
DFP	Delivery failure probability
DSP	Delivery success probability
EDF	Earliest deadline First
HW	hardware
SDMAC	Software-defined MAC
SDRet	Software-defined retransmissions
STA	Station
STD	Standard
SW	Software

2   Software-Defined Retransmissions

Software defined radios [7,8] make it possible to customize Wi-Fi operation. Unfortunately, this requires a non-trivial implementation of the related functions, which usually consists in the complex task of programming an FPGA [7]. Under the Linux operating system and for some Wi-Fi adapters, many new

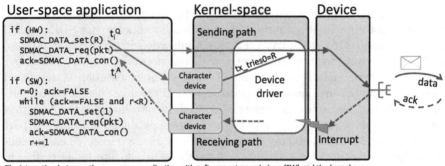

Fig. 1. Schema of the application used to manage HW and SW retransmissions.

features can be implemented and tuned directly by modifying the code of the device driver, leaving the hardware and the firmware of the adapter unchanged. This permits, with relatively low effort, to practically implement techniques like those based on TDMA [9], or Reactive Duplication Avoidance (RDA) methods used in seamless redundancy to improve both reliability and latencies [10,11], which require a fine control of the frames that are exchanged through the wireless medium.

In [5,6], a software implementation of SDMAC, which includes an API and the related mechanisms for managing frames transmission by means of a user-space application, was described, and the overhead (additional delays) it causes on communications was evaluated. One of the main purposes of SDMAC is to enable applications to access the basic transmission services offered by the wireless adapter, and to obtain the outcome of transmissions, i.e., *ACK* or *ACK-timeout* events, which correspond to a successful or unsuccessfully delivery of the frame, respectively. In this paper, SDMAC was employed as the interface to interact with the adapter. In particular, it was used to send a frame and to wait for the related outcome. Then, an application was implemented, which makes use of SDMAC to manage retransmissions in software.

Figure 1 sketches the relevant components of this application. In the sending path, SDMAC makes use of the function SDMAC_DATA_req() to send frames[1]. An *ACK* event is generated inside the device driver of the transmitting node each time it receives the *ACK* frame related to the frame it has previously sent. Conversely, each time an *ACKtimeout* timer expires (which implies that the *ACK* frame was not received timely) the corresponding *ACKtimeout* event is generated. To detect these two events, the code of the device driver needs to be slightly modified. For this reason, for the implementation of SDMAC and the subsequent experimental campaign, a wireless adapter managed by an open-source device

---

[1] The SDMAC_DATA_req() function, and consequently the sending path, relies on common Linux POSIX *raw sockets* and on the sendto() function.

driver was selected. In particular, this work relies on the popular `ath9k` device driver. The outcome of the event is then delivered from the device driver to the user-space level by means of a *character device*. A *character device* is one of the common software components made available by the Linux operating system to manage unbuffered communication between user and kernel spaces, and vice versa. Even if other more deterministic methods to transfer an event from user to kernel spaces exist [12], the use of a *character device* can be considered suitable for Wi-Fi [6]. The user-space application, which in the meanwhile was blocked on the `SDMAC_DATA_con()` function[2] waiting for the outcome of the last transmission, is released just after the outcome is written in the character device by means of a piece of code we added in a specific position of the device driver. The application manages retransmissions in software. In particular, each time the outcome is *ACKtimeout*, the application transmits again the same data, until the number of retries reaches the retry limit R. If the limit is reached and also the last retry is unsuccessful, the data transmission is labeled as lost.

In this new version of SDMAC, two functions were added to configure the values of the retry limit R and the contention window CW, respectively. In particular, the function `SDMAC_DATA_set()` is invoked, to set the retry limit R, just before the function `SDMAC_DATA_req()`, which is the one devoted to send the frame. It is worth remarking that the value of the retry limit R in `ath9k` device drivers is associated to the single packet (i.e., a different number of retransmissions can be associated to each packet). In this specific implementation, the `SDMAC_DATA_set()` function writes the value R for the next packet transmission inside a character device. In today's Wi-Fi adapters, the typical algorithm used to select the frame transmission rate is Minstrel [13]. Based on past statistics about the quality of the wireless channel, it configures for each packet queued in the adapter four TX series, i.e., four pairs of data containing the number of transmissions for a specific transmission rate. If all the transmissions of the first TX series fail (i.e., no *ACK* frame is received), the transmitter uses the setting of the second TX series, and so on. If, after the transmissions associated to the last TX series, the packet does not reach the destination, it is considered as lost. The device driver, in correspondence to the code devoted to set the number of transmission attempts for any of the rate series of the Minstrel algorithm, sets a number of transmissions equal to R for the first series, and 0 for the other three series. In details, we realized a software that sets the values of these four fields as `tx_tries0=R`, `tx_tries1=0`, `tx_tries2=0` and `tx_tries3=0`, by modifying the function `ath_buf_set_rate()` in the file `xmit.c` of the device driver.

Instead, the value of the contention window CW is modified by setting the values of the two fields `DATA_CW_MIN` and `DATA_CW_MAX` of the register `D_LCL_IFS` of the device driver to the same value CW. This operation can be performed in the function `ath9k_hw_resettxqueue()` in the file `mac.c` of the device driver.

---

[2] The `SDMAC_DATA_con()` function was implemented as a blocking `read()` system call executed on the file descriptor of the *character device*. In kernel-space, conventional kernel semaphores were used to make the `read()` system call blocking.

3   Testbed and Measurement System

The testbed is composed of a PC with the Intel® B86 Chipset, 4 GB of 1600 MHz DDR3 Dual Channel RAM, and an Intel® i3-4150 CPU running at 3.5 GHz. The PC executes the Linux kernel v. 3.14.61 compiled with the optimization reported in [6]. The wireless adapter is a dual-band TP-Link TL-WDN4800 managed by the version 4.4.2 of the ath9k device driver. It was configured to use channel 165 in the 5 GHz band. This channel was not in use by other Wi-Fi STAs in nearby networks, allowing us to precisely tune the amount of interfering traffic by purposely injecting it on the wireless medium.

A generic AP was configured in infrastructure mode and the Wi-Fi adapter of the PC was associated to it. The only role played by the AP in our analysis is to timely reply to data frames sent by the STA with the related ACK frame. Consequently, the results reported in this paper are valid also for other operation modes (e.g., ad-hoc).

In addition, we disabled the rate adaptation algorithm by fixing the transmission rate to 54 Mb/s. The main reason for this is that, we wished to obtain results for transmission latencies that do not include the jitter caused by changes of the transmission bit rate, and that are independent from the specific rate adaptation algorithm used to estimate the best transmission speed. In fact, it is known that the Minstrel rate adaptation algorithm is not the best solution for applications requiring low and bounded latencies [13].

It is worth remarking that the proposed testbed can be exploited for experimentation on rate adaptation algorithms as well. As a matter of fact, only minor modifications are needed to the function SDMAC_DATA_set() to allow SDMAC to regulate, on a per-frame basis, the transmission rate of exchanged frames.

In all the experiments, the payload size was set to 50 Bytes. This relatively small size was selected according to the typical width of process data exchanged in cyber-physical systems, which consist in small data packets that derive from digital/analogue signals acquired from sensors or set-points for actuators.

In all the experiments, the contention windows CW was set to a constant value. This is not a limitation, because transmission of real-time traffic likely benefits from a non-exponential increase of CW, so as to keep communication latencies bounded. The value of CW for this kind of traffic is typically changed in the transmission process (initial attempt and retries) of the same data packet between two possible values. For instance, for the highest priority traffic defined in the standard IEEE 802.11e (i.e., the AC_VO access category, which is used in Wi-Fi to provide a high quality of service), CW can assume only two values, namely $CW = 3$ and $CW = 7$. In fact, the defaults values for this AC are $CW_{Min} = 3$ and $CW_{Max} = 7$.

Latencies were obtain by reading a specific register of the CPU, i.e., the Time Stamp Counter (TSC). The TSC is increased by one on every CPU clock cycle and, since the operating system does not require any context switch to read its content, it represents a very precise and accurate way to acquire timestamps. The only important precaution, to obtain correct measures, is to disable CPU frequency scaling.

Each experiment consists in the transmission of $2N$ data packets $p_1, p_2, ...,$ p_{2N}, of which N packets are managed using HW retransmissions and N using SW retransmissions. To obtain results that do not depend on the characteristics of the channel, which could vary significantly across the whole experiment, in terms of the error rate, we decide to interleave HW and SW retransmissions. Consequently, the real sequence of packets on air is $p_1^{HW}, p_2^{SW}, p_3^{HW}, ..., p_{2N}^{SW}$.

Since each packet p_i can be retransmitted in the case of errors, the actual sequence of frames exchanged over the network is:

$$m_1^{HW,1}, m_1^{HW,2}, ..., m_1^{HW,r_1}, m_2^{SW,1}, m_2^{SW,2}, ..., m_2^{SW,r_2}, ... \qquad (1)$$

where the sequence of frames $m_1^{HW,1}, m_1^{HW,2}, ..., m_1^{HW,r_1}$ refers to packet p_1^{HW}, the sequence of frames $m_2^{SW,1}, m_2^{SW,2}, ..., m_2^{SW,r_2}$ to packet p_2^{SW}, and so on.

The latency for the transmission of packet p_i and the reception of the related outcome from the device driver, which consists on the whole of r attempts (the initial transmission m_i^1 plus any possible subsequent retransmissions $m_i^2, ..., m_i^r$, with $r \leq R$), is obtained as $d_i = t_i^Q - t_i^A$. It includes the network time to transmit data, the software time used to interface the device driver to the application running in user-space, the software for managing retransmissions, and delayes related to the hardware. The first timestamp t_i^Q is acquired when p_i is inserted in the transmitter queue, managed at the user-space level. The second timestamp t_i^A corresponds to the reception of the final ACK or $ACKtimeout$ outcome event concerning the transmission of packet p_i, and coincides with the event related to the transmission of frame m_i^r.

For any experiment and for any retransmission strategy (HW and SW), we computed, and presented as results, the most common statistical indices on the set of latencies d_i. They include minimum (d_{min}), average value $(\bar{d})$, standard deviation (σ_d), 99.9-percentile $(d_{p99.9})$, 99.99-percentile $(d_{p99.99})$, and maximum (d_{max}). Instead, the fraction of lost packets (i.e., losses l) is the number of frames m_i^r that experienced an $ACKtimeout$ event over the total number N of transmitted data packets.

As previously mentioned, to have full control on the traffic exchanged in the network, experiments were purposely performed on a channel not used by any other STAs. A number of STAs were then set up to inject specifically designed interfering traffic patterns on the communication medium. Behavior of any interferer periodically commutes between two states, idle and burst. The idle state is characterized by the absence of any network activity, and its duration is obtained by means of an exponential distribution with mean value 200 ms and truncated to 20 s. In the burst state, a burst of packets is generated with a generation period of 400 μs. The number of packets within the burst was obtained with an exponential distribution with mean value 300 packets and truncated to 1500 packets. Size of packets was 1500 bytes.

For the experimental campaign, we defined two load conditions: *low load* and *high load*. The first is characterized by only one interfering STA, while the second is characterized by 3 concurrent (identically configured but independent) interfering STAs.

4   Comparison with Conventional Wi-Fi

The first set of experiments was aimed at comparing retransmissions performed in SW in user-space by means of SDRet with those performed automatically in HW by the network adapter. In this experimental campaign, all the possible combinations of the following parameters have been analyzed: HW and SW, *low load* and *high load*; $CW = 31$ and $CW = 1023$; $R = 3$, $R = 5$ and $R = 7$. Each experiment consists in sending $N = 100,000$ data packets. Consequently, we performed on the whole 24 experiments, and about 2.5 million packets were sent.

Table 2. Comparison between software-defined retransmissions (SW) and hardware retransmissions (HW), by varying the interfering load, CW width, and number R of allowed retransmissions (Latency d and losses l).

	CW	R	Type	d_{min}	$\overline{d}$	σ_d	$d_{p99.9}$	$d_{p99.99}$	d_{max}	Losses l
						[ms]				[%] ([#])
Low load	31	3	HW	0.131	0.869	0.742	4.158	5.011	5.907	0.11 (114)
			SW	0.131	0.871	0.745	4.099	5.116	6.309	0.15 (149)
		5	HW	0.131	0.869	0.743	4.219	5.036	6.863	0.01 (5)
			SW	0.131	0.870	0.749	4.262	5.379	7.655	0.01 (8)
		7	HW	0.131	0.870	0.746	4.221	5.318	6.500	0.00 (2)
			SW	0.131	0.876	0.876	4.273	5.432	6.070	0.00 (3)
	1023	3	HW	0.131	20.285	20.900	113.545	144.007	162.595	0.10 (101)
			SW	0.131	20.324	20.890	113.505	140.408	160.205	0.14 (136)
		5	HW	0.130	20.399	21.079	115.686	155.560	203.182	0.00 (2)
			SW	0.131	20.258	20.986	117.965	154.709	186.483	0.00 (0)
		7	HW	0.131	20.328	21.105	123.963	158.378	188.546	0.00 (0)
			SW	0.131	20.396	21.090	119.506	150.200	171.149	0.00 (0)
High load	31	3	HW	0.131	2.224	1.724	10.013	12.015	13.480	1.33 (1328)
			SW	0.130	2.250	1.753	10.013	11.741	13.101	1.43 (1434)
		5	HW	0.131	2.240	1.784	11.226	14.188	19.345	0.09 (94)
			SW	0.131	2.276	1.817	11.311	13.989	16.626	0.07 (75)
		7	HW	0.131	2.248	1.796	11.162	14.468	17.543	0.00 (3)
			SW	0.131	2.271	1.831	11.493	15.113	17.729	0.01 (7)
	1023	3	HW	0.131	62.617	50.889	274.381	307.781	330.607	1.76 (1761)
			SW	0.131	63.150	51.138	274.244	307.961	326.883	1.72 (1724)
		5	HW	0.131	64.006	54.027	337.337	414.416	442.612	0.12 (117)
			SW	0.131	63.897	53.929	335.568	412.538	445.880	0.09 (94)
		7	HW	0.131	64.218	54.574	355.883	445.355	531.454	0.01 (10)
			SW	0.131	64.380	54.120	343.560	423.388	550.803	0.01 (5)

Results are reported in Table 2. As expected, in all the experiments the minimum measured latency (including SW overheads) is almost the same, i.e., $d_{min} = 131\,\mu s$. This corresponds to the condition where the channel is idle at the time of transmission and no retry is performed (i.e., $r = 1$). When the channel

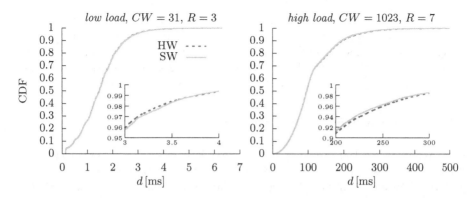

Fig. 2. CDFs for HW and SW retransmissions for the first and the last conditions of Table 2 (i.e., *low load, CW* = 31 and *R* = 3; *high load, CW* = 1023 and *R* = 7).

is sensed idle and the transmitter has already completed the backoff related to the previous transmission (this operation is sometimes called *post-backoff*), the transmitting node can immediately start the transmission of the frame, without waiting for any additional time.

In this case, the time needed to send the frame on air and to receive the corresponding ACK frame is composed of the three contributions, $T_{air} = T_{data} + T_{SIFS} + T_{ACK}$. In our experiments, $T_{data} = 36\,\mu s$, $T_{SIFS} = 44\,\mu s$ and $T_{ACK} = 16\,\mu s$, and hence $T_{air} = 96\,\mu s$. The minimum time taken by the software to manage SDRet operations is therefore $d_{min} - T_{air} = 131 - 96\,\mu s = 35\,\mu s$, which is relatively small if compared with the typical duration of frame exchanges on a wireless medium, when the payload is larger or the bit rate decreases.

As expected, both the use of large CW values (i.e., $CW = 1023$) and the amount of interfering load have a negative impact on latency. In particular, in the worst experimental condition from the point of view of latencies (i.e., *high load, CW* = 1023 and $R = 7$) the mean latency is $\bar{d} = \sim65\,ms$ and the worst-case latency d_{max} is slightly larger than 0.5s. The condition characterized by the highest number of lost data packets is obtained with *high load* and a reduced number of allowable retransmissions (i.e., $R = 3$). In this case, the fraction of losses is $l = 1.33\%$ and $l = 1.43\%$ for HW and SW retransmissions, respectively.

Regarding the main goal of this experimental campaign, that is the comparison between HW and SW retransmission mechanisms, we can notice from the results reported in the table that the two implementations are mostly indistinguishable, in terms of both latency and losses.

This is evidenced by the plots of the Cumulative Distribution Function (CDF) shown in Fig. 2, where the two most different experimental conditions reported in Table 2 (i.e., *low load, CW* = 31, $R = 3$ vs. *high load, CW* = 1023, $R = 7$) were analyzed. For any plot, the two curves associated to HW and SW retransmissions practically overlap. Taking into account specific parts of the plots, shown in the zoomed areas in the figure, it can be seen that the difference between the two curves is less than few tens of microseconds.

As expected, statistical values about the latency for SW retransmissions are always slightly larger than those referring to HW retransmissions. In fact, managing retransmissions in software has a (slight) cost from the performance point of view. Fortunately, the results in Table 2 and Fig. 2 show that SDRet remains a viable option for practically every possible application context.

5   SDRet for Real-Time Traffic

After verifying (in the previous section) that latencies for SW retransmissions (SDRet) are close to those obtained with standard (STD) HW retransmissions performed automatically by the network adapter, we analyzed the use of SDRet in a practical application. In cyber-physical systems, and in many Internet of Things (IoT) applications, data packets have typically to be delivered to destination within predefined deadlines. The transmission of deadline-constrained real-time traffic is needed, e.g., each time data acquired by sensors must be delivered to a specific node through the network within a predetermined maximum time.

To model the generation of this kind of traffic, we defined a set of real-time traffic flows $\mathcal{T} = \{\tau^1, \tau^2, ..., \tau^M\}$, where each flow τ^j is represented with the tuple of values $\tau^j = (t^j, \phi^j, \overline{T}^j, D^j)$. The queuing time of the first packet of flow j (i.e., packet p_1^j) is $t_1^{Q,j} = \phi^j$, where ϕ^j is the initial phase (or release time) and represents the time the first packet of the flow is queued in the transmission queue.

Table 3. Summary of the set of flows $\mathcal{T}$ used in the experimental campaign for the evaluation of SDRet for deadline-constrained real-time traffic.

j	Generation Pattern	ϕ^j	$\overline{T}^j$	D^j
			[ms]	
1	exp	0	50.000	5.000
2	per	1.000	50.030	10.000
3	exp	2.000	50.000	15.000
4	per	3.000	50.050	20.000
5	exp	4.000	50.000	25.000
6	per	5.000	50.070	30.000
7	exp	6.000	50.000	35.000
8	per	7.000	50.110	40.000

We modeled two generation patterns: *exp*, which follows an exponential distribution with mean value $\overline{T}^j$, and *per*, which represents a periodic generation pattern with period $\overline{T}^j$. Given the queuing time of any packet originated from flow j, in the case of an exponential (*exp*) distribution the queuing time of

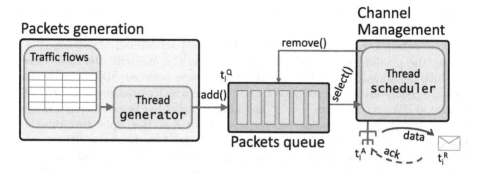

Fig. 3. Schema of the application used for the evaluation of SDRet for deadline-constrained real-time traffic.

the next packet is $t_{i+1}^{Q,j} = t_i^{Q,j} + exp(\overline{T}^j)$, where $exp(\overline{T}^j)$ represents a random value drawn from an exponential distribution with mean value $\overline{T}^j$. For the periodic (per) case, the queuing time of the next packet can be easily obtained as $t_{i+1}^{Q,j} = t_i^{Q,j} + \overline{T}^j$.

Finally, each packet of a specific flow j is characterized by a relative deadline D^j, which is related to the constraint that packet p_i^j has to be delivered to the destination within the absolute deadline $t_i^{Q,j} + D^j$.

Table 3 summarizes the set of traffic flows $\mathcal{T}$ used in this experimental campaign. In particular, for each flow we set a different initial phase ϕ^j to avoid that, at the beginning of the experiment, all packets are queued for transmission at the same time. We set different relative deadline D^j, ranging from $5ms$ to $40ms$, and for per flows we set periods $\overline{T}^j$ that are relatively primes to increase randomness of packet queuing times and order.

Figure 3 outlines the main components of the application we made for evaluating the use of SDRet to support deadline-constrained real-time traffic. In particular, a **generator** thread generates real-time traffic following the patterns defined by the traffic flows $\mathcal{T}$, and *adds* such packets to a transmission queue. Such **queue**, which is shared among the **generator** and the **scheduler** threads, is used to store packets and other information, such as the packet absolute deadline and the current number of transmission tries (i.e., how many times a packet has already been sent without obtaining a confirmation of successful delivery to destination through an *ACK* frame).

Finally, the **scheduler** thread, by applying a suitable scheduling policy, *selects* a packet from the queue and feeds it to the network adapter for transmission. Each time an *ACK* frame notifies the correct delivery of the packet, the packet is *removed* from the queue and another packet (provided that the queue is not empty) is selected for transmission. Access to the **queue** was managed by means of the typical *producer/consumer* paradigm of concurrent programming. In the context of the proposed application, there is only one producer and one consumer, i.e., the **generator** and the **scheduler** threads, respectively. The size of the queue has been configured in such a way that it never completely fills up in any of the experiments.

The scheduler is based on the EDF [14,15] scheduling algorithm that, among the pending packets in the queue, selects the one with the most close absolute deadline. The really important difference between SDRet (in which retransmissions are managed in SW), and STD (in which retransmissions are performed in HW) is that, in the latter case, after a packet has been selected it needs to complete its retransmission process (i.e., up to R retries, upon transmission failures) before other packets can be scheduled. Instead, in the case of SDRet, following a negative outcome of the previous transmission (failed attempt), another packet in the queue can be selected for transmission provided that it has a closer absolute deadline.

In this way, the transmission of a packet p_i can be interrupted by the transmission of other, more urgent packets (e.g., p_j). For instance, after two failed attempts related to packet p_i, it is possible to have an attempt for packet p_j, before transmission of p_i is finalized. A possible sample sequence could be $m_i^{SW,1}, m_i^{SW,2}, m_j^{SW,1}, m_i^{SW,3}$. This provides additional degrees of freedom from the point of view of the scheduling algorithms, and potential improvements from the point of view of the fraction of packets that manage to be transmitted within their deadline.

In the following two experiments, STD and SDRet are compared for the set of flows $\mathcal{T}$. Among the experimental conditions analyzed in the previous section, we selected the one for which this analysis is more appropriate, that is, *high load*, $CW = 31$ (a relatively small value that does not favour too much real-time traffic with respect to best-effort traffic), and $R = 7$ (a typical value for the maximum number of tries, often taken as the default choice). The same experiment was repeated for STD and SDRet, and each experiment consisted in 2.5 millions of samples.

The most important statistical indices for deadline-constrained real-time traffic are the Delivery Success Probability (DSP) and the Delivery Failure Probability (DFP). The DSP corresponds to the number of packets delivered within the deadline over the total number of packets that have been queued. Instead, the DFP can be obtained as DFP $= 1 - $ DSP.

Table 4. Comparison between standard HW retransmissions (STD) and SW retransmissions (SDRet) for the transmission of deadline-constrained real-time traffic.

Type	DSP	DFP		d_{min}	$\overline{d}$	σ_d	$d_{p99.9}$	$d_{p99.99}$	d_{max}	$\overline{r}$
	[%]	[%]	([#])				[ms]			
HW (STD)	97.79	**2.21**	(**55242**)	0.131	3.083	2.698	20.891	28.088	39.395	1.33
SW (SDRet)	98.17	**1.83**	(**45703**)	0.131	3.153	2.878	22.597	29.807	39.952	1.33

Results for the two experiments are reported in Table 4. In addition to the measured DSP and DFP, we also added results related to the latency, evaluated only on the packets that did not miss the deadline. In particular, and differently from Sect. 4, latency is calculated with the formula $d_i = t_i^Q - t_i^R$, where $t_i^R = t_i^A - T_{SIFS} - T_{ACK}$ was obtained by removing from the timestamp t_i^A, which is acquired on the reception of the ACK frame, the duration of the SIFS and the time needed to transmit the ACK frame (i.e., T_{SIFS} and T_{ACK}, respectively). This provides the exact delivery time of the packet to the destination node, which strictly precedes the time when the sender node is notified of the correct reception of the data packet by the destination node through the ACK frame.

Comparing STD and SDRet implementations from the point of view of the number of deadline misses, it can be seen that handling retransmissions in SW is advantageous. The DFP lowers from 2.21% to 1.83%, with a relative reduction on the fraction of deadline misses of about 17%. With SDRet, ~1000 more packets were delivered to destination within the deadline, obtaining a value of DSP equal to 98.17%. The better DFP shown by the SW solution is the direct consequence of the more degrees of freedom of SDRet in selecting which frames have to be transmitted in the network.

Improvements provided by SDRet are directly related to the average number of retransmissions ($\bar{r} = 1.33$ in our experimental conditions) and to the number of queued packets. In fact, the EDF scheduling algorithm has enough degrees of freedom to potentially enforce better sequences of transmission attempts (where different packets are interleaved) only if there is more than one packet pending in the queue and the channel is not error-free. Conversely, in the case all the flows in the set have the same relative deadlines (i.e., D^j are equal, $\forall \tau^j \in T$), the STD and SDRet techniques necessarily provide the same results.

The use of SDRet slightly increases latencies for timely delivered packets. This is no surprise, because both the management of retransmissions and the selection of the next frame to be sent are executed in SW in user-space. However, worsening of latencies is irrelevant if compared with the obtained benefits in terms of reduction of deadline misses. In particular, we performed a specific experiment aimed at evaluating the additional time due to the SW, and divided the analysis into two contributions, namely *selection delay* and *outcome management delay*. The *selection delay* (d^{select}) is the time taken by the SW to select the next frame to be transmitted from those pending in the queue, by using the EDF scheduling algorithm. Instead, the *outcome management delay* (d^{outcome}) refers to the code devoted to manage retransmissions and to remove frames from the queue.

Results obtained by considering $200,000$ samples show that mean values for above delays are $\overline{d}^{\text{select}} = 55\,\mu s$ and $\overline{d}^{\text{outcome}} = 78\,\mu s$, while 99.99-percentiles are $d_{p99.99}^{\text{select}} = 415\,\mu s$ and $d_{p99.99}^{\text{outcome}} = 2693\,\mu s$, respectively. This is a further indication that SW overheads are insignificant when compared with the transmission times of frames on air.

6 Conclusions

Managing frame retransmissions in software (SDRet), through an application implemented at the user-space level in a Linux operating system, is a viable direction that provides several benefits. With minor changes to the device driver of a commercial Wi-Fi adapter, we experimentally verified that it is possible to manage frame retransmissions in software directly at the application level. Worsening, in terms of mean latency, is confirmed to be really small (in the order of some tens of microseconds). This first interesting result is a main enabling achievement for a number of possible applications that take advantage of the possibility to manage the scheduling of frames with the granularity of the single frame.

In the second part of the paper, we validated SDRet by using it for the transmission of deadline-constrained real-time traffic, by employing the EDF scheduling algorithm to select the sequence of frames to be transmitted. As expected, results show several improvements in the case of SDRet, if compared with the automatic management of frame retransmissions performed in hardware by the Wi-Fi adapter.

Future work includes the use of SDRet, and the interface with the device driver on which it is based (i.e., SDMAC), for implementing new applications that potentially can exploit other SDMAC functions (i.e., signal quality of ACK frames, transmission rate, etc.) to provide better strategies for the scheduling of frames to be transmitted.

References

1. Kamruzzaman, M., Sarkar, N.I., Gutierrez, J., Ray, S.K.: A study of IoT-based post-disaster management. In: 2017 International Conference on Information Networking (ICOIN), pp. 406–410, January 2017. https://doi.org/10.1109/ICOIN.2017.7899468
2. Cambra, C., Díaz, J.R., Lloret, J.: Deployment and performance study of an ad hoc network protocol for intelligent video sensing in precision agriculture. In: Garcia Pineda, M., Lloret, J., Papavassiliou, S., Ruehrup, S., Westphall, C.B. (eds.) ADHOC-NOW 2014. LNCS, vol. 8629, pp. 165–175. Springer, Heidelberg (2015). https://doi.org/10.1007/978-3-662-46338-3_14. ISBN 978-3-662-46338-3
3. Sendra, S., Laborda, A., Díaz, J.R., Lloret, J.: A smart Bluetooth-based ad hoc management system for appliances in home environments. In: Guo, S., Lloret, J., Manzoni, P., Ruehrup, S. (eds.) ADHOC-NOW 2014. LNCS, vol. 8487, pp. 128–141. Springer, Cham (2014). https://doi.org/10.1007/978-3-319-07425-2_10. ISBN 978-3-319-07425-2
4. IEEE Standard for Information technology- Telecommunications and information exchange between systems Local and metropolitan area networks- Specific requirements-Part 11: Wireless LAN Medium Access Control (MAC) and Physical Layer (PHY) Specifications-Amendment 4: Enhancements for Very High Throughput for Operation in Bands below 6 GHz. IEEE Std 802.11ac-2013 (Amendment to IEEE Std 802.11-2012, as amended by IEEE Std 802.11ae-2012, IEEE Std 802.11aa-2012, and IEEE Std 802.11ad-2012), pp. 1–425. IEEE, December 2013. https://doi.org/10.1109/IEEESTD.2013.6687187
5. Cena, G., Scanzio, S., Valenzano, A.: A software-defined MAC architecture for Wi-Fi operating in user space on conventional PCs. In: IEEE 13th International Workshop on Factory Communication Systems (WFCS), pp. 1–10, May 2017. https://doi.org/10.1109/WFCS.2017.7991945

6. Cena, G., Scanzio, S., Valenzano, A.: SDMAC: a software-defined MAC for Wi-Fi to ease implementation of soft real-time applications. IEEE Trans. Ind. Informat. **15**(6), 3143–3154 (2019). https://doi.org/10.1109/TII.2018.2873205. ISSN 1551–3203

7. Kang, K., Zhu, Z., Liu, D., Zhang, W., Qian, H.: A software defined open Wi-Fi platform. China Commun. **14**(7), 1–15 (2017). https://doi.org/10.1109/CC.2017.8010965. ISSN 1673–5447

8. Sharma, A., Gelara, V., Singh, S.R., Korakis, T., Panwar, S.: Implementation of a cooperative MAC protocol using a software defined radio platform. In: 16th IEEE Workshop on Local and Metropolitan Area Networks, pp. 96–101, September 2008. https://doi.org/10.1109/LANMAN.2008.4675851

9. Louail, L., Felea, V.: Routing and TDMA joint cross-layer design for wireless sensor networks. In: Mitton, N., Loscri, V., Mouradian, A. (eds.) ADHOC-NOW 2016. LNCS, vol. 9724, pp. 111–123. Springer, Cham (2016). https://doi.org/10.1007/978-3-319-40509-4_8. ISBN 978-3-319-40509

10. Cena, G., Scanzio, S., Valenzano, A.: Seamless link-level redundancy to improve reliability of industrial Wi-Fi networks. IEEE Trans. Ind. Informat. **12**(2), 608–620 (2016). https://doi.org/10.1109/TII.2016.2522768. ISSN 1551–3203

11. Cena, G., Scanzio, S., Valenzano, A.: A prototype implementation of Wi-Fi seamless redundancy with reactive duplication avoidance. In IEEE 23rd International Conference on Emerging Technologies and Factory Automation (ETFA 2018), vol. 1, pp. 179–186, September 2018. https://doi.org/10.1109/ETFA.2018.8502636

12. Cereia, M., Scanzio, S.: A user space EtherCAT master architecture for hard real-time control systems. In: IEEE 17th International Conference on Emerging Technologies Factory Automation (ETFA 2012), pp. 1–8, September 2012. https://doi.org/10.1109/ETFA.2012.6489584

13. Xia, D., Hart, J., Fu, Q.: Evaluation of the minstrel rate adaptation algorithm in IEEE 802.11 g WLANs. In: 2013 IEEE International Conference on Communications (ICC), pp. 2223–2228, June 2013. https://doi.org/10.1109/ICC.2013.6654858

14. Toscano, E., Lo Bello, L.: Bandwidth-efficient admission control for EDF-based wireless industrial communication. In: IEEE International Symposium on Industrial Electronics (ISIE 2011), pp. 1186–1193, June 2011. https://doi.org/10.1109/ISIE.2011.5984212

15. Seno, L., Cena, G., Scanzio, S., Valenzano, A., Zunino, C.: Enhancing communication determinism in Wi-Fi networks for soft real-time industrial applications. IEEE Trans. Ind. Informat. **13**(2), 866–876 (2017). https://doi.org/10.1109/TII.2016.2641468. ISSN 1551–3203

RT-WiFi Approach to Handle Real-Time Communication: An Experimental Evaluation

José Betiol Júnior[1], Robson Costa[2(✉)], Ricardo Moraes[1], Luciana Rech[1], and Francisco Vasques[3]

[1] Federal University of Santa Catarina, Florianópolis, Brazil
roque.betiol@posgrad.ufsc.br,
{ricardo.moraes,luciana.rech}@ufsc.br
[2] Federal Institute of Santa Catarina, Lages, Brazil
robson.costa@ifsc.edu.br
[3] IDMEC, FEUP, University of Porto, Porto, Portugal
vasques@fe.up.pt

Abstract. WiFi (IEEE 802.11 standard) networks are widely used to support real-time (RT) applications, from home environment systems to complex networked control systems (NCS). Nevertheless, the Quality of Service (QoS) extensions incorporated into the standard are still unable to guarantee some relevant RT communications requirements. This paper presents an experimental validation of the RT-WiFi architecture that was recently proposed to deal with RT communication requirements and analysed through simulation. The experimental results demonstrate the feasibility of implementing the RT-WiFi architecture and improving the QoS level of communications through a comparative analysis with the EDCA (Enhanced Distributed Channel Access) mechanism, which is a mechanism incorporated in the IEEE 802.11 standard to provide different levels of transmission priority of different types of traffic.

Keywords: Real-time communication · IEEE 802.11 · Experimental evaluation

1 Introduction

The latest trends that are influencing automation technologies are the Internet of Things (IoT), the Cyber-Physical Systems (CPS) and the Tactile Internet [18]. These concepts are not entirely new and have emerged in the context of Information and Communication Technologies (ICT) for many years. However, they have recently penetrated in the industrial automation sector and are changing the way one looks at automation systems. The application of the CPSs and IoT ideas in this area leads to the definition of the Industry 4.0 concept, where 4.0 refers to the fourth industrial revolution, made possible by Internet technologies, to create intelligent products, intelligent production and intelligent services [18].

© Springer Nature Switzerland AG 2019
M. R. Palattella et al. (Eds.): ADHOC-NOW 2019, LNCS 11803, pp. 290–303, 2019.
https://doi.org/10.1007/978-3-030-31831-4_20

This term was originally created in Germany, but quickly became a buzzword on a global scale [6]. Currently several solutions exist in industrial systems, transportation, manufacturing processes [5], control and automation processes [16], health and biomedical systems [19], intelligent structures [11] and intelligent robotic systems [7].

From the perspective of communication systems, IoT and CPSs rely heavily on telecommunication networks, which have not played an important role in industrial communication until now. One of the main reasons is that most applications in industrial automation systems have RT requirements, which cannot be guaranteed by traditional telecommunication networks. A RT system is a computational system that must react to external triggers (events) within predefined deadline constraints. In a RT communication system, a message arriving at its destination after the deadline is considered as not useful (or even wrong). While the purpose of the traditional communication network is to minimize the average response time, the goal of a RT communication network will be to respect of the deadlines of each message.

More recent studies indicate that within a few years, there will be billions of devices connected to the Internet, forming the Web of Things (WoT), when the devices that make up the IoT will also be available on the World Wide Web [2]. The effective deployment of Industry 4.0 and WoT depends, amongst other things, on the development of 5G networks, which is a generation of telecommunication networks that will combine both wired and wireless communications from providers of public and private access [1].

To deal with the diversity of wireless IoT systems, 5G technology will need to integrate different networking technologies, ensuring the same level of Quality of Service (QoS) offered by the wired technologies. In this context, several wireless technologies are being addressed and it is likely that, in the near future, the wide availability of wireless networking solutions will also generate a standard for wireless communication, where the standard set of protocols IEEE 802.11 [9] and IEEE 802.15.4 [8] are the leading candidates.

One of the major problems of wireless technologies is the non-deterministic behaviour of medium access control mechanisms, where compliance with temporal constraints, imposed by RT-communication, is not guaranteed, so making these technologies inefficient. However, several improvements have been proposed in recent years to reduce the problems related to the non-determinism of wireless communication protocols. The mechanisms presented in the IEEE 802.11e amendment were incorporated into the IEEE 802.11 protocol to provide QoS guarantees, including different priorities for data packet transmissions. However, several papers evaluated these mechanisms [12,13], showing that it is not easy to find a suitable configuration for each scenario. Therefore, there is no guarantee that temporal constraints on IEEE 802.11-based RT communication systems will be achieved, even if the WiFi network is operating with the QoS capabilities enabled. Mechanisms based on virtual-token passing among RT stations have been proposed to deal with RT communication in non-deterministic medium access protocols [14]. Recently, it was also shown that the EDCA (*Enhanced Distributed Channel Access*) mechanism is not able to adequately support RT traffic when the environment is shared with non-RT alien devices, concluding that new communication approaches must be devised in order to use the EDCA mechanism to transfer RT packets, where the RT traffic may be disturbed by timing-unconstrained traffic from generic stations [10].

In this context, the authors proposed the RT-WiFi, a real-time communication architecture which uses the TDMA mechanism (*Time Division Multiple Access*) and a priority mechanism [15] to provide better QoS capabilities for RT applications, operating in Open Basic Service Set (OBSS) environments[1]. RT-WiFi was initially proposed in [4] and extended in [3], where it is detailed presented and compared to other solutions proposed in the literature that focus on increasing determinism in WiFi to enable RT communications. Therefore, the main objective of this paper is to present an experimental evaluation of the RT-WiFi architecture (never published before) when it is used in OBSS environments. Furthermore, the RT-WiFi results are compared with the EDCA results, also obtained by experimental evaluation.

2   EDCA - *Enhanced Distributed Channel Access*

The IEEE 802.11e amendment, published in 2005, incorporates an additional coordination function called HCF (*Hybrid Coordination Function*), intended to provide QoS guarantee in IEEE 802.11 networks. The HCF mechanism schedules the channel access by allocating TXOPs (*Transmission Opportunities*) to each of the stations. Each TXOP is defined by a starting time and a maximum duration, *i.e.* the TXOP defines a time interval during which the station keeps the medium access control. Consequently, within an acquired TXOP, multiple messages may be transmitted by the station. TXOPs may be allocated through one of two access mechanisms specified by HCF: the EDCA and the HCCA (*HCF Controlled Channel Access*) mechanisms.

The EDCA mechanism was designed to provide differentiated transmission services with four ACs (*Access Categories*). Each message arriving at the MAC sublayer is mapped into one of the four ACs, as follows: **(i)** background (BK); **(ii)** best-effort (BE); **(iii)** video (VI), and; **(iv)** voice (VO), that have the highest priority.

These different levels of service are provided to each of the ACs, based on three independent mechanisms: AIFS (*Arbitration Interframe Space*), TXOP and CW (*Contention Window*) size. For an EDCA station, each message will wait for an idle medium during an $AIFS_{[AC]}$ interval before contending for the medium access. Such a time interval is given by:

$$AIFS[AC] = AIFSN[AC] \times aSlotTime + aSIFSTime \qquad (1)$$

where $AIFSN_{[AC]}$ is a positive integer that must be greater than or equal to 2 for all *QoS Stations* (QSTA), except for the *QoS Access Points* (QAP), where

---

[1] In an open basic service set environment RT and non-RT (NRT) stations compete for access to the medium using the same communication channel and overlapping geographic area.

it shall be greater than or equal to 1. The default DCF and EDCA parameters depend on the physical layer. Table 1 shows the default parameters for a QSTA operating under IEEE 802.11a standard, where aCW_{min} and aCW_{max} values are equal to 15 and 1023, respectively.

Table 1. Default DCF and EDCA parameter set.

Parameters		CWmin	CWmax	DIFS/AIFS	TXOP
DCF		aCWmin	aCWmax	2	-
EDCA	AC_BK	aCWmin	aCWmax	7	0
	AC_BE	aCWmin	aCWmax	3	0
	AC_VI	(aCWmin+1)/2−1	aCWmin	2	3008 μs
	AC_VO	(aCWmin+1)/4−1	(aCWmin+1)/2−1	2	1504 μs

The admission control of the EDCA mechanism aims to limit the amount of traffic allowed by a service class to guarantee QoS in the previous existing communication and also to ensure greater use of available resources. It is only supported in voice and video ACs. An AP implementing these features requires that the set of EDCA stations implement this admission control, which is indicated through the Admission Control Mandatory (ACM) field, which remains fixed for the entire network.

Whenever a station wants to transmit a Traffic-Stream (TS), it requires a TXOP to AP sending an ADDTS (*Add Traffic Stream*) request, containing its AC and the EDCA access policy. When the AP receives this request (ADDTS), it can either accept or reject. If it is accepted, the transmission time in the medium should be calculated based on the information contained in the TSPEC (*Traffic Specification*). This value must be sent in the ADDTS request.

3 The RT-WiFi Architecture

The RT-WiFi architecture is composed of two layers as depicted in Fig. 1: Medium Access Control (MAC) and Admission Control Mechanism (ACM). At the lower layer, the MAC mechanism combines a FCR MAC [15] with a TDMA mechanism. The FCR (Forcing Collision Resolution) MAC prioritises RT traffic over NRT traffic, being the TDMA mechanism responsible for the access serialisation of RT stations to the communication medium. At the upper layer, an ACM manages the admission of RT traffic streams (TS) and is responsible for the scheduling tasks. It is assumed an infrastructured network interconnecting a set of RT stations through a central coordinator (AP_{RT}), where the lower layer mechanism must be implemented in both the RT stations and the AP_{RT}, where the upper layer mechanism must be just partially implemented in RT stations and fully implemented in the AP_{RT}. All the other stations supporting just NRT traffic, do not need to implement any of the proposed mechanisms. These mechanisms have been implemented using an open source wireless driver.

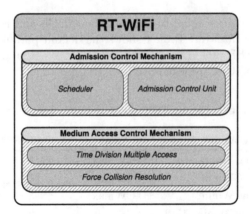

Fig. 1. RT-Wi-Fi architecture [3].

The use of a FCR MAC [15] ensures the highest priority level to the RT stations by managing the AIFS/CW parameters of both the RT stations and the AP_{RT}. Basically, whenever a collision between an RT station and one or more NRT stations occurs, all but the RT station will select a random backoff time. For NRT stations, the backoff time value will be set according to the default parameters for each access category. Conversely, the RT station will try to retransmit the message using the AIFS value of the highest priority access category (voice – VO), both for the uplink ($AIFS_{VO}^{QSTA} = SIFS + 2 \times SlotTime$) and the downlink traffic streams ($AIFS_{VO}^{QAP} = SIFS + SlotTime$), as defined in the IEEE 802.11 standard and illustrated in Fig. 2.

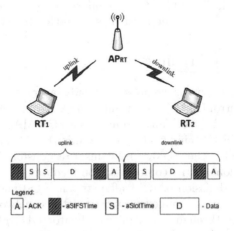

Fig. 2. Transmission flow.

Therefore, the main difference between NRT and RT traffic is that the latter is being transmitted with $aCW_{min} = aCW_{max} = 0$, meaning that its backoff

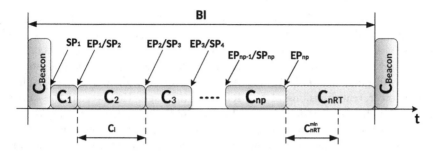

Fig. 3. TDMA rounds of RT-WiFi.

time is null. Therefore, whenever a collision occurs with an RT message involved, either the RT message is transferred before the other conflicting messages, or none of the messages is transferred at all.

The *Coordination Layer* organises the RT communication in TDMA rounds defined by a Beacon Interval (BI) (Fig. 3), during which it schedules the accepted traffic streams (TS).

The beginning of each TDMA cycle is defined by sending a beacon message from the AP. This message is used to synchronise the station clocks with the AP clock and also to disclose a scheduling list ($Sched_{List}$). Based on information retrieved from the Admission Control Unit (ACU), the scheduling list has, for each TS_i, the authorisation to transmit in the current cycle, the MAC address, the own ID[2] and the authorised transmission bounds SP_i and EP_i, respectively. Its content can be modified at each TDMA cycle (BI), ensuring a high flexibility for the RT-WiFi architecture.

A TS_i only can try to access the communication medium during the time interval defined between the bounds SP_i and EP_i (C_i), and send a unique data message. The C_i duration time is computed in order to allow multiple retransmissions of each TS_i, whether as uplink or downlink flows. However, in most cases, a successful transmission will occur before the end of assigned time for this TS_i. To ensure that RT stations transmit only one message per C_i slot, the respective TXOP is set to 0.

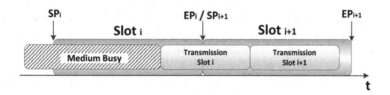

Fig. 4. Partial overlay of TDMA slots.

---

[2] The local ID (in the station) of an admitted TS can be different from ID assigned by ACU. Within this context, at stations level, the identifications are performed by the tuple [MAC address/local ID].

Importantly, even with the utilisation of the underlying FCR mechanism, there is a probability of multiple collisions between NRT devices. Thus, the RT stations perform the retransmissions until the assigned slot to TS_i ends or until a successful transmission. In a normal situation, the transmission of any RT message will ends before EP_i, since the duration of a TDMA slot (C_i) allows for multiple retransmissions of the RT data message. However, if the current transmission has not ended, it can be finalised during the next TDMA slot (Fig. 4). This situation does not lead to any conflict with a message wiling to use the next slot, since the communication medium is considered to be busy, temporarily blocking the beginning of any new transmission.

Finally, since each RT station can have one or more TS, the ACU assigns slots in an independent way for each TS admitted by the system. The oversizing of slots helps to avoid deadline misses of RT data messages and allows adequate opportunities for NRT message flows. However, it can be considered as an overhead, if a high occupation of medium is desired. In these cases, a resizing slots scheme can be used, which is beyond the scope of this paper.

3.1   Admission Control Mechanisms - ACM

To avoid an RT traffic overload, and consequently the degradation of the communication behaviour, the RT-WiFi architecture implements an Admission Control Mechanism (ACM), imposing that stations willing to transmit an RT traffic stream (TS) to previously request its admission. The ACM implements joining and leaving mechanisms, and has an Admission Control Unit (ACU) and a Schedulability test.

An RT station willing to set a TDMA slot for a TS firstly requests its association; only RT stations associated with the AP_{RT} have the right to join the group[3]. This request is realised by sending an ADDTS[4] message to the AP_{RT}, with the following parameters: generation period (P_k), nominal MPDU (MAC $Protocol\ Data\ Unit$) size (L_k), inactivity interval (II_k), request type (CT_k) and extra allocation time $(SurplusTime_k)$. Based on these traffic specifications, the AP_{RT} will verify whether the requested TS requirements can be supported. In this paper, only request type (CT_k) equal to HIGH is considered.

Additionally, the AP_{RT} receives from TCLAS ($Traffic\ Classification$) the MAC address of the RT station (Addr_STA) and the id of TS_k (TSID).

Each RT station determines the length of the TDMA slots for uplink and downlink data transmissions. It also defines the $SurplusTime$ to encompass an adequate number of retransmission attempts. In the case of a successful RT transmission, this $SurplusTime$ will enable the transmission of NRT messages. The AP_{RT} receives this message and is responsible for sending an ADDTS response message. When the ADDTS response is received, the station will verify

---

[3] This procedure can be used to avoid the association of non-authorised stations with the real-time network.

[4] The ADDTS ($Add\ Traffic\ Stream$) and DELTS ($Delete\ Traffic\ Stream$) messages are part of TSPEC element described in IEEE 802.11 standard.

whether the request was accepted or not. If the TS can be admitted, the AP_{RT} will add the station MAC address to a management list, to set subsequently values to the SP_{id} and EP_{id} parameters, performed by the *scheduler mechanism*. Otherwise, the TS is deleted.

As the joining procedure is performed only at the beginning of the RT TS transmission, no extra frames needs to be transmitted after the TS admission, avoiding communication overhead between RT stations and the AP_{RT}.

The ACU receives ADDTS messages and evaluates the required duration to transmit a message in the uplink and downlink flows (data link layer):

$$C_{attempt}^{uplink} = AIFS_{VO}^{QSTA} + C_{DATA}[L_k] + SIFS + C_{ACK} \tag{2}$$

$$C_{attempt}^{downlink} = AIFS_{VO}^{QAP} + C_{DATA}[L_k] + SIFS + C_{ACK} \tag{3}$$

where $C_{DATA}[L_k]$ is the time to perform the transmission of a message with L_k length and C_{ACK} is the time to perform the transmission of a ACK message. Then, the time to perform a transmission message is given by:

$$C_{attempt} = C_{attempt}^{uplink} + C_{attempt}^{downlink} \tag{4}$$

The ACU also defines the blocking duration ($Interf_k$) that a station can suffer until starting the transmission attempt, which are given by:

$$Interf_k = C_{DATA}[MPDU^{max}] + SIFS + C_{ACK} \tag{5}$$

where $C_{DATA}[MPDU^{max}]$ is the time to perform the transmission of a message with the maximum MPDU length.

As it is allowed multiple retransmission of each TS_i, this time is given by:

$$SurplusTime_k = C_{attempt}^{uplink} \times RN_k^{uplink} + C_{attempt}^{downlink} \times RN_k^{downlink} \tag{6}$$

where RN_k^{uplink} is the number of retransmission attempts in the uplink transmission flow and $RN_k^{downlink}$ in the downlink transmission flow. The time division of each element needed for the generation of a BI is illustrated at Fig. 5.

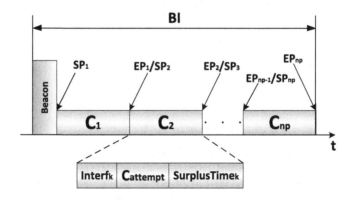

Fig. 5. Time division in the Beacon Interval.

4   Experimental Assessment

This section presents the implementation procedures of the RT-WiFi protocol in physical devices, the construction of an experimental setup and the obtained experimental results. The target of this experimental assessment is to demonstrate, through a comparative analysis of RT-WiFi versus the EDCA mechanism, the feasibility of implementing the RT-WiFi protocol, which improves the QoS level for applications with temporal constraints.

RT-WiFi protocol was implemented by modifying the driver of a TP-Link TL-WDN4800 wireless network adapter, which has the chipset Atheros AR9287 and the open source code module ath9k[5], which is compatible with framework mac80211[6]. Ubuntu operating system kernel version 3.13 and backports packet 3.13.2 were used in the stations. The RT-WiFi implementation was based on the fork, developed to implement the protocol, proposed by Wei et al. [17][7], which is also available at Github[8]. This project has already implemented the TDMA mechanism and a fixed scheduler, using similar components found in the RT-WiFi architecture, so it was necessary to make some modifications to ensure that its operation was compatible with the proposed RT-WiFi protocol.

4.1   Experimental Setup

The experimental validation of the protocol was performed in an environment where two networks (one RT and another NRT) operate in the same communication channel and in the same coverage area. The RT network consists of

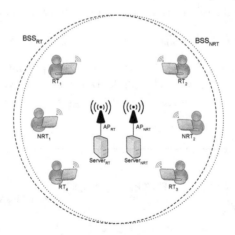

Fig. 6. Packet flow in the RT network.

---

[5] https://wireless.wiki.kernel.org/en/users/drivers/ath9k.

[6] https://www.kernel.org/doc/html/latest/driver-api/80211/.

[7] Although the name of the proposed architectures is the same (RT-WiFi), they are different works developed by different research groups.

[8] https://github.com/AlexisTM/RT-Wi-Fi.

four stations connected to AP_{RT}, such that all equipments use the RT-WiFi protocol or the EDCA mechanism defined by the IEEE 802.11 standard. The NRT network consists of two stations connected to an AP_{NRT} using the EDCA mechanism. In this way, both networks have their stations connected to their respective APs forming a star topology (Fig. 7).

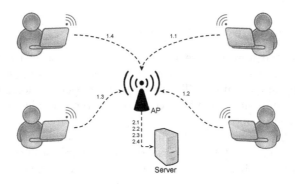

Fig. 7. Experimental setup topology.

RT stations are configured to transmit 45 byte of payload packets at data rates of 11.125 Kbps, 22.25 Kbps, 33.375 Kbps or 44.5 Kbps using the voice category of the EDCA mechanism or the RT-WiFi protocol. RT-WiFi stations used the default value for the number of retransmission attempts in the uplink flow ($RN_k^{uplink} = 4$), however, there is no downlink transmission flow in this experimental setup. NRT stations have the role of imposing network load, so each station transmits packets of 1470 bytes and the added transmission rate imposed by these stations varies from 0 to 32 Mbps, increasing by 3.2 Mbps for each evaluation scenario. For each assessment, 30 repetitions were performed with duration of ten seconds.

For the generation of RT and NRT traffic the *iperf*[9] tool was used, which can generate packets of different types and sizes, as well as determining the maximum transmission rate.

The transmission flow of the packets in the RT network during the experiments is represented in Fig. 6. Before running each experiment, the station and server clocks are synchronised. The RT stations transmit packets to the AP_{RT} within their respective assigned slots to transmit a TS_i (steps 1.1, 1.2, 1.3 and 1.4) and the AP routes the packets to the server (steps 2.1, 2.2, 2.3 and 2.4), where the packets are acknowledged. Since the AP and server are physically the same computer, no additional delay is considered in steps 2.1, 2.2, 2.3 and 2.4. Therefore, any observed delay is just due to wireless communication in the uplink flow.

The experiments were carried out at the Distributed Systems Research Laboratory (LaPeSD of the Federal University of Santa Catarina). As there are

---

[9] https://iperf.fr/.

several WiFi networks in operation, the channel in this coverage area that had the least possible interference was selected and the experiments were performed during periods of low use of WiFi networks (overnight and weekends) in order to reduce external interferences, that is, the RT-WiFi mechanism was evaluated in an open environment with the presence of an alien network (NRT), which was controlled during the tests to emulate an OBSS.

4.2 Experimental Results

The scenarios tested were represented by the combination of the transmission rate of the RT stations and the network load imposed by NRT stations, which resulted in forty-four variations. Thirty replications were performed on each of these variations and each repetition consisted of the periodic transmission of packets during ten seconds.

To perform the analysis, the following metrics were evaluated during the execution of the experiments: (i) *packet loss rate*, represents the average ratio of RT messages that miss their deadlines because either they have not been delivered (communication errors), or have been delivered late and the total number of packets transmitted; and (ii) *average delay*, represents the end-to-end average communication delay of the successfully received messages at the AP_{RT}. It is measured as the time interval between the instant when a message arrives at the RT station MAC layer to the instant when it is received from the $Server_{RT}$. As AP_{RT} and $Server_{RT}$ were implemented in the same computer, it represents the uplink end-to-end average communication delay.

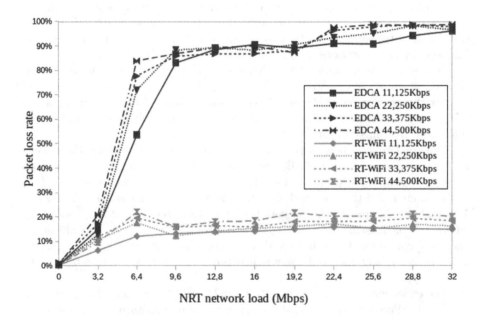

Fig. 8. Packet loss rate.

Analysing the packet loss rate criterion (Fig. 8), the behaviour of the scenarios, when the transmission rate of the RT stations was altered, was found to be similar. When there is no load on the NRT network, both the EDCA and RT-WiFi mechanisms have a low packet loss rate, the largest example being 1.22%. However, when the NTR network begins to impose network load, there was a noticeable difference between these protocols.

When the load imposed by the NRT network was 3.2 Mbps, the packet loss rate when using the EDCA was between 12.78% and 20.71%, whereas for the RT-WiFi it was between 9.63% and 14.69%. When the NRT network load was greater than 6.4 MBps, the difference becomes even more evident, with a difference of 81.20% in the scenario where the stations RT transmit at a rate of 22,250 Kbps and the NRT network load is 28.8 Mbps.

The average delay presented (Fig. 9) was lower in all cases using the RT-WiFi protocol as compared to the results obtained using the EDCA mechanism.

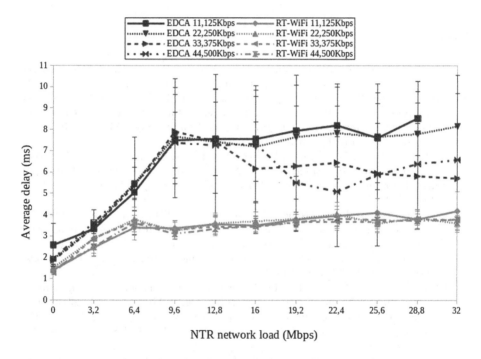

Fig. 9. Average delay.

The jitter can be observed indirectly from the standard deviation of each measured point at the average delay assessment. With the re-analysis of the graphs shown in Fig. 9, it is possible to observe, that in most cases, the standard deviation obtained when using the EDCA mechanism is considerably larger than when using the RT-Wi-Fi architecture. This behaviour was already expected, because the use of the TDMA mechanism in the RT-Wi-Fi protocol provides an almost deterministic behaviour in communication.

5   Conclusions

The results presented in this experimental assessment demonstrate that the RT-WiFi protocol provides higher QoS than the EDCA mechanism for soft real-time communications. While the average packet loss rate using the EDCA mechanism was 88.91%, the RT-WiFi protocol presented 15.89%. Even in the most extreme conditions, when the load imposed by the NRT network was 32 Mbps, the RT-WiFi protocol ensured a higher delivery of packages complying with the deadline. The most expressive case is presented when the transmission rate of the RT stations is 44.5 Kbps, where the average number of packet that have deadlines meet in the RT-WiFi network was 3898.97 and in the EDCA network was just 21.23.

Acknowledgments. This research was partially funded by CAPES Print Program (grant 698503P).

References

1. Akpakwu, G.A., Silva, B.J., Hancke, G.P., Abu-Mahfouz, A.M.: A survey on 5G networks for the Internet of Things: communication technologies and challenges. IEEE Access **6**, 3619–3647 (2018). https://doi.org/10.1109/ACCESS.2017.2779844
2. Botta, A., de Donato, W., Persico, V., Pescapé, A.: Integration of cloud computing and Internet of Things: a survey. Future Gener. Comput. Syst. **56**, 684–700 (2016). https://doi.org/10.1016/j.future.2015.09.021
3. Costa, R., Lau, J., Portugal, P., Vasques, F., Moraes, R.: Handling real-time communication in infrastructured IEEE 802.11 wireless networks: the RT-WiFi approach. J. Commun. Netw. **21**(3), 319–334 (2019). https://doi.org/10.1109/JCN.2019.000013
4. Costa, R., Portugal, P., Vasques, F., Moraes, R.: A TDMA-based mechanism for real-time communication in IEEE 802.11 e networks. In: 2010 IEEE Conference on Emerging Technologies and Factory Automation (ETFA), pp. 1–9. IEEE (2010)
5. Da Xu, L., He, W., Li, S.: Internet of Things in industries: a survey. IEEE Trans. Industr. Inf. **10**(4), 2233–2243 (2014)
6. Drath, R., Horch, A.: Industrie 4.0: hit or hype? [industry forum]. IEEE Industr. Electron. Mag. **8**(2), 56–58 (2014). https://doi.org/10.1109/MIE.2014.2312079
7. Han, S., et al.: Architecture of a cyberphysical avatar. In: Proceedings of the ACM/IEEE 4th International Conference on Cyber-Physical Systems, pp. 189–198. ACM (2013)
8. International Standard for low-rate wireless networks. IEEE 802.15.4-2015 (Revision of IEEE Std 802.15.4-2011), pp. 1–709. IEEE, April 2016. https://doi.org/10.1109/IEEESTD.2016.7460875
9. International Standard - information technology-telecommunications and information exchange between systems-local and metropolitan area networks-specific requirements-part 11: wireless LAN medium access control (MAC) and physical layer (PHY) specifications, IEEE 802–11, pp. 1–3538. IEEE, May 2018. https://doi.org/10.1109/IEEESTD.2018.8360794

10. Junior, J.R.B., Lau, J., de Oliveira Rech, L., Morales, A.S., Moraes, R.: Experimental evaluation of the coexistence of IEEE 802.11 EDCA and DCF mechanisms. In: IEEE Symposium on Computers and Communications (ISCC), pp. 00847–00852, June 2018. https://doi.org/10.1109/ISCC.2018.8538640

11. Li, B., et al.: Realistic case studies of wireless structural control. In: ACM/IEEE International Conference on Cyber-Physical Systems (ICCPS), pp. 179–188 (2013)

12. Mangold, S., Choi, S., Hiertz, G.R., Klein, O., Walke, B.: Analysis of IEEE 802.11e for QoS support in wireless LANs. IEEE Wirel. Commun. 10(6), 40–50 (2003)

13. Moraes, R., Portugal, P., Vasques, F.: Simulation analysis of the IEEE 802.11 e EDCA protocol for an industrially-relevant real-time communication scenario. In: IEEE Conference on Emerging Technologies and Factory Automation, pp. 202–209 (2006)

14. Moraes, R., Vasques, F., Portugal, P., Fonseca, J.A.: VTP-CSMA: a virtual token passing approach for real-time communication in IEEE 802.11 wireless networks. IEEE Trans. Industr. Inf. 3(3), 215–224 (2007)

15. Moraes, R., Vasques, F., Portugal, P., Souto, P.F.: A forcing collision resolution approach able to prioritize traffic in CSMA-based networks. Comput. Commun. 33(1), 54–64 (2010)

16. Song, J., et al.: WirelessHART: applying wireless technology in real-time industrial process control. In: Real-Time and Embedded Technology and Applications Symposium (RTAS), pp. 377–386 (2008)

17. Wei, Y.H., Leng, Q., Han, S., Mok, A.K., Zhang, W., Tomizuka, M.: RT-WiFi: real-time high-speed communication protocol for wireless cyber-physical control applications. In: IEEE 34th Real-Time Systems Symposium (RTSS), pp. 140–149 (2013)

18. Wollschlaeger, M., Sauter, T., Jasperneite, J.: The future of industrial communication: automation networks in the era of the Internet of Things and industry 4.0. IEEE Industr. Electron. Mag. 11(1), 17–27 (2017). https://doi.org/10.1109/MIE.2017.2649104

19. Zhang, W., Zhu, X., Han, S., Byl, N., Mok, A.K., Tomizuka, M.: Design of a network-based mobile gait rehabilitation system. In: IEEE International Conference on Robotics and Biomimetics (ROBIO), pp. 1773–1778 (2012)

A Passive Method to Infer the Weighted Conflict Graph of an IEEE 802.11 Network

Lafdal Abdewedoud[1], Anthony Busson[1], Isabelle Guérin-Lassous[1(✉)],
and Marion Foare[1,2]

[1] Univ Lyon, UCBL, EnsL, CNRS, Inria, LIP, 69342 Lyon Cedex 07, France
{Lafdal.Abdewedoud,Anthony.Busson,Isabelle.Guerin-Lassous,
Marion.Foare}@univ-lyon1.fr
[2] CPE, Lyon, France
Marion.Foare@cpe.fr

Abstract. Wi-Fi networks often consist of several Access Points (APs) to form an Extended Service Set. These APs may interfere with each other as soon as they use the same channel or overlapping channels. A classical model to describe interference is the conflict graph. As the interference level varies in the network and in time, we consider a weighted conflict graph. In this paper, we propose a method to infer the weights of the conflict graph of a Wi-Fi network. Weights represent the proportion of activity from a neighbor detected by the Clear Channel Assessment mechanism. Our method relies on a theoretical model based on Markov networks applied to a decomposition of the original conflict graph. The input of our solution is the activity measured at each AP, measurements available in practice. The proposed method is validated through ns-3 simulations performed for different scenarios. Results show that our solution is able to accurately estimate the weights of the conflict graph.

Keywords: Wi-Fi · Weighted conflict graph · Inference

1 Introduction

Wi-Fi networks in infrastructure mode are nowadays the most used technology to access the Internet. In public areas, campuses, or companies, Access Points (APs) are deployed in order to cover the areas of interest. A Wi-Fi network often consists of several APs and forms an Extended Service Set (named ESS). In order to simplify the management of an ESS, a centralized approach is often considered. Proprietary or standardized solutions [4] allow the network administrator to control the ESS through a centralized controller. The controller offers a single interface to manage the ESS but also helps to optimize network resources via channel allocation, user association [2], identifying configuration issues (like hidden terminal for instance), etc. These optimizations may significantly increase

© Springer Nature Switzerland AG 2019
M. R. Palattella et al. (Eds.): ADHOC-NOW 2019, LNCS 11803, pp. 304–316, 2019.
https://doi.org/10.1007/978-3-030-31831-4_21

the network performance like, for instance, throughput, fairness, and eventually the users' quality of experience.

In this context, an efficient network configuration relies on a deep and accurate knowledge of the current state of the Wi-Fi network. The parameters of interest can be the channels used on APs, the users' association with APs, the profile of traffic transmitted in the network, APs' load, etc. One key parameter, related to the network performance, is the **conflict graph**. The conflict graph is a model capturing the conflicts between devices in the Wi-Fi network. For instance, when two devices use the same channel, or overlapping channels, they may detect and/or interfere with each other. The nodes in the conflict graph represent the devices of the network and there is a link between two interfering devices in the conflict graph. The conflict graph is very useful to manage Wi-Fi networks (for instance to allocate channels, to choose the channel width, etc.) and to predict the network performance.

In the IEEE 802.11 standard, the signal detection is performed through the clear channel assessment (CCA) mechanism that indicates whether the radio medium is busy or idle. If two nodes do not detect each other, they may potentially transmit at the same time, otherwise they have to share the medium and transmit at different times. In recent IEEE 802.11 standards, in particular in the IEEE 802.11n/ac amendments, the CCA detection threshold is sufficiently high to ensure a proper reception of the frames, at least for the most robust Modulation and Coding Scheme (MCS). In this case, the detection area corresponds to the radio range. The radio range refers here to the area where frames may be correctly received when the most robust MCS is used. Two nodes in detection range (or radio range) are called neighbor nodes hereafter.

The CCA does not systematically detect the whole activity of a neighboring node. As we will show in this paper, when a node is at the edge of a detection area, only a part of its transmissions may be detected. In this case, the medium is not totally shared but **partially shared** between the two nodes. The classical conflict graph does not model such a phenomenon since a link in the conflict graph indicates that the two endpoint nodes are in conflict all the time. We think that a **weighted conflict graph** is more appropriate to represent the level of detection/conflict between nodes.

The notion of weighted conflict graph is not new, but, in this paper, we propose an original method to build, from any Wi-Fi network, its weighted conflict graph. More specifically, we design a method to infer the weight of the conflict graph based on measurements available in practice on most of the commercial products. Unlike previous solutions, our method does not rely on distances between nodes. The measurements concern the local activity and the busy time fraction. The local activity is the proportion of time a given node uses the channel for its own transmissions and receptions. The busy time fraction of a given node is the proportion of time this node detects the medium busy according to the CCA mechanism. Our method is based on a Markov network model that gives the theoretical busy time fraction for a given activity and a given weighted conflict graph. Then, the method searches the best weighted conflict graph minimizing the error between the measured busy times and the theoretical ones. Our approach is validated through a set of simulations performed with the network simulator ns-3.

The paper is organized as follows. In the next section, we present the problem statement and the state-of-the-art. The model is described in Sect. 3. The validation is performed through ns-3 simulations in Sect. 4. We conclude in the last section.

2   Problem Statement and State-of-the-art

2.1   Problem Statement

The conflict graph is a key parameter for radio networks as it is used to model the potential conflicts in terms of radio medium sharing. Many studies base their solutions on a conflict graph. This latter is very often considered as an input of the problem and most of the studies do not explain how to build this conflict graph from a given network topology.

In Wi-Fi networks, the radio medium sharing is ruled by the CSMA/CA (Carrier Sense Multiple Access with Collision Avoidance) principle. Two nodes share the radio medium when they are in detection range of each other and can not transmit at the same time except when their backoff simultaneously reaches zero. The random draw of the backoff limits these possibilities. Two nodes, that are not in detection range but whose transmissions interfere, are also considered as sharing the radio medium as their parallel transmissions may not lead to successful transmissions.

In this paper, our aim is to build the conflict graph that models the medium sharing due to the detection of the neighboring nodes' activity. We assume that the RTS/CTS mechanism is disabled. The activity detection by a Wi-Fi node is provided by the CCA mechanism. With the recent versions of IEEE 802.11, like 802.11n/ac, CCA assesses the medium occupancy according to three modes: (1) if the energy on the channel is greater than a given detection threshold (2) if a compliant IEEE 802.11 signal is detected (3) or if a combination of the first two modes appears. For most of the first Wi-Fi products based on the IEEE 802.11 standard of 1999, the detection range was almost two times the communication range induced by a use of a physical transmission rate of 2 Mb/s [7,8]. The CCA threshold for the IEEE 802.11n/ac versions has been raised compared with the first amendments. In the IEEE 802.11 standard version of 2016, the medium is considered as busy by the CCA mechanism if "the start of a valid OFDM transmission at a receive level greater than or equal to the minimum modulation and coding scheme sensitivity" or if "a received energy that is 20 dB above the minimum modulation and coding scheme sensitivity" is detected. It means that the detection range corresponds to, at most, the communication range when the most robust MCS is used.

With such a rule, one might think that the conflict graph can be simply deduced from the neighborhood graph. Indeed, two nodes can detect each other as soon as they can communicate by using the most robust MCS. To illustrate

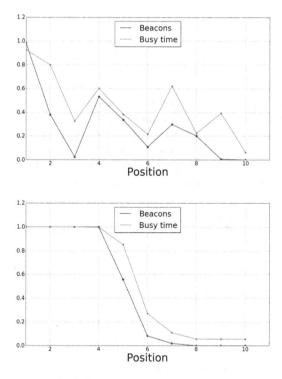

Fig. 1. Experimentations (up): busy time fraction and beacon reception rate for different distances. The different positions correspond to different distances given in an increasing order. Simulation ns-3 (down): we change the parameter of the ns-3 simulator to have a behavior close to the one obtained through experimentations. A log-normal fading has been added to the log distance propagation model and the level of noise has been increased.

that this is not so simple, we conducted a simple real experiment. We set up a first IEEE 802.11n AP, named AP1, that is always transmitting to a near station. The physical transmission rate is set by the default Wi-Fi manager. AP1 also periodically emits beacon frames to announce its network and some of its parameters. These beacon frames are sent with the most robust MCS at 6 Mbit/s. A second AP, named AP2, is located at different distances from AP1. AP2 measures two parameters: the busy time fraction and the percentage of received beacons. The obtained values are shown in Fig. 1. When AP2 is in the detection area and close to AP1, the measured busy time fraction is close to 1. When the distance increases between AP1 and AP2, the busy time fraction decreases and evolves between 0.8 and 0.2. When AP2 is far from AP1 and outside the detection area (position not shown in Fig. 1), the busy time fraction reaches 0. This experiment shows that, as soon as AP2 is not close to AP1, the CCA mechanism detects only a proportion of the transmissions but not all transmissions. It means that even if the two APs are in conflict, the medium is not totally exclusive and can be used, sometimes, at the same time by the two APs. Therefore, the links in the conflict graph are not binary. Two nodes can be sometimes in conflict and sometimes not. To model this property, we suggest to use a weighted conflict graph in which weights on links represent the partial radio medium sharing between neighbor nodes.

We initially thought that the percentage of received beacons could be used to estimate the link weights of the conflict graph. Nevertheless, with our simple experiment, we observe that the percentage of received beacons may be lower than the busy time fraction measured by the CCA mechanism. This is due to the fact that some beacons arrive in error, even if they are detected by the CCA mechanism. Also, we observe that as soon as the CCA detection is not 0, the proportion of received beacons is strictly positive. It may be one beacon over 1000 but it is always positive.

According to these different observations, we set up the conflict graph in the following way:

- The nodes of the conflict graph are the APs of the considered Wi-Fi network.
- An edge exists between two nodes of the conflict graph if one of the corresponding APs is able to at least detect one beacon of the other AP.
- We associate to each link (a, b) a weight $w_{a,b}$ corresponding to the busy time fraction due to the activity of node b detected via the CCA mechanism by node a. A weight of 1 means that the medium is always detected as busy due to the activity of the neighbor node.
- As radio links are generally not symmetric, the conflict graph is directional and a different weight may be assigned in each direction of a link $(w_{a,b} \neq w_{b,a})$.

Note that $w_{a,b}$ may be also interpreted as the probability for a to detect a transmission from b through its CCA mechanism. The main difficulty lies in the estimation of the weights of the conflict graph. Indeed, an AP, when communicating with its associated stations, do not always use the most robust MCS. On the contrary, it adapts the physical transmission rate to use in order to get the best throughput with each of its associated stations. When transmitting with a MCS corresponding to a fast transmission rate, a neighbor AP may decode the physical header of the frame sent with the most robust MCS and may not decode the MAC header and the payload of the frame sent with another MCS. In this case, the CCA mechanism will indicate to the node that the medium is busy for the intended duration of the transmitted frame (duration indicated in the frame physical header), but the node will be unable to know from which node the frame has been sent because it will be unable to decode the MAC (or the IP) address, and thus unable to infer the weight with this neighbor AP. Moreover, the busy time at a node cannot be computed as the sum of the activity of its neighbors. Indeed, these neighbors may not be in conflict and their transmission may overlap in time. The medium may then be detected as busy according to the CCA mode 1. In the following, we describe a passive method to infer the weights w of the conflict graph.

2.2 State-of-the-art

A large set of papers use a conflict graph to provision Wi-Fi networks or to estimate the Wi-Fi network performance. In most of these studies, the authors assume that the conflict graph is known and do not explain how to build this conflict graph (like for instance in [10]). Few papers are dedicated to the computation of the conflict graph. Moreover, most of these studies consider that nodes (or links), that are identified in conflict, are permanently in conflict, which is not true as shown in the previous section. This is for instance the case in [11,13,15].

In [3], the authors propose to investigate network traffic at wired routers that interconnect Wi-Fi networks to the Internet in order to infer which nodes interfere to each other and to which level. This method only concerns congested networks, whereas our solution can be applied whatever the load in the network. In [12], the authors also consider the notion of partial conflict. But, contrary to our approach that is focused on the neighbors' activity, this work aims at assessing the interference between nodes via received signal strength (RSS) measurements. Even if the RSS is a parameter of interest, it is difficult to infer, with this parameter, the performance, e.g. the throughput, of a Wi-Fi link as shown in [9]. In [14], the authors also propose a passive measurement framework to infer the neighbors' activity. Their approach requires to compare trace logs between any pair of nodes whereas our solution only needs to measure the busy time on each node. In [6,8], the authors build a weighted conflict graph from a Wi-Fi network in which overlapping channels may be used. In both solutions, the link weight is based among other things, on the distance between the two endpoints. Finally, in [5], the authors describe a method to measure the interference level on a node or a link and its impact on the network performance, but they do not build a conflict graph with their measurements.

As far as we know, our solution is the first one to consider the CCA measurements to determine the weights of a conflict graph.

3   Method to Infer the Weighted Conflict Graph

3.1 Inputs of the Proposed Method

We consider a weighted directed graph $G = (V, E)$ where V is the set of vertices representing the APs with $|V| = N$ and E is the set of directed edges. A directed edge (j, i) exists if AP_i is able to detect at least one beacon of AP_j. In this case, the weight w_{ij}, taking its value in the interval $[0, 1]$, is associated to the directed edge (j, i). An example of such a conflict graph is given in Fig. 2.

The weighted conflict graph can also be expressed through its matrix form:

$$W = \begin{pmatrix} 1 & w_{12} & w_{13} & w_{14} \\ w_{21} & 1 & w_{23} & w_{24} \\ w_{31} & w_{32} & 1 & w_{34} \\ w_{41} & w_{42} & w_{43} & 1 \end{pmatrix} = \begin{pmatrix} 1 & 1 & 0 & 0 \\ 1 & 1 & w_{23} & 0 \\ 0 & w_{32} & 1 & w_{34} \\ 0 & 0 & w_{43} & 1 \end{pmatrix} \tag{1}$$

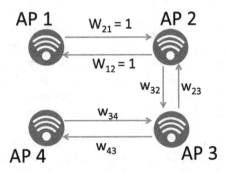

Fig. 2. The topology considered throughout this paper. AP_2 detects almost all beacons from AP_1. They are assumed to be permanently in conflict and the weight w_{21} is set to 1. AP_2 detects only a part of the beacons from AP_3. The weight is thus supposed unknown and denoted w_{23}. AP_2 does not receive any beacon from AP_4, the weight w_{24} is then set to 0. The same principles are applied to AP_1, AP_3, and AP_4.

In this matrix, each term w_{ij} is the weight of the directed edge (j, i) in the conflict graph. When AP_i does not receive any beacon from AP_j, the weight w_{ij} is set to 0 and there is no edge from AP_j to AP_i in the conflict graph.

If the proportion of received beacons is greater than a given threshold (close to 1), we set the weight to 1. It allows to reduce the number of unknown weights for a given topology.

The weights are inferred from the busy times. We assume that the busy times are measured on each AP during the same period. It corresponds to the proportion of time during which the medium is sensed busy by this AP according to its CCA mechanism. When the AP is transmitting, the medium is also assumed busy. The busy time measured on AP_i is denoted $\bar{b}_i$. The corresponding vector, denoted $\bar{B} = (\bar{b}_i)_{1 \leq i \leq N}$, gives the busy time measured by each AP of the network. The local activity (transmission/reception) of an AP_i is denoted x_i. It corresponds to its own contribution in terms of transmissions and receptions to $\bar{b}_i$ ($x_i \leq \bar{b}_i$).

To compute the weights of the conflict graph, we can not rely on the identity of stations occupying the radio medium with their transmissions, because, as explained in Sect. 2, the measurement of the busy times does not always allow to know which station causes this medium occupancy. Instead, we propose, in the next section, a model that computes a theoretical busy time at each AP for a given set of weights. These theoretical busy times are denoted $B(W) = (b_i(W))_{1 \leq i \leq N}$ for a given vector of weights $W = (w_{ij})_{1 \leq i \leq N; 1 \leq j \leq N}$. The inferred weights are then the ones that minimize the difference between the theoretical and the measured busy times.

$$\widehat{W} = \arg \min_{W} \| B(W) - \bar{B} \|_2 \tag{2}$$

where $\|.\|_2$ is the L^2 norm.

3.2   Theoretical Busy Time Calculation

Our method relies on the solution proposed in [2]. In this solution, the authors estimate the theoretical busy time for each AP with a Markov network model knowing the conflict graph of the network and the activity of each AP. The used conflict graph is undirected and no weight is considered in this study. It only models the detection activity between APs, which is assumed to be known. We extend this work to estimate the theoretical busy times at each AP for a directed weighted graph.

First, we propose to decompose the weighted conflict graph, given as an input, in all possible sub-graphs. The set of these sub-graphs is denoted SG. The directed edges with a weight of 1 are always present in all the sub-graphs. For all the other edges whose weight is not null and less than 1, they can be present in each sub-graph or not. When such an edge is present in a sub-graph, a weight of 1 is then given to this edge.

We define a probability of occurrence $p(g, W)$ to each sub-graph $g \in SG$ defined as $g = (V, E_g)$ where E_g is the set of directed edges present in g. To compute this probability, we associate to each directed edge $(j, i) \in E$ the probability w_{ij} if the edge (j, i) is present in the sub-graph and $1 - w_{ij}$ otherwise. The probability of occurrence of the sub-graph g is then the product of these probabilities for all possible edges $(i, j) \in E$, as follows (1 is the indicator function):

$$p(g, W) = \prod_{(j,i) \in E} \left(w_{ij} 1_{(j,i) \in E_g} + (1 - w_{ij}) 1_{(j,i) \notin E_g} \right) \tag{3}$$

For our example given in Fig. 2, some possible sub-graphs are described in Fig. 3. The computation of $p(g, W)$ for the presented sub-graphs is also given.

In each sub-graph, all link weights are set to 1. It is then possible, for each sub-graph, to estimate the theoretical busy time of each AP knowing the APs' activities in this sub-graph. A variant of the method in [2] is applied to the sub-graph to obtain these theoretical busy times. The only difference of this variant with the original method is that it takes into account the directed links in the computation of the busy time. More precisely, the busy time computation at a node i counts only links directed to i (all the links (j, i) but not (i, j)). The theoretical busy time estimated for node i in the sub-graph g is denoted b_i^g.

Finally, the theoretical busy time of a node i in the initial weighted directed conflict graph (given as an input) is then given by:

$$b_i(W) = \sum_{g \in SG} b_i^g \cdot p(g, W) \tag{4}$$

3.3   Weight Computation

The method, presented in the previous section, computes the theoretical busy time of each AP for a weighted conflict graph for which the link weights are given. But the link weights are not known and they must be inferred. As mentioned

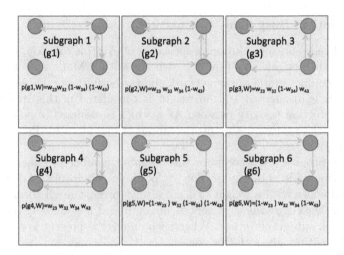

Fig. 3. Possible sub-graphs from the initial graph given in Fig. 2. The edges of weight 1 are present in all the sub-graphs (edges between AP_1 and AP_2). The number of possible sub-graphs for this example is then 2^4 (there are 4 unknown weights in the initial graph). Only 6 of these sub-graphs are represented with their probability of occurrence $p(g_i, W)$.

in Sect. 3.1, the inferred weights are the ones that minimize the error between the theoretical and the measured busy times as given in Eq. 2. To this end, we compute, for all the possible sets of weights, the theoretical busy times for all the APs and compare the estimated theoretical busy times with the measured ones. A step of 0.005 is considered to explore the weight space.

4   Numerical Results

Our approach is validated through simulations performed with the network simulator version 3 ns-3 [1]. We consider two scenarios simulating an IEEE 802.11n Wi-Fi network: the one presented in Fig. 2 where the weights are symmetric ($w_{23} = w_{32}$; $w_{34} = w_{43}$ and $w_{21} = w_{12} = 1$), and a second scenario with the same topology but with 6 weights to infer asymmetric links. The default path-loss function implemented in ns-3 has been modified to mimic the behavior observed in our experiments. It is described in bottom figure of Fig. 1. In order to get asymmetric weights for the second scenario, we set different antenna gain to the nodes. We perform 5 ns-3 simulations for each configuration and for a given network load, i.e. for each point in the figures. For each simulation, we measure the activity and the busy time for each node. The optimization problem is then solved for this input. Each point is then the mean of the 5 simulations shown with a confidence interval at 95%. The obtained weights are compared to the real ones that can be easily obtained from the simulator. The size of the considered networks in this section allows us to find the global optimum through an

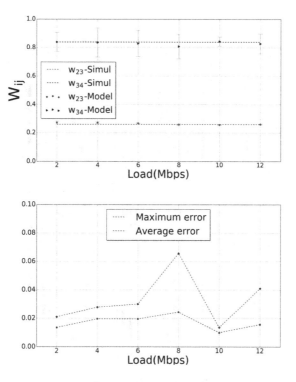

Fig. 4. Scenario 1 - comparison between the estimated and the real weights: values and errors. On top, the y-axis represents the values of the weights, $w_{23} = 0.25$ and $w_{34} = 0.83$. On the bottom figure, the error is computed as the absolute value between the inferred weight and the real weight. In the figure, we show the average and the maximum error for the 5 samples in each simulation.

exhaustive search, but any other approaches could be used instead, in particular for more complex scenarios.

4.1   Scenario 1: 4 Nodes with Symmetric Links

In Fig. 4, we show a comparison between the inferred and the real weights. Results show that our method is very accurate with a mean error approximately equals to 0.02 and a maximum error that does not exceed 0.07. In these two figures, we vary the load on the APs to observe its impact on our method. For this scenario, our approach is insensitive to the load and works for both unloaded and congested networks. 5 measures collected on the APs were sufficient to obtain accurate results. Nevertheless, we can observe on the obtained weights for each simulation and the confidence interval that a single measure does not always lead to accurate results. Instead, the computation of the mean of several samples is necessary to obtain more accurate weights. Therefore, the controller must regularly collect measures from the APs to refine its estimation.

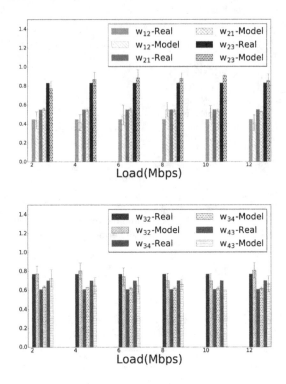

Fig. 5. Scenario 2 - comparison between the estimated and the real weights.

4.2   Scenario 2: 4 Nodes with Asymmetric Links

We consider a scenario with the same topology as the one described in Fig. 2. There are two differences with the previous scenario: the weights w_{12} and w_{21} are not 1 and must be inferred and the links are not symmetric. The asymmetry is created through different gains associated to the Wi-Fi cards. The real weights that we want to infer are $w_{12} = 0.45$, $w_{21} = 0.55$, $w_{23} = 0.83$, $w_{32} = 0.77$, $w_{34} = 0.61$, and $w_{43} = 0.7$.

We compare the values obtained with our method with the real weights in Fig. 5. The system load varies from 2 to 12 Mb/s. For this second scenario, it appears that the asymmetry between the weights of a same link does not impact the accuracy of our method. It is thus able to give accurate values of the weights even if the graph is undirected. It is a crucial feature of our method as Wi-Fi networks naturally introduce different behaviors at each node due to the radio environment and the wireless cards properties (gain for instance). As it is suggested by the confidence interval, a unique measurement was not enough to accurately estimate the weights. In Fig. 6, we show the errors (average and max) for the 5 simulations. The errors is not insensitive to this load. But, the mean error does not exceed 0.05 and the maximum error over the 5 samples is less than 0.1. It demonstrates that the controller must collect several measures from the APs at different times to obtain accurate estimations.

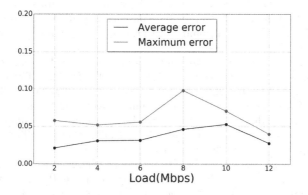

Fig. 6. Scenario 2 - The mean and maximum errors.

5   Conclusion

In this paper, we propose a passive method to infer the weights of a conflict graph modeling Wi-Fi networks based on recent IEEE 802.11 standards. The weight is defined as the proportion of the neighbor's activity detected by the Clear Channel Assessment mechanism. Our solution combines busy time measurements and the busy time estimations with an appropriate model. For the considered scenarios, the method has been shown very accurate and is able to infer the weights with approximately 2% of errors. Numerical results also suggest that the method is quite insensitive to the system load and the values of the weights. The numerical results show that it is necessary to collect AP measurements on different period of times to reach this level of errors. In a near future, we plan to validate the method through real experiments. Beside, the method has to be improved to take into account other sources, not belonging to the Extended Service Set.

References

1. Network simulator version 3 (ns-3). https://www.nsnam.org/
2. Amer, M., Busson, A., Guérin-Lassous, I.: Association optimization in Wi-Fi networks based on the channel busy time estimation. In: IFIP Networking (2018)
3. Cai, K., Blackstock, M., Feeley, M.J., Krasic, C.: Non-intrusive, dynamic interference detection for 802.11 networks. In: Proceedings of the 9th ACM SIGCOMM Internet Measurement Conference, IMC 2009, Chicago, Illinois, USA, 4–6 November 2009, pp. 377–383 (2009)

4. Calhoun, P., Montemurro, M., Stanley, D.: Control and provisioning of wireless access points (CAPWAP) protocol specification. RFC 5415, RFC Editor (2009). http://www.rfc-editor.org/rfc/rfc5415.txt

5. Chounos, K., Keranidis, S., Korakis, T., Tassiulas, L.: Characterizing the impact of interference through spectral analysis on commercial 802.11 devices. In: IEEE International Conference on Communications, ICC 2017, Paris, France, 21–25 May 2017, pp. 1–6 (2017)

6. Cui, Y., Li, W., Cheng, X.: Partially overlapping channel assignment based on "node orthogonality" for 802.11 wireless networks. In: 2011 Proceedings IEEE INFOCOM, pp. 361–365 (2011). https://doi.org/10.1109/INFCOM.2011.5935182

7. Dhoutaut, D., Guérin-Lassous, I.: Experiments with 802.11b in ad hoc configurations. In: Proceedings of the IEEE 14th International Symposium on Personal, Indoor and Mobile Radio Communications, PIMRC 2003, Beijing, China, 7–10 September 2003, pp. 1618–1622 (2003)

8. Ding, Y., Huang, Y., Zeng, G., Xiao, L.: Channel assignment with partially overlapping channels in wireless mesh networks. In: Proceedings of the 4th Annual International Conference on Wireless Internet, WICON 2008, pp. 38:1–38:9. ICST (Institute for Computer Sciences, Social-Informatics and Telecommunications Engineering), ICST, Brussels, Belgium, Belgium (2008). http://dl.acm.org/citation.cfm?id=1554126.1554173

9. Grünblatt, R., Guérin-Lassous, I., Simonin, O.: Study of the Intel WiFi rate adaptation algorithm. In: CoRes 2019, pp. 1–4 (2019)

10. Jang, S., Bahk, S.: A channel allocation algorithm for reducing the channel sensing/reserving asymmetry in 802.11ac networks. IEEE Trans. Mob. Comput. **14**(3), 458–472 (2015)

11. Kala, S.M., Reddy, M.P.K., Musham, R., Tamma, B.R.: Interference mitigation in wireless mesh networks through radio co-location aware conflict graphs. Wirel. Netw. **22**(2), 679–702 (2016)

12. Li, W., Zhang, J., Zhao, Y.: Conflict graph embedding for wireless network optimization. In: 2017 IEEE Conference on Computer Communications, INFOCOM 2017, Atlanta, GA, USA, 1–4 May 2017, pp. 1–9 (2017)

13. Magistretti, E., Gurewitz, O., Knightly, E.W.: Inferring and mitigating a link's hindering transmissions in managed 802.11 wireless networks. In: Proceedings of the 16th Annual International Conference on Mobile Computing and Networking, MOBICOM 2010, Chicago, Illinois, USA, 20–24 September 2010, pp. 305–316 (2010)

14. Paul, U., Kashyap, A., Maheshwari, R., Das, S.R.: Passive measurement of interference in WiFi networks with application in misbehavior detection. IEEE Trans. Mob. Comput. **12**(3), 434–446 (2013)

15. Zhou, X., Zhang, Z., Wang, G., Yu, X., Zhao, B.Y., Zheng, H.: Practical conflict graphs in the wild. IEEE/ACM Trans. Netw. **23**(3), 824–835 (2015)

SDNWisebed: A Software-Defined WSN Testbed

Jakob Schaerer[(⊠)], Zhongliang Zhao, Jose Carrera, Severin Zumbrunn,
and Torsten Braun

Institute of Computer Science, University of Bern, Bern, Switzerland
`jakob.schaerer@students.unibe.ch`

Abstract. Software-Defined Networking (SDN) is a promising approach to simplify the management of Wireless Sensor Networks (WSNs).
Many SDN frameworks for WSNs have been proposed, while real-world
testbeds to accelerate the development of SDN-based WSN applications
are still rare. In this work, we propose SDNWisebed: an SDN-empowered
WSN testbed management system that enhances the WSN management
functions with a stateful Software-Defined Networking solution. This
testbed was designed to evaluate various types of SDN-based WSN applications and enhance their performance, such as WSN routing protocols
and network applications, before deploying them in real-world infrastructures. To validate its efficiency, we conducted both functional and
performance evaluation. Real-world experiment results show that the
speed of integration of new SDN applications can be improved thanks to
the stateful feature awareness of SDNWisebed.

Keywords: Testbeds · Internet of Things ·
Software Defined Networking · Wireless Sensor Networks

1 Introduction

The rapid growth of the Internet of Things (IoT) has created new requirements for Wireless Sensor Networks (WSNs). In the IoT paradigm smart devices
exchange information. Therefore, smart devices of various manufacturers need to
be able to communicate with each other. To enable this interaction, it is essential that WSNs are easy to manage and have a unified management interface.
Software-Defined Networking (SDN) is a promising approach to simplify and
unify the management of WSNs. In the SDN paradigm the network is split into
the data plane and control plane [13]. The central controller of the control plane
provides global information about the WSN and, therefore, enables advanced
network applications which could anticipate the integration of IoT.

To design and evaluate new SDN-based WSN applications such as routing
protocols, a reliable and precise testing environment is needed. Simulators like
ns-3 [16], OMNeT++ [17] and Cooja [15] can be used for the simulation of
WSNs. With these simulations research projects can be tested, evaluated and

© Springer Nature Switzerland AG 2019
M. R. Palattella et al. (Eds.): ADHOC-NOW 2019, LNCS 11803, pp. 317–329, 2019.
https://doi.org/10.1007/978-3-030-31831-4_22

initially validated. But since these simulators are based on mathematical models, they always need to abstract the underlying physical system. The accuracy of the results always depends on the accuracy of the mathematical model. Consequently, to achieve realistic and precise WSN experiments that consider realistic environmental factors, the network applications also must be tested in a real testbed.

Many WSN testbeds have been created. For instance, TARWIS [11] enables easy WSN testbed reservation, fast deployment and testing of WSN applications. However, TARWIS lacks the opportunity for rapid SDN application deployment and testing. Even though the idea of using SDN for WSNs came up only recently, there are already some frameworks that put the concept of Software Defined Wireless Sensor Networks (SDWSN) into practice. Today, already many different SDWSN architectures exist, of which some already have been successfully implemented [14]. As one of the starting efforts of integrating SDN and WSN, SDN-Wise [2] provides a stateful SDN solution for WSNs. However, the current SDN-Wise works are mostly relevant to simulation-based studies, which limit their contributions to real-world SDWSN applications.

One of the main limitations of SDN-Wise is the complexity to set up a running real-world environment and to deploy an application to it. Especially, the deployment of multiple sensor nodes is very time consuming when all sensor nodes need to be programmed manually. Another limitation of SDN-Wise is addressed in this work, which is the limited information about the network that is collected at the controller. The SDN-Wise controller only collects information about the topology, but has no information about the traffic and other dynamic information in the sensor network. Therefore, the controller is not able to react to dynamic events in the network. SDN-Wise uses a tree-based routing protocol to route the control packets from the sensor nodes to the controller. As the routing tree of SDN-Wise does not have a version number it is not stable when the topology changes. That is why the original implementation of SDN-Wise is prone to failures in networks with mobile nodes or real-world deployments where sensor nodes fail and the topology can change quickly.

To solve these limitations of SDN-Wise, we extended TARWIS with SDN functions by using the SDN-Wise framework to create SDNWisebed: a real-world WSN testbed using SDN. SDNWisebed is a Multi-User Experimental Testbed (WSN-MXT)[8], which allows researchers to deploy and test their projects. SDNWisebed can be used for rapid research on various SDN-based network applications. Our main contributions are:

- Design and implementation of the multi-user experimental (WSN-MXT) testbed of SDNWisebed by integrating TARWIS with SDN-Wise to simplify the process of the environment setup and deployment of SDN-based WSN applications.
- Extension of SDN-Wise report packets with dynamic network information to provide the controller with information about what happens in the network and to pave the way for protocols that react to dynamic events like congestion in the network.

– Improvement of the control packet routing protocol of SDN-Wise to make it more stable and prevent cycles in the control packet routing.

The rest of the paper is organized as follows: We first discuss other SDN-based WSN testbeds in Sect. 2. Then, we introduce SDNWisebed and its core components in Sect. 3. Afterwards, we refer to the hardware and software platforms we used to implement SDNWisebed in Sect. 4. In Sect. 5 we present measurements of the characteristics of the testbed topology. Finally, we reflect our results and give a brief outlook for future work in Sect. 6.

2   Related Work

Many WSN testbeds have been built, but only a few are designed to support rapid SDN networking application deployment and testing. The EuWIn testbed [1] was used as a WSN testbed for SDN measurements [5]. 20 sensor nodes were used to measure the performance of SDWN, which is a SDN solution for WSNs [5]. To enable SDN, a controller, which can be positioned anywhere in the network and manages the network, was added to the EuWIn testbed [5]. The EuWIn WSN testbed provides up to 100 network nodes (50 are equipped with sensors) with fixed positions. It uses over the air programming to deploy the firmware [1]. Thanks to the fixed positions and the capability to run the experiment at a defined schedule, it is possible to perform repeatable experiments.

A small real-world testbed for SDN-Wise has also been proposed [10]. This testbed consists of five sensor nodes and a sink node deployed in a laboratory. EMB-Z2530PA based sensor nodes with an IEEE 802.15.4 wireless module have been used. The WISE-Visor and the controller of this testbed deployment were running on a single desktop computer. WISE-Visor is a virtualization layer that abstracts network resources and enables that different controllers can manage the same physical devices.

The study of the related work showed that already some testbeds were used to test the SDN paradigm in sensor networks. But these testbeds were rather built to show the advantages of using a specific SDN framework in WSNs than that they were designed to empower the research of SDN applications. None of the investigated SDN-based testbeds was designed as a Multi-User Experimental Testbed (WSN-MXT). Consequently, important tools that enable rapid prototyping of SDN-based network applications are missing in those testbeds.

3   SDNWisebed System Design

The main goal of the SDNWisebed testbed is it to provide researchers with a physical testbed environment, where they can easily and repeatably test and evaluate their projects and protocols. Therefore, it is essential to have a testbed management tool that is easy to use for the experiment management, firmware deployment, resource sharing and allocation, topology control, data collection and experiment execution.

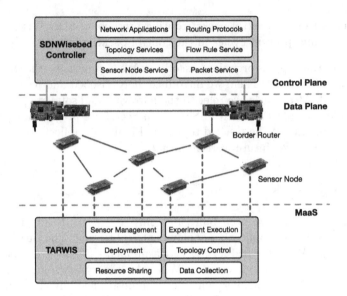

Fig. 1. The architecture of SDNWisebed

A SDN-based WSN network application normally consists of the sensor node firmware and a controller application. Therefore, a SDN managed sensor network additionally requires a SDN controller and a method to deploy network applications to the controller. Furthermore, a border router is needed to exchange information between the sensor nodes and the controller.

Figure 1 shows the architecture of the proposed SDN-Wisebed system. The architecture is split into three layers. The top layer is the control plane, known from the SDN paradigm. In the control plane the SDN controllers can be found. These controllers are used to gather network information and to run network applications.

In the middle layer the sensor nodes and border routers can be found. This layer is the data plane, known from the SDN paradigm. In this layer, topology information is gathered and sent to the controller. Packets are forwarded according to the controller directions. The third layer is used to manage the sensor nodes. It provides all the functionalities needed to deploy projects of different researchers to the sensor nodes, namely resource sharing and allocation, topology control, data collection, management and experiment execution. Providing all these services, this layer can be seen as a Metal as a Service (MaaS) for sensor nodes. In this Section more details of core components of SDNWisebed can be found.

3.1   SDNWisebed Controller

The controller builds the core component in a network following the SDN paradigm. The controller gathers information about the network topology, makes routing decisions and runs network applications. The controller used in SDN-Wisebed can be extended with network applications. The controller provides services that serve all information it has previously gathered from the network. With this information, the researcher can build its own network applications. The controller also provides services to change the behavior of the network. Those services enable traffic engineering on the WSN.

The topology information the controller has gathered from the WSN can be accessed over the Topology Service. This Topology Service provides a complete graph of the network. The flow rules can be managed with the Flow Rule Service. The Flow Rule Service keeps track of all routes installed in the network and provides the interface to install, update, or delete routes in the WSN. The Sensor Node Service provides all information like battery values and traffic statistics about the Sensors in the network to the network applications and routing protocols. The Packet Service provides functions to intercept and process inbound and outbound traffic.

To support researchers in the process of tweaking their algorithms and networking applications a fast redeployment method is crucial. The controller used by SDNWisebed allows to activate and deactivate applications at run-time, and therefore, the need for a fast development cycle is fulfilled. Furthermore, the controller allows to write log files about routing decisions, traffic statistics, sensor node states etc. These log files can later be analyzed to evaluate the network application under test.

3.2   SDN Network Application

The SDN network application is the piece of software that is tested in SDN-Wisebed. A SDN network application for WSNs is made of two components. The first component is the firmware that runs on the nodes. This firmware needs to implement the application and provides the controller with the information it needs for further processing.

The second component is the controller application plugin. This application has access to the complete information, which the controller has collected about the sensor network. The controller application plugin can access sensor node information from the Sensor Node Service or handle incoming packets with the Packet Service. Using the Topology Service, the shortest paths between two nodes can be calculated and the calculated routes can be installed on the sensor nodes by using the Flow Rule service.

When experiments are executed in a real testbed, it is important that the experiments are repeatable and that the wireless channel noise is as low as possible. Therefore, we focused on using components in SDNWisebed that allow repetitions of experiments with the same parameters, like network topology, time of execution etc. That rapid prototyping is possible, a fast research-feedback-loop is mandatory. Consequently, the controller and the operating system of the sensor nodes should provide libraries so that researchers can focus on the development of the network application of interest and the quick installation and re-installation of applications is compulsory.

3.3 Sensor Node

The sensor nodes of SDNWisebed fulfill two purposes. First, they need to forward packets through the WSN. In this case, they build the data plane of the
SDN paradigm. The sensor nodes match packets with their internal flow table
and execute the action of a matching flow entry. When a packet does not match
any flow entry, the sensor node sends a message to the controller to request a
new flow entry [10]. The second purpose of a sensor node is to interact with the
environment. This can either be the sensing of physical parameters or the execution of an action. This interaction with the environment is part of the application
layer and can be tested and evaluated with SDNWisebed. To integrate a new
program on the application layer of the sensor node, the hard- and software of
the sensor node can be extended with the needed functionality. This application
can exchange information with other sensor nodes or the controller.

3.4 Border Router

In SDNWisebed the data plane is formed by the sensor nodes. An ONOS server
is used as controller and forms the control plane [4]. Control information needs to
be exchanged between the sensor nodes and the ONOS controller. To exchange
this information between the wired controller and the wireless sensor nodes a
border router is required. In SDNWisebed we use a sensor node in sink mode,
connected to a Raspberry Pi as border router. This Raspberry Pi is connected
to the Internet and thus is able to send packets to the controller and the sensor
network. On the Raspberry Pi the WISE-Visor of SDN-Wise Java is running to
manage the flow of the control packets and data packets incoming or outgoing
the WSN. Figure 2 shows an example of a border router.

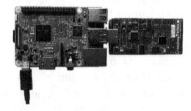

Fig. 2. Border router with Raspberry Pi and TelosB

In an SDN managed WSN, control packets always need to be sent to the
sink nodes. Thus, in large networks the sink nodes must handle a lot of traffic
and, therefore, the network is not scalable with a single sink. With the mobile
and cheap border routers it is possible to add multiple sink nodes to the WSN
to leverage the scalability of the network. When multiple sink nodes are added
to the network, control packets are always sent to the closest sink node. For
SDNWisebed it is possible to set up multiple border routers to be able to test
applications that require multiple sinks.

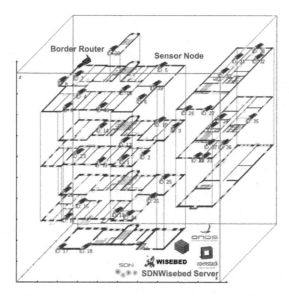

Fig. 3. Deployment of the sensor nodes, border router and controller of SDNWisebed

4 Implementation

4.1 Software Platform

Our testbed relies on open source SDN technologies, such as SDN-Wise [3,6,10] and TARWIS [11]. As controller the Open Network Operating System (ONOS) [4], provides well-defined interfaces between the different layers, and, therefore, enables a clear separation of networking applications and the access of the physical layer. ONOS also provides an easy to use plugin system, which enables rapid application development. To enable SDN-Wise on ONOS we use the SDN-Wise plugin for ONOS [3].

On the border router we use the WISE-Visor of SDN-Wise Java to manage the packet exchange between the wired and wireless network [6,9,10]. Especially, we define the ONOS Server as controller and forward all control packets to this server. To run the TelosB motes, we use Contiki OS [7] with the SDN-Wise application [10]. Contiki OS and SDN-Wise gives researchers the opportunity to focus on the development of the network application and removes the need to deal with the lower network layers. We use TARWIS [11] for management of the sensor nodes, firmware deployment, resource sharing and allocation, topology control, data collection and experiment execution.

4.2 Hardware Platform

SDNWisebed consists of 40 programmable sensor nodes based on the TelosB mote. The TelosB mote is an IEEE 802.15.4 compliant wireless sensor node equipped with temperature, humidity, and light sensors. All sensors are connected to TARWIS over the serial interface. The sensor nodes are fully controllable over TARWIS. Figure 3 shows the deployment of the TelosB sensor nodes in our institute [11].

For the border router we use a Raspberry Pi 3 Model B running Raspbian 4.14. This Raspberry Pi is connected to a TelosB sensor node running in sink mode. TARWIS and the controller are running in virtual machines on top of an OpenStack cluster.

4.3 SDN-Wise Framework Extensions

Separating the control plane from the data plane requires the nodes of the network to report their local information to the controller. The controller needs this information to build a global view of the network and to perform routing decisions. In SDN-Wise, report packets are sent periodically to update the controller with local changes. In the original version of SDN-Wise the battery level and RSSI levels to adjacent neighbors are reported to the controller. To enable dynamic network applications we have extended the report packet by adding the information that are relevant to dynamic traffic.

Header	Distance	Battery	Temperature	Humidity	Light1	Light2	
10 Bytes	1 Byte	1 Byte	2 Bytes	2 Bytes	2 Bytes	2 Bytes	...

#Neighbors	Address 1	RSSI 1	#RX 1	#TX 1	...	Address n	RSSI n	#RX n	#TX n
1 Byte	1 Byte	1 Byte	1 Byte	1 Byte	...	2 Bytes	1 Byte	1 Byte	1 Byte

Fig. 4. Extended Report Packet of SDN-Wise (Color figure online)

Figure 4 shows the structure of the updated report packet with the added information highlighted in green. We have added temperature, light, humidity, and rx/tx statistic values of the sensor nodes to the original report packet. This additional information gives us the opportunity to make more advanced routing decisions. For example, the light information can be used by a routing protocol to increase the routing cost over sensor nodes that are not exposed to light. Such a routing protocol might be advantageous when the sensor nodes are powered by solar cells and not all sensors have the same exposure to light. With our extension, we could include more relevant information that are helpful to design robust routing mechanisms.

In our updated version of the report packet, for each adjacent sensor node, two bytes are reserved for traffic statistic collection purposes. One byte is used for the ingress traffic from the adjacent node and the other for the egress traffic.

SDN-Wise uses a basic tree based routing protocol to route control packets from the sensor nodes to the controller. But, when the topology changes, the tree-building algorithm of SDN-Wise does not assign version numbers to the tree. Therefore, cycles could arise as a result of node mobility, failure, packet

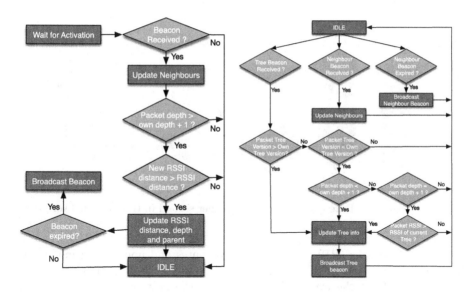

Fig. 5. Beacon processing of SDN-Wise (Left) and SDNWisebed (Right)

loss and packet propagation delays when the tree is updated and nodes accept routing information that is not recent.

Figure 5 shows the data flow diagrams of the beacon handling procedures in the SDN-Wise and SDNWisebed frameworks. As we can see, the major change is that the sink node issues new tree versions and broadcasts a new tree beacon. Tree versions are needed to improve the stability of the control packet routing. The tree versions ensure that sensor nodes only update recent tree information. A tree is disseminated through the network by re-broadcasting the tree beacon when a node was updated. Therefore, the sensor nodes do not have a fixed beacon interval and only the sink node is generating updates.

5   Evaluation

5.1   SDN Application Deployment and Evaluation

It is the major goal of SDNWisebed to provide a solid testing environment to researchers working on SDN-based applications. To show the functioning of SDNWisebed we have created an SDN-based test application, deployed it to SDNWisebed and used the reporting capabilities of SDNWisebed to evaluate this application. In this application, one node sends continuous data packets to another sensor node. To enable routing we have created a routing application that calculates the shortest path according to hop counts.

To evaluate the performance of this SDN-based routing protocol for sensor node to sensor node communication we have compared its performance with the Flooding routing protocol [12] and the Routing Protocol for Low-Power

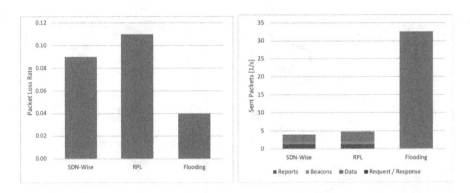

Fig. 6. Packet Loss Rate (a) and Packets sent per second in the whole network (b)

and Lossy Networks (RPL) with downward routes and non storing mode [18]. The logging functionalities of SDNWisebed enabled the collection of detailed information about the events that occured in the network. Therefore, it was possible to gather detailed information of all nodes in the network on a node level. These detailed reports enabled the evaluation of the tested routing protocols by different metrics. For example this information could be used to calculate the packet loss rate shown in Eq. 1 and the results shown in Fig. 6(a).

$$PLR = 1 - \frac{\#packets received}{\#packets sent} \tag{1}$$

The logging features of SDNWisebed even allow an analysis of the traffic in the WSN on packet level. Therefore, it is possible to use information like the packet type of every sent packet in the evaluation metrics of experiments. In Fig. 6(b) the results of a metric to research the overhead of routing protocols are shown. It also reveals another important strength of SDNWisebed. As SDNWisebed is built up on TARWIS it is possible to run SDN-based WSN applications and ordinary WSN applications with the same physical setup, under the same conditions and with the same reporting schema. Therefore, the comparison of the results of SDN and results of non SDN applications is much easier.

5.2   Control Packet Extension

By extending the report packet with additional dynamic information report packet overhead of the network is increased. In this section we discuss the impact of the addition of this auxiliary information to the report packet overhead. The overhead of the control packets consists of the report packets, the topology discovery packets, and the route and sensor node management packets. For the sake of space we concentrate on the report packet overhead only in this work. The original SDN-Wise packet size is $13 + 2 \cdot nBytes$, where n is the number of the neighbours of the reporting sensor node. Figure 4 shows that we have added $4 \cdot 2Bytes$ for sensor node and $2 \cdot nBytes$ for traffic statistics. Therefore, the packets size of our extended version is $21 + 4 \cdot nBytes$. In SDNWisebed with 40 sensor nodes and an average of 10 neighbours per node, this results in the addition of $28Bytes$ and almost doubles the report packet overhead. However, the added information is not redundant and enables a complete set of routing algorithms. Additionally, the overhead generated by the report packets is quite small and depends on the configuration of the network. For example in a setup with a data packet rate of one data packet per second, with a size of 22 Bytes (10 Bytes Payload), and a report interval of 1 report per minute the report packet overhead is 4.4%.

5.3   Tree Versions

To improve the stability of the routing tree that routes the report packet to the controller, we have added a tree version to the tree building packet and some restrictions when the tree should update. To evaluate these changes we measured the time needed to build the tree and tested the effect of removing sensor nodes during the tree building process. Table 1 shows the times needed to build the routing tree in a SDNWisebed scenario with 40 sensor nodes. The average of the time was build out of 50 experiments per algorithm. It can be seen that the addition of the tree version has no negative impact to the time needed to build the routing tree.

Table 1. Time needed to build the routing tree

Tree building method	Avg. time [ms]	Standard deviation [ms]
With tree versions	422	16
Without tree versions	417	19

To test the stability of the tree building algorithm, we removed 10% of the sensor nodes during tree building process without physically splitting the network and tested whether the network can recover. With the tree versions the network recovered in 100% of the tests. Without the tree versions the sensor network remained split in 15% of the cases. Therefore, we were able to show that we could improve the stability of the control packet routing.

6   Conclusions

In this work, we showed how to build an SDN-based WSN testbed: by integrating TARWIS with SDNWisebed. SDNWisebed allows the execution and evaluation of various SDN-based WSN applications with full sensor programmability. This new feature of supporting sensor programming enhances the possibility for fast and efficient WSN application prototyping with high flexibility. Therefore, with SDNWisebed, we are able to perform real-world WSN application with full sensor controllability and flexibility. The experiments showed that SDNWisebed enables multiple researchers to evaluate their SDN-based WSN applications in a real world testbed environment.

Additionally, we have extended the report packet of the SDN-Wise framework with dynamic information. This dynamic information contains traffic statistics of the sensor node. With the traffic statistics available on the SDN controller it is possible to design more sophisticated routing algorithms and networking applications. We also could show that the addition of the tree versions could improve the stability of the network, when sensor nodes fail or move during the tree building process. By running an example SDN-based application, we could not only show that it is possible to run experiments with SDNWisebed but also that tools provided by SDNWisbed improve the comparability of SDN and non SDN applications as the experiments can be executed within equal conditions.

References

1. Abrignani, M.D., et al.: The EuWIn testbed for 802.15.4/zigbee networks: from the simulation to the real world. In: ISWCS 2013, pp. 1–5 (2013)
2. Anadiotis, A.C.G., Galluccio, L., Milardo, S., Morabito, G., Palazzo, S.: Towards a software-defined network operating system for the IoT. In: 2015 IEEE 2nd World Forum on Internet of Things (WF-IoT), pp. 579–584 (2015)
3. Anadiotis, A.C.G., Milardo, S., Morabito, G., Palazzo, S.: Towards unified control of networks of switches and sensors through a network operating system. IEEE Internet Things J. **5**, 895–904 (2018)
4. Berde, P., et al.: ONOS: towards an open, distributed SDN OS. In: Proceedings of the Third Workshop on Hot Topics in Software Defined Networking, HotSDN 2014, pp. 1–6. ACM (2014)
5. Buratti, C., et al.: Testing protocols for the internet of things on the EuWIn platform. IEEE Internet Things J. **3**(1), 124–133 (2016)
6. Dio, P.D., et al.: Exploiting state information to support QoS in software-defined WSNs. In: Med-Hoc-Net 2016-Hoc-Net, pp. 1–7 (2016)
7. Dunkels, A., Gronvall, B., Voigt, T.: Contiki - a lightweight and flexible operating system for tiny networked sensors. In: 29th Annual IEEE International Conference on Local Computer Networks, pp. 455–462 (2004)
8. El-Darymli, K., Ahmed, M.H.: Wireless sensor network testbeds: a survey. In: Wireless Sensor Networks and Energy Efficiency: Protocols, Routing and Management, pp. 148–205 (2012)
9. Galluccio, L., Milardo, S., Morabito, G., Palazzo, S.: Reprogramming wireless sensor networks by using SDN-WISE: a hands-on demo. In: 2015 IEEE Conference on Computer Communications Workshops (INFOCOM WKSHPS), pp. 19–20, April 2015. https://doi.org/10.1109/INFOCOMW.2015.7179322
10. Galluccio, L., Milardo, S., Morabito, G., Palazzo, S.: SDN-WISE: design, prototyping and experimentation of a stateful SDN solution for WIreless SEnsor networks. In: INFOCOM 2015, pp. 513–521 (2015)
11. Hurni, P., Anwander, M., Wagenknecht, G., Staub, T., Braun, T.: TARWIS: a testbed management architecture for wireless sensor network testbeds. In: Proceedings of the 7th International Conference on Network and Services Management, CNSM 2011, pp. 320–323. International Federation for Information Processing (2011)

12. Jelasity, M.: Gossip-based protocols for large-scale distributed systems. Ph.D. thesis, szte (2013)
13. Kim, H., Feamster, N.: Improving network management with software defined networking. IEEE Commun. Mag. **51**(2), 114–119 (2013)
14. Kobo, H.I., Abu-Mahfouz, A.M., Hancke, G.P.: A survey on software-defined wireless sensor networks: challenges and design requirements. IEEE Access **5**, 1872–1899 (2017)
15. Osterlind, F., Dunkels, A., Eriksson, J., Finne, N., Voigt, T.: Cross-level sensor network simulation with COOJA. In: IEEE LCN 2006, pp. 641–648 (2006)
16. Riley, G.F., Henderson, T.R.: The $ns-3$ network simulator. In: Wehrle, K., Güneş, M., Gross, J. (eds.) Modeling and Tools for Network Simulation, pp. 15–34. Springer, Heidelberg (2010). https://doi.org/10.1007/978-3-642-12331-3_2
17. Varga, A.: OMNeT++. In: Wehrle, K., Güneş, M., Gross, J. (eds.) Modeling and Tools for Network Simulation, pp. 35–59. Springer, Heidelberg (2010). https://doi.org/10.1007/978-3-642-12331-3_3
18. Winter, T., et al.: RPL: IPv6 routing protocol for low-power and lossy networks. Technical report RFC6550, RFC Editor, March 2012

2.5 Layer Protocol for Traffic Regulation in Ultra-dense Nanonetwork
Traffic Regulation in Ultra-dense Nanonetwork

Lina Aliouat, Hakim Mabed$^{(\boxtimes)}$, and Julien Bourgeois

Univ. Bourgogne Franche-Comte - FEMTO-ST Institute, CNRS, Montbéliard, France
lina.aliouat@univ-fcomte.fr
{hmabed,julien.bourgeois}@femto-st.fr

Abstract. The nano terahertz networks represent one of the promising areas in the field of wireless telecommunications. Technological advances in miniaturization of antennas and terahertz communications have paved the way for new network applications such as the body network, the programmable material and multi-core processors. Some of these applications require the concentration of a very large number of tiny nodes in a limited space. In this ultra-dense context and in the absence of centralized access control units, we propose to implement a distributed strategy of spatial and temporal traffic regulation to guard against the risks of congestion, interference and energy over-consumption. In this paper, we propose a protocol for optimizing terahertz radio links using beam steering antenna, distributed time division technique and sleep mode in order to reduce the flow of redundant traffic over the network, smooth the volume of communications exchanged over time, and preserves the lifetime of the nodes.

Keywords: Terahertz nanonetwork · Ultra dense nanonetwork · Directional antenna · MAC Layer

1 Introduction

New network applications have emerged in recent years driven by major advances in the miniaturization of electronic devices and radio antennas. In ultra dense nanonetworks, a very large number of radio devices are confined in a small space. In this context, the Terahertz frequency band has the double advantage of combining a high bandwidth with a low energy and coverage range. The use of short-range terahertz communications finds many applications in the field of massively multi-core computer architectures [2] and programmable material [1].

Due to the limited computation and energy capabilities of the nanonetwork nodes (sub-millimeter scale), the multiple access protocols must meet simplicity and scalability requirements. Access to the channel must be done with a reduction of the number of control messages and without resorting to centralized entities. To this end, several innovative techniques have been proposed such as:

© Springer Nature Switzerland AG 2019
M. R. Palattella et al. (Eds.): ADHOC-NOW 2019, LNCS 11803, pp. 330–340, 2019.
https://doi.org/10.1007/978-3-030-31831-4_23

PHLAME [3], ASRH-TSOOK [4], HLMAC [7], DRIH-MAC [8], etc. However, in view of the extreme density of the network, the classical multiple access protocols are not sufficient to spread the traffic load and to control the multi-hop flows on the network. Indeed, given the density of the network, the message broadcast causes numerous feedback loops that saturate the system (broadcast storms).

The traffic regulation protocol is seen as a 2.5 networking layer that allows to extend the access control layer missions with some routing considerations. The traffic regulation amounts to defining a logical topology of the network starting from the physical topology where any two nodes can communicate when they are within range of each other. The logical topology designates a subset of neighboring nodes which can communicate in a predetermined direction and at predetermined time. Formally, the logical topology represents a directed sub-graph of the physical topology. The logical topology is said robust when the directed sub-graph is strongly connected. The connectivity degree of the sub-graph could be used as a measurement of the logical topology robustness. A directed graph is said k-connected if it remains connected whenever fewer than k nodes are removed.

Traffic regulation protocols for ad hoc networks have been widely studied in the literature [5,6,9]. One of the best known is the Optimized Link State Routing Protocol (OLSR) [5]. However the adaptation of this protocol in the case of an ultra-dense network is complicated. OLSR is based on the exchange of neighboring lists between nodes. Due to the density of the nanonetwork, those lists are heavy to transmit and difficult to store or to process. Other protocols aim to define a spanning tree over the network's nodes [10]. The logical topology of the network represents then a tree where the nodes close to the root concentrate more traffic then nodes near the leafs. Therefore these protocols are adapted when the physical structure of the network involves different types of nodes: simple nodes and super-nodes like in Wireless Body Sensor Nanonetwork architecture [11]. In addition, such protocols present only one path to link every two nodes, which makes the logical topology unreliable. By conclusion, few works from literature deal with traffic regulation in dense homogeneous ad hoc networks.

Our proposed protocol has three main objectives. First, traffic load evolution presents peaks that lead to congestion phenomena. The principle of communication by appointments allows to spread the traffic and to schedule communications in time. Secondly, dense networks present various path to transmit data from one node to another. In terms of routing (layer 3), this implies a greater complexity of choice. The risk of local congestion on the network is therefore higher and more redundancy is expected (multiple receptions of the same message by the same node). The use of electronically steerable antennas improves the control of the transmitted radio signals (interference). Moreover, each node selects the subset of neighboring nodes with which it can communicate directly. Finally, communication by appointment allows nodes to plan their waking and sleeping periods. In addition, the energy consumed by communications is reduced because the emission power is channeled in specific directions at given periods. Finally, only a subset of covered nodes are selected as sources or successors nodes and messages of not selected sources are ignored (not delivered to the layer 3).

In this paper, we propose an original procedure for the Layer 2.5 networking protocol that takes into account the terahertz frequencies particularities in a dense context. The idea is to extract a logical topology from a dense homogeneous nanonetwork that allows to both reduce the number of direct communication links and maintain the robustness against temporal nodes unavailability. This procedure exploits the available antenna steering techniques to schedule over time and space the data transmission. Unlike the other approaches, our method does not impose any conditions on the physical platform and presents, according to our knowledge, the first 2.5 networking layer protocol adapted for terahertz nanonetworks.

2   Traffic Regulation Problem Modeling

Let W be a nano wireless network composed of N nodes. Each node in the network has a reconfigurable directional antenna that can be steered dynamically to cover a particular direction. Let T_{ch} be the time needed to change the orientation of an antenna. Let $G(X, A)$ the connected graph describing the physical topology of the network with X the set of nodes ($|X| = N$) and A the communication links between the nodes. $(x, y) \in A$ means that there is a particular configuration of the x and y antennas that makes the two nodes communicate directly.

2.1   Traffic Regulation Constraints

The traffic control problem consists of calculating a directed sub-graph $G'(X, E)$ with $(x, y) \in E \rightarrow (x, y) \in A$ where the following conditions are satisfied:

- G' is strongly connected: given two nodes in the graph, there is a way to route the data from one node to the other in the two directions.

$$\forall x, y \in X^2, \exists \text{ a path from } x \text{ to } y \qquad (1)$$

- G' is robust: whatever the node, there are enough ways, p, to receive the data from the other nodes and enough means, s, for the node to broadcast its own data. The values p and s denote the desired level of robustness represented by the number of predecessors and successors of each node. Choosing a large value of p and s allows a higher level of robustness that derives from the reliability level of the nodes. When nodes are prone to a high risk of outages or if the energetic capacity of nodes makes it regularly in charging phase, then a high value of p and s is more suitable (Fig. 1).

 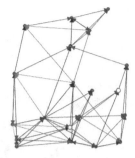

Fig. 1. Traffic regulation problem: from physical to logical topology

2.2 Antenna Steering and Sleeping Mode

Each directed edge (x, y) of the logical topology G' have two index values S_{xy} and S_{yx} designating the period of time (relatively to each node) during which x and y can communicate according to a particular orientation of their antennas. Each node changes its antenna configuration (orientation), in a cyclic manner and at a regular interval of time, $T_s; T_s \gg T_{ch}$. During the period S_1, the node x uses the configuration $C_{x,1} \in C$ then during the period S_2, it uses the configuration $C_{x,2}$ and so on. At the end of the period S_{NS} (NS being the number of slots in one cycle), the node x returns to the configuration $c_{x,1}$ for a new period S_1 and the cycle restarts as depicted in Fig. 2. The duration of a complete cycle T_{cycle} is identical for all the nodes (See Eq. 2). Certain periods S_i may correspond to periods of time during which the communication devices are deactivated. Moreover, the cycle of a node can have several periods with the same parameter $(i \neq j, C_{x,i} = C_{x,j})$.

$$T_c = NS \times T_s \qquad (2)$$

For a given period S_i, a node x is either in listening, transmitting or sleeping mode. For each listening period S_i of x, there is one and only one node $y \in X$ such that $(y, x) \in E$, and $S_{xy} = S_i$, which means that there is only one listened node at a time. If the period S_i is a transmission period of x, then there is at least one node y such that directed edge $(x, y) \in E$ and $S_{xy} = S_i$. Sleeping mode corresponds to periods of time where the node x has no directed edge $(x, y) \in E$ or $(y, x) \in E$ with $S_{xy} = S_i$, which means that the node is not listening and not transmitting.

Given the asynchronous nature of the network, the index of a period S_i of a given node has only a local signification. The Fig. 2 shows an example of traffic regulation involving 5 nodes. The node (A) has two active periods S_1 in transmission and S_2 in reception. The period $S_1 = S_{AC} = [0.3 - 0.4]$ covers $1/10$ of the cycle time T_c between instants $0.3 \times T_c$ and $0.4 \times T_c$. During this period, the node (A) covers the node (C) which is listening during its period $S_3 = S_{CA} = [0 - 0.1]$ as well as the node (E) which listens during its period $S_1 = S_{EA} = [0.7 - 0.8]$.

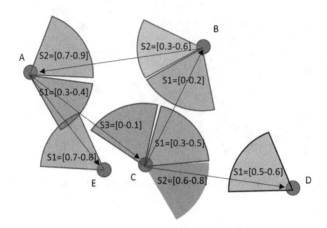

Fig. 2. Example of TDMA synchronization: each edge (x, y) is indexed by the index of the transmission period on x (S_i) and the index of the reception period on y (S_j). Each period $S[tb - te]$ is designated by its beginning and end time (the time is given relatively to the concerned node). The colored arcs display the antenna orientation at the corresponding period. (Color figure online)

When two edges $(x, y1)$ and $(x, y2)$ with the same tail have the same index value on x, the two incoming nodes $y1$ and $y2$ are then served by the same multicast stream. By the way, the edges $(x1, y)$ and $(x2, y)$ with the same head can not have the same period index on y in order to avoid interference. For all the edges $(x, y) \in G'$, the associated listening period on y must be equal to the duration of the transmitting time on x in order to maximize the sleep periods.

Along with the respect of traffic regulation constraints, in particular the connectivity and the robustness of the sub-graph G', the traffic control algorithm must take care to maximize the useful listening and transmission times, T_i, ($T_i \subset S_i$) as well as the sleep periods of the nodes. A transmission period of a node x is said to be useful when throughout all its duration, all nodes $y, (x, y) \in E$ are at listening mode. A listening period of a node y is said useful when throughout its duration, the listened node (there is only one) is in transmission phase to y.

2.3   Traffic Regulation in Terahertz Network

In DAMC modulation technique [12], the terahertz frequency band is mainly subdivided into three frequency windows which are allocated according to the transmitter-to-receiver distance which is either short, mid or long. To take into account this particularity, the traffic regulation protocol associates with each active period a coverage range: short, mid or long. Then, only nodes with a distance in the selected range are considered to be successors. At a given transmitting time slot, the successors of a given node are all in the same range, allowing to use the same optimal frequency window to serve them (See Fig. 3).

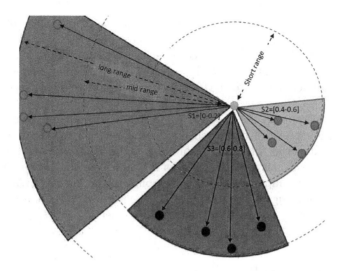

Fig. 3. At every period, the transmitting node selects its successors according their distance from the node in order to optimize the used frequency window. The colored arcs represent the orientation and coverage of the node at a given period. (Color figure online)

3   Distributed Algorithm of Traffic Regulation

The Algorithm 1 represents our traffic regulation protocol. The design of the algorithm aims to satisfy two main constraints: a reduced computation requirement and limited messages exchange. When a node wants to join the nanonetwork, it defines for each slot a covering range (short, mid or long). Then, the node alternates between two modes. In the first mode, the node listens to the channel and switches over the set of configurations $C = \{C_1..C_{NS}\}$ with a frequency of $1/T_s$. In the second mode, the node launches invitations in different directions looking for successor nodes and changes its configuration with a frequency of $1/T_c$. The use of two different reconfiguration speeds aims to prevent the hidden node problem.

In successor search mode, the node keeps the same antenna configuration during all a cycle T_c of NS slots T_s. The value of NS depends on several parameters such as the reconfiguration delay T_{ch}, the cycle duration and the number of needed sources and successors. In our tests, we have set $NS = 14$. At each period T_I, the node launches invitations. After each reception of an acceptance, the source updates its useful transmission period, its coverage list and sets the period mode to 'transmission' mode. Nodes in source search mode, listen for any invitations. Based on the target range of the source, the strength of the received signal and the remaining listening time, the node chooses to accept the invitation or not. In case of acceptance, the node registers the useful listening period. Once the number of necessary source nodes is reached (parameter p), the node stops using the source search mode.

To avoid a slow start when few nodes are active, the number of listening and announcement cycles is limited to M. After every M ordinary operating cycles, a node with not enough sources (resp. successors) listens (resp. re-sends invitations) during an entire cycle. These two procedures allow nodes that start very early or late compared to the other nodes to complete their lists of prefixed links.

The disconnection of the graph $G'(X, E)$ is avoided thanks to a long-term procedure which provides that each node, at a very important time interval, listens in all directions whether neighboring nodes belong to other connected components. For this purpose, the nodes of the same connected component share an identifier of the component which corresponds to the smallest MAC identifier of the nodes belonging to the component. When a node detects a neighboring node with a different component identifier, a connection procedure of the two nodes is started.

4   Tests and Results

To study the impact of the traffic regulation algorithm over dense nanonetworks, we have established several test scenarios, which are differentiated by the number of nodes, the spatial dimension of the network, the range of the radio signal and the density of the network. We first begin by evaluating the impact of traffic regulation on network performance in terms of interference. A first indicator of the impact on interference is the comparison of the number of edges in the graph $G(X, A)$ and the number of edges in the graph $G'(X, E)$. When $|E| \ll |A|$, the average number of signals arriving on each node is reduced considerably. Interference reduction also benefits from time division access mode, beam control antenna and selectivity of listened sources. All these factors make it possible to reduce the risks of massive arrival of communications at the same time on the same node.

Figure 4 presents three simulations of traffic regulation using different number of nodes 200, 500 and 1000 in the same area using Microsoft Excel VBA. For each scenario, on the left, the graph $G(X, A)$ shows the physical topology of the network and on the right the graph $G'(X, E)$ is obtained by the traffic control algorithm 1. The traffic regulation is carried out with the maximum number of sources equal to $p = 4$ and the maximum number of successors equal to $s = 10$. For Scenario 1, the traffic regulation algorithm reduces the density of the graph from 1202 edges to 744 edges, i.e. a reduction of 38%. For the Scenario 3, the traffic control algorithm reduces the graph from 30891 edges to 3997 edges, which corresponds to a reduction of 87%.

We also assess the impact of traffic regulation on network data broadcasting. To this end, we have selected three evaluation criteria: The total number of receptions including redundancies, the maximum number of receptions of the same message on one node and the time for a total broadcasting of the message. According to the first two criteria, the traffic regulation allows to improve the behavior of the network when a node broadcasts a message over the network.

Require: T_s, T_c, $t0$, NS, $P = \{C_1..C_{NS}\}$, $T = \emptyset$, $nbcycles = 0$, $t0 = now()$, $nbsec = 0$, $nbsrc = 0$

```
 1: for i ∈ {1 to NS} do
 2:    rng_i = rand(1..3); param_i = ∅;
 3:    cov_i = ∅; mode_i = ∅
 4: end for
 5: //research phase of the successors
 6: for i ∈ {1..NS each T_c } do
 7:    if nbsuc < s then
 8:       antenna parameters ← C_i
 9:       for j ∈ {1..NS each T_s} do
10:          if mode_j = NULL then
11:             left=t0 + nbcycles * T_c + j * T_s − now()
12:             send invit(me, left, rng_j) each T_I
13:             for each accept(n, t) do
14:                nbsuc + +; mode_j='trans'
15:                cov_j = cov_j ∪ n; param_j = i
16:                T_j.begin = now(); T_j.end = min(T_j.end, now() + t)
17:             end for
18:          end if
19:       end for
20:       nbcycles + +
21:    end if
22: end for
23: //research phase of sources
24: if nbsrc < p then
25:    for i=1 to NS with frequency T_s do
26:       begin=t0+nbcyles × T_c + (i − 1) × T_s
27:       end=begin+T_s
28:       antenna parameters ← C_i
29:       if mode_i = NULL then
30:          while end − now() > minCom do
31:             //remaining time is enough
32:             for each invit(node,t,rng) do
33:                if distance(node, me) ∈ rng then
34:                   send accept(me, min(t,end-now()))
35:                   nbsrc + +; mode_i='listen';
36:                   cov_i=node; param_i=i
37:                   useful time T_i = [now(), now + min(t,end − now())]
38:                end if
39:             end for
40:          end while
41:       end if
42:    end for
43:    if mode_i = NULL then
44:       mode_i='sleep'
45:    end if
46:    nbcycles + +
47: end if
```

Algorithm 1. Every M successive cycles

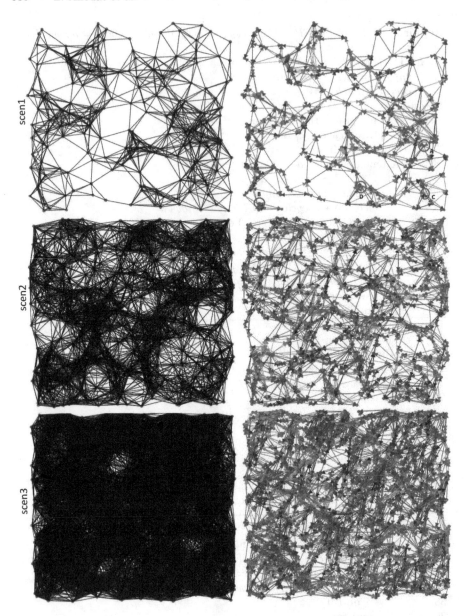

Fig. 4. Traffic regulation for 3 scenarios: 200 nodes, 500 nodes and 1000 nodes. Tests are implemented using Microsoft Excel VBA. (Color figure online)

Regarding the total number of messages received by the nodes, an approach without traffic regulation will generate for the scenarios 1, 2 and 3 respectively 2404, 15082 and 61618 messages. The number of receptions with traffic control decreases to 744, 1997 and 3997 messages respectively. The maximum number of reception of the same message varies in the approach without traffic regulation between 24, 45 and 96 for the three scenarios whereas with traffic control, it remains 4 for all three scenarios. This corresponds to the value of the maximum number of sources: parameter p.

The number of hops allowing all nodes to receive the message is also a crucial factor for the performance of the traffic control algorithm. The simulations show that the total diffusion of a message depends on the position of the source node in the network. We studied 4 different placement of the source nodes for the Scenario 1, shown in Fig. 4, circled in red and labelled A, B, C and D. Broadcasting without traffic regulation from node (A) requires 9 hops while 14 hops are required with traffic control. Similarly, the application of traffic control requires respectively 26, 18 and 22 hops to broadcast a message from the nodes (B), (C) and (D) instead of 12, 12 and 9 jumps without regulation traffic. For Scenario 1 which is the least dense, the number of hops for the total broadcast doubles with traffic regulation, a negligible additional cost in return for reducing the total number of exchanged messages.

5   Conclusion

In this paper, we have proposed a novel distributed protocol for optimizing the logical topology of homogeneous, ultra-dense terahertz nanonetworks. The objective of this optimization is to reduce the amount of interferences due to the concentration of numerous nodes transmitting in all directions at random instants. The logical topology we proposed fixes for each node the moments during which it can send data in a given direction to given selected destination nodes. Each node ignores messages sent by nodes that do not belong to the predefined subset of neighbors, which reduces the energy consumption.

Furthermore, the reduction of direct communication links between nodes does not impact data broadcasting coverage. Simulations show that the diminution of the broadcasting speed is limited compared to the gain in terms of transmission redundancy and generated interferences.

Finally, the traffic control protocol is adapted to the DAMC protocol used for terahertz communication. The successors of a given node in a specific direction are in the same range of distance from the transmitter. Therefore, all the nodes covered in the same direction are served by the same frequency channel. The distance between nodes and their successors varies according to the transmission direction leading to a better use of the terahertz band.

References

1. Bourgeois, J., et al.: Programmable matter as a cyber-physical conjugation. In: IEEE International Conference on Systems, Man, and Cybernetics (SMC), pp. 2942–2947. IEEE (2016)
2. Abadal, S., Alarcon, E., Cabellos-Aparicio, A., Lemme, M.C., Nemirovsky, M.: Graphene-enabled wireless communication for massive multicore architectures. IEEE Commun. Mag. **51**(11), 137–143 (2013)

3. Jornet, J.M., Pujol, J.C., Solé-Pareta, J.: PHLAME: a physical layer aware MAC protocol for electromagnetic nanonetworks, in Terahertz Band. Nano Commun. Netw. **3**(1), 74–81 (2012)

4. Mabed, H.: Enhanced spread in time on-off keying technique for dense Terahertz nanonetworks. In: IEEE Symposium on Computers and Communications (ISCC), pp. 710–716 (2017)

5. Jacquet, P., Muhlethaler, P., Clausen, T., Laouiti, A., Viennot, L.: Optimized link state routing protocol for ad hoc networks, HIPERCOM - INRIA Rocquencourt, Rapport de recherche, pp. 1–53 (2001)

6. Rodolakis, G., Naimi, A.M., Laouiti, A.: Multicast overlay spanning tree protocol for ad hoc networks. In: Boavida, F., Monteiro, E., Mascolo, S., Koucheryavy, Y. (eds.) WWIC 2007. LNCS, vol. 4517, pp. 290–301. Springer, Heidelberg (2007). https://doi.org/10.1007/978-3-540-72697-5_25

7. Jianling, C., Min, W., Cong, C., Zhi, R.: High-throughput low-delay MAC protocol for TeraHertz ultra-high data-rate wireless networks. J. China Univ. Posts Telecommun. **23**(4), 17–24 (2016)

8. Mohrehkesh, S., Weigle, M.C., Das, S.K.: DRIH-MAC: a distributed receiver-initiated harvesting-aware MAC for nanonetworks. T-MBMC **1**(1), 97–110 (2015)

9. Radhakrishnan, S., Racherla, G., Sekharan, C.N., Rao, N.S.V., Batsell, S.G.: Protocol for dynamic ad hoc networks using distributed spanning trees. J. Wirel. Netw. Arch. **9**(6), 673–686 (2003)

10. Rodolakis, G., Adjih, C., Laouiti, A., Boudjit, S.: Quality-of-service multicast overlay spanning tree algorithms for wireless ad hoc networks. In: Fdida, S., Sugiura, K. (eds.) AINTEC 2007. LNCS, vol. 4866, pp. 226–241. Springer, Heidelberg (2007). https://doi.org/10.1007/978-3-540-76809-8_20

11. Afsana, F., Asif-Ur-Rahman, M., Ahmed, M.R., Mahmud, M., Kaiser, M.S.: An energy conserving routing scheme for wireless body sensor nanonetwork communication. IEEE Access **6**, 9186–9200 (2018)

12. Han, C., Akyildiz, I.F.: Distance-aware multi-carrier (DAMC) modulation in Terahertz band communication. In: Proceedings of IEEE ICC, pp. 5461–5467 (2014)

Optimisation Schemes for Increasing Sensors Lifetime

Minimum Length Scheduling for Discrete Rate Based Full Duplex Wireless Powered Communication Networks

Muhammad Shahid Iqbal[1], Yalcin Sadi[2]([✉]), and Sinem Coleri Ergen[1]

[1] Electrical and Electronics Engineering, Koc University, 34450 Istanbul, Turkey
{miqbal16,sergen}@ku.edu.tr
[2] Electrical and Electronics Engineering, Kadir Has University,
34083 Istanbul, Turkey
yalcin.sadi@khas.edu.tr

Abstract. In this study, we consider a wireless powered communication network where multiple users with radio frequency energy harvesting capabilities communicate to a hybrid energy and information access point in full duplex mode. We characterize an optimization framework for minimum length scheduling to determine the optimal rate adaptation and transmission scheduling subject to energy causality and traffic demand constraints of the users considering discrete-rate transmission model. We first formulate the problem as a mixed integer nonlinear programming problem which is hard to solve for a global optimum in polynomial-time. Then, based on an analysis on the characteristics of the optimal solution, we derive optimality conditions for rate adaptation and scheduling using which we propose a fast polynomial-time complexity heuristic algorithm. We illustrate through numerical analysis that the proposed algorithm performs very close to optimal for various network scenarios.

Keywords: Energy harvesting · Wireless powered communication networks · Rate adaptation · Scheduling · Optimization

1 Introduction

Due to long range, full control on energy transfer, and small circuitry, Radio Frequency (RF) based energy transfer is a preferred choice to replenish the batteries of the nodes once they are depleted. Wireless powered communication networks (WPCNs) are becoming very popular for the low power networks in which a dedicated hybrid access point (HAP) transmits a continuous energy for the users in the downlink and users harvest this energy for their data transmission in the uplink. WPCN have been studied in many different scenarios and considering

This work is supported by Scientific and Technological Research Council of Turkey Grant #117E241.

© Springer Nature Switzerland AG 2019
M. R. Palattella et al. (Eds.): ADHOC-NOW 2019, LNCS 11803, pp. 343–354, 2019.
https://doi.org/10.1007/978-3-030-31831-4_24

different system models with the objective of total transmission time minimization and throughput maximization. *Harvest-then-transmit* is the first protocol in which the whole frame length is divided into two non-overlapping time durations dedicated for power and data transmission respectively and the data transmission interval is further divided into non overlapping slots allocated to each user [5] to maximize the sum throughput. The same system model is used to minimize the total transmission time in [1]. For throughput maximization, due to higher energy harvesting rates and low transmit power requirements, the near user dominate in the schedule which results in a doubly near far phenomenon. This unfair resource allocation motivated the authors for different objectives such as minimum throughput maximization [8], weighted sum throughput maximization [2] and common throughput maximization [6]. The authors in [1,2,5,6,8] have considered a half duplex WPCN model where all users have equal time for energy harvesting and hence the transmission order is not important. Furthermore, all of these models have considered continuous transmission rate models without a user transmit power constraint considering a simplistic model.

Some of the studies have recently started incorporating the full duplex technique for WPCN in which users can perform simultaneous energy harvesting and data transmission. For the full duplex model, [7] have presented the work for total time minimization in which the HAP is operating in full duplex mode and users are half duplex while [4] have considered full duplex users. In full duplex, users can harvest energy during both their own transmissions and the transmission of previously scheduled users which results in an uneven energy harvesting time for each user and hence making scheduling critical for the total time minimization. The authors in [3,9] have paid attention to scheduling but in a limited context, such as in [3], the authors have used Hungarian algorithm to schedule the users with an objective of total transmission time minimization. However, for such sequence dependent networks, Hungarian algorithm requires exponential computational complexity. On the other hand, authors in [9] have divided the whole frame into a constant number of equal length time slots allocated to the users yielding underutilization of the resources. Moreover, all existing studies have considered continuous rate transmission model; whereas, discrete rate transmission model is missing for minimum length scheduling which will be the main focus of this paper.

The goal of this paper is to determine optimal time allocation, rate adaptation and scheduling with the objective of minimizing the schedule length subject to the traffic requirements of the users, the maximum transmit power constraint, and the energy causality constraint considering initial battery levels and a realistic energy harvesting model, in an in-band full-duplex WPCN.

The original contributions of this paper are listed as follows:

- We characterize the minimum length scheduling problem for a discrete rate transmission model based full duplex WPCN and mathematically formulate as a mixed integer non-linear programming problem.

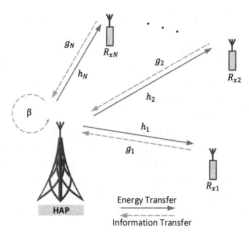

Fig. 1. Architecture of wireless powered communication network

- In order to solve the problem fast and efficiently, we propose a polynomial time complexity scheduling algorithm based on an analysis on the optimality conditions of the problem.
- We illustrate the performance of the proposed algorithm in comparison to a predetermined transmission order based heuristic algorithm and to the optimal solution.

The rest of the paper is organized as follows. The system model and assumptions are given in Sect. 2. The optimization problem for minimum length scheduling is presented in Sect. 3. In Sect. 4, we introduce the proposed scheduling algorithm. The numerical results are provided and discussed in Sect. 5. Finally, Sect. 6 presents the concluding remarks.

2   System Model and Assumptions

The system model and assumptions are described as follows:

1. The WPCN architecture, as depicted in Fig. 1, consists of a HAP and N users; i.e., sensors or machine type communications (MTC) devices. Both the users and the HAP are equipped with a full-duplex antenna. Full duplex antennas are used for simultaneous wireless energy transfer and data transmission on downlink and uplink channels, respectively. The channel gains for the downlink and uplink channels are assumed to be different. The downlink channel gain from the HAP to user i is denoted by h_i. The uplink channel gain from user i to the HAP is denoted by g_i. Both downlink and uplink channels are assumed to be block-fading, i.e., the channel gains remain constant over the scheduling frame. We assume that the HAP has perfect channel state information (CSI); i.e., the channel gains are perfectly known at the HAP.

2. The HAP has a stable power connection and continuously radiates a power P_h. On the other hand, the users are completely dependent on the harvested energy and no other supply is available for data transmission. All users harvest energy from the HAP and the harvested energy is stored in a battery with a large enough capacity such that no overflow will occur. The initial battery level is denoted by B_i which is the amount of energy already stored in the battery at the start of the transmission cycle.

3. Time division multiple access protocol is used as the medium access protocol for the uplink data transmission from the users to the HAP. Time is partitioned into possibly variable length scheduling frames and then each frame is further divided into variable length time slots for the user allocation.

4. The energy harvesting rate of user i, denoted by C_i, depends on the antenna efficiency η_i, downlink channel h_i and the power transmitted by the HAP P_h as follows:

$$C_i = \eta_i h_i P_h \tag{1}$$

5. We assume user i has a traffic demand D_i bits to be transmitted over the scheduling frame.

6. We use discrete rate transmission model, in which a finite set of rates $r = (r^1, r^2, \cdots, r^M)$ and a finite set of SINR levels $\gamma = (\gamma^1, \gamma^2, \cdots, \gamma^M)$ are determined such that user i can transmit at rate r^k successfully in the allocated time slot if the SINR achieved for user i is

$$\gamma_i = \frac{P_i g_i}{\sigma_o^2 + \beta P_h} \geq \gamma^k \tag{2}$$

where the term βP_h is the power of self interference at the HAP and σ_o^2 is the noise power.

7. We use continuous power model in which the transmission power of a user can take any value below a maximum level P_{max}, which is imposed by the regulatory authorities to avoid the interference to nearby systems.

3   Minimum Length Scheduling Problem

In this section, we introduce the Discrete Rate based Minimum Length Scheduling Problem, referred as DR-MLSP.

The joint optimization of the time allocation, power control, rate adaptation and scheduling with the objective of minimizing the schedule length is formulated as follows:

DR-MLSP:

$$\text{minimize} \qquad \sum_{i=0}^{N} \tau_i \qquad\qquad (3a)$$

$$\text{subject to} \qquad B_i + C_i \tau_0 + C_i \sum_{j=1}^{N} a_{ij} \tau_j - P_i \tau_i \geq 0, \qquad (3b)$$

$$P_i \leq P_{max}, \qquad\qquad (3c)$$

$$\tau_i \chi_i \geq D_i, \qquad\qquad (3d)$$

$$\chi_i = \sum_{k=1}^{M} z_{ik} r^k, \qquad\qquad (3e)$$

$$P_i g_i - \left(\sum_{k=1}^{M} z_{ik} \gamma^k \right) \left(\sigma_o^2 + \beta P_h \right) \geq 0, \qquad (3f)$$

$$\sum_{k=1}^{M} z_{ik} = 1, \qquad\qquad (3g)$$

$$a_{ij} + a_{ji} = 1, \qquad\qquad (3h)$$

$$\text{variables} \qquad P_i \geq 0, \ \tau_i \geq 0, \ a_{ij} \in \{0,1\}, \ z_{ik} \in \{0,1\}. \qquad (3i)$$

The variables of the problem are P_i, the transmit power of user i; τ_i, the transmission time of user i; a_{ij}, a binary variable that takes value 1 if user i is scheduled before node j and 0 otherwise; and z_{ik}, a binary variable which takes value 1 if user i is allocated rate r^k and 0 otherwise. In addition, τ_0 denotes an initial waiting time duration during which all users only harvest energy without transmitting any information.

The objective of the optimization problem is to minimize the schedule length as given by Eq. (3a). Equation (3b) gives the energy causality constraint: The total amount of available energy, including both the initial energy and the energy harvested until and during the transmission of a user, should be greater than or equal to the energy consumed during its transmission. Equation (3c) represents the maximum transmit power constraint. Equation (3d) represents the traffic demand constraint of the users where χ_i denotes the transmission rate of user i as given by Eq. (3e). Equation (3f) represents the SINR constraint of the users as presented in Eq. (2). Equation (3g) represents the rate adaptation; i.e., user can pick a single transmission rate from the specified finite set. Finally, Eq. (3h) represents the transmission order constraint for the users.

The optimization problem formulation presented in Eqs. (3a, 3b, 3c, 3d, 3e, 3f, 3g, 3h and 3i) is a Mixed Integer Non-Linear Programming (MINLP) problem which is generally hard to solve for a global optimum in polynomial-time. On the other hand, one straightforward solution is a brute-force search algorithm that enumerates all possible transmission orders and rate adaptations among which the one with minimum corresponding schedule length is determined as the optimal solution. However, this exact solution is intractable even for medium network sizes. In the following section, we propose a polynomial-time complexity algorithm based on the analysis on the optimality conditions of the DR-MLSP.

4 Scheduling Algorithm

In this section, we first analyze the optimality conditions for the DR-MLSP and then present a polynomial-time complexity algorithm.

We start by investigating the optimal rate adaptation policy for a single user. Initially, a user may not be able to transmit with even the minimum possible transmission rate level r^1 since the initial energy available B_i may not be able to support the corresponding transmit power that will satisfy the SNIR constraint given by Eq. (2). Each transmission rate level r^k requires certain amount of energy available to complete the required data transmission for the user. Let t_i^k be the first time instant at which user i can afford to use transmission rate r^k via satisfying the SNIR constraint $\gamma_i \geq \gamma^k$ using the harvested energy. Note that $t_i^1 \leq t_i^2 \leq ... \leq t_i^M$.

Consider Fig. 2 illustrating the transmission completion (end time) vs. allocation time (start time) for a user i. τ_0 denotes the initial waiting time for user i to be able to transmit with r^1 by satisfying $\gamma_i \geq \gamma^1$. Then, for a finite duration, user i can only transmit with r^1; i.e., r^1 region. At t_i^2, user i can support r^2 for the first time and r^2 is the maximum rate it can support for a specific duration; i.e., r^2 region. Figure illustrates regions for the transmission rate values r^ks. Let s_i be the start time of the transmission of user i. Then, the completion time of the transmission is given by $e_i = s_i + \tau_i$ where τ_i is the transmission time of user i such that $\tau_i = D_i/\chi_i$. Since, user i can support a higher transmission rate level at t_i^k instants, e_i is not a monotonically increasing function of s_i. At any $s_i = t_i^k$ value, e_i decreases discontinuously by an amount of $D_i/r^{k-1} - D_i/r^k$ since the transmission rate jumps from r^{k-1} to r^k. This suggests that waiting for the next transmission rate may decrease the completion time for a single user depending on the time instant at which the scheduling decision is given. In the following, we illustrate the optimal rate adaptation and scheduling policy for a single user.

We first start by the following definition.

Definition 1. *Let t_i^{dec} is the time instant at which a scheduling decision is made for a user i. Then, let $s_i^* \geq t_i^{dec}$ be the starting time for user i yielding the minimum completion time e_i^* such that $e_i^* = \min_{s_i \geq t_i^{dec}} s_i + \tau_i(s_i)$. Minimum length scheduling (MLS) slot for user i at time t_i^{dec} is then defined as the time slot for user i allocated in the interval $[s_i^*, e_i^*]$ where $s_i^* \geq t_i^{dec}$.*

Then, it is evident that for a single user, the DR-MLSP problem is solved by allocation of MLS slot at $t_i^{dec} = 0$. Figure 2 illustrates the MLS slot for a single user i. Note that the MLS slot for user i starts at t_i^2 where user i can afford rate r^2 for the first time. This suggests that even if user i can transmit with r^1 previously, the optimal policy is to wait until the time instant t_i^2 since the decrease in the transmission time due to this rate increase is larger than the waiting duration. Note that MLS slot for the user starts at a rate change

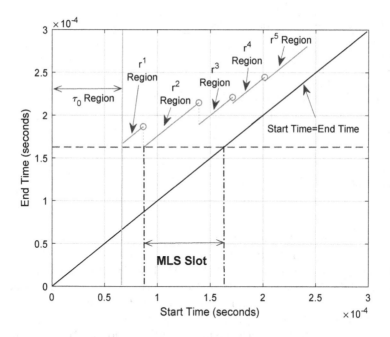

Fig. 2. Illustration of rate regions and MLS slot

instant t_i^k which is not a coincidence for this specific scenario. The following lemma illustrates this behaviour.

Lemma 1. *MLS slot for user i at t_i^{dec} starts at either t_i^{dec} or $t_i^k \geq t_i^{dec}$ for some $k \in [1, M]$.*

Proof. Let starting time for the MLS slot of user i be s_i^* such that $s_i^* \neq t_i^{dec}$ or $s_i^* \neq t_i^k$ for $k \in [1, M]$. Then, let the completion time be e_i^*. Suppose that s_i^* is inside r^l region; i.e., $t_i^l < s_i^* < t_i^{l+1}$. If $t_i^{dec} \leq t_i^l$, then starting the transmission time of user i at t_i^l decreases the completion time by $s_i^* - t_i^l$ since the transmission rate remains the same within r^l region. If $t_i^{dec} > t_i^l$, then starting the transmission time of user i at t_i^{dec} decreases the completion time by $s_i^* - t_i^{dec}$. This is a contradiction by definition of MLS slot.

Lemma 1 illustrates that for a single user, the optimal scheduling policy is allocation of the user at either the time instant where the scheduling decision is made or at one of the time instants where the transmission rate changes for the user. Then, MLS slot determination can be made by evaluating at most $M + 1$ time instants where M is the number of rate levels. Furthermore, Lemma 1 shows that for a predetermined transmission order of users, the optimal scheduling policy is simply determining the MLS slots for the users in the predetermined order.

In the following, we propose a polynomial-time algorithm based on the foregoing discussion.

Algorithm 1. Minimum MLS Slot Algorithm

1: **input:** $\mathcal{F}$
2: **output:** $\mathcal{S}$, $t(\mathcal{S})$
3: $\mathcal{S} \leftarrow \emptyset$, $t^{dec} \leftarrow 0$,
4: **while** $\mathbf{F} \neq \emptyset$ **do**
5:     determine MLS slots for all $i \in \mathcal{F}$ at t^{dec},
6:     $k \leftarrow \mathrm{argmin}_{i \in \mathcal{F}}\, s_i^*(t^{dec})$,
7:     $\mathcal{S} \leftarrow \mathcal{S} + \{k\}$,
8:     $\mathcal{F} \leftarrow \mathcal{F} - \{k\}$,
9:     $t^{dec} \leftarrow e_k^*(t^{dec})$,
10: **end while**
11: $t(\mathcal{S}) \leftarrow t^{dec}$,

The Minimum MLS Slot Algorithm (MMSA), given in Algorithm 1, is described next. Input of MMSA algorithm is a set of users, denoted by $\mathcal{F}$, with the characteristics specified in Sect. 2 (Line 1). The algorithm starts by initializing the schedule $\mathcal{S}$ where the ith element of $\mathcal{S}$ is the index of the user scheduled in the ith time slot and the scheduling decision time t^{dec} (Line 3). At each step of the algorithm, MMSA determines the MLS slots for the unallocated users at t^{dec} (Line 5), and picks the user with the minimum MLS slot starting time s_i^* (Line 6). Then, this user is allocated to its MLS slot starting at s_k^* and completed at e_k^* (Lines 7–8). Algorithm continues by updating the scheduling decision time (Line 9) and giving scheduling decisions for the remaining users (Lines 4–10). MMSA terminates when all users in $\mathcal{F}$ are scheduled and outputs the schedule $\mathcal{S}$ with schedule length $t(\mathcal{S})$ (Line 11).

5   Performance Evaluation

The goal of this section is to evaluate the performance of the proposed algorithm MMSA in comparison to the optimality and a predetermined transmission order based heuristic algorithm, denoted by PDO. PDO aims at minimizing the schedule length for a given transmission order of the users by allocating each user as early as possible, without considering scheduling. The optimal solution is obtained by a brute force algorithm, denoted by BFA, enumerating all possible transmission orders and then picking the best schedule with minimum length.

5.1   Simulation Setup

Simulation results are obtained by averaging over 1000 independent random network realizations. The attenuation of the links considering large-scale statistics are determined using the path loss model given by

$$PL(d) = PL(d_0) + 10\alpha log_{10}\left(\frac{d\cdot}{d_0}\right) + Z \tag{4}$$

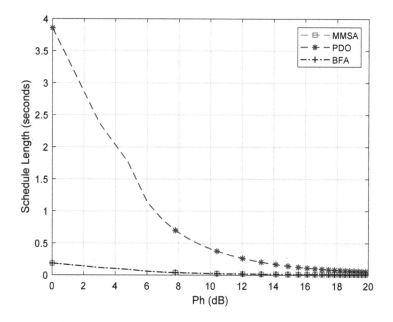

Fig. 3. Schedule Length vs. HAP transmit power P_h

where $PL(d)$ is the path loss at distance d in dB, d_0 is the reference distance, α is the path loss exponent, and Z is a zero mean Gaussian random variable with standard deviation σ. The small-scale fading has been modelled by using Rayleigh fading with scale parameter Ω_i set to mean power level obtained from the large-scale path loss model. The parameters used in the simulations are $\eta_i = 1$ for $i \in [1, N]$; $D_i = 100$ bits for $i \in [1, N]$; $W = 1\,\text{MHz}$; $d_0 = 1\,\text{m}$; $PL(d_0) = 30\,\text{dB}$; $\alpha = 2.76$, $\sigma = 4$. The self interference coefficient β is taken as $-70\,\text{dBm}$. We use $M = 5$ discrete rate and corresponding SNIR levels.

5.2 Scheduling Performance

Figure 3 illustrates the performance of the proposed algorithm for different values of the transmit power of the HAP. Figure illustrates that the proposed algorithm performs very close to the optimal solution. MMSA outperforms PDO significantly for a wide range of P_h. It can be observed that for low values of P_h, scheduling is more critical because the users with low energy require more time to achieve a particular rate level. However, for higher values of the P_h the users can harvest energy at a higher rate so they can reach to the desired SNR levels quickly hence less waiting time is required. Therefore, the superiority of MMSA over PDO is really significant for low values of P_h whereas the performance improvement decreases as P_h increases.

Figure 4 illustrates the performance of MMSA for different number of users. Note that due to exponential complexity of the brute force enumeration used

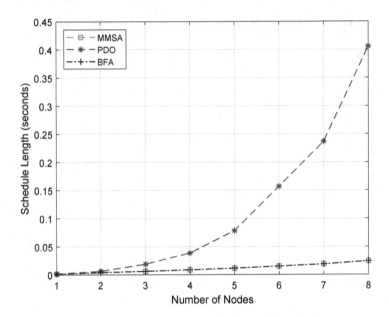

Fig. 4. Schedule Length vs. Number of nodes

in BFA, simulation results are obtained up to 8 users. Similar to Fig. 3, MMSA performs almost optimal while outperforming PDO significantly. As the number of users increases, scheduling becomes more critical since an arbitrary transmission order may result in delays in the transmission of high rate users even if these users do not need large energy harvesting durations. Moreover, increasing number of users puts an arbitrary transmission order further away from the optimality hence increasing the suboptimality of PDO. On the other hand, if the users are scheduled properly by eliminating the unnecessary waiting intervals for achieving higher rates as in MMSA, the optimality performance is preserved showing the robustness of MMSA to the network size. Note that robustness to the network size is very important for future networks with high number of machine type devices or sensors.

Finally, Fig. 5 illustrates the behaviour of the network for different required SNR levels for minimum rate transmissions. It can be observed that for lower values of SNR, the users can start transmission earlier since the amount of energy required for that SNR value will be harvested earlier. This yields smaller schedule length. On the other hand, as the required SNR increases, users need to wait longer to harvest enough energy and achieve successful transmissions increasing the overall schedule length. MMSA performs again close to optimal while significantly outperforming PDO illustrating the importance of a proper scheduling decision.

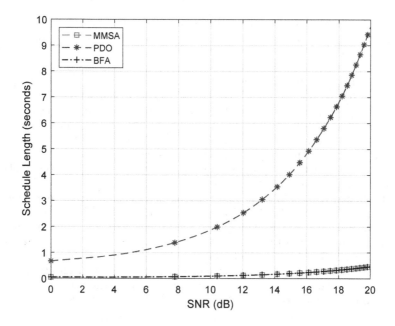

Fig. 5. Schedule length vs SNR values

6   Conclusion and Future Work

In this paper, we have investigated minimum length scheduling problem considering discrete rate transmission model in a full duplex wireless powered communication network. We have characterized an optimization framework to determine the optimal time allocation, rate adaptation and scheduling subject to maximum transmit power, traffic demand and energy causality requirements of the users. First we have mathematically formulated the problem as a mixed integer nonlinear programming problem which is difficult to solve for the global optimum in polynomial time. In order to solve the problem fast and efficiently, then, we have proposed a polynomial time algorithm based on an optimality analysis on the optimization problem. Through numerical analysis, we have shown that the proposed algorithm performs almost optimal while outperforming a predetermined order based heuristic algorithm significantly.

For future work, we plan to extend this work to propose optimal polynomial-time algorithm for the investigated system model. Besides, we aim at extending the system model incorporating multiple hybrid access points and beamforming technology.

References

1. Chi, K., Zhu, Y., Li, Y., Huang, L., Xia, M.: Minimization of transmission completion time in wireless powered communication networks. IEEE Internet Things J. **4**(5), 1671–1683 (2017). https://doi.org/10.1109/JIOT.2017.2689777

2. Di, X., Xiong, K., Fan, P., Yang, H., Letaief, K.B.: Optimal resource allocation in wireless powered communication networks with user cooperation. IEEE Trans. Wirel. Commun. **16**(12), 7936–7949 (2017)
3. Hu, J., Xue, Y., Yu, Q., Yang, K.: A joint time allocation and UE scheduling algorithm for full-duplex wireless powered communication networks. In: 2017 IEEE 86th Vehicular Technology Conference (VTC-Fall), pp. 1–5, September 2017
4. Ju, H., Chang, K., Lee, M.: In-band full-duplex wireless powered communication networks. In: 2015 17th International Conference on Advanced Communication Technology (ICACT), pp. 23–27, July 2015
5. Ju, H., Zhang, R.: Throughput maximization in wireless powered communication networks. In: 2013 IEEE Global Communication Conference (GLOBECOM), pp. 4086–4091, December 2013
6. Ju, H., Zhang, R.: Throughput maximization in wireless powered communication networks. IEEE Trans. Wirel. Commun. **13**(1), 418–428 (2014)
7. Kang, X., Ho, C.K., Sun, S.: Full-duplex wireless-powered communication network with energy causality. IEEE Trans. Wirel. Commun. **14**(10), 5539–5551 (2015)
8. Liu, L., Zhang, R., Chua, K.: Multi-antenna wireless powered communication with energy beamforming. IEEE Trans. Commun. **62**(12), 4349–4361 (2014)
9. Pathak, K., Kalamkar, S.S., Banerjee, A.: Optimal user scheduling in energy harvesting wireless networks. IEEE Trans. Commun. **66**(10), 4622–4636 (2018)

Energy Efficient Naming in Beeping Networks

Ny Aina Andriambolamalala$^{(\boxtimes)}$ and Vlady Ravelomanana$^{(\boxtimes)}$

Université de Paris, IRIF, CNRS, 75013 Paris, France
Ny-Aina.Andriambolamalala@irif.fr, vlad@irif.fr

Abstract. A single-hop beeping network is a distributed communication model in which each station can communicate with all other but only by $1 - bit$ messages called beeps. In this paper, we focus on resolving two fundamental distributed computing issues: the naming and the counting on this model. Especially, we are interested in optimizing energy complexity and running time for those issues. Our contribution is to have design randomized algorithms with an optimal running time of $O(n \log n)$ and optimal $O(\log n)$ energy complexity whether for the naming or the counting for a single-hop beeping network of n stations.

Keywords: Distributed · Initialization · Naming · Energy · Optimal · Beep

1 Introduction

Introduced by Cornejo and Kuhn in 2010 [8], the beeping model makes little demands on the devices which need only to be able to do carrier-sensing, differentiating between silence and the presence of a jamming signal on the network (considered as $1 - bit$ message or one beep). Such devices have unbounded local power computation [6]. They note in [8] that carrier-sensing can typically be done much more reliably and requires significantly less energy and other resources than message-sending models. Minimizing such energy consumption per node arises as all nodes are battery-powered. Since sending or receiving messages costs more energy than internal computations, the energy consumption is measured by the maximal waking time of any node (beeping or listening to the network) [6,16,17,19,21,29]. It is more realistic when the nodes have no prior information about the topology of the network and are initially indistinguishable (have no identifier denoted ID). To break such symmetry, researchers designed various protocols such as leader election ([6,11,12,15,17–19,23,26]) Maximal Independent Set ([1,28]) and naming protocols ([2,7,13,20,21]). In this paper, we consider the naming problem on the single-hop[1] beeping networks which consists in assigning a unique label $\ell \in \{1, 2, ...n\}$ to each node. On the previously described model, we design an energy optimal randomized naming algorithm succeeding

---

[1] The underlying graph of the network is a complete graph.

© Springer Nature Switzerland AG 2019
M. R. Palattella et al. (Eds.): ADHOC-NOW 2019, LNCS 11803, pp. 355–369, 2019.
https://doi.org/10.1007/978-3-030-31831-4_25

in $O(n \log n)$ time slots with high probability[2] (*w.h.p.*), having $O(\log n)$ energy complexity. We start by presenting a deterministic algorithm naming M nodes ($M \leq n$) in $O(M \log n)$ time slots with $O(M + \log n)$ energy (Sect. 2). We then consider the case when n is unknown in Sect. 3. This is then adapted to solve the counting problem, consisting in assigning their exact number to all nodes (Sect. 3). Thereafter, we use derandomization techniques to adapt our algorithm in order to have a deterministic one if n is known beforehand (Sect. 4) terminating with $O(\log n)$ energy complexity. As customary in deterministic settings, we assume that the nodes have unique ID $\in \{1, 2, ...N\}$ (N is a polynomial upper bound of n). Finally, we prove a lower bound of $\Omega(\log n)$ on the energy complexity for naming a beeping network in Sect. 5 and present maple simulation results illustrating our works in Sect. 6.

1.1   The Models

In a single-hop beeping network, nodes communicate with each other via a shared beeping channel.

As shown in the following Figure, this can be used for modeling an ad hoc network where all nodes are in each other's communication range. The nodes can send $1-bit$ messages and do a carrier sensing in order to detect any transmission.

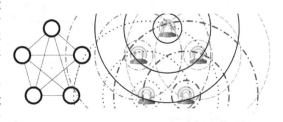

At each synchronous discrete time slot, a node independently decides whether to transmit a beep, to listen to the network or to remain idle (asleep). Only listening nodes can receive the state of the common channel which can be, BEEP if at least one node is transmitting or NULL when no node transmits. This model is also called BL or Beep Listen model. In this paper, we use in general the BL except for the randomized counting protocol for which we use the $B_{\text{CD}}L$ model (Beep with Collision Detection Listen) where transmitters can detect collisions [1,28].

1.2   Related Works and New Results

As a fundamental distributed computing problem [20], many results exist for the naming problem. Let us first consider the simplest model, the single-hop network, where the underlying graph of the network is complete. In [13], Hayashi, Nakano and Olariu presented a $O(n)$ running time randomized protocol for radio networks with collision detection (RNCD). Later, Bordim, Cui, Hayashi, Nakano and Olariu [2] presented an algorithm terminating *w.h.p.* in $O(n)$ time slots, and $O(\log n)$ energy complexity. In [22], for radio network with no collision detection

---

[2] An event ε_n occurs with high probability if $\mathbb{P}[\varepsilon_n] \geq 1 - \frac{1}{n^c}$ for any constant $c > 0$.

(RNnoCD), Nakano and Olariu designed a protocol terminating in $O(n)$ time slots *w.h.p.* with $O(\log \log n)$ energy complexity. The results on beeping model appeared very recently when Chlebus, De Marco and Talo [7] presented their algorithm terminating in $O(n \log n)$ time slots *w.h.p.* for the BL model and provided $\Omega(n \log n)$ lower bound on the time complexity. Moreover, Casteigts, Métivier, Robson and Zemmari [4] presented a counting algorithm for the $B_{\mathrm{CD}}L$ model terminating in $O(n)$ time slots *w.h.p.* They noticed that adapting their algorithm to the BL model will cost a logarithmic slowdown in time complexity. The following Table shows our results on single-hop networks (Table 1).

Table 1. Our results

Problem and model	Time complexity	Energy complexity	Succeed with probability
Randomized naming in BL network Indistinguishable nodes, n unknown, Theorem 2, 5	$O(n \log n)$	$\Theta(\log n)$	$1 - O(\frac{1}{n^c})$ $c > 0$
Unconditional Deterministic naming in BL Unique ID $\in \{1, N\}$, n unknown, Theorem 1	$O(n \log n)$	$O(n)$	-
Derandomized Deterministic naming in BL Unique ID $\in \{1, N\}$, n unknown, Theorem 4	$O(n \log n)$	$O(\log n)$	$1 - O(\frac{1}{n^c})$ $c > 0$
Randomized Counting in BL Theorem 3, 5	$O(n \log n)$	$\Theta(\log n)$	$1 - O(\frac{1}{n^c})$ $c > 0$

The more realistic model where the underlying graph of the network is an arbitrary connected graph (it is called the multi-hop network model) also gained in importance as subject of researches [24]. The only analysis for the initialization protocol in such a multi-hop case was given in [27] and was restricted to a set of nodes randomly thrown in a square. It will then be very interesting to adapt our designed protocols to work on such a model.

2 New Approach: Deterministic Naming of M Nodes

Let N be a polynomial upper bound of n known by the nodes, each node having a unique identifier denoted ID $\in \{1, 2, ...N\}$. In the next sections, N is randomly approximated by the nodes if unknown and the nodes randomly generate unique ID *w.h.p.* In this section, we use a known method consisting in representing ID by its binary encoding and sending the obtained bits one by one in reverse order [14]. If M nodes ($M \leq n$) hold such unique ID, they firstly encode their ID into a binary code-word denoted CID $= [\mathrm{CID}[1]\mathrm{CID}[2]...\mathrm{CID}[\lceil \log_2 N \rceil]]$ such that $\mathrm{CID}[i] \in \{0, 1\}$ ($\mathrm{CID}[1]$ corresponds to $2^{\lceil \log_2 N \rceil}$ and $\mathrm{CID}[\lceil \log_2 N \rceil]$ corresponds to 2^0). Each participant then sends its CID bit by bit during $\lceil \log_2 N \rceil = O(\log n)$ time slots in order to know if it has the largest ID of all participants. If a node detects that one of its neighbors has a higher ID, it gets eliminated (it is no longer a candidate to take the next available label). Then, the unique node holding the largest ID gets such next available label. Such an algorithm can be considered as M deterministic seasons $S_1, S_2, ...S_M$ (the nodes do not know M). In one season S_j, each node sends its CID bit by bit during $\lceil \log_2 N \rceil$ steps $t_1, t_2, ...t_{\lceil \log_2 N \rceil}$. We define the TEST($i$) protocol, called at a step t_i and taking the step number 'i' as parameter. It encodes one bit CID[i] into two communication steps $t_{i,0}$ and $t_{i,1}$ and outputs a status $\in \{\text{ELIMINATED}, \text{ACTIVE}, \text{NULL}\}$.

-TEST(i): If the node s running TEST(i) has CID[i] = 0, then it beeps at $t_{i,0}$ and listens to the network at $t_{i,1} = t_{i,0} + 1$. If it hears beep at $t_{i,1}$, TEST(i) returns ELIMINATED. Otherwise, it returns NULL. If s has CID[i] = 1, then it listens at $t_{i,0}$. If it hears beep at $t_{i,0}$, TEST(i) returns ACTIVE, otherwise it returns NULL.

Then at any step t_i, by executing TEST(i), each participant knows if at least one of them has CID[i] = 1. In such case, each node s having CID[i] = 0 gets eliminated until the next season S_{j+1}. At the end of the season S_j, the last non-eliminated node takes the label j. By looping these computations until no node remains unlabeled, this method produces a naming algorithm terminating in $O(M \log n)$ time slots.

Energy Optimization Principle: The latter algorithm is not energy efficient because all nodes have to be awake during the whole $O(M \log n)$ time slots. To improve such energy consumption, we remark that each node s must be awake only during two specific set of steps in order to know if any of its neighbors has a higher ID. Thus, we introduce the following two definitions of such steps.

Definition 1 (Step To Listen: STL). *A STL is one step t_i recorded by the node s during any season S_j. A node s receiving TEST(i) = ELIMINATED records i into STL and on the next seasons $S_{j+1}, ...S_M$, s wakes up and listens at $t_{i,0}$ in order to verify if it is still eliminated at this step. s may not sleep after t_i.*

Definition 2 (Steps To Notify: STN). *A STN is a set of steps $\{t_i, t_k, ...\}$ recorded by the node s_1 during any season S_j. A node s_1 receiving TEST(i) = ACTIVE knows there is at least one node s_2 having CID[i] = 0 while it has CID[i] = 1. It saves i into STN because at the next seasons, it has to beep at $t_{i,1}$ in order to notify that s_2 is still eliminated at this step. When s_1 adds i into STN, it has no more active neighbor holding CID[k] = 1, $k > i$. Thus, s_1 empties STL.*

Description of the Energy Efficient Algorithm: All nodes are initially sleeping and run the following computations during some seasons $S_1, S_2, ...$ until being labeled. For any season S_j ($j \in \{1, 2, ..., M\}$ and the nodes do not know M), a node s wakes up only at the first step t_i found in its STL or STN. If such $i \in$ STN, then s sleeps before moving at t_{i+1}. Otherwise, if $i \in$ STL and s has TEST(i) = ELIMINATED, then it sleeps until the next season. s stays awake and moves on t_{i+1} if TEST(i) = ACTIVE. At the end of season S_j, the last remaining awake node sets $\ell = j$, empties STN and STL and sleeps. For a better comprehension, we represent the execution of the algorithm by a binary tree as done in [10]. One path of such a tree represents the CID of a device and one of its edges represents one bit of such CID. In the figures showing such representation, we consider the execution of the naming algorithm for only one device. In such figures, the hexagons represent the STL, the squares represent the STN and the circles represent the other waking steps. The number inside these shapes represents the season during which the node wakes up.

Algorithm 1. DETERMINISTICNAMING(N) on any node s

Input   : Upper bound N of n, unique ID $\in \{1, 2, ...N\}$
Output: Node s has unique label $\ell \in \{1, 2, ...M\}$

1 encode ID into binary code-word CID $= \{0, 1\}^{\lceil \log_2 N \rceil}$;
2 $\ell \leftarrow 0$; STL $\leftarrow$ NULL; STN $\leftarrow$ NULL; $S \leftarrow 1$; $Test \leftarrow$ NULL.
3 **while** $\ell = 0$ **do**
4   **for** $i \leftarrow 0$ *to* $\lceil \log_2 N \rceil$ **do**
5   **if** $i \in$ STL **then**
6   wake up at t_i; $Test \leftarrow$ TEST(i)
7   **if** $Test =$ ELIMINATED **then**
8   sleep
9   **end**
10   **end**
11   **if** $i \in$ STN **then**
12   wake up at t_i, run TEST(i) and sleep
13   **end**
14   **if** *s is awake and* $i \notin$ STL **then**
15             $Test \leftarrow$ TEST(i)
16   **if** $Test =$ ACTIVE **then**
17   add i into STN and empty STL
18   **end**
19   **if** $Test =$ ELIMINATED **then**
20   add i into STL and sleep
21   **end**
22   **end**
23   **end**
24   **if** *s is awake* **then**
25         $\ell \leftarrow S$; STL $\leftarrow$ NULL; STN $\leftarrow$ NULL; $Test \leftarrow$ NULL; sleep
26   **end**
27     $S \leftarrow S + 1$
28 **end**

The presented example in the following Figure is for 9 devices having ID $\in$ {15, 14, 13, 12, 11, 10, 9, 8, 7}. The black leaf represents the device having CID = [1010]. s wakes up at step t_1 of season S_1 (1 inside a circle for the root node in the figure). It has CID[1] = 1 and hears that some nodes have CID[1] = 0 then saves 1 into its STN (Fig. 1).

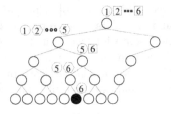

Fig. 1. Example of execution of Algorithm 1

It wakes up at t_2 (1 inside a circle for the next node in the left of the root). As CID[2] = 0 and s hears that some nodes have CID[2] = 1, it adds 2 into its STL and sleeps until the end of S_1. s wakes up at t_1 of S_2 because 1 is in its STN (2 inside a square for the root). Then it wakes up at t_2 as 2 is in its STL (2 inside an hexagons for the left node after the root). As there remains a node having CID[2] = 1, it sleeps until the end of the season S_2. s do the same computations for seasons $S_3, \ldots, S_6$ and gets labeled at S_6.

Lemma 1. *In single hop beeping networks of size n, there is a deterministic algorithm naming some M participating nodes in $O(M \log n)$ time slots with no node being awake for more than $O(M + \log n)$ steps.*

Proof. Algorithm 1 terminates deterministically in $M \times \lceil \log N \rceil = O(M \log n)$ time slots. In the following, let W_s be the total waking times of any node s in the previously defined Algorithm 1, W_{STN}, W_{STL} and W_{other} correspond to STN total waking time, STL and other total waking times. Similarly, $(W_{STN})_{worst}$, $(W_{STL})_{worst}$ and $(W_{other})_{worst}$ are the worst waking times of all nodes. We have

$$W_s = W_{STN} + W_{STL} + W_{other} \leq (W_{STN})_{worst} + (W_{STL})_{worst} + (W_{other})_{worst}. \quad (1)$$

In order to find $(W_{STN})_{worst}$ and $(W_{STL})_{worst}$, we can simulate a complete binary tree to be the tree representation of the networks devices as done in [10]. For a better comprehension, we illustrate how we obtained the two following figures in Appendix 1 and Appendix 2.

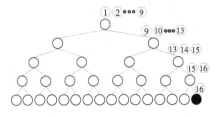

Fig. 2. Worst case for STL.

The node s having $(W_{STL})_{worst}$ (the black node in this Figure) wakes up T times (T Seasons) at any step t_i of STL until no other node has a higher ID. This value T is at most half of participants on t_1 and gets halved every i. We can see (by the hexagons shapes), that s wakes up $\frac{M}{2} + 1$ times in season S_1 (Fig. 2).

Furthermore, as for STL, a node s wakes up at $t_i \in$ STN during as many times (Seasons) as the number of nodes with a higher ID. I.e., half the number of participants at step t_1. This value gets halved every i and we have (Fig. 3)

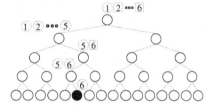

Fig. 3. Worst case for STN.

$$(W_{STN})_{worst} \sim (W_{STL})_{worst} \leq \sum_{i=1}^{M} \left(\frac{M}{2^i} + 1 \right) \leq O(M) \tag{2}$$

A node s wakes up just once at any step t_i not in STN and STL (we can see that by the round shapes in the Figures). Hence, we have

$$(W_{other})_{worst} \leq \sum_{i=1}^{\log N} O(1) \leq O(\log N) \leq O(\log n). \tag{3}$$

$\square$

A Maple simulation illustrates our results in Sect. 6.

Theorem 1. *In single-hop beeping networks of size n, if no node knows n but a polynomial upper bound N of n is given in advance to all nodes and the nodes have a unique ID $\in \{1, 2, ...N\}$, there is an energy efficient deterministic naming algorithm, assigning unique label to all nodes in $O(n \log n)$ time slots, with no node being awake for more than $O(n)$ time slots.*

Proof. Applying Lemma 1 to $M = n$, we reach the desired result. $\square$

In Sect. 3, we use Algorithm 1 as a subroutine to design a randomized energy efficient naming protocol, having $O(\log n)$ energy complexity. To do so, we distribute the nodes into $O\left(\frac{n}{\log n}\right)$ groups in order to have $\Theta(\log n)$ nodes in each group. The main idea is to make $\Theta(\log n)$ nodes running the DETERMINISTIC-NAMING(N) protocol $O\left(\frac{n}{\log n}\right)$ times (each group executes DETERMINISTIC-NAMING(N) one time) instead of n nodes calling DETERMINISTICNAMING(N) one time. This leads us to a $O(\log n)$ waking time per node.

3   Energy Efficient Randomized Algorithms

We assume that the total number of nodes is unknown and that the nodes are initially indistinguishable. All the nodes then have to know a linear approximation u of n. This approximation problem was well studied in the distributed computing area. Brandes, Kardas, Klonowski, Pająk and Wattenhofer [3] designed a randomized linear approximation algorithm, terminating *w.h.p.* in $O(\log n)$ rounds. Our main idea is to make all nodes approximating u in $O(\log n)$ time slots using algorithm presented in [3], which can be parameterized in order to have $u \in [\frac{1}{2}n, 2n]$ in $O(\log n)$ time slots (*i.e.* $2u \in [n, 4n]$ is locally known by the nodes). Then each node chooses uniformly at random to enter into one of $\lceil \frac{2u}{\log(2u)} \rceil = O(\frac{n}{\log n})$ groups.

Lemma 2. *As a classical result (see for instance [25]), if n nodes randomly and uniformly choose to enter into $\lceil \frac{n}{\log n} \rceil$ groups, there is at most $4 \log n$ nodes in each group with high probability.*

Proof. The probability to enter any group G_i is $O\left(\frac{\log n}{n}\right)$. As a consequence, if $|G_i|$ denotes the number of nodes in a group G_i, then $\mathbb{E}[|G_i|] = O(\log n)$. Hence, by means of Chernoff bound, $|G_i| \leq O(\log n)$ with probability at least $1 - O\left(\frac{1}{n}\right)$. $\square$

After that, each node takes a unique ID uniformly from $\{1, 2, ...(2u)^2\}$. We then sequentially run DETERMINISTICNAMING$((2u)^2)$ on each group one group at a time. Firstly, each node in the group G_1 works during at most $\lceil \log(2u)^2 \rceil = O(\log n)$ time slots to name itself. Then, during extra $O(\log n)$ time slots, the last labeled node in G_1 sends its label bit by bit to the next group G_2. In parallel, all the nodes in G_2 wake up and listen to the network during $O(\log n)$ time slots. Those nodes save the received value into a variable ℓ_{prev}. By running DETERMINISTICNAMING(N), all nodes in G_2 have a label $\ell \in \{1, 2, \ldots, |G_2|\}$. Then, each of them has to update $\ell \leftarrow \ell + \ell_{prev}$ in order to make a labeling $\in \{1, 2, \ldots, n\}$. We apply these computations to each couple of groups $\{\{G_1, G_2, \}, \{G_2, G_3\}, \ldots\}$ one by one.

To know if any node s has the last label of its group, we modify the DETERMINISTICNAMING(N) algorithm such that a node labeled at a season S_j wakes up during the entire season S_{j+1} and listens to the network, finding out if there remain unlabeled nodes. This extra $O(\log n)$ waking time doesn't affect our $O(\log n)$ energy complexity.

Theorem 2. *In single-hop beeping networks of size n, if n is unknown by all nodes and nodes are initially indistinguishable, there is an energy efficient randomized naming algorithm, assigning a unique label to all nodes in $O(n \log n)$ rounds w.h.p, with no node being awake for more than $O(\log n)$ time slots.*

Proof. The latter described algorithm uses DETERMINISTICNAMING(N) and is therefore quasi deterministic. As by [3], $u = \Theta(n)$, if we note the time complexity of DETERMINISTICNAMING$(N = (2u)^2)$ algorithm by T_D, our naming algorithm terminates in $\lceil \frac{2u}{\log(2u)} \rceil \times T_D$ time slots. Then by Lemma 2, the number of participants is at most $O(\log n)$ *w.h.p.* Thus, by using $M = O(\log n)$ in Lemma 1 we get $T_D = O(\log^2 n)$, implying the $O(n \log n)$ time complexity of our randomized naming algorithm.

Therefore, each node s is awake only during the execution of the DETERMINISTICNAMING$((2u)^2)$ protocol and $O(\log n)$ extra times for checking if s has the last label as well as sending it to the next group. Consequently, the energy complexity is $O(\log n)$. $\square$

Using such an algorithm, we can design a counting algorithm with $O(n \log n)$ time complexity and $O(\log n)$ energy complexity on the single-hop BL network. To do so, we add the following computations. As it terminates after at most $\lceil \frac{2u}{\log(2u)} \rceil \times \lceil \log^2(2u) \rceil = \lceil 2u \log(2u) \rceil$, all nodes wake up after $\lceil 2u \log(2u) \rceil$ time slots (counted from the first time slot of the Season S_1 for the first group) and the last labeled node send its label bit by bit.

Theorem 3. *In single-hop beeping networks of size n, if n is unknown by all nodes and nodes are initially indistinguishable, there is an energy efficient randomized counting algorithm allowing all the nodes to know the exact number of the participants, terminating in $O(n \log n)$ rounds w.h.p, with no node being awake for more than $O(\log n)$ time slots.*

Proof. If at the end of the last group $G_{\lceil \frac{2u}{\log(2u)} \rceil}$, all nodes wake up and the last labeled node sends its label bit by bit, this value corresponds *w.h.p.* to the exact number of nodes on the network.   □

4   Deterministic Energy Efficient Naming Algorithm

The randomized part of our algorithm consists in the assignment of all nodes to $O\left(\frac{n}{\log n}\right)$ groups of size $O(\log n)$ each. Then, the nodes execute the DETERMINISTICNAMING(N) protocol one group at a time in order to have each node awake for at most $O(\log n)$ time slots. In this Section, we consider a network of n nodes that know the exact value of n. Each node has a unique ID taken from $\{1, N\}$ where N is a polynomial upper bound of n. Our goal is to do the previous group assignment in a deterministic manner, with a very small error rate. To do so, we use a hash function in order to map each node's ID into $\lceil \frac{n}{\log n} \rceil$ values, such that the nodes holding the same value belong to the same group.

Celis, Reingold, Segev and Wieder [5] construct such hashing function, by encoding integer values into binary code-words of length $O(\log n \log \log n)$, such that there is at most $O(\frac{\log n}{\log \log n})$ integers mapped to the same code-word with a probability greater than $1 - O\left(\frac{1}{n^c}\right)$, c being a positive constant. Having this in mind, each node firstly maps its ID into a code-word, using the hashing function described in [5]. The nodes having the same code-word are in the same group. Then, the nodes having the first code-word (the nodes in the first group) execute DETERMINISTICNAMING(N) in order to be labeled. The last labeled node sends ℓ bit by bit to the next group during $O(\log n)$ time slots when the nodes having the second code-word listen to the network. Those nodes in the second group run DETERMINISTICNAMING(N) and add the previously received label to the latter computed label. The last labeled node in the group 2 sends ℓ to the next group and so on.

With such adaptations, we have the following result.

Theorem 4. *In single-hop beeping networks of size n, if n is known in advance by all nodes and nodes have a unique ID $\in \{1, 2, ...N\}$ (N is a polynomial upper* bound of n), there is an energy efficient deterministic naming algorithm, assigning unique label $\ell \in \{1, 2, ...n\}$ to all nodes in $O(n \log n)$ time slots, having no node being awake for more than $O(\log n)$ time slots, with a probability of error less than $O\left(\frac{1}{n^c}\right)$, for some constant $c > 0$ independent of n.

5   Lower Bound on Energy Complexity

In [7], the authors presented an $\Omega(n \log n)$ lower bound for the running time of any randomized naming algorithm. We use such a lower bound in order prove the following result.

Theorem 5. *The energy complexity of any randomized algorithm solving the naming problem with constant probability is $\Omega(\log n)$.*

Proof. It was proved in [7] that any randomized algorithm for naming n stations requires $\Omega(n \log n)$ expected time slots to succeed with a probability of error smaller than $\frac{1}{2}$. Their proof uses the Yao's minimax principle and is combined to Shannon's entropy [9]. We use such running time lower bound to prove the Theorem 5 by contradiction. Let us first remind that the time complexity of any distributed algorithm is measured by the communication time instead of local computations and that the energy complexity is measured by the maximal waking (communication) time of any node. We suppose that there is a randomized naming algorithm with $o(\log n)$ energy complexity. *i.e.* each node communicates on the network during at most $o(\log n)$ time slots when running such an algorithm. It is then straightforward to see that the total communication time (*i.e.* time complexity by definition) of such algorithm is at most $o(n \log n)$. This contradicts the given lower bound of $\Omega(n \log n)$ for time complexity in [7].   □

6   Maple Simulation

In this Section, we present a maple simulation of Algorithm 1: DETERMINISTIC-NAMING(N) where n, the total number of nodes, varies from 10^5 to 10^{10}, 10^6 by 10^6. The $X - axis$ corresponds to the values of n while the $Y - axis$ corresponds to the waking time numbers.

For each value of n, $N = n^2$ and M nodes participate to the naming task (for sake of simplicity, we fix $M = \lceil \log_2 N \rceil$). For each value of n, we randomly choose one of the M participating nodes in order to count the total number of its waking time. In the following Figure, the green (or grey) graph represents the total waking time of any node s_i taken randomly from the M participating nodes $s_1, s_2...s_M$ for each values of n. The blue (or bold black) graph is the values of M for each value of n and the red (or black) graph represents $c \times M$ (here $c = 3.6$) (Fig. 4).

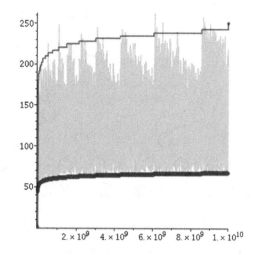

Fig. 4. The energy complexity of nodes taken randomly from a set of $\lceil \log N \rceil$ nodes. (Color figure online)

The maple codes are available in

https://www.irif.fr/~nixiton/initLoop.mw or in
https://www.irif.fr/~nixiton/initLoop.pdf

7 Conclusion

In this paper, we focus on the naming problem in single-hop beeping networks. We start by a deterministic version, when the nodes known N, a polynomial upper bound of n and all nodes have a unique ID $\in \{1, N\}$. Such a protocol has $O(n \log N)$ time complexity and $O(n)$ energy complexity. Then, when the nodes do not know the exact value of n and are initially indistinguishable, we design a randomized algorithm terminating in optimal $O(n \log n)$ time slots *w.h.p.*, and optimal $O(\log n)$ energy complexity. We have also established that for the same task, $\Omega(\log n)$ waking time slots are necessary for any randomized algorithm to succeed with a constant probability. Our algorithm can be used for the counting problem, returning the exact number of the nodes in $O(n \log n)$ time slots, with $O(\log n)$ energy complexity. By means of derandomization, we devise an energy-efficient deterministic naming algorithm that errs with probability less than $O\left(\frac{1}{n^c}\right)$ terminating in $O(n \log n)$ time slots with $O(\log n)$ energy complexity. Our protocols has optimal time and energy complexity for the single-hop network. It will be then interesting to consider how to adapt such a protocol to work on the multi-hop beeping network model which is much more realistic than the single-hop one.

Appendix 1: Worst Case for STL

Here, we show a simulation of the execution of Algorithm 1 on the worst case
for STL in a complete binary Tree to count the number of waking time of this
node.

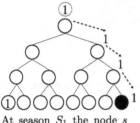

At season S_1 the node s
wakes up once at step t_1,
gets eliminated and sleeps
until season S_2. Node 1
gets labeled.

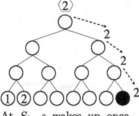

At S_2, s wakes up once
at step $t_1 \in$ STL, gets
eliminated and sleeps
until S_3. Node 2 gets
labeled.

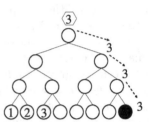

At S_3, s wakes up at step
$t_1 \in$ STL, gets eliminated
and sleeps until S_4. Node
3 gets labeled.

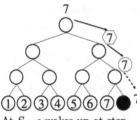

At S_4, s wakes up at step
$t_1 \in$ STL, gets eliminated
and sleeps until S_5. Node
4 gets labeled.

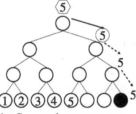

At S_5, s wakes up at step
$t_1 \in$ STL. Since there is
no more node that can
eliminate it, s remain
awake until t_2, gets eliminated there and sleeps
until S_6. Node 5 gets
labeled.

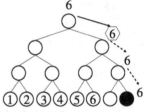

At S_6, s wakes up at step
$t_2 \in$ STL, gets eliminated
and sleeps until S_7. Node
6 gets labeled.

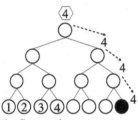

At S_7, s wakes up at step
$t_2 \in$ STL, remains awake
until t_3, gets eliminated
at t_3 and sleeps until S_8.
Node 7 gets labeled.

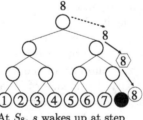

At S_8, s wakes up at step
$t_3 \in$ STL, remains awake
until t_4. s gets labeled at
t_4.

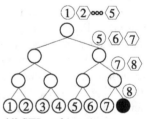

All STL waking times

Legends: hexagons represent the STL waking steps of the node, squares are the
STN waking steps and circles represent the other waking steps. The numbers

inside these shapes represent the season where the node wakes up. Numbers without any shape represent the sleeping steps of the node. Dotted lines represents the transition between two steps t_i, t_{i+1} on any season where the node starts to sleeps or remains sleeping. And solid lines the transition between two steps t_i, t_{i+1} on any season where the node wakes up or remains awake.

Appendix 2: Worst Case for STN

In this section, we show a simulation of the execution of Algorithm 1 on the worst case for STN in a complete binary Tree to count the number of waking time of this node.

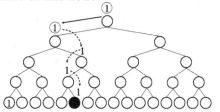

At season S_1 the node s wakes up once at step t_1, remains awake until t_2, gets eliminated at t_2 and sleeps until season S_2. Node 1 gets labeled.

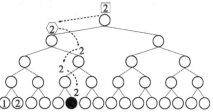

At S_2, s wakes up at step $t_1 \in$ STN, sleeps and wakes up at $t_2 \in$ STL, gets eliminated at t_2 and sleeps until season S_2. Node 2 gets labeled.

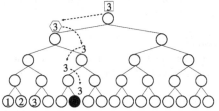

At S_3, s wakes up at step $t_1 \in$ STN, sleeps and wakes up at $t_2 \in$ STL, gets eliminated at t_2 and sleeps until season S_4. Node 3 gets labeled.

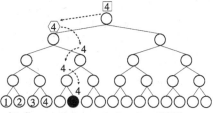

At S_4, s wakes up at step $t_1 \in$ STN, sleeps and wakes up at $t_2 \in$ STL, gets eliminated at t_2 and sleeps until season S_5. Node 4 gets labeled.

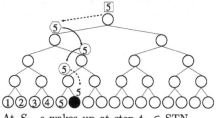

At S_5, s wakes up at step $t_1 \in$ STN, sleeps and wakes up at $t_2 \in$ STL, Since there is no more node that can eliminate it there, s remain awake until t_4 where it gets eliminated, and sleeps until S_6. Node 4 gets labeled.

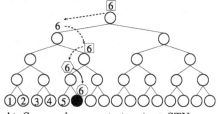

At S_6, s wakes up at step $t_1 \in$ STN, sleeps and wakes up at $t_3 \in$ STN, sleeps an wakes up at $t_4 \in$ STL. Since there is no more node that can eliminate it there, s remain awake until t_6 and gets labeled.

References

1. Afek, Y., Alon, N., Bar-Joseph, Z., Cornejo, A., Haeupler, B., Kuhn, F.: Beeping a maximal independent set. Distrib. Comput. **26**(4), 195–208 (2013)
2. Bordim, J.L., Cui, J., Hayashi, T., Nakano, K., Olariu, S.: Energy-efficient initialization protocols for ad-hoc radio networks. ISAAC 1999. LNCS, vol. 1741, pp. 215–224. Springer, Heidelberg (1999). https://doi.org/10.1007/3-540-46632-0_23
3. Brandes, P., Kardas, M., Klonowski, M., Pająk, D., Wattenhofer, R.: Approximating the size of a radio network in beeping model. In: Suomela, J. (ed.) SIROCCO 2016. LNCS, vol. 9988, pp. 358–373. Springer, Cham (2016). https://doi.org/10.1007/978-3-319-48314-6_23
4. Casteigts, A., Métivier, Y., Robson, J.M., Zemmari, A.: Counting in one-hop beeping networks. Theoret. Comput. Sci. (2016, to appear)
5. Celis, L.E., Reingold, O., Segev, G., Wieder, U.: Balls and bins: smaller hash families and faster evaluation. SIAM J. Comput. **42**(3), 1030–1050 (2013)
6. Chang, Y.J., Kopelowitz, T., Pettie, S., Wang, R., Zhan, W.: Exponential separations in the energy complexity of leader election. In: Proceedings of the 49th Annual ACM SIGACT Symposium on Theory of Computing, pp. 771–783. ACM (2017)
7. Chlebus, B.S., De Marco, G., Talo, M.: Naming a channel with beeps. Fundamenta Informaticae **153**(3), 199–219 (2017)
8. Cornejo, A., Kuhn, F.: Deploying wireless networks with beeps. In: Lynch, N.A., Shvartsman, A.A. (eds.) DISC 2010. LNCS, vol. 6343, pp. 148–162. Springer, Heidelberg (2010). https://doi.org/10.1007/978-3-642-15763-9_15
9. Cover, T.M., Thomas, J.A.: Elements of Information Theory. Wiley Series in Telecommunications and Signal Processing, 2nd edn. Wiley, Hoboken (2006)
10. Fuchs, M., Hwang, H.K.: Dependence between external path-length and size in random tries. arXiv preprint arXiv:1604.08658 (2016)
11. Ghaffari, M., Haeupler, B.: Near optimal leader election in multi-hop radio networks. In: Proceedings of the Twenty-Fourth Annual ACM-SIAM Symposium on Discrete Algorithms, pp. 748–766 (2013)
12. Ghaffari, M., Lynch, N., Sastry, S.: Leader election using loneliness detection. Distrib. Comput. **25**(6), 427–450 (2012)
13. Hayashi, T., Nakano, K., Olariu, S.: Randomized initialization protocols for packet radio networks. In: ipps, p. 544. IEEE (1999)
14. Jacquet, P., Milioris, D., Mühlethaler, P.: A novel energy efficient broadcast leader election. In: 2013 IEEE 21st International Symposium on Modelling, Analysis and Simulation of Computer and Telecommunication Systems, pp. 495–504. IEEE (2013)
15. Jurdziński, T., Kutyłowski, M., Zatopiański, J.: Efficient algorithms for leader election in radio networks. In: Proceedings of the Twenty-First Annual Symposium on Principles of Distributed Computing, pp. 51–57. ACM (2002)
16. Jurdziński, T., Kutyłowski, M., Zatopiański, J.: Energy-efficient size approximation of radio networks with no collision detection. In: Ibarra, O.H., Zhang, L. (eds.) COCOON 2002. LNCS, vol. 2387, pp. 279–289. Springer, Heidelberg (2002). https://doi.org/10.1007/3-540-45655-4_31
17. Kardas, M., Klonowski, M., Pajak, D.: Energy-efficient leader election protocols for single-hop radio networks. In: 2013 42nd International Conference on Parallel Processing (ICPP), pp. 399–408. IEEE (2013)

18. Kutten, S., Pandurangan, G., Peleg, D., Robinson, P., Trehan, A.: Sublinear bounds for randomized leader election. In: Frey, D., Raynal, M., Sarkar, S., Shyamasundar, R.K., Sinha, P. (eds.) ICDCN 2013. LNCS, vol. 7730, pp. 348–362. Springer, Heidelberg (2013). https://doi.org/10.1007/978-3-642-35668-1_24

19. Lavault, C., Marckert, J.F., Ravelomanana, V.: Quasi-optimal energy-efficient leader election algorithms in radio networks. J. Inf. Comput. **205**(5), 679 (2007)

20. Nakano, K.: Optimal initializing algorithms for a reconfigurable mesh. J. Parallel Distrib. Comput. **24**(2), 218–223 (1995)

21. Nakano, K., Olariu, S.: Energy-efficient initialization protocols for radio networks with no collision detection. In: 2000 International Conference on Parallel Processing, pp. 263–270 (2000)

22. Nakano, K., Olariu, S.: Energy-efficient initialization protocols for single-hop radio networks with no collision detection. IEEE Trans. Parallel Distrib. Syst. **11**(8), 851–863 (2000)

23. Nakano, K., Olariu, S.: Uniform leader election protocols for radio networks. IEEE Trans. Parallel Distrib. Syst. **13**(5), 516–526 (2002)

24. Perkins, C.E., et al.: Ad Hoc Networking, vol. 1. Addison-Wesley, Reading (2001)

25. Raab, M., Steger, A.: "Balls into Bins" — A Simple and Tight Analysis. In: Luby, M., Rolim, J.D.P., Serna, M. (eds.) RANDOM 1998. LNCS, vol. 1518, pp. 159–170. Springer, Heidelberg (1998). https://doi.org/10.1007/3-540-49543-6_13

26. Ramanathan, M.K., Ferreira, R.A., Jagannathan, S., Grama, A., Szpankowski, W.: Randomized leader election. Distrib. Comput. **19**(5–6), 403–418 (2007)

27. Ravelomanana, V.: Randomized initialization of a wireless multihop network. In: Proceedings of the 38th Annual Hawaii International Conference on System Sciences, pp. 324b–324b. IEEE (2005)

28. Scott, A., Jeavons, P., Xu, L.: Feedback from nature: an optimal distributed algorithm for maximal independent set selection. In: Proceedings of the 2013 ACM Symposium on Principles of Distributed Computing, pp. 147–156. ACM (2013)

29. Vlady, R.: Time-optimal and energy-efficient size approximation of radio networks. In: 2016 International Conference on Distributed Computing in Sensor Systems (DCOSS), pp. 233–237. IEEE (2016)

Optimisation of Energy Consumption in Traffic Video Monitoring Systems Using a Learning-Based Path Prediction Algorithm

Papa Samour Diop[✉], Ahmath Bamba Mbacké[✉], Gervais Mendy[✉], Ibrahima Gaye[✉], and Jeanne Roux Ngo Bilong[✉]

Laboratoire d'Informatique et de Réseaux Télécommunications (LIRT), École Supérieure Polytechnique de Dakar (ESP/UCAD), Dakar, Senegal
{papasamour.diop,ahmathbamba.mbacke,gervais.mendy,gaye.ibrahima, jeanneroux}@esp.sn

Abstract. The number of CCTV video surveillance systems has grown rapidly over the past decade. As CCTV systems are large energy consumers, the problem of optimising the energy consumption of CCTV systems is urgently needed. In this study, we analyse with mathematical models the energy balance consumption for an architecture that implements a path-by-learning prediction algorithm that predicts the path and destination of a mobile in a CCTV network in order to reduce energy consumption. This method significantly reduces the energy consumption of the CCTV system in real time. An experimental system is designed to evaluate the method and experiments are carried out to demonstrate the validity of the method. The experimental results show that the method has not only significantly improved resource use and reduced energy consumption.

Keywords: Data transmission · Mobile · Monitoring · Forecasting perception · Distributed learning · Smart city · CCTV system · Energy consumption

1 Introduction

While the major contradiction between energy demand and supply is gradually increasing, energy conservation has become an increasingly important concern worldwide, particularly in Senegal. With the improvement of people's standard of living, the proportion for which the energy consumption of buildings represents the total consumption of society is constantly increasing. HVAC (heating, ventilation and air conditioning) and lighting systems consume the vast majority of the daily energy consumption of buildings (more than 50%) and have considerable potential for energy savings.

© Springer Nature Switzerland AG 2019
M. R. Palattella et al. (Eds.): ADHOC-NOW 2019, LNCS 11803, pp. 370–387, 2019.
https://doi.org/10.1007/978-3-030-31831-4_26

Much of the irrational energy consumption is due in large part to the fact that conventional video surveillance systems and the processing systems for these data from video surveillance cameras. One way to save energy is to use a closed loop feedback control strategy involving real-time information to allow a video surveillance system to only film scenes where there are events. When the number of cars in a road decreases, some cameras must be automatically set to standby to reduce unnecessary energy consumption. Therefore, the presence detection of objects in a scene is a necessary support. Previous research has shown that good occupancy detection can save up to 50% energy for lighting and 20% energy for HVAC.

The document is structured as follows: Firstly, we will presented a related works in Energy Optimization Methods in CCTV (closed circuit monitoring systems). Secondly, we will proposed our learning path prediction algorithm in a video monitoring architecture. Thirdly, we will presented energy balance results and we will analysed comparing a centralized and distributed architecture. End, we present the conclusion and our future research.

2   Related Works

Today, energy optimization methods for CCTV are mainly divided into two categories: methods based on scale models and methods based on piecemeal models. Methods based on reduced models should adjust server parameters, such as processor voltages and disc rotation speeds, according to load requirements [1]. Methods reduce the power consumption of servers to a scale close to the number of inactive servers, if the parameters are adjustable. Since this type of method ignores inactive energy consumption, it is difficult to significantly improve the efficiency of energy savings. Clearly, the methods cannot work in the CCTV if the server configurations are not able to adjust the given parameters. In addition, it is difficult to significantly improve the efficiency of energy savings because the power consumption of resting servers is still important in the virtual storage system. Bulk model methods take into account inactive energy consumption and can be classified into three types of methods: virtual machine migration methods, task migration methods and planning methods. Methods of migration of virtual machines empty the servers by moving the virtual machines that are run there to the other servers, and then turn the inactive servers off to save energy. A new server is only opened when the number of servers is not sufficient to meet the requirements of the current loading operation. The issue of energy optimization can be framed as a packaging problem for mapping virtual machines to servers. It is part of a difficult problem to solve (non-deterministic polynomial time) and has been widely studied [1,2]. The principle of energy optimization of task migration methods is identical to that of VM migration methods, with the exception of migrating objects for energy optimization, but these are tasks for VM. However, real-time migration of virtual computers and tasks requires a great deal of computation, communication and energy consumption. In addition, as the real-time and high-reliability task requirements in the CCTV become increasingly stringent, it is difficult to ensure the continuity of all in-progress video surveillance tasks during real-time mobile tracking. As a result, virtual machine and task migration methods are not adapted to the nature of the CCTV system; task planning methods assign tasks to the appropriate virtual computers to perform in the overall objective of reducing the number of virtual computers started while ensuring that all tasks in progress are qualified. As a result, the number of live servers is reduced, potentially reducing energy consumption. Our proposal will use this model for video surveillance cameras to reduce the overall consumption of the system.

3   Power Supply, Various Configurations

- 220 V Network
  If our cameras are electrically powered by the 220 V network and connected to it by a processor, there is no specific problem with consumption. Aside from the installation of the power grid, we will only need to know how much electricity is consumed.
- CPL (power lines online)
  If CPL technology is used, it does not have a particular point when used indoors but can be difficult to implement outdoors, as equipment (transfo, Plug) can be strenuous, especially at temperature extremes.
- POE (Power Over Ethernet)
  On the other hand, we do not use the POE technique in our video surveillance architecture what is POE. Many people are now using the POE system. The advantage is that you are free of a power supply and the power supply to the camera passes through the rj45 cable. So a single cable for data and power supply is simple, economical and available to all. In addition, in the event of an electrical power outage, the POE allows you to operate your cameras in combination with an inverter. There are two standards:

  - 802.3af: Injector or Switch have a maximum power of 15.4 W under 48 V
  - 802.3at: power goes from 24 W mini to 30 W under 48 V [1,3].

3.1   Using a POE Switch Correctly

A POE switch has a maximum power, also known as Budget, and a maximum power per POE port. The IEEE802.3af Power Power over Ethernet standard defines how power will be provided on CAT5 lines. Despite the differences between existing devices and those that adhere to the new standard, there is no need to completely replace existing systems. The 48 V nominal voltage required by the Powered Devices (PD) can be provided by medium-sized energy source equipment (PES), which is connected to the serial frontal interface with legacy routers and switches. The LTC4259A controller is a fourfold PSE controller designed for the final and mid-range PES that integrates PD signature detection, power level classification, AC and DC disconnect detection, and current limit without microcontroller requirement.

3.2   The Responsibilities of an PSE

The responsibilities of the PSE are to detect if a compliant PD is connected to a port, eventually classify the PD and properly feed the PD while protecting the port from failures. Once the PD is activated, the PSE monitors its presence and cuts power when the device is removed. An SSE must also provide overstress protection to avoid damage to the SSE and DP.

Traditional PSE solutions use a microcontroller to perform measurements, detect calculations and control additional circuits that switch power to a PD. The LTC4259A in Fig. 1, on the other hand, does not require any microcontroller and independently performs signature detection. It automatically interprets loading conditions and energizes a valid PD.

The median PSE does not either have to hamper the functioning of a full stop. A PSE of extremity feeds the pairs of signals or the spare pairs of the cable CAT5, whereas the PSE of middle of the range has to feed only the spare pairs. If a PSE of middle of the range or extremity is capable of detecting a valid signature 25 KO(KB) (RSIG) and of feeding the PD, a compatible PD will not post any more the RSIG to prevent any other detection of good signature detected and switched on from the second PSE. The material implementation of the timer of protection eliminates the need for a routine of software schedule of the microcontroller.

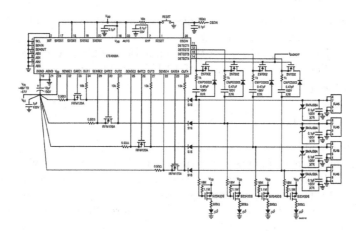

Fig. 1. Autonomous 4-port power over Ethernet midspan PSE

3.3   Detection of Disconnect

When a PD is disconnected from a powered port, the IEEE standards specify that a PES shall implement at least one of the two modes of power disconnect detection for the removal of power from the port: DC disconnect and/or sector disconnect. The DC disconnect measures the minimum current taken from a port to determine if a PD is present and requires power. Although this is easier to implement, CA disconnect is considered a more accurate detection of the presence of a DP. The AC disconnect measures the impedance of the PD and keeps a port powered, even for PDs that are inactive at low power The automatic LTC4259A mode uses the default CA disconnect method. The LT1498 in Fig. 2 is a double rail-to-rail amp used to emit a sine wave to control the LTC4259A OSCIN. The LTC4259A applies the AC signal to the lines and detects its presence when a PD has been removed and the port power must be turned off [7].

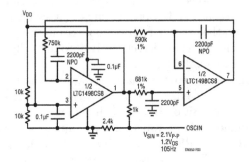

Fig. 2. Sine wave circuit for AC disconnect

3.4 Supply of 3,3 V from −48 V

A 3.3 V power supply supplies the digital portion of the LTC4259A. LTC3803 converts 48 V to 3.3 V, eliminating the use of a second power supply. This overvoltage controller circuit achieves a tight regulation of 2% and delivers outputs of 400 mA, sufficient for a maximum of 12 LTC4259As and port lights in a 48 port application [7].

3.5 Options of the LTC4259A

The LTC4259A also offers a big flexibility during the conception of a PSE of full or intermediate stop. The internal registers are accessible via I2C for a control and additional regulations, including the option of disconnection DC. The LTC4259A facilitates the management of the supply in compliance with IEEE by supplying a classification PD (method more effective than to guess via a current of surveillance) of devices presenting a class, such as a controller of interface LTC4257 PD.

Example: for 4 ports POE, if the maxi power by port is of 15 w, it does not mean that you can connect 4 cameras of 15 w, or 15 w × 4 = 60 w.

Most of the time, the maxi power of Switch is lower, 53 w for example. It means that you can connect cameras of a power = in 15 w but on condition that the sum of the powers of cameras is = in 53 w.

Or for example: 2 cameras of 15 w, 1 camera of 10 w and a camera of 13 w.

Some Switch has a function of priority of port. The most priority port being the port 1, the least priority the port 4 for example. In case of overload, the system cuts the supply of the least priority port [7].

- If the POE power of my Switch is insufficient, this may be the case for more energy consuming PTZ cameras (40 w for example). In this case, you will need to use a POE injector with power that is adapted to or greater than that of your camera.
- My camera is not POE: In this case and if you still want to use the POE technique, you will need to acquire a Splitter. The latter is an adapter that allows you to receive data and power via a rj45 cable and then return data and power separately by two cables adapted to your camera's connectivity.

3.6   State of the Art of Video Sensors

Nowadays, various video sensors are used from surveillance systems. The technical specifications of video sensors playing an essential role in the potential of a surveillance system, we describe in this section the technical characteristics of the sensors.

The oldest and most widely used types of video sensors are analogy video sensors used in CCTV surveillance systems (closed circuit television). The resolution of analogy cameras is measured in vertical and horizontal line dimensions and is generally limited by the camera and recorder capabilities used by the video surveillance system.

Until five years ago, the higher resolution for analogy systems came from the D1 format. However, since 2015, AHD CCTV (Analogy High Definition) cameras, as well as the corresponding recorders, have been introduced to the market. For the specification of analogy video sensors in images per second (FPS), it can vary between 30 FPS, 15 FPS, 7,5 FPS, 5 FPS and 1 FPS. The majority of systems use either 15 FPS or 7,5 FPS, as higher values require a high storage volume, if recorded.

Over the past 15 years, digital video sensors have gained market share over analogy technology. While analogy sensors transmit captured data without compression, digital sensors digitize the input stream and can therefore benefit from compression algorithms and advanced video codecs. As a result, these sensors can interface directly with network infrastructures and transmit their data via switches and routers. This is why digital sensors are often referred to as IP cameras. The resolution and pace of digital sensors are adjustable. Common IP cameras, now in the HD (high definition) category, can capture 1920 1080 and 30 SPF videos and reduce to 1280 720 or D1 for 15 SPF's. Ultra HD (UHD) video sensors were also introduced into monitoring systems, pushing the available resolutions to 4K (3840 2160, generally less than 15 SPF) or 2048 1536 to less than 30 SPF [4].

Finally, since the beginning of year 2010, a new type of video camera was introduced, the video sensors HDR (High Dynamic Range). These sensors, who work generally in a resolution HD, are capable of capturing the same scene several times by using various exposure times (interval of time during which the shutter of the camera remains open and data collection), then these images in a single image organize. This technique, which is at present available only for video cameras top of the range, darkens the clear zones of the scene and the clearer dark zones, so improving the quality of the video flow.

Camera HDR (as well as cameras HD and UHD) uses the video codec an Hour 264. Furthermore, the community of the researchers suggested during the last years using the video high-efficiency coding (HEVC) as standard of video coding suited for the contents HDR. Recently, several organizations, among which the Association of Blu-ray discs (BDA), the Forum of the high-definition multimedia interface (HDMI) and the alliance (wedding ring) UHD (Ultra-High Definition) decided to adopt a size of distribution based on HEVC hand 10. "HDR10", for the contents HDR of compression and delivery.

4   Prediction Principle

The architectures of our model have been validated in the articles [5,6].

The road network will be represented by a graph $G = (V, E)$ where V is a set of vertices and E the set of edges.

$$V = \{x_1, x_2, ...x_n\} \ and \ E = \{e_1, ...e_2, ...e_m\} \tag{1}$$

We have a graph G of order n and size m. The goal is to predict the road $P_j = x_1 e_1 ... x_i e_i ... e_{j-1} x_j$ that the mobile has to take. We assume that at each node in the network, we have a camera.

The vertices x_i denotes the cameras and e_i denotes the edge connecting the cameras x_i and x_{i+1}.

It is assumed that there is a succession of nodes (cameras) and the edges (e_i) the links between two cameras. For predicting a path, we can either consider a succession of nodes or a succession of edges. A vehicle that passes through this circuit will take one path (it will move from one edge to another).

$$G = (V, E) \tag{2}$$

We pose:

$N_i =$ node or camera
crossing Edge = The next edge
$NberVehicle =$ The number of vehicles crossed and detected at each camera
$Prob_0 =$ The probability of passing at each node.
$Prob_{N_i} =$ The probability of passing from the node N_i to an edge E_i as a function of time
$Card_{N_i E_j(t)} =$ Number of vehicles crossed on a node.

Theoretically, it is supposed to take an optimal path (V_{op}). We define V_{op} according to time and energy consumption. Thus, we define an optimal path, the path whose duration is the smallest.

V_{op} the path whose duration of travel $<<<$:
$T_{op} = Min\{T(Ch)\} = \sum T_{E_{i_{(E_i \in Ch)}}}.$

The optimal path between two nodes is the path on which the midway point is the lowest. Let us consider all the paths that connect a starting point x to an end point y. We have: $V_{op} \in \{V_k\}_{Cost(Vop) \leqslant Cost(V_k)}$.

It is assumed that the starting point (x) and the destination (y) where x and y are the ends of the path are known and will certainly analyse this network in terms of cost (the most traditional approaches). Drivers commonly seek to optimize this path in terms of cost V_{op}. Classical predictive solutions are better-way algorithms. So you can have variable costs and even distances from a road depending on time. So you can have variable costs and even distances of a road depending on the time (Fig. 3).

$$Cost(V_{op}) = T_{op} \qquad (3)$$

In our case, the strong assumption is that the vehicles know their way and their destination. As we try to have a tracking system, we have to be able to predict where the motive goes in order to be able to get it before it gets there. Our system must be able to receive a vehicle at the entrance and predict the way. $N_i\{outgoingEdge : Nber.Vehicle\}$. The strategy adopted is the use of a learning process: For each vehicle that arrives at a node (N_i) (a camera), we will learn the probability of passing each edge

$$Prob_0 = (E_i, N_j, t) = \frac{\sum NberVehicle/E_i, t}{\sum NberVehicle/E_j, t} \qquad (4)$$

$$Prob_{N_i}(E_j, t) = \frac{Card_{N_i E_j(t)}}{\sum_{k=0}^{nberEdgeN_i} Card_{N_k E_j(t)}} \qquad (5)$$

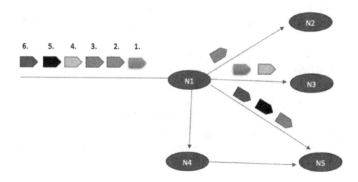

Fig. 3. Prediction on an N1(camera) node of the video surveillance system

Either N4: The knot

- **Simple Scenario:** Prediction without prior knowledge of nodes:

In this case, we have a prediction based on learning how to distribute the preceding passages. We have a prediction that's limited to a ridge.

Next $Edge/Node_{N_i}$:

$$Prob_1 = N_i \in \{V_{N_j}\}/Prob_{N_i}(V_{N_j}, t) = Max(Prob_{N_i}(V_{N_j}, t) \text{ and } Prob_{N_i}(V_{N_j}, t) \neq 0 \quad (6)$$

with V_{N_j} = the neighbouring nodes of Ni

$$N_1 \in \{N_2, N_4\} = Prob_{N_1}(E, t) = Max \begin{cases} Prob_{N_1}((N_2, t) = 1/6 \\ Prob_{N_1}((N_3, t) = 2/6 \\ Prob_{N_1}((N_4, t) = 0/6 \\ Prob_{N_1}((N_5, t) = 3/6 \end{cases} \quad (7)$$

Data representation (camera level knowledge) or shared mental map: Tab' [node, TimeStamp, Destination_Node] = Global Matrix.

- **Complex Scenario:** Prediction with knowledge of path before

By linking the prediction based on the probability on each node and on the history we can not only predict the prediction on the next ridge but on the whole path it will take.

$$Prob_2 = (V_i, N_j, t) = \prod Prob_1 i/k \in [Edge_1, \ldots., Edge_j] \quad (8)$$

- **Complex Scenario:** Prediction with knowledge of previous path

By linking the probability-based prediction to each node and to the history, we can not only predict the prediction on the next ridge but the whole path it will take.

- **Distributed Learning Prediction:** Presentation of Data Models. Representation of data (knowledge at the level of each camera) local. We pose:

Timestamp (At which point the node was last refreshed)
Knot: Knot where the motive is located
$Destination_{Node}$: Next Node
VehicleNber = Number of times a mobile has passed.
We put the timestamp like a time slot on an interval of 1 h
Tab [timestamp, $Destination_{Node}$] = NberVehicle
Tab [timestamp, $Preceding_{Path}$, $Destination_{Node}$] = NberVehicle

N_5:
$$\begin{aligned} V &= [8h - 9h, < N_1, N_3, N_4 >, N_6] = 3 \\ &= [8h - 9h, < N_1, N_2, N_4 >, N_6] = 1 \\ &= [8h - 9h, < N_1, N_3, N_4 >, N_7] = 0 \end{aligned} \quad (9)$$

Data representation (camera level knowledge) or shared mental map: Tab[Node] [timestamp, $Preceding_{Path}$, $Destination_{Node}$] = NbrVehicule.

- **Presentation of the used Algorithm:** In this case, we will need an information processing model to be able to predict the path according to the video surveillance architecture (Fig. 4).

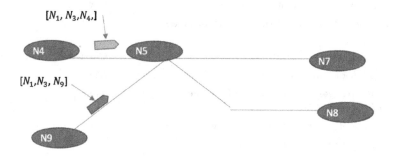

Fig. 4. Knowledge prediction of previous node history

$NextNode_{N_i}(Vehicle) = N \in \{N_j\}/Prob_{N_i}(N, t, Vh) = Max(Prob_{N_i}(N_j, t, Vh))$ and $Prob_{N_i}(N, t, Vh) \neq 0$
with $Vehicle \mapsto NumberVehicle$
$Vh \mapsto Historicvector = < Node_{Origin}, \ldots\ldots, Node_{Destination} >$

we'll have:

$NextNode_{N_i}(Vehicle) \mapsto Node_{Next}$
$Vehicle.vh \longleftarrow Vehicle.vh + N_i$
Path prediction algorithm
$NextNode_{N_i}(Vehicle) \mapsto Node_{Next}$
$VehicleTest \longleftarrow Vehicle;$
$VehicleTest.Vh \longleftarrow VehicleTest.Vh + N_i;$
For i $\leftarrow$ 0 To n Do
$\quad NextNode_{Next}(VehicleTest) \mapsto Node_{Next'}$
$\quad VehicleTest.Vh \longleftarrow VehicleTest.Vh + Node_{Next}$
$\quad Node_{Next} \longleftarrow Node_{Next'}$

- **Energy Balance Sheet:** Know the consumption of its network of cameras. The electric consumption of an element of the network expresses himself in kilowatt-hours (KWH). To estimate the annual consumption, you have to take into account the following 2 points:

  - the power of your device, expressed in watts
  - the number of hours a day in the course of which the device works

Generalization: in Table 1, we have the used values reference in our model.

Table 1. Reference values

Time of decision-making	Td
Time of activation camera	Tap
Consumption in energy of the processing center	Ct
Consumption in energy of the switch	Cew
The number of sections of the network of video surveillance	NbrT
Field of vision will be on drugs	Carried by the camera
The number of will be on drugs by section	NbrCt
The time averages of functioning of a camera in the entry of the network	Tmc
The consumption on average of energy of a camera	Cec
The number of vehicle on average by section	NbrVt
Speed of the mobile (constant speed)	Vm
Consumption in central energy of the processing center for centralized architecture	Ctc
Consumption in energy of the network equipment's	Cer
Distance between two will be on drugs	Dc
Waiting time after activation before arrival of the mobile	Tat
Duration of functioning camera	Dfc
Duration of functioning of the system	Dfs
The consumption on average of energy of camera 1 (who is in the entry of our CCTV)	Cec1
The consumption on average of energy by sections	Cet
The consumption in energy of the system for distributed architecture	Cesd
The consumption in energy of the system for centralized architecture	Cesc
The consumption in energy of the system for distributed/year architecture	Cesd
The consumption in energy of the system for centralized/year architecture	Cesc

Application: In our case, we use the CPL technology and the camera is POE. The case CPL passes on the data and the supply of the camera passes by an injector POE. We are going to take into account the consumption of a camera IP (Cn), that of the previous plan and the consumption of Switch.

Consumption Camera Cn (case Ccn), where D = the duration of functioning. For the global consumption (Cg) in energy of it will be on drugs Cn we shall have:

$$Cg = Ccn + Csw + Csv$$

For them will be on drugs Cn + 1, we suppose that the normal traffic, by the result [5, 6], we have:

We have $Speed = \frac{distance\ travelled}{time\ put}$

Thus $Time\ put = \frac{distance\ travelled}{Speed}$

Duration total of treatment = Duration of decision-making + duration of next activation will be on drugs + time put to take out of the field of vision of it will be on drugs + time of arrived wait transport

Daily consumption (Cj) = Ci * D

For the global consumption (Cg) in energy of it will be on drugs Cn we shall have:

Cg = Ccn + Csw + Csv

We shall have the global consumption in energy (Cge) = Consumption Cn + (Nbr camera * consumption /camera)

For a global consumption in energy we have:

Cg = Ci + Csw number of will be on drugs.

- **Case of Architecture Centralizes with Permanent Activation of will be on Drugs:** the consumption in global energy of the system is:
  Cesc = (Cec + Ctc) * NbrCt * NbrT * cte + Cer with cte = 1, 2, 3, ..., 24 h
- **Case of Architecture Distributed with Algorithm of Prediction of Path by Learning:**

  Cec1 = (Cec + Cew + Ct) * cte with cte = 1, 2, ... 24 h
  Dfc (n + 1, n + 2 ... n + N) = Td + Tac + Tt + Tat
  Dfs = Dfc * NbrCt * NbrT
  Cet = Cec * Dfs * NbrVt + Cer
  Cesd = Cet + Cec1

5   Results and Discussion

5.1   Energy Balance Sheet

We're going to talk about a couple of key points in terms of power and power. But before discussing the calculation of the electrical power of our installation, a few remarks on the configurations that can be found among users of IP cameras.

IP camera network architecture (Figs. 5 and 6).

The network of cameras illustrated by our distributed video surveillance architecture

Case N°1: the camera is connected on a port not POE of Switch and the supply is assured by the sector + Transformer.

Case N°2: the camera PTZ is connected on Switch POE but its power is too important for this one. We use then an adapted Injector POE and we do not pass by a port POE of Switch.

Case N°3: we wish to use the POE technology but the camera is not POE. Splitter allows the connection. The power of the camera does not have to overtake that admitted by the port POE.

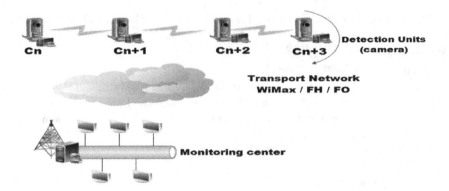

Fig. 5. Distributed architecture

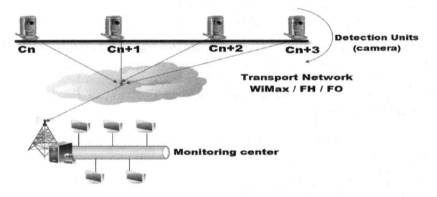

Fig. 6. Centralized architecture

Case N°4: the camera is POE and its power is compatible with that of Switch, we connect directly the camera on a port POE.

Case N°5: we use the CPL technology but the camera is not POE. The case CPL passes on the data but the supply of the camera passes by its electric transformer.

Case N°6: we use the CPL technology and the camera is POE. The case CPL passes on the data and the supply of the camera passes by an injector POE.

Know the consumption of its network of cameras.

The electric consumption of an element of the network expresses himself in kilowatt-hours (KWH).

To estimate the annual consumption, you have to take into account the following 3 points:

- the power of your device, expressed in watts (*)
- the number of hours a day in the course of which the device works
- the number of days a year in the course of which the device works.

(*) the power of the device is not still mastered when it is about cameras. Indeed, if the power is indicated well on the march in the daytime and at night for cameras to focal fixed, it is more difficult to know the power of cameras PTZ when is mentioned only the maxi power.

For a PTZ, the commands of movement and zoom owed only during some time assist or. Unless using a wattmeter, we shall content ourselves with an estimation of on the march normal power, without movements.

Application:

In our case, we use the CPL technology and the camera is POE. The case CPL passes on the data and the supply of the camera passes by an injector POE. We are going to take into account the consumption of a camera IP (Cn), that of the previous plan and the consumption of Switch.

Consumption Camera Cn (case Ccn)

Power: 8 W

Power with infrared activated: 10 W from 7 pm till 7 am in the morning

8 W: time of functioning estimated at 12 am? (8/1000) × 12 = 0.096 KWH

10 W: time of functioning estimated(esteemed) at 12 am? (10/1000) × 12 = 0.12 KWH

Electric/day consumption: 0.096 + 0.12 = 0.216 KWH

Electric/year consumption: 0.216 × 365 = 78.84 KWH

Annual cost (base 114,2 cfa the KWH): 78.84 × 114,2 = 9003.528 FCFA.

Consumption Switch (Csw)

We will also take into account the power of the Switch on which these cameras are connected. If the consumption is not indicated, we will make an estimate of the order of 2 W for example for the Switch of our installation.

Power: 2 W

Operating time: 24 h

Annual power consumption: (2/1000) × 24 × 365 = 17.52 KWh

Annual cost (base 114.2 FCFA per KWh): 17.52 × 114.2 = 2000.784 FCFA.

Consumption Treatment Server (csv):

In our case, we will take the following configuration:

Raspberry Pi 3 Model A+

When we look on the intelligent taking at the consumption is 10 watts This. It is the consumption without screen, because he too consumes, even in sleep mode.

Or D = the duration of functioning

We are thus going to compare both types of functioning's over one year of 365 days.

Daily consumption (Cj) = Ci * D

Cj=10 * 24 240 W

For an average use of 24 h (12 pm) a day, the PC consumes: 240 * 365 = 87 600 W that is 87,6 KW.

With a basic rate which is 114,2 FCFA by kWh consumed at SENELEC for a regulated Price Rate, this is what we can spend:

- permanent Consumption: $87,6 \times 114,2 = 10\ 003,92$ FCFA is $27,408$ FCFA a day.

For the global consumption (Cg) in energy of it will be on drugs Cn we shall have:

Cg = Ccn + Csw + Csv
Cg = 78.84 KWH + 17.52 KWH + 87,6 KWH
Cg = 183,96 KWH for it will be on drugs in the entry of the network.

For them will be on drugs Cn + 1, we suppose that the normal traffic.

If we take into account 100 mobile detected during the day by the camera which is in the entry of the network.

By the result [17, 18], we have:

We have Speed $= \frac{distance\ travelled}{time\ put}$

Thus Time put$= \frac{distance\ travelled}{Speed}$

Duration total of treatment = Duration of decision-making + duration of next activation will be on drugs + time put to take out of the field of vision of it will be on drugs + time of arrived wait transport

Daily consumption (Cj) = Ci * D

For the global consumption (Cg) in energy of it will be on drugs Cn we shall have:

Cg = Ccn + Csw + Csv

We shall have the global consumption in energy (Cge) = Consumption Cn + (Nbr camera * consumption/camera)

For architecture centralized standard we shall have.

For a global consumption in energy we have:

Cg = Ci + Csw * number of will be on drugs

Consumption energy central processing center

When we look on the intelligent taking at the consumption is 118 W. It is the consumption without screen, because he too consumes, even in sleep mode. We are thus going to compare both chaps of functioning's over one year of 365 days.

For an average use of 24 h (12 pm) a day, the PC consumes:

Daily consumption (Cj) = Ci * D

Generalization:

We have:

- Time of decision-making = Td
- Time of activation camera = Tap
- Consumption in energy of the processing center = Ct
- Consumption in energy of the switch = Cew
- The number of sections of the network of video surveillance = NbrT
- Field of vision will be on drugs = Carried by the camera
- The number of will be on drugs by section = NbrCt
- The time averages of functioning of a camera in the entry of the network = Tmc

- The consumption on average of energy of a camera = Cec
- The number of vehicle on average by section = NbrVt
- Speed of the mobile (constant speed) = Vm
- Consumption in central energy of the processing center for centralized architecture = Ctc
- Consumption in energy of the network equipment's = Cer
- Distance between two will be on drugs = Dc
- Waiting time after activation before arrival of the motive(mobile) = Tat
- Duration of functioning camera = Dfc
- Duration of functioning of the system = Dfs
- The consumption on average of energy of camera 1 (who is in the entry of our video surveillance system) =Cec1
- The consumption on average of energy by sections = Cet
- The consumption in energy of the system for distributed architecture = Cesd
- The consumption in energy of the system for centralized architecture = Cesc
- The consumption in energy of the system for distributed/year architecture = Cesd
- The consumption in energy of the system for centralized/year architecture = Cesc.

The consumption in global energy of the system is:

Cesc = (Cec + Ctc) * NbrCt * NbrT * cte + Cer with cte = 24 h
2. Case of architecture distributed with algorithm of prediction of path by learning
Cec1 = (Cec + Cew + Ct) * cte with cte = 24 h
Dfc (n + 1, n + 2 ... n + N) = Td + Tac + Tt + Tat
Dfs = Dfc * NbrCt * NbrT
Cet = Cec * Dfs * NbrVt + Cer
Cesd = Cet + Cec1.

5.2   Results Analysis

The analysis of this curve (Sect. 5.1) shows us the variation of the energy consumption according to the number of sections of a network of video surveillance with an average of 4 four cameras by sections and a distance of separates 500 m them will be on drugs. We notice that with architecture where the treatment is centralized and what all the cameras must be active to visualize all which takes place in their own environment, we have a strong energy consumption of the system which evolves with the increase of the number of sections (more cameras increase) (Fig. 7).

This gives some explanation (is understandable) in the first one, that the processing center has to have a rather powerful unit of treatment because it belongs to him to analyse all the scenes filmed since them will be on drugs to make the treatment and the follow-up of the mobile. What means that the processing center has to assure all the treatments stemming from various cameras

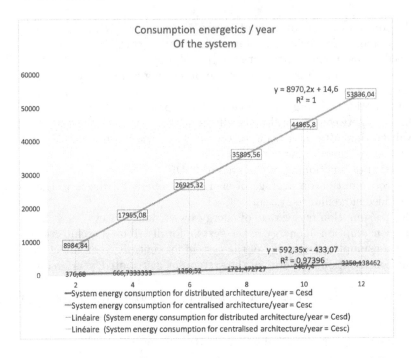

Fig. 7. Curve of correspondence between both architectures and their difference

of all the sections. Besides, because all the cameras have to work in real time to assure the real time surveillance and the follow-up of the mobile at the level of the video surveillance system, thus use some energy continues it to assure the real time follow-up of the mobile. For distributed architecture, we have a low consumption in energy of the system and a low increase of this energy consumption with the increase of the number of sections (increase of the number of cameras). This gives some explanation (is understandable) because we use mini Pc with a low energy consumption because every device takes care only of the treatment of a camera at the same time. In addition, the cameras are only active if there is a mobile that is headed for it. That is, the previous camera detects a mobile in its field of view and predicts the path and segment on which the mobile must follow its path and become alert if it is not the input camera of the system until it is activated in turn by a camera to indicate that there is a mobile in its direction. In this architecture, the increase in the energy consumption of cameras and the local processing centre is proportional to the increase in the number of cars passing through the network. The system is operational if and only if a mobile is detected by one of the network cameras.

6   Conclusion

In this study, we examined the problem of the energy consumption of energy in the architectures of road video surveillance. In the first place, we proposed an algorithm of prediction of path by learning. Then, we formulated the problem of the energy consumption in classic models and apply our model of prediction of path to optimize the energy consumption at the level of cameras and of local processing center.

Then, by taking into account the requirement of the real time video surveillance and the characteristics of the tasks of video, we applied our algorithm of prediction which is going to deactivate by default all the cameras of the network of video surveillance has the exception of the one who is in the entry of the network of video surveillance. Once the realized prediction, it is going to activate the following camera (the one who supposed to receive the mobile in its field of vision). The follow-up and the activation of cameras at the level of the section will be made in parallel with the prediction of the knot following (camera). This method reduces considerably the energy consumption which is 376,68 watts a year against 8984,84 as well as a reduction of the financial cost.

Experiments have demonstrated the effectiveness of our method by increasing the number of sections of video surveillance networks as well as the traffic at each section. It would be very important to analyse bandwidth occupancy between our predictive model and existing models. It will be implemented in the near future.

References

1. Song, M., Kim, M.: Solid state disk (SSD) management for reducing disk energy consumption in video servers. In: Proceedings of the 9th USENIX Conference on File and Storage Technologies, pp. 1–2 (2011)
2. Mohan Raj, V.K., Shriram, R.: Power aware provisioning in cloud computing environment. In: Proceedings of the International Conference on Communication and Electrical Technology (ICCCET), pp. 6–11. IEEE (2011)
3. Beaumont, O., Eyraud-Dubois, L., Thraves Caro, C., Rejeb, H.: Heterogeneous resource allocation under degree constraints. IEEE Trans. Parallel Distrib. Syst. **24**(5), 926–37 (2013)
4. Hsu, W.H., Shieh, Y.P.: Virtual network mapping algorithm in the cloud infrastructure. J. Netw. Comput. Appl. **36**(6), 1724–34 (2013)
5. Diop, P.S., Mbacke, A.B., Mendy, G.: Centralized and distributed architectures: approximation of the response time in a video surveillance system of road traffic by logarithm, power and linear functions. In: Puliafito, A., Bruneo, D., Distefano, S., Longo, F. (eds.) ADHOC-NOW 2017. LNCS, vol. 10517, pp. 314–327. Springer, Cham (2017). https://doi.org/10.1007/978-3-319-67910-5_26
6. Diop, P.S., Mbacké, A.B., Mendy, G.: Predictive assessment of response time for road traffic video surveillance systems: the case of centralized and distributed systems. In: Hsu, C.-H., Wang, S., Zhou, A., Shawkat, A. (eds.) IOV 2016. LNCS, vol. 10036, pp. 34–48. Springer, Cham (2016). https://doi.org/10.1007/978-3-319-51969-2_4
7. Reyes, D.: Fully autonomous IEEE 802.3af Power over Ethernet midspan PSE requires no microcontroller, p. 576 (2016)

eLoBaPS: Towards Energy Load Balancing with Wake-Up Radios for IoT

Sebastian L. Sampayo$^{(\boxtimes)}$, Julien Montavont, and Thomas Noël

ICube Laboratory, University of Strasbourg, 67412 Illkirch, France
{sampayo,montavont,noel}@unistra.fr

Abstract. In an effort to extend the lifetime and reliability of multi-hop wireless sensor networks we recently presented LoBaPS, a protocol to select opportunistic parents and achieve load balancing. This algorithm takes advantage of the wake-up radio for its ultra-low power consumption and always-on feature. Moreover, it overcomes an open problem in the routing layer: achieving both stability and efficient parent selection at the same time. However, the random load balancing strategy and the energy wastage in listening mode still limits the network lifetime. In this article, we present eLoBaPS, a significant modification of LoBaPS that distributes better the energy among the parents improving around 17% the lifetime of the network towards the ideal case. In a nutshell, the next hop is selected in a decentralized way and it is the parent that issues a shorter back-off period before attempting to retransmit. In addition, the nodes overhear all the traffic in the wake-up radio channel and adapt the protocol parameters to the current state of the battery of the neighbors. We perform simulations with a network of ContikiOS nodes running eLoBaPS, LoBaPS and W-MAC, a reference protocol that uses the wake-up radio.

Keywords: WSN · Wake-up radio · Opportunistic routing · Contiki · Load balancing

1 Introduction

The global smart city market was valued at five hundred billion dollars in 2017 and is projected to reach two thousand billion by 2025 [1]. Wireless Sensor Networks (WSN) with low power and resource-constrained devices are generally used for those IoT applications. The energy consumption was traditionally controlled in these networks by some form of duty-cycle in the communication protocol at the MAC layer trading off latency for energy efficient operations. Recently, the Wake-Up Radio (WuR) technology has advanced with increasing acceptance as a promise to the end of this tradeoff [7]. Its fundamentals are explained in Sect. 2.

On top of that, the nodes need to compute a path towards a collecting station (called the sink) in order to deliver their data in a multi-hop fashion. This is

© Springer Nature Switzerland AG 2019
M. R. Palattella et al. (Eds.): ADHOC-NOW 2019, LNCS 11803, pp. 388–403, 2019.
https://doi.org/10.1007/978-3-030-31831-4_27

the role of the routing protocol generally operating at the layer 3 of the network stack. When the system starts operating, the nodes exchange control packets to generate a routing structure in order to reach the sink, and eventually, other peer-nodes. In general, the implementation of this structure is based on a tree, where each node defines a preferred parent to forward its data packets towards the sink. However, it is difficult to achieve both stability and efficient parent selection at the same time in these routing protocols. A simple implementation can provide stability but at the cost of using sometimes bad links, thus degrading the performance. On the other hand, a more complex protocol can improve the parent selection for good links, but usually, this leads to an increase in the number of control packets and degraded stability, since each node may change its preferred parent very frequently. In addition, the underlying duty-cycle in the MAC layer increases the latency in an effort to reduce the energy consumption, thus limiting the performance for high traffic loads.

Load Balancing Parent Selection (LoBaPS) [9] has been presented in previous works leveraging the power efficiency and always-on feature of WuR. It proposes a solution to the tradeoff between stability and efficient parent selection. Once the routing structure is built, the preferred parent is not exclusively used to forward data packets. Instead, all available feasible parents compete in order to share the load. This approach presents a first step into load balancing with WuRs in order to extend the network lifetime. However, LoBaPS balances the load in a random way and therefore can not achieve the best energy balancing among nodes. LoBaPS is described in Sect. 4.1.

In this article, we present Energy LoBaPS (eLoBaPS), an improvement over LoBaPS that takes a step forward into the ideal energy balancing in WSN. In this protocol, the backoff period is proportional to the battery consumed by each parent. In addition, the nodes that are consuming a lot stop competing for a while and let other feasible forwarders spend their batteries. In Sect. 3 we provide a review of the related publications and how the present work stands out. Our contribution, eLoBaPS, is described in Sect. 4.2. The energy savings achieved are reflected in the resulting lifetime that is compared to that of W-MAC and LoBaPS. In addition, we look at the packet delivery ratio of the network over time to compare the stability and final decline of the operation performance, where eLoBaPS has a longer stable operation and a shorter decline. This metric, together with the latency and the productivity of the network are compared to that of W-MAC and LoBaPS in Sect. 6 based on the simulation framework presented in Sect. 5. Finally, the conclusions of the article are presented in Sect. 7.

2   Wake-Up Radio

The Wake-Up Radio (WuR) is a secondary hardware module that contains a Wake-Up Receiver (WuRx) and is connected to the microcontroller (MCU) of the main node. This receiver is highlighted by the Ultra-Low Power (ULP) consumption in listening mode around 5 orders of magnitude less than that of the traditional radios [7]. This is usually achieved by using a simple On-Off Keying (OOK) modulation and a low data rate up to 10 kbps [7]. As a result of this architecture, there are two communication channels. On the one hand, the communication in the Main Radio (MR) channel is performed by the traditional transceiver of the node (e.g. CC2420). On the other hand, the node uses the WuRx to continuously listen to the WuR channel thanks to the ULP feature. However, the transmissions on the WuR channel do not involve a dedicated chip, but generally use the same as that of the MR provided that it supports OOK modulation and low data rate.

Having said that, the W-MAC protocol presented in [8] is an example of how this architecture might work. In that case, the WuR is controlled at the MAC layer. To initiate the communication, a node sends a message (called thereafter wake-up signal) over the WuR channel to wake up the MR of the layer 2 destination. Shortly after, the source sends the data packet over the MR channel. Upon reception of this packet, the receiver sends back an ACK on the MR channel. As a result, there is no need of duty-cycling the activity/sleeping period nor continuous synchronization as destinations will only wake up their MR on-demand via the WuR channel.

Optionally, the WuR hardware block might contain a module to decode the wake-up signal received. This task is performed normally by a ULP microcontroller (MCU) that is placed between the WuRx circuit and the main MCU through some sort of digital connection such as SPI or I2C [6]. It is common to transmit the address of the destination node in the wake-up signal so that a receiver node maximizes the sleeping period of the MR and only wakes up if there is a match between its own address and the received wake-up signal. This is the reason why the WuR is particularly interesting for asynchronous communications.

3   Related Work

eLoBaPS is an improvement of LoBaPS [9], providing a solution to its main drawbacks: random load balancing and energy wastage in listening mode. To the best of our knowledge, LoBaPS was the first work leveraging the WuR to overcome some of the routing challenges (presented in Sect. 1) in multi-hop scenarios. It is a further step towards the energy load balancing in WSN with WuR based on the work of W-MAC [8], OPWUM [3], WHARP [4] and GreenRoutes [5], briefly described below.

In Sect. 2 we briefly described W-MAC [8]. Although it achieves a great power efficiency, latency and reliability in comparison to the duty-cycled approach, it does not tackle the problems of the routing layer summarized in Sect. 1. OPWUM [3] allows opportunistic forwarding using the WuR and is based on the well-known RTS/CTS paradigm. A source can reserve the MR channel by exchanging 3 broadcast messages over the WuR channel. However, OPWUM was evaluated at a very small-scale (with 4 nodes - 1 source, 1 destination, and 2 relays). We already showed [9] that increasing the WuR channel usage is prone to collisions and errors because transmission opportunities are very limited due to the time over the air required to transmit wake-up signals (most of the current prototypes work at 1 kbps). By contrast, eLoBaPS minimizes the usage of the WuR channel (if the path between a source and the sink includes n nodes, eLoBaPS sends n wake-up signals instead of $3(n-1)$ for OPWUM).

In [4] and [5], the authors presented WHARP and GreenRoutes. In those solutions, the next relay is opportunistically selected by taking into account the energy, obtaining great performance. However, those schemes are cross-layer solutions including their own routing solution. In consequence, they are less generic as it is not possible to use a well-known routing protocol. In addition, they use the RTS/CTS paradigm on the WuR channel increasing the channel utilization.

4 LoBaPS and eLoBaPS

4.1 LoBaPS

LoBaPS was presented in [9] featuring the Wake-Up Radio (WuR) to select opportunistic parents in the layer 3 of the communication stack. This protocol operates only under convergecast data traffic and when the routing layer has converged so there is a stable topology where each node knows its own metric with respect to the sink. For example, this metric could be how many hops away it is from the sink. We are going to call this metric r.

Whenever a source node generates an application packet, it initiates the communication by transmitting a packet over the WuR channel: the Wake-Up Request (WREQ), as depicted in Fig. 1. This packet contains the metric r of the transmitting node. The nodes are continuously listening to the WuR channel, so all the nodes inside the communication range of the sender will receive this WREQ. Upon reception, the received metric is compared with the r of the node, so that only nodes that have a better metric (i.e. nodes that are closer to the sink) wake up their MR, avoiding routing loops. Shortly after the transmission of the initial WREQ, the data packet is sent by the source on the MR channel. Then the source turns off its MR and starts a timer waiting for the acknowledgment. When the sink wakes up its MR and receives a data packet, it sends back an acknowledgment via the WuR channel. Conversely, when an intermediate node receives the data packet, it tries to forward it by transmitting a new WREQ with its own metric r. This WREQ has three purposes: to wake up next hops towards the sink, to acknowledge data reception for the sender, and to stop other competitors.

A data packet may be received by several nodes, since a single node may have multiple parents (cf. R1 and R2 in Fig. 1). In order to mitigate collisions, a random backoff period is calculated by the Carrier Sense Multiple Access (CSMA) layer of each relay before the transmission of the new WREQ. The first one whose backoff expires will send a WREQ and cancel the ongoing backoff of the others.

Given that the WuR works at low data rates, the time over the air for wake-up signals is significant and can be longer than the one of the main data. This way, transmission opportunities over the WuR channel are very limited, which

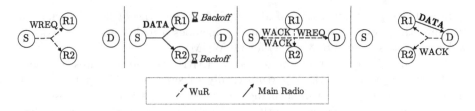

Fig. 1. Example of LoBaPS/eLoBaPS operations

results in a high sensitivity to collisions. For this reason, LoBaPS includes a Clear Channel Assessment (CCA) function in the WuR driver. When a node wants to transmit, it calls first the CCA function, and if the WuR channel is not clear a collision error is passed to the CSMA layer.

4.2   eLoBaPS: Improved Load Balancing

The main problems with LoBaPS are the way in which the load is balanced and the energy wastage in listening mode. The load is balanced randomly, so it is not the best effort towards energy efficiency. On top of that, there is a significant amount of energy wasted in listening mode when all the feasible successors wake up their MR, limiting the network lifetime. In this article, we present eLoBaPS, an improvement of LoBaPS that increases the network lifetime and provides better energy balancing. In this extension, the general behavior is also described by Fig. 1. In this case, the backoff period is proportional to the energy consumed by the node, so that nodes with more remaining battery have more chances to win the competition. The first approach in order to calculate a backoff period aware of the energy consumption is to make it directly proportional to the amount of consumed battery percentage:

$$B_j(t) = Ke_j(t) + C \tag{1}$$

where $e_j(t)$ is the energy percentage consumed by the node j at time t, and K is a constant parameter to adjust the units to milliseconds. A small random contention window C uniformly distributed with range $[0, T_c]$ is added to mitigate the case where more than one node has the same amount of energy. However, the battery discharges as the time goes by, so $e_j(t)$ is proportional to t. In consequence, the backoff period will increase over time as the battery discharges. Notice that the backoff period adds latency to the protocol, so it would increase the end-to-end delay of the application. In order to keep it stable as the battery discharges, we came up with a slight modification of Eq. 1:

$$B_j(t) = K[e_j(t) - e_{dj}(t)] + C \tag{2}$$

where $e_{dj}(t)$ is the desired energy consumed at time t. This variable is such that if all the relays consume this energy, the load is balanced and the network lifetime is maximized. In order to estimate it, the nodes include their energy consumption in all the packets sent on the WuR channel (WREQs and WACKs) so that they overhear the current energy of all their neighbors. Then the value is estimated for node j with a metric r as:

$$e_{dj}(t) = \min_{i \in R}\{e_i(t)\} \tag{3}$$

where R is the set of all nodes i with a metric of r.

Although this may balance the energy by controlling the transmissions, it is not reducing the energy consumed by the listening mode every time a node requests several relays to wake up and listen to the packet (see node R2 in Fig. 1). With this in mind, another feature is included in the algorithm to reduce the listening mode energy: if the current energy consumed by the node is above a certain threshold on top of the desired energy consumption, then the node does not wake up and listen to the MR channel whenever it receives a WREQ. However, this feature can create problems when a node is the only parent possible for some nodes for example. In such a situation, the packet will be delayed until the parent saves enough energy to keep up with $e_d(t)$. For these reasons, this threshold should be chosen carefully to not degrade the performance. In this work, it has been set to the energy consumed by the node that has consumed the most among all its neighbors in R, that is:

$$e_{thresholdj}(t) = \max_{i \in R}\{e_i(t)\} \quad . \tag{4}$$

Figures 2, 3, 4, and 5 may help to understand the overall behavior of the protocol. Figure 2 shows the overall finite state machine of a generic node running the eLoBaPS protocol. Besides, Figs. 3, 4, and 5 describe the internals of each mode. When the application layer of the node wants to send a message, it issues a transmission request to the lower layers. The CSMA layer receives this request and performs the algorithm described in Fig. 3, calling the routine of the TRANSMIT mode, detailed in Fig. 4. Notice that the COLLISION output of the TRANSMIT routine is a flag to prevent from a collision. In such a case, the TRANSMIT routine does not get to transmit the DATA on the MR. This is the classic behavior of the CSMA protocol. Its implementation in ContikiOS was not significantly modified. The values of the constant parameters used in our implementation can be found in Table 1. On the other hand, when a node receives a WREQ, an interrupt is triggered and the RECEIVE mode is activated, following the steps in Fig. 5.

5   Simulation Framework

For the performance evaluation of eLoBaPS, we used WaCo [8]. This is a simulation framework that is an extension of ContikiOS and Cooja that reproduces the firmware that runs on real devices. WaCo is publicly available and has been validated with a WuR prototype.

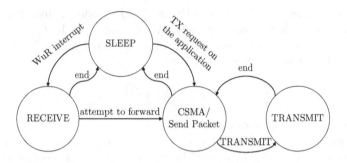

Fig. 2. Finite state machine of the entire system

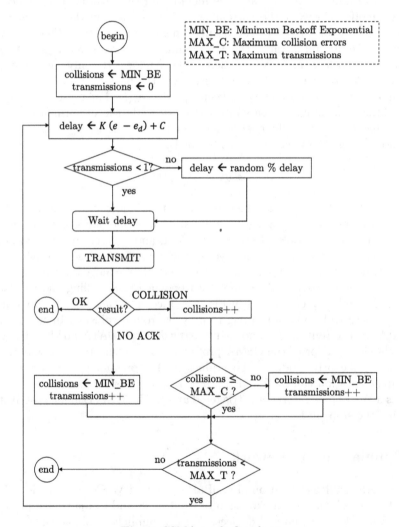

Fig. 3. CSMA mode flowchart

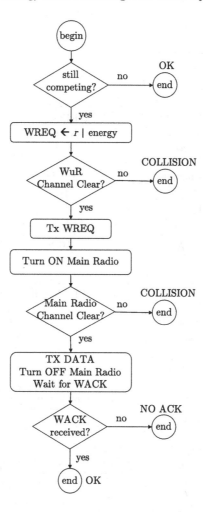

Fig. 4. TRANSMIT mode flowchart

5.1   Simulation Setup

Table 1 depicts the main simulation parameters. The simulations are carried out in a triangular grid topology as depicted in Fig. 6. The nodes are not more than 2 hops away from the sink and each leaf can have between 2 and 7 feasible parents. In this figure, we can see the links, represented by arrows, of each node to all its feasible next hops. However, for legibility purposes, dot line arrows are the links to the sink of the nodes that are just 1 hop away from it, and solid line arrows are the links to the parents of the nodes that are 2 hops away from the sink. Notice that some nodes have more chances to listen and forward packets since they have more children, in particular nodes 5, 8, and 9. To simulate the battery lifetime, each node keeps track of the energy consumed with a linear model, so that it is

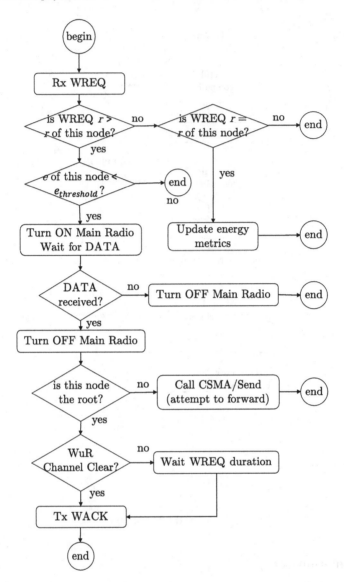

Fig. 5. RECEIVE mode flowchart

killed when it reaches some threshold level. This value is defined so that the sink receives around 1000 packets when the first node dies. At this point, we find two different scenarios that follow. First, some children might be temporarily unreachable (in the case of W-MAC with a routing protocol that is based on a preferred parent), but after a repair mechanism is triggered, a new parent can be found and all the living nodes can reach the sink again. Second, some nodes might be left far away from any other one, becoming absolutely unreachable,

Table 1. Simulation parameters

Parameter	Value
Number of nodes	15
Repetitions of each simulation	50
eLoBaPS T_c	30 ms
eLoBaPS K	11.6 ms
MIN_BE	3
MAX_C	7
MAX_T	4
Inter Packet Interval (IPI)	1, 5, 10, 60 s
WuR packet length	16 bits
WuR data rate	10 kbps
Main radio RX success ratio	80%
WuR RX success ratio	80%

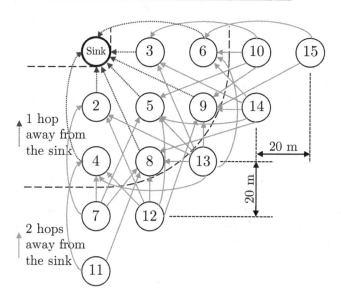

Fig. 6. Test topology

and no mechanism can get the network graph connected again. The simulation finishes immediately and exclusively when the second scenario is found. This way, we can analyze the behavior of the network after the first node dies and during the process of parent changes.

We use an optimized version of W-MAC that supports the Routing Protocol for Low Power and Lossy networks (RPL) with Objective Function 0 and Min-Hop metric, as well as CCA capability in the WuR channel. In RPL OF0 RFC

[11] there is no clear explanation on how to detect that the preferred parent of a node is no longer available. For this reason, we implement the parent change trigger when a fixed number of communication attempts fail consecutively (which in our implementation is set to 4). This means that every time a parent dies, it takes some time to the W-MAC solution to return to its correct operations. This routine is triggered after MAX_T transmission attempts on the CSMA layer.

6   Results

6.1   Lifetime

Figure 7 shows the results for the relative network lifetime under different traffic loads with respect to the lifetime of W-MAC. The network lifetime is defined in this work as the time elapsed when the first node dies. We show the relative value of the lifetime so that the results can be appreciated on the same scale for all protocols and all values of the Inter Packet Interval (IPI). However, to get a rough idea of the absolute values when using two AA batteries, the lifetime of W-MAC is 90 days when the IPI is 1 s and 3 years when the IPI is 60 s in mean values.

The Inter Packet Interval (IPI) between the generation of application packets has been varied from 1 s (high traffic) up to 60 s (low traffic) which are typical values in smart cities applications [10]. The bar plot shows the median values for each scenario over the 50 repetitions and the confidence intervals of 95%. The results show the superiority of eLoBaPS over its predecessor LoBaPS (up to 17%) and the reference W-MAC (up to 40%) in all scenarios. Studying the maximum and minimum outcomes for all the repetitions (not shown in the figure), we can affirm that the lifetime improvement can actually go up to 77% in the best case of eLoBaPS compared to the worst case of W-MAC. This is because of the two main features of the protocol: the energy consumption due to packet transmissions is well distributed among all the feasible parents and the nodes that are excessively consuming energy turn off their MR till they keep up with the energy consumption of their neighbors.

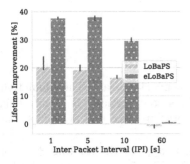

Fig. 7. Lifetime improvement over W-MAC for different traffic loads

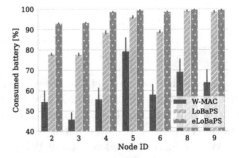

Fig. 8. Consumed battery of nodes at 1 hop from the sink when the first node dies

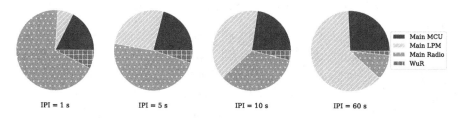

Fig. 9. Energy profile for different IPIs for the W-MAC protocol

At the same time, it is interesting to remark that in low traffic scenarios almost all the protocols present very small differences in the resulting lifetime. The reason behind this is that as the IPI increases, the impact of the radio communications on the overall energy consumption decreases. Figure 9 supports this fact by depicting the contribution to the overall energy consumption of the different power states of an average node running W-MAC: main MCU in active mode, main MCU in Low Power Mode (LPM), main radio, and wake-up radio. The radio contributions (Main Radio and WuR) comprise transmission, reception and listening for each one. In this figure, it can be noticed that the contribution of the radio modes (Main Radio and WuR) is the most significant to the total only for high traffic scenarios (1 s IPI). On the contrary, in low traffic scenarios, the major contribution to the overall energy is just the LPM, that is, because of the silent power consumption when the node is sleeping.

6.2 Battery Consumption

The battery consumption of each node at only one hop away from the sink is depicted in Fig. 8 at the instant when the first node of the network dies, for a 10 s IPI as an example of the general behavior. The topology of the network imposes constraints to the amount of load balancing that can be achieved with good performance. Leaf nodes (2 hops away from the sink) do not consume the same order of energy than relays, because they do not wake up often to listen to the MR channel. This is the reason why we do not show their battery consumption in this figure. However, the topology still generates more energy consumption on some nodes (nodes 8 and 9) because they have more chances to be woken up by some child and waste energy listening to the MR channel. The point of this figure is to analyze how equally distributed is the energy among the network. The goal is to have all nodes consuming approximately the same amount of battery when the first one dies. In the ideal case where the network consumes all the batteries in a balanced way we would expect that all the nodes die at the same time, that is, showing 100% battery consumption. However, we can see that in W-MAC there are nodes that have only consumed half of their batteries when the first node that dies consumed it all. That amount of remaining battery not used is the reason why the lifetime is shorter because the load is not equally shared. On the contrary, in LoBaPS, the maximum remaining battery for a node at one hop

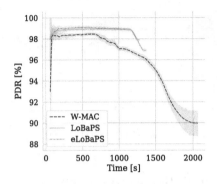

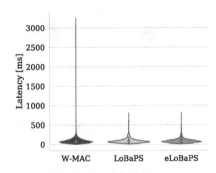

Fig. 10. Packet delivery ratio for IPI =
10 s

Fig. 11. Latency for IPI = 10 s

from the sink is of 22%, while in eLoBaps it is of 7%, proving the improvement
of the load balancing algorithm in terms of energy efficiency.

6.3 Packet Delivery Ratio

The reliability is studied in Fig. 10 by analyzing the evolution of the Packet
Delivery Ratio (PDR) over time for a 10 s IPI in mean values and with the
95% confidence interval. Previous works [9] have shown the benefits of LoBaPS
in contrast to W-MAC because of the stable behavior in steady state and the
better final PDR. In addition, it is possible to see the decline of the PDR after
the first node dies, which happens between 750 s and 1200 s for W-MAC, and
around 1200 s in LoBaPS and eLoBaPS. In W-MAC protocol, the PDR decreases
fast and with high variability after this point, while in LoBaPS there is good
stability during the network lifetime and a precise and controlled decline slope.
eLoBaPS improves this point by reducing the length of the decline, so there is
a better ratio of stable time over decline time.

6.4 End-to-End Latency

Figure 11 shows the end-to-end latency as a violin plot that takes into account
every successful packet transmission in all repetitions for an IPI of 10 s. In
eLoBaPS, the latency is similar to the one achieved by LoBaPS, but in this
case, it only depends on the number of retransmissions because there is no backoff exponential. The actual amount of time of the backoff period in eLoBaPS
is adjusted so that it is similar to that of the average CSMA backoff period in
LoBaPS. In this plot, we can also see that the lack of precision and the inefficient parent selection after a parent dies in W-MAC can lead to extremely high
maximum values of latency, while in LoBaPS and eLoBaPS, the maximum is
three times smaller.

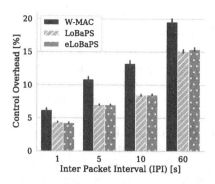

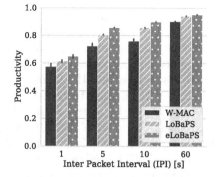

Fig. 12. Control overhead   **Fig. 13.** Throughput for different IPIs

6.5   Control Overhead

We also consider a metric to measure the number of control packets transmitted on the whole network:

$$c = 100\frac{\#network\ control\ packets}{\#\ app\ packets\ at\ the\ sink} \tag{5}$$

The results are shown in Fig. 12 evidencing a low control overhead for both LoBaPS and eLoBaPS compared to W-MAC. The main cause of this is that in W-MAC, whenever a backup parent dies, its children need to repair the routing structure by generating new control packets. In contrast, in both LoBaPS and eLoBaPS, this is not necessary since the initial routing structure can still be used as long as there is still connectivity in the network graph.

6.6   Productivity

Naturally, the overall application data received at the sink is different for each traffic scenario, thus making somehow doubtable the comparisons for both the PDR and the lifetime. For this, we have come up with a productivity formula that divides the number of application packets correctly received at the sink by the simulation elapsed time, so-called *simulation disconnectivity time* because the network stops being a connected graph. In addition, it is scaled by the scenario parameters (IPI and network size) so that the value can be compared between all the simulations.

$$Productivity = \frac{\#\ app\ packets\ at\ the\ sink}{disconnectivity\ time}\frac{IPI}{\#\ nodes} \tag{6}$$

This way we conceive a metric of the productivity of the network that somehow combines the notion of latency, reliability and lifetime in a single value: productivity. Clearly, we want this value to be as higher as possible. We can also see this formula in an equivalent way, as the ratio of the expected disconnectivity time (calculated based on the number of application packets received at the sink, the IPI and the number of nodes) and the simulation disconnectivity time:

$$Productivity = \frac{expected\ disconnectivity\ time}{simulation\ disconnectivity\ time} \qquad (7)$$

Notice that the maximum in mean values is 1 since the simulation disconnectivity time cannot be shorter than the expected one since the nodes can not generate packets faster than the IPI in mean values. So smaller values of productivity mean that it takes more time than expected to deliver the packets to the sink.

The results of this metric are illustrated in Fig. 13, where we can see a trend of improvements between W-MAC, LoBaPS, and eLoBaPS, for all the traffic loads. The reason for this is linked to the reduced number of retransmissions that are required in eLoBaPS as well as its shorter decline slope (described in Sect. 6.3) which turns into a smaller disconnectivity time. Couple with this result, we can see that the productivity increases as the IPI increases too for all protocols. The reason is that with low IPI there are more collisions and so fewer packets are successfully delivered to the sink.

7   Conclusions and Future Work

This article introduces eLoBaPS, an improvement of LoBaPS towards the ideal load balancing in wireless sensor networks exploiting the always-on feature of the wake-up radio. The main idea is to allow all feasible successors to compete for a packet forwarding when a node transmits a packet, prioritizing the ones with more remaining battery. At the same time, it mitigates the main radio listening energy wastage by turning off the most consuming nodes until they keep up with the energy consumption of their neighbors. Moreover, the same idea can be applied with a different metric instead of the energy in order to optimize a different parameter of the network, for instance, the packet queue size. By improving the load balancing towards the ideal case, it extends the network lifetime up to 77%. In addition, the network behavior becomes more stable over its lifetime and the decline with degraded performance is shorter.

An important point that can be concluded based on the results with varying IPI, is that it is not necessary to make an effort on the design of the protocol for low traffic scenarios (high IPI). In those scenarios, the radio communication power is not significant. In contrast, research efforts should focus on high traffic scenarios (that is, with an IPI of 10 s or less as suggested by our results), thus emphasizing the importance of the CCA function already discussed in our past and present works.

Although in the long run, the parents with the best quality links probably win the competition more often than parents with bad links, the main drawback of this proposal is that nothing ensures that the most reliable end-to-end route is chosen. In our next steps, we plan to investigate this and focus on the third layer of the communication stack as well as performing real experiments in the FIT-IoT lab [2].

Acknowledgments. This work is part of the project *WakeUp* funded by the French National Research Agency (ANR).

References

1. Allied Market Research. https://www.alliedmarketresearch.com/smart-cities-market
2. Adjih, C.: FIT IoT-LAB: a large scale open experimental IoT testbed. In: 2015 IEEE 2nd World Forum on Internet of Things (WF-IoT), pp. 459–464, December 2015
3. Ait Aoudia, F., Gautier, M., Berder, O.: OPWUM: opportunistic MAC protocol leveraging wake-up receivers in WSNs. J. Sens. (2016). https://doi.org/10.1155/2016/6263719, https://hal.inria.fr/hal-01244800
4. Basagni, S., Valerio, V.D., Koutsandria, G., Petrioli, C., Spenza, D.: WHARP: a wake-up radio and harvesting-based forwarding strategy for green wireless networks. In: 2017 IEEE 14th International Conference on Mobile Ad Hoc and Sensor Systems (MASS), pp. 257–265, October 2017
5. Basagni, S., Valerio, V.D., Koutsandria, G., Petrioli, C.: Wake-up radio-enabled routing for green wireless sensor networks. In: 2017 IEEE 86th Vehicular Technology Conference (VTC-Fall), pp. 1–6, September 2017
6. Magno, M., Jelicic, V., Srbinovski, B., Bilas, V., Popovici, E., Benini, L.: Design, implementation, and performance evaluation of a flexible low-latency nanowatt wake-up radio receiver. IEEE Trans. Ind. Inf. **12**(2), 633–644 (2016)
7. Piyare, R., Murphy, A.L., Kiraly, C., Tosato, P., Brunelli, D.: Ultra low power wake-up radios: a hardware and networking survey. IEEE Commun. Surv. Tutorials **19**(4), 2117–2157 (2017)
8. Piyare, R., Istomin, T., Murphy, A.L.: WaCo: a wake-up radio COOJA extension for simulating ultra low power radios. In: EWSN (2017)
9. Sampayo, S.L., Montavont, J., Noel, T.: LoBaPS: load balancing parent selection for RPL using wake-up radios. In: 2019 IEEE Symposium on Computers and Communications (ISCC) (IEEE ISCC 2019), Barcelona, Spain, June 2019
10. Shukla, S.N., Champaneria, T.A.: Survey of various data collection ways for smart transportation domain of smart city. In: 2017 International Conference on I-SMAC (IoT in Social, Mobile, Analytics and Cloud) (I-SMAC), pp. 681–685, February 2017
11. Thubert, P.: Objective function zero for the routing protocol for low-power and lossy networks (RPL). RFC 6552, RFC Editor, March 2012

Vehicular and UAV Networks

Comparative Evaluation Study of GLOSA Approaches Under Realistic Scenario Conditions

Mouna Karoui[✉], Antonio Freitas[✉], and Gerard Chalhoub[✉]

LIMOS-CNRS - University Clermont Auvergne, Clermont-Ferrand, France
{mouna.karoui,antonio.freitas,gerard.chalhoub}@uca.fr

Abstract. Cooperative Intelligent Transport Systems (C-ITS) are a promising solution to enhance road management, traffic efficiency, fuel consumption and road safety. Green Light Optimal Speed Advisory (GLOSA) is one of the traffic efficiency ITS services that can significantly cut fuel consumption and decrease waiting time while crossing intersections. When approaching a signalized intersection, GLOSA allows to inform the driver of an advisory speed to respect in order to reach the intersection while the traffic light is green. In this paper, we propose a multiple segments approach algorithm for GLOSA that allows the driver to anticipate multiple intersections ahead and adopt a speed that allows him to cross the consecutive traffic lights while their state is green. We simulated our approach using Artery framework under realistic communication and traffic conditions based on a wireless communication simulator and a real life map. Results show that taking into account multiple intersections while adopting the speed allows the driver to better optimize the crossing of intersections. Results also show the impact of activation distance and sending frequency on each approach. We show that an activation distance of 400 m allows a significant stop time gain of about 100% for both approaches.

Keywords: C-ITS · ETSI ITS-G5/IEEE 802.11p · GLOSA

1 Introduction

The fuel consumption economy is an important issue in our efforts towards a green and clean environment. C-ITS (Cooperative Intelligent Transport Systems) systems can be used to contribute in the resolution of this problem. C-ITS are a special type of VANETs (Vehicle AdHoc NETworks) that is based on cooperation amongst vehicles, and between vehicles and infrastructure in order to exchange and broadcast information related to traffic management. Potential benefits of C-ITS systems are also studied today in different aspects such as road safety, traffic management and driving comfort.

© Springer Nature Switzerland AG 2019
M. R. Palattella et al. (Eds.): ADHOC-NOW 2019, LNCS 11803, pp. 407–419, 2019.
https://doi.org/10.1007/978-3-030-31831-4_28

Several European projects[1] are conducted in the field of C-ITS such as SAFESPOT (Cooperative systems for road safety "Smart Vehicles on Smart Roads"), CVIS (Cooperative Vehicle-Infrastructure Systems) and DRIVE C2X. These projects were a great opportunity for the design of C-ITS standards, the test and the validation of architectures as well as the development of test methodologies and the examination of the impacts of cooperative systems on users, environment and society. C-Roads European project[2] is one of the recent projects that aim to make C-ITS a step closer to reality. This project is mainly focusing on the deployment and the wide assessment of innovative road C-ITS solutions through field operational tests (FOTs). Using vehicle-to-vehicle (V2V), vehicle-to-infrastructure (V2I), and infrastructure-to-vehicle (I2V) communications, these systems show a great promise in helping the driver to take the right decisions and ensure a better driving assistance. Moreover, the ability of mutually exchanging information allows to improve road environment and reduces traffic congestion. Furthermore, C-ITS is offering multiple services which play an important role to save energy and make the world less polluted. One such application called Green Light Optimal Speed Advisory (GLOSA) is a C-ITS traffic efficiency service that can reduce excessive stop-and-go driving on urban areas. Based on I2V communications, GLOSA service uses received information about traffic light position and its signal phase timing to calculate an advisory speed that enables the driver to pass at green phase. It updates the advisory speed periodically according to the current situation. In previous research work, two approaches of GLOSA were proposed: (i) simple segment approach which consists of giving an advisory speed dedicated to pass the upcoming traffic light at green phase, (ii) and multiple segment approach which provides an advisory speed taking into account all next intersections parameters in order to pass more than one traffic light at green phase with minimum speed variation.

The main contribution of our work is summarized in two aspects. First, we aim to investigate the performance of GLOSA approaches in different traffic conditions especially in congested traffic flow scenario. Second, both aspects are evaluated through realistic simulations based on communication emulation and a real-world urban map. The remainder of this paper is organized as follows: In Sect. 2, we give an insight of related work on main contributions about GLOSA strategies. Then, we propose a multi-segment approach called SABIN-MS in Sect. 3. The setup and details of our scenario simulations along with the evaluation will be presented in Sect. 4. In this section, we will also study the network parameters impact on GLOSA. In Sect. 5, we conclude and we present some perspectives.

2   Related Work

Many papers studied different algorithms for GLOSA service proving its benefits and potentials in reducing stop-and-go driving phenomena and saving energy.

---

[1] https://cordis.europa.eu/projects/en.
[2] https://www.c-roads.eu.

Paper [1] compared single and multi-segment approaches of GLOSA in terms of travel time and fuel consumption. The authors proposed a solution based on genetic algorithm to solve speed optimization problem, which consists of finding speed that minimizes travel time or fuel consumption. In this paper, authors compared different strategies. The ones that aim to optimize fuel consumption and others in which the goal was to reduce trip time. Their results showed that multi-segment approach outperforms single-segment approach. In this study authors made the results with the assumption of non-congested traffic flow.

In paper [2], authors also evaluated both GLOSA approaches and results showed similar conclusion, where multi-segment approach is more efficient for fuel consumption. In addition, the paper discusses the impact of the activation distance on GLOSA. The main drawback of this paper is the used simulation platform that does not include a realistic driver model nor a realistic communication model.

In paper [3], authors evaluated GLOSA benefits and its limitations in different traffic densities states. In free-flow conditions, authors found that GLOSA meet all its expected goals of reducing CO_2 emissions and waiting time. For a penetration rate of 100% and free-flow conditions, they observed an improvement of about 11% of CO_2 emissions, a gain of 17% in terms of waiting time . and 13.7 % of fuel consumption gain. However, in a congested traffic scenario, authors noticed a deterioration of GLOSA performances. They also observed that dense traffic scenario can cause longer waiting time, more CO_2 emissions and more frequent stop number.

Paper [4] proposed a performance study for GLOSA in urban areas. Authors used both simulation environment and field operational test measurements. For this evaluation, they used algorithm in paper [5]. They evaluated waiting time and average of CO_2 emissions for GLOSA and without GLOSA considering different penetration rate levels. Authors observed reliability between simulated results and real measurements. For a penetration rate of 100%, they achieved a reduction of CO_2 emission of about 10%. They concluded that a penetration rate of 50% is sufficient to give significant results in terms of fuel consumption and waiting time.

In paper [6], authors proposed an estimation of optimal late deceleration for GLOSA application. It is based on calculating the needed deceleration to reach the stop line at the estimated time of departure. Then, they evaluated the CO_2 emission in free flow situation and peak-hour scenarios. In peak-hour situation, they achieved a reduction of CO_2 emission of about 7%. They also observed that the number of stopping vehicles is increasing during peak-hour conditions.

Paper [7] proposed an optimal acceleration advice algorithms. In this paper, Authors presented a set of acceleration advice algorithms that aim to minimize speed changes. Through the evaluation of different metrics such as vehicle stop number ratio and fuel consumption, they proved the multiple benefits acquired from using their proposed acceleration advice algorithms. In free-flow conditions, they achieved an improvement of fuel consumption of about 25%. They also compared average delay for GLOSA and without GLOSA using simple traffic models and an Intelligent Driver Model (IDM). In this paper, authors gave an insight of comparison between cases where advisory speed is given only to the lead vehicle and when it is given both to the leader and the flower vehicle. Their results showed an enhancement between 31% and 32% of average delay using a simple traffic model and they noticed that their algorithm enables to save an average of fuel consumption between 21% and 23%. However, using IDM traffic model they obtained an improvement of 48% of average delay and 17% of fuel consumption reduction.

In paper [8], authors proposed a solving method for multiple segment speed optimization based on genetic algorithm. They applied the proposed solution in the context of electric cars. In this paper, the authors achieved a gain of 46% in terms of total number of stops. They also showed a gain of fuel consumption of about 30%. They tested their algorithm under real traffic topology composed of a set of three traffic lights using different traffic conditions.

Paper [9] proposed an algorithm for GLOSA based on calculating the distance that the vehicle will need to travel during the remaining red signal time or the remaining green time called respectively NOGO and GO indicators according to the paper terminology. If the vehicle is already travelling during GO indicator, there is no need to decelerate. Contrary to the NOGO indicator which advises vehicle to decelerate at $1\,\mathrm{m/s^2}$ until it reaches the green zone indicator. The authors showed that their proposed GLOSA approach performs well for traffic demand between 400 veh/h to 500 veh/h. In other traffic situations, the efficiency level of the proposed solution was worse than unequipped vehicle.

We observe that most cited papers have made their evaluation using simple traffic topology. In addition, the majority of them didn't take into account the impact of network communications parameters on GLOSA. In what follows, we will present our algorithms for single segment and multiple segments approaches for GLOSA and evaluate these proposal under realistic scenarios.

3   Multiple Segment Approach Algorithm (SABIN-MS)

In paper [10], we proposed a simple segment approach called Speed Advisory Boundary fInder (SABIN). It allows to find two possible speeds (v_1, v_2) to pass the green phase as fast as possible using v_1 or as slow as possible using v_2. SABIN algorithm takes the following parameters as inputs:

– t_1 and t_2 are respectively the start and the end of the green phase.
– distance to traffic light d
– current time t_0
– initial speed v_0.

SABIN Simple Segment (SABIN-SS) algorithm starts by calculating arrival time using maximum authorized speed and compares its value with the end of the green phase (time $t2$). This test is necessary to define cases in which driver can't pass during the current green phase. In this case, we need to repeat the algorithm in order to get an adequate advisory speed for the upcoming green phase. The output result of this algorithm is both speeds v_1 and v_2. These speeds are always between minimum and maximum authorized speeds[3].

In this paper, we extend SABIN-SS and we propose a multiple segments approach (SABIN-MS) as illustrated in Algorithm 1. The goal of this algorithm is to keep the speed as constant as possible in order to reduce fuel consumption and avoid unnecessary acceleration or deceleration every time we pass a consecutive set of traffic lights. First, we start by collecting data from available RSUs in the coverage area of communication. Second, we calculate speed Bounds ($v1$ and $v2$) for each segment. Third, we examine if a common speed exists between segment i and segment $i + 1$. If the segment i is not yet passed, the obtained common speed will be adopted. If the segment i is already passed, we shift the counter and we restart the search process. If there is no possible common speed, we use simple segment approach.

Algorithm 1. Multiple segments algorithm (SABIN-MS)

Data: N: Segments number, Advisory speeds :$[v_1, v_2]_j$,
id : sender id
Result: Common speed to pass a set of traffic lights

1 Collect data from different RSUs.
2 Calculate (v_1, v_2) for each detected segment
3 **for** ($i = 0;\ i < N;\ i++$)
   ;   // try to find a common speed enabling to pass more than one segment
4   **if** $(intersection([v_2, v_1]_i, [v_2, v_1]_{(i+1)})$=$true)$ **then**
5   **if** (segment "i" is not yet passed) **then**
6   s=UpperBound($[v_2, v_1]_i \cap [v_2, v_1]_{(i+1)}$)
7   Use speed "s" to pass the segment i and i+1
8   **else**
9   i=i-1 ;   // If segment i is passed, we shift the counter to not consider passed segments and we restart search process to find a common speed for the rest of segments
10   **else**
    ;   // In this case there are no intersections between consecutive speed intervals
11   Use the single segment approach

---

[3] We suppose that at every location there are two speeds that drivers need to respect: maximum authorized speed over which drivers will be fined, and minimum authorized speed below which drivers are not allowed to drive in order not to block traffic.

4   Impact of Traffic Flow on GLOSA

In this section, we compare different approaches: without GLOSA, SABIN single-segment (SABIN-SS) and SABIN-multiple segment (SABIN-MS) in terms of speed evolution, stop delay, and fuel consumption in different traffic flows.

4.1   Simulation Environment

In our study, we chose Artery framework[4] that enables vehicles to be equipped with ETSI ITS-G5 protocol stack as shown in Fig. 1. Single vehicles can hold multiple ITS-G5 applications through Artery's ITS-G5 middleware. Artery middleware operates as an abstraction and data provisioning layer for VANET applications, called services in Artery's terminology. It also implements Geo-networking routing protocol, Basic Transport Protocol (BTP) and the Decentralized Congestion Control (DCC) mechanism as specified in ETSI ITS-G5 requirements [11]. This framework uses OMNeT++ as a network simulator and SUMO as a road traffic simulator. It offers the possibility to produce a coupled simulation between both simulators. This is insured by Traffic Control Interface (TraCI). TraCI uses a TCP based client/server architecture to provide access to SUMO. It also allows to retrieve values from simulated objects, namely, positions and speeds.

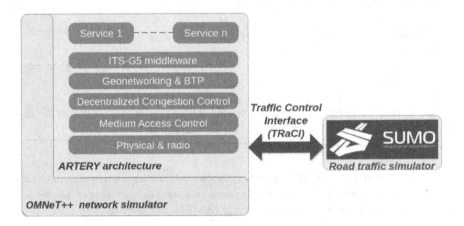

Fig. 1. Simulation environment architecture.

4.2   Simulation Scenario

Field Operational Tests (FOTs) of GLOSA service are challenging due to their cost and deployment complexity. For this reason, we used a communication network and road traffic coupled-simulator to evaluate GLOSA performances. We

---

[4] https://github.com/riebl/artery.

chose a realistic simulation scenario which consists of an urban road section of Bordeaux city in France as shown in Fig. 2. The total length of this section is about 2.7 km and it is composed of a set of five traffic lights. We set five RSUs, one RSU for each traffic light. Assuming that the position of the RSU and traffic light are the same. Our evaluation is done in case of autonomous driving, in which advisory speed is applied immediately after reception of the necessary information from the RSU. In this simulation scenario, the default sending period is fixed to 0.5 s as recommended in ETSI specification [12]. Communication range of both RSU and vehicle is also fixed to 900 m. As for propagation model, we use two rays interference model which is an adapted version of two-ray ground-reflection model for V2X communications [13]. In our study, we use ITS-G5/802.11p protocol stack in which the MAC layer is mainly based on IEEE 802.11-2012 standards including features of 802.11p such as the avoidance of channel scanning and association operations required for establishing a BSS. This mode is known as 'outside the context of BSS' (OCB) which is adopted by ITS-G5/IEEE 802.11p standard. Moreover, the MAC layer of ITS-G5 uses the basic Distributed Coordination Function (DCF) with CSMA/CA algorithm. Furthermore, ITS-G5 implements Decentralized Congestion Control (DCC) mechanism which ensures fair allocation between different stations located in the same zone [14].

We also assume that traffic lights change their phases at the same time with periodic cycle of 60 s composed of the three following states: red (30 s), green (25 s) and amber (5 s). We will measure speed, as well as the gain in terms of fuel consumption and stop delay of both approaches according to different traffic demands. Table 1 summarizes with more details the road traffic configuration.

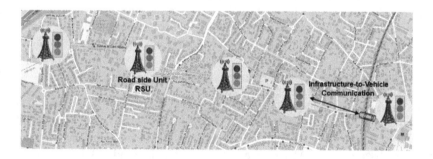

Fig. 2. Traffic network topology.

Table 1. Mobility traffic simulation parameters.

Car following model settings	
Car following Model	Krauss
Minimum gap between vehicles	0.5 m
Driver time headway τ	0.5 s
Step length of simulation	0.1 s
Vehicle settings	
Vehicle category	Passenger
Vehicle length	5m
Max speed	50 km/h
Min speed	20 km/h
Acceleration	$1\,m/s^2$
Deceleration	$2\,m/s^2$
Emission model	PHEMlight Gasoline Euro 4

4.3   Results Analysis

In this part, we study the impact of traffic flow on GLOSA approaches in terms of stop time and fuel consumption gain. The gain of both these metrics is calculated as follow:

$$Gain(\%) = \frac{(X - Y)}{X} * 100$$

where X and Y are respectively metrics for non equipped and equipped vehicles.

In Fig. 3, we observe the evolution of fuel consumption for each approach. For non equipped vehicle (without GLOSA), fuel consumption increases in every acceleration and deceleration due to stop and go behavior behind the traffic light. For SABIN-SS and SABIN-MS, we observe that the vehicle avoids stopping behind the traffic light due to the speed regulation according to the reception of information about the traffic light state.

As illustrated in Table 2, SABIN-MS outperforms SABIN-SS in terms of fuel consumption achieving a gain of about 18.4% in the case of single leader vehicle.

Figure 4 illustrates stop time gain against traffic flow. In unsaturated conditions, we observe that SABIN-SS achieves a stop time gain of 100% for traffic flow varying from 300 veh/h to 1000 veh/h. However, the stop time gain of SABIN-MS reaches a value of 90% for a traffic flow between 300 and 600 veh/h. For a medium traffic flow between 600 veh/h and 800 veh/h, stop time gain scales between 85% and 60%. In high traffic flow of about 1000 veh/h, stop time gain decreases for both approaches, but it influences SABIN-MS more than SABIN-SS which achieves a respective gain of 15% and 62%. This important difference

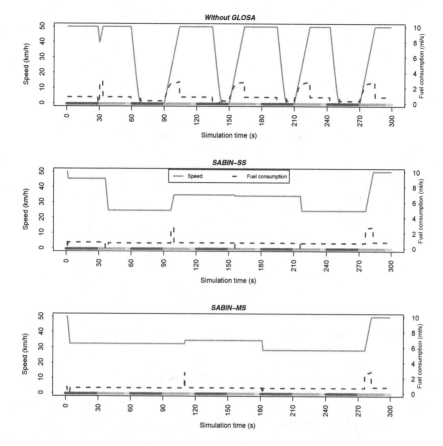

Fig. 3. Instantaneous speed and fuel consumption of a single traveling vehicle.

Table 2. Fuel consumption gain GLOSA per single leader vehicle.

GLOSA approaches	Fuel consumption gain (%)
SABIN-SS	17.02
SABIN-MS	18.44

is explained by the fact that driver speed in multi-segment approach is lower than advisory speed in simple-segment approach. Thus, with low speeds high traffic densities is rapidly reached. This is proved by the relationship between traffic density k, speed V and traffic demand Q ($k = \frac{Q}{V}$).

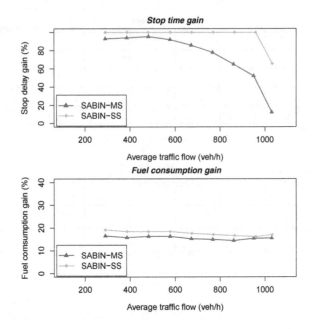

Fig. 4. Impact of traffic flow on stop delay and fuel consumption.

4.4   Network Parameters Impact on GLOSA

In this section, we study network parameters impact on SABIN-SS and SABIN-MS algorithms in terms of stop delay and fuel consumption gain. We choose to study the impact of network parameters in the case of a medium traffic flow of about 600 veh/h which is equivalent to a traffic demand of about one vehicle every 6 s. Figure 5 illustrates stop delay gain against activation distance variation. The activation distance is defined as the distance from the intersection at which GLOSA service is activated.

The following test is done using a sending period of 0.5 s. Under traffic flow of 600 veh/h, we observe that stop delay gain of SABIN-SS and SABIN-MS reaches around 100% for a communication range greater than 400 m. This can be explained by the fact that the speed regulation is closely related to distance to traffic light. To sum up, the selection of an optimal activation distance for GLOSA can be calculated for each intersection according to traffic light phases duration. For our scenario, we observe an optimal activation distance of about 400 m which is adequate for stop time minimization. In the case of SABIN-SS, an optimal activation distance of about 500 m gives a maximum fuel consumption gain of about 18%. However, the fuel consumption of SABIN-MS reaches its maximum value with an activation distance of about 1000 m. Indeed, this is an expected result since the optimal speed adaptation when dealing with multiple segments requires a greater distance in order to allow for multiple light phases to reach the right sequence. Figure 6 shows the impact of sending period on

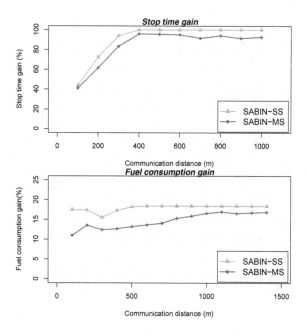

Fig. 5. Activation distance impact on GLOSA using a sending period of 0.5 s.

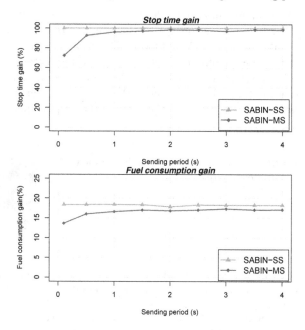

Fig. 6. Impact of sending period on GLOSA using a communication range of 900 m.

GLOSA gain in terms of stop delay and fuel consumption. For SABIN-SS, both gains are constant against the variation of sending period. For SABIN-MS, a slight improvement is obtained passing from a sending period of 0.5 to 1 s.

5   Conclusion and Perspectives

GLOSA service is expected not to be only an eco-friendly C-ITS service that reduces fuel consumption and emissions, but also to be a driving assistance service that aim to widely improve the driving user experience comfort through decreasing stop time behind traffic intersections. In this paper, we proposed a comparative study of two GLOSA approaches using a realistic traffic topology.

First of all, we studied the impact of traffic flow on GLOSA approaches. In free flow traffic conditions, we achieved a gain of stop delay that reaches 95% and a fuel consumption gain of about 18%. In dense traffic scenarios, performances of both algorithms decrease while reaching a traffic flow of 1000 veh/h which is equivalent to a traffic demand of one vehicle every 3.6 s. In this study, we also investigated the impact of network communication parameters on GLOSA. As a conclusion, we noticed that it is important to select a suitable communication range according to the used GLOSA approach as well as an adequate sending period. These network parameters systematically influenced stop delay and fuel consumption.

In the future work, we aim to made our work a step closer to reality by adjusting the driver behavior according to the results from FOTs. We want to further focus on evaluating GLOSA and more ITS services using a heterogeneous vehicular network topology combining both a short-range wireless communication standard and a cellular technology. Using long range communications allows better coverage and enhanced connectivity. We would be interested in investigating the impact of cellular communications on the effectiveness of real time messages of GLOSA.

Acknowledgement   This work is partially funded by C-ROADS France European project.

References

1. Seredynski, M., Dorronsoro, B., Khadraoui, D.: Comparison of Green Light Optimal Speed Advisory approaches. In: 2013 16th International IEEE Conference on Intelligent Transportation Systems-(ITSC), pp. 2187–2192. IEEE (2013)
2. Sharara, M., Ibrahim, M., Chalhoub, G.: Impact of network performance on GLOSA. In: 2019 16th IEEE Annual Consumer Communications & Networking Conference (CCNC), pp. 1–6. IEEE (2019)
3. Eckhoff, D., Halmos, B., German, R.: Potentials and limitations of Green Light Optimal Speed Advisory systems. In: 2013 IEEE Conference on Vehicular Networking Conference (VNC), pp. 103–110. IEEE (2013)

4. Lebre, M.A., Mouël, F.L., Ménard, E., Garnault, A., Bradaï, B., Picron, V.: Real scenario and simulations on GLOSA traffic light system for reduced CO_2 emissions, waiting time and travel time. arXiv preprint arXiv:1506.01965 (2015)
5. Katsaros, K., Kernchen, R., Dianati, M., Rieck, D.: Performance study of a Green Light Optimized Speed Advisory (GLOSA) application using an integrated cooperative its simulation platform. In: 2011 7th International Wireless Communications and Mobile Computing Conference (IWCMC), pp. 918–923. IEEE (2011)
6. Van Katwijk, R.T., Gabriel, S.: Optimising a vehicle's approach towards an adaptively controlled intersection. IET Intell. Transp. Syst. **9**(5), 479–487 (2015)
7. Stebbins, S., Hickman, M., Kim, J., Vu, H.L.: Characterising Green Light Optimal Speed Advisory trajectories for platoon-based optimisation. Transp. Res. Part C Emerg. Technol. **82**(43–62), 3 (2017)
8. Luo, Y., Li, S., Zhang, S., Qin, Z., Li, K.: Green Light Optimal Speed Advisory for hybrid electric vehicles. Mech. Syst. Sign. Process. **87**, 30–44 (2017)
9. Suzuki, H., Marumo, Y.: A new approach to Green Light Optimal Speed Advisory (GLOSA) systems and its limitations in traffic flows. In: Ahram, T., Karwowski, W., Taiar, R. (eds.) IHSED 2018. AISC, vol. 876, pp. 776–782. Springer, Cham (2019). https://doi.org/10.1007/978-3-030-02053-8_118
10. Karoui, M., Freitas, A., Chalhoub, G.: Efficiency of Speed Advisory Boundary finder (SABIN) strategy for GLOSA using ITS-G5. In: 2018 IFIP/IEEE International Conference on Performance Evaluation and Modeling in Wired and Wireless Networks (PEMWN), pp. 1–6. IEEE (2018)
11. Riebl, R., Günther, H.J., Facchi, C., Wolf, L.: Artery: extending VEINS for VANET applications. In: 2015 International Conference on Models and Technologies for Intelligent Transportation Systems (MT-ITS), pp. 450–456. IEEE (2015)
12. ETSI: Intelligent Transport Systems (ITS); vehicular communications; basic set of applications; part 2: Specification of cooperative awareness basic service (2011)
13. Sommer, C., Joerer, S., Dressler, F.: On the applicability of two-ray path loss models for vehicular network simulation. In: 2012 IEEE Vehicular Networking Conference (VNC), pp. 64–69. IEEE (2012)
14. Strom, E.G.: On medium access and physical layer standards for cooperative intelligent transport systems in Europe. Proc. IEEE **99**(7), 1183–1188 (2011)

Quality of Context for VANETs: QoC Metrics for Connectivity in VANETs

Margarete Sá and Sérgio Gorender[(✉)]

Distributed Systems Laboratory (LaSiD),
Graduate Program in Mechatronics (PPGM), Federal University of Bahia (UFBA),
Salvador, BA 40.170-110, Brazil
{magsa,gorender}@ufba.br
http://www.lasid.ufba.br

Abstract. Context describes the status of a system and of the environment in which it operates. In context-aware systems, contextual information is obtained by monitoring the environment with various sensors. Applied to a vehicular network, the context describes the state of the network, considering its various components and requirements for running applications. The context is used by the network to decide about routing, about fault correction and about recovery and the adequacy of services. This adapts the network to changes that occur in the environment. Due to the high dynamicity of the network, context information changes frequently, and old information should no longer be used for system decisions. It is therefore important that the information collected by the context is presented, along with indications of validity time, adding quality to this information. The validity time of context information is one of the parameters that characterize Quality of Context (QoC). In this article we present a context definition for vehicular networks and QoC parameters for this context. In particular, as QoC parameters we present the validity of the status of communication between pairs of vehicles, the timeliness of this context information, and the confidence, which indicates the reliability of the context. We programmed the context conditions into a simulator to generate results. The results show the efficiency of the context and the QoS metrics, and that these metrics are applicable and provide relative reliability to the context.

Keywords: VANETs · Context-aware · Quality of Context

1 Introduction

Traffic applications executing over a vehicular ad hoc network (VANETs) provide traffic information in real time for human drivers. This information helps drivers to decide on the better route to a specific place, considering traffic, gas station, conditions of roads and others. These applications may demand for the satisfaction of distinct time requirements. Applications for autonomous vehicles being developed may demand stronger time requirements.

M. R. Palattella et al. (Eds.): ADHOC-NOW 2019, LNCS 11803, pp. 420–431, 2019.
https://doi.org/10.1007/978-3-030-31831-4_29

On the other hand, Ad hoc Vehicular Networks (VANETs) are dynamically constructed, based on the distance between the vehicles, making communication between them possible. Due to their mobility, vehicles may be closer and establish a communication link (a connection). Or they can be distant from one another and can't directly communicate with each other. The mobility of the vehicles makes it difficult to provide guarantees for the communication links between them. Consequently it is necessary to constantly monitor the network to obtain information about the status of the connection between vehicles and then change network configuration to provide more stable connections.

We adopt the concept of context, which has been developed for pervasive systems, based on information collected from sensors. We developed a context for VANETs, to be part of the I-Car architecture, presented in [15]. A context for vehicular communication can be defined as a set of information collected in the environment of the vehicular network, and from the vehicles themselves, and which forms the current state of the operation of the network. The concept of context awareness has been used in pervasive, ubiquitous and other systems, based on sensor information, as a way of characterizing the information collected through these sensors [2,21]. The proposed context describes the situation of vehicular communication, correlating communication, mobility, traffic conditions, devices and protocols of the network.

A frequent update of the context would bring such information closer to the actual situation of the network. If the context update does not occur with the necessary frequency, the information can become old and obsolete. To improve the reliability of the obtained context information, it is possible to define metrics about the quality of this context [3,10]. The concept of quality of context (QoC) is based on different metrics and parameters, which are defined using characteristics of sensors and application requirements. Different context information may present different quality parameters. Quality of context has also been developed for pervasive systems and systems based on sensors, in general. In this paper we propose the use of QoC as a way to qualify the context information collected and calculated for the I-Car VANET Context.

The validity time is a calculated metric which indicates a period of time during which it is expected that the connection between two vehicles is stable and functioning. We provide an estimated validity, which is closer to the actual status of the vehicles and their mobility, but without stronger guaranties. This information may indicate that the communication will be possible in sufficient time to execute applications and protocols.

It is also interesting to calculate the confidence of information, considering that vehicles constantly change their mobility characteristics. The confidence metric, as we propose in this paper, is based on the age of the context, and can be used to determine when to collect new context and quality of context information.

In this paper we present a proposal for the context of vehicular networks (context-aware VANETs) including quality metrics. In this proposal, based on the definition of context information for vehicle networks, we define how to calculate the validity time for the connectivity between a pair of vehicles. We also define how to calculate the confidence for this information. The context and its quality metrics are part of the I-Car architecture, presented in [15]. Both the context and the calculation of the validity period and of the confidence of this information are presented in their equations and concepts. We also introduce an implementation of our vehicular network with quality of context in a simulation environment, with some results.

The paper is organized as follows: Sect. 2 presents Related Works in the use of context-awareness and quality-of-context in VANETs; in Sect. 3 we define our system model; Sect. 4 presents our proposal of context for vehicular communication; Sect. 5 defines the quality of context metrics adopted and present the calculation for the metrics; Sect. 6 describes an implementation of the system and simulation results; and Sect. 7 presents some conclusions.

2 Related Works

The concepts of Context-Awareness and Quality of Context, have been used in the field of pervasive systems, in works such as [2,3,11]. In these papers we have both the definition of the context based on information obtained from sensors being used, and the definition of quality of context parameters, which considers both the characteristics of the sensors and the requirements of the applications.

Some papers have proposed the use of Context in VANETs such as [1,4,13]. These papers consider information collected in a vehicular network, such as position, direction and speed of vehicles, and characteristics of wireless communication, including hardware and software.

Quality of context applied to VANETs is really recent. In [20] quality of context parameters are defined relative to messages being exchanged by applications over the vehicular network. Parameters such as temporal relevance of messages, completeness of information, priority of information and spatial relevance are defined, relative to the messages being exchanged, and used to calculate the quality of context of each message being sent. The article also presents the concept of peer reputation based on confidence in the information provided by a node, using previous interactions. The quality of context associated with the reputation of the people, are used in the decision on the priority given to the processing of each message.

In [12] it is proposed the use of QoC metrics in an Ambient Assisted Living e-Health System. Int this paper QoC metrics are calculated from the average of up-to-dateness, precision, completeness, and coverage metrics.

Distinct from [20] and [12], we propose the use of QoC applied to the context of communication links, based on information from the network itself, and the status of each vehicle.

3 System Model

We assume a vehicular ad-hoc network (VANET) in which each vehicle has communication, processing, data storage capabilities, a GPS (Global Positioning System) and sensors to measure speed and acceleration. Several vehicular applications run over the VANET. The vehicular agents maintain information about their physical situation and about the communication environment. This information forms a context for the VANET.

We also assume that when two agents can communicate on the network, it works as if there is a connection between them. These connections are unstable, and they can be created, lost and/or restored at all times. Communication links are asynchronous and messages delivery can be incomplete or messages can be lost. The geographic extension of the network and the number of nodes in the system are unknown and it can vary throughout the execution.

In each vehicular agent the GPS provides an information about the location of the vehicle in terms of latitude and longitude. The GPS also provides the updated global time, which is used for the synchronization of the agent's clock. In the vehicles there are no restrictions on the use of energy, once the batteries are charged at all times by the operation of the vehicle's engine.

It is not purpose of this paper to discourse this matter, however it is important to mention that the system has a failure detector oracle that identifies the fault agents.

4   A Context for Vehicular Communication

The communication context for the I-Car system [15] represents the status of the communication environment as perceived by each agent. This context includes information about network devices and protocols, distributed communication services, vehicle position and mobility, and conditions of routes, among other factors. Each agent has a distinct view of the communication context.

A context monitoring system uses information obtained directly from sensors such as GPS, accelerometer and others, communication hardware and software, and messages exchanged between agents. It may use application messages or messages sent periodically by the monitor system itself depending on the frequency of application messages. Agents inform each other about their current location, direction and speed of vehicle mobility and the state of communication with other agents.

The context for a vehicle contains information about the vehicle and its systems and about the communication between the vehicle and other vehicular agents in the network (agent pairs). Communication context informs the status of the communication between the local agent (l) and a remote agent (r) according to the perception of the local agent. It includes a set of information such as mobility data between agents, neighborhood condition and the mode of interaction between agents.

As in this paper we focused specifically on communication context, we do not include other context information, which will be presented in another paper.

4.1 Context Information About Mobility

Each agent maintains context information about its mobility and about other vehicles movements. A vehicle uses its GPS and other sensors, such as accelerometer, to periodically obtain information such as: vehicle speed (v_l), vehicle direction (dir_l), geographic longitude (lon) and latitude (lat) of the vehicle and the time when the information has been collected (ts). In addition, in each agent, the value of the maximum possible speed of the vehicle $(vMax_l)$ is considered as the highest speed the vehicle can perform during its movements - it is emphasized that $vMax_l \geq v_l$. It can be used as maximum speed, the maximum speed value of a street or highway, or the maximum speed indicated by the vehicle manufacturer.

The mobility between pairs of vehicles (vehicular agents l and r) deals with information, such as: distance between agents (d_{rl}) which is calculated based on the Euclidean geometry $d_{rl} = \sqrt{(lon_r - lon_l)^2 + (lat_r - lat_l)^2}$ and the relative speed between l and r, which depends on the speed and direction of the vehicles [6]. This information is calculated and updated when l receives information about the individual movement of r or when l updates its own individual motion data.

4.2 Context Information About Neighborhood Conditions

Two agents are considered neighbors if they have a communication connection between them, and they can communicate directly. Neighboring agents are within the reach of their communication signals and can communicate without the presence of forwarding nodes. The neighborhood condition has two situations:

- Neighbors - remote agent (r) is considered a neighbor of the local agent (l) if the agents are within their range of communication.
- Non-neighbor - r is considered non-neighbor to l, when during the communication among them, it is necessary to use forwarding nodes, because the agents are out of the reach of their communication signals.

This context is constructed using local information about the position and mobility of the local agent, and using this same information obtained from a remote agent, through exchanged messages. The context also uses information about the reach of communication signals.

4.3 Status of the Interaction Between Two Agents

The context regarding the status of the communication between pairs of agents indicates the status of a remote agent. This context is obtained through messages received from the remote agents, or the absence of this messages. A failure detector oracle monitors remote agents and informs a set of faulty ones.

- Communicating - a remote agent r is receiving and transmitting messages from and to the local agent. The remote agent is alive and communicating.

– Faulty - the remote agent r is in the faulty set maintained by the failure detector oracle. It is not communicating with the local agent.

The behavior of the failure detector oracle, and its implementation is out of the scope of this paper, and will be presented in another article.

5   Quality of Context for Communication Links

We assume a local agent (l) and a remote agent (r). Agent r is classified as Communicating by l's context. The communication status between two agents in a VANET can change when they move outside their communication signals, or when agents which are part of a route between the communicating agents move and leave the range of their signals. As the movement of these vehicles can't be predicted, because vehicles can change their speed and directions, we calculate the QoS metrics Validity, Timeliness and Confidence.

5.1   Validity for the Connection Between Neighbor Agents

The validity time for neighbor agents defines a period of time during which it is ensured that the communication context is valid. It is calculated based on information such as the reach of the vehicles communication signals and the position and mobility of the vehicles. This metric is a estimation for a period of time when it is expected for the vehicles to continue communicating, maintaining their neighborhood condition. A local agent calculates the validity time for each remote neighbor agent. It is considered that there is a high probability that, during this period of time, the agents are not going to leave their respective communication limits, being no longer neighbors. This time is based on the quality of the communication signal from the remote agent r, the geographic positions of both agents and the possibility of movements, considering direction and speed.

$$VT_{rl}^i = \frac{s_{rl}}{rv_{rl}} \tag{1}$$

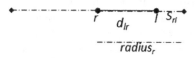

Fig. 1. Distance for local and remote agents (l and r) to go out of the limits of their communication signals

We assume, as a simplification, that a circumference represents the reach of the communication signal, expressed in Fig. 1 as $radius_r$. When l receives a message from r, l measures the power of r's signal and estimates $radius_r$. There are several approaches in the literature to estimate the reach of the communication signal. In this paper we adopt the Free Space [14] technique, which is a classic approach in MANET (Mobile Ad Hoc Network). We define that S_{rl} is the shorter distance for a local agent to be out of the range of communication of a remote agent ($s_{rl} = radius_r - d_{rl}$). In this formula, d_{rl} is the distance between agents r and l considering the latest GPS measurement.

In Eq. 1, VT_{rl}^i is the validity time for the connection between two vehicles, corresponding to an estimated amount of time for the agents to travel the distance S_{rl} and change its context. This formula considers that rv_{rl} is the relative speed between the agents, calculated based on the current direction and speed of the vehicles. The calculation of the relative speed uses information collected at the latest measurement for the two involved agents.

5.2   Validity for the Connection Between Non-Neighbor Agents

When two agents are not neighbors but are communicable (the agents classify each other as Non-Neighbor and Communicating in their contexts), the exchange of messages between them occurs through a route formed by intermediary nodes, which forward the message to its destination. Each forwarding agent retransmits the message to the next node on the route, considering that these two agents must be neighbors. Figure 2 shows a route with forwarding nodes $f1$ and $f2$, where s is the origin of the message and d its destination.

Fig. 2. Route for a message to be transmitted between agents s and d

Each agent that is involved in transfer messages in a route ($route_{sd}$), calculates the validity time for the next agent in this route. The sender of the message, agent s, knows the validity time of its communication link with the next selected agent, to which it must send the message. Thus, the validity of a route between a pair of agents ($routeVT_{sd}$) is the shortest validity period between the pairs of agents in the path for transmitting the message.

Considering the communication between two agents, source (s) and destination (d), it is possible that exists more then one path, forming a list of valid routes - $routeList_{sd}$. We consider the validity time between non-neighboring agents as the longer validity time between the routes existing in $routeList_{sd}$. The calculation of the validity time (VT_{sd}) for non-neighboring agents is presented in Algorithm 1.

5.3   Timeliness

The QoC metric Timeliness represents how recent is the update of the context. We define the timeliness metric qualifying the communication context.

Algorithm 1. Context Validity for non-neighbor agents

---

1 $VT_{sd} \leftarrow 0$;
2 **for** *each* $route_{sd}$ *in* $routeList_{sd}$ **do**
3   **if** $routeVT_{sd} > VT_{sd}$ **then**
4         $VT_{sd} \leftarrow routeVT_{sd}$

$$T^i_{rl} = \begin{cases} 1 - \frac{age^i_{rl}}{VT^i_{rl}} & : \text{if } (age^i_{rl} < VT_{rl}) \\ 0 & : \textit{otherwise} \end{cases} \tag{2}$$

Equation 2 computes the Timeliness rate - T^i_{rl}, which relates the age (age^i_{rl}) of the context of the pair of agents (r e l), with the estimated validity of the pair r and l (VT_{rl}). The calculation for the age (age^i_{rl}) is represented in Eq. 3 and corresponds to the difference between the current time instant ($actualTime$) and the latest instant of time when context information has been collected.

$$age^i_{rl} = actualTime - min(mobilityDataTime^i_l, mobilityDataTime^i_r) \tag{3}$$

5.4   A Confidence Metric for Communication Context

The estimated validity time is based on the behavior of the communication signal and the mobility of the vehicles involved. It is observed that the dynamics of these behaviors in the environment may interfere with the value of the calculated validity time. In this sense we proposed the confidence coefficient of the validity (α^i_{rl}) - presented in Eq. 4. It indicates the degree of confidence with respect to the age of the context (age^i_{rl}), the estimated validity (VT^i_{rl}) and the minimum validity (VT^{min}_{rl}), that is the validity time assuming the vehicles are running in their maximum speeds.

$$\alpha^i_{rl} = \begin{cases} 1 - \frac{(age^i_{rl} - VT^{min}_{rl})}{(VT^i_{rl} - VT^{min}_{rl})} & : \text{if } (VT^{min}_{rl} \le age^i_{rl} \le VT^i_{rl}) \\ 1 & : \text{if } (age^i_{rl} < VT^{min}_{rl}) \\ 0 & : \textit{otherwise} \end{cases} \tag{4}$$

The confidence is equal to 1 (100%) when the age is less than the minimum validity time. In this period we assume that the information is really reliable. With the age between VT^{min}_{rl} and VT^i_{rl}, the metric varies from 1 to 0, decreasing the confidence of the information as age^i_{rl} approximates to the validity time. The minimum validity time is calculated with $VT^{min}_{rl} = \frac{S_{rl}}{rv^{max}_{rl}}$.

6   Implementation, Simulation, Setup Scenario and Results

The implementation was performed in C++ in the OMNeT++ (Objective Modular Network Testbed in C++ – network simulator environment). The experiments were performed using the VEINS Framework [17], which integrates the platforms OMNET++ [19] used to simulate communication protocols, and SUMO [8] used to simulate vehicular traffic on roads. We used a common simulation scenario with the aim of characterizing the concepts presented here. The driver model is the SUMO standard Krauss based on [9]. The vehicles are queued in a predefined path, avoiding collisions between them. The scenario uses a road of the Erlangen city map in Germany available at the VEINS framework. The vehicles move in different bands, in opposite directions. We assume a typical driving speed of 16–24.4 m/s. The vehicles communicate with each other using the IEEE 802.11p protocol [7,16]. We adopted the model implemented in [5], using a rate of 6 Mbits/s, a transmission power of 20 mW and a receiver sensitivity of −89 dBm. Each vehicle measures the power of the received signal considering the model of obstacles in [18].

The aim of the simulations is to verify in what conditions the proposed validity time adequately represents the period of time when the neighborhood condition between pairs of vehicles is maintained. Considering this objective, two evaluations were carried out: one which analyzes the relation between the validity period, estimated and measured in the environment; the other verifies the effects of the expiration time and its coefficient. Each simulation experiment lasted a maximum of 200 s.

6.1   Simulation Results

To analyze the validity period estimated and measured in the environment, we observed the time instant when the pair of agents lose connectivity and calculate the duration of this connectivity $period_{rl}$.

In Fig. 3, the graph shows, in many different moments of the simulation, the behavior of the difference between the time when the communication has been lost and the estimated validity time ($VTDiff = period_{rl} - VT_{rl}$). It also shows the same difference applied to the minimum validity period ($VTDiff^{min} = period_{rl} - VT_{rl}^{min}$). The X-axis represents the time instant in which the VT_{rl} and VT_{rl}^{min} were updated ([110 s, 121 s]). Such values are updated when the local agent (l) receives new information from the remote agent (r) and when l receives its mobility information from GPS. In Fig. 3, the smaller the difference (y-axis), the closer the estimated value is to the measured value. Note that the difference of the minimum validity is greater than the difference applied to the estimated validity. The minimum validity (VT_{rl}^{min}) is always less than the measured time period ($period_{rl}$). The estimated validity (VT_{rl}) is quite always less than the measured time period ($period_{rl}$), being a good and relatively secure estimate.

Table 1 presents a sample of QoC metric values obtained by the simulation. The columns present the maximum relative speed (rv_{rl}^{max}), the instantaneous rel-

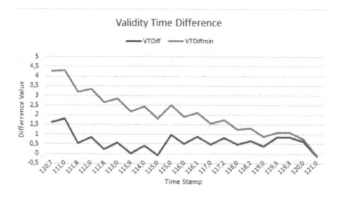

Fig. 3. Validity time error

ative speed (rv_{rl}^i), the age of the last information collection (age^i), the Timeliness metric (T_{rl}^i), the Confidence metric (α_{rl}^i), the minimum validity time (VT_{rl}^{min}) and the instantaneous validity time (VT_{rl}^i). The Table 1 shows the coefficient values in relation to the age of the context. When T_{rl}^i (timeliness) is negative, and consequently, α_{rl}^i is equal to zero, it indicates that the context may be obsolete and unreliable in relation to the environment. When $0 < \alpha_{rl}^i < 1$ and, consequently we have that $VT_{rl} > age^i > VT_{rl}^{min}$, it indicates that the context information is usable by applications, in relation to the environment. When the age is less than VT_{rl}^{min}, the confidence is equal to 1, and it is not necessary to collect new context. The confidence helps define when it becomes necessary to monitor the context again, considering also application requirements.

Table 1. A data sample of metrics values

rv_{rl}^{max}	rv_{rl}^i	age^i	T_{rl}^i	α_{rl}^i	VT_{rl}^{min}	VT_{rl}^i
48.8	33.8819	1.07431	0.87614	1	6.02207	8.674
48.8	33.88	1.10001	0.872752	1	6.00165	8.645
48.8	33.8539	1.03569	0.869558	1	5.50808	7.94
48.8	33.8252	1.08999	0.845687	1	4.89599	7.064
48.8	33.8081	1.1	0.779607	1	3.45778	4.991
48.8	33.9097	1.07431	0.73293	1	2.79519	4.023
48.8	33.8479	1.0457	0.654983	1	2.10221	3.031
48.8	33.9503	1.8954	0.249266	0.819	1.7565	2.524
48.8	33.888	1.09	0.477758	1	1.44938	2.087
48.8	33.8453	1.06432	−0.250784	0	0.590155	0.851

7 Conclusions

In this paper we discussed the concept of context-awareness and quality of context (QoC) for vehicular networks. We also presented a definition of context for communication status between pairs of vehicular agents as a service of the I-Car system. We described this context, and we presented QoC metrics characterizing parameters for the quality of this context. We propose validity time, the timeliness and also the confidence to determine the validity of information of vehicular communication context.

The context informs a communication status for pairs of agents, which can be neighbors and communicate directly or non-neighbors and communicate through routes. For neighboring agents, we presented a formula to calculate a period of time during which the connection is expected to be maintained. This formula can be also used to calculates the validity time for routes. This information can be used by users or user applications. They can analyze the possibilities to execute services and protocols. The confidence QoC metric is based on the age of the context and validity information. It can help to define when it would be necessary to collect new information context. It is important considering the dynamics of the traffic, with vehicles changing their mobility status.

The formulas presented here have been implemented in a simulation environment, obtaining results that prove its efficiency and that the definition of the validity period can be of great value for the management of networks. The use of the concept of quality-of-context in vehicular networks is still recent and there are few proposals with this approach. In this article we take these ideas forward, showing how we can use quality of context embedded in a network architecture, the I-Car.

Due to lack of space, we presented a common scenario and its results, with the aim of characterizing the concepts developed in this paper. The results using other scenarios and situations related to traffic and vehicular communication are going to be published in other papers.

References

1. Alagar, V., Wan, K.: Context-aware trust-based management of vehicular ad-hoc networks (VANETs). In: 2015 IEEE 12th International Conference on Ubiquitous Intelligence and Computing and 2015 IEEE 12th International Conference on Autonomic and Trusted Computing and 2015 IEEE 15th International Conference on Scalable Computing and Communications and Its Associated Workshops (UIC-ATC-ScalCom). IEEE (2015)
2. Baldauf, M., Dustdar, S., Rosenberg, F.: A survey on context-aware systems. Int. J. Ad Hoc Ubiquitous Comput. 2(4), 263–277 (2007)
3. Buchholz, T., Küpper, A., Schiffers, M.: Quality of context: what it is and why we need it. In: Proceedings of the Workshop of the HP OpenView University Association, vol. 2003 (2003)
4. Dressler, F., Klingler, F., Sommer, C., Cohen, R.: Not all VANET broadcasts are the same: context-aware class based broadcast. IEEE/ACM Trans. Netw. 26, 17–30 (2017)

5. Eckhoff, D., Sommer, C., Dressler, F.: On the necessity of accurate IEEE 802.11 p models for IVC protocol simulation. In: 2012 IEEE 75th Vehicular Technology Conference (VTC Spring), pp. 1–5. IEEE (2012)
6. Halliday, D., Resnick, R., Krane, K.: Física 4a edição. Livros Técnicos e Científicos SA, Rio de Janeiro, 1 (1983)
7. Jiang, D., Delgrossi, L.: IEEE 802.11 p: towards an international standard for wireless access in vehicular environments. In: Vehicular Technology Conference, 2008. VTC Spring 2008, pp. 2036–2040. IEEE (2008)
8. Krajzewicz, D., Hertkorn, G., Rossel, C., Wagner, P.: Sumo (simulation of urban mobility), pp. 183–187 (2002)
9. Krauß, S.: Microscopic modeling of traffic flow: investigation of collision free vehicle dynamics. Ph.D. thesis, Dt. Zentrum für Luft-und Raumfahrt eV, Abt. Unternehmensorganisation und ... (1998)
10. Manzoor, A., Truong, H.-L., Dustdar, S.: On the evaluation of quality of context. In: Roggen, D., Lombriser, C., Tröster, G., Kortuem, G., Havinga, P. (eds.) EuroSSC 2008. LNCS, vol. 5279, pp. 140–153. Springer, Heidelberg (2008). https://doi.org/10.1007/978-3-540-88793-5_11
11. Manzoor, A., Truong, H.L., Dustdar, S.: Quality of context: models and applications for context-aware systems in pervasive environments. Knowl. Eng. Rev. **29**(02), 154–170 (2014)
12. Nazário, D.C., Todesco, J.L., Dantas, M.A.R., Tromel, I., Neto, A.: A quality of context evaluating approach in an ambient assisted living e-health system. In: 2014 IEEE 16th International Conference on e-Health Networking, Applications and Services (Healthcom), pp. 158–163. IEEE (2014)
13. Paridel, K., et al.: Analyzing the efficiency of context-based grouping on collaboration in VANETs with large-scale simulation. J. Ambient Intell. Humaniz. Comput. **5**(4), 475–490 (2014)
14. Petterson, L.L., Dave, B.S.: Computer Networks: A Systems Approach, 4th edn. Morgan Kaufman (2007)
15. Sá, M., Gorender, S.: Uma arquitetura de rede para serviços de comunicação autonômicos. In: III Workshop em Sistemas Distribuídos Autônomo (WoSiDA) - 31o Simpósio Brasileiro de Redes de Computadores e Sistemas Distribuídos, May 2013
16. Schwartz, R.S., Ohazulike, A.E., Sommer, C., Scholten, H., Dressler, F., Havinga, P.: On the applicability of fair and adaptive data dissemination in traffic information systems. Ad Hoc Netw. **13**, 428–443 (2014)
17. Sommer, C., German, R., Dressler, F.: Bidirectionally coupled network and road traffic simulation for improved IVC analysis. IEEE Trans. Mob. Comput. **10**(1), 3–15 (2011)
18. Sommer, C., Eckhoff, D., German, R., Dressler, F.: A computationally inexpensive empirical model of IEEE 802.11 p radio shadowing in urban environments. In: 2011 Eighth International Conference on Wireless on-Demand Network Systems and Services, pp. 84–90. IEEE (2011)
19. Varga, A., et al.: The OMNeT++ discrete event simulation system. In: Proceedings of the European Simulation Multiconference (ESM2001). pp. 319–324 (2001)
20. Yasar, A., Paridel, K., Preuveneers, D., Berbers, Y.: When efficiency matters: towards quality of context-aware peers for adaptive communication in VANETs. In: 2011 IEEE Intelligent Vehicles Symposium (IV), pp. 1006–1012. IEEE (2011)
21. Zimmermann, A., Lorenz, A., Oppermann, R.: An operational definition of context. In: Kokinov, B., Richardson, D.C., Roth-Berghofer, T.R., Vieu, L. (eds.) CONTEXT 2007. LNCS (LNAI), vol. 4635, pp. 558–571. Springer, Heidelberg (2007). https://doi.org/10.1007/978-3-540-74255-5_42

Performance Analysis of MANET Routing Protocols in Urban VANETs

Antonio Di Maio[1(✉)], Maria Rita Palattella[2], and Thomas Engel[1]

[1] SnT - University of Luxembourg, Luxembourg City, Luxembourg
antonio.dimaio@uni.lu
[2] Luxembourg Institute of Science and Technology, Esch-sur-Alzette, Luxembourg

Abstract. Infrastructure-less communications between moving vehicles present emblematic challenges because of high node mobility and link volatility, which may harm the performances of different categories of emerging vehicular applications. In order to move data between vehicles that are not in direct communication range, several distributed routing protocols have been proposed and tested in vehicular networks, highlighting their strengths and weaknesses. Some previous works report disagreeing claims about routing protocol performances in similar vehicular scenarios. Therefore, in this work, we evaluate the performances in terms of Packet Delivery Ratio (PDR), packet delay, frame collision rate, and signaling rate of three well-known routing protocols (AODV, DSDV, and GPSR), simulating them in a realistic Manhattan scenario. Furthermore, we evaluate the impact of typical urban obstacles (e.g. buildings) on the considered performance metrics. We observed that, in the proposed urban scenario, AODV provided the best PDR, GPSR the best packet delay, and DSDV failed to provide satisfactory performances due to signaling-induced congestion. Simulations showed that considering the shadowing effects induced by the buildings in an urban scenario drastically changes the observed performances, i.e. reduces the frame collisions, decreases the PDR, and increases the packet delay.

Keywords: Mobile ad-hoc networking · Vehicular networks · Routing · AODV · DSDV · GPSR · Simulation · Performance evaluation

1 Introduction

Connected vehicles of the future will provide users with a wide range of different applications that will need to exchange information with high data rate, high reliability, and low communication delay. For example, some modern vehicular applications that aim at improving the users' safety (e.g. emergency remote control [10]) require a video data throughput of up to 4 Mbit/s and a control packet

This work was supported by the FNR CONTACT project, CORE/SWISS/15/IS/ 10487418.

M. R. Palattella et al. (Eds.): ADHOC-NOW 2019, LNCS 11803, pp. 432–451, 2019.
https://doi.org/10.1007/978-3-030-31831-4_30

delay in the order of milliseconds. The incoming revolution in vehicular networks brought by 5G will heavily rely on heterogeneous and Device-to-Device (D2D) communications, which will have the potential to offload a substantial part of vehicular data traffic from the core network infrastructure to the Vehicular Ad-Hoc Network (VANET). VANETs are a particular class of Mobile Ad-Hoc Networks (MANETs), in which the network nodes are extremely mobile and the communication links are very volatile. Vehicles in a VANET will be able to exchange data over multi-hop routes when they are not in direct communication range, and several protocols to compute these routes have been proposed so far. Due to the specific characteristics of dynamicity and instability of VANETs, we would expect that applying traditional MANET routing protocols to VANETs, without special adjustments, would lead to suboptimal network performances. This issue has already been addressed in literature, yet without reaching a unanimous understanding about the achievable performances in these scenarios. For this reason, we conducted further simulations and analyses to determine whether MANET routing protocols are able to satisfy vehicular applications' requirements.

Among all the proposed routing protocols, we chose to compare Ad-hoc Online Distance Vector (AODV) [18], Destination-Sequenced Distance-Vector Routing (DSDV) [19], and Greedy Perimeter Stateless Routing (GPSR) [11] because they are the best-known protocols belonging to their own categories: reactive, proactive table-driven, and proactive position-based protocols, respectively [4]. Since they have been the most studied routing protocols, they are also the ones about which the highest number of contrasting claims has been reported (see Sect. 3).

The rest of the article is organized as follows. In Sect. 2, we will describe the operation and characteristics of the selected MANET routing protocols. In Sect. 3, we will present some previous studies about their performances and discuss their similarities, strengths, and limitations. In Sect. 4, we explain the rationales behind the choice of the simulation parameters and their expected impact on the performance. In Sect. 5, we analyze and present the findings originated from the data collected from the simulations. Section 6 concludes the article and highlights future research questions.

2   Routing Protocols for MANETs

There exist several distributed routing protocols for MANETs, whose main aim is to provide *next-hop* information to the intermediate nodes along the path between source and destination. Routing protocols can be classified into *reactive* and *proactive* protocols, according to the events that trigger the exchange of signaling traffic [4,16]. Reactive protocols exchange signaling packets to establish a valid route between source and destination only when the source needs to send information. Conversely, proactive protocols exchange signaling packets regardless of the presence of active data traffic between nodes. In the category of proactive protocols, some algorithms exchange periodic signaling packets to update the local network view, whereas others rely on external mechanisms (e.g. Link-Layer Acknowledgements) to trigger network-wide network status updates.

Hereafter, we will describe the operation and the characteristics of the selected routing protocols: AODV, DSDV, and GPSR.

2.1 AODV

Operation—AODV [18] is a reactive routing protocol for MANETs, thus the routes from source to destination are created upon request. When a source node needs to send data to a destination node and does not have a valid route entry in its routing table, it initiates a route discovery by broadcasting a Route Request (RREQ) message to its neighbors. Upon reception of the RREQ, each neighbor checks whether it has already received a RREQ for the same route discovery and, if not, it checks if it has a route entry in its routing table to reach the destination. If the node cannot find a valid entry, it rebroadcasts the RREQ to its neighbors. Otherwise, if it has a valid entry to reach the destination (or the node is the final destination itself), it unicasts a Route Reply (RREP) message to the route discovery originator. The route discovery process is represented in Fig. 1b. The unicast route gets finally established when the RREP reaches the source node, because each intermediate node creates reverse and forward path entries in its routing table as the RREQ and RREP messages cross the network. If any of the intermediate nodes along the active route diappears, the node upstream of the link break will detect the topology change (e.g. with missing Link-Layer Acknowledgements) and unicast a Route Error (RERR) message back to the source. This RERR message informs every intermediate node about the topology change, and they will accordingly modify their routing tables. At this point, the source node can reinitiate a route discovery process.

Features—The routes generated by AODV are guaranteed to be loop-free because of the node sequence numbers that are associated to each signaling packet. The protocol offers many techniques for optimizing its operations, such as a local repair for broken routes or gratuitous RREPs for efficient bidirectional route instantiation. For sake of simplicity, they have not been considered and studied in the present work.

2.2 DSDV

Operation—DSDV [19] is a proactive table-driven routing algorithm for MANETs. Each mobile node periodically broadcasts information about viable routes to reach every other destination node in the network to their one-hop neighbors (Fig. 1c). In particular, the distributed information is a set of route entries, each of them associated with the distance in number of hops (or any other metric) between the sender and the route destination, accompanied by a *sequence number*. This data structure is referred to as the *distance vector* (DV).

The *sequence number* is needed to maintain only the freshest route entry received by a node, and to guarantee that the computed routes are loop-free.

Its value is determined exclusively by the destination node, and it is an even number when the associated route is viable. When a link break occurs, all the route entries towards destinations that were routed through the unreachable hop are modified by setting their metrics to $+\infty$ and setting the relative sequence number to the next odd number. After having done this, the intermediate node must immediately advertise the event to the neighbors by broadcasting an update that contains the new route entries.

In order to reduce network signaling traffic, the routing-protocol updates can be incremental, rather than full dumps. Full dumps happen less regularly than incremental updates, and convey all of the information stored in the routing table of a node to its neighbors. Incremental updates happen more frequently than full dumps and can be either periodic or triggered by significant events (e.g. immediately after a link break).

Features—One of the biggest drawbacks of applying traditional DV-based routing protocols to highly dynamic MANETs is that the routing tables in the mobile nodes could contain stale network information status. Furthermore, small inaccuracies of the network state contained in each router can lead to routing loops. Nevertheless, DSDV is immune to routing loops because of the embedded sequence numbers in its signaling packets. DSDV suffers from low scalability: each node is required to maintain a routing table entry for every destination in the network, determining a linear space complexity $\mathcal{O}(n)$ of the protocol.

2.3   GPSR

Operation—GPSR [11] is a proactive position-based routing algorithm for MANETs. Each vehicle encapsulates its address and geographical position in a *beacon* and broadcasts it to its one-hop neighbors, which use it to build a *neighbors list*. When a node does not receive a beacon from a neighbor after an expiration time, it deletes that neighbor from its neighbor list. When a node needs to send a packet to a destination, it forwards it to the neighboring node that is closest to the destination. In case there is no node closer to the destination than the sender, the packet goes in *perimeter mode*. When a packet enters the perimeter mode, it temporarily gets routed further from the destination with the hope of finding a route that goes around the void area (Fig. 1d).

In specific cases, the perimeter mode might fail to find an existing route to the destination. This might happen especially when the graph is *non-planar*, i.e. with crossing edges. For this reason, GPSR must employ some *planarization* techniques. The first naive approach is applying the *no-crossing* heuristic, in which a random crossing edge is removed from the graph. The disadvantage of this technique is the possibility of partitioning the graph. More sophisticated approaches are the *Relative Neighborhood Graph* (RNG) and the *Gabriel Graph* (GG) planarizations. In short, they work by checking, per each couple of nodes in the network, if a third node is present in an area between them. If this is the case, the edge between the two considered nodes is removed from the graph. For RNG, the area is shaped as the intersection of two circles centrered on the selected nodes. For GG, the area is a circle centered at the median point of the segment connecting the two selected edges, with a diameter equal to the distance between the two nodes.

Features—GPSR is more scalable than other table-driven routing protocols because it needs and stores only local information regarding the network topology. The protocol's signaling rate is (i) constant per each node in the network, (ii) depends uniquely on the beaconing frequency, and (iii) is unrelated to the network traffic load, vehicular mobility, and vehicular density. The reaction speed to topology changes is influenced by the beaconing frequency and the vehicular density and mobility. When the beaconing frequency is low, the signaling rate is low but the network registers topology changes slowly. When the beaconing frequency is high, the signaling rate is higher but the neighbors lists are updated more promptly. In case the local product of beaconing frequency and vehicular density is very high, the contention-based access to the channel can influence the *freshness* [12] of the neighbors' positions stored in the local neighbors list.

One further foreseeable problem of stateless routing protocols like GPSR is that they do not remember poor routing decisions. If a packet enters a local maximum and travels around a void in perimeter mode, so will all the subsequent packets. Each packet will run through the same suboptimal route discovery, leading to longer paths and lower PDR.

2.4 Signaling Traffic Analysis

The signaling rate of proactive protocols like GPSR and DSDV depends exclusively on the beaconing frequency or on how dynamic and large the network topology is, and never on the rate of creation and duration of new network flows. On the contrary, reactive protocols like AODV have a signaling rate that depends on the mobility of the relay nodes along active routes, but also on the rate of creation and duration of new network flows. This is because every time a route is disrupted, the route discovery process is restarted or the route repair procedure is initiated. For reactive protocols, the neighborhood of the active routes is flooded with information on how to update routing tables at each new flow instantiation or disconnection of active relay nodes. For proactive protocols, the whole network is flooded with information on how to update the routing tables of every node for each topology change in the network.

The overall signaling traffic is much higher for DSDV because local topology-change information must be iteratively spread throughout the whole network, whereas for reactive protocols the topology changes trigger signaling traffic in the vicinity of the route (i.e. route repair mechanisms or route discovery repetition). However, we mostly care about the signaling traffic that is generated in the vicinity of the active routes, as it might induce congestion and application packet loss. Under this point of view, the signaling rates of DSDV and of reactive protocols become comparable, even though we still expect reactive protocols to produce lower signaling traffic.

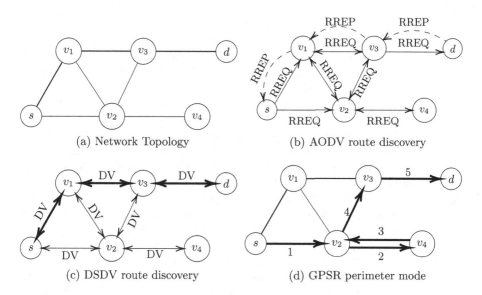

Fig. 1. Features of AODV, DSDV, and GPSR. On (a) an example of VANET connectivity graph, with a source vehicle s and a destination vehicle d, (b) illustrates the AODV's route discovery process, (c) shows the DSDV's distance vector broadcasting, with the computed route in bold, and (d) shows the route of a packet in GPSR perimeter mode to bypass a void area, where the numbers are the sequence of links on which the data packet is forwarded.

3   Related Works

Broch et al. [5] simulate AODV and DSDV in a MANET scenario, and evaluate their performances in terms of PDR and signaling traffic. This work does not consider the presence of obstacles (e.g. buildings) that might shadow wireless transmissions and that would have a dramatic impact on networking performances (as we show in Sect. 5). The mobility model used in this study is the Random Waypoint (RWP) model [3], in which nodes pick random destinations, move towards them at a constant speed and, after reaching the target, wait for a constant number of seconds defined as the *pause time*. This work studies the influence of pause time on the different aforementioned metrics, per each evaluated routing protocol. The results obtained by this pioneering piece of work are not directly applicable to VANETs because the RWP mobility model is not suitable to approximate realistic vehicular mobility patterns [24]. It is therefore indispensable to perform simulations based on realistic vehicular mobility models, such as those offered by Simulation of Urban MObility (SUMO) [14].

Karp and Kung [11] propose, describe, and evaluate GPSR in a simulated 1500 m × 300 m scenario without obstacles, in which nodes move according to a RWP mobility model and have a 250 m transmission range. Several other works (e.g. [5]) also use this scenario for their evaluations. The study compares GPSR and Dynamic Source Routing (DSR) [9] in terms of PDR and signaling traffic, showing the superior scalability and performances of their protocol for both metrics. As claimed by the authors, an elongated, rectangular scenario *forces the use of longer routes between nodes, compared to a square scenario with identical node density*. However, the lack of physical obstacles, combined with the high ratio between the fixed transmission range and the length of the smaller edge of the scenario, generates mono-dimensional routes and hardly allows GPSR to go into *perimeter mode*. This means that, in this scenario, the source can almost always reach the destination with greedy forwarding alone. This justifies why in both evaluations [5,11], the routes generated by the evaluated protocols are almost always as short as physically possible. From these two articles it is not evident how the authors evaluated the behavior of MANET routing algorithms when the data packets must route around an obstacle or a void area. For this reason, in our work, the scenario's aspect ratio and the vehicles' transmission ranges are set so that the routes have a higher degree of freedom and are more likely to be forced to route around a void area.

Naumov et al. [17] compare the performances of AODV and GPSR for the RWP mobility model and for a realistic vehicular mobility model. The study shows that the performances of both routing protocols are dramatically lower when considering realistic vehicular mobility models. GPSR outperforms AODV in the RWP mobility scenario and the opposite happens in the realistic vehicular mobility scenario. In both scenarios, 550 vehicles move at urban speeds within an area of 6 km^2. Shadowing effects are taken into account through analytical models that ignore the specific location of the obstacles. GPSR's beaconing interval is set to 3 s (a relatively high value) because the authors claim that higher values would significantly increase frame collisions. Unsurprisingly, they also report that nodes' neighbor tables are often stale, causing up to 80% of next-hop forwarding decisions to be incorrect. The majority of the currently-standardized protocol stacks for vehicular networks (i.e. IEEE WAVE and ETSI ITS-G5) do not recommend any specific beaconing frequency but, for several delay-sensitive applications in the literature, the beaconing frequency typically ranges from 10 Hz [21]. For this reason, for our performed simulations, GPSR's beaconing interval is set to 100 ms without observing any detrimental congestion effects.

In [20], the authors compare the packet delay performances of AODV and DSDV in the context of vehicular safety applications in VANETs. The article proposes a cooperative collision avoidance application on highways: the overtaking of a vehicle at the end of a line of vehicles is canceled if another vehicle occupies the lane in the opposite direction. The simulation lasts 10 seconds and the highway scenario contains from 3 to 12 vehicles, each provided with a 1 Mbit/s IEEE 802.11b interface and a 250 m nominal transmission range. The authors claim that DSDV is the only protocol able to support safety applications in VANETs and they discourage the use of AODV.

Ali et al. [1] measure PDR, packet delay, and packet burst loss for AODV and GPSR both in a Manhattan grid and in a section of London's map. The simulated fading model (Nakagami Two Ray), MAC Layer (IEEE 802.11p), and vehicular mobility (SUMO) are realistic. The scenarios contain 100 vehicles that move at urban speeds and share between 200 and 1000 data flows containing 100 packets each, with a duration of 10 s/flow. The study claims that GPSR provides the most stable PDR and lowest packet delay under different traffic load scenarios.

In [2], the authors evaluate PDR, packet delay, throughput, and signaling traffic of AODV, DSDV, and GPSR in a realistic urban map of Oujda, Morocco. The vehicular density ranges between 20 and 90 vehicles over an area of 1.7 km × 1.5 km, with realistic mobility and moderate urban speeds. The data flow is modeled as a UDP CBR stream of 5 packets/s and 512 B/packet. The study claims that DSDV provides a high PDR and a high throughput, whereas GPSR provides the lowest signaling traffic and packet delay. AODV shows the highest signaling traffic among all the evaluated protocols.

Inconsistent Claims About Routing Performances—Many of the cited performance studies [1,2,11,17,20] unanimously claim that proactive protocols provide the best packet delay in a variety of scenarios. However, we also notice that several works claim discordant findings regarding PDR, throughput, and signaling rate for the selected routing protocols, even in similar vehicular scenarios and network conditions. For example, [5,17] claim that reactive routing protocols provide a better PDR and a better throughput than proactive protocols, whereas [1,2,11] claim the opposite. Regarding signaling rate, [5] claims that reactive protocols outperform proactive protocols, whereas [2,11,17] claim the opposite. In order to provide new evidence to solve the disagreement, we hereby investigate the performances of some of the most widely studied MANET routing protocols to verify the claims reported in previous articles, and check whether traditional MANET routing protocols can satisfy the performance requirements of future VANET applications.

4 Simulation Setup

The present work aims at comparing MANET routing algorithms in urban scenarios. Therefore, we designed a set of suitable simulation scenarios that emphasized strenghts and weaknesses of the evaluated protocols. To provide statistical relevance to the results, we repeated the simulation for each configuration 20 times, each time setting a different seed for the random number generators that control the randomness of the network and mobility simulators.

Road Network, Obstacles, and Vehicular Mobility—We perform our simulations in Manhattan grids, with characteristics defined in Table 1. We fixed the road topology and the maximum vehicular speed in an urban area, and we generated different vehicular densities to test the performances of the selected routing protocols in different vehicular traffic conditions. The vehicular mobility is highly realistic: each vehicle is modeled with its own physical characteristics such as its unique acceleration, deceleration, size, and category. Drivers are modeled with different driving skills and respect for the road rules. Each vehicle enters the scenario at a random location and plans a trip to reach a random arrival point

Table 1. Road network and vehicular mobility parameters

Manhattan grid	1 km × 1 km, 6 roads × 6 roads
Inter-road distance	200 m
Road width	6 m (Two 3 m lanes)
Road features	No traffic lights, 2 opposite-directional lanes
Buildings' base dimensions	180 m × 180 m
Inter-building distance	20 m
Vehicular mobility generator	SUMO Netgen, Discretization 1 s
Vehicular density	20 to 200 veh/km^2, increments of 20 veh/km^2
Vehicular maximum speed	Uniformly distributed from 30 to 50 km/h
Car-following model	Krauss [15]
Starting and arrival points	Random trips, minimum distance 500 m
Road path choice	Shortest path (Dijkstra)

on the map, provided that the starting and arrival points are at least 500 m apart. The road path to reach the arrival point from the starting point is computed using the Dijkstra shortest-path algorithm, where the edge weight is the road segment's length. The vehicles chosen as data source and destination do not move and are geographically fixed at the opposite corners of the simulation scenario. This is to ensure that the vehicles keep the same distance from one another and remain in the simulation for the whole duration of the data flow. This also prevents the length of the computed routes from varying according to the geographical distance between source and destination vehicles, consequently altering the performance of the routing protocols.

Inter-vehicular Communications—Our scenario features a single data flow from the data-source vehicle to the data-destination vehicle, respectively located at the top-left and bottom-right corners of the simulation scenario (Fig. 2). The transmission power of their wireless network interfaces, and the presence of shadowing objects (i.e. buildings), prevent them from communicating directly. Therefore, a multi-hop path must be established between them by one of the selected routing protocols. The characteristics of the application data flows and the parameters of the MAC/PHY layers are reported in the respective sections of Table 2.

We chose to evaluate the performances of the selected routing algorithms in scenarios with a single data flow. When the network is not congested, simulating multiple simultaneous flows instead of a single flow would not affect the signaling rate for the proactive routing algorithms, but would increase AODV's signaling rate proportionally with the number of simultaneous flows. This is because, unlike proactive protocols, AODV's signaling rate depends also on the number of active flows. The increased signaling traffic, generated by AODV for routing multiple flows, would decrease the PDR due to a high amount of frame collisions.

Table 2. Networking parameters

Application Layer	
Application packet size	1200 B = 9600 bit
Application interpacket interval	512, 128, 32 ms
Application data rates	18.75, 75, 300 kbit/s
Number of flows	1
Flow duration	180 s
MAC and PHY Layers	
Protocol	IEEE 802.11p single channel, no priority
Transmission power	15 mW
Receiver sensitivity	−89 dBm
Transmission capacity	6 Mbit/s
MAC queue capacity	100 frames

Furthermore, none of the compared routing protocols implement congestion-avoidance, load-balancing, or flow-distribution techniques. Therefore, simulating multiple flows instead of a single flow in different scenarios would not provide a meaningful discrimination element to compare the performances of the evaluated protocols. In addition, the performances of the routing algorithms would be influenced by the spatial allocation and the uncontrolled overlapping of the allocated flows, which could direct multiple flows over the same path and congest the network.

Simulating multiple flows could aggravate the congestion induced by application-layer messages and consequently show worse PDR and packet delay. Considering that the selected routing protocols are not designed for multi-flow management, the congestion induced by application-layer

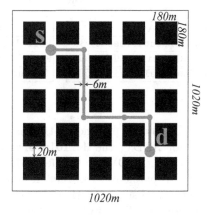

Fig. 2. Representation of the simulated Mahattan scenario. The larger gray nodes are the fixed source and destination vehicles, while the smaller nodes are the intermediate relays selected by the routing protocol. We observe an example of an established unicast route over 6 hops.

messages is unrelated to the protocols' intrinsic performances. Therefore, we focus our analyses on the congestion generated by the signaling packets at the network layer and leave application-induced congestion out of the scope of this work.

We fix source and destination nodes' positions at the opposite corners of the simulation scenario and we simulate realistic urban mobility between them, with different vehicular densities per each scenario (Table 1). The source node sends a Constant Bit Rate (CBR) stream of fixed-size UDP packets to the destination, with a bitrate never higher than a twentieth of the transmission capacity of the wireless channel (Table 2). This is because we do not want the application-layer packets to generate congestion, as it is not the focus of the present study. We are interested in comparing the signaling rates of the different routing protocols and measuring the data packet loss due to route reestablishments and due to the congestion induced by network-layer signaling packets.

Choice of MANET Routing Parameters—For each investigated routing protocol, a parameter study has been performed in order to detemine the configurations that would lead to the highest PDR for each scenario. For sake of brevity, we omit the details of this preliminary parameter study and we report, in Table 3, the best parameter configurations that we chose to perform the comparative simulations. The parameters that have not been reported in Table 3 are set to the default values as indicated in the relative implementations.

Table 3. Parameters of routing protocols

AODV		DSDV		GPSR	
ActiveRouteTimeout	3 s	HelloInterval	2048 ms	BeaconingInterval	100 ms
AskGratuitousRREP	false	RouteLifetime	4096 ms	NeighborValidity	450 ms
UseLocalRepair	false	UseFullDumps	false	Planarization	GG

Notably, the parameters that have been optimized are the `ActiveRouteTimeout` for AODV, the `HelloInterval` for DSDV, and the `BeaconingInterval` for GPSR. AODV's `ActiveRouteTimeout` is the maximum time interval during which a route entry can remain unused. After its expiration, the route becomes inactive and subsequently deleted. An overly short `ActiveRouteTimeout` would increase signaling traffic and packet loss, as routes that are still valid would be rediscovered during temporary periods in which the source does not send any data to the destination. An overly long `ActiveRouteTimeout` could make nodes store a route to an unreachable destination, due to the mobility of the network nodes. DSDV's `HelloInterval` is the time that elapses between two consecutive one-hop broadcasts of a *distance vector* containing local routing-table information. Decreasing the `HelloInterval` would increase the signaling rate but also increase the reliability of the local network-connectivity-status information, and vice versa. GPSR's `BeaconingInterval` is the time that elapses between two consecutive one-hop broadcasts of a beacon containing the node's address and geographical position. Decreasing the `BeaconingInterval` would increase the signaling rate but reduce the error between the list of neighbors maintained by the node and the neighbors that are actually reachable. In order to avoid synchronization effects [7], GPSR beacons are randomly delayed with a maximum jitter of 50 ms.

DSDV's `RouteLifetime` is the maximum time interval a route entry can be inactive before being deleted, and it has been set to double the `HelloInterval`. Due to implementation limitations, DSDV does not provide periodic full dumps as indicated by the protocol specifications [19], therefore each variation of a route entry will trigger a network-wide signaling broadcast. For GPSR, a node v removes a neighbor w from its neighbor list if v has not received a beacon from w for at least 4.5 times the duration of the `BeaconingInterval`, as suggested in [11]. The planarization mode is Gabriel Graph (GG) [8] and we assume that the precision of the vehicle's geographical position can be represented with 8 B. Assuming that a vehicle's L3 address is 4 B, the GPSR beacon will be 4 B+8 B = 96 bit long.   •

Implementation Details—The implementations of the evaluated routing protocols are based on the INET[1] library. In particular, AODV's implementation does not provide route repair, so every time a route is interrupted, the route discovery procedure is restarted from the source. The implementation of DSDV does not distinguish between full dumps and incremental updates of routing tables. Therefore, each node that receives a *useful* distance vector (called *hello message* in the implementation) from a neighbor, propagates it to its neighbors with a uniformly randomized delay between 10 ms and 500 ms without aggregation, causing a substantial signaling traffic increase.

The vehicular mobility was simulated with SUMO[2] [14], and the network protocols were simulated with Objective Modular Network Testbed in C++ (OMNeT++)[3] [23]. These two tools communicate through a TraCI interface wrapped by Veins INET[4] [22].

5   Performance Evaluation

Performance Metrics—In this work, we use *Packet Delivery Ratio (PDR)*, *packet delay*, *frame collision rate*, and *signaling rate* to compare the performances of the evaluated routing protocols in each scenario. The PDR is defined as the ratio between the number of packets that have been correctly received by the destination over the number of packets sent by the source. The frame collision rate is defined as the total number of frames incorrectly decoded by the network interfaces of every vehicle in the simulation, divided by the duration of the data flow. The signaling rate is defined as the total volume of transmitted signaling messages, specific to each routing protocol, divided by the duration of the data flow. For the three abovementioned metrics, each plotted point shows the average and the standard deviation of the metric computed for each simulation repetition. The packet delay is defined as the total time needed for a packet to travel from source to destination across the network. For this metric, each

---

[1] INET-v4.1.1 (hash *ce69d08*), https://github.com/inet-framework/inet.
[2] SUMO-v1.2.0 (hash *1d09773*), https://github.com/eclipse/sumo.
[3] OMNeT++-v5.5 (hash *6942b44*), https://github.com/omnetpp/omnetpp.
[4] Veins-v4.7.1 (hash *550e246*), https://github.com/sommer/veins.

plotted point shows the average and the standard deviation of the packet delay of all the received packets in all the simulation repetitions. The *goodput* provided by the different routing protocols is proportional to the PDR by a factor equal to the transmission data bitrate at the source (e.g. 300 kbit/s for the PDR in Figs. 3 and 4).

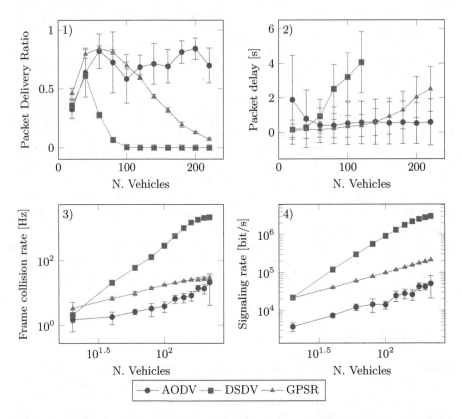

Fig. 3. Performances of the selected routing algorithms (AODV, DSDV, and GPSR) for a 300 kbit/s data flow, ignoring the shadowing effects caused by the buildings.

Figures 3 and 4 show the performance of the evaluated routing algorithms in terms of the aforementioned metrics for a data bitrate of 300 kbit/s, respectively ignoring and considering the shadowing effects induced by the presence of the buildings in the Manhattan grid. More simulations were performed for other data bitrates (75 kbit/s and 18.75 kbit/s), but the obtained results were similar to those displayed in Figs. 3 and 4, and are omitted for brevity.

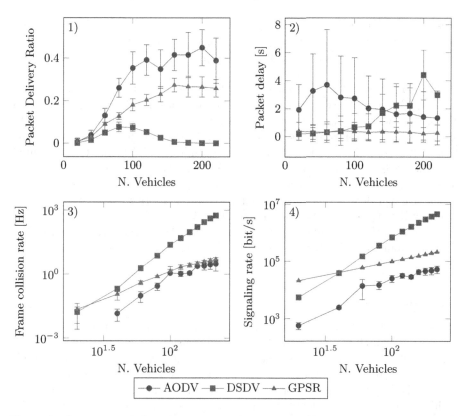

Fig. 4. Performances of the selected routing algorithms (AODV, DSDV, and GPSR) for a 300 kbit/s data flow, considering the shadowing effects caused by the buildings.

5.1 Signaling and Frame Collision Rate

From Figs. 3.4 and 4.4, we notice that the signaling rate of all the considered routing protocols is positively correlated to the vehicular density, although with different coefficients. AODV's and GPSR's signaling rates have similar sensitivity to vehicular density, i.e. comparable ratios of signaling rate increment to vehicular density increment. This can be justified because GPSR's signaling rate is linearly bound to vehicular density and beaconing frequency (which is fixed in this work), whereas AODV's signaling rate for a single flow depends on the route break frequency and on the vehicular density. For AODV, a higher vehicular density means a higher average number of neighbors that must forward a RREQ during a route discovery phase. However, a higher vehicular density leads to lower average vehicular speeds, and therefore to more stable routes.

DSDV displays a much higher sensitivity to vehicular density compared to the other two protocols. In fact, DSDV's signaling rate depends on two factors. The first factor is the network nodes' mobility, because each node must immediately inform its neighbors about link breaks. The second factor is the vehicular density, because each vehicle broadcasts a distance vector to its one-hop neighbors and each topology change must reach every node in the network. DSDV's signaling rate can be up to two orders of magnitude greater than the signaling rates of the other protocols.

We can observe that the signaling rate of each routing protocol does not dramatically vary between scenarios in which we consider shadowing effects and scenarios in which we ignore them. This suggests that the degree of connectivity of the network graph has a moderate impact on the amount of signaling traffic *transmitted* by each node. For GPSR, it has no effect at all because the beaconing frequency is fixed. Both AODV's and DSDV's signaling rate curves are slightly shifted upwards for the scenario without building shadowing because the higher nodes' average degree increases the number of neighbors that must forward an AODV's RREQ or a DSDV link-break notification.

We notice that the signaling rate of the three protocols is correlated to the relative frame collision rate (Figs. 3.3 and 4.3) which, in turn, influences the PDR.

5.2 Packet Delivery Ratio

From Figs. 3.1 and 4.1, we can observe that the PDR is generally lower for scenarios in which the shadowing effects are considered, as the routes become longer and more difficult to establish and maintain (even though there are relatively fewer frame collisions). For particularly low vehicular densities (e.g. 20 vehicles/km^2), PDRs are low for all protocols and configurations. This is because, with such low vehicular densities and having fixed the transmission power for all the network interfaces, there is a relatively low probability of having enough vehicles that can form a route from source to destination.

DSDV's PDR peaks when the frame collision rate is slightly below 10 Hz, which corresponds to a vehicular density of 20 vehicles/km^2 when we ignore shadowing effects, and a vehicular density of 80 vehicles/km^2 when we consider them. When the vehicular density increases, so does the frame collision rate, and the PDR of DSDV quickly converges to zero. Nodes running DSDV must broadcast their distance vectors to one-hop neighbors and propagate important network-update information across the whole network. This generates an enormous amount of signaling packets that congest the wireless medium, increasing the chances of frame collisions involving a data packet, and therefore decreasing the PDR. As an additional side effect, in congested-medium scenarios, signaling packets get queued and therefore delayed, slowing down the convergence of the protocol. Due to the slow convergence of the protocol, network nodes are likely to keep stale routing table entries or delete expired but valid entries. This would make nodes forward data packets to incorrect intermediate nodes or drop data packets when the correct intermediate node is still in range. As a consequence, we notice that the PDR drops for high vehicular densities and high signaling rates.

AODV's PDR increases proportionally to the vehicular density up to a moderate density and then converges to a steady-state value for higher vehicular densities. This is because, for lower vehicular densities, packets get dispersed due to unstable links and sporadic route establishments. For higher densities, routes become easier to set, but the increased signaling traffic hinders the data packet delivery.

As the vehicular density increases, GPSR's PDR first increases, then converges to a steady-state value, and then decreases. For low vehicular densities it is hard to find a set of vehicles that can offer a route between source and destination, whereas for high vehicular densities the beacons congest the wireless medium and collide with data packets, consequently decreasing the PDR. This phenomenon is clearly visible for the scenario in which the shadowing effects are ignored, and not present at all in the scenarios in which shadowing effects are taken into account. This happens because the presence of buildings in the Manhattan grid shadows the nodes from hearing excessive signaling traffic from their neighbors, therefore preventing the data packets from colliding with signaling packets.

5.3 Packet Delay

The curves in Figs. 3.2 and 4.2 report the average and standard deviation of the correctly-delivered packets' delay. Considering that the number of delivered packets varies per each simulation, the stability of the reported averages and standard deviations is not uniform for all the vehicular densities. For some simulations in which no packet was correctly delivered, no packet delay data could be displayed.

The average delay of packets routed by DSDV and GPSR increases as the vehicular density, signaling rate, and frame collision rate increase. This is because when the wireless medium is congested and very busy, the transmission of the frames containing the data packets are deferred. The packet delay curves increase faster in the scenarios without building shadowing than in the scenarios with shadowing, due to the missing protective effect of the physical obstacles against interference.

For AODV, we notice that the average packet delay decreases as the vehicular density increases. This is due to easier route establishment in scenarios with higher vehicular densities. In scenarios with building shadowing, the packet delay decays slower than in scenarios without building shadowing. This phenomenon can be justified because, under the same vehicular density, routes are longer and more difficult to set.

We notice that some of the packet delay curves are highly heteroscedastic. This means that the standard deviation of the packet delay varies across scenarios with different vehicular densities. A high packet delay variance means that the length of the packet queues in the network nodes are very variable over time, which also means that the packets' transmission is bursty. In the designed scenario, this may happen (i) because the routes are established and interrupted frequently, (ii) because the packets are routed over paths of very variable length, or (iii) because of dishomogeneous zones of congestion that migrate over time according to vehicular mobility.

AODV establishes a single route per data flow. In the case of a highly-dynamic network topology, such as in VANETs, this path is frequently broken. Each time a path is broken, the route discovery must be restarted from the source. When a route is interrupted, the packets received by the intermediate node without a valid next hop are queued and accumulate delay until a route is re-established. Upon route re-establishment, the queued packets are transmitted and leave the queue. If the network is not congested, the packets are cleared from the queue in bursts and the newly arrived packets are forwarded with low delay until the next path break happens. Proactive protocols do not show this behavior: for GPSR, the concept of a route does not exist at all, and for DSDV, the local information of the global connectivity status is constantly refreshed and therefore the routes are locally repaired. The packet delay variance of GPSR is particularly low because there is no route establishment phase and no routing table buildup; all the routing decisions are made only according to the node's and the node's neighbors' current locations.

6   Conclusion and Future Work

In this work, we investigated the applicability of some well-known MANET routing protocols to VANETs in realistic urban scenarios. We found out that using DSDV as a routing protocol in VANETs is unfeasible because, even for modest vehicular densities, the signaling traffic generated for updating the routing tables is unsustainably high. When using DSDV as a routing protocol, the PDR peaks for a medium-low vehicular density and decreases sharply after that due to intense signaling-induced congestion. AODV provided the best PDR, especially for higher vehicular densities. We also noticed that AODV's packet delay decreased as the vehicular density increased. GPSR offered intermediate PDR and signaling rate, with an overall low packet delay that showed a moderate sensitivity to vehicular density. This is because GPSR's beaconing congests the network only when network nodes have a very high average number of neighbors. In terms of signaling rate, DSDV has turned out to be up to two orders of magnitude more demanding than the others. None of the evaluated routing protocols could satisfy modern vehicular application requirements in all the generated scenarios, therefore further development of vehicular routing protocols is desirable.

With this study, we observed that reactive protocols provide a higher PDR and throughput compared to proactive protocols, as claimed in some of the previous works [5,17]. We also observed that proactive protocols provide the best packet delay, as stated by the majority of the cited previous works. In the proposed single-flow scenario, AODV outperformed the proactive protocols in terms of signaling rate. For reactive protocols, the signaling traffic is highly dependent on the data traffic load, therefore we cannot extend this claim to multi-flow scenarios.

Future Work—For each of the evaluated routing protocols, the packet delays are too high to satisfy the strict requirements of modern vehicular applications.

One reason for this is the complexity of the traditional TCP/IP stack, which features some functions that are non-essential or even detrimental [13] for ad-hoc networks. These functions increase packet delay because of unnecessary MAC address resolutions, unicast packet acknowledgments, and various other operations. Therefore, a new architecture to provide a high PDR and a low packet delay in ad-hoc networks is needed.

One way to achieve such a challenging goal is to delegate some routing intelligence from the ad-hoc network to the network infrastructure, which has a global view of the ad-hoc network state and can make globally-optimal routing decisions. One paradigm that has been proposed to improve performances in VANETs is Software-Defined Vehicular Networking (SDVN) [6]: in this view, each vehicle becomes a simple L2 forwarding device, delegating all the routing decisions to a centralized controller.

The literature about SDVN is still young and its benefits not yet fully explored. For example, there is a lack of studies regarding the minimum requirements for the signaling traffic between vehicles and the SDVN controller to ensure such improved performances. In ultra-dense SDVNs (e.g. in road congestion scenarios), controllers could quickly become overloaded in terms of computational and network traffic loads, as every managed node reports its information to the controller at a fixed frequency.

In modern 5G-assisted ultra-dense SDVNs, vehicles communicate with the SDVN controller via valuable cellular links. The scarcity of bandwidth between vehicles and the controller makes it even more important to study the signaling traffic features of modern SDVNs architectures, and to devise novel techniques that can reduce the signaling rate requirements between vehicles and the controller while maintaining high network performances.

From an architectural standpoint, not enough studies consider scenarios in which the controller's knowledge domain covers only part of the total amount of connected vehicles. Therefore, it is important to study a hybrid approach that can benefit from the controller's coordination when it is available and fall back on a distributed routing scheme when it is not.

References

1. Ali, A.K., Phillips, I., Yang, H.: Evaluating VANET routing in urban environments. In: 2016 39th International Conference on Telecommunications and Signal Processing (TSP), pp. 60–63, June 2016. https://doi.org/10.1109/TSP.2016.7760829
2. Bengag, A., Elboukhari, M.: Performance evaluation of VANETs routing protocols using SUMO and NS3. In: 2018 IEEE 5th International Congress on Information Science and Technology (CiSt), pp. 525–530. IEEE (2018)
3. Bettstetter, C., Resta, G., Santi, P.: The node distribution of the random waypoint mobility model for wireless ad hoc networks. IEEE Trans. Mob. Comput. **2**(3), 257–269 (2003)
4. Boukerche, A., Ahmad, M.Z., Turgut, D., Turgut, B.: A taxonomy of routing protocols for mobile ad hoc networks. Algorithms and Protocols for Wireless and Mobile Ad Hoc Networks, p. 129 (2009)

5. Broch, J., Maltz, D.A., Johnson, D.B., Hu, Y.C., Jetcheva, J.G.: A performance comparison of multi-hop wireless ad hoc network routing protocols. In: MobiCom., vol. 98, pp. 85–97 (1998)
6. Di Maio, A., Palattella, M.R., Engel, T.: Multi-flow congestion-aware routing in software-defined vehicular networks. In: 2019 IEEE 90th Vehicular Technology Conference (VTC Fall). IEEE (2019)
7. Floyd, S., Jacobson, V.: The synchronization of periodic routing messages. IEEE/ACM Trans. Netw. **2**(2), 122–136 (1994). https://doi.org/10.1109/90.298431
8. Gabriel, K.R., Sokal, R.R.: A new statistical approach to geographic variation analysis. Syst. Zool. **18**(3), 259–278 (1969)
9. Johnson, D.B., Maltz, D.A.: Dynamic source routing in ad hoc wireless networks. In: Mobile computing, pp. 153–181. Springer, Boston (1996). https://doi.org/10.1007/978-0-585-29603-6_5
10. Kang, L., Zhao, W., Qi, B., Banerjee, S.: Augmenting self-driving with remote control: challenges and directions. In: Proceedings of the 19th International Workshop on Mobile Computing Systems & Applications, pp. 19–24. ACM (2018)
11. Karp, B., Kung, H.T.: GPSR: greedy perimeter stateless routing for wireless networks. In: Proceedings of the 6th Annual International Conference on Mobile Computing and Networking, MobiCom 2000, pp. 243–254. ACM, New York (2000). https://doi.org/10.1145/345910.345953, http://doi.acm.org/10.1145/345910.345953
12. Kaul, S., Yates, R., Gruteser, M.: Real-time status: how often should one update? In: 2012 Proceedings IEEE INFOCOM, pp. 2731–2735, March 2012. https://doi.org/10.1109/INFCOM.2012.6195689
13. Klingler, F., Dressler, F., Sommer, C.: IEEE 802.11p unicast considered harmful. In: 2015 IEEE Vehicular Networking Conference (VNC), pp. 76–83. IEEE (2015)
14. Krajzewicz, D., Erdmann, J., Behrisch, M., Bieker, L.: Recent development and applications of SUMO - Simulation of Urban MObility. Int. J. Adv. Syst. Meas. **5**(3&4), 128–138 (2012)
15. Krauß, S., Wagner, P., Gawron, C.: Metastable states in a microscopic model of traffic flow. Phys. Rev. E **55**(5), 5597 (1997)
16. Lee, K.C., Lee, U., Gerla, M.: Survey of routing protocols in vehicular ad hoc networks. In: Advances in vehicular ad-hoc networks: Developments and challenges, pp. 149–170. IGI Global (2010)
17. Naumov, V., Baumann, R., Gross, T.: An evaluation of inter-vehicle ad hoc networks based on realistic vehicular traces. In: Proceedings of the 7th ACM International Symposium on Mobile Ad Hoc Networking and Computing, MobiHoc 2006, pp. 108–119. ACM, New York (2006). https://doi.org/10.1145/1132905.1132918
18. Perkins, C.E., Royer, E.M.: Ad-hoc on-demand distance vector routing. In: Proceedings WMCSA 1999 Second IEEE Workshop on Mobile Computing Systems and Applications, pp. 90–100, February 1999. https://doi.org/10.1109/MCSA.1999.749281
19. Perkins, C.E., Bhagwat, P.: Highly dynamic destination-sequenced distance-vector routing (DSDV) for mobile computers. In: Proceedings of the Conference on Communications Architectures, Protocols and Applications, SIGCOMM 1994, pp. 234–244. ACM, New York (1994). https://doi.org/10.1145/190314.190336
20. Santoso, G.Z., Kang, M.: Performance analysis of AODV, DSDV and OLSR in a VANETs safety application scenario. In: 2012 14th International Conference on Advanced Communication Technology (ICACT), pp. 57–60, February 2012
21. Sommer, C., Dressler, F.: Vehicular Networking. Cambridge University Press, Cambridge (2015)

22. Sommer, C., German, R., Dressler, F.: Bidirectionally coupled network and road traffic simulation for improved IVC analysis. IEEE Trans. Mob. Comput. **10**(1), 3–15 (2011). https://doi.org/10.1109/TMC.2010.133

23. Varga, A., Hornig, R.: An overview of the OMNeT++ simulation environment. In: Proceedings of the 1st International Conference on Simulation Tools and Techniques for Communications, Networks and Systems & Workshops, Simutools 2008, pp. 60:1–60:10. ICST (Institute for Computer Sciences, Social-Informatics and Telecommunications Engineering), Brussels, (2008). http://dl.acm.org/citation.cfm?id=1416222.1416290

24. Yoon, J., Liu, M., Noble, B.: Random waypoint considered harmful. In: IEEE INFOCOM 2003 Twenty-second Annual Joint Conference of the IEEE Computer and Communications Societies (IEEE Cat. No. 03CH37428), vol. 2, pp. 1312–1321. IEEE (2003)

Initial Placement Optimization
for Multi-channel UAV Networks

Dorin Rautu[1,2], Riadh Dhaou[1,2(✉)], and Emmanuel Chaput[1,2]

[1] Université de Toulouse, INP, 31071 Toulouse, France
[2] IRIT, 31062 Toulouse, France
{dorin.rautu,dhaou}@enseeiht.fr

Abstract. Unmanned Aerial Vehicles (UAV) can be used to deploy communication networks by acting as access points for ground users. Taking advantage of the lightness and the high maneuverability of drones, such a network can be implemented quickly and inexpensively in situations where network infrastructures are damaged or overloaded (emergency situations), or nonexistent (wild life observation). To mitigate these issues, an off-loading network based on UAVs carrying radio access points was proposed in our previous work. The goal is to temporarily provide multiple services, voice, video, data, etc., over a specific zone.

The design of the aerial network was formulated as a self-deployment method built on a Coulomb's law analogy where users and UAVs act as electrical charges. In this paper, we go beyond the proposed scheme by considering a multi-channel model taking into account the interference. We set up association and channel switching schemes that boost the overall performance of the network.

Keywords: Unmanned Aerial Vehicle (UAV) · Drone · Deployment · Channel switching · Ad-hoc network

1 Introduction

The use of flying aircraft such as unmanned aerial vehicles (UAVs), also known under the name of drones, is fast growing in a wide range of networking applications. In particular, with their ingrained attributes such as mobility, adaptive altitude and flexibility, UAVs concede several key applications in wireless systems.

Benefiting of these characteristics, future generation networks can integrate UAVs to improve the quality of service provided as well as implementing novel functionalities. Drones can be used to extend and support terrestrial networks in information dissemination, [1]. D2D (Device-to-Device) networks offer an efficient solution to alleviate terrestrial networks by offloading some traffic, but their benefits are limited as the communications are short-ranged. Drones can play a major role, as they can offer a rapid dissemination platform. As suggested in [2], UAVs can take a major part in vehicular networks as they can facilitate the information spreading by reducing the number of links needed at ground level.

© Springer Nature Switzerland AG 2019
M. R. Palattella et al. (Eds.): ADHOC-NOW 2019, LNCS 11803, pp. 452–466, 2019.
https://doi.org/10.1007/978-3-030-31831-4_31

With the rapid expansion of the IoT (Internet of Things) market, the network operators have to rethink how conventional networks operate, to incorporate the massive number of IoT devices (smart-city sensors, health-care wearables, smartphones, vehicles). In poorly covered areas, IoT devices may have a hard time sending messages, as the device energy constraints limit the transmission power. In [3], UAVs could be deployed to act as base stations and to provide an energy efficient link for these kind of communications. Thanks to the line-of-sight communications and variable altitude, the signal attenuation can be reduced and the coverage area can be increased.

Natural catastrophes, apart of the devastating material destruction, can bring forth massive communication disruptions as the terrestrial communication networks can be damaged or destroyed. In such events, reliable public safety communications are needed to facilitate first responders deployment, victim search and rescue operations. The use of drone based aerial networks can be a promising solution as for the fast deployment, high coverage and flexibility [4].

All of these applications, heterogeneous as may seem, have an important common issue : the drone placement. In order to work efficiently, the UAVs have to be at the right spot at the right time.

We believe that a versatile solution needs to be dynamic (as the users could move) distributed (in order to be resilient to any loss of device or link capability) and independent of users position (as we believe that the UAV fleet cannot know the actual users position). The aim of this paper is then to propose an efficient solution. Our technique, introduced in [5], is based on a Coulomb's law analogy. Of course, in dense areas, a single UAV cannot provide network access to a large number of users. The IEEE 802.11 standard, used in our network, offers several orthogonal channels to mitigate interference. So in this paper, we improve the coverage ratio with the use of multiple channels. For this purpose, we have to tackle two new issues: how can a drone select the channel to use? and how can a user select the drone to use as access point?

The remainder of this paper is organized as follows: Sect. 2 introduces a brief state of the art for channel allocation and optimization problems, Sect. 3 presents the system description, Sect. 4 introduces the interference management mechanism and its associated algorithms, Sect. 5 introduce the performance evaluation and Sect. 6 concludes the paper and proposes some potential extensions.

2   Related Works

Several works have already been done to take up similar issues.

In [6,7] the goal is to restore the network connectivity. Drones are used to fill the gaps serving as bridges between the disrupted infrastructures. UAVs are sent over the affected areas to interconnect terrestrial networks by relaying the messages between them. In [6], the authors use Delaunay triangulation to improve connectivity and in [7], they use a game theory approach to interconnect partitions of a network by using drones to drop relays in pre-computed spots. None of them can be used in dynamically changing networks due to the complexity needed to determine the positions of the temporary access points.

Several propositions exist in the literature as for how to optimally assign channels to reduce or eliminate the interference. Authors in [8] have studied the assignment of channels in the Multiple Radios, Multiple Channels Wireless Mesh Networks (MRMC WMN), and proposed a cross–layer mathematical formulation of joint channel assignment and multicast tree construction designed to minimize the total number of links by forming a multicast tree and thus minimize the total interference.

All these propositions cannot be used in our network as the approaches are centralized. A drone has to make decisions based on local information. In [9], the authors have proposed a distributed algorithm called Efficient Wireless Multicast (EWM) which builds a tree in which channels are assigned to the transmission for next hop in function of the used channels.

In [3], the authors efficiently collect data and recharge sensors by the aim of drones. The network is separated in multiple clusters. Unfortunately, this publication offers an overview over a static sensor network and does not look into the optimal deployment of the UAVs.

The optimal placement of UAVs in order to cover targets on-the-ground is already researched form different perspectives.

In [10,11], the authors assume that the devices evolve in a 2D space. Therefore their problem is simplified because the coverage radius is fixed for each mobile devices. In the former article, the authors consider a mathematical model to maximize the amount of information collected based on a greedy approach and in the latter, the authors present a decentralized model for optimal positioning of sensors in order to track a target.

In [12], the authors aim to find UAV positions in order to minimize the number of drones used ensuring the surveillance of all the targets, by defining a mixed integer non-linear optimization models.

Nonetheless, the difference between the works presented above and ours is related to the constraints. Indeed, we consider that not all users have to be covered by a drone and introduce it as a constraint in our problem.

3   System Description

3.1   Scenario

The purpose of our work is to use a fleet of UAVs to set up a backbone network which provides communication means for a particular event such as a public gathering or a disaster situation when the traditional infrastructure is overloaded or wiped out. This network should be quick to deploy and inexpensive to implement, so that implicated parties (organizers, firefighters, public services) could use it rapidly. We will assume that the UAVs can communicate with each other, *eg* with the help of directional antennas. The primary objective of this work is to implement the best coverage with the minimal number of drones and with the most extended battery life possible for the UAVs.

Users position cannot be known with precision, so we will assume that we only know some specific points close to which users are more likely to be found (*eg* checkpoints).

Our main objective is to define the *initial position* of each UAV in order to maximize the number of associated users. A user can be associated to a drone if the reception power is strong enough and if the UAV can provide the required service.

3.2   Modeling Users Position

The scenario we focus on is depicted in Fig. 1. Let $\mathcal{D}$ be the set of available drones and $\mathcal{U}$ the set of users to cover. Each user $u \in \mathcal{U}$ has a fixed position at (x_u, y_u, h_u), where x_u and y_u represent the positions in $2D$ plane and h_u the altitude of the user, fixed at 0.

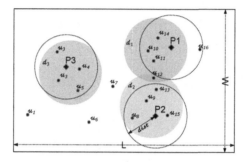

Fig. 1. Our scenario's model

Each UAV, $d \in \mathcal{D}$ is free to move into a $3D$ plane, having the coordinates (x_d, y_d, h_d). The altitude of the drone is fixed at $h_d = 100\,\mathrm{m}$. We assume that each drone has a fixed sensing range s. A user u found in this range is then detected and can be associated to a drone. The radius of the sensing range is computed based on the UAVs altitude and its directional antenna half beam-width, in our model, $s = 50\,\mathrm{m}$.

We consider that a drone $d \in \mathcal{D}$ covers a user $u \in \mathcal{U}$ if the distance (1) between the drone and the user is $\mathcal{L}_d^u \leq s$.

$$\mathcal{L}_d^u = \sqrt{(x_d - x_u)^2 + (y_d - y_u)^2 + (h_d - h_u)^2} \tag{1}$$

As already stated, we have already proposed an initial UAV placement strategy based on a statistical knowledge of users positions [5]. For this purpose, we have introduced a *Point of Interest* or POI as a point close to which users are more likely to be found. We have also introduced p, the probability that a user is at most at a distance d of one of the N_p POIs, named $P_1, \ldots, P_{N_p}$.

In Fig. 1, $N_p = 3$ and $p = 0.75$. Distance $dist$ has been arbitrarily chosen to match the sensing range of a drone.

3.3   Modeling UAV Behavior

UAVs are supposed to get as close as possible to a maximum number of users while preserving a minimal distance to each other (in order to mitigate interference). We have thus chosen to represent their interactions with the help of a model inspired by Coulomb's law [5]. In this model, a user is described as a positive electric charge and a UAV as a negative electric charge. Drones are then attracted by users within their sensing range.

On the other hand, UAVs using the same channel have to repel one another to avoid interference. As can be seen in Fig. 2, if γ is the ratio between a user charge and a UAV charge, a low value of γ will induce a high ratio of "interfered" users (users within the range of several UAVs, that could then suffer from hidden terminal situations). Of course a high value for γ is more difficult to implement and could lead to a lower association ratio. Users are not affected by this force, being able to move freely.

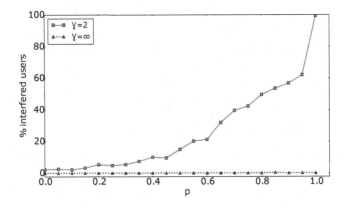

Fig. 2. Association ratio for high and low values of γ

In our simulations, UAVs are activated above POIs and aim at reaching an initial position with an optimal coverage. Such a position must be reached as soon as possible to improve battery life.

3.4   Traffic Model

In this paper, we focus on an initial UAV positioning, seeking an optimal coverage. We will not study traffic scheduling, so we will not implement a sophisticated data traffic. To bring our model closer to reality, we will however assume that each user has the same communication needs, with limited resources available on each drone. Each UAV has a fixed capacity equal to $\kappa = 50$ users. In these conditions, more UAVs are needed to cover users concentrated in the same region. A typical example, when p values are high, users will gather tightly in a small area around the POIs.

3.5   Observed Metrics

Our objective is to provide the best network access to a large number of users. We will thus measure the following parameters. The coverage ratio is the ratio of users with a high enough reception power from at least one UAV. The interfered ratio is the ratio of users covered by more than one UAV using the same channel. The associated ratio is the rate of non-interfered users, associated with a UAV. The reception power is evaluated for each user with the help of a propagation model. The battery capacity will be described with a simple model.

3.6   Path Loss Model

UAVs are situated above the users at a constant altitude $h = 100\,\text{m}$, and we assume that they are in line-of-sight so, we used the Friis transmission formula [13] to calculate the received power P_R :

$$P_R = \frac{P_T G_T G_R c^2}{(4\pi R f)^2} \tag{2}$$

Equation 2 allows acquiring a magnitude of radio power sensed by a receiver located at a certain distance of a transmitter, in free space. P_T represents the transmission power, G_T represents the transmitting antenna gain, and G_R represents the receiving antenna gain. R and f symbolize the distance between transmitters and the used frequency respectively. The simulation parameters used are displayed in Table 1.

Table 1. Scenario parameters

Characteristics	Value
UAV transmission power P_{T_d}	27 dBm
User transmission power P_{T_u}	27 dBm
Transmission gain G_T	5.2 dBi
Reception gain G_R	2 dBi
Transmission frequency f	5150 Mhz
Received power threshold T_R	−65 dBm

3.7   Energy Management

A simple energy model was also integrated into the model. The purpose is to estimate the mean lifetime of a drone participating in the deployment and operation of the network. To compute the energy consumption, we took into consideration only the main equipment embarked on an UAV such as the propeller motors, the CPU (central processing unit) and the Wi-Fi antennas.

A precise model of motor consumption depends on weather conditions (temperature, atmospheric pressure, winds), propeller diameter and pitch, internal

resistance and motor efficiency. We choose to use the measurements presented in
[14]. The authors did an extensive study on the energy consumption in various
discrete movement states of a UAV. The Wi-Fi consumption is also based on
other experiments done in [15]. In this paper, the authors measured, in detail,
the energy consumption for wireless nodes. The last piece of equipment took
into consideration in our energy model is the CPU. We imagined that the UAVs
would embark an on-board computer, like Raspberry Pi, that will run our model.
In [16] the authors measured the power consumption of a Raspberry Pi based on
different CPU utilization. A summary of different power consumption utilized
in our simulation is given in Table 2.

Table 2. Energy consumption parameters

Characteristics	Value
One motor - hoovering	3 Amps
One motor - in move	5 Amps
One Wi-Fi antenna - idle/RX	300 mAmps
One Wi-Fi antenna - TX	400 mAmps
CPU - 50% utilization	600 mAmps
Battery capacity C_b	6200 mAh

To determine the battery lifetime we used the following equation: $T_r = \frac{C_b}{C_e}\epsilon$,
where T_r is the remaining battery lifetime in hours, C_b the battery capacity
in mAh, C_e the current in the drone's load. ϵ takes into account the external
factors that can affect the autonomy of the battery, being equal to 0.7 in our
simulations.

A UAV replacement mechanism was already studied in [17]. When a drone's
battery is about to be depleted, it will send a replacement request over the control
plane. A replacement UAV will come alongside the depleted drone permitting
the routing algorithm to adapt the routes. When traffic is rerouted, the end-life
drone will depart to the control center to recharge its batteries.

3.8   Implementation Concerns

As mentioned, we will use IEEE 802.11 as our communication protocol between
drones and between UAVs and users. To adapt our method to real life, Wi-Fi
beacons and probe requests come in handy. Two different discovery approaches
are proposed by the standard, passive or active scanning. In passive scanning,
a station will scan all possible channels, one by one and listen to beacons. A
beacon frame is sent by every access point to announce its presence.

For active scanning, a station still goes through each channel in turn, but
instead of passively listening to the signals on that channel, It will send to the
broadcast address a Probe Request management frame asking what network is
available on that channel.

We use these two frames to implement the interactions in our network. As the access points mounted on UAVs send beacons to the broadcast address, other drones will receive them. By receiving the beacon on one of the directive antennas the UAV can approximately determine the direction of the neighboring drone. Moreover, as each UAV is equipped with GPS (Global Positioning System), we can use the beacon's timestamp to roughly determine the relative distance between drones.

Regarding the user detection, we use the probe requests that user equipment send to detect the presence in the drone's sensing range. After that, by using the information on signal and noise level, the UAV will try to determine the relative position of the user.

4   Interference Management

As presented in [5], our network performs very well without having the exact users positions. But when taking into account the interference that can be produced by neighboring drones, we notice a slight decrease in association ratio. If two or more drones are needed to cover the same area, user communications are disturbed by the nearby drone, if they use the same radio channel. As already stated, it is possible to reduce interference by increasing γ (minimal distance between drones), but in the same time, the association ratio decreases as some users will not be covered anymore.

4.1   Introducing Multi-channel

Figure 3 depicts the percentage of associated, non-interfered users for several numbers of channels. We notice that our assumptions where founded. Of course, using the same frequency on each drone, creates massive interference with more than 50% of users interfered when p is high, as UAVs are trying to cover as many users as possible.

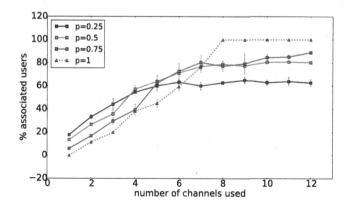

Fig. 3. User association ratio based on the number of channels

The overlapping can be managed by altering the ratio between repulsive and attraction forces. In fact, this allows us to state a trade-off between covering users and reducing interference.

4.2   Interference Management and Channel Switching

One of the improvements is related to the usage of multiple radio channels. As explained before, the system becomes interfered when multiple UAVs try to cover the same area. The main purpose is to offer an interference-free environment reducing the risk of frame collisions and reduced throughput. For this, we added a multi-channel reuse scheme to reduce interference.

Luckily, physical specifications for IEEE 802.11 standard allow for simultaneous operation of several orthogonal (non-overlapping) channels. As an example, in the 2.4 GHz Wi-Fi band, three channels can be used concurrently. As to IEEE 802.11a standard, introducing the 5 GHz band, a total of twelve orthogonal channels are set forth.

By deploying antennas which allow the usage of multiple channels and affecting different non-overlapping channels when they are located in proximity, the UAVs can provide services to user on-the-ground simultaneously with minimum interference. Therefore, the association capacity of our proposed network can be increased.

Drones are collaborating, when in the immediate vicinity, to change the used channel. Each one exchanges, with its neighbors, information on the used channels. Accordingly, they adapt their own to eliminate local interference. In the beginning, every drone starts with the same Wi-Fi channel. At each iteration all UAVs will search for potential neighbors. Once found, it will choose a channel not used by another UAV in the vicinity.

As simple as it may look, it is very efficient, as it provides complete decentralized channel management. The flip-flopping between channels is mitigated as only the newest interfering drone will change the channel, bringing the neighborhood to a stable state. Besides that, as only one drone can send messages over the same Wi-Fi channel at one time, there cannot be two or more UAVs changing the channel at the same time as they have to notify the neighbors and the associated clients.

4.3   Association Strategy

As a user may be within the range of several UAVs (each one using a different channel), the question of the channel (and thus the drone) to use arises.

When a new user is covered by several UAVs (still with available capacity), then it can be associated to any of them. We have studied three different UAV association strategies:

- The simplest strategy is to use any of them, for example the first one from which a beacon is received. Let us call this the random strategy.
- The first real strategy is to implement a very simple load balancing algorithm. Users can be transferred between UAVs to reach a fair share.

- The second one is to transfer a user from a UAV to another one only if this improves the received power for this user.

If the drone capacity can be clearly stated and depends only on the number of associated users, then the random strategy is relevant. However, if the back-haul link provided by the UAV is a bottleneck, then the simple load balancer seems more appropriate. Finally, if the bottleneck is the Wi-Fi capacity, then the last one can be thought as suitable as it aims at improving transmission conditions.

Through an extensive set of simulations, we have noticed that these metrics are not really sensitive to the choice of the algorithm. As depicted in Fig. 4, the ratio of covered users is merely the same. The reception power for the users, described in Fig. 5 is not really affected neither, mainly because of the UAV altitude (in our model, the reception power depends on the distance from the UAV, and thus on its altitude). Finally, we can see in Fig. 6 that for high values of p, the random solution is more energy efficient. The reason is that it avoids some UAV movements that would follow a client transfer.

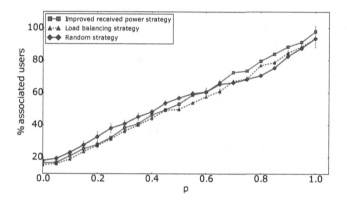

Fig. 4. Association ratio for different association strategy

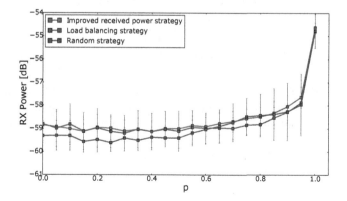

Fig. 5. Reception power for different association strategy

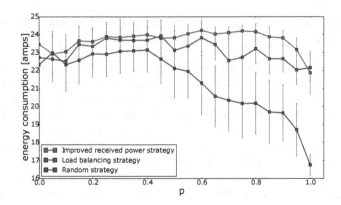

Fig. 6. Energy consumption for different association strategy

5   Simulation Performance Evaluation

In this section, we evaluate the performance of our proposed schemes with the help of a simulator that we developed.

The simulation parameters are presented in Table 3.

Table 3. Simulation parameters

Characteristics	Value
$card(u)$	500
$card(d)$	10
κ	50
$dist$	50 m
N_p	5
$(L \times W)$	1 km × 0.8 km
γ	2
h	100 m

As depicted in Fig. 7, using only one channel produces massive interference when the users are gathered around the POIs. In this cases, frame collisions and a reduced throughput can be expected. By taking into account these limitations we refined our simulator to include these new features.

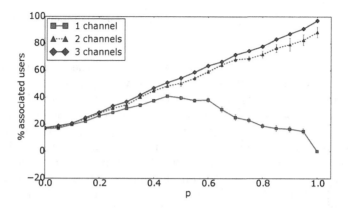

Fig. 7. User association ratio comparison when adding multiple channels

The interference that a user can sustain when multiple drones, operating on the same channel, are in its vicinity is also analyzed. To consider a user as interfered, the power received from the interfering AP (Access Point) must be higher than the receiving threshold, in our case $T_R = -65\,\text{dBm}$. All the following results are taking into account the interference. Only non-interfered users are counted as associated.

In Fig. 7 we compared the association rates for 500 users when using one, two and three channels. For low values of p, users are disseminated and the association rate is about 20%. For high values of p, because of the high user density, one channel is not enough. We see that the use of multiple channels dramatically enhances the performance for high values of p. We can also notice that for p close to 1, the number of channels needed is roughly equal to (3) where N_u is the total number of users, N_p is the total number of POIs in the network and κ is the maximum number of users that a drone can cover.

$$N_C = \frac{N_u}{N_p * \kappa} \tag{3}$$

For example, using the values from Table 3 we obtain 2 channels, $N_C = 2$. Even with this number of channels, we cannot reach a 100% user association rate for the following reasons:

- The users are not evenly distributed among POIs so that if a point of interest has 110 users, 10 of them will not be covered, with only 2 drones.
- Two POIs can be close enough so that 2 channels are not sufficient, some users being interfered by neighbor UAVs.

Taking our model to a higher scale, we analyzed the performance when a larger number of users is present. We looked into the association rates by varying the number of channels available when $n = 2000$ and have to be covered with only 40 UAVs. In Fig. 3 we depicted the association ratio when $p = 0, 25, p = 0, 5$,

$p = 0,75$ and $p = 1$. When disposing of only a small number of channels it is better when the users are more dispersed than gathered around a POI. As users are concentrated in a small area, p is high, the number of drones that can cover them without creating interference will be limited by the number of channels. When the number of channels is sufficient to cover everyone, as users are more dispersed, the number of drones needed to provide a 100% association rate grows to be inefficient to deploy that many resources to increase the association rate.

Table 4 shows the energy consumption of a drone in our network. Based on the model described before, we compared the mean battery lifetime and the mean energy consumption. We evaluate the impact of the p value and the number of channels on the energy consumption. The number of channels does not impact the battery lifetime. However, as expected, the users position has a tremendous effect on battery depletion. For $p = 1$, i.e., users are all gathered around POIs, UAVs do not have to move a lot, which saves the battery lifetime, offering approximately 16 minutes of flight time. As users are more dispersed in the given area, the drones have to travel longer distances to find them, using more power. When $p \neq 1.0$, 30% more energy is consumed by the drone decreasing the mean lifetime, as we expected. We believe that it worth adding the antennas to the UAV, battery lifetime not being drastically impacted.

Table 4. Mean energy consumption and mean battery lifetime

p	Battery lifetime	Energy consumption
$p = 1.0$	16 mn	16 amps
$p \neq 1.0$	12 mn	24 amps

Our proposed network performs remarkably well, the interference management and association schemes improve drastically the ground association rates offering better quality, not interfered transmissions and better resource allocation between users.

6   Conclusion and Future Works

We are currently working on optimizing drone placement taking into account our constraints. This optimization will allow us to observe the efficiency and performance of our self-deploying distributed network. User mobility is another critical point in our study. Being distributed and easy to implement, our solution should be efficient in a mobile scenario.

This paper proposed several novel enhancements to our network of UAVs used as access points. The network deployment is based on Coulomb's law, with users being represented as positive charges and drones as negative charges, being attracted by users. After detailing this model, we introduced two mechanisms that boost the user association ratio of the network, an interference management, and several association mechanisms. Allowing each drone taking part in the network to choose in a distributed manner the best channel to use by taking into account local interference, we point out that the non-interfered association rate of users increases remarkably. Furthermore, an analysis of energy consumption is done. Adding extra weight to drones (antennas, additional on-board computer) does not impact the energy consumption, overall battery consumption remaining reasonably acceptable, contributing to the feasibility of our proposed model in real life.

In this paper, users are evenly distributed among the POIs, they all have the same communication needs and all the UAVs have the same capacity κ. We plan to run more simulations to study the impact of these parameters.

We have shown that p is an important parameter, but its value is probably unknown in actual scenarios. We can imagine the use the UAVs discovering users position to dynamically compute an estimator of p that could be helpful to improve their behavior. Improving the performance for low values of p is also a challenge.

Finally, this work was dedicated to the initial placement of UAVs. The next step is to study how our system behaves with moving users.

References

1. Zeng, Y., Zhang, R., Lim, T.J.: Wireless communications with unmanned aerial vehicles: opportunities and challenges. IEEE Commun. Mag. **54**(5), 36–42 (2016). https://doi.org/10.1109/MCOM.2016.7470933
2. Orsino, A., et al.: Effects of heterogeneous mobility on D2D-and drone-assisted mission-critical MTC in 5G. IEEE Commun. Mag. **55**(2), 79–87 (2017). https://doi.org/10.1109/MCOM.2017.1600443CM
3. Pang, Y., Zhang, Y., Gu, Y., Pan, M., Han, Z., Li, P.: Efficient data collection for wireless rechargeable sensor clusters in harsh terrains using UAVs. In: Global Communications Conference (GLOBECOM), pp. 234–239. IEEE (2014). https://doi.org/10.1109/GLOCOM.2014.7036813
4. Merwaday, A., Guvenc, I.: UAV assisted heterogeneous networks for public safety communications. In: Wireless Communications and Networking Conference Workshops (WCNCW), pp. 329–334. IEEE (2015). https://doi.org/10.1109/WCNCW.2015.7122576
5. Rautu, D., Dhaou, R., Chaput, E.: Crowd-based positioning of UAVs as access points. In: Consumer Communications and Networking Conference (CCNC). IEEE (2018). https://doi.org/10.1109/CCNC.2018.8319279
6. Han, Z., Swindlehurst, A.L., Liu, K.R.: Optimization of manet connectivity via smart deployment/movement of unmanned air vehicles. IEEE Trans. Veh. Technol. **58**(7), 3533–3546 (2009). https://doi.org/10.1109/TVT.2009.2015953
7. Senturk, I.F., Akkaya, K., Yilmaz, S.: Relay placement for restoring connectivity in partitioned wireless sensor networks under limited information. Ad Hoc Netw. **13**, 487–503 (2014). https://doi.org/10.1016/j.adhoc.2013.09.005
8. Jahanshahi, M., Dehghan, M., Meybodi, M.R.: On channel assignment and multicast routing in multi-channel multi-radio wireless mesh networks. Int. J. Ad Hoc Ubiquit. Comput. **12**(4), 225–244 (2013). https://doi.org/10.1504/IJAHUC.2013.052866

9. Nargesi, A., Bag-Mohammadi, M., Haghighat, A.T.: Efficient multicast and channel assignment in multi-channel wireless mesh networks. In: Information and Communication Technology Convergence (ICTC), pp. 404–409. IEEE (2012). https://doi.org/10.1109/ICTC.2012.6387163

10. Wang, Q., Xu, K., Takahara, G., Hassanein, H.: Wsn04-1: deployment for information oriented sensing coverage in wireless sensor networks. In: Global Telecommunications Conference (GLOBECOM), pp. 1–5. IEEE (2006). https://doi.org/10.1109/GLOCOM.2006.482

11. Martínez, S., Bullo, F.: Optimal sensor placement and motion coordination for target tracking. Automatica **42**(4), 661–668 (2006). https://doi.org/10.1016/j.automatica.2005.12.018

12. Zorbas, D., Pugliese, L.D.P., Razafindralambo, T., Guerriero, F.: Optimal drone placement and cost-efficient target coverage. J. Netw. Comput. Appl. **75**, 16–31 (2016). https://doi.org/10.1016/j.jnca.2016.08.009

13. Friis, H.T.: A note on a simple transmission formula. Proc. IRE **34**(5), 254–256 (1946). https://doi.org/10.1109/JRPROC.1946.234568

14. Dietrich, T., Krug, S., Zimmermann, A.: An empirical study on generic multicopter energy consumption profiles. In: Systems Conference (SysCon), pp. 1–6. IEEE (2017). https://doi.org/10.1109/SYSCON.2017.7934762

15. Zhao, Z., Mao, Y., Shi, G., Dou, Z., Shu, Y.: Energy-efficient data gathering in high-voltage transmission line monitoring system. In: Mobile Ad-hoc and Sensor Networks (MSN), pp. 45–51. IEEE (2011). https://doi.org/10.1109/MSN.2011.34

16. Kaup, F., Gottschling, P., Hausheer, D.: Powerpi: measuring and modeling the power consumption of the raspberry pi. In: Local Computer Networks (LCN), pp. 236–243. IEEE (2014). https://doi.org/10.1109/LCN.2014.6925777

17. Rautu, D., Dhaou, R., Chaput, E.: Maintaining a permanent connectivity between nodes of an air-to-ground communication network. In: Wireless Communications and Mobile Computing Conference (IWCMC), pp. 681–686. IEEE (2017). https://doi.org/10.1109/IWCMC.2017.7986367

Body Area Networks, IoT Security and Standardisation

Reliable Cross-Layer Protocol for Broadcast in Wireless Body Area Networks

Wafa Badreddine$^{(\boxtimes)}$ and Maria Potop-Butucaru

Sorbonne Université, CNRS, LIP6, 75005 Paris, France
`wafa.badreddine@lip6.fr`

Abstract. Wireless Body Area Networks (WBAN) open an interdisciplinary area within Wireless Sensor Networks (WSN) research, with a tremendous impact in healthcare area where sensors are used to monitor, collect and transmit biological parameters of the human body. We propose the first network-MAC cross-layer broadcast protocol in WBAN. Our protocol, evaluated in the OMNET++ simulator enriched with a realistic human body mobility and channel model issued from a recent research on biomedical and health informatics, outperforms existing flat broadcast strategies in terms of network coverage, sensors energy consumption and correct reception of FIFO-ordered packets. We investigate the resilience of both existing flat broadcast strategies and our new cross-layer protocol face to various transmission rates and human body mobility. Existing flat broadcast strategies, without exception, start to have a drastic drop of performance for transmission rates above 11 Kb/s while our cross-layer protocol maintains its good performance for transmission rates up to 190 Kb/s.

Keywords: Wireless Body Area Networks · Broadcast · Mobility model · Cross-layer

1 Introduction

In the healthcare area, WBAN (Wireless Body Area Networks) [10,17] emerged as a viable solution in response to various disadvantages associated with wired sensors commonly used to monitor patients in hospitals and emergency rooms. Recent medical reports predict that the number of people using home health technologies will enormously increase from 14.3 to 78 million consumers from 2014 to 2020 [2], respectively. Additionally, body sensors shipments will hit 3.1 million units every year.

In WBAN tiny devices with low computing power and limited battery life, deployed in/on or around human body, are able to detect and collect physiological phenomena of the human body (EEG (Electroencephalography), ECG (Electrocardiography), SpO2, lactic acid, etc.), and transmit this information to a collector point (i.e *Sink*) that will process it, take decisions, alert or record.

© Springer Nature Switzerland AG 2019
M. R. Palattella et al. (Eds.): ADHOC-NOW 2019, LNCS 11803, pp. 469–482, 2019.
https://doi.org/10.1007/978-3-030-31831-4_32

Note that the current needs in surgery rooms [3] are: ECG is measured every millisecond, body temperature is measured each minute, blood pressure is measured every millisecond, CO_2 is measured every 200 ms and aspirator every 10 ms.

WBANs [11] differ from typical large-scale Wireless Sensor Networks (WSN) in many aspects: the size of the network is limited to a dozen of nodes, in-network mobility follows the body movements and the wireless channel has its specificities. Links have, in general, a very short range and a quality that varies with the wearer's posture, but remains low in the general case. Indeed, the transmission power is kept low, which improves devices autonomy and reduces wearers electromagnetic exposition. Consequently, the effects of body absorption, reflections and interference cannot be neglected and it is difficult to maintain a direct link (one-hop) between a data collection point and all WBAN nodes. Although, recent research [19] advocates for using *multi-hop* communication in WBAN, very few multi-hop communication protocols have been proposed so far and even fewer are optimized for the human body mobility.

Contributions. The current work extends in several ways the results in [5, 6] where the authors evaluate in multi-hop WBAN existing broadcast strategies adapted from Adhoc, DTN (Delay Tolerant Network) and WSN literature. Moreover, they present new efficient broadcast strategies for WBAN.

We propose the first *network-MAC cross-layer broadcast protocol, CLBP*, designed for multi-hop topologies and resilient to realistic human body mobility. Our protocol exploit the human body mobility by carefully choosing the most reliable communication paths (i.e paths with the highest success transmission probability) in each studied posture. Moreover, our protocol includes a slot assignment mechanism that reduces the energy consumption, collisions, idle listening and overhearing. Additionally, *CLBP* includes a light synchronization scheme that helps nodes to resynchronize with the *Sink* on the fly.

We stressed all strategies with various transmission rates up to 544 Kb/s in seven different postures (walk, run, sleep, weak walk, etc) ranging from static to high mobility postures. Our evaluation has been conducted in OMNET++ simulator that we enriched with realistic human body mobility model and channel model issued from the recent research on biomedical and health informatics [19].

With no exception, the existing flat broadcast strategies register a dramatic drop of performance when the transmission rate is superior to 11 Kb/s.

Our cross-layer broadcast protocol outperforms existing flat broadcast strategies in terms of reliability and correct reception of FIFO-ordered packets (i.e. packets are received in the order of their sending). Furthermore, our protocol maintains its good performance up to 190 Kb/s transmission rates.

Roadmap. This paper is organized as follows: Sect. 2 presents the related work. Section 3 presents the channel model and the realistic human body mobility model. In Sect. 4 we detail CLPB, our new functional cross-layer broadcast protocol. In Sect. 5, we extensively evaluate protocols in [5, 6] and our new cross layer protocol. Section 6 concludes the paper.

2   Related Work

There are very few cross-layered protocols specifically designed for WBAN [15, 20]. The proposed WBAN cross-layer approaches prove that there is still a need for further optimization of such networks and that cross-layering is efficient to accomplish that.

In the following we will discuss mainly multi-hop cross-layer protocols that involve MAC and Network layers.

Lahlou et al. present EEAWD [13], a MAC-Network cross layer energy optimization model for WBAN. With EEAWD, authors introduce two traffic classes (normal and emergency), and consider a pseudo mobility model. Authors only focused on energy efficiency parameter despite others.

In [7], Braem et al. propose WASP: Wireless Autonomous Spanning tree Protocol, a converge-cast cross-layer protocol for multi-hop WBAN. WASP is a slotted protocol that uses a spanning tree for medium access coordination and traffic routing. Each node will tell its children in which slot they can send their data using a special packet called WASP-scheme. WASP-scheme is also used as acknowledgement to each node's parent and as resources request if needed. However, for some parent nodes sleep period is shorter because they have to handle more children than other parent nodes. In addition, latency is correlated to the number of levels of the spanning tree. WASP is not resilient to realistic human body mobility due to parent-child definition, parent forward data packet from its child only. Scalability is also an issue since each node has only one packet to send per cycle and increasing number of nodes decreases throughput.

Latre et al. propose CICADA [14] as an improvement of WASP. CICADA sets up a network tree in a distributed manner. It aims to reduce energy consumption with the use of a spanning tree and an assignment of transmission slots to ensure collision free medium access. A cycle is divided into a control sub-cycle (used for schemes transferring) and a data sub-cycle. These two schemes are both sent in the control sub-cycle. When all nodes have received schemes from their parents, the control sub-cycle ends and the data sub-cycle starts. To remedy the delay issue with WASP protocol, in CICADA, nodes at the bottom of the tree start sending and all nodes send data to the Sink node in one cycle. CICADA has not been evaluated against realistic human body mobility and various transmission rates. Moreover, the medium access control scheme proposed in CICADA is specifically designed to handle converge-cast. Its adaptation to broadcast was reported as open question.

Nadeem et al. introduce SIMPLE-Stable Increasing-throughput Multi-hop Protocol for Link Efficiency in WBAN [18]. A cost function is used to select the parent node with high residual energy and minimal distance to the Sink node. The Sink node broadcasts a packet which contains its position while the other nodes broadcast a packet which contains their ID, position and energy status. Then, Sink node computes the cost function of each node based on the received information from the hello packet. The cost function is transmitted to all nodes and only nodes with minimum cost function are selected as forwarder. This selection is processed for each round. Finally, forwarder nodes assign TDMA schedule to other nodes hence nodes with data to transmit wake up only in their assigned time slot.

Elhadj *et al.* present a cross-layer based data dissemination algorithm for IEEE 802.15.6 [9]. Authors considered a two-hop extended star topology since their work is based on IEEE 802.15.6 standard. Authors adopt a simple reverse tree route discovering approach rooted at the coordinator for a two-hop topology network using hello beacons exchange. The coordinator (i.e *Sink* node) starts with a beacon broadcast. Beacon messages are then forwarded only once by all sensors. Each node that received one or more beacons will choose a next hop to the coordinator based on the shortest path in terms of delay. In addition, authors introduce data traffic priorities and a pre-emptive queuing model at a WBAN node. However, high priority packets can contend resources and low priority packets can be blocked at the MAC buffer. To cope with this problem authors define the maximum time that a packet can wait in the buffer. Even so, latency stills an issue.

Note that cross-layer approach showed a good compromise between reliability, energy efficiency, QoS requirements, etc. However, proposed protocols, discussed earlier, focus only *converge-cast* (multiple source nodes send packets to a unique destination *Sink*). To the best of our knowledge, no paper has discussed broadcast in WBAN exploiting a cross-layer approach. In addition, these proposals handle body mobility by reconstructing and updating the tree topology used for packet routing.

2.1   Broadcast in WBAN

Broadcast has been studied for the first time in WBAN in [5] and [6]. The authors propose a set of multi-hop broadcast strategies and extensively evaluate them against realistic human body mobility. Inspired by the tremendous work in WSN, adhoc networks and DTN, broadcasting in multi-hop networks can be divided into two major categories: *dissemination* (or *flooding*) algorithms which require no particular knowledge of the network, and, *knowledge-based* algorithms which use knowledge of the network mobility to predict spatio-temporal connectivity and use this information to reduce the number of transmissions. A precise characterization of the mobility pattern leads to a better efficiency, however acquiring this information has a cost and there is a subtle balance to find between duplicate data packets and control messages.

Authors of [5,6] adapted, implemented and compared various broadcasting strategies with different levels of knowledge. The following 7 broadcast strategies were considered in our evaluation and to compare with a cross-layer approach:

- Flooding In *Flooding* strategy nodes rebroadcast each received packet as long as its TTL is greater than 1, decreasing its TTL value by 1 unit every time.
- Plain Flooding *Plain flooding* is more restrictive: using sequence number, a received packet is rebroadcasted only once. Other copies are discarded.
- Pruned Flooding Each node forwards a received packet to K neighbors, chosen randomly, according to an uniform distribution. We run simulations with different K values.

- Probabilistic flooding ($P = 0.5$) Nodes decide to broadcast packets according to a constant probability, P. For our simulations, we chose $P = 0.5$.
- Probabilistic flooding ($P_{new} = P_{old}/2$) Nodes decide to broadcast according to a probability P that is divided by 2 every time a packet is broadcasted. In our simulations, the initial forwarding probability is set to 1.
- MBP: Mixed Broadcast Protocol [5] MBP is a mix between the *dissemination-based* and *knowledge-based* approaches. The broadcast begins as a basic flooding algorithm (i.e *Flooding* strategy). When a node receives a message, it checks the number of hops NH this message has traveled since its emission by the *Sink*, either stored as an explicit value, or based on the TTL, and compares it to a threshold, Δ. As a result, nodes choose either to broadcast to its neighbors in range, to wait for acknowledgements or to acknowledge (an acknowledgement is a specific third layer packet from a receiver).
- OptFlood: Optimized Flooding [6] It builds up on classical flooding, which exhibits excellent performance in terms of network coverage and completion delay, while attempting to keep the number of transmissions and receptions low to preserve energy and channel resources. OptFlood maintains, associated to each packet, two counters: *cptGlobal*, embedded into the packet itself (or in all its copies) and the node increases this counter value to reflect the fact that the packet reached a new node, and *CptLocal*, which is a per-packet variable local to each node and it is a local copy of the maximum value of *cptGlobal* that the node has seen so far.

3   Channel Model

We integrated to our simulator Omnet++ a realistic channel model published in [19] over the physical layer implementation provided by the Mixim framework [12]. This channel model of an on-body 2.45 GHz channel between 7 nodes, that belong to the same WBAN, using small directional antennas modeled as if they were 1.5 cm away from the body. Nodes are assumed to be attached to the human body on the head, chest, upper arm, wrist, navel, thigh, and ankle. Considering the application of vital sensor monitoring for medical and health-care, these nodes are selected based on the possible vital sensors.

Nodes positions are calculated in 7 postures: walking (walk), walking weakly (weak), running (run), sitting down (sit), wearing a jacket (wear), sleeping (sleep), and lying down (lie). Walk, weak, and run are variations of walking motions. Sit and lie are variations of up-and-down movement. Wear and sleep are relatively irregular postures and movements.

Channel attenuation is calculated between each couple of nodes for each of these postures as the average attenuation (in dB) and the standard deviation (in dBm). The datasets we used to integrate the mobility model are presented in [4]. The model takes into account: the shadowing, reflection, diffraction, and scattering by body parts.

4 *CLPB*: Cross Layer Protocol for Broadcast in WBAN

In this section, we introduce our new cross layer broadcast protocol *CLPB*.

CLPB handles both the control medium access and the broadcast process. *CLPB* is a slotted protocol that builds on top of a pruned communication graphs constructed based on the channel model [19] described in Sect. 3.

In order to include the channel model specificities in the broadcast process, *CLPB* needs a *preprocessing* phase (see Sect. 4.1). The preprocessing phase is only handled at the beginning and only at the *Sink* node level.

After this preprocessing phase, *Sink* broadcasts packets that will carry both data and control information (e.g. slots assignment, synchronization information, etc) (see Sect. 4.2).

Each node wakes up on each slot on reception mode, RX, for a period of time that equals to a half time slot. During this period, there are two possible cases:

- no packet is received: The node goes back to sleep mode and wakes up (on reception mode RX) next time slot.
- a packet is received:
  - if it is allowed to transmit (based on time slots schedule), then it schedules a transmission.
  - if more packets are expected, based on *Sink* node transmission rate, then it computes the next cycle and goes back to sleep at the end of the current cycle. Otherwise, it sleeps definitely.

4.1 Preprocessing Phase

The aim of preprocessing phase is to identify, for each posture and for each node, one or more reliable paths from *Sink* node, i.e paths with the highest success transmission probability. This phase is executed only by *Sink* node before starting the broadcast process.

First, *Sink* node computes, based on the mean attenuation and the standard deviation of each link between a couple of nodes, the Cumulative Distribution Function (CDF) of the random attenuation $x : F(X) = P[x < X]$ where X is a threshold. X represents the maximum acceptable attenuation referring to the transmission power $-55\,\text{dBm}$ and the reception sensibility $-100\,\text{dBm}$. X is equal $(-55 - (-100)) = 45\,\text{dB}$ and $F(45)$ represents the probability of a successful transmission at this link. A similar approach is used by the authors of [8].

Then, *Sink* computes a pruned communication graph. Nodes in this graph are the nodes in the network, the edges correspond to the links with success transmission probability greater than 0.5.

Figure 1 shows 3 pruned communication graphs, for walking, walking weakly and sleeping postures, obtained by applying the procedure described above.

Sink selects a set of *senders*, for each posture, starting from top to down. A sender is a node that presents a link with a high transmission success probability with a node other than the *Sink*.

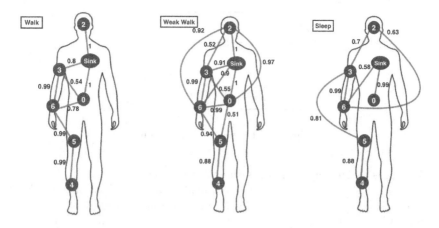

Fig. 1. The resulting communication graphs (a graph per posture)

We suppose that *Sink* node knows in advance the postures of the body. Postures detection is out of the scope of our study. Note that several works [16,21] addressed the posture detection.

At the end of the preprocessing phase, *Sink* assigns a slot to each sender outputted by the preprocessing phase. A node is allowed to forward previously received packets only if it is a sender and the current slot was assigned to it. When a node wakes up on its assigned time slot to transmit previously received data, it transmits until the end of its slot. After this point, it delays the remaining packets to be broadcasted in the next cycle.

4.2 Medium Access and Synchronization Scheme

Sink node divides time into *cycles*. A cycle corresponds to a fixed number of time slots i.e. a sequence of time slots equals to the number of senders including *Sink* node.

In a cycle, during its corresponding time slot, each sender node is allowed to forward data received in the previous time slot or in the previous cycle.

Nodes synchronize with *Sink* node via the scheduling and synchronization scheme (Fig. 2). We also show that nodes are able to resynchronize even though some packets are lost.

Our new cross layer approach minimizes coordination overhead. No exchange of control packets is needed because *Sink* node broadcasts packets which include data and a *medium access and synchronization scheme*.

Our protocol assumes that nodes execute in synchronized time-slots. Furthermore, it is assumed that the boundaries of slots are also synchronized.

Each received packet is considered as a reference for the current time slot. A *sender* includes in packets it forwards its slot number called **current slot**.

1. **Slots Assignment:** is the result of the preprocessing phase and describes what time slot did the *Sink* node assigned to each sender.

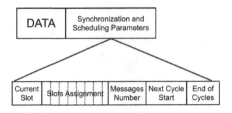

Fig. 2. CLPB packet description

2. **Messages Number:** represents the total number of packets to be sent by *Sink* node and that should be received by all nodes. This parameter refers to sequence number and enable nodes to recognize missing packets.
3. **Next Cycle Start:** Depends on the transmission rate of *Sink* node. This transmission rate allows to compute the time between two consecutive cycles: the *CyclesInterleave* parameter presented below.

$$CyclesInterleave = \begin{cases} 0, \text{if } Sink \text{ Transmission rate * Cycle Duration } > 1 \\ \\ (\lceil Transmission rate/SlotDuration\rceil) \\ *SlotDuration] - CycleDuration, \text{otherwise.} \end{cases}$$

$$(1)$$

If the transmission rate is such that *Sink* node receives an application packet while previous packet is still in broadcast (the current cycle is not finished), then *CyclesInterleave* is null. In this case, *Sink* node waits the end of the current cycle and then immediately starts a new cycle.

If *Sink* node receives an application packet much later. For example, *Sink* node receives an application packet every 8 time slots, which is greater than a cycle duration equals to 5 time slots for example. In this case, nodes enter in a sleep mode waiting for the next cycle.

Next Cycle Start is a key parameter that optimizes nodes duty cycle. Instead of alternating between reception and sleep mode each time slot, nodes will go back to sleep and schedule wake up when more packets are available.

4. **End of Cycles:** Nodes have to wake up each cycle in order to receive data packets. However, in case of packet loss, nodes will keep waiting for lost packets. To avoid such scenario, *Sink* node computes, based on traffic parameter, an end of communication time that we call *End of Cycles*. Then, when a node reaches the estimated time, it decides to sleep definitely (another alternative could be chosen regarding the application requirements specified by the concerned entity: a return to the initial state i.e half of the slot awake the other half sleep, or a wakeup after x seconds, etc.)

5　Performance Analysis

In this section, we compare flat broadcast strategies published in [5] (and its companion technical report [6]) and the new cross layer protocol *CLPB*.

Our evaluation targets the parameters below:

- **Reliability: Network coverage.** *Sink* node is our unique source of packets. We therefore compute the number of nodes that have received the message and present results as the percentage of covered nodes.
- **FIFO Order: Percentage of de-sequencing.** The percentage of packets received in a different order than the sending order.

Section 5.2 presents simulation results when strategies are stressed with a *Sink* node transmission rates from 2 to 1000 packets/s.

More results are available in [4]. We extend our evaluation to the impact of MAC buffer sizes on protocols' performance. The goal of studying strategies performance with various transmission rates and different MAC buffer sizes is to highlight the hidden impact of some parameters like MAC buffer size on the performance of the different strategies. Our simulation confirms that a cross-layer approach offers the best performance.

5.1   Simulation Settings

We use the discrete event simulator Omnet++ [1] and the Mixim framework [12] enriched with the described channel and mobility model in Sect. 3.

Above the channel model, we used standard protocol implementations provided by the Mixim framework [12]. In particular, we used, for the medium access control layer, the IEEE 802.15.4 implementation (2006 version, non-beacon mode). Sensitivity levels, packets header length and other basic information and parameters are based on IEEE 802.15.4 standard.

Each data point is the average of 50 simulations run with different seeds. We used Omnet++ default internal random number generator, i.e. the Mersenne Twister implementation (cMersenneTwister; MT19937) for the uniform distribution, with different initialization seeds for each run, and the normal distribution generator (cNormal) for the signal attenuation.

The transmission power is set at the minimum limit level -55 dBm [6] that ensures a limited energy consumption, reduces wearers electromagnetic exposition and allows an intermittent communication given the channel attenuation and the receiver sensitivity -100 dBm. For *CLPB* protocol, slot duration is set to 5 ms with a bitrate equal to 1 Mb/s.

5.2   Simulation Results

In this section, we stress the different strategies with *Sink* node transmission rate up to 1000 packets/s and a MAC buffer size equals to 100 which is the default value in the IEEE 802.15.4 standard.

In all body postures, *CLPB* strategy outperforms the flat strategies. Moreover, *CLPB* good performance is maintained up to 200 packets/s while the other strategies percentage drops starting from 10 packets/s.

Network Coverage. Figure 3 presents the percentage of covered nodes in function of *Sink* transmission rate. This rate is presented as the number of broadcasted packets per second.

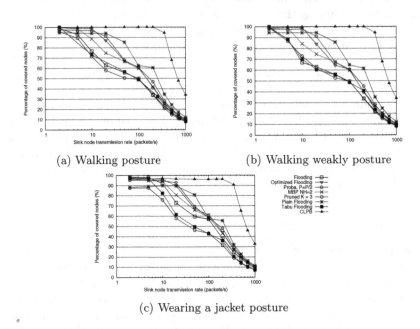

(a) Walking posture   (b) Walking weakly posture

(c) Wearing a jacket posture

Fig. 3. Percentage of covered nodes for walk, walking weakly and wearing a jacket postures for flat broadcast strategies and CLPB – MAC buffer size 100

All flat broadcast strategies behave similarly: Going to 1000 packets/s, the percentage of covered nodes almost linearly decreases to reach 10%. At 100 packets/s, only 50% of the network is covered.

With *Flooding* strategy, nodes broadcast each received packet without restrictions hence, the important amount of packets overloads the network and creates collisions and loss of packets.

With *Pruned Flooding*, even if nodes are restricted to broadcast to only K nodes, still, with $K = 3$ many copies are generated and the network is overloaded. Also, because of the random choice of the next hops, some nodes are not qualified for forwarding.

With *MBP*, broadcast is only delayed to give time for the other nodes to receive and acknowledge correct reception. This delay allows *MBP* to avoid network overloading and hence limits collisions and ensures a better percentage of covered nodes than *Flooding* and *Pruned Flooding* strategies.

CLPB maintains a good percentage, greater than 90%, up to 350 packets/s. Indeed, with 350 packets/s, *Sink* has one packet to send every 2.85 ms. In our settings, a cycle lasts 5 time slots with a time slot duration equals to 5 ms. At the end of the cycle, *Sink* node has 8 packets waiting in buffer for broadcast. Or, with a bit rate equals to $1Mbs$, *Sink* node can send up to 5 Kbs during its time slot. A packet size is equal to 544 bits then *Sink* node can send up to (5 Kbs/544 bits) packets i.e 9 packets per time slot. Beyond the rate 350 packets/s, performance falls to 30% of covered nodes by 1000 packets/s. Nodes are no more able to broadcast all waiting packets, then new received packets are dropped because buffer is saturated at MAC level.

FIFO Order: Percentage of De-sequencing. Figure 4 presents the percentage of de-sequencing in function of *Sink* node transmission rate.

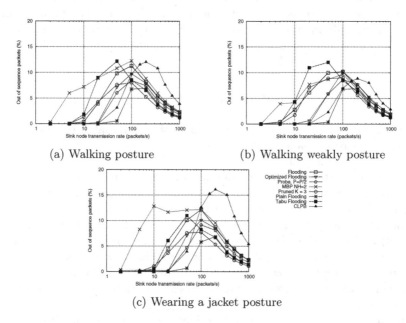

(a) Walking posture   (b) Walking weakly posture

(c) Wearing a jacket posture

Fig. 4. Percentage of de-sequencing for walk, walking weakly and wearing a jacket postures for flat broadcast strategies and CLPB

Three zones can be observed:

- At the beginning, all strategies present 0% of de-sequencing. At this point, strategies are able to handle more than one packet in the network.
- Then, from a given rate (depending on the strategy), the percentage increases. Here, based on Fig. 3, the percentage of covered nodes decreases due to collisions. Therefore, sequencing is no longer ensured.
- Finally, the percentage decreases to converge to 0% again due to the fact that few packets are received.

We observe that, for flat broadcast strategies, the inflection points of different curves have the same abscissa. This abscissa corresponds to a transmission rate equal to 100 packets/s. Looking deeper to different set parameters, 100 is the default value of the buffer size at the MAC level.

MBP strategy presents the highest percentage of de-sequencing for all postures, starting from 2 packets/s. In this strategy, nodes can whether broadcast immediately received packet or put it in the buffer and delay broadcast depending on threshold values.Thus, de-sequencing is more feasible.

Percentage of de-sequencing increases starting from 5 packets/s for *Flooding* and *Pruned Flooding* and from 20 packets/s for *Optimized Flooding, PlainFlooding* and *Probabilistic Flooding. Flooding* and *Pruned Flooding* have difficulties to handle transmission rate increase due to collisions and packets loss.

CLPB reacts as the other strategies and we observe de-sequencing in the received sequence. This is due to the mobility model. That is, unreliable links may occur, thus allowing reception of one of several packets from the broadcasted sequence. The links then disappear and the complete sequence will be received through a more reliable link.

6   Conclusion and Future Works

This paper is, to the best of our knowledge, the first that proposes a MAC-network cross-layer broadcast in WBAN.

Our work was motivated by results obtained after an extensive set of simulations where we stressed the existing network layer broadcast strategies [4–6] against realistic human body mobility and various transmission rates.

With no exception, the existing flat broadcast strategies register a dramatic drop of performance in terms of percentage of covered nodes, end-to-end delay and energy consumption when the transmission rates are superior to 11 Kb/s. We therefore, propose a new MAC-network cross-layer broadcast that exploits communication graph defined by the body postures in order to optimize medium access and nodes synchronization. Our protocol maintains its good performance up to 190 Kb/s transmission rates.

Our work opens several research directions. In the following we discuss two of them. First, we plan to investigate the slot synchronization in WBAN. The cross-layer protocols designed so far for WBAN assume a strong slot synchronization. Efficiently synchronizing slots in WBAN with realistic human body postures and mobility is an open issue. Second, we intend to extend our study to cross-layer converge-cast protocols. Although, there are several proposals in the WBAN literature, none of them has been stressed with realistic human body mobility and peaks of transmission rates.

Acknowledgment. This work was funded by SMART-BAN project (Labex SMART) http://www.smart-labex.fr.

References

1. The omnet home page (2014). https://omnetpp.org. Accessed 02 Aug 2019
2. Tractica.com . More than 78 Million Consumers Will Utilize HomeHealth Technologies by 2020 — tractica (2015). https://www.tractica.com/newsroom/press-releases/more-than-78-million-consumers-will-utilize-home-health-technologies-by-2020/

3. Personal communication. Fabien Koskas Professor Head of the Vascular Surgery Department at Salpetriere Hospital Paris France (2017)
4. Badreddine, W.: Wafa badreddine-thesis-communication protocols in wireless body area networks (wban). researchgate (2018). https://www.researchgate.net/publication/330442252_Wafa_Badreddine-Thesis-Communication_Protocols_in_Wireless_Body_Area_Networks_WBAN/comments
5. Badreddine, W., Chaudet, C., Petruzzi, F., Potop-Butucaru, M.: Broadcast strategies in wireless body area networks. In: Proceedings of the 18th ACM International Conference on Modeling, Analysis and Simulation of Wireless and Mobile Systems, MSWiM 2015, pp. 83–90 (2015). https://doi.org/10.1145/2811587.2811611
6. Badreddine, W., Chaudet, C., Petruzzi, F., Butucaru, M.P.: Broadcast strategies and performance evaluation of ieee 802.15.4 in wireless body area networks wban. Technical report, Sorbonne University, Laboratoire d'Informatique de Paris 6, LIP6, F-75005 Paris, France (2016)
7. Braem, B., Latré, B., Moerman, I., Blondia, C., Demeester, P.: The wireless autonomous spanning tree protocol for multihop wireless body area networks. In: 3rd Annual International ICST Conference on Mobile and Ubiquitous Systems: Computing, Networking and Services, MOBIQUITOUS 2006, San Jose, California, USA, 17–21 July 2006, pp. 1–8 (2006)
8. Bu, G., Potop-Butucaru, M.: Total order reliable convergecast in WBAN (2016). CoRR abs/1609.06862. http://arxiv.org/abs/1609.06862
9. Elhadj, H.B., Boudjit, S., Fourati, L.C.: A cross-layer based data dissemination algorithm for IEEE 802.15.6 wbans. In: 2013 International Conference on Smart Communications in Network Technologies (SaCoNeT), vol. 01, pp. 1–6 (2013). https://doi.org/10.1109/SaCoNeT.2013.6654578
10. Javaid, N., Khan, N.A., Shakir, M., Khan, M.A., Bouk, S.H., Khan, Z.A.: Ubiquitous healthcare in wireless body area networks - a survey (2013). CoRR abs/1303.2062, http://arxiv.org/abs/1303.2062
11. Johny, B., Anpalagan, A.: Body area sensor networks: requirements, operations, and challenges. IEEE Potentials **33**(2), 21–25 (2014). https://doi.org/10.1109/MPOT.2013.2286692
12. Köpke A, et al.: Simulating wireless and mobile networks in omnet++ - the mixim vision. In: 1st International Workshop on OMNeT++ (hosted by SIMUTools 2008), Marseille, France (2008)
13. Lahlou, L., Meharouech, A., Elia,s J., Mehaoua, A.: Mac-network cross-layer energy optimization model for wireless body area networks. In: 2015 International Conference on Protocol Engineering (ICPE) and International Conference on New Technologies of Distributed Systems (NTDS), pp. 1–5 (2015). https://doi.org/10.1109/NOTERE.2015.7293512
14. Latré, B., et al.: A low-delay protocol for multihop wireless body area networks. In: 2007 Fourth Annual International Conference on Mobile and Ubiquitous Systems: Networking Services (MobiQuitous), pp. 1–8 (2007). https://doi.org/10.1109/MOBIQ.2007.4451060
15. Laurie, H., Xinheng, W., Tao, C.: A review of protocol implementations and energy efficient cross-layer design for wireless body area networks. Sensors **12**(11), 14730 (2012). https://doi.org/10.3390/s121114730. https://www.mdpi.com/1424-8220/12/11/14730
16. Quwaider, M., Biswas, S.: (2008) Physical context detection using wearable wireless sensor networks. In: Journal of Communications Software and Systems, vol. 4 (2008). https://doi.org/10.24138/jcomss.v4i3.219

17. Movassaghi, S., Abolhasan, M., Lipman, J., Smith, D., Jamalipour, A.: Wireless body area networks: a survey. IEEE Commun. Surv. Tutorials **16**(3), 1658–1686 (2014). https://doi.org/10.1109/SURV.2013.121313.00064
18. Nadeem, Q., Javaid, N., Mohammad, S.N., Khan, M.Y., Sarfraz, S., Gull, M.: Simple: stable increased-throughput multi-hop protocol for link efficiency in wireless body area networks. In: 2013 Eighth International Conference on Broadband and Wireless Computing, Communication and Applications, pp. 221–226 (2013). https://doi.org/10.1109/BWCCA.2013.42
19. Naganawa, J.I., Wangchuk, K., Kim, M., Aoyagi, T., Takada, J.I.: Simulation-based scenario-specific channel modeling for wban cooperative transmission schemes. IEEE J. Biomed. Health Inf. **19**(2), 559–570 (2015). https://doi.org/10.1109/JBHI.2014.2326424
20. Ullah, F., Abdullah, A.H., Zubair, M., Rauf, W., Junaid, J., Qureshi, K.N.: The role of cross-layered designs in wireless body area network. In: EMERGING 2010 The Second International Conference on Emerging Network Intelligence (2016). https://doi.org/10.11113/jt.v78.8260
21. Xu ,W., Zhang, M., Sawchuk, A.A., Sarrafzadeh, M.: (2012) Co-recognition of human activity and sensor location via compressed sensing in wearable body sensor networks. In: 2012 Ninth International Conference on Wearable and Implantable Body Sensor Networks, pp. 124–129 (2016). https://doi.org/10.1109/BSN.2012.14

MTM-MAC: Medical Traffic Management MAC Protocol for Handling Healthcare Applications in WBANs

Rim Negra[1]([✉]), Imen Jemili[1,2], Abdelfettah Belghith[1,3], and Mohamed Mosbah[4]

[1] ENSI, University of Manouba, 2010 Manouba, Tunisia
rim.negra@gmail.com
[2] Bizerte Faculty of Science, University of Carthage, Carthage, Tunisia
[3] College of Computer and Information Sciences, Riyadh, Saudi Arabia
[4] Bordeaux INP, Bordeaux, France

Abstract. Wireless Body Area Networks (WBANs), designed especially for healthcare applications require a strict guarantee of quality of service (QoS), in terms of latency, error rate and reliability. Generally, medical applications have different kinds of data traffic which may be classified into periodic, urgent or on-demand. Each type has its own requirements and constraints. The IEEE 802.15.6 WBAN specific standard, designed especially to handle healthcare applications, proposes different channel access mechanisms and superframe structures but does not specify how to handle the different types of medical traffic. The present paper describes MTM-MAC protocol, a new traffic aware MAC protocol which adapts the IEEE 8021.15.6 and exploit network context-awareness to satisfy the specific requirements of each traffic type. Through simulations, the proposed protocol proved its efficiency in comparison with IEEE 802.15.6 in terms of delay, energy and throughput.

Keywords: Wireless Body Area Networks · Traffic-awareness · Reliability · Context-awareness · Medical traffic

1 Introduction

Recently, Wireless Body Area Networks (WBANs) have emerged as a key enabling low cost technology for provisioning of healthcare applications. A WBAN is a collection of low-power, miniaturized and invasive/non-invasive lightweight bio sensors, which are collecting vital signs, such as heartbeat, body temperature and blood pressure, for a remote or a local process by the Body Node Coordinator (BNC). In ubiquitous WBAN environments, sensor nodes may request different channel resources under different scenarios. For example, within the monitoring context of a patient with heart disease, many vital signs could be transmitted with the same priority for a daily data collection. When this patient is doing exercise and suffers from potential danger to his/her health, heart rate

M. R. Palattella et al. (Eds.): ADHOC-NOW 2019, LNCS 11803, pp. 483–497, 2019.
https://doi.org/10.1007/978-3-030-31831-4_33

and Electrocardiography (ECG) signals are most time-critical and should be transmitted in a real-time manner. In such scenario, real-time transmission of other unconcerned data, like blood glucose or Electroencephalography (EEG) signals, is usually not necessary. Thus, the medical traffic in WBANs has several aspects. In fact, data generated by bio sensors in health monitoring are correlated with each other. For example, if a patient falls sick due to fever, his/her body temperature will rise together with heart rate and possibly blood pressure [16]. Besides, it is heterogeneous since each sensor may have a different data rate, a different context priority, etc. In fact, WBANs are usually designed for supporting medical applications generating different kinds of traffic, having various constraints and requirements. This medical traffic is generally classified into three categories: Periodic, urgent and on-demand. The periodic traffic is the data collected periodically in normal conditions. The urgent traffic is relative to critic situations and occurs when sensors data is out of normal ranges. The on-demand traffic is initiated generally by the BNC to collect additional information from bio sensors in ambiguous situations. For developing WBAN medical applications, several technologies can be adopted [18]. Yet, the standard IEEE 802.15.6 [1] was primarily established for healthcare promotion. It proposes a superframe structure with different sub periods and different channel access mechanisms to support heterogeneous traffics, but does not specify how to handle the different types of medical traffic with these available resources. Besides, since its appearance on 2012, the different features of the IEEE 802.15.6, especially MAC ones, are still under analysis and performance evaluations [2,4,8,17]. In addition, the IEEE 802.15.6 standard does not specify any retransmission strategy.

However, due to the sensitivity and criticality of the data carried and handled by WBANs, achieving a reliable network communication is crucial, mainly in emergency situations, as any packet loss could be fatal. In fact, several external factors may degrade the network reliability such as packets collision during contention phases, interference, channel deep fading or body shadowing caused by user postures changes and body movements. Through context-awareness paradigm, the system can adjust itself to user preferences and perform tasks according to the user nature. Moreover, the more knowledge an application has of each user and his/her context, the better it can adapt itself to assist that user [13]. In this context, depending on network and nodes constraints, we try to adapt the nodes behavior to fit with each traffic kind in order to satisfy its specific requirements.

Our main focus in this paper is to adapt the IEEE 802.15.6 standard by leveraging its proposed sub periods and channel mechanisms to appropriately handle the three kinds of medical traffic. The main contributions in this paper are:

- Exploit the different access mechanisms and the proposed sub periods of IEEE 802.15.6 standard in order to handle the heterogeneity of the different sensor kinds.
- Adapt the MAC mechanisms to the context of the heterogeneous sensors in order to support the three kinds of traffic relative to medical applications (Periodic, Urgent and On demand) and satisfy their QoS needs.

– Optimize the use of the network resources by minimizing the unnecessary management packets and adjusting the length of the different subperiods.

The structure of the following paper is as follow. In Sect. 2, we provide a general highlight of the IEEE 802.15.6 standard, especially MAC mechanisms. In Sect. 3, we review the state of the art relative to traffic-aware protocols in WBANs. In Sect. 4, we introduce our traffic-aware MAC protocol. We evaluate its performances in Sect. 5. Finally, we conclude the paper.

2   IEEE 802.15.6 Standard

IEEE 802.15.6 standard covers both physical and MAC layers [1]. It defines a MAC layer supporting three Physical (PHY) layers, namely Narrow Band (NB), Ultra Wide Band (UWB) and Human Body Communication (HBC). For organizing channel access, the time axis is divided into superframes. However, the IEEE 802.15.6 network can operate in one of the following modes: (1) Beacon mode with superframes boundaries, (2) non beacon mode with superframes boundaries and (3) non beacon mode without superframe boundaries. Generally, the first mode, in which the entire channel is divided into superframe structures, is the most adopted. As exposed in Fig. 1, the superframe begins with a beacon phase, as beacons are transmitted by the hub in each superframe, except inactive ones. This phase is followed by an Exclusive Access Phase (EAP1) relative to emergency traffic, a Random Access Phase (RAP1) necessary for handling network management traffic and a Managed Access Period (MAP1) generally used for improvised, scheduled and unscheduled accesses. These periods can be repeated once within the same superframe. A second beacon B2 must be sent before a last Contention Access Phase (CAP). Any of these periods can be disabled when the hub sets them to zero, unless for RAP1. EAP periods are only reserved for the traffic having the highest user priority, mainly 7 according to the standard user priority mapping varying from 0 to 7 as depicted in Table 1. RAP and CAP periods are based on prioritized contention access, while MAP periods may be used for periodic data traffic. For these different sub periods, the IEEE 802.15.6 standard provides different access modes, which are:

Table 1. IEEE 802.15.6 user priorities

UP	Traffic designation	Frame type
0	Background (BK)	Data
1	Best Effort (BE)	Data
2	Excellent Effort (EE)	Data
3	Voice	Data
4	Video	Data
5	Medical Data or Network Control	Data or Management
6	High priority Medical Data or Network Control	Data or Management
7	Emergency or Medical Implant Event Report	Data

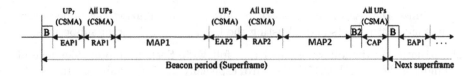

Fig. 1. IEEE 802.15.6 superframe structure

- **Random Access Mode (Contention Based)**: It uses either slotted CSMA/CA or slotted Aloha for channel access in EAP1, EAP2, RAP1, RAP2 and CAP. The size of the Contention Window (CW) is set according to the frame priority. The high priority frame uses a small CW as compared with the low priority frame.
- **Improvised, Unscheduled Access**: It is generally used for Post (a hub instruction) or Poll (a data request from the hub). During this access mode, sensor nodes must be awake and wait for a poll or post frame from the hub, before they can transmit. Improvised transfers occur in MAP1 and MAP2.
- **Scheduled Access (Contention free)**: It is relative to 1-periodic allocations where devices exchange frames with the hub in every superframe or m-periodic allocations where devices and hub exchange frames every m superframes allowing the device to sleep between transfers. In this mode, sensor nodes can start their transfer exactly on their reserved slots. Scheduled transfers occur in the MAP1 and MAP2.

Scheduled-based and contention-based MAC are the most used channel access mechanisms for such networks. A scheduled-based approach is usually more efficient in WBAN star topology than a contention-based approach. However, the complex time-varying channel in WBANs, caused by several factors such frequent body movements, are not considered in IEEE 8021.15.6. Transmitted data may sometimes suffer deep fading and cannot be detected by the receiver. Deep fading usually lasts for 10–50 ms, during which several packets can be transmitted. In a scheduled based design with continuous slots allocation, packets from one sensor may experience consecutive losses and a simple retransmission mechanism is insufficient to recover all these lost packets. In the other hand, contention access is vulnerable to packets collisions, especially with an increasing number of nodes.

3   Related Work

Work relative to WBAN traffic-awareness can be divided into three main categories. In the first category, authors adopted IEEE 802.15.4 for building their own strategies and protocols. In [9], authors proposed a traffic-aware protocol for saving network energy while considering the three kinds of traffic, namely periodic, urgent and on demand. They rely on two mechanisms: A traffic-based wakeup mechanism to accommodate normal traffic and a wakeup radio mechanism to accommodate emergency and on-demand traffic. The IEEE 802.15.4

based protocol described in [15] is based on node requirements. It dynamically modifies the duty cycle and data rate of sensor nodes in order to adapt their sampling rate and assigned bandwidth. Only two states are considered which are normal and emergency. Otherwise, the proposed protocol is only for fixed star topology and does not consider body movements and the context description is kept very general. CA-MAC [10], an hybrid Context-Aware and traffic adaptive MAC protocol, is proposed essentially to improve energy efficiency and to reduce delay. CA-MAC dynamically changes the sampling rate and the scheduled-based slots of each type of sensors and it designs a polling-based access to manage time-critical contexts. The context awareness of CA-MAC is based on channel and traffic-aware functions without taking more specific contextual information [14]. ATLAS MAC [12] is based on a multi-hop cluster topology while considering different traffic loads. The protocol modified the superframe structure of IEEE 802.15.4, however, no priority is given for traffic classes. It includes a simplified traffic load estimation technique, where the load is derived based on nodes radio capacity usage; the proposed categories of loads are: Low-load, Moderate-load, High-load and Over-load. ATLAS MAC improves energy efficiency but ignores traffic prioritization. PLA-MAC [3] modifies also the superframe structure of IEEE 802.15.4. PLA-MAC has a dynamic superframe structure depending on the variation of traffic loads. Based on the delay and reliability constraints of data packets, the protocol performs a traffic classification and combines it with sensors data generation in order to calculate the different priority and back-off values. The back-off values are used by the sensor nodes in order to perform prioritized random back off before transmitting their data packets. PLA-MAC is inefficient when dealing with traffic heterogeneity, traffic load and network synchronization.

The second category of work considers researches which have adopted the IEEE 802.15.6 reference standard. In [6], authors considered a simplified form of the IEEE 802.15.6 superframe, based only on a EAP, RAP and MAP in order to reduce complexity. MDTA-MAC [7], which is IEEE 802.15.6 based, performs traffic classification and prioritization. It classifies traffic into four classes namely: Critical data packet, Reliability-driven data packet, Delay-driven data packet and Ordinary data packets. In MDTA-MAC, traffic load is categorized as low load, moderate load, high load, and overload. MDTA-MAC modifies the IEEE 802.15.6 duty cycle and uses different frame structures depending on load type. However, this protocol offers network complexities and requires additional synchronization tasks. In CL-RRS [15], also based on IEEE 802.15.6 standard, four kinds of superframes were proposed. The switch from one kind to another is done according to predefined conditions.

Other work adopting traffic awareness adopted their own superframes. In [16], the superframe is composed of a beacon followed by a First Round Reservation Period (FRRP) and a Second Round Reservation Period (SRRP), and a Sleep Period (SP). The first round reservation period aims to transmit the periodic data. The second round is dedicated for nodes requesting to sample additional data to record the variation more accurately. The second round reservation period takes charge of the burst data transmission. In [11], based on

WBAN channel status and application context, authors proposed a MAC protocol which dynamically adjusts the transmission order and transmission duration of the nodes.

4   MTM-MAC: Medical Traffic Management MAC Protocol

In order to guarantee the required QoS for WBAN medical applications, we propose a Medical Traffic Management MAC protocol (MTM-MAC) which exploits context-awareness to acquire additional information relative the node and traffic contexts in order to improve the channel access. Our main objective is to handle the various kinds of traffic, mainly periodic, urgent and on demand, in the context of medical applications while referring to the IEEE 802.15.6 standard [1]. It assigns a different treatment based on traffic type (Periodic/Urgent) and criticality (data priority) and enhances the network reliability through recovering lost packets.

To this end, our approach requires an initialization phase, during which we collect the network information. During this phase, the superframe is composed of a beacon phase and only a RAP phase, as exposed in Fig. 2, in order to allow hub to acquire some knowledge from exchanged control packets sent by the nodes already present in the network. Each node sends a **connection request** frame including the **node context**. The **node context** represents the node's contextual information related to its application requirements, such as the traffic type (periodic/urgent), the data criticality through providing the data priority, the data rate determined by the node sampling rate and the data packet size, as illustrated in Table 2.

Table 2. MTM-MAC node's context

Feature	Description
Priority	From 0 to 7 according to Table 1
Traffic kind	Urgent or Periodic
Data size	The application payload length
First packet arrival	The reception time of the first packet from the Application Layer (only for Periodic Traffic)
Time received beacon	The beacon reception time after receiving the first packet from the Application layer (only for Periodic Traffic)
Packet rate	The node application Rate

The hub stores the context of each node in a Table called *Nodes-Table*. The structure of this table is as described in Table 3.

Then, based on the acquired contextual information, we apply the appropriate mechanisms to select the most adequate superframe structure, calculate the subperiods sizes to allow all nodes to have enough time in the adequate subperiod to send their traffic and handle appropriately each type of traffic.

Table 3. MTM-MAC Nodes-Table Structure

Fields	ConnNID	Priority	SlotLength	StartSlot	EndSlot	DataSize	FirstpktArrival
NextPktArrival	Context	IsPresent	period	bufferSize	InitialWakeup	Ack-Notification	NextWakeup

Selection of the Superframe Structures. According to MTM-MAC, the different superframe subperiods are selected relatively to number of nodes known during the initialization phase and their contexts. EAP period is available only if there is an urgent traffic, while a MAP scheduled phase is available when there is a periodic traffic on the WBAN. A MAP polling period is required when the hub needs additional information. However, a RAP period is always present in each superframe for handling management traffic. According the contextual information acquired, the network adopts one of the following superframes as illustrates in Figs. 2, 3, 4 and 5:

- **Superframe 1**: It is the superframe relative to the initialization phase. It includes only a beacon and a RAP periods as depicted in Fig. 2. The RAP period is a contention-based access period. A RAP period is always present in each superframe in order to allow new nodes to connect to the network. The length of the RAP may be estimated according to the charge of traffic as well as the events history, etc.
- **Superframe 2**: It used for general periodic traffic; this superframe is composed of a beacon, a RAP and a MAP periods as illustrated in Fig. 3. The RAP period is used for nodes slot requests or general management traffic and the MAP scheduled period allows nodes to send their frames in the reserved slots, allocated by the hub.
- **Superframe 3**: When there is an emergency traffic, we add an EAP period for emergency traffic, after the beacon period, as illustrated in Fig. 4. For the urgent traffic, the EAP is a prioritized contention based period allowed only for nodes having the highest priority.
- **Superframe 4**: When an abnormal situation occurs; i.e, a node is sending erroneous values, the BNC needs some additional information from the other communicating sensors for a better understanding of the current situation in order to resolve the network ambiguity. The superframe in this case is formed by a beacon, a MAP for the on demand traffic, an EAP, a RAP and a MAP, as depicted in Fig. 5. The MAP for on demand traffic is polling based period. Since additional information is requested by the hub, it specifies the nodes which have to be active during this MAP period. During this MAP polling phase, the hub sends a polling frame and the node sends the requested data.

Adjustment of Subperiods Lengths. In MTM-MAC, the length of the different sub periods are dynamically adjusted in order to fit with the current situation in terms of number of nodes, their relative context, etc.

EAP period, the hub dynamically calculates its length L_{EAP}, according to the number of emergency nodes in the network using the Eq. 1, where L_{EAP}

Fig. 2. Initialization superframe.

Fig. 3. General MTM-MAC super-frame

Fig. 4. General MTM-MAC super-frame with emergency traffic.

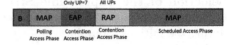

Fig. 5. General MTM-MAC super-frame in presence on demand traffic.

represents the number of slots of the EAP period. $Treq_i$ is the time required by each node, having an urgent traffic and contending to access the channel during EAP to send its frame. L_{slot} is the length of slot of the considered superframe. $Treq_i$ is calculated according to Eq. 2.

$$L_{EAP} = \lceil \frac{\sum_1^n Treq_i}{L_{slot}} \rceil \tag{1}$$

$$Treq_i = CW_{max} + T_{Data} + 2 * p_{SIFS} + T_{Ack} \tag{2}$$

Where n is the number of nodes having urgent or critic traffic, CW_{max} is the maximal back-off time before accessing to the channel, T_{Data} is the required time for sending the data and T_{Ack} is the required time for sending the acknowledgment frame. p_{SIFS} represents the time to start the transmission a frame after the reception of another one. Adjusting the length of EAP allows to guarantee enough time for the urgent nodes to send their packets and to increase the chance of successful transmissions, since this kind of traffic is correlated.

For the periodic traffic, the hub computes the slots requested by each node during MAP scheduled phase as follows:

$$T_{Ei} = T_{Data} + 2 * p_{SIFS} + T_{Ack} \tag{3}$$

Where T_{Ei} is the estimated time for a node to send one packet. The total number of slots required by a node T_{Toti} is calculated according to Eq. 4

$$T_{Toti} = \lceil \frac{T_{Ei} * \frac{L_{SF}}{Rate_i}}{L_{slot}} \rceil \tag{4}$$

Where L_{SF} is the length of the considered superframe and $Rate_i$ is the packet rate generation of the node i.

For the on demand traffic, the length of MAP polling is calculated as follows:

$$L_{MAP_{poll}} = \lceil \frac{\sum_1^m T_{Poll_i}}{L_{slot}} \rceil \tag{5}$$

$$T_{Poll_i} = T_{POLL} + p_{SIFS} + T_{Data} + 2 * p_{SIFS} + T_{Ack} \tag{6}$$

Where $L_{MAP_{poll}}$ is the total length of $MAP1$. m is the number of the designed nodes to access MAP1. T_{Poll_i} is the required time for each node allowed to access this phase to send its data. It is calculated according to Eq. 6 where T_{POLL} is the time of sending POLL frame by the hub.

Handling Traffic Types. At the end of each superframe, the hub updates the *Nodes-Table* using the information exchanged during the current superframe.Based on this information, the hub treat appropriately the different kinds of traffic of the following superframes:

Periodic Traffic: Since the majority of medical traffic is periodic, allocating slots in MAP scheduled access phase should be carried on carefully by the BNC. The slot allocation algorithm used in IEEE 802.15.6 MAC protocol is a simple algorithm with using First In First Out (FIFO) mechanism. Our dynamic slot allocation strategy (DSA) strategy allocates slots to nodes while taking into account their requirements, mainly priority, packet data arrivals, data size and traffic rates. Thus, DSA takes into account both low and high traffic rates. First, the slot allocation is based on nodes priorities. If considered nodes belong to the same priority class, the slots allocation will be according the packet generation time in order to reduce the un-avoided queuing delay in overloaded environments. In MTM-MAC, the periodicity of each node is calculated by the hub relatively to the node application data rate and the generation time of the first packet. If there is no enough slots for a node in the current superframe, the hub allocates slots for this node in the next superframe, before others. Besides, in order to enhance the network reliability, the hub allocates slots in the subsequent superframe for nodes which failed to send in the current one. When the node sends the packet in the designed slot, but the packet failed to reach the hub; certainly, the packet has to be retransmitted. But, if the hub receives correctly the frame and the node does not receive the I-ACK, the node will consider this case as a packet loss and retransmit it. In this case, the hub has to inform the node that there is not need to resend the packet thanks to the additional field called Ack-Notification, in the beacon. If this field is set to O, all frames were received correctly in the previous superframe. When it is set to 1, there is lost frames which need to be retransmitted in the current superframe. But, if the hub receives correctly the frame and the node does not receive the I-ACK, the node will consider this case as a packet loss and wants to retransmit it. In this case, the hub has to inform the node that there is not need to resend the packet.

Emergency Traffic: Meeting the constraints of emergency traffic in the presence of other traffics with diverse QoS requirements is a great challenge. The proposed MAC protocol privileges the urgent traffic over the other types of traffic. While the IEEE 802.15.6 provides a contention period EAP for the traffic with highest priority (UP=7), in MTM-MAC urgent traffic delivery approach, data is delivered instantly without any delay. If the urgent packet arrives during EAP, it contends with other nodes having (UP=7), if any. If the urgent packet arrives during RAP, it also contends with the lower priorities nodes using prioritized backoff based on a reduced contention window. When the packet arrives during an empty slot, it will be send immediately. If the packet arrives in MAP scheduled access, it can take the slots assigned to a periodic traffic node. This later can postpone its packet transmission on any empty slot in the current Superframe or sends it in the next superframe as its data is not as important as the urgent one. To allow this functional behavior, a node with periodic traffic has to wait for a guard time before sending its packet during its allocated slot. If the channel is not busy, the node begins its transmission, otherwise, it has to differ its transmission since it was preempted by a node with an urgent traffic.

On Demand Traffic: In MTM-MAC, the hub, receiving data from different sensors, analyses it in its application layer. The hub may receive a strange or an erroneous value, while other values are normal. The ambiguous value can be caused by a device breakdown, a quick variation caused by patient context change or a serious health danger. In order to avoid false alerts and confuse the medical staff, it is worth to locally treat these kinds of ambiguous situations. In such cases, the hub requests additional information from some concerned sensors in order to get a general view of the patient healthcare. In the beacon of the next superframe, the hub informs the nodes about the duration of the polling-based MAP1 and the nodes which have to be awake in this sub period. Each node, receiving a POLL message, has to provide a sample and sends it to the hub. Then, the hub tests the value. If there is more abnormal values, its sends immediately an alert to the gateway via its second interface. If all other values are normal, the hub considers this ambiguous value as temporary and non-critic.

5 MTM-MAC: Performance Evaluation

In this section, we will point out the ability of MTM-MAC protocol and its effectiveness for handling different kinds of medical traffic; we compare it with IEEE 802.15.6 MAC standard using Castalia simulator [5]. For IEEE 802.15.6, we adopt a fixed superframe, including a beacon, EAP, RAP and MAP periods. EAP period is for urgent traffic, while RAP period is for management traffic. Periodic traffic is sent only during MAP using contention free access. Simulation parameters of the IEEE 802.15.6 are summarized in Table 4.

Table 4. Simulations parameters IEEE802.15.6

Parameters	Value
EAP length	5 slots
RAP period	5 slots
Superframe length	32 slots
Slot size	10 msecs
Contention slot size	0.36 msecs
pSIFS	0.03 msecs

To validate MTM-MAC performances, we focus essentially on periodic and urgent traffics. To this end, we use the following performance metrics:

- **Packet Delivery Ratio**: It corresponds to the rate of packets delivered correctly among the packets generated by all the nodes.
- **Waiting Time**: It represents the delay spent before the transfer of a packet begins. It is measured in seconds.
- **The average energy consumed per packet**: It represents the total energy consumed divided by the total number of delivered data packets;
- **Latency (end-to-end delay)**: It is the time taken by a packet to travel from node to the hub.

We will consider one hop star topology composed of a hub and a number of nodes having periodic and/or urgent traffic, placed around the body. We realize simulations in an ideal environment and a realistic environment, prone to human body shadowing, collision and interference.

Periodic Traffic. In this scenario, we will consider only periodic traffic, mainly low and high, while varying the number of nodes during simulations. Their relatives simulation parameters are summarized in Table 5.

Table 5. Simulations parameters of periodic low and high traffic

Parameters	Value
Number of sensor nodes	1–12
Data size	10 bytes
Data rate	10 s
Priority	5
Simulation time	100 s

As exposed in Fig. 6(c) and (d), in an ideal environment, both protocols can send all the data packets correctly to the hub. However, in a non ideal environment, we observe a remarkable degradation of the packet delivery ratio for IEEE 802.15.6. Despite the throughput decrease for MTM-MAC, it still outperforms IEEE 802.15.6. From Fig. 6(c) and (d), we observe that throughput has decreased for MTM-MAC from 100% in an ideal environment to approximately 70% in a non ideal environment. Generally, shadowing caused by body movements has a big impact on the scheduled access. However, thanks to the notification acknowledgment strategy proposed by MTM-MAC, packet losses are recovered rapidly. MTM-MAC assigns additional slots in the subsequent superframe first to the nodes which have failed to transmit during the current superframe. This functional behavior contributes to enhance the waiting time as exposed in Fig. 6(a). In fact, MTM-MAC improves considerably the delay of periodic traffic. For low traffic, the average waiting time for MTM-MAC is about 0.05 s, while it is about 6 s for IEEE 802.15.6. For the high periodic traffic, the average waiting time is

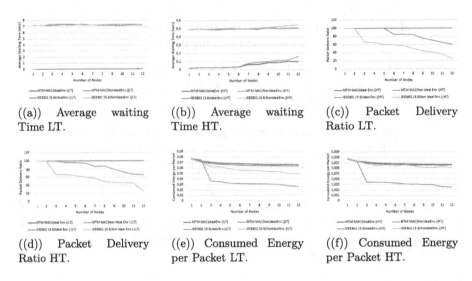

((a))   Average   waiting Time LT.

((b))   Average   waiting Time HT.

((c))   Packet   Delivery Ratio LT.

((d))   Packet   Delivery Ratio HT.

((e))   Consumed   Energy per Packet LT.

((f))   Consumed   Energy per Packet HT.

Fig. 6. Results of scenario 1 relative to low and high periodic traffics in both ideal and non ideal environments

about 0.04 s for MTM-MAC against 0.5 s for the standard. The knowledge of nodes contexts allows MTM-MAC to allocate adequately the slots in the appropriate superframes. Assigning slots based on packet priority and packet arrival times for nodes with the same priority reduces considerably the waiting time, and consequently the overall delay for both kinds of traffic. In this way, we reduce the energy waste. As illustrated in Fig. 6(e) and (f), we remark that the MTM-MAC consumed energy per packet is lower than the IEEE 802.15.6. In fact, the standard adapts a superframe with a fixed structure where periodic traffic is sent during scheduled-based MAP with a fixed size. So, with high demands, the hub may deprive some nodes to have scheduled access slots. In addition, the EAP is always present in each superframe even there is no urgent traffic. In MTM-MAC, the selection of subperiods is according to nodes context, number, etc. So, we will have only required subperiods in each superframe.

Urgent Traffic. We consider a one hop star topology with three urgent nodes and a varying number of periodic nodes. Simulations parameters of urgent traffic are summarized in Table 6.

Simulations parameters of the periodic traffic are summarized in Table 7. Results of urgent traffic simulations are summarized in Fig. 7. As illustrated in Fig. 7(a), the end to end delay for urgent traffic is considerably reduced in comparison with IEEE 802.15.6 standard. In fact, in MTM-MAC, the urgent traffic is essentially managed to be transmitted during EAP. However, it is allowed in to be transmitted during other subperiods. Thus, we observe, in Fig. 7(b), the increase of end-to-end delay for periodic traffic with the increase in the number of nodes, as allocated slots may be taken by urgent nodes and periodic nodes will have to postpone their transmissions.

Table 6. Simulations parameters of urgent traffic

Nodes	Node 1	Node 2	Node 3
Priority	7	7	7
Traffic	Urgent	Urgent	Urgent

Table 7. Simulations parameters of periodic traffic

Parameters	Value
Number of sensor nodes	0–10
Data size	10 bytes
Data rate	1 s
Priority	5

As expected, the IEEE 802.15.6 end-to-end delay of urgent traffic is much bigger than in MTM-MAC, this delay is due to the time the packets have to wait in the queue until the next EAP.

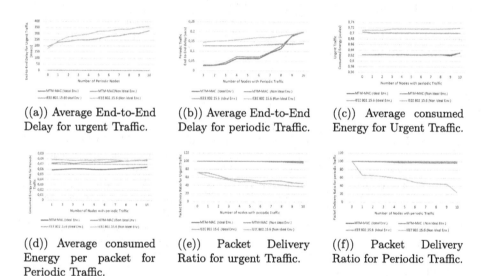

((a)) Average End-to-End Delay for urgent Traffic.

((b)) Average End-to-End Delay for periodic Traffic.

((c)) Average consumed Energy for Urgent Traffic.

((d)) Average consumed Energy per packet for Periodic Traffic.

((e)) Packet Delivery Ratio for urgent Traffic.

((f)) Packet Delivery Ratio for Periodic Traffic.

Fig. 7. Results of scenario 1 relative to urgent and periodic traffic in both ideal and non ideal environment

Figure 7(c) shows a lower energy consumption for MTM-MAC. In fact, urgent nodes in IEEE 802.15.6 consumes more energy since all the traffic is sent using contention. However, for periodic traffic, energy consumption for MTM-MAC, which is initially lower than in IEEE 802.15.6, increases slowly with the increase in the number of nodes in bad channel environments. In reality, in such conditions, the periodic nodes consume more energy due to retransmissions and additional waiting times, as we privilege the urgent nodes to access during their reserved slots. Besides, periodic nodes have to retransmit their packets in case of loss due to body shadowing. Hence, in Fig. 7(f), we observe a slight decrease in the packet delivery ratio for periodic traffic which is initially 100%, while it is always 100 % for urgent traffic in both channel environments. In contrary, we observe a packet delivery ratio varying from 80% to 40% in IEEE 802.15.6 for this critic traffic.

6 Conclusion

Guaranteeing reliability in WBAN is crucial task due to several factors such as the channel characterization, the channel conditions, the nodes heterogeneity, etc. In order to achieve the required level of reliability in such networks and enhance the overall network performances, MTM-MAC assigns the appropriate treatment to each traffic types, mainly periodic, urgent and on demand. the key strategy of MTM-MAC protocol is to acquire knowledge about node context then exploit these information for realizing a dynamic superframe structure and a personalized treatment. The proposed protocol satisfies the WBAN medical traffic while adopting the IEEE 802.15.6 mechanisms. Performance evaluation showed that MTM-MAC protocol outperforms the IEEE 802.15.6 standard in terms of delay, energy and throughput.

References

1. http://www.ieee802.org/15/pub/TG6.html
2. An, N., Wang, P., Yi, C., Li, Y.: Performance analysis of CSMA/CA based on the IEEE 802.15. 6 MAC protocol. In: 2013 15th IEEE International Conference on Communication Technology (ICCT), pp. 539–544. IEEE (2013)
3. Anjum, I., Alam, N., Razzaque, M.A., Mehedi Hassan, M., Alamri, A.: Traffic priority and load adaptive MAC protocol for QoS provisioning in body sensor networks. Int. J. Distrib. Sens. Netw. 9(3), 205192 (2013)
4. Benmansour, T., Ahmed, T., Moussaoui, S.: Performance evaluation of IEEE 802.15. 6 MAC in monitoring of a cardiac patient. In: 2016 IEEE 41st Conference on Local Computer Networks Workshops (LCN Workshops), pp. 241–247. IEEE (2016)
5. Boulis. http://castalia.npc.nicta.com.au/
6. Fukuya, T., Kohno, R.: QoS-aware superframe management scheme based on IEEE 802.15. 6. In: 2016 10th International Symposium on Medical Information and Communication Technology (ISMICT), pp. 1–4. IEEE (2016)
7. Hossain, M.U., Kalyan, M., Rana, M.R., Rahman, M.O., et al.: Multi-dimensional traffic adaptive energy-efficient MAC protocol for wireless body area networks. In: 2014 9th International Forum on Strategic Technology (IFOST), pp. 161–165. IEEE (2014)
8. Khan, P., Ullah, N., Ullah, S., Kwak, K.S.: Analytical modeling of IEEE 802.15. 6 CSMA/CA protocol under different access periods. In: 2014 14th International Symposium on Communications and Information Technologies (ISCIT), pp. 151–155. IEEE (2014)
9. Kwak, K.S., Ullah, S.: A traffic-adaptive MAC protocol for WBAN. In: 2010 IEEE Globecom Workshops, pp. 1286–1289. IEEE (2010)

10. Liu, B., Yan, Z., Chen, C.W.: CA-MAC: a hybrid context-aware MAC protocol for wireless body area networks. In: 2011 13th IEEE International Conference on e-Health Networking Applications and Services (Healthcom), pp. 213–216. IEEE (2011)

11. Liu, B., Yan, Z., Chen, C.W.: Medium access control for wireless body area networks with QoS provisioning and energy efficient design. IEEE Trans. Mob. Comput. **16**(2), 422–434 (2017)

12. Rahman, M.O., Hong, C.S., Lee, S., Bang, Y.C.: Atlas: a traffic load aware sensor MAC design for collaborative body area sensor networks. Sensors **11**(12), 11560–11580 (2011)

13. Tentori, M., Favela, J., Rodriguez, M.D.: Privacy-aware autonomous agents for pervasive healthcare. IEEE Intell. Syst. **21**(6), 55–62 (2006)

14. Tobón, D.P., Falk, T.H., Maier, M.: Context awareness in WBANs: a survey on medical and non-medical applications. IEEE Wirel. Commun. **20**(4), 30–37 (2013)

15. Tseng, H.W., Wu, R.Y., Wu, Y.Z., Chou, S.C.: An efficient cross-layer reliable retransmission scheme for the human body shadowing in IEEE 802.15. 6-based wireless body sensor networks. In: Proceedings of the 2015 Conference on Research in Adaptive and Convergent Systems, pp. 216–222. ACM (2015)

16. Yang, L., Li, C., Song, Y., Yuan, X.: An energy-efficient 2r MAC based on IEEE 802.15. 6 for health monitoring. In: 2015 IEEE Globecom Workshops (GC Wkshps), pp. 1–6. IEEE (2015)

17. Yang, L., Li, C., Song, Y., Yuan, X., Lei, Y.: Performance evaluation of IEEE 802.15. 6 MAC with user priorities for medical applications. In: Park, J., Pan, Y., Kim, C., Yang, Y. (eds.) Future Information Technology-II. Lecture Notes in Electrical Engineering, vol. 329, pp. 233–240. Springer, Dordrecht (2015). https://doi.org/10.1007/978-94-017-9558-6_27

18. Yuce, M.R., Khan, J.: Wireless Body Area Networks: Technology, Implementation, and Applications. CRC Press, Boca Raton (2011)

Secure Provisioning for Achieving End-to-End Secure Communications

Patrícia R. Sousa(✉), João S. Resende, Rolando Martins, and Luís Antunes

DCC-FCUP/CRACS-INESC TEC, Porto, Portugal
{patricia.sousa,jresende,rmartins,lfa}@fc.up.pt

Abstract. The growth of the Internet of Things (IoT) is raising significant impact in several contexts, e.g., in cities, at home, and even attached to the human body. This digital transformation is happening at a high pace and causing a great impact in our daily lives, namely in our attempt to make cities smarter in an attempt to increase their efficiency while reducing costs and increasing safety. However, this effort is being supported by the massive deployment of sensors throughout cities worldwide, leading to increase concerns regarding security and privacy. While some of these issues have already been tackled, device authentication remains without a viable solution, specially when considering a resilient decentralized approach that is the most suitable for this scenario, as it avoids some issues related to centralization, e.g., censorship and data leakage or profit from corporations. The provisioning is usually an arduous task that encompasses device configuration, including identity and key provisioning. Given the potential large number of devices, this process must be scalable and semi-autonomous, at least. This work presents a novel approach for provisioning IoT devices that adopts an architecture where other device acts as a manager that represents a CA, allowing it to be switched on/off during the provisioning phase to reduce single point of failure (SPOF) problems. Our solution combines One Time Password (OTP) on a secure token and cryptographic algorithms on a hybrid authentication system.

1 Introduction

Internet of Things (IoT) is an umbrella concept detailing how technology will interact with users in the coming years. The highly paced technological development surrounding it is exposing several novel challenges, namely on privacy and security. In particular, there is a need to adopt secure solutions for IoT devices characteristics due to their intrinsic limitations [1] (e.g., battery life and memory space). Among the set of security and privacy requirements necessary to securely support IoT, we highlight the user and device identity management, authentication, the confidentiality of data exchanged in communications, network access control to allow only authorized devices, and the availability of resources and systems [2].

© Springer Nature Switzerland AG 2019
M. R. Palattella et al. (Eds.): ADHOC-NOW 2019, LNCS 11803, pp. 498–507, 2019.
https://doi.org/10.1007/978-3-030-31831-4_34

Most past systems base their identity and authentication through the use of Public Key Infrastructure (PKI) [3]. However, there are known limitations of this technology as it depends on a centralized Certification Authority (CA), which once compromised, the entire system is compromised as well. On top of this, many security and privacy issues are caused by human configuration errors [19], and to solve them, we need systems with better interfaces to users and better tools to help with the provision of new devices.

Nowadays, PKI-based solutions are still unable to provide security by default, as systems rely on user-provided security through manual device provisioning configurations. For this reason, the paper presents a decentralized secure device-to-device communications solution in which device provisioning is focused on improving usability while providing security by default. The solution focuses on the use of a PKI where the CA is represented by a manager device that can be switched on/off to reduce single point of failure (SPOF) problems. Our solution combines public key cryptography and symmetric keys with the One Time Password (OTP) concept using a secure token. Device identity is guaranteed by physical access to this physical token. In addition to generating an OTP, the physical token also stores a public key to be transmitted to target devices only, eliminating attacks such as impersonation or man-in-the-middle. It also improves usability as we exclude configuration errors and difficulty choosing the right settings while provisioning the device. Although there is manual interaction to use the secure token, the process itself, is as simple as finding the device to be provisioned and plugging in the secure token.

Section 2 presents the related work with some systems related with our approach. Section 3 describes an overview of the proposed system and the characteristics of the system. The implementation details of the system is described in Sect. 4. Section 5 defines a threat model and an attack model, in order to see the vulnerabilities from the point of view of defender's and attacker's. Lastly, Sect. 6 presents the conclusions of this work and some future work.

2 Related Work

There are many applications that provide identity, authentication and authorization across multiple contexts.

PKI provides important core authentication technologies for IoT. A study by *Ponemon* [11] claims that, 42% of devices will continue to use digital certificates for authentication and identification in the next two years. The *SSL/TLS* [13] or *Kerberos* [12] are some examples of authentication systems based on a PKI.

Some of the current solutions have scalability limitations regarding their authentication protocols. For example, the author Sousa et al. [15] solves peer-to-peer authentication in a decentralized way by using Short Authentication Strings, but it does not scale well for multiple devices (M-to-N authentication).

The following papers from the authors Solano et al. [14] and Hirmer et al. [16] are focused on the provisioning of IoT devices but are not focused on usability, because the authors propose manual solutions where all device data must be entered manually by the users.

There are several end-to-end solutions more related with OTP solutions. Some of them, are based on temporary passwords and/or unique numbers (OTP-based solutions [4–6], for example), as well as Physically Unclonable Functions (PUF)-based solutions [7,8]). Kelly et al. [5] claim that IoT devices with single factor authentication are not sufficient for secure communication. A solution presented by Shivraj et al. [4] creates a lightweight, robust and scalable OTP technique developed by using the principles of IBE-Elliptic Curves Cryptography (ECC) allowing two-factor authentication. The work done in [6] also has an authentication through OTP to the application level information security.

3   System Overview

This section describes all components of the architecture, as well as the different phases to achieve a decentralized secure end-to-end communications. The description includes the provisioning phase, authentication mechanisms and scalability extension.

3.1   Manager Setup Phase

The manager device represents the system CA that plays an essential role in a certification system by signing public keys (or certificates). This device should be assumed to be trusted and controlled only by trusted persons (such as the network owner). All certificates signed by the device will be implicitly trusted. Currently, systems that manage a PKI require a high degree of security and are installed on an isolated machine. In this proposed system, the PKI is installed on the manager device that is hybrid, meaning it may be offline from the network when not in use, to prevent the possibility of the private key being stolen in a possible network intrusion.

For added security, the manager device can use Intel SGX [22] in order to secure all the cryptographic assets in a Trusted Execution Environment (TEE).

The manager begins by setting a CA using 256-bit Elliptic Curve Digital Signature Algorithm (ECDSA) and a 256-bit Elliptic Curve Integrated Encryption Scheme (ECIES) key pair to generate a shared key without the need for Diffie-Hellman exchange. This option was chosen because the ECC is better for low resource devices as ECC requires fewer resources and provides the same level of security as Rivest-Shamir-Adlema (RSA) cryptography with a smaller key [17]. In brief, it is possible to use RSA also at this stage, but as the focus of the approach is on IoT, ECC was chosen.

The manager device also features an OTP manager for allowing authentication through the use of a secure token, i.e., "something that you have". It works like a key to a door in a house where the key holder has access to the house. For this reason, anyone who has access to this secure token can authenticate with the manager. This secure token is not limited to generating OTPs, as the idea is also to store the manager's public key for transmission to trusted devices.

3.2   Alice and Bob Device Authentication

The authentication between a new device and the manager is essential for ensuring that it is added to the trusted device pool. To do this, the owner inserts the secure token into the target device and then the new device is added to the pool (Alice and Bob device) (Fig. 1).

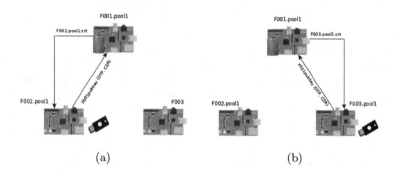

Fig. 1. Alice (a) and Bob (b) Device authentication

As previously described, the secure token also has the manager's device public key. The new device starts by sending the Certificate Signing Request (CSR) of itself (which contains only the public key, not the private key, so the private key has not been compromised). When the new device sends the CSR to the manager, the later will produce a signed x509 Certificate. Furthermore, it also sends OTP to verify that the new device is in physical presence with the secure token and is therefore the correct device to authenticate. All this information is sent encrypted with the shared key (ECDHE) generated for both parties (client and manager) to encrypt a message that can only be decrypted by the manager. After the authentication is successful, the manager device sends back the signed certificate to certify that the client is a secure device that can be added to the trusted device pool. These certificates are used to establish trust between client devices and provide decentralized secure communication between them without the intervention of the manager device.

3.3   Unique Service Name

The manager needs to have a well-known service domain to offer to their users so that he can be discovered by them. At first, only the manager has his URL like identifier (Unique Service Name (USN)) along with the domain "pool1" chosen only for example purposes in this paper. USN is a unique identifier that serves to uniquely identify a specific service to allow identical services to be differentiated. Once a device is authenticated with the manager, it gains its domain, and therefore the USN is modified from "F002" to "F002.pool1", for example, to add the domain to which it now belongs. Thus, for example, when the device "F001.pool1" wants to communicate with the "F002.pool1", it can use a peer discovery protocol Simple Service Discovery Protocol (SSDP), to discover the device with this USN to authenticate with it.

3.4   Decentralized Secure End-to-End Communications

After the discovery process, devices need to authenticate with each other. For mutual trust, both devices must exchange manager's signed certificates. After verifying the authenticity of certificates, a symmetric key is generated between both devices to establish secure communication.

Symmetric key generation needs authentication so that the nodes know each other. ECDSA was chosen for signing and verification and ECIES was chosen for encryption. Then, Diffie-Hellman Ephemeral (DHE) or Elliptic-curve Diffie-Hellman Ephemeral (ECDHE) is used for key exchange. Ephemeral mode is important because if the key pair is used for more than a few hours, it must be stored somewhere because devices can be turned off. There is always some risk that a stored key pair may be compromised, although a wide variety of methods can be and are used to mitigate this issue. This mode avoids this type of attack by not storing key pairs and generating a new key pair every millisecond, thus ensuring Perfect Forward Secrecy.

After the establishment of a shared secret using ECDHE, the devices can exchange data with symmetric encryption using the secure cipher AES256 to encrypt messages.

When all devices are provisioned, the manager can be turned off until a new device needs to be added to the pool or there is a change on the device pool, such as certificate revocation or renewal.

3.5   Merge Two Trusted Devices Pools

An identity and authentication system must be flexible and highly scalable enough to handle billions of device infrastructures in multiple environments such as smart home and smart cities in general. This system must support different types of environments, given the heterogeneity of applicability that exists in IoT scenarios.

For greater scalability, there needs to be a usable way to integrate different device pools to make the system more practical as it would not be feasible to re-provision devices already provisioned with another manager, so that devices from different pools can communicate with each other.

To address this issue, the system replicates the traditional mechanisms of having multiple CAs supported by a client. It is essential to ensure two points to deploy this in a real world configuration: Use a secure token authentication scheme to enable enrollment and trust between different managers; and information dissemination on new pools among all new devices.

To allow two pools to connect to each other, the authentication between managers (Fig. 2 in 1) uses the same mechanism described in (Sect. 3.1). After

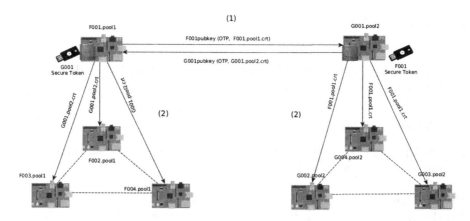

Fig. 2. Trust between two device pools

both managers perform mutual authentication, the next step is to spread the information across devices among different pools. To do this, the manager must send the signed and encrypted information to the devices. This allows any of the devices to read the information and verify the manager's signature. Figure 2 represents the agreement between both managers and the corresponding spread of information from managers to their peers when they begin to trust each other and can announce on the network that others should move to include these new trusted colleagues in their trusted network.

4   Implementation

In order to implement the system, it is used *Raspberry PI*'s to represent all devices and the secure token is represented by the Yubikey NEO and USB pen drive. The OTP generator is the Yubikey NEO and the USB pen drive replicates the extra storage that contains the public key.

The secure token needs to be configured with the manager's public key and with an OTP server. The manager's public key is generated through ECDSA based on a GitHub repository [21]. The OTP Server is represented by *privacyIDEA* [9] that is a modular authentication system. To enroll the secure token on *privacyIDEA*, it is used a test account and the *"Enroll Token"* in the *"Yubico AES mode: One Time Passwords with Yubikey"* option. This system allows the administrator to revoke or disable registered tokens so that there is a security guarantee in case of stealing or losing tokens.

After the enrollment, it is possible to authenticate with the secure token. The exchange of OTP and public key to authenticate is done through ECIES. The implementation is based on a Python implementation - *Elliptic Curve Integrated Encryption Scheme (ECIES) with Rabbit* [18].

For the device-to-device authentication, it is implemented the ECDHE algorithm.

5   Security Analysis

In this section, it is defined a threat and an attack model with a security analysis of the proposal, exploring the vulnerabilities from the defender's and attacker's point of view.

5.1   Threat Model

From the defender's perspective, this section identifies system (assets) and potential threats against the proposed system.

Physical Devices

The device manager acts as a dynamic validation point in the device provisioning phase. Devices must be reliable to ensure that they are not broken or stolen. The network owner is supposed to avoid exposing the device. In addition, the fact that it is not an Internet-wide exposed CA and that it is possible to turn off the manager when there are no new peers to join the network, makes it less exposed to potential attacks eliminating the SPOF.

If the secure token is used as a first factor authentication, it means that all accounts configured with this token are vulnerable to theft of that physical token. To mitigate this situation, it is possible to revoke the secure token on the OTP manager if it is lost and with an expiration time.

Cloning a device is a problem for current IoT devices. When there is a physical access to any device, security can be compromised. Current research challenges are focusing on deploying trust zones (such as Intel SGX), where parts of the code can safely compute secrets and store authentication keys and device identity. Future work will focus on this to mitigate and ensure device integrity.

On the other hand, using secure token helps protect against hacking as physical access to the secure token is required to generate OTP.

Unique Service Name

A USN is theoretically easily changeable and it is possible for an attacker to register a fake name to impersonate another device. However, in this proposal, the attacker must have a certificate signed by the manager to ensure that the USN belongs to him, in addition to changing the USN, to be able to impersonate another device.

Configurations for Mitigation of Attacks

There is an option in *privacyIDEA* which is the Maximum Fail Counter to avoid brute force attacks when an authentication request occurs. If the fail-counter exceeds this number, the token cannot be used unless the fail-counter is reset. This system has a fail counter of 5 and this option must be manually reset to prevent this type of Brute Force attack.

5.2   Attack Scenarios

This section identifies attack modeling from an attacker's point of view to analyze how the system could be exploited in terms of vulnerabilities in IoT solutions.

Tag impersonation attacks are safe because the secure token generates OTPs and also stores the manager's public key for transmission to trusted devices. This prevents the manager from being impersonated even if the attacker could change his name. An attacker must have their data (authenticated OTP and its public key) in the physical secure token, which is impractical.

Also, the system is safe from replay attacks because the secure token uses a set of volatile and non-volatile counters that ensures that an OTP can no longer be used after validating once [10].

For man-in-the-middle attacks, there are two options: unknown peers and peers that are already authenticated. The first issue is resolved because this approach uses a secure token with the receiver's public key, so it is transmitted only over USB. This mitigates the unknown attacker's access to the public key. For authenticated peers, as already described in the replay attack, the problem is solved using an OTP that can no longer be used after validating once [10].

6   Conclusions and Future Work

This work presents a design and implementation of a new approach to IoT device provisioning, giving an identity to a *thing*, eliminating the risk of impersonating attacks and allowing devices to be authenticate. In addition, in terms of security, the single point of failure problem is mitigated with a hybrid solution to allow the manager device to shut down when not needed.

Device provisioning is based on a secure token proposed in this paper. In addition to generating an OTP, this secure token stores a public key to be transmitted only to the target devices, to improve security.

Although using a secure token requires a USB port, it can be adapted to other technology such as RFID or similar. However, given the study by authors *Singh, Kiran Jot, and Divneet Singh Kapoor* [20], there are USB ports on most devices that are used in IoT.

This work proves the feasibility of the solution by presenting a wide range of options needed in order to be deployed in real-world scenarios.

In future work, we plan to deploy this architecture on a Porto street to fully understand the impact on IoT devices in a smart city deployment. It is necessary to analyze the energy impact of the solution on low resource devices and measure authentication latency between devices. Revocation and information dissemination protocols should be developed and tested in a real environment to analyze the associated capacity and delay.

Acknowledgment. This work of Patrícia R. Sousa and João S. Resende was supported by Fundação para a Ciência e Tecnologia (FCT), Portugal
(SFRH/BD/135696/2018, PD/BD/128149/2016).

This work is financed by National Funds through the Portuguese funding agency, FCT - Fundação para a Ciência e a Tecnologia within projects: UID/EEA/50014/2019 and CMU/CS/0042/2017.

This work has been supported by the EU H2020-SU-ICT-03-2018 Project No. 830929 CyberSec4Europe (cybersec4europe.eu).

References

1. Yang, Y., et al.: A survey on security and privacy issues in Internet-of-Things. IEEE Internet Things J. **4**(5), 1250–1258 (2017)
2. Sundmaeker, H., Guillemin, P., Friess, P., Woelffle, P.: Vision and challenges for realising the Internet of Things. Cluster Eur. Res. Proj. Internet Things **3**(3), 34–36 (2010)
3. Kuhn, D.R., et al.: Introduction to public key technology and the federal PKI infrastructure. National Inst of Standards and Technology Gaithersburg MD (2001)
4. Shivraj, V.L., et al.: One time password authentication scheme based on elliptic curves for Internet of Things (IoT). In: 2015 5th National Symposium on Information Technology: Towards New Smart World (NSITNSW). IEEE (2015)
5. Kelly, D., Hammoudeh, M.: Optimisation of the public key encryption infrastructure for the nternet of things. In: Proceedings of the 2nd International Conference on Future Networks and Distributed Systems. ACM (2018)
6. Rajagopalan, S., et al.: IoT framework for secure medical image transmission. In: 2018 International Conference on Computer Communication and Informatics (ICCCI). IEEE (2018)
7. Aman, M.N., Chua, K.C., Sikdar, B.: Physically secure mutual authentication for IoT. In: 2017 IEEE Conference on Dependable and Secure Computing. IEEE (2017)
8. Aman, M.N., Chua, K.C., Sikdar, B.: Mutual authentication in IoT systems using physical unclonable functions. IEEE Internet Things J. **4**(5), 1327–1340 (2017)
9. Kolbel, C.: privacyIDEA Authentication System, Release 2.17. Accessed 23 Jan 2017
10. Popp, N.: Token authentication system and method. U.S. Patent No. 8,639,628. Accessed 28 Jan 2014
11. Ponemon, 2018 global PKI trends study. https://bit.ly/2EEkQjJ. Accessed 13 Nov 2018
12. Neuman, B.C., Ts'o, T.: Kerberos: an authentication service for computer networks. IEEE Commun. Mag. **32**(9), 33–38 (1994)
13. Rescorla, E.: SSL and TLS: Designing and Building Secure Systems. Addison-Wesley, Reading (2001)
14. Solano, A., et al.: A self-provisioning mechanism in OpenStack for IoT devices. Sensors **16**(8), 1306 (2016)
15. Sousa, P.R., et al.: pTASC: trustable autonomous secure communications. In: 20th International Conference on Distributed Computing and Networking (2019)
16. Hirmer, P., et al.: Automating the provisioning and configuration of devices in the Internet of Things. CSIMQ **9**, 28–43 (2016)
17. Gueron, S., Krasnov, V.: Fast prime field elliptic-curve cryptography with 256-bit primes. J. Cryptogr. Eng. **5**(2), 141–151 (2015)
18. Elliptic Curve Integrated Encryption Scheme (ECIES) with Rabbit. https://bit.ly/2JPoNGv. Accessed 29 May 2019

19. Hwang, Y.H.: Iot security & privacy: threats and challenges. In: Proceedings of the 1st ACM Workshop on IoT Privacy, Trust, and Security. ACM (2015)
20. Singh, K.J., Kapoor, D.S.: Create your own Internet of Things: a survey of IoT platforms. IEEE Consum. Electron. Mag. **6**(2), 57–68 (2017)
21. A set of tools and scripts useful to learn the basics about Elliptic Curve Cryptography (2015). https://github.com/andreacorbellini/ecc. Accessed 29 July 2019
22. Brekalo, H., Strackx, R., Piessens, F.: Mitigating password database breaches with Intel SGX. In: Proceedings of the 1st Workshop on System Software for Trusted Execution. ACM, New York (2016)

An Intrusion Detection System for the OneM2M Service Layer Based on Edge Machine Learning

Nadia Chaabouni[1,2]([✉]), Mohamed Mosbah[1], Akka Zemmari[1],
and Cyrille Sauvignac[2]

[1] Univ. Bordeaux, CNRS, Bordeaux INP, LaBRI, UMR 5800, 33400 Talence, France
chaabouni.nadia14@gmail.com, {mosbah,zemmari}@u-bordeaux.fr
[2] Atos Innovation Aquitaine Lab - Atos, 33600 Pessac, France
cyrille.sauvignac@atos.net

Abstract. The number of connected Things is growing at a frantic pace, which has led to vertical, proprietary Internet of Things (IoT) solutions. To ensure a horizontal IoT cross-industry interoperability, eight of the word's leading ICT standards bodies introduce the oneM2M standard. Its main goal is to satisfy the need for a common M2M Service Layer that guarantees the communication between heterogeneous devices and applications. Various security mechanisms have been proposed in the oneM2M specifications to protect the IoT solutions. As a complementary security level, we propose the first generic Intrusion Detection System (IDS) for the oneM2M Service Layer based on Edge Machine Leaning (ML). This oneM2M-IDS can be added to the basic architecture of oneM2M or can be added as a plugin to existing systems based on oneM2M. In this work, we define and implement oneM2M attack scenarios related to the service availability. Moreover, we propose an edge IDS architecture and we detail ML features selection. The performance of the proposed IDS is studied through multiple experiments with different ML algorithms.

Keywords: Internet of Things · IoT · Standardization · OneM2M standard · Security · Intrusion detection · IDS · Machine learning · ML

1 Introduction

OneM2M [20] is a global standard initiative designed to converge towards an horizontal common platform for the multi-industry M2M applications such as e-Health, intelligent transportation, industrial automation, smart homes, etc. Today, many industries from different sectors rely on proprietary solutions with customized hardwares and softwares for Machine-To-Machine (M2M) systems hence Internet of Things (IoT) applications. Such vertical, mono-industry solutions reinvent the wheel independently with non-interoperable technologies. Hence, eight of the word's leading ICT standards bodies [20] initiated the international partnership project oneM2M in 2012. OneM2M main goal is to satisfy the

M. R. Palattella et al. (Eds.): ADHOC-NOW 2019, LNCS 11803, pp. 508–523, 2019.
https://doi.org/10.1007/978-3-030-31831-4_35

need for a common M2M Service Layer which enables the communication of heterogeneous devices and applications with each other, regardless of their manufacturer or technical specifications with no need to redevelop common components. Therefore, deploying IoT and M2M solutions becomes less expensive in terms of money, time and complexity. It is important to mention that oneM2M takes into consideration the existing worldwide networks and standards. It extends and standardizes the IoT ecosystem by interworking with other standards and protocols like Open Mobile Alliance (OMA) [4] and Message Queuing Telemetry Transport (MQTT) [1] as a protocol.

The pervasive growth of IoT across the globe has not only affected the security of IoT, but has also threatened the complete Internet ecosystem including web-sites, applications, social networks and servers. Therefore, one of the main concerns of researchers and industrialists is the security of IoT systems. Since oneM2M is an international standard for IoT, its security implies the security of the IoT ecosystem. Hence, we focus our work on the security aspect of the oneM2M standard. Besides the various described security specifications in oneM2M [19], our approach does not only provide security threats avoidance but also enables attacks detection. We propose the first generic intrusion detection system (IDS) for the oneM2M Service Layer based on Edge Machine Learning (ML). Generic in our case indicates that the IDS is independent of the implementation of the oneM2M standard. This oneM2M-IDS can be added to the basic architecture of oneM2M or can be added as a plugin to existing systems based on oneM2M. Such an IDS enables a fast threats detection (as soon as they are carried out) so that the actions can be taken before the system is affected. We choose to use ML techniques since they show better detection results in IDS state of art [5] compared to the traditional IDS. We propose an edge intelligence to guarantee a lightweight detection since we are in the IoT context.

This paper offers the following contributions: (i) we propose the first generic IDS for the oneM2M Service Layer based on Edge ML; (ii) We define oneM2M Service Layer attacks as well as different related scenarios (for the dataset creation); (iii) We provide a standard abstraction of the oneM2M flows to enable IoT security datasets creation.

The rest of the paper is structured in five sections. Section 2 presents an overview of the oneM2M standard: its architecture and the specified security measures. Then, in Sect. 3, we cite some works related to the IoT IDS. We explain the importance of an IDS by defining a set of oneM2M attack scenarios related to the service availability in oneM2M. Moreover, we present our attacks taxonomy and implementation. Furthermore, we detail, in Sect. 4, our oneM2M-IDS proposal; its ML approach and its integration to the oneM2M architecture. In Sect. 5, we present our evaluation environment as well as the ML experiments and results. Finally, we end our paper with a conclusion and future directions.

2 OneM2M Standard

OneM2M project defines a set of specifications for the standardization approach. It covers architecture details, security mechanisms, communication protocols, etc. In this section, we focus on the oneM2M architecture and its security.

2.1 OneM2M Architecture

The functional architecture of oneM2M is mainly composed of three layers as presented in Fig. 1. First, the application layer provides functions related to the logic of the end-to-end M2M applications (e.g. remote blood sugar monitoring). Hence, an application is represented by an Application Entity (AE). Furthermore, the common services layer exposes all the functions specific to the machine-to-machine (M2M) environment such as data management, notification and subscription management, message handling,etc. The service layer relies on the Common Services Entity (CSE) as defined by the oneM2M team (with no dependence with the underlying networks). CSE takes a request as input (RequestPrimitive) and gives a response as output (ResponsePrimitive). Finally, the network layer relates the underlying network services (e.g. device management) to the layer of common services with the Network Services Entities (NSE).

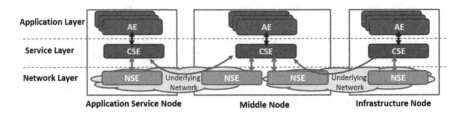

Fig. 1. OneM2M architecture

A set of these layers forms a node which is the key component of M2M/IoT systems. Thus, a node is composed of a network layer, an application layer consisting of zero to several AE(s) and optionally a common services layer. However, a node without a CSE must be connected to another node that has one. Nodes only communicate together through the service layer or the application layer. Thus, there are several types of nodes: (i) Infrastructure Node (IN) is the main node in a oneM2M domain and is unique in a multi-node architecture. Therefore, it contains all three functional layers and is characterized by additional features, such as its capacity to manage identifiers for all other nodes that are linked to it; (ii) Middle Node (MN) represents a transition node and has all three layers; (iii) Application Service Node (ASN) is like the MN except that no other node can connect to it (but it can connect to other nodes); and (iv) Application Dedicated Node (ADN) looks like ASN but without the service layer. An M2M/IoT system is composed of a unique IN (as a main server), one or more MN (as gateways), many ASN (as devices) and many ADN (as constrained/small devices). Figure 1 schematizes the main node types.

As detailed earlier, oneM2M is mainly about the service layer. Hence, at this point, we concentrate on the CSE. It allows to manage the resources of the node through oneM2M requests that follow the CRUD+N model (C for CREATE, R

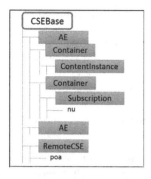

Fig. 2. OneM2M resource tree

for RETRIEVE, U for UPDATE, D for DELETE and N for NOTIFY). There are several types of resources in oneM2M [18] that are disposed in a resource tree model as illustrated in Fig. 2. OneM2M logic is based on a resource data model. Hence, each service is represented as a uniquely identified resource (data structure). A resource has a set of attributes (e.g. resourceName, content, etc.) and a set of child resources (represented with rectangles in Fig. 2). Below, we detail some of the characteristics of the resources we will need in the following sections:

- The CSEBase shall represent a CSE. It represents the root for all resources that are residing in the CSE. A CSEBase can have a list of points of access (poa). A poa is used by the M2M system to communicate with a CSE on a M2M node. Typically, a poa contains information related to the network address.
- The AE refers to an application registered to a CSE. It has a poa attribute and can only have a CSEBase as a parent.
- The Container controls the data of an application. It is used to share information with other entities. Possible parents are AE and other containers.
- The ContentInstance is a data instance that contains the useful data of a container resource. The content of the contentInstance can be encrypted. Unlike other resources, this resource shall not be modified once created. It can only be created, retrieved or deleted. Its only parent is a container.
- The Subscription resource concerns subscription information about the oneM2M resource to which it is subscribed. NotificationURI (nu) refers to the list of one or more targets that the hosting CSE shall send notifications to when the corresponding container has new data.
- The RemoteCSE is a representation of the CSE of a remote node. It can only have a CSEBase as a parent.

After having detailed the oneM2M architecture structure, we summarize the available security mechanisms proposed in the specifications of the project.

2.2   OneM2M Security

The goal of oneM2M is to define, approve and maintain a number of requirements and specifications to standardize the M2M and IoT ecosystem. Among these specifications, oneM2M community focuses on security and privacy aspects in TS-0003 [19]. The oneM2M security strategy is based on six main categories:

(a) identification to verify the validity of the identity that asks to authenticate then authentication to associate a trustworthy credentials to the valid identity,

(b) authorization to regulate services and data access authorizations for the authenticated entities,
(c) identity management to guarantee the anonymity of the entities,
(d) security association to ensure the confidentiality and the integrity of the exchanged information,
(e) sensitive data handling to enable secure storage, cryptographic operations and bootstrapping methods for the application layer,
(f) security administration to manage the sensitive resources: data and functions.

Indeed oneM2M provides a large panel of security mechanisms to protect the service layer itself as well as the communication between the oneM2M architecture layers. However, none of the specified techniques detect the intrusions in the oneM2M architecture. The security aspect is treated in a protection point of view to avoid security threats and not to detect them. Surely this aspect is fundamental and crucial, but what may be also interesting is a detection strategy of the security attacks/threats to analyze them and to have a better understanding of the attackers goals and strategies. Therefore, the proposed IDS represents a second security line to complement and strengthen the mechanisms from (a) to (f). In the next phase, we study and propose a oneM2M IDS.

3 OneM2M Intrusion Detection

Intrusion detection is an interesting security mechanism that detects threats to the systems and networks and may mitigate them. It can detect intrusions as soon as they are carried out on the target system. Intrusion detection systems (IDS) [5] are mainly used for networks protection. However, in our proposal, we study and suggest an IDS for the oneM2M standard whose main goal is to provide M2M and IoT ecosystem with a common M2M service layer. Hence, our IDS concentrates on the service layer. To implement the IDS, we start this section by presenting some IDS related to the IoT security since there is no previously proposed IDS for the oneM2M standard. Moreover, we define categories of the oneM2M security threats related to the service layer exchanges. Then, we detail our security threats scenarios that we will detect as well as their implementation.

3.1 State of Art of IDS for IoT

Many IoT IDS have been proposed in the state of art [5]. The first network IDS for IoT (SVELTE) was designed by Raza et al. [21]. It is a real time IDS for the IPv6-connected IoT devices. SVELTE is based on signature and anomaly detection techniques and concentrates on routing attacks. Raza et al. deploy lightweight IDS modules in resource constrained nodes and resource-intensive IDS modules at the Border Router. Moreover, Kasinathan et al. [13,14] detect Denial of Service attack (DoS) attacks at the 6LoWPAN protocol[1]. Their IDS is

---

[1] Kasinathan et al. in [14] define 6LoWPAN as "a standard protocol designed by IETF as an adaptation layer for low-power lossy networks enabling low-power devices (LLN) to communicate with the Internet".

centralized and signature-based. One of the first IDS for IoT that does not target an individual protocol or application is the one proposed by Midi et al. [15]. It is an online network-based with a signature and anomaly detection strategy. Its architecture is considered hybrid centralized and distributed that adapts to different environments. Hodo et al. [10] used Multi-Layer Perceptron (MLP) which is a type of supervised Artificial Neural Network (ANN) in an off-line IoT IDS. It analysis internet packet traces and tends to detect DoS attacks in IoT network. Many other studies suggested an IoT IDS based on machine learning like Hosseinpour et al. [11], Bonstani and Sheikhan [2,23], Diro et al. [6] and Moustafa et al. [16].

The intrusion detection in IoT systems is an important research topic. Many IDS have been proposed for the different IoT layers. However, to the best of our knowledge, our IDS is the first proposition to secure the oneM2M service layer.

3.2   OneM2M Attack Scenarios

In order to protect the oneM2M standard, we decide to concentrate on threats related to the service availability in oneM2M which is, first and foremost, about services for M2M and IoT systems. Consequently, we decide to implement an IDS for the service layer. Hence, we need to distinguish the related security threats. To do that, we specify attacks by analogy with DoS taxonomy [7,24] since this type of attack is the one that corresponds to the availability of services in the network layer. We propose a taxonomy for service threats of the oneM2M standard. These attacks are based on legitimate behaviors that were exploited in malicious strategies. An attacker or a defective device could overwhelm, consciously or unconsciously, the resources and/or the network until bringing down the system. Hence, we assume in the attack descriptions that the malicious user has previously gained access to the system.

- Flooding attacks are typically explicit attempts to disrupt legitimate users' access to services. It leads to services unavailability hence it costs time and data loss as well as money to mitigate the attacks and restore the services. In critical IoT systems, such as emergency fleet management (ambulance, police, etc.) or smart traffic signal systems, failures or delays in information exchange may cause serious problems. In oneM2M, we describe flooding attacks (Fig. 3(a)) as the submerge of the service layer with the legitimate oneM2M CRUDN operations. It is about bombarding a node with one or multiple types of operations. For example, a person with malicious intent can manipulate the different devices of an IoT network to create or retrieve a huge number of AE or Container resources in a target node thus, a target will dedicate all its resources to respond to the fake operations instead of real legitimate needs.
- Amplification attacks have the same goals as the flooding attacks. However, they differ in terms of strategy. In flooding attacks we specify direct actions that will occur during the attack, although in the amplification attacks, we put in place simple legitimate actions that will be later amplified to generate

massive service operations. This could be based on amplification or reflection tactics. Let's take the example of "announceTo" mechanism in the oneM2M standard. An announced resource (let's say AE1, we consider AE1 as a child resource of CSE1) [18] is a representation (that we name (AEAnnc1)) of the resource (AE1) at a remote CSE (that we name CSE2) that is linked to the original resource (CSE1). AEAnnc1 maintains some of the characteristics of AE1. Hence, changes in these AE1 characteristics will be transfered/notified to all the remote presentations of AE1 which means to all the elements of the list in the "announceTo" (in our example to AEAnnc1). Consequently, as represented in Fig. 3(b), if we put a large list in the "announceTo" and each element of the list will announce, in cascade, to another list, this will amplify the traffic when changes will be made on the first resource AE1.

– Protocol Exploit Attacks have a different strategy to consume resources. They exploit specific features or implementation bugs of the oneM2M protocol operations to overwhelm and/or bring down the device. An example of protocol exploit is the creation of loopholes in the notification system. It occurs when two resources register to the changes of each other. Hence, if a resource A has changes, a notification will be sent to resource B that will make changes as a result to the notification received from A. Since B has been changed, a notification will be sent to A to make new changes as well. Such a loop will consume resources in vain.

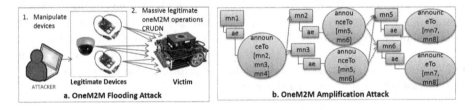

Fig. 3. OneM2M attacks

– Zero-day Attacks correspond to unknown or new abnormal behaviors which are not previously seen or at least analyzed. This term is widely used in the security community since it refers to unpredictable threats.

3.3   Attack Implementation

In this part, we propose examples of the implementation of each oneM2M attack category presented previously. These examples were set up to create our oneM2M security dataset, as well as to implement and test our IDS oneM2M solution proposal later. Concerning flooding attacks and amplification attacks, two parameters have been changed over the executions to have different instances in each type: N_OP which corresponds to the number of actions and N_TH which refers to the number of threads running the attack. Each type of attacks was running in centralized and distributed environments. Some of the attacks cause slowdown in the response to legitimate requests, others bring the target down.

Flooding Attacks: For this category of attack, we develop six types. The symbol N_OP α N_TH stands for the expression "N_OP times with N_TH threads".

- *Ae Flooding (AF):* In this attack we retrieve an AE resource N_OP α N_TH.
- *Containers Flooding (CsF):* In this attack we retrieve all the container resources of a given AE N_OP α N_TH.
- *Container Flooding (CF):* In this attack we retrieve one container resource of a given AE N_OP α N_TH.
- *ContentInstance Flooding (CIF):* We retrieve one contentInstance resource of a given container of a given AE N_OP α N_TH.
- *Subscription Flooding (SF):* In this attack we retrieve one subscription resource of a given container of a given AE N_OP α N_TH.
- *Various Flooding (VF):* In this attack we retrieve various resources from a given CSEBase N_OP α N_TH.

Amplification Attacks: For this category of attack, we need each time at least two AE resources under the same CSEBase or in two different related CSE nodes (e.g. A and B). We develop three types:

- *Amplify One Ae One Container (AOAOC):* In this type, B will subscribe n times to the same container of A with N_TH threads. These subscriptions are possible since each subscription has a different identifier. After that, we create N_OP contentInstance under the corresponding container of A. Consequently, each new creation of a contentInstance will be notified to B. Since we have n subscriptions for the same container then, for each new contentInstance creation, we have $n * N\_TH$ generated notifications.
- *Amplify One Ae Multiple Containers (AOAMC):* This type is similar to AOAOC but concerns not only one container but N_OP containers.
- *Amplify Discovery Ae (ADA):* This attack is also based on the same principle as AOAOC, however it concerns all the contained AE under the same CSEBase resource as A. Thus B subscribes to all the containers of all the AE resources at the same level as A.

Protocol Exploit Attacks: For this category, we implement a loophole attack that is based on the *poa* attribute. We have an AE resource A with a *poa* value for example "http://toto:8181". A is registered under a CSEBase with the same value of *poa* as A ("http://toto:8181"). We have also another AE resource named B (under the same CSEBase as A or in a remote CSE nodes). A will subscribe to a container of B. Hence, for each new value under this container, A will be notified thanks to the declared *poa* address. Since both the CSEBase and the AE node A have the same *poa*, the notification will be received by the AE A that will redirect it to the CSEBase and hence we create a loop (Fig. 4).

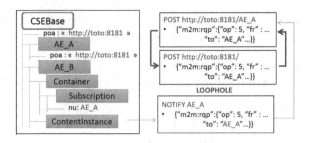

Fig. 4. OneM2M loophole attack

4   OneM2M-IDS Architecture and Implementation

After having presented the different categories of oneM2M attacks that we intend to detect, we introduce in this section our intrusion detection proposal. The previously detailed threats as well as the proposed IDS concern mainly the messaging mechanism of the oneM2M service layer. Hence, most of the attacks can not be detected at the underlying communication networks.

4.1   Proposed Method for Intrusion Detection

After having previously analyzed the different mechanisms used in IoT Network IDS (NIDS) [5], we decide to use machine learning (ML) algorithms in our solution since: (i) supervised ML has better results in zero day attacks detection than traditional IoT NIDS; (ii) ML equipped IDSs learn continuously the traffic pattern from recent past; hence they identify minor variation in traffic pattern to detect minor changes. In other words, ML algorithms are efficient in detecting attack variants; (iii) ML algorithms in IoT NIDS improve the detection rate, the detection accuracy in a reduced detection time, in the one hand. In the other hand, they reduce the high false attacks recognition of the traditional NIDS [5].

Consequently, we analyze the communication model of the oneM2M service layer to decide about inputs of the ML algorithms that will be evaluated in the intrusion detection. OneM2M information exchange is based on a pair of Request and Response messages referenced as a flow in the oneM2M specifications [18]. Requests from an originator to a receiver contain mandatory and optional parameters depending on the requested operation and the involved oneM2M tree resources. Since ML algorithms need fixed features to analyze, our ML features are only built on the mandatory parameters.

- *requestIdentifier (rqi)* is a string key that enables the correlation between a request and its corresponding response.
- *From (fr)* is a string parameter that identifies the originator of the request. It is needed for the receiver to verify the originator identity in terms of access privilege.
- *To (to)* refers to the identity of the receiver.

- Operation (op) integer parameter reflects the operation to be executed at the receiver: CREATE, RETRIEVE, UPDATE, DELETE and NOTIFY.
- *responseStatusCode* indicates the result status of the requested operation if it has been successfully or unsuccessfully processed. For example 2000 corresponds to *OK* status, 2001 refers to *CREATED*, 2002 is *DELETED*, etc. There is a large amount of values of *responseStatusCode* that are specified in the oneM2M specifications [17].

In analogy with the network IDS [5], we notice that considering only basic features (only the mandatory attributes of each request/response) will not give a global and detailed information about the attacks being processed. Consequently, we introduce a new abstraction of the oneM2M standard flows that we named *GFlows* for *Generated Flows*. We built these *GFlows* on the messaging mechanism. *GFlows* will be the inputs to our ML based IDS. A *GFlow* encompasses multiple oneM2M original flows on the basis of the key from, to, op and responseStatusCode. For each n exchanged flows, a set of *GFlows* is generated. Besides the *GFlow* key attributes, we generate the properties detailed in Table 1. To propose this flow abstraction, we have tried to cover as many combinations and properties as we think relevant to allow maximum attack detection.

4.2   Integration of OneM2M IDS in OneM2M Architecture

Our IDS proposal is based on edge ML. In this part, we will deal with our IDS architecture and placement in the IoT systems.

To have an efficient intrusion detection in terms of scalability and autonomy in local attack detection, we decide to use a distributed placement. Hence, we include our IDS in each Application Service Node (ASN), Middle Node (MN) and Infrastructure Node (IN) having a CSE layer (Fig. 1) on the basis of an edge computing strategy. In other terms, our IDS will be integrated in powerful IoT devices (ASN and not ADN), gateways and servers. We tend to push intelligence and processing logic employment down near to data sources (which means as close as possible to sensors and actuators). Consequently, each IDS instance analyzes its corresponding local flows exchange (both outgoing and incoming traffic) which leads to an autonomous and lightweight intrusion detection processing suitable for the IoT systems that have challenges related to resource constraints [5]. We represent our IDS architecture on a general design of a oneM2M system in Fig. 5.

5   Experimental Evaluation

In this section, we detail the test environment then we compare the results of the different ML algorithms used for the experiments. In this section, we focus only on two categories of attacks which are the flooding and the amplification.

Table 1. OneM2M *GFlows* properties

Property name	Type	Description
counterKey	Integer	The number of request/response sharing the same key in NB flows
isSameFromTo	Boolean	To check if (From) and (to) have the same values in the *GFlows* key
isFromRemote	Boolean	To check if the request is from a remote CSE
isToRemote	Boolean	To check if the request is to a remote CSE
fromResourceType	Integer	The type of (from) resource: (1-AE), (2-Container), (3-ContentInstance), etc.
toResourceType	Integer	The type of (to) resource: (1-AE), (2-Container), (3-ContentInstance), etc.
counterSameFromRequests	Integer	The number of *GFlows* sharing the same (from) resource in NB flows
counterSameToResponses	Integer	The number of *GFlows* sharing the same (to) resource in NB flows
counterSameTypeResponses	Integer	The number of *GFlows* having the same responseStatusCode type in NB flows
counterSameCategoryResponses	Integer	The number of *GFlows* having the same responseStatusCode category in NB flows
duration	Long	The duration of the registered *GFlows*
counterFlows	Integer	The ranking of the *GFlows* in NB flows
counterSameOperations	Integer	The number of *GFlows* sharing the same (op) attribute in NB flows
counterSameFromTo	Integer	The number of *GFlows* sharing the same (from-to) attribute in NB flows
counterSameFromOp	Integer	The number of *GFlows* sharing the same (from-op) attribute in NB flows
counterSameFromResponseType	Integer	The number of *GFlows* sharing the same (from-responseType) attribute in NB flows
counterSameFromResponseCategory	Integer	The number of *GFlows* sharing the same (from-responseCategory) attribute in NB flows
counterSameFromOperationResponseType	Integer	The number of *GFlows* sharing the same (from-op-responseType) attribute in NB flows
counterSameFromOperationResponseCategory	Integer	The number of *GFlows* sharing the same (from-op-responseCategory) attribute in NB flows
counterSameToOperation	Integer	The number of *GFlows* sharing the same (to-op) attribute in NB flows
counterSameToResponseType	Integer	The number of *GFlows* sharing the same (to-responseType) attribute in NB flows
counterSameToResponseCategory	Integer	The number of *GFlows* sharing the same (to-responseCategory) attribute in NB flows
counterOperationResponseType	Integer	The number of *GFlows* sharing the same (op-responseType) attribute in NB flows
counterSameOperationResponseCategory	Integer	The number of *GFlows* sharing the same (op-responseCategory) attribute in NB flows

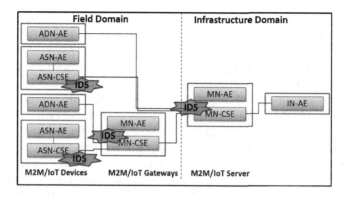

Fig. 5. OneM2M IDS architecture

5.1 Test Environment

To generate the attacks dataset that will be used later in the ML experimentation, we apply the different types of flooding and amplification attacks (previously detailed) on a Raspberry Pi 3 Model B (Quad Core 1.2GHz Broadcom BCM2837 64bit CPU and 1GB RAM). We equipped the Raspberry Pi with a oneM2M instance to play the role of an ASN where we have deployed the proposed IDS. The used oneM2M implementation is *Atos Standardized IoT Platform (ASIP)* initiated in May 2017 by Atos Innovation Aquitaine Lab. By running multiple attack instances (launched from one or many computers/devices), we generate a dataset composed of 223273 of *GFlow* inputs (165253 lines of attacks and 58020 of benign flows). We summarize the number of *GFlow* generated for each type of attack: 22258 of AF, 18867 of CsF, 13489 of CF, 9569 of CIF, 14922 of SF, 25356 of VF, 24449 of AOAOC, 17865 of AOAMC and 18478 of ADA. The generated dataset will be published soon. A *GFlow* is tagged as an attack if it causes more than 6 seconds of delay in the oneM2M response acquisition or if it causes errors/shutdown of the oneM2M platform. Otherwise, it is labeled as benign. To run the ML algorithms, we consider all the *GFlow* properties except for *From* and *To* to respect anonymity. So in total we ended up with 26 features plus the label. For the ML algorithms, we use Weka 3 tool [9] which offers a collection of ML algorithms for data mining tasks.

5.2 Machine Learning Algorithms Experimentation

Since we have generated labeled data, we experiment supervised ML algorithms in two modes; (i) a binary mode where the inputs are labeled as attacks or benign and (ii) a multi-classification mode where inputs are labeled as benign or as the corresponding attack type. We choose five ML algorithms to evaluate our generated dataset: (i) NaiveBayes (NB) [12] is a probabilistic classifier based on Bayes' theorem; (ii) MultilayerPerceptron (MLP) [8] classifies inputs using a simple feedforward artificial neural network; (iii) J48 [22] in Weka tool is an open source Java implementation aiming to generate a pruned or unpruned decision tree; (iv) RandomForest (RF) [3] is an ensemble learning used for classification, regression, etc. It is constructed on a multitude of decision trees at training phase; (v) SMO [25] in Weka is the implementation of John Platt's sequential minimal optimization algorithm for the Support Vector Machine (SVM) classifier.

We use the introduced ML algorithms with their default parameters as proposed by Weka. We only change the epsilon parameter of SMO since it takes a lot of time to train with default configuration (even when using kernels). We choose epsilon, which is for round-off error, as 1.0/(mean squared distance between our sample points). Each algorithm was trained on 66% randomly chosen inputs and tested on the remaining values (34%). Moreover, our results comparison is based on six metrics (the most used in network IDS [5]); (i) the recall which is the detection rate, (ii) the accuracy, (iii) the precision, (iv) false/incorrect classifications, (v) false positive rate (FPR), (vi) model size, (vii) CPU training time and (viii) CPU testing time. The higher the first three metrics are, the better the ML model is. The lower the last five metrics are, the better the ML model is. We study the model sizes since we are in the context of IoT (small devices). The last two metrics are presented to give an idea about the needed time to train and test the ML models which are important metrics for security. The faster we detect threats the best is. The false negative rate (FNR) is also an important measure to consider. However, we will not present it in our results since it can be deduced with the following formula $FNR = 1 - Recall$. The ML classifications were made offline (on a machine with Intel(R) Xeon(R) CPU E3-1225 v3 @ 3.20 GHz and 16Go of RAM).

Binary Classification Results. In the following experiments, datasets are labeled as attacks or benign behaviors. In Table 2, we compare results of the different ML algorithms for the binary classification. As we notice, SMO achieves the best attack detection rate (recall) of 98.60%. However, it has the worst CPU training time. J48 has the best result in terms of accuracy, precision, false classifications and FPR with 87.81%, 88.9%, 12.19% and 34% respectively. It achieves also the best CPU testing time of about 160ms. However, to have a faster learning phase with the smallest model, NB algorithm reaches 800 ms with 10 Ko.

Table 2. Comparison of binary classification results

ML algorithm	Recall (%)	Accuracy (%)	Precision (%)	False classifications (%)	False positive rate (%)	Model size (Ko)	CPU training time (ms)	CPU testing time (ms)
NB	79.70	71.05	80.90	28.95	53.70	**10**	**800**	800
MLP	97.40	87.04	86.70	12.96	42.60	36	629 640	320
J48	95.40	**87.81**	**88.90**	**12.19**	**34.00**	301	27 490	**160**
RF	89.90	83.84	88.50	16.16	**33.50**	307 673	138 010	6 290
SMO	**98.60**	84.14	83.20	15.86	57.10	15	36 968 840	190

Multi-classification Results. In this part, datasets are labeled depending on the attack types. In Table 3, we compare the results (the average of the results of the different attacks) of the different ML algorithms for the multi-classification experiments. J48 achieves the best recall, accuracy and precision of 77.07%, 74.80% and 74.80% respectively with the lowest false classifications value of 25.02%, the lowest FPR of 2.31% and the fastest CPU testing time of 170 ms. However, NB has the fastest CPU training time (700 ms) and the smallest model (24 Ko). Meanwhile, it has the worst false detection rate of about 63%.

Table 3. Comparison of multi-classification results

ML algorithm	Recall (%)	Accuracy (%)	Precision (%)	False classifications (%)	False positive rate (%)	Model size (Ko)	CPU training time (ms)	CPU testing time (ms)
NB	63.22	48.00	56.13	52.00	5.94	**24**	**700**	3 620
MLP	68.97	65.71	69.43	34.29	3.40	56	1 229 360	480
J48	**77.07**	**74.98**	**74.80**	**25.02**	**2.31**	3 677	60 850	**170**
RF	71.41	70.42	71.30	29.58	2.61	952 810	134 070	7 900
SMO	65.92	63.76	63.10	36.24	3.79	34	4 343 370	280

6   Conclusion and Future Directions

IoT is increasingly widespread. Hence, industrials tend to put in place proprietary solutions. In this paper, we propose an IDS for the security of the oneM2M standard. OneM2M is an international standard created to ensure horizontal IoT cross-industry interoperability. Our IDS uses edge ML to detect security attacks at the service layer of oneM2M. In our work, we define and implement the attacks scenarios. We propose oneM2M features abstraction for IoT datasets creation. Then, we experiment different ML algorithms to detect these threats as soon as possible. We consider both binary and multi-class classification. Binary classification results show good detection rate of 95.40% with the J48 algorithm. It achieves the best accuracy, precision, false classifications and FPR with 87.81%, 88.9%, 12.19% and 34% respectively. It has also the lowest CPU testing time (160 ms) for a model of 301 Ko.

In the future, we will explore more in detail dimension reduction and feature selection for the dataset features since we notice that, for example, J48 excludes 5 features with the entropy theory to improve the detection time. Moreover, we will consider other ML algorithms like deep learning. We also intend to focus more on the design and the implementation of the IDS. Furthermore, we plan to extend our oneM2M-IDS to take into consideration the different layers of the IoT stack such as the network layer.

Acknowledgement. The authors would like to thank the "Association Nationale de la Recherche et de la Technologie" (ANRT) for CIFRE funding (N° 2017/0122).

References

1. MQTT, April 2019. http://mqtt.org/
2. Bostani, H., Sheikhan, M.: Hybrid of anomaly-based and specification-based IDS for Internet of Things using unsupervised OPF based on MapReduce approach. Comput. Commun. **98**(Suppl. C), 52–71 (2017)
3. Breiman, L.: Random forests. Mach. Learn. **45**(1), 5–32 (2001)
4. Brenner, M., Unmehopa, M.: The Open Mobile Alliance: Delivering Service Enablers for Next-Generation Applications. Wiley, Hoboken (2008)
5. Chaabouni, N., Mosbah, M., Zemmari, A., Sauvignac, C., Faruki, P.: Network intrusion detection for IoT security based on learning techniques. IEEE Commun. Surv. Tutor. **21**(3), 2671–2701 (2019)
6. Diro, A.A., Chilamkurti, N.: Distributed attack detection scheme using deep learning approach for Internet of Things. Future Gener. Comput. Syst. **82**, 761–768 (2017)
7. Douligeris, C., Mitrokotsa, A.: DDoS attacks and defense mechanisms: classification and state-of-the-art. Comput. Netw. **44**(5), 643–666 (2004)
8. Gardner, M.W., Dorling, S.R.: Artificial neural networks (the multilayer perceptron)-a review of applications in the atmospheric sciences. Atmos. Environ. **32**(14), 2627–2636 (1998)
9. Hall, M., Frank, E., Holmes, G., Pfahringer, B., Reutemann, P., Witten, I.H.: The WEKA data mining software: an update. SIGKDD Explor. Newsl. **11**(1), 10–18 (2009)
10. Hodo, E., et al.: Threat analysis of IoT networks using artificial neural network intrusion detection system. In: 2016 International Symposium on Networks, Computers and Communications (ISNCC), pp. 1–6 (May 2016)
11. Hosseinpour, F., Vahdani Amoli, P., Plosila, J., Hämäläinen, T., Tenhunen, H.: An intrusion detection system for fog computing and IoT based logistic systems using a smart data approach. Int. J. Digit. Content Technol. Appl. **10**, 34–46 (2016)
12. John, G.H., Langley, P.: Estimating continuous distributions in Bayesian classifiers. In: Proceedings of the Eleventh Conference on Uncertainty in Artificial Intelligence, UAI 1995, pp. 338–345. Morgan Kaufmann Publishers Inc., San Francisco (1995)
13. Kasinathan, P., Costamagna, G., Khaleel, H., Pastrone, C., Spirito, M.A.: DEMO: an IDS framework for Internet of Things empowered by 6LoWPAN. In: Proceedings of the 2013 ACM SIGSAC Conference on Computer & Communications Security, CCS 2013, pp. 1337–1340. ACM, New York (November 2013)
14. Kasinathan, P., Pastrone, C., Spirito, M.A., Vinkovits, M.: Denial-of-Service detection in 6LoWPAN based Internet of Things. In: IEEE 9th International Conference on Wireless and Mobile Computing, Networking and Communications, pp. 600–607 (2013)
15. Midi, D., Rullo, A., Mudgerikar, A., Bertino, E.: Kalis a system for knowledge driven adaptable intrusion detection for the Internet of Things. In: 2017 IEEE 37th International Conference on Distributed Computing Systems (ICDCS), pp. 656–666 (June 2017)
16. Moustafa, N., Turnbull, B., Choo, K.R.: An ensemble intrusion detection technique based on proposed statistical flow features for protecting network traffic of Internet of Things. IEEE Internet Things J. **6**(3), 4815–4830 (2019)
17. OneM2M: TS-0004-V2.7.1 Service Layer Core Protocol Specification, p. 427, August 2016
18. OneM2M: TS-0001-V2.18.1 Functional Architecture, p. 427, March 2018

19. OneM2M: TS-0003-V2.12.1 Security Solutions, p. 427, March 2018
20. OneM2M: oneM2m - Home, April 2019. http://www.onem2m.org/
21. Raza, S., Wallgren, L., Voigt, T.: SVELTE: real-time intrusion detection in the Internet of Things. Ad Hoc Netw. **11**(8), 2661–2674 (2013)
22. Salzberg, S.L.: C4.5: programs for machine learning by J. Ross Quinlan. Morgan Kaufmann Publishers Inc, 1993. Mach. Learn. **16**(3), 235–240 (1994)
23. Sheikhan, M., Bostani, H.: A security mechanism for detecting intrusions in Internet of Things using selected features based on MI-BGSA. Int. J. Inf. Commun. Technol. Res. **9**(2), 53–62 (2017)
24. Sonar, K., Upadhyay, H.: A survey: DDOS attack on Internet of Things. Int. J. Eng. Res. Dev. **10**(11), 58–63 (2014)
25. Zeng, Z.Q., Yu, H.B., Xu, H.R., Xie, Y.Q., Gao, J.: Fast training support vector machines using parallel sequential minimal optimization. In: 2008 3rd International Conference on Intelligent System and Knowledge Engineering, vol. 1, pp. 997–1001. IEEE, November 2008

Efforts Towards IoT Technical Standardization

Shyam Wagle$^{(\boxtimes)}$ and Johnatan E. Pecero

ANEC-GIE, Luxembourg 1, Avenue du Swing, 4367 Belvaux, Luxembourg
{shyam.wagle,johnatan.pecero}@ilnas.etat.lu

Abstract. Internet of Things (IoT) refers to business process and applications of sensed data, information and content generated from interconnected world by means of connected devices that exist in the Internet infrastructure. Every day thousands of additional devices are connected to the Internet. The rapid growth of connected devices to the Internet as well as adoption of IoT technology across business sectors have led to a careful study and development of technical standards. IoT success is highly dependent on the elaboration of inter-operable global standards within and across application domains. For example, common language (vocabulary) and standard reference architecture are a prerequisite to develop cost-effective business solutions and enable cooperation between various applications, to cover a wide range of disciplines. This paper intends to summarize the major efforts of Standards Development Organizations (SDOs) and alliances towards IoT technical standardization. In particular, it identifies the implementation challenges in IoT ecosystem mainly from the perspective of technical, business, and societal. Then, it provides the level of focus of major SDOs and alliances in IoT related technical standardization on identified areas of challenges.

Keywords: Internet of Things · Challenges · Standards · Need of standardization · Standards development organizations · SDO efforts · Standardization gap analysis

1 Introduction

Internet of Things (IoT) is a promising topic of technical, societal and economic significance [1,2]. It has a potential to significantly drive business, technology, and economic growth over next decade [3]. The IoT is intended for ubiquitous connectivity among different entities, which are also called **things** [4,5]. Today, these entities become a part of our life that communicate intelligently with one another to execute daily operations or businesses. Adoption of IoT technology in various applications, such as industries, transport systems, agriculture, logistics

The standardization department of ANEC-GIE implements national standardization strategy established by ILNAS, National Standards Body in Luxembourg, in order to support the development of technical standardization at national level.

and supply chain, energy meters, health & well-being, etc. improves their current operational efficiency and interaction with the people [6]. The data generated across applications helps to create valuable insights for optimizing operations and quality standards of the IoT service users [7]. In the context of growing number of connected devices and applications, the IoT is going to be a dominant technology, where any devices can be connected to another devices all over the world. This growth of the IoT is mainly attributed to (i) creation of new applications; (ii) advancement of communication technology and; (iii) massive growth of low cost devices [8]. Existing Internet standards does not sufficiently support IoT technology. On the other hand, IoT architecture, use cases and devices are still evolving. In this context, this paper intends to provide insights to the need of technical standardization in IoT, and efforts of Standard Development Organizations (SDOs) and alliances in it. Moreover, it also guides current gaps on IoT technical standardization. In particular, it identifies the implementation challenges in IoT ecosystem mainly from the perspective of technical, business, and societal. Then, provides the current status of major SDOs and alliances involved in IoT related technical standardization about their level of involvement in identified areas. The rest of the paper is organized as follows: Sect. 2 provides the necessity of IoT standardization in the context of current challenges in the IoT deployment. Technical standardization efforts by several SDOs and alliances are provided in Sect. 3. Section 4 provides the level of focus of SDOs and alliances related to IoT technical standardization on challenges identified in Sect. 2. Finally, Sect. 5 concludes the paper with the issues to be addressed by related stakeholders in the context of IoT technical standardization.

2   Standardization and Its Necessity in IoT

Information and Communication Technology (ICT) is the infrastructure and components that enable modern computing, where standards play an essential role in achieving interoperability of complex ecosystem of ICT technologies and can bring significant benefits to both industry and consumers [6,9,10]. The standards also guarantee to work such technologies smoothly and reliably together. Furthermore, they help to make ICT markets remain open and allow consumers the widest choice of products. In the context of digitization of the global economy and society, ICT standards are more relevant where the world tends to become all digitized and everything become connected. In fact, the digitization of the global economy and society affects all sectors.

The success of every technology is eventually highly dependent on the elaboration of such complex interoperable global standards within and across applications. Not only now, it will become increasingly important in the future. For example, more and more devices will be connected to each other ranging from cars and transportation systems, to appliances and e-Health systems. For the European market, the European Commission has proposed, in its latest rolling plan for ICT standardization [10], to focus standard-setting resources and communities on five priority areas including IoT and 5th Generation Mobile (5G) as essential technologies for wider European Union competitiveness. Before providing IoT specific standardization initiatives, a concept of standards and technical standardization is provided here:

2.1 Concept of Technical Standardization

Standards are effective economic tools for achieving various objectives, such as mutual understanding, reduction of costs, elimination of waste, improvement of efficiency, achievement of compatibility between products and components or access to knowledge about technologies [11]. In this context, technical standardization is a keystone to ensure interoperability of complex ICT systems and it will contribute to minimize the barriers that may exist to build the future of the digital world. European commission's ICT rolling plan defines that technical standardization is an essential component of industrial competitiveness [10]. Regulation 1025/2012 on European standardization [12] sets the legal framework in which the actors in standardization (the European Commission, European standardization organizations, industry, SMEs and societal stakeholders) operate. More significantly, the role of standardization is to support the stakeholders of the various economic sectors, such as developers, researchers, government, regulators and users all over the world.

Technical standards are developed within standardization bodies, also called SDOs that bring together all interested stakeholders and are active at different geographical levels in their own areas of competency. In particular, technical standardization is important [13–15] to ensure (i) interoperability across products, services and applications that helps to avoid vendor lock-in, (ii) interoperation across physical communication systems, protocol syntax, data semantics as well as domain information, (iii) security and privacy of data and users including physical security of products, services and systems. Moreover, technical standards can help to establish and maintain digital trust to ICT technologies. For example by setting up appropriate information security management systems, providing common communication protocols, allowing interoperability between different applications and technologies, etc.

2.2 Need of Technical Standardization in IoT

Technical standardization is one of the most critical part of the IoT evolution [16,17]. The growing complexity of devices or services that need to connect and communicate each other remains the same or even more without global standards [18]. That complexity is associated to interfaces, quality of service, communication, security, related addressing, and many more. In this context common standards provide guidelines for billions of connected things in order to operate with an acceptable, manageable and scalable level of complexity. In current model, most of the IoT solution providers have been building all components of the stacks naming as IoT solutions from the hardware devices to the relevant services, for example cloud services. As a result, there is a lack of consistency and standards across the services used in different IoT solutions. As the organization or structure of the industry evolves, the need for a standard model (e.g. IoT reference architecture) becomes more relevant to perform common IoT backend solutions, such as processing or storage [19]. In the new model, it is expected to work different IoT solutions with common backend services. It provides levels of guarantee of interoperability, portability, manageability, etc., which are still missing in the current generation of IoT solutions.

Let's take an example: data is collected by sensors within IoT devices and transmitted through networks (wired or wireless), warehouses store in the cloud, and aggregated for the analysis through analytics and related intelligence applications. In this case, technical standardization is important to solve the issues of interoperability or interconnectivity. Apart from this, it is also equally important to reduce the gaps between protocols and associated security issues and other loop holes. In general, technical standardization enables more compatible components, which leads to reduce the cost of design, manufacturing, implementation and reduce a time to the market. Prior to providing overall challenges in IoT ecosystem, composition of various components of the IoT solution will be provided to understand how technical standardization is important for components of IoT implementation [19] (see Fig. 1).

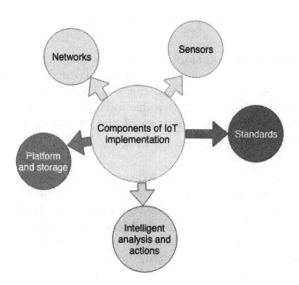

Fig. 1. Components of IoT implementation [19] and need of standards

Sensors. New trends in technology facilitate manufacturer to produce sensors cheaper, smarter and smaller, which drives increasing number of sensors installed by IoT solutions providers. But due to multiple vendors and technologies used, IoT sensors are facing problems of interoperability, power consumption, and security and privacy.

Networks. The networks with high data rate, high availability, cheaper cost on data usage, virtualization etc. are the some of the prerequisite for wide adoption of the IoT technology. As mentioned earlier, networks are used to transmit data collected by sensors over the networks with different components including routers, bridges in different IoT implementations. Now, connecting different parts of the networks to the sensors are being done by different technologies (e.g. WiFi, cellular networks). But smooth interconnectivity and heterogeneity of the networks, availability of networks coverage, power consumption, security etc. are still missing in the context of the enormous growth in the connected devices to the IoT.

Platform and Storage. The platform in the IoT includes the form and design of the products, analytics tools used to deal with the massive data streaming from all products in a secure way. Most of the IoT data (structured or unstructured) will get preserved and perform analytics functions to generate insights. The storage in IoT should accommodate an increasing number of data files generated from sensors. Cloud-integrated storage or cloud storage is ideal for IoT specific data. In addition to cloud computing specific issues, such as security & privacy, control, performance etc., smooth interoperability among cloud providers is still missing from technical standardization point of view.

Intelligent Analysis and Actions. The components include the tools, which extract insight from data for analysis. Generally, IoT analysis is driven by cognitive technologies and related models. But IoT implementation is still facing problems because of inaccurate analysis due to flaws in the data source, limited ability to analyze and manage unstructured and real-time data, missing data extraction guidelines, etc.

Standards. As discussed before, the IoT has complex and fragmented landscape. The components mentioned before are inter-related, all of them are important to make the system operable. Missing one of them will break the entire system and stop the standardization process. Many stakeholders (e.g. SDOs, manufacturer, developers, researchers, government, regulators) have their own role to smoothly run the entire IoT ecosystem. In this context, standards help entities work together ranging from sensing to networking, cloud services to different application domains and verticals including intelligent analysis and actions, providing vendor independent common guidelines applicable for all concerned stakeholders. Following these challenges of IoT components implementation, a list of challenges in the entire IoT ecosystem mainly from the perspective of technical, business, and societal [14] from the view of technical standardization has been identified in Table 1. On the basis of these challenges, efforts of the SDOs and gaps in IoT technical standardization will be further analyzed.

Table 1. Need of IoT technical standards

IoT challenges	Need of related standards
Common language (vocab.)	There should be a common understanding about the technology and an acceptable common reference architecture to its stakeholders for the implementation. As the IoT is broad and applicable most of the sectors of the society, there is a need of common understanding about the technology as well as well-defined reference architecture acceptable from different perspective across the sectors
Interoperability (interop.)	The IoT is growing across the sectors. Seamless interoperability with different devices operating in different technology is a major challenge. In addition to this, interoperation of the network protocol stacks at higher layers involving domain specific operation, and semantic level is another challenge
Connectivity (connect.)	Connecting billions of devices is a major challenge in IoT. Apart from this, various communication technologies: WiFi, Zigbee [20], LoRa [21], Low-Power Wide Aera Network (LPWAN), Long Term Evolution (LTE), LTE-advanced, 5G, etc. are ruling the current IoT paradigm and other technologies yet to come. Seamless connectivity among connecting devices across the sectors and communication technologies is a major challenge
Security and privacy (sec. & priv.)	Today, security and privacy are the prime concerns for the IoT deployment. Most of its deployments are prone to security and privacy at device, edge, cloud platform level. It is necessary to consider appropriate deployment architecture to overcome all the related issues
Trustworthiness (trust.)	Trustworthiness reflects the degree of confidence one has that the system performs as expected with regard to characteristics including safety, security, privacy, reliability and resilience, etc. [22]. Trustworthiness of IoT systems will require active management of risks for all these characteristics
Reliability (relia.)	Reliability of the services is also another major concern in specific sectors, such as in health care, connected vehicles. These sectors require utmost reliability (99.9999% or better) to get the appropriate service
Scalability and agility (scal.)	The IoT is referred as a network of networks. The future applications or networks should be both scalable and agile to the user demands. System should be dynamically scaled up and down without sacrificing basic requirements, such as Quality of Service (QoS), security/privacy, reliability, etc. The IoT is more heterogeneous than the Internet. In the context of tremendous challenges due to unbounded, unplanned, and unregulated growth of networks in the Internet leads to significant improvements also in the IoT technology
Intelligence and analytics (intel.)	By nature, the IoT is to collect information and to react based on it. Information is collected at the devices and communicated to the cloud with or without the support of edge. The factors: delay, jitter, cost, regulatory issues, etc., play significant role to place the appropriate analytic platform; i.e. whether at edge/fog or at the cloud. Inaccurate analysis due to flaws in the data source, limited ability to analyze and manage unstructured and real-time data, missing data extraction guidelines, etc. are critical issues in the current context
Sector-specific requirements (sector.)	Deployment decision can impact the vertical, horizontal or end customer markets of the IoT. In particular, they can be consumer, industrial, and commercial IoT. In this context, specific guidelines for specific sectors of deployment are very important, which is missing in the current context for the most of the sectors
Societal (socie.)	The services of IoT should satisfy consumers, developers, regulators etc. as stakeholders of the society. This societal challenges includes the mode of usage, the energy consumption, environment impact and other related societal impact, which play a vital role in the IoT deployment

3   Technical Standardization Efforts for the IoT

Several SDOs and alliances are focusing on to maintain the seamless operations of the IoT systems. Particularly, International Organization for Standardization (ISO), the International Electrotechnical Commission (IEC) and joint collaboration between them (ISO/IEC JTC 1) [23], the European Telecommunications Standards Institute (ETSI) [25], the International Telecommunication Union's Telecommunication Standardization Sector (ITU-T) [26], etc. are well-known SDOs. They are developing standards, guidelines, specifications to support its stakeholders to the ICT deployment. SDOs can be broadly categorized into two classes from the perspective technological offering: generic and application specific. The organizations of the first category play a pivotal role in defining technology standards to cover overall problem space [14]. The organizations of the second category, on the other hand, are created in the interest of standardizing technologies for some specific domain of applications. This paper intends to provide an overview of SDOs and alliances who provide generic standards. In the context of the IoT, ISO/IEC JTC 1, ETSI and ITU-T, etc. cover most of the areas in technical standardization for generic standards. The rest of the section provides a short summary of the efforts of these SDOs and other alliances related to the IoT standards.

3.1   ISO/IEC JTC 1

This is a joint technical committee of ISO and IEC. It is created to develop, maintain and promote standards in the fields of information technology (IT) and Information and Communications Technology (ICT). A subcommittee under JTC 1, SC 41 [24], serves as the focus and proponent for JTC 1's standardization programme on the IoT and related technologies, including Sensor Networks and Wearable technologies. This subcommittee is addressing most of the issues listed in Table 1. In particular, it has three working groups (WGs) for different areas of IoT standardization to address these issues:

ISO/IEC JTC 1/Working Group 3 - IoT Architecture provides standardization in the area of common language - IoT vocabulary, architecture and frameworks. An international standard ISO/IEC 20924:2018 IoT - Vocabulary[1] developed by this working group provides a definition of IoT for a common understanding about IoT within its stakeholders along with a set of terms and definitions forming a terminology foundation for the IoT. Similarly, another international standard ISO/IEC 30141:2018 - IoT Reference Architecture[2] provides a standardized IoT reference architecture using a common vocabulary, reusable designs and industry best practices. It has used a top down approach, deriving a high level system based reference with subsequent dissection of that model

---

[1] https://webstore.iec.ch/publication/60582.
[2] https://webstore.iec.ch/publication/60606.

into five architecture views from different perspectives, beginning with collecting the most important characteristics of IoT. The need of security, privacy and requirement for trustworthiness framework and methodologies while deploying IoT is also addressing by this working group forming different ad-hoc groups and liaison coordination groups;

ISO/IEC JTC 1/Working Group 4: IoT Interoperability provides standardization activities in the area of interoperability, connectivity, platform, middle-ware, conformance and testing. This working group recently published an international standard ISO/IEC 21823-1:2019 - Interoperability for IoT systems - Part 1: Framework[3] provides an overview of interoperability framework for IoT systems. It facilitates IoT stakeholders to be built in such a way that the entities of the IoT system are able to exchange information and mutually use the information in an efficient way. Apart from this, it is also working to define transport and semantic interoperabilty for IoT systems;

ISO/IEC JTC 1/Working Group 5: IoT Applications is dealing with standardization in the area of IoT applications, uses cases, tools, and implementation guidance. A technical report ISO/IEC TR 22417:2017[4], published by this working group, identifies IoT scenarios and use cases based on real-world applications and requirements. These use cases provide a practical context for considerations on interoperability and standards based on user experience. In addition to this, it clarifies where existing standards can be applied and highlights where standardization work is needed.

Apart from it, this subcommittee is also considering societal aspects of IoT, relationship of the IoT with new technologies, such as Blockchain, Artificial Intelligence (AI), Cloud/Edge technology through various ad-hoc groups and liaison coordination groups. Furthermore, ISO/IEC JTC 1/SC 41 also jointly works together with ISO/IEC JTC 1/SC 27[5] - Information security, cybersecurity and privacy protection for the security and privacy related standards for IoT. For example, an international standard ISO/IEC 27030 - Guidelines for security and privacy in IoT is being developed to provide security and privacy guidelines in IoT under ISO/IEC JTC 1/SC 27.

3.2   ETSI

The ETSI is a standardization organization for ICT standards fulfilling European and global market needs. It has long been involved on IoT related technical standardization. It develops several standards (specifications, reports) in the area of interoperability and use cases. In particular, standards related to Machine to Machine (M2M), IoT, Smart cities, Smart meters, Intelligent Transport Systems,

---

[3] https://webstore.iec.ch/publication/60604.

[4] https://webstore.iec.ch/publication/60605.

[5] https://www.iso.org/committee/45306.html.

Low power supplies, Radio spectrum etc. and related security issues are main focus of this organization. Some technical committees more relevant for the IoT are highlighted below:

ETSI/TC Smart M2M is responsible to provide specifications to IoT, Smart Cities related applications. In the beginning, ETSI special task force 505 - IoT Standards landscaping and IoT European Large Scale Pilots (LSP) gap analysis provided two technical reports, ETSI TR 103 375 and ETSI TR 103 376 to provide the roadmaps of the IoT standards, and gap analysis in the IoT technical standardization. In particular, ETSI TR 103 375 - IoT Standards landscape and future evaluations is to provide standards landscape for IoT and identification of potential frameworks for interoperability and ETSI TR 103 376 - IoT LSP use cases and standards gaps is to identify standardization gaps and proposals on how to address them in standardization respectively. For cyber security guidelines related to IoT, the ETSI technical committee on Cybersecurity - TC Cyber has recently released a standard, ETSI TS 103 645, for cybersecurity in IoT aiming at establishing a security guideline for internet-connected consumer products and providing a basis for future IoT certification schemes;

ETSI/TC Earth Station and Systems (SES) is responsible for standardization relating to all types of satellite communication systems, services and applications but still needs to be discovered many issues, for example, applicability of current satellite communication scenario for the IoT, efficient M2M/IoT protocols suitable for future services, etc.

3.3   ITU-T

ITU is the United Nations specialized agency for ICTs. The Study Groups of ITUś Telecommunication Standardization Sector (ITU-T) gather experts from around the world to develop international standards known as ITU-T Recommendations, which act as defining elements in the global infrastructure of ICTs. ITU-T put forward a vision of IoT in the landmark "Internet of Things" report published in 2005 as part of a series of ITU reports on the Internet. It was defined in recommendation ITU-T Y.2060 (06/2012) as a global infrastructure for the information society, enabling advanced services by interconnecting (physical and virtual) things based on existing and evolving interoperable information and communication technologies. Some relevant study groups of ITU-T related for the IoT are highlighted below:

SG 20 - IoT & Smart Cities, and Communities (SC&C) is working to address the standardization requirements with an initial focus on IoT applications in Smart Cities and communities. This study group is responsible from ITU-T to put forward the vision of IoT defined in Recommendation ITU-T Y.2060 (06/2012). A central part of this study is the standardization of end-to-end architectures for IoT, and mechanisms for the interoperability of IoT applications and data sets employed by various vertical industry sectors. This study group has also addressed the issue of defining application specific reference architecture, such as in smart manufacturing and Industrial IoT, e-health and e-agriculture, wearable device and services, and cooperative applications and transportation safety services;

SG 17 - Security coordinates security-related work across all ITU-T SGs together with a broad range of standardization issues. In particular for the IoT, it is working for the security of applications and services for the IoT and smart grid.

A few examples of standards developed by above-mentioned SDOs are listed in Table 2.

Table 2. Some examples of IoT standardization deliverables

SDOs	IoT related standards	Description
JTC 1/SC 41	-TR 22417:2017 IoT - IoT use cases	-Examples and template for IoT usecase analysis
	-20924:2018 IoT - Vocabulary	-Basic IoT terminologies
	-30141:2018 IoT - Reference Architecture	-Generic IoT reference architecture
	-21823-1:2019 IoT - Interoperability systems framework - Part 1–Framework	-Interoperability framework for IoT
ETSI	-TR 103 375 - IoT standards landscape and future evolutions	-Requirements, protocols, tests, etc.
	-TR 103 376 - IoT LSP use cases and standards gaps	-Recommendations
	-TS 103 645 - Cyber Security for Consumer IoT	-High-level provisions for IoT security
ITU-T	-Y.2060 (06/2012) - Overview of the Internet of things	-Clarifies the concept and scope of the IoT
	-Y.4203 - Requirements of things description in the IoT	-Introduction and requirements of things
	-Y.4459 - An architecture for IoT interoperability	-Digital Objective Architecture (DOA) features and its capabilities
	-Y.4204 - Accessibility requirements for the IoT applications and services	-Accessibility requirements for IoT applications and services

3.4 Other SDOs and Alliances

In addition to previous list of SDOs, several other SDOs and alliances are working to maintain seamless operations of the IoT. oneM2M [27] is a joint alliance of eight SDOs active in ICT standardization including ETSI. This alliance is playing an important role in developing interoperability related standards and specifications within and out of the IoT system. Basically the specifications developed by oneM2M address the need for a common M2M Service Layer that can be readily embedded within various hardware and software, and relied upon to connect the myriad of devices in the field with M2M application servers. The Institute of Electrical and Electronics Engineers (IEEE) [28] has been producing standards for local/personal area connectivity, which play a vital role in forming a physical and Medium Access Control (MAC) layer related standards. The project P2413 [29] aims to develop an architectural framework to cover the needs of different applications. Similarly, considering market growth of the IoT, the third Generation Partnership Project (3GPP) [30] is working on and has already provided set of specifications to Long Term Evolutions (LTE), Narrow-Band IoT (NB-IoT), and 5G related radio specifications and standards related for the IoT. The Internet Engineering Task Force (IETF) [31] is an another leading organization in standardizing protocols for the Internet at different layers of the network stack. It is also working to optimize the IETF's protocols offerings for the lower level on LPWAN from SigFox, LoRA Alliance, 3GPP etc. as well as to define the upper layer exchanges and signaling of existing protocol offerings. Likewise, Message Queuing Telemetry Transport (MQTT) [32], an ISO standard, submitted by Organization for the Advancements of Structured Information Standard (OASIS) [33] provides a standardized mechanism to connect devices. It helps cloud based architectures to be developed with common protocol semantics for the inter-connectivity. Apart from this, there is a huge list of alliances who are actively working on technical standardization to maintain seamless operations of the IoT, namely Alliance for Internet of Things Innovation (AIOTI) [34], Association for Automatic Identification and Mobility (AIM) [35], Industrial Internet Consortium (IIC) [36], Global Standards One (GS1) [37], Open Connectivity Foundation (OCF) [38] World Wide Web Consortium (W3C) [39], Open Geospatial Consortium (OGC) [40], etc.

Further analysis related to level of focus in IoT technical standardization of SDOs and alliances, on identified challenges in Table 1, is provided in Sect. 4.

4   Current Status in IoT Technical Standardization

This section provides the current status of the IoT standardization from the view point of selected challenges identified in Table 1. Based on our involvement to the various technical committees, and publicly available information of different SDOs and alliances, Table 3 provides a summary of analysis concerning technical standardization efforts to the various areas related to IoT. Rather than comparing the work of SDOs or alliances, Table 3 is dedicated to provide their areas of focus on identified challenges in Table 1 related to IoT.

In this observation, it is seen that ISO/IEC JTC 1 addresses most of the challenges identified in Table 1. For example, this committee has well addressed the need of a common understanding about the technology and a common implementation architecture acceptable for related stakeholders from different aspects across the sectors providing its definition, a set of terms and definitions forming a terminology foundation for the IoT as well as a common IoT reference architecture. This committee has also put a lot of efforts to define interoperability framework within and out of the IoT system. Security & privacy, and

Table 3. Efforts towards IoT technical standardization

SDOs/alliances	Covered area of efforts through technical standardization									
	Vocab.	Interop.	Connect.	Sec & Priv.	Trust.	Relia.	Scal.	Intel.	Sector.	Socie.
ISO/IEC JTC 1	xxx	xx	x	xx	xx	x	x	x	xx	x
ETSI	x	xxx	xxx	xx	x	x	x	xx	xx	x
ITU-T	xx	xx	xxx	xxx	x	x	xx	xxx	xx	x
oneM2M	-	xxx	xx	xx	-	-x	xx	x	x	-
IEEE	xx	xx	xxx	xx	-	x	x	xx	x	x
3GPP	x	xx	xxx	x	-	x	x	xx	x	-
IETF	xxx	xx	xx	xx	-	x	x	xxx	x	x
OASIS	x	xx	xx	xxx	-	xx	xx	xxx	x	-
AIOTI	x	x	x	x	-	x	xx	xxx	xxx	xx
AIM	x	xx	xx	x	-	-	-	-	-	-
IIC	xxx	xx	x	xx	xx	x	x	x	x	x
GS1	xx	x	xx	x	-	-	x	-	xx	-
OCF	x	xx	x	xx	-	x	xx	-	x	-
W3C	xx	xx	x	x	-	x	x	-	x	-
OGC	-	x	x	-	-	x	x	-	x	-

- x represents level of involvement: x - low, xx - medium, xxx - high, - N/A

trustworthiness issues in IoT are also well covered topics under ISO/IEC JTC 1/SC 41. In addition to this, this committee is currently working on through JTC 1/AG 7 - Trustworthiness to define trustworthiness concept applicable for every field of IT and ICT technologies. Similarly, it is intended to cover variety of deployment sectors while developing standards. For example, ISO/IEC JTC 1/SC 41 has recently identified industrial and consumer IoT sector to initiate standardization activities. However, connectivity, reliability, scalability, intelligence and analytics as well as societal aspects are the least covered areas in IoT standardization by this committee compared to others.

The ETSI's main focus as a standard development organization is in the telecommunications industry, for example for equipment makers, and network operators. It also supports to create an environment for timely development, ratification and testing of globally applicable standards for ICT-enabled systems, applications and services. It is significantly contributing to develop standards related to connectivity and interoperability for the IoT. Security & privacy, intelligence and analytics, and sector specific standards are other focus areas of the ETSI. As shown in Table 3, defining common language and reference architecture, trustworthiness issues, reliability, scalability, and societal aspects are the least covered areas by the ETSI compared to others.

Similarly, the ITU-T has main focus on providing recommendations standards defining how telecommunication networks operate and interwork. It is significantly contributing to develop standards related to connectivity, security & privacy, and intelligence and analytics for the IoT. Similarly, providing common understanding about IoT technology, interoperability framework, scalability, sector specific standards are other focus areas of the ITU-T. However, trustworthi-

ness, reliability, and societal aspects in technical standardization issues in IoT
are the least covered areas by ITU-T compared to others.

As shown in Table 3, concerning other alliances related to the IoT technical standardization, most of them are focused in specific areas. For example,
oneM2M is basically addressing interoperability related standards in IoT and
M2M. Connectivity, security & privacy, scalability are secondary focus area of
this committee. Similarly, IEEE and 3GPP are primarily focused on connectivity
related standards for the IoT. Likewise, IIC and IETF are primarily focused to
provide related terminologies and definitions concerning IoT. IIC has also put its
effort to provide interoperability, security & privacy, and trustworthiness related
issues whereas IETF is focused on connectivity, intelligence and analytics related
standards in IoT in addition to terminologies, and interoperability. OASIS is primarily focused on security & privacy, intelligence and analytics as well as interoperability, connectivity, reliability, and scalability related standards. AIOTI is
primarily focused on sector specific as well as intelligence and analytics related
standards. It is also involved in scalability and societal aspects. Similarly, AIM
is primarily focused on interoperability and connectivity related standards for
IoT. Providing common terminologies as well as addressing security & privacy
issues related to IoT are secondary focused areas of this organization. Likewise,
GS1 is primarily focused on vocabulary, connectivity and sector specific related
standard for IoT compared to others. The primary focus of OCF related to
IoT standardization are on interoperability, security & privacy, and scalability.
Similarly, W3C is actively addressing the technical standardization issues on
vocabulary as well as interoperability for the IoT. On the other hand, OGC is
addressing sector specific standards as well as interoperability, connectivity, reliability, scalability related standards for IoT. Fo global understanding, Table 3
provides the status of technical standardization related to the IoT of selected
SDOs and alliances (non-exhaustive list) on identified technical standardization
issues in Table 1.'x' represents level of involvement in particular areas related to
IoT standardization (x represents low, xx represents medium, and xxx represents
high).

5   Conclusions and Future Steps Toward IoT Technical Standardization

Today, the Internet of Things become a part of our life that communicate intelligently with one another to execute daily operations or businesses. Adoption of
IoT technology in various applications improves their current operational efficiency and interaction with the people. Every day thousands of additional connected devices are connected to the Internet as well as growing adoption of IoT
technology across business sectors have led to a careful study and development of
technical standards because they are effective economic tools for achieving various objectives, such as mutual understanding, reduction of costs, elimination
of waste, improvement of efficiency, achievement of compatibility between products and components or access to knowledge about technologies. In this context,

this paper identified deployment challenges in IoT and observed the efforts of SDOs and alliances to minimize these challenges through the help of technical standardization.

In our observation, it is seen that multiple efforts are undergoing related to IoT standardization by several SDOs and alliances. Vocabulary and reference architecture for common understanding about the technology, interconnectivity and related protocols specifications, connectivity, and IoT data & device security are some of the common issues being addressed by most of the SDOs and alliances. Since IoT is a completely heterogeneous system in terms of technologies and applications, there are still a lot of issues, which need to be addressed to make the IoT ecosystem seamlessly deployable. As IoT system is capable to access and gather sensitive data of users, data security and privacy issues are being more concerned to the IoT ecosystem in the current context. Various Machine Learning (ML) and Artificial Intelligence (AI) tools are used to extract and identify users behavior, where there are possibilities of mishandling of private information. In this scenario, a proper guidance concerning exposer and use of private information, regardless of the technology enhancement, to ensure that such data are not mishandled without compromising their privacy and performance.

Not only security and privacy issues, it is equally important to address by SDOs about trustworthiness issues, which reflects the degree of confidence to the users for the use of IoT service. Trustworthiness of the IoT systems will require active management of risks of security, privacy, safety, etc. In the emerging context of traditional society to the connected society, SDOs should carefully consider the issues of reliability, and scalability. This observation (see Table 3) also shows that trustworthiness, reliability, scalability and agility, societal related issues are the least focused areas of IoT technical standardization by SDOs and should be equally addressed as others, which help for the smooth deployment of the IoT technology. Satellite connectivity is another potential sector for widening IoT deployment. Several vertical standardization efforts are undergoing on satellite communication systems considering new technologies, however a lot of issues across domains still need to be carried out by SDOs, particularly to the IoT, 5G and connected vehicles.

References

1. The Internet of Things: An Overview, understanding the Issues and Challenges of a More Connected World, October 2015. www.internetsecurity.org
2. The European Research Cluster on Internet of Things (IERC), IoT definition. http://www.internet-of-things-research.eu/aboutiot.html
3. Market Pulse Report, Internet of Things (IoT) Discover Key Trends & Insights on Disruptive Technologies & Innovations, GrowthEnabler, April 2017
4. Mendez, D., Papapanagiotou, I., Yang, B.: Internet of Things: Survey on Security and Privacy. Cornell University Library, Ithaca (2017)
5. Bandyopadhyay, D., Sen, J.: Internet of Things: applications and challenges in technology and standardization. Wirel. Pers. Commun. **58**(1), 49–69 (2011)

6. ILNAS IoT White Paper, 2018. https://portail-qualite.public.lu/fr/publications/normes-normalisation/etudes/ilnas-white-paper-iot.html

7. ILNAS Data Protection and Privacy White Paper, 2018. https://portail-qualite.public.lu/fr/publications/normes-normalisation/etudes/ilnas-white-paper-data-protection-privacy-smart-ict.html

8. Greenough, J.: The Internet of Things is Rising: How the IoT Market will Grow across sectors. Business Insider Intelligence, New York (2014)

9. Gazis, V.: A survey of standards for machine-to-machine and the Internet of Things. IEEE Commun. Surv. Tutorials **19**(1), 482–511 (2017)

10. Rolling Plan for ICT Standardization 2019. https://ec.europa.eu/docsroom/documents/34788

11. CEN-CENELEC, Standards and your business, 2013. https://www.cencenelec.eu/news/publications/Publications/Standards-and-your-business2013-09.pdf

12. Regulation (EU) No. 1025/2012 - General framework of European standardisation policy. https://ec.europa.eu/growth/single-market/european-standards/policy/frameworken

13. European Commission, COM (2016) 176 final - Commission Staff working document - Advancing the Internet of Things in Europe (2016)

14. Pal, A., et al.: IoT Standardization: The Road Ahead, Book chapter, 2018. https://doi.org/10.5772/intechopen.75137

15. Marques, G., Garcia, N., Pombo, N.: A survey on IoT: architectures, elements, applications, QoS, platforms and security concepts. In: Mavromoustakis, C.X., Mastorakis, G., Dobre, C. (eds.) Advances in Mobile Cloud Computing and Big Data in the 5G Era. SBD, vol. 22, pp. 115–130. Springer, Cham (2017). https://doi.org/10.1007/978-3-319-45145-9_5

16. Guillemin, P., et al.: Internet of Things Standardisation - Status, Requirements, Initiatives and Organisations. https://www.academia.edu/29074933/InternetofThingsStandardisation-StatusRequirementsInitiativesandOrganisations

17. Saleem, J., et al.: IoT standardisation - challenges, perspectives and solution. In: The International Conference on Future Networks and Distributed Systems (ICFNDS) (2018)

18. e-Tech News and Views from the IEC, Why the IoT needs standardization. https://iecetech.org/Technical-Committees/2017-01/Why-the-IoT-needs-standardization

19. Banafa, A.: IoT standardization and implementation challenges (2016)

20. Zigbee Alliance. https://www.zigbee.org/

21. Lora Alliance. https://lora-alliance.org/

22. IIC definition: The Industrial Internet of Things, Volume G8: Vocabulary Industrial Internet Consortium, 2017. http://www.iiconsortium.org/pdf/IICVocabTechnicalReport2.0.pdf

23. ISO: IEC joint technical committee (JTC 1). https://www.iso.org/isoiec-jtc-1.html

24. ISO/IEC JTC 1/SC 41 - Internet of Things and related technologies. https://www.iec.ch

25. The European Telecommunications Standards Institute (ETSI). https://www.etsi.org

26. The International Telecommunication Union's Telecommunication Standardization Sector. https://www.itu.int/en/Pages/default.aspx

27. oneM2M, Standards for M2M and the Internet of Things. http://www.onem2m.org/

28. The Institute of Electrical and Electronics Engineers (IEEE). https://www.ieee.org/

29. IEEE: Standard for an architectural framework for the Internet of Things (IoT). http://grouper.ieee.org/groups/2413/
30. The third Generation Partnership Project (3GPP). https://www.3gpp.org/
31. The Internet Engineering Task Force (IETF). https://www.ietf.org/
32. MQTT organization. http://mqtt.org/
33. The Advancements of Structured Information Standard (OASIS). https://www.oasis-open.org/
34. Alliance for Internet of Things Innovation (AIOTI). https://aioti.eu/
35. Association for Automatic Identification and Mobility (AIM). https://www.aimglobal.org/
36. Industrial Internet Consortium (IIC). https://www.iiconsortium.org/
37. Global Standards One (GS1). https://www.gs1.org/
38. Open Connectivity Foundation. https://openconnectivity.org/
39. World Wide Web Consortium (W3C). http://www.w3.org/
40. Open Geospatial Consortium (OGC). http://www.opengeospatial.org/

Posters and Demos

5G Satellite Communications Services Through Constellation of LEO Satellites

Vahid Joroughi$^{(\boxtimes)}$ [iD], Lars K. Alminde [iD], and Eduardo Cruz [iD]

GomSpace Luxembourg S.a.r.l, 9 Avenue des-Alzette, Esch-sur-Alzette, Luxembourg
vajo@gomspace.com
https://gomspace.com/home.aspx

Abstract. Satellite communication systems are a promising solution to extend and complement terrestrial communication networks in un-served or remote area. This aspect is reflected by recent commercial and standardisation endeavours. In particular, 3GPP recently initiated a study item for new radio-based, i.e. 5G, non-terrestrial communication networks aimed at deploying satellite systems to integrate with terrestrial networks in mobile broadband and machine-type communication scenarios. In this context, employing a constellation of small satellites in Low Earth Orbit (LEO) adsorbs lots of attractions duo to their ability to provide cost-efficient communications with lower service latency compared to traditional geostationary satellite networks. Here, we aim at showing the potential of our new constellation of BroadBand GomSpace (GOMBB) LEO satellites which are able to integrate by future terrestrial communication networks, i.e. 5G and beyond.

Keywords: 5G satellite · Broadband communication · LEO satellite constellation · 5G LEO satellites

1 Introduction

5G is set to radically transform our lives with providing new types of applications and services in the domains of health, transport, entertainment, machine-to-machine communications, and security, to name just a few. Comparing to the 4G network, it is expected that 5G can provide increased computing power, scalability, reduced operation costs, and creative business models to enable differentiation. 5G will also lead to a huge shift towards a landscape dominated by broadband mobile data connectivity. Mobile broadband data traffic is expected to grow annually at a rate of 31% over the next five years to reach 136 exabytes per month by end 2024, at which time 5G networks will carry 25% of mobile data traffic globally, according to the latest Ericsson Mobility Report [1]. By 2024, smartphones will consume four times more broadband data on average than they do today, reaching an average 21 GB of data per month, driven primarily by video apps [2]. Satellite communication is becoming an important element in the 5G ecosystem, complementing fixed and wireless terrestrial communication

© Springer Nature Switzerland AG 2019
M. R. Palattella et al. (Eds.): ADHOC-NOW 2019, LNCS 11803, pp. 543–548, 2019.
https://doi.org/10.1007/978-3-030-31831-4_37

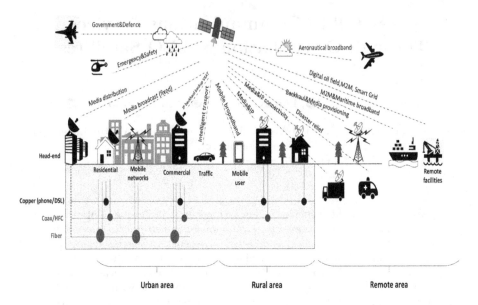

Fig. 1. Selected use cases for satellite communication in 5G.

(see Fig. 1). Cost-effective global service delivery is only possible via satellite networks. A constellation of LEO satellites can offer services such as fine-grained geo-location ubiquitous access or effective global transit so that virtual operator business models based on satellite resources could be more effective and efficient in space than on the ground. In addition, while the service latency is one of important factor in 5G connectivity, LEO satellites intuitively support lower service latency than geostationary satellites [3].

2   GOMBB LEO Satellites

GomSpace is a globally leading designer, integrator and manufacturer of high-end nanosatellites located in LEO for customers in the academic, government and commercial markets. Its positions of strength include systems integration, nanosatellite platforms and advanced miniaturised radio technology. GomSpace business model allows to provide turn-key projects to customers to deliver the business solution needed. GomSpace R&D team delivers these projects based on their strong in-house portfolios of established products and a wealth of capabilities. These include

(1) subsystems in all relevant product categories,
(2) payloads – off-the-shelf and mission tailored,
(3) platform designs from 1U[1] and up,
(4) reference designs for relevant business solution cases

---

[1] nU refers to a rectangular space of size $n10cm \times n10cm \times n10cm$.

GomSpace is currently working on a Constellation of GOMBB LEO satellites communication network which will aid to the terrestrial networks in following services

- **Ubiquitous coverage,** a constellation of GOMBB satellites can cover virtually all the inhabited Earth's surface. Even one satellite can cover a much vaster number of potential subscribers than any terrestrial network. Therefore, GOMBB network can help terrestrial communications by enlarging the coverage area.
- **Broadband IoT services,** as IoT scales to massive connectivity in future communication networks, e.g. 5G, the constellation of GOMBB satellites will deliver the ubiquitous broadband service continuity needed for the IoT users as well as future industrial control applications.
- **Edge server connectivity,** a constellation of GOMBB satellites can provide high-capacity backhaul connectivity and multicasting a service, i.e. distribute software updates, to a large numbers of edge servers over wide areas, thereby complementing the terrestrial network with cost-effective scalability.
- **Moving platforms,** due to resilience and ubiquitous coverage, constellation of GOMBB satellites networks is a proper broadband communication solution for providing connectivity to aboard moving vehicles, such as planes, trains and ships. In addition, these networks can support applications for fleet management, navigation and over-the-air software updates for connected cars anywhere in the world which is a key part of 5G IoT strategic plans [4].
- **Fixed backhaul to remote locations,** establishing satellite broadband connectivity to underserved areas where it is not feasible to deploy terrestrial infrastructure, such as remote villages, islands or mountainous regions, disaster relief services, support emergency response teams as well as connectivity for one-off entertainment or sports events anywhere in the world.
- **Broadcast and multicast communication,** a constellation of GOMBB satellites can transmit multimedia content via broadcast and multicast streams not only for consumer multimedia services, but also a variety of applications that require edge caching and local distribution.

2.1   Pragmatic Sample

Obviously, in 5G communication for some users and applications even very short variances of transmission delays or service interruption can be critical, e.g. communication between two stock markets which are located geographically in different premises. In addition, these applications might require high reliability and security as well as acceptable Quality of Service (Qos). A constellation of GOMBB satellites could work as an alternative for current terrestrial communications, e.g. fiber connection, via hiring multiple inter-satellite connections. These inter-connections can offer

- *Reliable communication,* multiple number of inter-satellite routes with advanced real-time performance monitoring facilities and a satisfied privacy

can be established. Then, in case of unsafety or link failure, the data traffic
can be rerouted through other links.

- *High QoS connectivity,* multiple inter-satellite connections allow selecting a
  link with acceptable quality and lower latency between origin and destination
  to transmit data.
- *Secure communication,* to connect two 5G core networks which are geographically distributed within different locations, the service providers require costly
  mutual agreements with local operators to establish corresponding connection. Instead, a constellation of GOMBB satellites can provide a private and
  secure communication with high privacy between two core networks.

Fig. 2 depicts a 5G network encompasses a LEO satellite constellation.

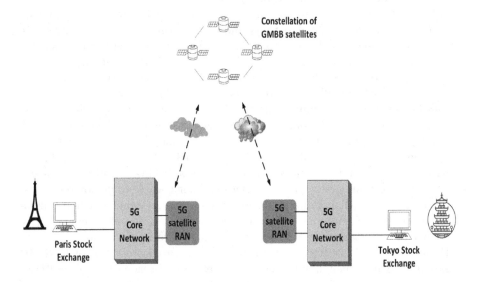

Fig. 2. GOMBB satellites path between two 5G core network.

2.2   GOMBB Technical Facilities

The GOMBB satellites will embed the following on-board unit
(1) *Low cost services,* using miniaturized GOMBB satellites in LEO can decrease
the cost level up to 1000 times cheaper than traditional satellites in higher orbits,
e.g. GEO satellite (2) *Service with low latency,* the GOMBB LEO satellites are
35 times closer to Earth than traditional GEO used for current satellite communications. Due to the closeness and shorter data paths, LEO based networks
have latency close to terrestrial networks, leading to have high potential to integrate with terrestrial communication, e.g. 5G.
(3) *Global coverage with scalability,* several GOMBB small satellites located in
a constellation around the Earth can pick up signal from any point of the Earth
and transfer it to its destination site via inter-connection with other satellites in

the constellation, or by inter-connection to a series of Earth stations, i.e. gateway, on the ground. In addition, the coverage area can be easily extended by employing additional small GOMBB satellites since the network extension in GEO and MEO requires launching costly new satellites.

(4) *Up to date technology*, GOMBB satellites life time (up to 5 years) is shorter than traditional GEO satellites with the lifetime of 15 years. Therefore, communication technology platform can be updated every 5 years in GOMBBx satellites. It leads to high possibility to integrate with fast growing terrestrial communication networks or even work solely with upgraded technologies.

(5) *High service diversity*, multibeam coverage can be established employing multiple GOMBB satellites where each satellite can generate multiple number of beams. In this context, the following benefits can be realized: (i) Each beam can guarantee a larger antenna gain-to-noise (G/N) ratio at each user terminal. This is due to fact that each satellite can generate narrow beam with high pointing possibility toward each user terminal. (ii) Since the frequency resources are scare in satellite communication, the available frequency can be reused between spatially separated beams. (iii) Multiple users may be simultaneously served within the coverage area, with individual data stream per beam or broadcasting a data stream to different beams, leading to high data distribution flexibilities.

(7) *High throughput connectivity*, using recent high throughput satellite standard, i.e. high throughput DVB-s2x transmission standard, each satellite can provide realtime high data rate connectivity (up to Gbps), video, voice, data, etc, to fixed and mobile user terminals.

(8) *Flying global data routing possibilities,* in the current satellite communication technology, to establish communication between different GEO satellite networks which serve different geographical areas, on-ground terrestrial inter-GEO-network connectivity is required. However, it suffers: (i) Satellite service providers shall make multiple costly mutual agreements with different terrestrial service operators to establish an inter-GEO-network communication. (ii) Even with having mutual agreement expressed in (i), involving with different terrestrial service operators might increase service outage probability in rush hours and decrease data privacy protection. In contrast, a constellation of GOMBB LEO satellites can fulfil a global connectivity and service delivery, either traffic data stream, between two geographically separate service points without touching any intermediate ground point. For this GOMBB satellite embeds a dynamic on-board routing scheme whose role is to exchange data between GOMBB satellites as well as an inter-GOMBB satellite link is established to provide physical interface for data routing scheme.

(9) *Dynamic resource allocation*, satellite on-board resources, i.e. power and bandwidth, are scarce and employing these resources in optimal way is essential. Therefore, GOMBB satellites will use different fancy resources allocation techniques, e.g. dynamic on-board beamforming, beam-hopping [5], which are widely discussed in literature of communication networks.

Concretely, the main perspective of deploying constellation of GOMBB satellites is to aid or even replace with current High Throughput Service (HTS)-

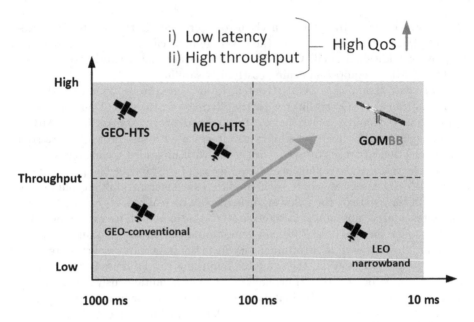

Fig. 3. Perspective on deploying constellation of GOMBB satellite networks.

GEO/MEO satellites. In very rough estimation, *it implies that the constellation of GOMBB satellites shall stand on a performance similar to HTS-GEO/MEO with lower latency and cost which can intuitively come from behaviours of LEO communication services* (see Fig. 3).

References

1. Ericsson Mobility Report. https://www.ericsson.com/en/mobility-report/reports/november-2018
2. Militano, L., Orsino, A., Araniti, G., Iera, A.: TNB-IoT for D2D-enhanced content uploading with social trustworthiness in 5G Systems. J. Future Internet **9**(3), 31 (2017). https://doi.org/10.3390/fi9030031. http://www.mdpi.com/1999-5903/9/3/31
3. Kodheli, O., Guidotti, A., Vanelli-Coralli, A.: Integration of satellites in 5G through LEO constellations. In: GLOBECOM- IEEE Global Communications Conference (2017)
4. Rupendra Nath, M., Agrawal, D.P.: 5G mobile technology: a survey. In: ICT Express (2017). https://doi.org/10.1016/j.icte.2016.01.003
5. Joroughi, V., et al.: Deploying joint beam hopping and precoding in multibeam satellite networks with time variant traffic. In: IEEE Global Conference on Signal and Information Processing (GlobalSIP) (2018)

On the Interplay Between 5G, Mobile Edge Computing and Robotics in Smart Agriculture Scenarios

Giovanni Valecce[1,2,3], Sergio Strazzella[2], and Luigi Alfredo Grieco[1,3(✉)]

[1] Department of Electrical and Information Engineering (DEI),
Politecnico di Bari, Bari, Italy
{giovanni.valecce,alfredo.grieco}@poliba.it
[2] Sf System srl, Carosino, TA, Italy
s.strazzella@solarfertigation.com
[3] CNIT, Consorzio Nazionale Interuniversitario per le Telecomunicazioni,
Politecnico di Bari, Bari, Italy

Abstract. The relentless growth of the human population over the time is driving an exceptional rise in food demand. Improving the efficiency of farming processes is the only way to face the so called Malthusian catastrophe. This objective could be pursued by automating production processes in farms. Robots can play a key role in this context, especially when they can execute tasks on collaborative basis. At the same time, low latency communication capabilities are required to translate in reality the robotic-aided smart agriculture vision. This contribution explores the interplay of 5G, Internet of Things (IoT), and Mobile Edge Computing (MEC) as enabling drivers for technology spread in the agriculture domain, based on Industry 4.0 principles. In particular, some key performance indicators have been investigated for a rural-area scenario, exploring different technological configurations.

Keywords: Smart agriculture · Robotics · 5G · MEC, IoT

1 Introduction

Food security has become a global concern. Governments worldwide are facing an exceptional rise in demand for food, and a significant human population growth. Moreover, limits on the exploitation of natural and human resources cause debates about the actual sustainability of the current economic model [1]. This has led to the rise of precision agriculture methods, which focus on harvest and production maximization, while fully optimizing the available land resources. Just as with any industry, production efficiency requires automation and elimination of human factor issues, which brings great interest in robotics integration into the agriculture supply chain. Many technological and engineering challenges need to be addressed in the context of agriculture mobile robots and precision autonomous farming [2].

© Springer Nature Switzerland AG 2019
M. R. Palattella et al. (Eds.): ADHOC-NOW 2019, LNCS 11803, pp. 549–559, 2019.
https://doi.org/10.1007/978-3-030-31831-4_38

The introduction of autonomous agricultural systems fosters a new range of flexible equipments able to reduce waste, improve economic profitability, cut environmental impact and increase food production sustainability [3]. The Agriculture Robots market is expected to rise to more than $16 billion by 2020 [4], and the use of robotics in this sector will employ a manpower larger than the automotive and aerospace sectors combined [5]. However, costs and technological obstacles to the adoption of such technologies on a large scale could be prohibitive [6]. It is, therefore, necessary to find a new economic and reliable approach to deploy a feasible infrastructure for agricultural robotics.

In this context, IoT and 5G technologies, combined with MEC, can become key drivers. 5G will be the dominant technology providing large area connectivity in the coming years with extremely large throughput coupled with low latency communications [7]. IoT is a definite paradigm for many industrial contexts, widely spread for information sharing and decision coordination [8]. MEC enables the network architecture to move cloud computing capabilities at the edge of a cellular network, reducing network congestion and optimizing applications execution [9]. Combining these technologies makes it possible to take decisions and execute functions more accurately, reliably, and quickly.

In this paper an overview on 5G-MEC and robotics is provided, proposing a use case architecture for precision agriculture environment as an emblematic paradigm for Industry 4.0 applications [10]. In addition, two demonstratives use case examples have been conceived using ground and aerial robots for agricultural operations. Key features of the envisioned domain support many automation improvements for monitoring, harvesting, and remote sensing.

The rest of the paper is structured as follows: Sect. 2 proposes an overview on Smart Agriculture state of the art, with the current trends in agricultural robotics. Section 3 reports the chosen enabling technologies, focusing on key aspects for the proposed architecture requirements. Section 4 presents the proposed framework focusing on the application areas of the aforementioned technologies. Two representative use cases are described in Sect. 5. In Sect. 6, an outline of the work is given, thus envisaging further research activities.

2 Smart Agriculture

The current challenge of agriculture industry is to produce more food to feed a growing population with a smaller rural labor force [11]. As a consequence, in many agriculture-dependent developing countries, the adoption of more efficient and sustainable production methods, and climate change adaptation strategies become mandatory. Within this context, farming technologies will be crucial to the evolution of this industry. Modern agricultural tools have eased the work of many farmers worldwide, and many instruments such as data analysis, detection systems, telecommunication networks, hardware, and software systems are involved into the environment referred to as "Smart Agriculture".

The typical IoT architecture implemented here, entails the deployment of an array of sensors on the field, a gateway that collects information and a cloud-processing service [12].

2.1 Agricultural Robotics

The large scale adoption of robotics in agriculture certainly requires the following technological features: navigation tools, image processing, real-time control of physical extensions, and reliable walk on rough terrain [2]. Many works and prototypes have been put in place in recent years: *agricultural robot partners* facilitating harvesting and pest control, remotely controlled by human operator [13]; Controller Area Network (CAN-bus)-based robot using vision positioning systems to identify and locate the fruit to harvest [14]; autonomous Agriculture Robot designed for seed sowing tasks [15]. Moreover, other studies focus on human-machine interaction, regulations, safety, ethics, and human comfort [16].

The aforementioned requirements has led to a growing demand in terms of both tools and connectivity that recent technologies struggle to satisfy. To this end, the rise of 5G and Software Defined Networking (SDN)-based edge computing interplay can be a keystone for effectively boosting robotics adoption in agriculture, even more on a large scale.

3 Enabling Technologies and Key Features

A description of the involved technologies is proposed herein, thus highlighting their most effective features for the proposed environment.

3.1 5G Technology

As reported in [17], 5G networks are expected to provide Enhanced Mobile Broadband (eMBB) with a peak data rate up to 20 Gbps, massive Machine Type Communication (mMTC) bringing long range and low data rate capabilities and Ultra Reliable Low Latency Communication (URLLC) for ultra responsive connections offering less than 1 ms air interface latency (Fig. 1).

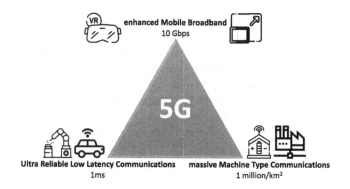

Fig. 1. 5G fundamental pillars and use cases

In addition, 5G technology adopts Cloud based Radio Access Network (CloudRAN) supplying massive connections of multiple standards and deploying on-demand functions of Radio Access Network (RAN) with a simplified core network architecture. Robotics can certainly take advantages from this framework, especially looking at high data rate, for high-definition video streaming, virtual or augmented realit, very low latency (about 1ms) for real-time interaction, and reliability for errors and delays reduction in communication.

Compared to the current 4G standard, 5G connectivity brings higher energy efficiency, more possible connections, higher data volumes, and a lower latency, essential features in the robotics domain [18]. The high number of possible connections provides a mainstay for massive industrial IoT applications where a large sensor network can communicate via 5G modules. 5G also incorporates a direct machine-to-machine mode of communication without the base station as an intermediate waypoint [19]. In Smart Agriculture context, the combination of 5G and Global Positioning System (GPS) will completely unbind robots from manual or near-field control, allowing them to foster innovative farming techniques.

3.2   Mobile Edge Computing

Currently, cloud computing represents an efficient way for data processing, since the computing power on the cloud outclasses the one at the network gateways. However, with the growing quantity of data that IoT and automation systems produce, the network bandwidth has come to an impasse, particularly when compared to the fast developing data processing speed. This represents a bottleneck for the cloud-based computing paradigm [20].

In this context, MEC can represent a step-forward for network design.

The Edge computing model (Fig. 2) refers to the capability of moving computation precisely at the *edge* of the network.

MEC servers are implemented on a generic computing platform within the RAN and allow the execution of applications near end devices. This policy can lighten the backhaul enabling low latency, high bandwidth and enhanced mobile services. Specifically, some key performance indicators within peculiar use cases for MEC technological interplay can be highlighted.

The first is about the benefits of using edge nodes in robotics environments for computation offloading over remote processing platforms or local robot controllers. Specifically, computationally expensive robotic Simultaneous Localization and Mapping (SLAM) task can be offloaded. For instance, in [21] a SLAM offloading algorithm in a multi-tier edge+cloud setup is proposed. The proposed scheme outperformed the static offloading strategies thus demonstrating performance enhancement of robotic SLAM using servers at network edge.

The second, highlights the scalability perspectives through edge analysis integration. The growing number of IoT devices is demanding significant cloud input bandwidth for data processing. This can be remarkably lower if data analysis is moved at the edge, uploading only light metadata and information. As shown in [22], the proposed cloudlet-based framework runs computer analytics of high-data-rate sensors streams in near real time reducing ingress bandwidth into the cloud by three to six orders of magnitude.

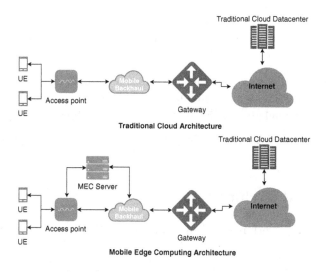

Fig. 2. MEC vs Traditional architecture.

The third considers the adoption of wireless interconnected Virtual Reality (VR) in a 5G/MEC network.

Authors in [23] envisage the migration of computationally intensive activities from VR devices to more resource-rich edge servers, thus increasing the computational capacity of low-cost devices while saving energy. For VR applications, both radio access and computational resources are brought closer to users, taking advantage from small cell base stations near to computing, storage, and memory resources. Experimental results show a 16 percent more immersive experience gains in MEC/FOG configuration compared to other. The immersive experience is defined as the percentage of tasks that are executed and carried out under a specific deadline.

3.3 Key Features

Looking at a classic smart agriculture pattern, the leading requirement is to bring automation to the different phases of an agricultural process. However, the full adoption of these solutions on a large scale by precision farming systems is of complex implementation. Farming techniques lacks of actual automation and control in several tasks, still conducted by humans. To this end, robotics certainly represent an enabling technology but unplugging robots from human control requires a strong technological set. As previously mentioned, next generation of 5G networks can meet these needs, ensuring high throughput for bandwidth intensive applications, low latency for real-time control, high scalability to enable a massive number of devices, energy efficiency and ubiquitous connectivity for end-users. Furthermore, considering that IT Infrastructure, data gathering, and Decision Support Systems (DSSs) activities, all access to cloud computing services, the implementation of this pattern into rural areas is often not feasible without a reliable Internet connection and area coverage by local telecommunications infrastructure. As a result, the following topics should be examined to straight out above issues:

- real-time and reliable connections for robotics equipment;
- rural areas coverage by telecommunication networks;
- solid computing capabilities for real-time decision support.

In this paper a Smart Agriculture 5G-robotics architecture is proposed in order to address above queries.

4   Envisioned Architecture

The proposed framework is sketched in Fig. 3. The involved entities are:

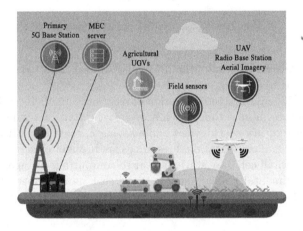

Fig. 3. 5G-MEC-Robotics Smart Agriculture scenario

- Unmanned Aerial Vehicle (UAV)
- Agricultural Unmanned Ground Vehicle (UGV)
- Field sensors
- 5G primary Base Station (BS)
- MEC application server

Thanks to the adoption of these tools, it is possible to accomplish UAV-based monitoring and connectivity, field machineries automation, and MEC-based fast processing. More details are provided in the following subsections.

4.1 UAV-Based Monitoring and Connectivity

The advent of low-cost UAVs will enable a large adoption of remote sensing applications for precision agriculture. Indeed, in the proposed architecture the UAV can carry out two main tasks: area patrolling and analysis through image processing and 5G coverage extension.

The first task is executed through high-resolution image capture by using on-board cameras. This pictures, together with the information gathered from soil sensors, can trigger a more precise crop management. As reported in many studies [24–26] and applications [27] a possible alternative to aerial images could be satellite-based captures. On one hand, the accessibility of this type of images is limited and high-priced. On the other hand, open-access multispectral imagery has very low resolution. In this context, aerial imaging campaigns can be convenient even though they require sophisticated camera systems and sturdy hardware. UAV images can address many of the imaging needs of the agriculture context, such as mixed cropping analysis, low area landholding, and variable planting cycles observation.

The second task is fulfilled by the presence of an UAV refers to the need for a 5G platform able to bring rural areas coverage with no infrastructures for Internet connection. To this end, as foreseen in [28,30] an UAV-aided 5G network architecture can be designed. This solution allows the UAV to carry on a mobile 5G base station, thus providing radio connectivity to the targeted area and connecting itself to a primary base station. In this way, UAV-aided wireless communications can supply ubiquitous coverage, relaying, and data collection. The proposed framework accomplishes the so-called 5G BS offloading through the use of drones.

4.2 Field Machineries Automation

In the proposed environment, real-time control and autonomous driving capabilities can enable field robots to assist workers by carrying payloads and conduct agricultural operations. Image processing, combined with data gathering from sensors, can be used for instant evaluation of the phenological phases, control weeds, detect the presence of insects, and diagnose diseases. The reported features will increase automation in the field and reduce the reliance on human action in farming management, planning, and decision making.

4.3 MEC Application Server

All the aforementioned applications, from data gathering to real-time processing, can not be efficiently executed if they are still based on the current cloud-computing paradigm. In autonomous vehicles and robotics systems, gigabytes of data are generated every second, requiring real-time processing to take correct decisions. Classic cloud-computing architecture poses a serious time-response issue in this environment, especially if the use case presents a large number of devices/vehicles to serve in one area. Executing the data processing at the edge can speed up response time, optimize processing, and avoid network congestion [31]. The proposed pattern envisages a MEC server at the edge, in order to manage requests and process information. In particular, it acts as a low-latency aggregation point, allowing applications to respond in real-time. In the following sections some case studies are described where techniques and scenarios are proposed to take advantage of MEC systems, in the smart agriculture environment.

5   Use Case Configurations

In order to provide examples of how the proposed architecture can be applied, two use case configurations are presented herein.

The first case is about the implementation of an autonomous harvesting robot (Fig. 4). The main goal for this type of robot is to execute an unmanned patrolling while having a stable walk on raw terrains and avoiding obstacles. To this end, in the proposed architecture, the robot could employ both real-time processing capabilities and low-latency response to process corrective measures instantly. Moreover, the robot can carry on a high-resolution camera that, powered by MEC high computational capabilities, will be able to process 3D imaging of fruits, vegetables, and plants, thus properly driving a real-time decision policy for the harvesting process based on color detection, dimension, and shape.

Fig. 4. First use case: Robot patrolling the area and harvesting with image processing-driven decision policy

The second example, reported in Fig. 5, concerns the use of the UAV for monitoring purposes. In particular, the drone can periodically execute an unmanned patrolling of the area, providing soil imagery and sensor data. Moreover, thanks to high throughput and bandwidth of the envisioned 5G architecture, farmers can exploit a First Person View (FPV) system for drone navigation through a VR head-mounted display, experiencing immersive teleoperation capabilities. In Table 1 some of the differences for use case requirements are listed. Bandwidth and latency requests, and error tolerance characteristics are highlighted for each

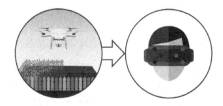

Fig. 5. Second use case: Drone monitoring and VR teleoperation

Table 1. Use case requirements

	Task	Bandwidth	Latency	Error tolerance
UGV	Harvesting	High	Low	Very low
	Patrolling	Low	Low	Low
UAV	Monitoring	High	High	High
	VR Teleoperation	Very high	Very low	Very low

task. Despite the advanced applications of the proposed use cases, there are some serious drawbacks that have to be investigated. In particular, energy question is primary. An autonomous recharge policy should be provided and UGVs and UAVs have to return periodically to a charge station, thus requiring job scheduling optimization for charging phases. Furthermore, research on robots physical extensions for seeding and harvesting (e.g. extensible arms, prehensile manipulators and automatic drills) still presents many open issues. Indeed, these tools must be reliable and cost-effective to allow a large scale adoption of these solutions.

6   Conclusions and Perspectives

This work proposed a reference architecture for Smart Agriculture environments based on 5G, MEC and robotics technologies. The main objective for this solution is to design a system suitable for a large scale adoption of robotics in the agriculture domain. To this end, use case configurations have been provided, highlighting benefits and open issues of employed technologies. The challenge for future research will be to execute modeling and simulations, proving the feasibility of this technological interplay. Moreover, solid business models and attractive pricing strategies can help the wide diffusion of this model. For this reasons, further research activities will consider the application of telecommunication network economics theory within this context.

Acknowledgment. This work was partially founded by Italian MIUR PON projects Pico&Pro (ARS01_01061), AGREED (ARS01_00254), FURTHER (ARS01_01283), RAFAEL (ARS01_00305) and by Apulia Region (Italy) Research Project E-SHELF (OSW3NO1).

References

1. Bruinsma, J.: World agriculture: Towards 2015/2030: An FAO Study. Routledge, Abingdon (2017)
2. Hajjaj, S.S.H., Sahari, K.S.M.: Review of research in the area of agriculture mobile robots. In: Mat Sakim, H., Mustaffa, M. (eds.) The 8th International Conference on Robotic, Vision, Signal Processing & Power Applications. Lecture Notes in Electrical Engineering, vol. 291, pp. 107–117. Springer, Singapore (2014). https://doi.org/10.1007/978-981-4585-42-2_13
3. Duckett, T., Pearson, S., Blackmore, S., Grieve, B., Smith, M.: White paper-agricultural robotics: the future of robotic agriculture (2018)
4. U. S. D. of Agriculture, Usda agricultural projections to 2024. (2015)
5. Duckett, T., Pearson, S., Blackmore, S., Grieve, B.: Agricultural robotics: the future of robotic agriculture. arXiv preprint arXiv:1806.06762 (2018)
6. Hajjaj, S.S.H., Sahari, K.S.M.: Review of agriculture robotics: practicality and feasibility. In: 2016 IEEE International Symposium on Robotics and Intelligent Sensors (IRIS), pp. 194–198, December 2016
7. Agiwal, M., Roy, A., Saxena, N.: Next generation 5G wireless networks: a comprehensive survey. IEEE Commun. Surv. Tutorials 18(3), 1617–1655 (2016)
8. Al-Fuqaha, A., Guizani, M., Mohammadi, M., Aledhari, M., Ayyash, M.: Internet of things: a survey on enabling technologies, protocols, and applications. IEEE Commun. Surv. Tutorials 17(4), 2347–2376 (2015)
9. Dinh, H.T., Lee, C., Niyato, D., Wang, P.: A survey of mobile cloud computing: architecture, applications, and approaches. Wirel. Commun. Mob. Comput. 13(18), 1587–1611 (2013)
10. Kagermann, H., Helbig, J., Hellinger, A., Wahlster, W.: Recommendations for implementing the strategic initiative INDUSTRIE 4.0: Securing the future of German manufacturing industry; final report of the Industrie 4.0 Working Group. Forschungsunion (2013)
11. Global agriculture towards 2050, in How to Feed the World in 2050. FAO High-Level Expert Forum, Rome (2009)
12. Ray, P.P.: A survey on Internet of Things architectures. J. King Saud Univ. Comput. Inf. Sci. 30(3), 291–319 (2018)
13. Kashiwazaki, K., Sugahara, Y., Iwasaki, J., Kosuge, K., Kumazawa, S., Yamashita, T.: Greenhouse partner robot system. In: ISR 2010 (41st International Symposium on Robotics) and ROBOTIK 2010 (6th German Conference on Robotics), pp. 1–8, June 2010
14. Feng, Q., Wang, X., Wang, G., Li, Z.: Design and test of tomatoes harvesting robot. In: 2015 IEEE International Conference on Information and Automation, pp. 949–952, August 2015
15. Naik, N.S., Shete, V.V., Danve, S.R.: Precision agriculture robot for seeding function. In: 2016 International Conference on Inventive Computation Technologies (ICICT), vol. 2, pp. 1–3, Augut 2016
16. Cheein, F.A., et al.: Human-robot interaction in precision agriculture: sharing the workspace with service units. In: 2015 IEEE International Conference on Industrial Technology (ICIT), pp. 289–295, March 2015
17. Shafi, M., et al.: 5g: a tutorial overview of standards, trials, challenges, deployment, and practice. IEEE J. Sel. Areas Commun. 35(6), 1201–1221 (2017)
18. Akpakwu, G.A., Silva, B.J., Hancke, G.P., Abu-Mahfouz, A.M.: A survey on 5g networks for the internet of things: communication technologies and challenges. IEEE Access 6, 3619–3647 (2018)

19. Voigtländer, F., Ramadan, A., Eichinger, J., Lenz, C., Pensky, D., Knoll, A.: 5g for robotics: ultra-low latency control of distributed robotic systems. In: 2017 International Symposium on Computer Science and Intelligent Controls (ISCSIC), pp. 69–72, October 2017

20. Porambage, P., Okwuibe, J., Liyanage, M., Ylianttila, M., Taleb, T.: Survey on multi-access edge computing for internet of things realization. arXiv preprint arXiv:1805.06695 (2018)

21. Dey, S., Mukherjee, A.: Robotic slam: a review from fog computing and mobile edge computing perspective. In: Adjunct Proceedings of the 13th International Conference on Mobile and Ubiquitous Systems: Computing Networking and Services, pp. 153–158. ACM (2016)

22. Bastug, E., Bennis, M., Médard, M., Debbah, M.: Toward interconnected virtual reality: opportunities, challenges, and enablers. IEEE Commun. Mag. **55**(6), 110–117 (2017)

23. Tran, T.X., Hajisami, A., Pandey, P., Pompili, D.: Collaborative mobile edge computing in 5g networks: New paradigms, scenarios, and challenges. arXiv preprint arXiv:1612.03184 (2016)

24. Ryu, C., Suguri, M., Iida, M., Umeda, M., Lee, C.: Integrating remote sensing and gis for prediction of rice protein contents. Prec. Agric. **12**(3), 378–394 (2011)

25. Zhang, C., Walters, D., Kovacs, J.M.: Applications of low altitude remote sensing in agriculture upon farmers' requests-a case study in northeastern ontario, Canada. PloS one **9**(11), e112894 (2014)

26. Gevaert, C.M., Suomalainen, J., Tang, J., Kooistra, L.: Generation of spectral-temporal response surfaces by combining multispectral satellite and hyperspectral UAV imagery for precision agriculture applications. IEEE J. Sel. Top. Appl. Earth Obs. Rem. Sens. **8**(6), 3140–3146 (2015)

27. Manna irrigation — remote sensing - manna irrigation. https://manna-irrigation. com/remote-sensing/

28. Chiaraviglio, L., Amorosi, L., Blefari-Melazzi, N., Dell'Olmo, P., Natalino, C., Monti, P.: Optimal design of 5g networks in rural zones with UAVs, optical rings, solar panels and batteries. In: 2018 20th International Conference on Transparent Optical Networks (ICTON), pp. 1–4. IEEE, (2018)

29. Merwaday, A., Guvenc, I.: Uav assisted heterogeneous networks for public safety communications. In: 2015 IEEE Wireless Communications and Networking Conference Workshops (WCNCW), pp. 329–334. IEEE (2015)

30. Mozaffari, M., Saad, W., Bennis, M., Debbah, M.: Efficient deployment of multiple unmanned aerial vehicles for optimal wireless coverage. IEEE Commun. Lett. **20**(8), 1647–1650 (2016)

31. Shi, W., Cao, J., Zhang, Q., Li, Y., Xu, L.: Edge computing: vision and challenges. IEEE Internet Things J. **3**(5), 637–646 (2016)

The Agromet Project: A Virtual Weather Station Network for Agricultural Decision Support Systems in Wallonia, South of Belgium

Damien Rosillon[1]([⊠]), Jean Pierre Huart[1]([⊠]), Thomas Goossens[1]([⊠]),
Michel Journée[2]([⊠]), and Viviane Planchon[1]([⊠])

[1] Agriculture and Natural Environment Department,
Walloon Agricultural Research Centre, 5030 Gembloux, Belgium
{d.rosillon, j.huart, t.goossens,
v.planchon}@cra.wallonie.be
[2] Royal Meteorological Institute of Belgium, Brussels, Belgium
michelj@meteo.be

Abstract. Weather-based forecasting models play a major role in agricultural decision support systems but warnings are usually computed at regional level due to a limited amount of automatic weather stations. Farmers have to refer to the nearest AWS but recommendations are not always adapted to their situation. Agromet project aims to set up an operational web-platform designed for real-time agro-meteorological data dissemination at high spatial (1 km $\times$ 1 km grid) and temporal (hourly) resolution in Wallonia, southern part of Belgium. This paper focuses on the interpolation of hourly temperature and daily maximum temperature. Five learners are tested: multilinear regression, inverse distance weighted, one nearest neighbor, ordinary kriging and kriging with external drift. All interpolation methods except ordinary kriging perform better than taking the nearest station to predict air temperature. Multilinear regression is the best one. The size of the dataset is a limit to data interpolation. IoT is an opportunity to improve the quality of the interpolated data by increasing the size of our training dataset. Either by developing our own low price and robust sensors to measure air temperature and humidity or by exploiting data measured by non-meteorological devices monitoring temperature (e.g. tractors or cars).

Keywords: Interpolation · Meteorology · Agricultural decision support system

1 Introduction

Since a long time, weather-based forecasting models play a major role in agricultural decision support systems (DSS). Those systems aim to control plant diseases and to reduce spraying intensity. Usually, DSS are fed with meteorological data recorded on a limited amount of automatic weather stations (AWS). Warnings are computed at a regional level. Farmers have to refer to the nearest AWS but recommendations are not

© Springer Nature Switzerland AG 2019
M. R. Palattella et al. (Eds.): ADHOC-NOW 2019, LNCS 11803, pp. 560–565, 2019.
https://doi.org/10.1007/978-3-030-31831-4_39

always adapted to their situation. With the development of smart farming, it is important to provide DSS with real-time and local weather data.

In Germany, interpolation of hourly weather data provide more detailed and more accurate data to feed potato late blight decision support system [1, 2]. A reduction in spraying intensity can then be achieved guaranteeing an economical and environmentally friendly crop production strategy.

The Agromet project aims to transpose the concept in Wallonia, southern part of Belgium, and to improve the methodology by testing new algorithms and including weather forecasts as a dynamic explanatory variable. The output of the project is an operational web-platform designed for real-time agro-meteorological data dissemination at high spatial (on a 1 km × 1 km grid) and temporal (hourly) resolution to provide DSS with locally predicted weather data. Spatialization will result in a gridded dataset corresponding to a virtual network of 16 000 virtual stations uniformly spread on the whole territory of Wallonia.

Usually, meteorological data interpolation is performed on low temporal resolution data (e.g. monthly [3] or yearly) or on climatic data [4]. Interpolate hourly or daily data is much more uncommon and is a real challenge.

This paper focuses on the interpolation of hourly temperature and daily maximum temperature. Interpolation of air humidity and leaf wetness duration will be analyzed in next step. Spatialized rainfall will be directly imported from RMI's radars and imported on the web-based platform.

2   Materials and Methods

2.1   Datasets

Two datasets of meteorological data are used in this study. A first dataset comes from the Pameseb network from the Walloon Agricultural Research Centre CRA-W referred in this paper as 'Pameseb network'. This network is composed of 30 AWS recording hourly data. For this study, 28 stations were selected. Two stations were left out because they are located in singular environment: a forest and an industrial zone. It generates a micro climate which is not representative of the region. The dataset used in this study comes from Pameseb database. The dataset contains two years, from 01/01/2016 00h UTC+2 to 31/12/2017 23h UTC+2, of hourly air temperature data.

The second dataset comes from the Royal Meteorological Institute network referred in this paper as 'RMI network'. This network is composed of 14 synoptic AWS. For this study, 8 AWS were selected for their location in or close to Wallonia our region of interest. The dataset contains two years, from 01/01/2016 00h UTC+2 to 31/12/2017 23h UTC+2, of hourly air temperature data.

2.2   Interpolation Methods

Spatialization creates a continuous surface from values measured at discrete locations to predict values at any location in the interest zone with the best accuracy. The principle is to find a relationship between a meteorological data to explain (i.e.: air temperature) and an explanatory variable (i.e.: elevation).

Five learners (or algorithms) are tested: multilinear regression (MultiReg), inverse distance weighted (IDW), one nearest neighbor (NN1), ordinary kriging (OK) and kriging with external drift (KED).

This choice is based on studies dealing with interpolation of meteorological data at high temporal [1, 2] and high spatial [5] resolution. The spatial interpolation of hourly mean and daily maximum air temperature has been performed on a regular grid of 1 km by 1 km.

Data analysis is conducted with R software [6] based on mlr (Machine Learning in R) [7]. This package provides a unified interface to more than 160 basic learners [7]. It provides all required interpolation algorithms except kriging. For the purpose of our study, we integrated gstat functions to mlr.

2.3 Explorative Constructions and Benchmarks

A huge amount of possibilities can be tested in machine learning based on a combination of a learner (algorithm), one or several explanatory variables, a defined dataset, … To give a structure to our analysis, we define several "explorative constructions" (EC). One EC is a unique combination of a learner, hyper-parameters (if required for the learner e.g. semi-variogram parameters for kriging), one or several explanatory variables (if relevant for the learner) and a dataset. For example, ec1 is a multiregression analysis with longitude, latitude and elevation as explanatory variables conducted with Pameseb dataset. ec14 is an ordinary kriging analysis conducted with Pameseb and RMI datasest, semivariogram parameters are range = 800, psill = 200000, nugget = 0, semivariogram is a spherical type.

The Table 1 described the ECs tested in this study.

Table 1. Explorative constructions tested

id	Learner	Hyper parameters	Explanatory variables	Datasets
ec1	MultiReg	–	lon, lat, elev	Pameseb
ec2	MultiReg	–	lon, lat, elev	Pameseb, RMI
ec7	IDW	–	lon, lat	Pameseb
ec8	IDW	–	lon, lat	Pameseb, RMI
ec10	NN1	set = list(idp = 0), nmax = 1	lon, lat	Pameseb
ec11	NN1	set = list(idp = 0), nmax = 1	lon, lat	Pameseb, RMI
ec13	OK	range = 800, psill = 200000, model.manual = Sph, nugget = 0	lon, lat	Pameseb
ec14	OK	range = 800, psill = 200000, model.manual = Sph, nugget = 0	lon, lat	Pameseb, RMI
ec15	KED	range = 800, psill = 200000, model.manual = Sph, nugget = 0	lon, lat, elev	Pameseb
ec16	KED	range = 800, psill = 200000, model.manual = Sph, nugget = 0	lon, lat, elev	Pameseb, RMI

3   Results and Discussion

Each EC is tested by conducting a benchmark. Models are trained on a 2 years of hourly and daily measurement dataset. Training period is from 01/01/2016 00h UTC+2 to 31/12/2017 23h UTC+2. Quality of the prediction models is assessed by a leave-one-out cross validation. Two quality indicators are computed: Root mean square error (RSME) and predicted residuals.

RMSE is calculated for the dataset as:

$$RMSE = \sqrt{\frac{1}{n}\sum_{j=1}^{n}(y_j - \hat{y}_j)^2}$$

where:

- y = the observed value
- $\hat{y}$ = the predicted value.

Predicted residuals are calculated for the dataset as:

$$e = y - \hat{y}$$

where:

- e = the predicted residual
- y = the observed value
- $\hat{y}$ = the predicted value.

Table 2 shows the results for the 5 learners to interpolate air. According to our first results, multilinear regression with latitude, longitude and elevation as explanatory variables is the best method to interpolate hourly air temperature (see Table 2). This method gives the best accuracy in predictions with a median RMSE equals to 0.47 °C. This method is also the most robust with lowest whisker equals to −1.89 °C and highest whisker equals to 1.85 °C for predicted residuals. All interpolation methods except ordinary kriging perform better than taking the nearest station (NN1) to predict hourly mean air temperature on a 1 km × 1 km grid.

When we increase our dataset from 28 AWS (Pameseb network only) to 36 AWS (Pameseb + RMI network), prediction quality and robustness slightly increases. Median RMSE changes from 0.47 °C to 0.46 °C. For residuals, lowest whisker changes from −1.89 °C to −1.86 °C and highest whisker changes from 1.85 °C to 1.82 °C.

As expected, predictive ability of the interpolation is better for daily than for hourly temperatures. For multilinear regression, median RMSE changes from 0.46 °C to 0.42 °C. For residuals, lowest whisker changes from −1.86 °C to −1.67 °C and highest whisker changes from 1.82 °C to 1.71 °C.

Table 2. Summary statistics for air temperature interpolation

Quality indicator	ec	Learner	wl* [°C]	Q25 [°C]	Median [°C]	Q75 [°C]	wh** [°C]	Dataset	Time step
RMSE	ec1	MultiReg	0	0.21	0.47	0.91	1.96	Pam	Hourly
RMSE	ec7	IDW	0	0.27	0.6	1.1	2.35	Pam	Hourly
RMSE	ec10	NN1	0	0.3	0.7	1.2	2.5	Pam	Hourly
RMSE	ec13	OK	0	0.47	0.95	1.61	3.32	Pam	Hourly
RMSE	ec15	KED	0	0.23	0.52	1.02	2.2	Pam	Hourly
RMSE	ec2	MultiReg	0	0.20	0.46	0.90	1.94	Pam +RMI	Hourly
RMSE	ec2	MultiReg	0	0.19	0.42	0.77	1.63	Pam +RMI	Daily
Residuals	ec1	MultiReg	−1.89	−0.49	0	0.45	1.85	Pam	Hourly
Residuals	ec7	IDW	−2.4	−0.6	−0.03	0.6	2.4	Pam	Hourly
Residuals	ec10	NN1	−2.6	−0.7	0	0.6	2.5	Pam	Hourly
Residuals	ec13	OK	−3.8	−1	−0.2	0.88	3.69	Pam	Hourly
Residuals	ec15	KED	−2.11	−0.54	−0.01	0.5	2.07	Pam	Hourly
Residuals	ec2	MultiReg	−1.86	−0.48	−0.01	0.44	1.82	Pam +RMI	Hourly
Residuals	ec2	MultiReg	−1.67	−0.41	0.03	0.44	1.71	Pam +RMI	Daily

*wl: "lower whisker" = lowest value within 1.5 times interquartile (Q25–Q75) range below 25th percentile.

**wh: "higher whisker" = highest value within 1.5 times interquartile (Q25–Q75) range above 75th percentile.

4   First Conclusions

This paper presents the first conclusions of our ongoing project. So far, only the air temperature at hourly and daily step was interpolated and only five learners were explored. However, we can see that even at high temporal resolution of one hour, interpolate data with geostatistical analysis increase the quality of field level air temperature prediction and is better than taking the nearest automatic weather station. Multilinear regression is the best method for both hourly and daily air. Increasing the dataset from 28 to 36 observations points slightly increases the quality of interpolation.

The next steps in the project to go further in interpolation analysis are: to check the value of short-term gridded weather forecast as a dynamic explanatory variable; to check the value of other prediction methods as artificial neural network; to perform interpolation of relative humidity and leaf wetness duration and to implement an automatic check to assess data reliability and to filter out wrong data.

The size of the dataset is a limit to data interpolation. IoT is an opportunity to improve the quality of the interpolated data by increasing the size of our training dataset. Either by developing our own low price and robust sensors to measure air temperature and humidity or by exploiting data measured by non-meteorological devices monitoring temperature (e.g. tractors or cars). Unknown quality of the measurement should be balanced with the amount of data. A new study should be conducted to know how to take benefit from a huge amount of data of unknown quality and how to work with an heterogeneous dataset composed of few observations of high quality (Pameseb and RMI AWS) and loads of observation of unknown precision.

References

1. Zeuner, T., Kleinhenz, B.: Use of geographic information systems in warning services for late blight*. EPPO Bull. **37**(2), 327–334 (2007). https://doi.org/10.1111/j.1365-2338.2007.01134.x
2. Racca, P., Kleinhenz, B., Zeuner, T., Keil, B., Tschöpe, B., Jung, J.: Decision support systems in agriculture: administration of meteorological data, use of geographic information systems (GIS) and validation methods in crop protection warning service (2011). https://doi.org/10.5772/20809
3. Perry, M., Hollis, D.: The generation of monthly gridded datasets for a range of climatic variables over the UK. Int. J. Climatol. **25**, 1041–1054 (2005)
4. Dobesch, H., Dumolard, P., Dryas, I. (eds.): Spatial Interpolation for Climate Data: the Use of GIS in Climatology and Meteorology. Geographical Information Systems Series. ISTE Ltd., London (2007)
5. Appelhans, T., Mwangomo, E., Hardy, D.R., Hemp, A., Nauss, T.: Evaluating machine learning approaches for the interpolation of monthly air temperature at Mt. Kilimanjaro, Tanzania. Spat. Stat. **14**, 91–113 (2015)
6. R Core Team: R: A language and environment for statistical computing. R Foundation for Statistical Computing, Vienna, Austria (2018). https://www.R-project.org/
7. Bischl, B., et al.: mlr: machine learning in R. J. Mach. Learn. Res. **17**(170), 1–5 (2016). http://jmlr.org/papers/v17/15-066.html

Prototype of a LPWA Network for Real-Time Hydro-Meteorological Monitoring and Flood Nowcasting

Audrey Douinot[1]([⊠]), Alessandro Dalla Torre[2], Jérôme Martin[2],
Jean-François Iffly[1], Laurent Rapin[2], Claude Meisch[3],
Christine Bastian[3], and Laurent Pfister[1]

[1] ERIN Department, Catchment and Eco-Hydrology Research Group,
Luxembourg Institute of Science and Technology,
5 Avenue des Hauts-Fourneaux, Esch-sur-Alzette, Luxembourg
audrey.douinot@list.lu
[2] IoT Business Solutions, POST Telecom, 1 rue Emile Bian,
Luxembourg City, Luxembourg
[3] Administration de la gestion de l'eau,
1 avenue du Rock'n'Roll, Esch-sur-Alzette, Luxembourg

Abstract. Over the past decade, Luxembourg has experienced an increase in extreme precipitation events during the summer season. As a direct consequence of this evolution, increasingly flashy hydrological responses have been observed in the river network – eventually leading to several flash flood events. In an area that has been historically prone to large scale winter floods, the current flood forecasting and monitoring chain is not adapted to this specific type of events, characterized by small spatial extents (<200 km^2), short time scales (<6 h) and high magnitudes. The SIGFOX network deployed in Luxembourg since 2016 provides a unique opportunity to leverage the potential for a Low-Power Wide-Area Network (LPWAN) to implement and operate a hydro-meteorological monitoring system of unprecedented spatial and temporal density. The restricted message size (12 bytes) supported by this technology is suited for the small data sets that are to be transmitted from each monitored hydro-meteorological site. In addition, the inter-connection of the different sensing devices allows for an immediate adaptation of the data acquisition and transmission frequencies – according to rapidly changing hydro-meteorological states. The entire network is able to switch from a sleep and low power consumption mode to a warning mode, with high frequency recordings and transmissions. The initial limit of 140 daily transmissions is eventually compensated for by a systematic compression of the numeric data on the one hand and the switch to cellular transmission during flash flood warning mode. Here we present the prototype implemented in the Ernz Blanche catchment (102 km^2), which was successively exposed to flash flood events in 2016 and 2018. The overall set-up consists of 4 raingauges, 4 streamgauges, and 4 soil moisture sensors. The first three months of operation of the prototype monitoring and transmission system on the Ernz Blanche catchment are assessed for validating the data transmission, acquisition, and emergency warning system.

Keywords: IOT · LPWAN · Flood monitoring · Flood forecasting · Emergency triggering thresholds

© Springer Nature Switzerland AG 2019
M. R. Palattella et al. (Eds.): ADHOC-NOW 2019, LNCS 11803, pp. 566–574, 2019.
https://doi.org/10.1007/978-3-030-31831-4_40

1 Status Quo: The Challenge of Forecasting Flash Flood Events in Luxembourg

1.1 Inter-annual Climate Variability and Trends in Europe

Investigations on future climate scenarios for the coming decades have reached a consensus on the intensification of extreme precipitation events in Europe [1, 2]. Despite remaining uncertainties in predictions of precipitation amounts and rates [3], the consensus among climate scientists relates to expected climate states, expressing through a warmer atmosphere with higher saturation vapor pressure – eventually paving the way for convective cells [4].

Long-term observations of precipitation have already confirmed to a large extend the forecasted climate trends. In Europe, several national studies based on long-term rainfall observations spanning 50 to 100 years, show evidence of an increase in heavy precipitation magnitude and frequency: in Switzerland [5], Czech Republic [6] and Poland [7] to name only a few. In addition to the climate shift, climate oscillation, associated with more or less persistent atmospheric circulations, lead to an inter annual variability of extreme precipitation [8–10] and consecutively to particular drought-rich and flood-rich periods [11, 12].

Luxembourg is not sheltered from these climate trends and climate variability [13]. As an example, Fig. 1 shows the records of maximum daily precipitation for 20 raingauges located in Luxembourg - illustrating several heavy precipitation-rich periods spread across nearly 60 years. The increase in heavy precipitation is demonstrated by a shift from an average of 3.1 days per year with precipitation intensities locally exceeding 50 mm per day during the 1957–1977 period to an average of 4.7 days per year during the 1989–2009 period for the same daily precipitation intensity. Eventually, the last decade has the highest frequencies of heavy precipitation.

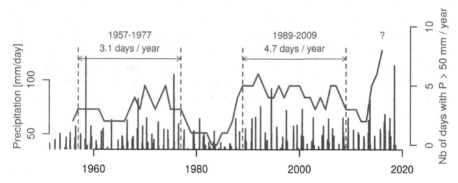

Fig. 1. Blue bars: days with precipitation exceeding 35 mm per day during the April-October season of the 1954 – 2018 period, for at least 1 out of 20 long-term raingauge records in Luxembourg. Red line: 5-year moving average of the number of days with precipitation exceeding 50 mm per day. Periods with heavy precipitation are highlighted by horizontal dotted lines. (Color figure online)

1.2   Flash Floods as an Emerging Natural Risk in Luxembourg

As a result of extreme precipitation, Luxembourg experienced successively two flash flood events of unprecedented magnitude in 2016 and 2018 [13]. A flash flood is characterised by a fast increase in discharge, up to an extreme flood peak in less than 6 h. The flash floods typically occur after strong convective events over medium sized catchments (<250 km^2). Due to their magnitude and sudden occurrence, flash floods are a major natural risk in Europe, each event causing important economic losses and sometimes fatalities [14].

In Europe, flash floods usually occur on the foothills of the largest mountain ranges (i.e. the Alps, the Pyrenees and the Carpathian mountains [15, 16]), as the topographical features allow both highly humid air coming from the Mediterranean sea to condensate, generate extreme precipitation and subsequently flashy runoff responses. In the last decade, several flash flood events have been reported in Western Central Europe (Belgium, Netherlands, Luxembourg and West Germany) [13, 17–20]. While this area had not been identified as prone to flash floods until recently, the successive events corroborating the increase in heavy precipitation has the stakeholders of this region face a new issue.

1.3   Limitations of the Conventional Hydro-Meteorological Monitoring Network for Forecasting Flash Flood Events

In a historical context, floods in Luxembourg have typically been triggered by large advective precipitation events during the winter season. Therefore, the local flood forecast system was designed for large-scale riverine floods (triggered mostly by moderate long-lasting precipitation spread over large areas). Consequently, this set-up was not suited for grasping the specific short spatial and temporal scales that had characterized the 2016 and 2018 flash flood events.

Current meteorological forecasting tools are not able to exactly locate a convective rainfall event [21]. To complete the meteorological forecast, the stakeholders require real-time observations. National authorities currently have at their disposal a 1 min time-step raingauge network and 5 min time-step radar observations from the German Weather Service (RADOLAN products), each one transmitted every 15 min and every hour respectively. These data sets have some limitations, the raingauge network being spatially too coarse to catch the extreme values of local convective events (Fig. 2a), and the radar products suffering from uncertainties when estimating high intensities (Fig. 2b, [22]).

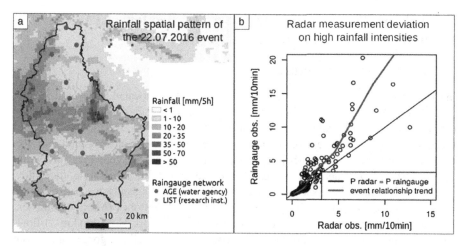

Fig. 2. (a) Example of localized rainfall patterns related to flash flood processes against the current conventional raingauge network density. (b) Typical underestimation of high rainfall intensities as obtained from radar assessments when compared to raingauge measurements. Rainfall observations relate to the 22.07.2019 event.

1.4 Opportunities Provided by a Low-Power Wide-Area Network (LPWAN)

In 2016, a Low Power Wide Area Network (LPWAN) was rolled out in Luxembourg by the national telecommunication company (POST) and RMS who owns the Sigfox licence in Luxembourg. A LPWA network supports communication between devices without the need of human interaction (Machine to Machine communication, [23]). The key feature of LPWAN networks is to enable a fixed and short range communication, but requiring low power consumption (up to 1000 times less than an usual wireless connection [24]) and supporting a massive number of Internet of Things (IoT) devices. The proprietary SIGFOX [25] LPWAN, that was set up in Luxembourg, uses the 8–900 MHz unlicensed bands to transmit up to 140 12-bites-limited messages.

The SIGFOX LPWAN provides the opportunity to increase the density of the raingauge network, and to ensure a confident nearly real-time connection, without requiring extensive power consumption (and consecutive extensive maintenance in remote areas). In addition, this perspective allows to go back over the monitoring network concept and to design it not as a passive recording device network, but rather as an active 'operator' thanks to POST Cumulocity IoT Platform, which manage all the sensors and the way they communicate with each other. This platform ables to immediately warn the public authorities of heavy precipitation and to adapt its own functioning according to the rapidly changing meteorological conditions. Here, we present a test facility of a hydro-meteorological network relying on the SIGFOX LPWAN network.

2   The Ernz Blanche Catchment as a Test Bed for a LPWAN-Connected Flood Monitoring Set-Up

2.1   The Ernz Blanche Catchment

The Ernz Blanche catchment covers an area of 102 km^2, located in Central-Eastern Luxembourg (Fig. 3). The Ernz Blanche has been chosen as: (i) it is located in a region that has been repeatedly affected by recent extreme summer precipitation; (ii) 2 out of the 3 recent flash flood episodes have occurred within the close vicinity of this catchment; (iii) the stretched shape, the topographical and the geological properties support fast runoff generation processes and are suited for monitoring local flow processes. Catchment bedrock is characterised by calcareous sandstone (Luxembourg sandstone), covered nearly half by residual marls and limestones (Marls of Strassen, 37%), forming impermeable plateaus [26]. The river network (1.24 km.km^{-2}) flows northward and cuts deep into the sandstone, designing cliffs, gorges and steep hillslopes.

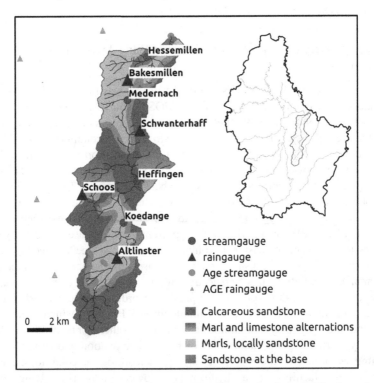

Fig. 3. Location and geological properties of the Ernz Blanche catchment and sub-catchments in Luxembourg: calcareous sandstone (Luxembourg sandstone, 43%), marls and locally sandstone, dolomite (37%); Marls and limestone alterations (Marls of Strassen, 20%). The proposed flood monitoring network is covering four subcatchments: Koedange (31 km^2), Heffingen (49 km^2), Medernach (79 km^2), Hessemillen (93 km^2).

The LPWAN-connected flood monitoring set-up consists of 4 streamgauges and 4 raingauges, combined with pairs of soil moisture sensors. The devices have been dispatched (Fig. 3) in order to equally cover the catchment, rendering its combined geological–pedological diversity. Finally, for each station, the low-power consumption is additionally supported by solar panels.

2.2 Operating Mode

The raingauge stations are inter-connected through the SIGFOX network, while the streamgauge stations, as located in the populated valley floors, remain connected through the conventional cell phone network. In addition, the raingauge stations are able to switch to the cell network, in case of 3 successive failed transmissions.

The network transmits the relevant variables for flood forecasting (i.e. soil moisture, water levels and rainfall rates) but also useful information for carrying out the station maintenance (battery level and temperature of the datalogger, see Fig. 4). In a standard operation mode, the network transmits at 15-minute time step. However, the entire network is able to switch from the standard and low power consumption mode to a warning mode, with higher frequency recording and transmissions. In case of emergency situations the stations communicate at 5 min time step through the cell phone network. Similarly, the critical recorded data, i.e. the rainfall rate and the river water levels are recorded with higher frequency during the warning mode. The Table 1 summarizes the recorded variables and the respective acquisition/transmission frequencies.

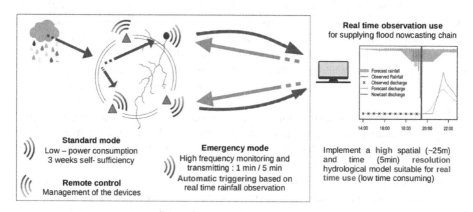

Fig. 4. Scheme of the LPWAN-connected flood monitoring set up.

The transition to a warning mode is automatically done according to the network records: when a high rainfall intensity ($I_{indiv} > 4.5$ mm/15 min) at one raingauge or a moderate rainfall intensity ($I_{cat} > 2.8$ mm/15 min) but at all the raingauges is recorded, the network automatically switches to the warning mode. For convenience, the stakeholders may also manually activate the emergency mode. The rainfall intensity thresholds are fixed according to a statistical analysis of 20 years worth of rainfall time series observed in the vicinity of the Ernz Blanche catchment, with the aim to trigger the warning mode 10 times during the test period (2 summers). The high frequency monitoring mode of the system is maintained during 2.5 h after the last warning mode trigger.

Table 1. Observed variables and acquisition/transmission frequencies

	Standard mode	Warning mode
Streamgauges		
Water level [m]	5 min/15 min	1 min/5 min
Battery [V]	5 min/15 min	1 min/5 min
Raingauges and soil moisture sensors		
Rainfall accumulation [mm]	5 min/15 min	1 min/5 min
Soil water content [%]	15 min/15 min	15 min/15 min
Battery [V]	30 min/30 min	1 min/5 min

3   Conclusion and Perspectives

Our contribution presents a proof-of-concept of an innovative flood monitoring system relying on a LPWAN network. This set-up has been motivated by: (i) the current deficiency of the conventional flood warning system in Luxembourg, not adapted for the more frequent summer flash flood events, and (ii) the opportunity provided by the LPWAN facilities, allowing for an increase in the density of the hydro-meteorological network, and to implement an adaptive smart system for intense rainfall occurrences.

We have designed and deployed a dense hydro-meteorological network on the mesoscale Ernz Blanche catchment – prone to flash floods. Four streamgauges, four raingauges, combined with eight soil moisture sensors, have been installed on the Ernz Blanche catchment (102 km^2). The different sensing devices have adaptive data acquisition and transmission frequencies – according to immediate rainfall records. The first operated month has proven the network's robustness, with no failed connection, nor battery loading issue. In addition, during this period two high-intensity rainfall events have triggered the emergency mode and the overall system has alternatively switched to the expected transmission protocols.

The assessment of the proposed flood monitoring system will be pursued further to test its functioning under strong intensive convective storms. This larger assessment period will allow us to adjust the rainfall triggering thresholds related to the soil wetness condition, taking then into account the critical complexity of the catchment's response to rainfall events. At a later stage, joint reflections between hydrologists, public stakeholders and telecommunication professionals will be organized to find out the adequate way to communicate flood warnings to different stakeholders (i.e. safety officers, rescue services, inhabitants), ultimately implementing and deploying a complete flood warning chain adapted for flash flood events.

References

1. Filippo, G., Raffaele, F., Coppola, E.: The response of precipitation characteristics to global warming from climate projections. Earth Syst. Dyn. **10**, 73–89 (2019). https://doi.org/10.5194/esd-10-73-2019
2. Pfahl, S., O'Gorman, P.A., Fischer, E.M.: Understanding the regional pattern of projected future changes in extreme precipitation. Nat. Clim. Change **7**, 423–428 (2017). https://doi.org/10.1038/NCLIMATE3287
3. Sillmann, J., et al.: Understanding, modeling and predicting weather and climate extremes: challenges and opportunities. Weather Clim. Extremes **18**, 65–74 (2017). https://doi.org/10.1016/j.wace.2017.10.003
4. Tandon, N.F., Zhang, X., Sobel, A.H.: Understanding the dynamics of future changes in extreme precipitation intensity. Geophys. Res. Lett. **45**, 2870–2878 (2018). https://doi.org/10.1002/2017GL076361
5. Scherrer, S.C., Fischer, E.M., Posselt, R., Liniger, M.A., Croci Maspoli, M., Knutti, R.: Emerging trends in heavy precipitation and hot temperature extremes in Switzerland. J. Geophys. Res. Atmos. **121**, 2626–2637 (2016). https://doi.org/10.1002/2015JD024634
6. Hanel, M., Pavlásková, A., Kyselý, J.: Trends in characteristics of sub-daily heavy precipitation and rainfall erosivity in the Czech Republic. Int. J. Climatol. **36**, 1833–1845 (2016). https://doi.org/10.1002/joc4463
7. Pińskwar, I., Choryński, A., Graczyk, D., Kundzewicz, Z.W.: Observed changes in extreme precipitation in Poland: 1991–2015 versus 1961–1990. Theoret. Appl. Climatol. **135**(1), 773–787 (2019). https://doi.org/10.1007/s00704-018-2372-1
8. Marani, M., Zanetti, S.: Long-term oscillations in rainfall extremes in a 268 year daily time series. Water Resour. Res. **51**(1), 639–647 (2015). https://doi.org/10.1002/2014WR015885
9. Irannezhad, M., Marttila, H., Chen, D., Kløve, B.: Century-long variability and trends in daily precipitation characteristics at three Finnish stations. Adv. Clim. Change Res. **7**(1), 54–69 (2016). https://doi.org/10.1016/j.accre.2016.04.004
10. Gregersen, I.B., Madsen, H., Rosbjerg, D., Arnbjerg-Nielsen, K.: Long term variations of extreme rainfall in Denmark and Southern Sweden. Clim. Dyn. **44**(11), 3155–3169 (2015). https://doi.org/10.1007/s00382-014-2276-4
11. Blöschl, G., et al.: Increasing river floods: fiction or reality? Wiley Interdiscip. Rev. Water **2**(4), 329–344 (2015). https://doi.org/10.1002/wat2.1079
12. Merz, B., et al.: Spatial coherence of flood-rich and flood-poor periods across Germany. J. Hydrol. **559**, 813–826 (2018). https://doi.org/10.1016/j.jhydrol.2018.02.082
13. Pfister, L., Douinot, A., Meisch, C., Bastian, C., Tamez, C.: Recent extreme hydro-meteorological events in North-Western Central Europe (Luxembourg): extreme hydrological features, meteorological factors and atmospheric conditions. In: EGU (2019). https://meetingorganizer.copernicus.org/EGU2019/EGU2019-13457.pdf
14. Barredo, J.I.: Major flood disasters in Europe: 1950–2005. Nat. Hazards **42**(1), 125–148 (2007). https://doi.org/10.1007/s11069-006-9065-2
15. Marchi, L., Borga, M., Preciso, E., Gaume, E.: Characterisation of selected extreme flash floods in Europe and implications for flood risk management. J. Hydrol. **394**(1–2), 118–133 (2010). https://doi.org/10.1016/j.jhydrol.2010.07.017
16. Amponsah, W., et al.: Integrated high-resolution dataset of high-intensity European and Mediterranean flash floods. Earth Syst. Sci. Data **10**(4), 1783–1794 (2018). https://doi.org/10.5194/essd-10-1783-2018

17. Van Campenhout, J., et al.: Flash floods and muddy floods in Wallonia: recent temporal trends, spatial distribution and reconstruction of the hydrosedimentological fluxes using flood marks and sediment deposits. Belgeo. Revue Belge de Géographie (1) (2015)

18. Brauer, C.C., et al.: Anatomy of extraordinary rainfall and flash flood in a Dutch lowland catchment. Hydrol. Earth Syst. Sci. **15**(6), 1991–2005 (2011). https://doi.org/10.5194/hess-15-1991-2011

19. Piper, D., et al.: Exceptional sequence of severe thunderstorms and related flash floods in May and June 2016 in Germany – Part 1: Meteorological background. Nat. Hazards Earth Syst. Sci. **16**(12), 2835–2850 (2016). https://doi.org/10.5194/nhess-16-2835-2016

20. Ruiz-Villanueva, V., Borga, M., Zoccatelli, D., Marchi, L., Gaume, E., Ehret, U.: Extreme flood response to short-duration convective rainfall in South-West Germany. Hydrol. Earth Syst. Sci. **16**(5), 1543–1559 (2012). http://www.hydrol-earth-syst-sci.net/16/1543/2012/hess-16-1543-2012.html

21. Davolio, S., Buzzi, A., Malguzzi, P.: High resolution simulations of an intense convective precipitation event. Meteorol. Atmos. Phys. **95**(3–4), 139–154 (2007). https://doi.org/10.1007/s00703-006-0200-0

22. Jacobi, S., Heistermann, M.: Benchmarking attenuation correction procedures for six years of single-polarized C-band weather radar observations in South-West Germany. Geomat. Nat. Hazards Risk **7**(6), 1785–1799 (2016). https://doi.org/10.1080/19475705.2016.1155080

23. Lauridsen, M., Nguyen, H., Vejlgaard, B., Kovacs, I.Z., Mogensen, P., Sorensen, M.: Coverage comparison of GPRS, NB-IoT, LoRa, and SigFox in a 7800 km² area. In: 2017 IEEE 85th Vehicular Technology Conference (VTC Spring), pp. 1–5 (2017). https://doi.org/10.1109/VTCSpring.2017.8108182

24. ICT Experts Luxembourg, Rapin, L.: Iot: La guerre des réseaux aura t'elle lieu? https://ictexpertsluxembourg.lu/digital-media/iot-guerre-reseaux-aura-t-lieu/. Accessed 01 May 2019

25. SigFox. https://www.sigfox.com. Accessed 01 May 2019

26. Kausch, B., Maquil, R.: Landscapes and landforms of the Luxembourg Sandstone, Grand-Duchy of Luxembourg. In: Demoulin, A. (ed.) Landscapes and Landforms of Belgium and Luxembourg. WGL, 1st edn, pp. 43–62. Springer, Cham (2018). https://doi.org/10.1007/978-3-319-58239-9_4

Efficient Wireless Sensor Deployment at Minimum Cost

Francesca Guerriero[1], Luigi Di Puglia Pugliese[1], and Nathalie Mitton[2(✉)]

[1] Department of Mechanical, Energy and Management Engineering,
University of Calabria, Rende, Italy
{francesca.guerriero,luigi.dipugliapugliese}@unical.it
[2] Inria, Villeneuve-d'Ascq, France
nathalie.mitton@inria.fr

Abstract. We address the problem of defining a wireless sensor network by deploying sensors with the aim of guaranteeing the coverage of the area and the connectivity among the sensors. The wireless sensor networks are widely studied since they provide several services, e.g., environmental monitoring and target tracking. We consider several typologies of sensors characterized by different sensing and connectivity ranges. A cost is associated with each typology of sensors. In particular, the higher the sensing and connectivity ranges, the higher the cost. We formulate the problem of deploying sensors at minimum cost such that each sensor is connected to a base station with either a one- or a multi-hop and the area is full covered. We present preliminary computational results by solving the proposed mathematical model, on several instances. We provide a simulation-based analysis of the performances of such a deployment from the routing perspective.

Keywords: Sensor deployment · Routing · Wireless · Cost efficiency

1 Introduction

These last years have witnessed the development of several wireless sensors deployment strategies, to be applied in many different fields. A large part of them focus on environmental monitoring and surveillance operations [4]. When deploying such a sensor network, the following main challenges arise. How many sensors need to be deployed to ensure the full area coverage at a minimum cost? Where to deploy them to keep not only the proper monitoring of the area, but also to ensure the existence of a wireless multi-hop path between any pair of nodes in the network? Then, once sensors deployed, how good is the quality of the communicating network yet constructed beyond the plain connectivity?

Covering problems have been investigated for several years by different research communities: robotics, networking and optimization groups. Most of robotics researchers mainly couple coverage with path planning and friction efforts; networking researchers mainly consider energy costs and connectivity

© Springer Nature Switzerland AG 2019
M. R. Palattella et al. (Eds.): ADHOC-NOW 2019, LNCS 11803, pp. 575–587, 2019.
https://doi.org/10.1007/978-3-030-31831-4_41

while optimization researchers have generally neglected the connectivity issues. To the best of our knowledge, only very few approaches [2,11,12] from the literature consider jointly connectivity and quality of monitoring coverage. These approaches propose mixed integer linear programs to formulate the problem of deploying sensors ensuring coverage and connectivity. Efficient solutions are obtained, achieving very interesting and performing results, but they do not take into account the deployment cost. In addition, the solutions obtained by using the existing approaches are considered satisfactory if they achieve connectivity, whereas none of them evaluates the quality of the communication network obtained.

In this paper, we assume to have a limited number of sensors of different typologies, each characterized by a sensing range, a communication range and an operational cost. We add communication constraints in order to force sensors to be connected (permanently or intermittently) and form a communication network, allowing them to dynamically self-adapt to any environment aspect. We also consider the energy consumption and the travelled distance.

The main contributions of our work are reported in what follows:

- We address a generalized sensors deployment problem with coverage and connectivity constraints, considering different typologies of sensors.
- We formulate the problem as a mixed integer program and we provide a deep evaluation of the solutions obtained, analyzing the efficiency and the effectiveness with respect to the deployment cost.
- We assess the obtained sensor deployment, in terms of quality of communication topology.

The remainder of this paper is organized as follows. Section 2 summarizes the state of the art. In Sect. 3 we formally describe the addressed problem along with the mathematical formulation. Section 4 provides the numerical results collected on meaningful instances. Section 5 concludes the paper.

2   State of the Art

The coverage and monitoring of a point or an area of interest have been studied by different research communities. i.e., networking, robotics, and optimization.

The robotics community refers to the techniques set up to cover an area as "formation control". They generally do not consider connectivity issues [14,16].

In the optimization field, some works focus on multi-objective mathematical models, to determine the best placement of mobile nodes for different tasks; we cite, for example, the papers of Guerriero *et al.* [5] and Lambrou *et al.* [8]. Guerriero *et al.* [5] focus on the optimal sensor displacement to allow the network to achieve high performance in terms of energy consumption and travelled distance.

In Lambrou *et al.* [8], the authors provide a collaborative architecture between mobile and static sensors. The coverage objective described in [8] is the same as the one taken into account in the present work. However, they do not consider the communication constraints. Yu et al. [17] applied Genetic

Particle Swarm Optimization (GA-PSO) techniques to solve the optimal sensor deployment problem. However, the authors do not pursue the same goal as in this paper and do not address communication aspects.

Several challenging issues arise when quality of coverage and connectivity issues are considered simultaneously [7]. From the networking perspective, self-deployment distributed and localized protocols are generally proposed to address these specific aspects. These protocols broadly aim at a single objective which is either cover a point of interest/target [6] or a whole area of interest [1], that might be mobile [10]. Such approaches used different tools such as Virtual Forces [13], Swarm Optimization [9] or graph theory tools [3,15].

Very few works, addressing jointly communication connectivity and quality of coverage, have been published by researchers operating in the optimization field. The main goal considered in [2,11,12] is very similar to the one taken into account in the present paper, since the authors aim at covering a sensing area, by deploying the minimum number of wireless sensors, while maintaining the connectivity between the deployed sensors. In [11,12], the authors address the problem by reducing it to a two-dimensional critical coverage problem (an NP-Complete problem), and developing an integer linear programming formulation to obtain an optimal solution. In [2] standard mixed integer linear programs are used to represent several variants of the problem. Although these works achieve very interesting results, they do not consider the cost of the deployment.

Most of the existing approaches that consider the cost of a wireless sensor network only focus on the deployment phase (cost of a sensor, number of sensors and sometimes distance to drop it), but, to the best of our knowledge, none of them take into account the operational cost (energy sensors will consume to send and forward data) and quality (quality of links).

3   Problem Definition

Given a field, the objective is to deploy a set of sensors at minimum cost, such that full coverage and full connectivity are ensured.

We assume the availability of K different typologies of sensors. Each sensor $k \in K$ is characterized by a sensing range r_k, a communication range R_k and a cost c_k. In addition, we assume a limited number of sensors for each typology, i.e., n_k. We assume a point is covered if it is within a sensing range of at least one sensor.

The full connectivity is guaranteed if each sensor is connected to a sink node o with either a 1-hop or multi-hop communication. In the latter case, the other sensors play the role of relay.

We formulate the problem over a complete graph $G(N, A, C)$ where N is the set of possible location points in the field where the sensors could be deployed, A is the set of arcs connecting each point $i \in N$ to the other points $j \in N \setminus \{i\}$, C is the set of locations to be covered (so that are in sensing range of at least one sensor). The Euclidean distance d_{uv} is associated with each pair of positions $u, v \in N \cup C$.

3.1   Mathematical Formulation

To formulate the problem, we introduce the following decision variables:

$x_{ij}, \forall (i,j) \in A$. Continuous variables taking value greater than zero if a communication between position i and j is active, zero otherwise.

$w_{ij}, \forall (i,j) \in A$. Binary variables taking value equal to one if a bilateral communication between i and j can be activated, i.e., $d_{ij} \leq \min\{R_k, R_{k'}\}$, where k and k' are the typologies of sensors located in position i and j, respectively, zero otherwise.

$y_i^k, \forall i \in N, k \in K$. Binary variables that assume value equal to one if a sensor of typology k is deployed in position i, zero otherwise.

$z_h^i, \forall h \in C, i \in N$. Binary variables taking value equal to one if point h is covered by a sensor deployed in position i, zero otherwise.

The problem can be formulated as follows:

$$\min \sum_{i \in N} \sum_{k \in K} c_k y_i^k$$

s.t.   (1)

$$\sum_{i \in N} y_i^k \leq n_k, \quad \forall k \in K, \tag{2}$$

$$\sum_{k \in K} y_i^k \leq 1, \quad \forall i \in N, \tag{3}$$

$$w_{ij} \leq \frac{\sum_{k \in K} y_i^k R_k}{d_{ij}}, \quad \forall (i,j) \in A, \tag{4}$$

$$w_{ij} \leq \frac{\sum_{k \in K} y_j^k R_k}{d_{ij}}, \quad \forall (i,j) \in A, \tag{5}$$

$$x_{ij} \leq M w_{ij}, \quad \forall (i,j) \in A, \tag{6}$$

$$\sum_{(i,j) \in A} x_{ij} - \sum_{(j,i) \in A} x_{ji} = \begin{cases} \sum_{k \in K} \sum_{j \in N} y_j^k & \text{if } i = o \\ -\sum_{k \in K} y_i^k & \text{otherwise} \end{cases} \quad \forall i \in N, \tag{7}$$

$$z_h^i \leq \frac{\sum_{k \in K} y_i^k r_k}{d_{ih}}, \quad \forall h \in C, i \in N, \tag{8}$$

$$\sum_{i \in N} z_h^i \geq 1, \quad \forall h \in C, \tag{9}$$

$$x_{ij} \in \mathbb{R}_+^{|A|}, w_{ij} \in \{0,1\}, \forall (i,j) \in A, y_i^k \in \{0,1\}, \forall i \in N, k \in K,$$
$$z_h^i \in \{0,1\}, \forall i \in N, h \in C. \tag{10}$$

Equation (1) minimizes the cost of deployed sensors. Equation (2) allows the deployment of at most n_k sensors for each typology $k \in K$. Equation (3) imposes that at most one sensor is deployed for each position $i \in N$. Equations (4) and (5) define the variables w_{ij}. In particular, w_{ij} is imposed to be zero in the case either the distance between the sensors deployed in positions i and j

is greater than the minimum communication range between both sensors or no sensor is deployed in either position i or j. Equations (6) ensure that each arc (i, j) is active if and only if it is able to connect sensors deployed in positions i and j, where M is a big positive number. If $w_{ij} = 1$ means that the sensors deployed at positions i and j can communicate. Since the value of x_{ij} is not upper bounded, then it can assume any positive value $\leq M$. Equations (7) represent flow constraints aiming at defining the communication between the sink node o and all the deployed sensors. Equations (8) define the coverage of position $h \in C$. In particular, if the sensing range of a sensor of typology k located in position i is less than the distance d_{hi} between $h \in C$ and $i \in N$, then variable z_h^i is forced to assume the value zero. Equation (9) impose that each point $h \in C$ is covered by at least one sensor. Equation (10) defines the domain of the decision variables. We observe that Equation (7) represent flow conservation constraints. Once a solution is determined, variables x_{ij} define a possible communication tree among the deployed sensors. It is as if we considered that each sensor sent one unit of data, thus all variables $x_{ij} > 0$ define the quantity of data that traverses arc (i, j). In the worst case, the data of all deployed sensors are sent through a single arc. It follows that the value that each variable x_{ij} can assume is upper bounded by $\min \left\{ |N|, \sum_{k \in K} n_k \right\}$. The value of M can be set to this value, i.e., $M = \min \left\{ |N|, \sum_{k \in K} n_k \right\}$.

We highlight that the proposed model can couple the case where a target has to be covered by at least $S > 1$ sensors. Indeed, it is sufficient to introduce the parameter S in the right-hand-side of constraints (9) for the point that needs to be covered by the S sensors (possibly all points).

4   Computational Results

In what follows, we analyze the behaviour of the proposed mathematical model, referred in the sequel as GMc, on randomly generated instances.

We have considered also the case in which the number of sensors is minimized. In particular, the objective function (1) has been modified in $\sum_{i \in N} \sum_{k \in K} y_i^k$. The model with the latter objective function is referred in the sequel as GMs.

The models have been implemented in Java language and solved by CPLEX 12.51. The tests were carried out on an Intel(R) core(TM) i7-4720HQ CPU 2.60 GHz 8 GB RAM machine.

The main aim of this section is to present the numerical results obtained and to show the bi-objective nature of the considered problem, with the respect to the minimization of the overall cost, i.e., function (1) and the minimization of the number of deployed sensors (i.e., $\sum_{i \in N} \sum_{k \in K} y_i^k$). We suppose that the higher the sensing range, the higher the cost. On the one hand, when minimizing the number of sensors, those with higher sensing range are chosen, on the other hand, sensors with low sensing range are preferred because they have lower cost than those with high sensing range. The numerical results confirmed the conflicting nature of the two objectives. A sensitivity analysis on the number of available typologies of sensors is also carried out. Finally, we evaluate the effectiveness of the solutions from a communication point of view.

We deploy a varying number of nodes at position $<x, y>$ such that $X_{min} \leq x \leq X_{max}$ and $Y_{min} \leq y \leq Y_{max}$ in a field with varying size.

The results are collected on instances generated by considering the following characteristics:

- $X_{min} = Y_{min} = 0$
- $X_{max} = Y_{max} \in \{10, 12, 14, 20\}$
- $n_k = 100, \forall k \in K$
- each point $i \in N$ has integer coordinates (X_i, Y_i) in the defined field.

The testing phase has been carried out by considering four scenarios that differ from each other for the dimension of the (square) field, i.e., $(10, 10)$, $(12, 12)$, $(14, 14)$, and $(20, 20)$. The instances are characterized by the following parameters:

- $|K| \in \{2, 3, 4, 5\}$
- r_k randomly chosen in the interval $[2, 6]$
- $R_k = R * r_k$ with $R = \max\{1, \alpha f\}, \alpha \in [0, 1], f = \sqrt{3}$ meaning that $1 \leq \frac{R_k}{r_k} \leq \sqrt{3}$
- $c_k = r_k^2$
- each point $h \in C$ has coordinates associated to the centre of the cell. Each corner is a point in N.
- the sink is located at coordinate $(0, 0)$.

We follow the scientific literature to generate the instances. The dimensions of the field and the sensing range values refer to [2], whereas, the connectivity range values satisfy the property described in [7]. Indeed, $\frac{R_k}{r_k} \leq \sqrt{3}$ guarantees that the full coverage does not imply the full connectivity. Fixing the number of typologies of sensors, we generate 5 different configurations varying the seed for the randomly generated parameters.

4.1 Numerical Results

In this section, we analyze the results obtained by solving GMc, aimed at minimizing the overall cost, and the model GMs in which the objective function, to be minimized, represents the number of deployed sensors (i.e., $\sum_{i \in N} \sum_{k \in K} y_i^k$).

First of all, we analyze the efficiency of the proposed model and give some insights on the conflicting nature of the two criteria, i.e., cost and number of sensors. Secondly, we analyze the solutions obtained by both GMc and GMs under a communication point of view. In particular, we investigate how good the network topology built by the sensor deployment is for routing protocols, in terms of path diversities and energy consumption.

Models Evaluation. The results obtained with MGs and MGc are shown in Table 1. We report, for each dimension of the field and number of typologies of sensors $|K|$, the number of deployed sensors under column #sensors, the cost, i.e., the value of (1), under column cost, the execution time of CPLEX for solving the instances in seconds under column time. We impose a time limit of 1800 s to the solver for solving each instance, for both models. The superscript near to the time indicates the number of instances that are not solved to optimality within the imposed time limit. We notice that each line of Table 1 reports average results over the five instances generated by varying the seed.

Table 1. Average results obtained with GMc and GMs, varying the dimension of the field and the number of available typologies of sensors.

	$|K|$	GMc			GMs		
		#sensors	cost	time	#sensors	cost	time
(10, 10)	2	8.80	54.00	953.36[2]	3.20	75.40	1.28
	3	6.40	53.00	749.78[2]	2.60	71.00	1.08
	4	10.20	54.00	1800.00[5]	2.20	79.20	1.42
	5	8.20	43.80	1494.98[4]	2.20	79.20	1.80
AVG		8.40	51.20	1249.53[13]	2.55	76.20	1.39
(12, 12)	2	9.80	76.20	1433.52[3]	4.60	110.80	23.82
	3	8.20	77.40	1528.67[4]	3.60	100.80	57.80
	4	11.80	75.40	1800.00[5]	3.00	99.60	71.88
	5	10.80	68.60	1800.00[5]	3.20	104.20	126.51
AVG		10.15	74.40	1640.55[17]	3.60	103.85	70.00
(14, 14)	2	14.20	110.20	1800.00[5]	5.20	124.40	387.56[1]
	3	11.60	104.00	1800.00[5]	4.60	130.60	112.57
	4	12.00	117.40	1800.00[5]	4.40	158.40	173.58
	5	13.80	101.00	1800.00[5]	4.20	151.20	135.83
AVG		12.90	108.15	1800.00[20]	4.60	141.15	202.38[1]
(20, 20)	2	24.40	284.20	1800.00[5]	21.60	554.20	1684.00[4]
	3	36.40	388.80	1800.00[5]	11.40	319.60	1800.00[5]
	4	22.60	262.60	1800.00[5]	10.20	367.20	1800.00[5]
	5	32.00	239.00	1800.00[5]	9.80	352.80	1800.00[5]
AVG		28.85	293.65	1800.00[20]	13.25	398.45	1771.00[19]
AVG2	2	14.30	131.15	1496.72[15]	8.65	216.20	524.16[5]
	3	15.65	155.80	1469.61[16]	5.55	155.50	492.86[5]
	4	14.15	127.35	1800.00[20]	4.95	176.10	511.72[5]
	5	16.20	113.10	1723.75[19]	4.85	171.85	516.04[5]
AVG3		15.08	131.85	1622.52[70]	6.00	179.91	511.20[20]

Row AVG reports the average results on the instances with the same dimension of the field, row AVG2 shows the average results over the instances with the same value of $|K|$, and row AVG3 reports the average results over all instances.

The results reported in Table 1 highlight that the model GMc is more difficult to solve than GMs. Indeed, 13, 17, 20, and 20 instances with the field $(10, 10)$, $(12, 12)$, $(14, 14)$, and $(20, 20)$ are not solved to optimality by the solver within the time limit, respectively. We highlight that 20 instances are considered for each field dimension. Thus, more than a half of instances are not solved for each field dimension. For the biggest ones, the optimal solution is not available for all the instances. It follows that solving GMc requires 3.17 times higher computational time than that needed by the solver to handle GMs, on average (see row AVG3).

Comparing the performance of the two models varying the dimension of the field, we observe that the higher the field dimension the lower the difference in term of computational effort between GMc and GMs. Indeed, GMs is 897.53, 23.44, 8.89, and 1.02 times faster than GMc for the fields $(10, 10)$, $(12, 12)$, $(14, 14)$, and $(20, 20)$, respectively. It is worth noting that these results are highly influenced by the imposed time limit. Indeed, GMs is able to obtain the optimal solution for all the instance, excluding the one with field $(14, 14)$ and the 9 with field $(20, 20)$. In addition, solving GMs requires, on average, 1.39, 70.00, 202.38, and 1771.00 s. Thus, a high increase in the computational effort is observed. This trend is not evident for GMc since the time limit imposes an upper bound on the computational cost. The same conclusion can be drawn from the results obtained varying the values of $|K|$. In this case, GMc is 2, 86, 2.98, 3.52, and 3.34 times slower than GMs for $|K|$ equals to 2, 3, 4, and 5, respectively.

Table 1 highlights the conflicting nature of the two objective functions, i.e., the minimization of the cost and the minimization of the number of sensors.

On the one hand, GMs provides solutions with 6.00 deployed sensors and cost equals to 179.91, on average. On the other hand, the solutions obtained by solving GMc are characterized by 15.08 deployed sensors with a cost of 131.85, on average. Thus, GMc provides solutions that are 1.56 less expensive than those obtained with GMs, but they require 2.51 times more sensors than those deployed by GMs.

This is an expected trend since the higher the coverage r, the higher the cost. Thus, when the number of sensors is minimized, those with higher values of r are preferred with a consequent increase in the cost. On the other hand, when the cost is minimized, sensors with low values of r are chosen. This implies the use of a higher number of such sensors, in order to guarantee the coverage of the field.

Referring to the number of available typologies of sensors $|K|$, we do not observe a clear trend of the difference, in terms of cost, between GMc and GMs (see row AVG2 for each value of $|K|$ of Table 1). Indeed, the solutions obtained by solving GMs are, on average, 1.65, 1.00, 1.36, and 1.52 times more expensive that those obtained by solving GMc for $|K|$ equals to 2, 3, 4, and 5, respectively. This behaviour is due to the fact that GMs does not provide the optimal solution for almost all the instances with field $(20, 20)$. This implies that the number of sensors deployed is not minimized, then the cost tends to decrease (by the conflicting nature of the two objectives). As a matter of this fact, if we consider only the fields $(10, 10)$, $(12, 12)$, and $(14, 14)$, the difference in terms of cost between GMc and GMs increases when $|K|$ increases. Indeed, GMs provides solutions that are 1.29, 1.29, 1.37, and 1.57, times more expensive than those provided by GMc for $|K|$ equal to 2, 3, 4, and 5, respectively.

Considering the number of deployed sensors, the higher the value of $|K|$, the higher the difference between the two models (see row AVG2 for each value of $|K|$ of Table 1). Indeed, GMs provides solutions with a number of deployed sensors that is 1.65, 2.82, 2.86, and 3.34 times lower than that deployed by the solutions obtained by GMc, on average, for values of $|K|$ equals to 2, 3, 4, and 5, respectively.

Topology Evaluation. The set of sensors yet deployed aims to efficiently cover and monitor the full area and to constitute a connected network. This property ensures that the base station can communicate with every single sensor and vice-versa. However, this communication is multihop and relies on different routing protocols. In this section, we evaluate the properties of the topologies obtained in the previous sections globally and with regards to the communication and routing costs. We have compared the topologies obtained previously using a home-made C simulator.

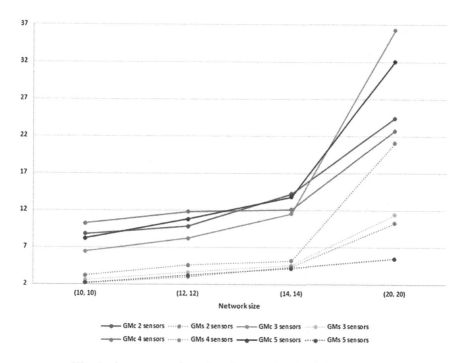

Fig. 1. Average number of nodes varying the field dimension.

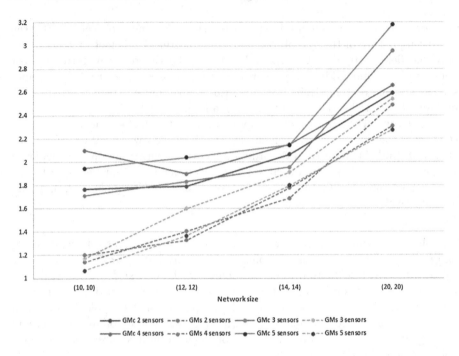

Fig. 2. Average node degree varying the field dimension.

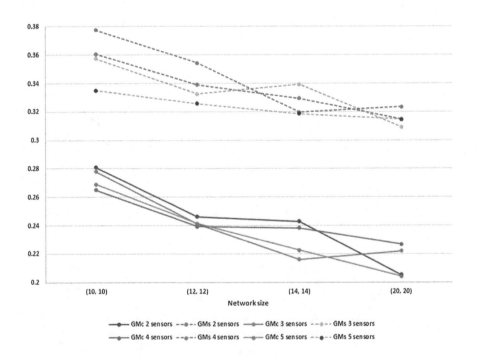

Fig. 3. Average edge length varying the field dimension.

Figure 1 shows the average number of nodes selected by each model for several numbers of available typologies of sensors. We can observe that as expected, the number of nodes selected increases with the area size. Naturally, the solutions obtained with GMs present less nodes than observed for those provided by GMc but also (not shown on the figure), it tends to select only one kind of sensors, the ones with the longer ranges, unlike the GMc that selects several types of sensors to cover the full area at a better cost.

Figure 2 shows the average degree of nodes, i.e., the average number of nodes a node can directly communicate with. It tends to increase with the size of the area. This is due to the fact that the area is bounded and to cover all single small area in the border, we need to increase the density over these points. The node degree increases quicker with GMs than with GMc, which makes GMc potentially more scalable. The mean degree obtained with GMs is very low (between 1 and 2 neighbors in average), which also implies a single communication path between two nodes. This can be a cause of unreliability since all traffic will take the same path and provokes potential bottlenecks. Each node represents a point of failure on the path since there is no possible alternative path.

Figure 3 shows the average length edge. Obviously, since there are less nodes in the solution provided by GMs than in GMc over a same area, the edges are longer in average with GMs. Thus, they are thus more energy-consuming.

Figures 4 and 5 show some topology examples obtained by model GMc and GMs, respectively, for different number of sensor typologies. In particular, we depict the solutions to the instances with field dimension $(20, 20)$ and $(14, 14)$ for GMc and GMs, respectively. The edges represent the possible communication among the deployed sensors. Each color corresponds to a typology of sensor.

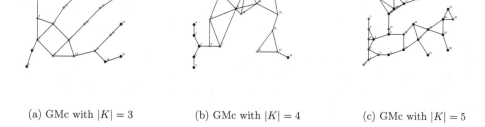

(a) GMc with $|K| = 3$ (b) GMc with $|K| = 4$ (c) GMc with $|K| = 5$

Fig. 4. Topologies obtained with GMc for different numbers of sensor typologies. (Color figure online)

Although the deployment cost could be reduced with GMs since there are less sensors to deploy, the solutions obtained with the GMc ensure a better cost operation. First, it has been designed to provide the lowest operation cost

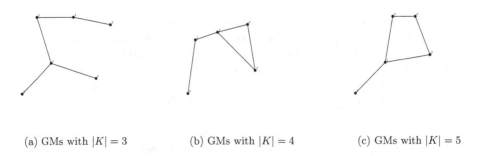

(a) GMs with $|K| = 3$ (b) GMs with $|K| = 4$ (c) GMs with $|K| = 5$

Fig. 5. Topologies obtained with GMs for different numbers of sensor typologies.

but also, the topologies that GMc generates provide a better basis for routing data between the different nodes, offering more routing options and lower energy consumption for data transmission.

5   Conclusions and Future Work

In this paper, we have addressed a generalized deployed sensors problem with coverage and connectivity constraints, considering different typologies of sensors. We have formulated the problem as a mixed integer program and we provide a deep evaluation of the solutions obtained, analyzing the efficiency and the effectiveness with respect to the deployment cost. We have compared the solutions obtained with those determined by minimizing the number of deployed sensors. Since the cost increases with the increase of the sensing range, the objectives of minimizing the cost and that of minimizing the number of sensors are in conflict one with the other. Finally, we have assessed the obtained sensor deployment from a quality of communication topology perspective. The numerical results suggest that the solutions obtained when the cost is minimized present a high potential in terms of quality of communication. To the best of our knowledge, we are the first to propose such a study. Our model can be easily extended to ensure a k-coverage of every point (each point of the grid is in sensing range of at least k different sensors). As a future work, we will investigate further the impact of the so-built topology on routing utilisation together with the global cost (deployment and hardware cost together with software cost).

References

1. Al-Karaki, J.N., Gawanmeh, A.: The optimal deployment, coverage, and connectivity problems in wireless sensor networks. IEEE Access **5**, 18051–18065 (2017)
2. Elloumi, S., Hudry, O., Estel, M., Martin, A., Plateau, A., Rovedakis, S.: Optimization of wireless sensor networks deployment with coverage and connectivity constraints. Ann. Oper. Res. (2018). https://doi.org/10.1007/s10479-018-2943-7
3. Erdelj, M., Razafindralambo, T., Simplot-Ryl, D.: Covering points of interest with mobile sensors. IEEE Trans. Parallel Distrib. Syst. **24**(1), 32–43 (2013)

4. Farsil, M., Elhosseini, M.A., Badawy, M., Ali, H.A., Eldin, H.Z.: Deployment techniques in wireless sensor networks, coverage and connectivity: a survey. IEEE Access **7**, 28940–28954 (2019)
5. Guerriero, F., Violi, A., Natalizio, E., Loscri, V., Costanzo, C.: Modelling and solving optimal placement problems in wireless sensor networks. Appl. Math. Model. **35**(1), 230–241 (2011)
6. Kaur, D., Kaur, M.: An approach of mobile wireless sensor network for target coverage and network connectivity with minimum movement. Int. Res. J. Eng. Tech. (IRJET) **04**(01), 1275–1280 (2017)
7. Khoufi, I., Minet, P., Laouiti, A., Mahfoudh, S.: Survey of deployment algorithms in wireless sensor networks: coverage and connectivity issues and challenges. Int. J. Auton. Adapt. Commun. Syst. (IJAACS) **10**(4), 341–390 (2017)
8. Lambrou, T.P., Panayiotou, C.G.: Collaborative area monitoring using wireless sensor networks with stationary and mobile nodes. EURASIP J. Adv. Signal Process. **7**, 1–16 (2009)
9. Laturkar, A.P., Malathi, P.: Coverage optimization techniques in WSN using PSO: a survey. Int. J. Comput. Appl. **975**, 19–22 (2014)
10. Razafindralambo, T., Erdelj, M., Zorbas, D., Natalizio, E.: Spread and shrink: point of interest discovery and coverage with mobile wireless sensors. J. Parallel Distrib. Comput. (11) (2016)
11. Rebai, M., Le berre, M., Snoussi, H., Hnaien, F., Khoukhi, L.: Sensor deployment optimization methods to achieve both coverage and connectivity in wireless sensor networks. Comput. Oper. Res. **59**, 11–21 (2015)
12. Rebai, M., Murat Afsar, H., Snoussi, H.: Exact methods for sensor deployment problem with connectivity constraint in wireless sensor networks. Int. J. Sens. Netw. (IJSNET) **21**(3), 157–168 (2016)
13. Reynaud, L., Guérin Lassous, I.: Improving the performance of challenged networks with controlled mobility. In: EAI International Conference on Ad Hoc Networks (ADHOCNETS), Ottawa, Canada, September 2016
14. Renzaglia, A., Dibangoye, J., Le Doze, V., Simonin, O.: Multi-UAV visual coverage of partially known 3D surfaces: Voronoi-based initialization to improve local optimizers. Computing Research Repository (2019)
15. Tolba, F., Tolba, C., Lorenz, P.: Topology control by controlling mobility for coverage in wireless sensor networks. In: IEEE International Conference on Communications (ICC), Kuala Lumpur, Malaysia, May 2016
16. Wang, Z., Chen, P., Song, Z., Chen, Y., Moore, K.L.: Formation control in mobile actuator/sensor networks. In: SPIE 2005, no. 435, pp. 706–717 (2005)
17. Yu, Z., Shan, G., Xu, G., Duan, X.: Method of multi-sensor optimal deployment for area coverage. In: International Conference on Electronics Technology (ICET), Chengdu, China (2018)

Traffic Monitoring on City Roads Using UAVs

Mouna Elloumi[1,2]([✉]), Riadh Dhaou[1]([✉]), Benoit Escrig[1], Hanen Idoudi[2],
Leila Azouz Saidane[2], and Andrei Fer[1,3]

[1] IRIT-ENSEEIHT, University of Toulouse, Toulouse, France
`mouna.elloumi@etu.enseeiht.fr`, {`Riadh.Dhaou,Benoit.Escrig`}`@enseeiht.fr`,
`andreifer20@gmail.com`
[2] National School of Computer Science, University of Manouba, Manouba, Tunisia
{`hanen.idoudi,leila.saidane`}`@ensi.rnu.tn`
[3] Military Technical Academy, Bucharest, Romania

Abstract. Unmanned Aerial Vehicles (UAVs) based systems are a suitable solution for monitoring, more particularly for traffic monitoring. The mobility, the low cost, and the broad view range of UAVs make them an attractive solution for traffic monitoring of city roads. UAVs are used to collect and send information about vehicles and unusual events to a traffic processing center, for traffic regulation. Existing UAVs based systems use only one UAV with a fixed trajectory. In this paper, we are using multiple cooperative UAVs to monitor the road traffic. This approach is based on adaptive UAVs trajectories, adjusted by moving points in UAVs fields of view. We introduced a learning phase to search for events locations with a frequent occurrence and to place UAVs above those locations. Our approach allows the detection of a lot of events and permits the reduction of UAVs energy consumption.

Keywords: Unmanned Aerial Vehicles (UAVs) · Traffic monitoring · UAVs trajectories · Events detection process · Learning strategy

1 Introduction

Unmanned aerial vehicles (UAVs) are gaining popularity in civil and commercial applications. They are considered as a new traffic monitoring technology used to collect information about road traffic conditions. This paper addresses the design of a UAV-based system for the management of road traffic within a city.

Several road traffic monitoring systems already exist. They have many objectives, among them the detection of infractions like speeding violations and the discovery of congestion. To fulfill these goals, monitoring systems should first collect traffic data from deployed devices. Traffic data consist of the number of vehicles, their position, and their speed. The data should then be transmitted to a processing center. The processed data can be used offline or online. For example, notification can be sent online to vehicles owners to avoid congested

M. R. Palattella et al. (Eds.): ADHOC-NOW 2019, LNCS 11803, pp. 588–600, 2019.
https://doi.org/10.1007/978-3-030-31831-4_42

roads, or emergency measures can be triggered automatically like calling rescue in the case of cars accidents [1–3]. For the regulation of traffic offline, statistics are generated using the collected data, then, for example, red lights and traffic displays are reorganized [2,4].

A lot of researches treated the congestion detection [5–7] and the early congestion detection [8–11] to overcome the low efficiency of transportation, which is a significant problem on roads in urban cities. The numbers of vehicles in an area and their velocities are the two main parameters that indicate whether there is congestion or not.

Several road traffic monitoring systems exist, they can be mobile or fixed. Fixed systems are for example sensors, detectors, and fixed cameras [12]. They enable the monitoring of a specific and limited area, their implementation and maintenance costs are very high, and they are generally affected by bad weather conditions. While for mobile systems, UAVs is the best solution for traffic monitoring [13]. In fact UAVs are mobile and equipped with cameras, sensors, and detectors. Using UAVs in the context of traffic monitoring have many advantages. UAVs can cover large areas and access specific locations; they can be deployed in any area, at any time, for any duration, and at no additional cost. UAVs can also perform vehicle identification, positions, and velocities estimation because they are equipped with cameras and have image processing capabilities.

For traffic monitoring systems based on UAVs, UAVs trajectories are predefined in advance by fixed points of interest. Those fixed points of interest can be intersections where there is a lot of traffic, critical areas, or positions of sensors placed on the ground. UAVs move from a fixed point of interest to another to get information about the traffic and vehicles. One or multiple UAVs can be used to collect data from various ground sensors placed on city roads [3,14]. UAVs fly over the sensors and collect the data after establishing a connection with them. Also, the UAV can receive data only from clusters heads nodes [15]. In other systems, a single UAV with image processing capabilities is responsible for the measurement of relevant vehicles parameters [16,17].

In [18], we proposed a road traffic monitoring solution based on the use of multiple cooperative UAVs with image processing capabilities. The goal is to detect as many events as possible. UAVs trajectories are adapted according to the position of vehicles in their field of view, which is not enough to detect all events, and which is consuming a lot of energy due to unnecessary movements. Vehicles trajectories are not from real traces; they were generated according to a mobility model, this can cause the computation of events detection percentages far from the reality.

So in this paper, we propose to adjust the position of UAVs not only according to the position of vehicles in their fields of view but also according to the position of events. We propose to place some UAVs at positions where events frequently occur. The choice of UAVs to place can be according to the distance that separates them from those positions, or according to the number of targets in their fields of view. This solution is applied to all types of events like speeding violations and congestion. For that, we introduced a learning phase to predict event positions with frequent occurrences, that we call Strategic Points (SPs). Because we want to group events positions that happened close to each other, we choose the unsupervised learning as the learning method to work with. The unsupervised learning is used to learn more about the data by exploring it and finding some structure or distribution within. After the learning phase, we propose to place UAVs above some SPs, to increase percentages of events detection, and to reduce the total traveled distance by UAVs. We also propose to use real vehicles traces to work on real conditions and to get realistic results while applying our approach. Finally, we improve the events detection process by better defining the conditions for events detection. We are interested mainly in the congestion detection and the speeding violation detection. For congestion detection, we use a vehicles clustering approach. For speeding violation detection, we use a velocity threshold approach.

The purpose is to show the positive impact of applying our approach on events detection percentages, on the number of covered vehicles, and on the UAVs total traveled distance, while using real vehicles traces. In fact, due to the limited number of UAVs, and due to their limited autonomy, having some moving UAVs and others placed above SPs is a good solution.

The rest of the paper is organized as follows. In Sect. 2, we present the system model. In Sect. 3, we present our contributions. In Sect. 4, we analyze simulation results for real traces and mobility model traces. We conclude in Sect. 5.

2   System Model

The system consist of multiple UAVs $(U_1, U_2, ..., U_i)$, characterized by their positions $(P_1, P_2, ..., P_i)$, velocities $(V_1, V_2, ..., V_i)$, and labels i with $1 \leq i \leq U_{max}$, where U_{max} is the maximal number of UAVs. We assume that all UAV are flying at the same altitude (A) and have the same radius (R) of fields of view. They are monitoring the road traffic during an observation time (St).

The system consist also of multiple targets $(T_1, T_2, ..., T_j)$, characterized by their positions $(Pt_1, Pt_2, ..., Pt_j)$, velocities $(Vt_1, Vt_2, ..., Vt_j)$, and label j with $1 \leq j \leq T_{max}$, where T_{max} is the maximal number of targets. Targets are vehicles moving on city road, their positions and velocities are updated according to a mobility model or updated from real traces for the period St. St is divided into times slots. Updates, instructions, and decisions are made at each time slot.

We assume that all UAVs have image processing capabilities. They are capable of detecting targets in their field of view and estimating relevant targets parameters (label, position, and velocity). A processing delay Du can occur at UAVs. Targets information are used to detect events and to adjust UAVs trajectories. Those information are processed at a processing center. We assume that there is a processing delay Dp at the processing center.

All UAVs send the collected information to the processing center, it deduces if events occur and send new positions to UAVs for the adjustment of their trajectories. The control is centralized because decisions are made at a single point. LTE connections are used for the exchange of information. Some delays can occur while transmitting (Dt) and receiving (Dr) information.

Delays differ from a time slot to another because the distance between the processing center and UAVs vary. UAVs transmit new information to the processing center at each time slot. While the processing center sends back new instructions to UAVs only when they arrive at destination, because it can take several times slots for UAVs to reach the final destination.

We assume that no obstacle is obstructing UAVs line of sight and that they temporarily change their altitude to avoid collisions between each other. While changing the altitude, the minimal and the maximal altitude (A_{min}, A_{max}) must be respected.

3   Contributions

3.1   Events Detection

UAVs are deployed over an area to monitor the traffic and to detect abnormal events. Several parameters are observed and measured: vehicles positions, vehicles speeds, and vehicles number. Specific events are detected through value changes of the above mentioned parameters [5–7]. We propose algorithms to perform the congestion detection and the speeding violation detection. We assign a speed threshold V_{max1} and a density threshold N_{min} to detect congestion, and another speed threshold V_{max2} to detect speeding violations.

The Congestion Detection is performed according to a clustering approach. First, vehicles in the field of view (FoV) of UAVs with a velocity lower than the velocity threshold V_{max1} are selected. Then, for each selected vehicle, we search for neighbors within a radius equal to the radius of the FoV of UAVs. For each constituted group, if the number of vehicles is equal to or higher than the density threshold (N_{min}) we consider that the group is in congestion. Centers of congested areas are centers of gravity of groups in congestion. We form a list of congested vehicles, updated with members of the congested group. It is necessary to have that list for each time slot. In fact, the duration of congestion increases if from, one time slot to another, a vehicle still in the list of congested vehicles.

For the Speeding Violation Detection, first we select vehicles in the FoV of UAVs, then we compare their velocity to V_{max2}. If the velocity of a vehicle exceeds the threshold, we consider that there is a speeding violation and we tag the vehicle. For the next time slots, the velocity of a tagged vehicle can still be higher than the threshold or can go under it. If the vehicle keeps traveling with a high velocity, we do not consider that there is another speeding violation, only the duration of speeding violation increases. If the velocity goes under the threshold we remove the tag. That way, the number of infraction increases only if the velocity of a non-tagged car exceeds the threshold. Also, when a tagged car goes out from the FoV of UAVs, we remove the tag.

3.2   UAVs Trajectories

Now we address the design of UAVs trajectories and placement. UAVs position and trajectories have an impact on the number of covered vehicles, on the number of detected events, and on detected events duration.

The proposed methods are based on the use of multiple cooperative UAVs. UAVs are capable of detecting and identifying vehicles in their field of view, perfectly estimating their positions and velocities values, and exchanging relevant information with each other and with a processing center.

Opportunistic Method. We proposed this approach in [18]. UAVs trajectories are adapted by mobile points. Those mobile points are centers of gravity of vehicles groups in the field of view of UAVs. The motion of UAVs depends on the motion of their groups of vehicles, so they adjust their position and fly over the centers of gravity of their groups. In this method, the goal is that every UAV keeps in its field of view the maximum number of targets, keeps tracking them, and detect as many events as possible for as long as possible. UAVs keep tracking and monitoring the same group of targets while considering the new targets entries. If from one observation to another groups disappear, UAVs randomly choose other groups to track and supervise.

Opportunistic Method with Learning. The Opportunistic Method with learning is based on the Opportunistic Method because UAVs are moving according to this method. However, some UAVs will be placed above Strategic Points (SPs) after a learning phase. SPs are locations where events frequently occur. So, this method is characterized by a learning phase performed at the beginning. During this phase, all UAVs are mobile. They are collecting information about vehicles, detecting abnormal events, and estimating the positions of those events.

At the end of this phase, all events positions are processed by a processing center. The goal is to find the SPs. In our case, SPs are locations where congestion or speeding violation frequently occur. To find the SPs, the processing center uses a machine learning approach to process the data, and make decisions and predictions regarding it. Two of the most adopted machine learning methods are the supervised learning and the unsupervised learning [19,20]. We choose the unsupervised learning because we want to explore the data and split it into groups.

In our learning method, the data that we want to split into group is all events positions that were collected during the learning phase. The clustering criterion is the distance. Indeed, the position of each event is compared to the positions of all other events of the same nature. If the distance between them is less than a given value, this means that they are part of the same group. The occurrence frequencies of events are equal to the number of positions in the groups. For example, for a given event position p_1, if other events were observed in the same position or in a circular area with a radius r_a and with a center p_1, the occurrence frequency of events at this position will increase. If the frequency of occurrence is higher than a given threshold, the center of this group will be considered as a SP. The frequency threshold is not fixed in advance, but it must be at least equal to 2 to consider that the center of a group is a candidate SP. Indeed, an event must have occurred at least twice in a circular area with a radius r_a. The frequency of occurrence depends on the total number of vehicles, the observation period and the number of deployed UAVs.

At the end of the learning phase, a certain number of UAVs are placed above the previously calculated SPs. UAVs are placed in priority above SPs with the highest frequency of occurrence, so that they can observe more events.

The choice of UAVs to place can be:

- Random: UAVs are randomly assigned to SPs.
- According to a distance criterion: the distance here refers to the distance between UAVs and SPs. For each SP, the closest UAV to it will be placed above it.
- According to a coverage criterion: the coverage here refers to the number of vehicles in the field of views of UAVs. UAVs with the smallest number of vehicles under their coverage will be placed above SPs.

The non-placed UAVs continue moving according to the Opportunistic Method, and all UAVs, fixed and mobile, continue monitoring the traffic.

The idea behind this proposal is to reduce the energy consumption of UAVs and to ensure better performances in terms of events detection than in the case where all UAVs are mobile. In fact, when UAVs are fixed the energy consumption due to movement decreases and the battery lives longer, and when they are fixed above points where events frequently occur the chance to observe more events is better.

4 Simulation

For the computation of events rates and events duration, we do simulation for real vehicles traces and for vehicles traces generated by a mobility model. We opted for the Opportunistic Network Environment (ONE) simulator to generate car mobility traces based on roads of the city of Helsinki, Finland [21]. For the real mobility traces, we opted for mobility traces of cars moving on the city of Cologne, Germany [22]. Using real traces of vehicles is very important to see how our approaches react in real conditions.

UAVs are flying over the areas, trying to collect as much data as possible. We evaluate the coverage percentage of vehicles, the percentage of occurrence of the abnormal events (congestion and infractions), and the duration of detected events. Also, we study the impact of two types of traces on the performances criteria.

4.1 Parameters

For the mobility model, we work on the Helsinki downtown to generate car mobility traces using the ONE simulator. The total surface of the area is

(4500 m × 3400 m) and we consider scenarios with 1000 cars spread over that area. We use the Shortest Path Map-Based Movement model (SPMBM), which is integrated into the simulator, to compute the path between a starting point and a point of arrival. Paths are computed according to the Dijkstra's shortest path algorithm. Vehicle velocities are uniformly distributed between 0 m/s and 15 m/s. The wait time when vehicles arrive at their destination is null. For our observations, we only consider the central area (1600 m × 1500 m).

For real traces, we work on Cologne city area to investigate real traces of cars. The total surface of the city is 400 km², with more than 700000 cars passing by. Real cars data is available for 24 h in a typical working day. For our investigations, we only consider the central area (225 km²). We did observations in a rush period (at 4 pm). A rush period is a period where we observe a lot of cars transiting. The total number of cars transiting in the selected area is 25800 cars in the rush period.

The observation time is only 1000 s because it approximately the autonomy duration of a commercial UAV. The radius of UAVs field of view is related to the maximal authorized altitude of UAVs flying on a city. Velocities, density thresholds, and velocities intervals are related to the nature of the city roads and the traffic. Other parameters are presented in Table 1.

The processing center is placed in the center of areas to monitor. In the case of Helsinki city, the maximal distance between the processing center and an UAV is approximately 1 km. In the case of Cologne city, the maximal distance between the processing center and an UAV is about 15 km.

UAVs send information about vehicles (positions, velocities, and number) and information about events (positions and duration) to the processing center using LTE links. When the processing center receives the data, it processes it and sends back positions to UAVs for their positions adjustments using also LTE link.

The transmission delay and the propagation delay depend on the distance between the processing center and UAVs and the speed of the light. For Helsinki city, the maximal transmission delay is about 3.33×10^{-6} s. For Cologne city, the maximal transmission delay is about 5×10^{-5} s. UAVs observe the traffic, they detect vehicles and estimate their velocity and position. So, part of the processing delay in UAVs is due to the detection process and the other part is due to the state estimation process. When using the Extended Kalman filter, the execution time is around 3.69×10^{-2} s [23]. When using new detection techniques like Wave3D, the execution time is around 6.306×10^{-3} s [24].

The processing center processes the position, the speed, and the number of vehicle to deduce new positions (centers of gravity of vehicles in UAVs Field of View that they are tracking) of UAVs and positions of strategic points (centers of gravity of vehicles in UAVs Field of View that verify conditions of events detection).

Table 1. Parameters.

Parameters	Helsinki	Cologne
Observation time	1000 s	1000 s
Cars velocity interval	[0–15 m/s]	[0–50 m/s]
Maximal velocity for congestion (V_{max1})	8 m/s	5 m/s
Maximal velocity on roads (V_{max2})	12 m/s	20 m/s
Minimal congested group members (N_{min})	10	20
Radius of the field of view of UAVs (R)	100 m	100 m
UAVs altitude (A)	200 m	200 m
Supervised area	2.4 km^2	225 km^2

4.2   Performances of UAVs Monitoring Methods

In this section, we study the performance of the Opportunistic Method with learning in terms of events detection, coverage percentage and UAVs total traveled distance. We study the influence of parameters like the learning duration, UAVs placement criteria, and the number of UAVs to place.

Then, we compare the performance of the Opportunistic Method, the Opportunistic Method with learning, and the Fixed Method in terms of congestion detection. The Fixed Method is an existing method [16,17]. In this method, only one UAV is used to monitor the traffic. The UAV trajectory is predefined in advance, the UAV moves from one fixed Point of Interest (PoI) to another to do the monitoring task. PoIs are intersections where there is a lot of traffic.

For the Opportunistic Method with learning, the placement of UAVs above SPs can be done according to the Distance Criterion (DC) or to the Coverage Criterion (CC). In the Fixed Method, in the case of our simulations, to be fair, the number of UAVs will be equal to the number of PoIs. UAVs move from their initial locations to their respective closest PoI, and hover over those points with a null speed. For all methods, initially, all UAVs are randomly placed.

We use the following metrics:

- Coverage percentage: the percentage of vehicles in the UAV's field of view.
- Percentage of detection of the number of speeding violations: speeding violations are detected when vehicles velocities exceed V_{max2}.
- Percentage of detection of congestion duration: congestion events occur in a group of vehicles, so when members velocities are lower than V_{max1} and members number is at least equal to N_{min}, we conclude that a group of vehicles is in congestion.

We did simulations offline to compute the number of UAVs to deploy. When using the Opportunistic Method, we observed a stabilisation of the performance criteria for 25 UAVs in the case of the mobility model, and for 150 UAVs in the case of the real traces. UAVs velocity will be 5 m/s which is a typical velocity of a commercial UAV.

Performances of the Opportunistic Method with Learning. For the next simulations, SPs will be positions where congestion frequently occur, and the radius r_a of the area that allows as to split events positions into groups will be equal to the radius of the UAVs field of views.

In the case of the mobility model traces, with observations made by 25 UAVs, the processing center computed a maximum number of SPs equal to 6. In the case of the real traces, the processing center calculated up to 20 SPs with data collected from 150 UAVs. The processing center collects during the learning phase all congestion positions and computes positions where congestion frequently occur.

Because hovering consumes less energy than flying, fixing UAVs lead to less energy consumption and longer battery lifetime. To evaluate the gain when using the Opportunistic Method with learning rather than the Opportunistic Method, we introduce another criterion: the UAVs total traveled distance. The less traveled distance, the less energy consumed.

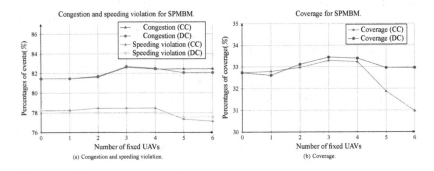

Fig. 1. Influence of UAVs placement on events detection and coverage.

For real and mobility model traces (Fig. 2(a) and (b)), we observe that when the learning phase is shorter the traveled distance is lower, thus, the energy consumption decreases. We compute the total traveled distance for the two criteria of UAVs placement above SPs: the Distance Criterion (DC) and the Coverage Criterion (CC).

From Figs. 1(a) and 3(a), Figs. 1(b) and 3(b), we observe that the percentages of coverage, congestion detection, and speeding violation detection are better when using the DC rather than the CC. For SPMBM, we can select 3 SPs, because we got better performance with this number. While, for the real traces, we can select 20 SPs.

We observe that when we choose the DC, less distance is traveled because the closest UAVs to the selected SPs are placed above them. We observe fluctuations especially when we use the CC because sometimes the selected UAV can be close to the SP and sometimes not.

We choose 200 s as a possible duration of the learning phase, because for that duration the traveled distance is the lowest comparing to other learning

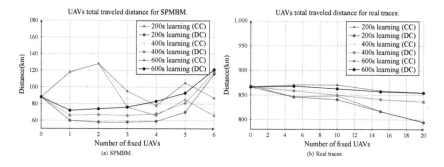

Fig. 2. Influence of the learning on the total travelled distance.

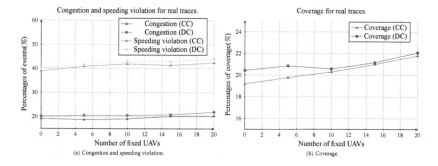

Fig. 3. Influence of UAVs placement on events detection and coverage.

duration. For UAVs placement, it is better to do it according to the DC because less distance is traveled and the performances criteria are better than for the CC.

For 200 s of learning, for the SPMBM, with 3 fixed UAVs, we got 12 km less traveled distance when the CC is applied. While, when the DC is applied, we got 30 km less traveled distance. For real traces, the total UAVs traveled distance is 70 km lower in the Opportunistic Method with learning because we placed 20 UAVs above SPs at the end of the learning phase.

Comparison of Performances of Monitoring Methods Based on UAVs. SPs are positions where congestion frequently occurs. So, we will compute percentages of congestion detection. We compare the performance of Opportunistic Method with learning to the performance of the Opportunistic Method, and to the performance of the Fixed Method regarding congestion detection.

For mobility model traces (Fig. 4(a)), we observe that the performance of the Opportunistic Method with learning and the performance of the Opportunistic Method are almost the same regarding congestion detection. The performance of the Fixed Method become the worst at the end of the simulation, because UAVs will be monitoring fixed PoI and miss a lot of vehicles and events, while

UAVs are all mobile in the Opportunistic Method, and placed above SPs in the Opportunistic Method with learning.

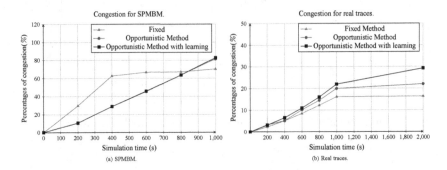

Fig. 4. Influence of the simulation time and the monitoring method on congestion detection.

For real traces (Fig. 4(b)), the performance of the Opportunistic Method with learning is the best regarding congestion detection. In fact, 20 UAVs are placed above positions where congestion frequently occur, so the discovery of this event is better. Also, mobile UAVs are tracking groups of vehicles, and probably they follow them much longer when they are moving with low velocities.

We observe that, in the Fixed Method after a certain period of observation, the percentage of congestion detection becomes almost stable. This method becomes inefficient because in the fixed PoI no more congestion can be observed after 400 s for SPMBM and 1000 s for real traces.

5   Conclusion

In this paper, we used multiple UAVs to monitor the road traffic. We proposed a method characterized by a learning phase and by adaptive UAVs trajectories. During the learning phase, UAVs collect events positions, after this phase, positions where events frequently occur are computed, and UAVs are placed above some of them. We defined also a process for the detection of speeding violations and a process for the detection of congestion. Our method has two goals, the first one is to detect the highest number of events and the second one is to save the energy of UAVs by limiting their traveled distance. To evaluate the performance of our proposal, we used real vehicles traces and traces generated by a mobility model. We observed, especially for real vehicles traces, better events detection comparing to the Opportunistic and the Fixed Methods, and less traveled distance comparing to the Opportunistic Method.

References

1. Kim, N.V., Chervonenkis, M.A.: Situation control of unmanned aerial vehicles for road traffic monitoring. Modern Appl. Sci. **9**(5), 1 (2015)
2. Coifman, B., McCord, M., et al.: Roadway traffic monitoring from an unmanned aerial vehicle. In: IEE Proceedings-Intelligent Transport Systems, IET 2006, vol. 153, no. 1, pp. 11–20 (2006)
3. Rasmussen, S., Kalyanam, K., et al.: Field experiment of a fully autonomous multiple UAV/UGS intruder detection and monitoring system. In: 2016 International Conference on Unmanned Aircraft Systems (ICUAS), pp. 1293–1302. IEEE (2016)
4. Ke, R., Li, Z., et al.: Real-time bidirectional traffic flow parameter estimation from aerial videos. IEEE Trans. Intell. Transp. Syst. **18**, 890–901 (2016)
5. Pattanaik, V., Singh, M., et al.: Smart real-time traffic congestion estimation and clustering technique for urban vehicular roads. In: IEEE Region 10 Conference (TENCON), pp. 3420–3423. IEEE (2016)
6. Pongpaibool, P., Tangamchit, P., et al.: Evaluation of road traffic congestion using fuzzy techniques. In: 2007 IEEE Region 10 Conference, TENCON 2007, pp. 1–4. IEEE (2007)
7. Abdelhafid, Z., Harrou, F., et al.: An efficient statistical-based approach for road traffic congestion monitoring. In: 2017 5th International Conference on Electrical Engineering-Boumerdes (ICEE-B), pp. 1–5. IEEE (2017)
8. More, R., Mugal, A., et al.: Road traffic prediction and congestion control using artificial neural networks. In: International Conference on Computing, Analytics and Security Trends (CAST), pp. 52–57. IEEE (2016)
9. Fouladgar, M., Parchami, M., et al.: Scalable deep traffic flow neural networks for urban traffic congestion prediction. In: 2017 International Joint Conference on Neural Networks (IJCNN), pp. 2251–2258. IEEE (2017)
10. Al Najada, H., Mahgoub, I.: Anticipation and alert system of congestion and accidents in VANET using big data analysis for intelligent transportation systems. In: 2016 IEEE Symposium Series on Computational Intelligence (SSCI), pp. 1–8. IEEE (2016)
11. El Khatib, A., Mourad, A., et al.: A cooperative detection model based on artificial neural network for VANET QoS-OLSR protocol. In: 2015 IEEE International Conference on Ubiquitous Wireless Broadband (ICUWB), pp. 1–5. IEEE (2015)
12. Leduc, G.: Road traffic data: collection methods and applications. Working Papers on Energy, Transport and Climate Change, vol. 1, no. 55 (2008)
13. Wang, L., Chen, F., et al.: Detecting and tracking vehicles in traffic by unmanned aerial vehicles. Autom. Constr. **72**, 294–308 (2016)
14. Reshma, R., Ramesh, T., et al.: Security situational aware intelligent road traffic monitoring using UAVs. In: 2016 International Conference on VLSI Systems, Architectures, Technology and Applications (VLSI-SATA), pp. 1–6. IEEE (2016)
15. Abdulla, A.E., Fadlullah, Z.M., et al.: An optimal data collection technique for improved utility in UAS-aided networks. In: 2014 Proceedings IEEE INFOCOM, pp. 736–744. IEEE (2014)
16. Guido, G., Gallelli, V., Rogano, D., Vitale, A.: Evaluating the accuracy of vehicle tracking data obtained from Unmanned Aerial Vehicles. Int. J. Transp. Sci. Technol. **5**, 136–151 (2016)
17. Rosenbaum, D., Kurz, F., et al.: Towards automatic near real-time traffic monitoring with an airborne wide angle camera system. Eur. Transp. Res. Rev. **1**(1), 11–21 (2009)

18. Elloumi, M., Dhaou, R., et al.: Monitoring road traffic with a UAV-based system. In: 2018 IEEE Wireless Communications and Networking Conference (WCNC), pp. 1–6. IEEE (2018)

19. Ongsulee, P.: Artificial intelligence, machine learning and deep learning. In: 2017 15th International Conference on ICT and Knowledge Engineering (ICT&KE), pp. 1–6. IEEE (2017)

20. https://towardsdatascience.com/supervised-vs-unsupervised-learning-14f68e32ea8d . Accessed 22 May 2018

21. http://crawdad.org/ . Accessed 06 Apr 2018

22. http://kolntrace.project.citi-lab.fr/ . Accessed 06 Apr 2018

23. Shu, W., Zheng, Z.: Performance analysis of Kalman-based filters and particle filters for non-linear/non-Gaussian Bayesian tracking. IFAC Proc. Vol. **38**(1), 1131–1136 (2005)

24. Martín, F., Veloso, M.: Effective real-time visual object detection. Prog. Artif. Intell. **1**(4), 259–265 (2012)

An Automotive Cooperative Collision Avoidance Service Based on Mobile Edge Computing

A. García Olmos, F. Vázquez-Gallego, R. Sedar$^{(\boxtimes)}$, V. Samoladas, F. Mira, and J. Alonso-Zarate

Centre Tecnològic de Telecomunicacions de Catalunya (CTTC/CERCA),
Av. Carl Friedrich Gauss 7, 08860 Castelldefels, Barcelona, Spain
{agarcia,francisco.vazquez,roshan.sedar,vsamoladas,fermin.mira,
jesus.alonso}@cttc.es

Abstract. Even before 5G is rolled out, Mobile Edge Computing (MEC) can be considered as a key driver towards the deployment of vehicular use cases, which pose stringent latency and bandwidth requirements to the underlying Vehicle-to-Everything (V2X) communication infrastructure. In this paper, we present a MEC-enabled cooperative Collision AVoidance (CAV) service designed to anticipate the detection and localization of road hazards by extending vehicles' perception range beyond the capabilities of their own sensors. The CAV service is a software application that runs on MEC servers allocated at the roadside and at Mobile Network Operators' (MNO) infrastructures. The CAV service receives ETSI ITS-G5 standard-compliant messages transmitted by vehicles: periodic Cooperative Awareness Messages (CAM), which include the position, velocity and direction of the vehicle; and event-triggered Decentralized Environmental Notification Messages (DENM), which include the position of detected road hazards. The CAV service creates a distributed dynamic map using all the received information, and sends unicast messages to each vehicle with the relevant information within its collision risk area. We have implemented and validated the operation of the CAV service using vehicles' On-Board Units (OBU) based on OpenC2X, an open-source experimental platform supporting the ETSI ITS-G5 standard.

Keywords: V2X · MEC · Collision Avoidance · OpenC2X

1 Introduction

In recent years, the road safety has received much attention in the wake of alarming figures by the World Health Organization[1] showing that 1.4 million people were killed by road accidents in 2016. In order to improve road safety,

---

[1] https://www.who.int/news-room/fact-sheets/detail/the-top-10-causes-of-death.

© Springer Nature Switzerland AG 2019
M. R. Palattella et al. (Eds.): ADHOC-NOW 2019, LNCS 11803, pp. 601–607, 2019.
https://doi.org/10.1007/978-3-030-31831-4_43

vehicles are becoming more aware of their environment thanks to the integration of smart sensors (i.e., cameras, radar, lidar, ultrasonic sensors, etc.) and their level of automation is rapidly increasing. In addition, in near future the use of Vehicle-to-Everything (V2X) communication will allow vehicles to exchange information with other vehicles (V2V), roadside infrastructure (V2I), pedestrians (V2P) or communication networks (V2N). Therefore, V2X communication will facilitate vehicles to cooperate with each other and to extend their perception range beyond the capabilities of their sensors, supporting vehicular services that increase traffic efficiency and road safety, and it will pave the way for future Cooperative-Intelligent Transportation Systems (C-ITS) and fully-automated driving.

The deployment of vehicular services will impose very strict requirements to the underlying communication infrastructure, which must guarantee that information reaches its destination in a secure and timely manner. Mobile Edge Computing (MEC) can be considered as a key enabler for V2X communication [1]. This is due to the fact that MEC brings processing, storage and networking resources closer to the network edge and facilitates the compliance of low-latency and high-bandwidth requirements. Furthermore, MEC servers can be easily installed at the roadside infrastructure and integrated within the Radio Access Network, deployed between the core network and cellular base stations [2].

Motivated by this context, we have designed and implemented a MEC-based Collision AVoidance (CAV) service that allows to anticipate the detection and localization of road hazards. The CAV service is a software application that runs on the MEC infrastructure with the aim of facilitating smooth vehicle reactions in order to avoid hard braking and collisions. Vehicles send their status information and detected hazards to the CAV service, which stores all collected information and sends to each vehicle the relevant data within its collision risk area. In this work, we describe the functionalities, networking and software architecture of the CAV service, and we present the implementation and validation of a proof-of-concept. This work is an extension of the demo presented in [3].

The remainder of this paper is organized as follows. Section 2 provides an overview on V2X communication, open-source implementations of the ITS-G5 protocol stack and field trials of vehicular use cases implemented with the support of MEC. Section 3 describes the scenarios of the cooperative collision avoidance use case. Sections 4 and 5 describe the design and implementation of the CAV service, respectively. Finally, Sect. 6 concludes this paper.

2 Related Work

In the context of C-ITS, two standards have been developed for direct short-range communications (DSRC): the ITS-G5 standard developed in Europe [4] and the IEEE WAVE standard developed in North America [5]. ITS-G5 and WAVE are based on IEEE 802.11p, which facilitates the formation of wireless ad-hoc networks whenever vehicles or roadside units are within the range of each other, thus enabling vehicles to directly communicate with each other (V2V) and with the roadside infrastructure (V2I).

The realization of the ITS-G5 protocol stack can be found in open-source implementations such as Vanetza[2] and OpenC2X [6]. These two experimental and prototyping platforms implement the majority of modules of the ITS-G5 reference architecture. For instance, OpenC2X does not include the security and GeoNetworking modules, but implements all the other modules and includes an interface to access the vehicle's CAN bus using an OBD2 adapter, whereas Vanetza leaves out the implementation of the Local Dynamic Map (LDM) and the interface to the vehicle's CAN bus. Both OpenC2X and Vanetza support the Cooperative Awareness Messages (CAM) and Decentralized Environmental Notification Messages (DENM) defined in the ITS-G5 facilities layer. CAM messages are transmitted periodically, including the vehicle's position, speed and direction, and DENM messages are event-triggered to disseminate cooperative awareness information like the position of road hazards.

In the absence of short-range wireless connectivity based on IEEE 802.11p, vehicles could be opted to communicate over the cellular networking infrastructure. Recently, 3GPP has developed the first set of cellular standards for V2X communication. Today's realization of Cellular-V2X (C-V2X) is based on LTE-V2X (3GPP Release 14, March 2017) and it will evolve into future 5G-V2X (3GPP Release 16, to be completed by end of 2019), also known as 5G New Radio, to support both cellular V2N and V2V communication. C-V2X is gaining support from the leaders of automotive and telecom industries, which has led to worldwide trials [7] of C-V2X, whereas the trials of DSRC have been limited to Europe, North America, and Japan.

As ETSI MEC outlines [8], the amount of data is expected to increase rapidly from connected vehicles and, therefore, these data sets can be conveniently collected and processed closer to the user, i.e., at the edge of the network. Clearly, such an architecture is ideal for building real-time situational awareness and High Definition maps by effectively using real-time data collection and fusion from multiple available sources, e.g., vehicles' on-board sensors and road-side units. To this end, a number of MEC-based architectures have already been proposed in the existing literature. The works in [9,10] suggest that MEC-assisted network architectures will likely contribute to reduce end-to-end latency in V2X communication. The authors of [11] propose a MEC-based architecture for cellular V2N networks where MEC servers are integrated within the Radio Access Network and deployed between the core network and base stations.

Recently, several field trials have demonstrated some vehicular use cases with the support of MEC [7]. A real use case deployment of MEC-based architecture can be found in the Car2MEC [12] project, in which a MEC infrastructure has been deployed covering 30 Km on the A9 motorway in Germany to demonstrate time-critical use cases like emergency warning, end of jam warning and variable speed limit assistant, sending information from one car to another with a delay below 20 ms using LTE. Another field trial presented in [13] demonstrated the use case of assistance in road intersections.

---

[2] https://github.com/riebl/vanetza.

3   Cooperative Collision Avoidance Use Case

The Cooperative Collision Avoidance use case refers to the detection of road hazards that are beyond the perception range of vehicles' on-board sensors as well as keep vehicles informed on potential collision risk events ahead of time. Under certain conditions, typical sensors (e.g., radar, camera and Lidar) may not be able to detect some hazardous events with enough level of anticipation, which may lead to dangerous maneuvers or hard braking of vehicles and potentially cause a collision. As an example, typical scenarios of this use case are the situations where there is an incident (e.g., car accident, traffic jam, etc.) which is not clearly visible because of a downhill or behind a curve, or there is an obstacle like a building that blocks the view of approaching vehicles to an intersection.

In this Cooperative Collision Avoidance use case, vehicles cooperate with each other through the dissemination of their own status information (i.e., position, velocity and direction) as well as the location of the events detected by the sensors. This cooperation enabled by V2X communication that allows vehicles to anticipate the detection and localization of such dangerous events, and facilitates smooth vehicle reactions to avoid hard braking or to escape potentially from a collision.

4   Architecture of the Collision Avoidance Service

In this work, we consider cellular base-stations (BS) that provide wireless connectivity to the vehicles driving within their coverage area. Each cellular BS is connected to one MEC server where the CAV service is deployed. MEC servers are connected to a centralized public cloud Data Center (DC) through the core network, and the DC keeps MEC servers with up-to-date information. To this end, we implement a centralized MQTT[3] broker service from which the MEC servers communicate via the broker deployed in the Cloud Data Center.

Each vehicle is equipped with a cellular User Equipment (UE), a computer, a Human Machine Interface (HMI) and a set of sensors that allow detecting road hazards in the proximity, such as icy surfaces, unexpected manoeuvres, traffic jams, emergency braking, etc. The communication between the CAV service and vehicles is based on V2N with the use of ITS-G5 standard-compliant messages: periodic CAMs and event-triggered DENMs. Vehicles are able to receive up-to-date information through frequent communication with the MEC server where the CAV service is deployed.

Figure 1 illustrates the software modules of the CAV service. The communication between the modules is realized using the ZeroMQ[4] asynchronous messaging library. The CAV service performs the following operations: (1) it receives and decodes CAM and DENM messages transmitted by vehicles, (2) it stores vehicles' status and hazards related information in a database, (3) it calculates distances between vehicles, and between vehicles and hazards, and (4) it encodes

---

[3] http://mqtt.org/.
[4] http://zeromq.org/.

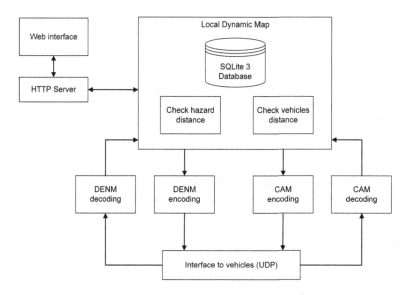

Fig. 1. Software architecture of the Collision Avoidance service

and transmits CAM and DENM messages only to those vehicles that are either approaching road hazards or other vehicles. As shown in Fig. 1, incoming messages are received at the CAV service through a UDP server included in the Interface-to-Vehicles module. At the UDP server, the incoming CAM and DENM messages are handled separately and forwarded into their respective CAM and DENM modules, which decode the messages and forward the extracted information to the LDM module. The LDM module stores the most recent information in a SQLite[5] database system to keep up-to-date events.

Two parallel threads are executed concurrently inside the LDM module. One thread computes the distance between each pair of vehicles, while the other thread computes the distance between each vehicle and each road hazard. If the distance between any two vehicles is smaller than a pre-defined threshold, e.g., 100 m, the CAV service will transmit a CAM message to both vehicles. If the distance between a vehicle and a hazard is below a certain threshold, e.g., 50 m, the CAV service will transmit a DENM message to the vehicle. The CAM and DENM messages are transmitted over UDP through the Interface-to-Vehicles module.

The CAV service integrates a web interface module (over HTTP) that allows to visualize the positions of vehicles and hazards over OpenStreetMap[6], configure the distance threshold of the collision risk area of each vehicle, and clear the information stored in the database.

---

[5] https://www.sqlite.org.
[6] https://www.openstreetmap.org/.

5   System Validation

We have implemented and validated a proof-of-concept of the CAV service in a small scale testbed using WiFi. The testbed is arranged using two Intel NUC[7] computers. The CAV service runs on Ubuntu 16.04 environment in one of the NUC computers, which operates as the MEC server and the WiFi access point. In the other NUC computer we have deployed three separate Virtual Machines (VMs) with Ubuntu 16.04. Each VM runs one vehicle application in it. In this way, we have deployed three virtualized vehicles and they communicate with the CAV service via WiFi.

We have developed a vehicle application based on OpenC2X which implements the ITS-G5 protocol stack, including a graphical user interface (GUI) with an LDM and allows to manually trigger simulated events. We have extended OpenC2X with a new software component that encapsulates the CAM and DENM messages over UDP in the transport layer. Since we use virtualized vehicles, instead of acquiring real positions from a GNSS receiver, the vehicle application reads the position of the vehicle from a trajectory file that contains a sequence of geographical coordinates with associated time-stamps. The vehicle application allows to select a trajectory file, start, pause and stop the movements of the vehicle. The vehicle application transmits CAM messages to the CAV service every 100 ms and sends a DENM when it is manually triggered.

We have demonstrated that if two vehicles approach at a distance below a predefined threshold, the CAV service transmits CAM messages to both vehicles, which show the position of the other vehicle on their LDM. Finally, we have generated simulated events and validated that if a vehicle approaches to any hazard at a distance below a certain threshold, the CAV service transmits a DENM message to that vehicle, which shows a warning on its GUI.

6   Conclusions

In this paper, we have presented a new MEC-based cooperative Collision Avoidance (CAV) service for vehicular networks. The CAV service is a software application deployed in the MEC infrastructure. Using Vehicle-to-Network (V2N) communication, vehicles exchange information with the CAV service in the form of unicast CAM and DENM messages over UDP. The incoming messages from vehicles are processed by the CAV service, which disseminates to each vehicle only the relevant information within its collision risk area (e.g., dangerous events, presence of other vehicles, etc.). We have implemented a proof-of-concept of the CAV service and demonstrated its functionalities under different traffic conditions in a small scale testbed. As a future work, a field trial of the CAV service will be deployed in the city of Barcelona using LTE Small Cells at 3.5 GHz in order to evaluate key performance metrics under different real road traffic conditions. We plan to evaluate the performance of the CAV service in terms of latency, scalability and robustness against failures in the MEC servers.

---

[7] https://www.intel.com/content/www/us/en/products/boards-kits/nuc.html.

Acknowledgment. This work is part of 5GCroCo project that has received funding from the European Union H2020 Research and Innovation Programme under grant agreement No. 825050. It has also been partially funded by SPOT5G (TEC2017-87456-P) and by Generalitat de Catalunya under Grant 2017 SGR 891.

References

1. Shah, S.A.A., et al.: 5G for vehicular communications. IEEE Commun. Mag. **56**, 111–117 (2018)
2. Li, L., et al.: A novel mobile edge computing-based architecture for future cellular vehicular networks. In: IEEE WCNC, pp. 1–6, March 2017
3. Vázquez-Gallego, F., et al.: Demo: a MEC-based collision avoidance system for future vehicular networks. In: CNERT INFOCOM Workshop, April 2019
4. Wevers, K., et al.: V2X communication for ITS - from IEEE 802.11p towards 5G, June 2017. https://futurenetworks.ieee.org/tech-focus/march-2017/v2x-communication-for-its
5. Task Group p: IEEE P802.11p: Wireless Access in Vehicular Environments (WAVE). draft standard ed. (2006)
6. Klingler, F., et al.: Field testing vehicular networks using OpenC2X. In: 15th ACM International Conference on Mobile Systems, pp. 178–178, June 2017
7. 5GAA: Toward fully connected vehicles: edge computing for advanced automotive communications. White Paper (2017)
8. Reznik, A., et al.: Developing software for multi-access edge computing. ETSI White Paper, September 2017
9. Emara, M., et al.: MEC-assisted end-to-end latency evaluations for C-V2X communications, pp. 1–9. IEEE (2018)
10. Datta, S.K., et al.: Vehicles as connected resources: opportunities and challenges for the future. IEEE Veh. Technol. Mag. **12**, 26–35 (2017)
11. Li, L., Li, Y., Hou, R.: A novel mobile edge computing-based architecture for future cellular vehicular networks. In: 2017 IEEE Wireless Communications and Networking Conference (WCNC), pp. 1–6, March 2017
12. Car2MEC Project, September 2018. https://www.nokia.com/about-us/news/
13. Press release: Comba Telecom and ASTRI demonstrate Mobile Edge Computing system (MEC) with Vehicle-to-Everything (V2X) system prototype at Mobile World Congress 2017 in Barcelona

A Demonstration of Low Power Wide Area Networking for City-Scale Monitoring Applications

Sebastian Barillaro[1,2](✉) 🆔, Dhananjay Anand[1] 🆔,
Avi M. Gopstein[1] 🆔, and Julian Barillaro 🆔

[1] National Institute of Standards and Technology,
Gaithersburg, MD 20899, USA
sebastian.barillaro@nist.gov
[2] Instituto Nacional de Tecnología Industrial,
C.A. Buenos Aires 1001, Argentina

Abstract. Networks of sensors are key components of an Internet of Things. This paper outlines a demonstration of a wireless technology called LoRa/LoRaWAN that may be used to network sensors over a range of several kilometers. LoRa is an example of a Low Power Wide Area Network (LPWAN) and features hardware, software and network protocols especially designed to achieve wide area coverage with exceptionally low power consumption. However, these features constrain effective data rate and multiplexing capabilities. Our demonstration applies LoRa to an Environment Monitoring and Electrical Power System application where these tradeoffs are justified.

Keywords: IoT · Internet of Things · LPWAN · Environment monitoring · LoRa · LoRaWAN · Sensor network

1 Introduction

Internet of Things (IoT) is a broad concept that addresses the advantages and concerns of connected 'Things' such as computers, devices, sensors, etc. These Things can be diverse in terms of function and core technology, necessitating an equally diverse set of connectivity solutions differing in range, data rate, and energy consumption. In the case of wireless connectivity solutions, fundamental limits prevent a single wireless networking panacea to cover all possible connectivity application requirements. Consequently, expansion of IoT applications has created opportunities for innovation in wireless technologies to address application specific tradeoffs. LPWANs (Low Power Wide Area Networks) are class of networking technologies that aim to minimize energy consumption while retaining wide area coverage. Typical LPWAN applications include sensors which must operate for years with an operational range of several kilometers, but with batteries that cannot be easily replaced.

The tradeoffs addressed by LPWANs are not new: For example, NASA's Voyager 1 and Voyager 2 spacecraft launched in 1977, are still transmitting to earth from beyond our solar system despite being constrained by the limited onboard energy

M. R. Palattella et al. (Eds.): ADHOC-NOW 2019, LNCS 11803, pp. 608–618, 2019.
https://doi.org/10.1007/978-3-030-31831-4_44

supply. The LPWAN options discussed in this paper and the example application presented are low cost, terrestrial use cases in which the hardware involved is barely larger than a postage stamp.

2   LPWAN Solutions

Numerous LPWAN solutions exist, in various stages of maturity. The Internet Engineering Task Force (IETF) published a Request for Comments (RFC) 8376 [1] describing four LPWAN options: LoRaWAN, NB-IoT, Sigfox and Wi-SUN. It is unclear why the IETF selected a subset of those four LPWAN options for RFC-8376. We decided to evaluate a larger set of LPWAN solutions prior to developing our demonstration, including:

- LTE-M
- NB-IoT
- Sigfox
- Wi-SUN (FAN, RLMM, JUTA, ECHONET)
- IngeNU (formerly On-Ramp Wireless)
- Weightless (N, P, and W)
- DASH7
- LoRa/LoRaWAN
- LoRa/M.O.S.T.
- LoRa/Symphony Link

2.1   Selection of a Representative Technology for Demonstration

For this demonstration, it was decided to use a technology with the following properties:

1. It provided visibility into the network stack (i.e., was not a proprietary and closed end-to-end solution).
2. It included security protocol specifications.
3. It integrated all the components needed for a sensor network application.
4. It did not require access to the public internet for operation.
5. It had a mature design with established evidence of end-user adoption.

Many of the options we evaluated did not fully meet these criteria and were not considered for this demonstration. The technology we selected for our demonstration is LoRa/LoRaWAN. LoRa is a proprietary wireless technology, but LoRaWAN is an open communication standard. It does not require the public internet for operation and it can be deployed entirely using private infrastructure. LoRaWAN also has security specifications included and appears to be widely adopted [2].

The LPWAN demonstration described in this paper uses LoRa/LoRaWAN for an environment monitoring use case in the electrical power system.

3 LoRa/LoRaWAN Overview

Figure 1 provides a simplified overview of the LoRa/LoRaWAN topology. Note that a full implementation requires four major components: the End-Nodes (such as sensors) to be wirelessly networked; a Gateway that communicates wirelessly with the End-Nodes; a Network Server to handle low level logical networking functions such as producing and verifying network session keys; and lastly an Application Server to handle user-controlled higher level data pipeline functions such as application session keys and data schemas.

In a real deployment, there may be more than one Gateway. Multiple Application Server instances may also exist to handle different End-Node data schemas/types. Figure 1 adequately represents the core operating principles of the majority of competing solutions to LoRa/LoRaWAN. Note that LoRa is a specification for the sub-GHz radio frequency link between a Gateway and End-Nodes while LoRaWAN is a specification for the data pipeline between the End-Nodes and the Application Server. This distinction is outlined in the following two sub-sections.

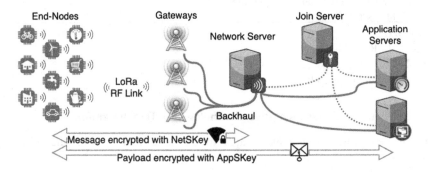

Fig. 1. LoRa/LoRaWAN topology

LoRa. Although sometimes used interchangeably, LoRa and LoRaWAN refer to different concepts. LoRa (Long Range) is a chirp spread spectrum (CSS) modulation technique [3]. LoRa Modulation operates in sub-GHz license free ISM bands [4] with variable Spreading Factor (SF). Radio modules vary SF automatically to optimize between data rate and range while keeping radiated power constant. Depending on the SF and bandwidth in use, bit rate varies between 250 bps and 21.9 Kbps. At longer range, the effective data rate is reduced resulting in longer transmit times and the proportional increase in total energy needed per bit.

Most ISM bands are duty-cycle restricted resulting in a limit on payload size at a given SF. Maximum duty-cycle is 1% in Europe, thus each frame may be between 51 and 222 bytes. In the United States, restrictions on the dwell time to under 400 ms [4] effectively limit the maximum payload to between 11 bytes and 242 bytes.

Range is estimated to be about 2 km in urban areas, and 10 km in suburban areas with unobstructed line-of-sight [5].

LoRaWAN. This is the specifications for the (Media Access Control) MAC protocol [6]. The specification is open and maintained by the LoRa-Alliance [7] comprised of industry, academia and research institutions. The logical network has a star-of-stars topology with an addressing scheme that is not Internet Protocol compatible due to optimizations applied with the aim of reducing transmission time. LoRaWAN features end-to-end encryption with two keys: the Network Session Key which encrypts LoRa frames to secure addressing and routing information and the Application Session Key which encrypts payloads, this key is owned by the application developer/user.

Advanced power optimization is achieved by integrating End-Node sleep and transmitter synchronization functions within the specification. To save power, an End-Node enters a power saving 'sleep' state and 'wakes' to transmit a message. During sleep, the End-Node is unable to receive messages from Gateways- increasing latency. Three modes of operation balance energy consumption with reception latency by regulating when an End-Node opens a reception window: always receiving thus never sleeping (called Class C); receiving after each transmission and sleeping for the rest of the time, (called Class A); and periodically opening reception windows (called Class B).

Just like Wi-Fi—where the end-user is able to buy Wi-Fi adapters, access points; and deploy, use, and manage a wireless local area network—LoRa/LoRaWAN allows the end-user to own, deploy, and manage the hardware for a wireless wide area network. It is unique in that it lets the end user the freedom to control both the wireless infrastructure as well as the data pipeline. For those users who prefer not to deal with network deployment, there are several network service providers offering LoRaWAN based IoT solutions. Cellular telecommunications companies are rolling out nationwide coverage [8] and there are community network operators offering non-comprehensive global coverage [9].

4 LPWAN Demo

For this demonstration, an entire LoRaWAN based infrastructure is deployed on premises with the aim to demonstrate an application of LPWANs in monitoring the environment across a city. This demonstration shows how both static sensors and mobile sensors may be integrated to build a sensor network that can be used to optimize the dispatch of distributed photovoltaic generators.

4.1 LPWAN Demo Architecture

The LPWAN Demo Architecture is illustrated in Fig. 2. One static End-Node consisting of a set of environmental sensors is placed within Gateway coverage range, with data reported from the End-Node over the LoRaWAN infrastructure to a web-based dashboard. The LPWAN infrastructure is shared with another parallel data pipeline from a mobile End-Node reporting its Global Navigation Satellite System (GNSS) coordinates periodically. These coordinates are displayed on a continuously updated map showing the mobile End-Node's last location.

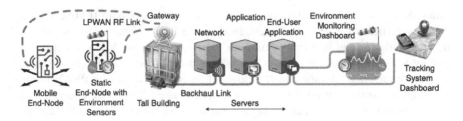

Fig. 2. LPWAN Demo Architecture based on LoRa/LoRaWAN showing both static and mobile End-Nodes and their respective dashboards.

End-Nodes. Both static and mobile End-Nodes are based on the same prototyping platform called a Pycom FiPy Development module. It has an Espressif ESP32 SoC, five network interfaces: Bluetooth, Wi-Fi, LTE-M, Sigfox, and LoRa. FiPy development module has a Micro-Python interpreter to execute software.

For the mobile End-Node a Pycom PyTrack is added to the prototyping platform. The PyTrack board includes a 3-axis accelerometer and a GNSS receiver to compute location, shown in Fig. 3-left.

For the static End-Node, a Pycom PySense expansion board is added that provides environmental measurements like Temperature, Humidity, Barometric Pressure, Ambient Light, and 3-axis accelerations. Specifications for the Pycom products used are available on the Pycom website [10].

Each End-Node is adequately powered by a 5 VDC, 0.5 A power supply and is connected to a 4 dBi whip antenna.

Fig. 3. Equipment used in Demo. Left: Pycom FiPy Development Module mounted on PyTrack (as Mobile End-Node). Center: Gateway module RisingHF RHF0M301 mounted on Raspberry Pi. Right: 4 dBi Antenna. Images are not to scale.

Gateway. The LoRaWAN Gateway is an interface between LoRa and an Internet Protocol Switching Network. The Gateway maintains two independent network interfaces, a LoRa interface to communicate wirelessly with End-Nodes and an independent Ethernet interface to maintain a backhaul connection with the Network Server.

The backhaul connection may be alternatively served by a cellular data link or WLAN link.

The LoRa interface on a Gateway has more functionality than the interface on End-Nodes. Each Gateway has two LoRa transceivers. Together they cover eight 125 kHz bandwidth channels and one overlapped 500 kHz LoRa Channel. Behind these two transceivers there is a digital signal processor (DSP) that demodulates received signals. Each 8 + 1 channel set is called a sub-band. There are 8 sub-bands in the US-915 spectrum allocation. Gateway implementations vary on how many sub-bands are utilized. Digital multiplexing between channels enables Gateways to maintain simultaneous connections across all channels in all available sub-bands.

A packet forwarding program is used to maintain an uplink where all valid LoRA frames are forwarded to the Network service. The program also maintains the downlink sending packets from the Network Server to the appropriate Gateway for transmission.

For this demonstration, a packet forwarder made by Semtech is used. The forwarder runs on Raspbian OS on a Raspberry Pi 3 single board computer. The Gateway used is comprised of a RisingHF RHF0M301 [11] LoRA interface mounted on a Raspberry Pi 3, shown in Fig. 3-center. This gateway module covers 8 + 1 channels in a sub-band. The Gateway uses a weather proof 4dBi antenna with a magnetic base (see Fig. 3-right). The same kind of antenna is used for the End-Nodes as well.

Network Server. The Network Server manages the LoRaWAN network by registering Gateways and End-Nodes. The Network Server receives LoRa frames wrapped in IP packets from the Gateway. If the same LoRa frame is received by more than one Gateway, the Network Server discards duplicate frames. The Network Server also decrypts messages using the Network Session Key while retaining the encrypted message payload. Finally, the Network Server routes encrypted payloads to the respective Application Server based on header information.

For outbound messages (downlink), the Network Server receives encrypted payloads from Application Servers and doubly-encrypts the message using the Network Session Key. Then, the network server assigns the transmission of the LoRa frame to the Gateway that received the most recent uplink with the strongest signal.

When End-Nodes allow it, the Network Server also regulates the data rate for the network by sending MAC-commands to End-Nodes to adapt their modulation increasing the spreading factor – a mechanism called Adaptive Data Rate (ADR).

There are a plenty of options for Network Servers. For this demonstration, a free opensource Network Server called LoraServer [12] is used.

Application Server. From the perspective of the LoRa/LoRaWAN topology, the Application Server is the terminal end for LoRaWAN traffic. This server owns the Application Key and is able to encrypt/decrypt message payloads, protecting it from the rest of the LoRaWAN infrastructure. Once decrypted, payload has to be decoded to obtain sensor data. Message coding is out of scope of LoRaWAN specification. It is up to System Infrastructure Designer to decide whether to use a custom coding, or to adopt a de-facto standard like the CayenneLPP codec [13]. Sensor data may be passed to a diverse set of user applications through System Integrations, according to system functional specifications.

For this demonstration, the Application Server module (part of LoRaServer implementation) decodes payloads (using CayenneLPP codec) and transfers sensor data through an InfluxDB integration.

End-User Application Server. Beyond the LoRaWAN Specification, but present in any LPWAN implementation, there is at least an End-User Application. This could be a software application, or combination of several software applications working collaboratively on one or more computers according to system functional specifications.

For this demonstration, sensor data received from Application Server is persisted in an InfluxDB [14] database. Stored sensor data is represented using a dashboard visualization tool called Grafana [15].

4.2 Demo Deployment

This demonstration uses all the components described above to build an integrated LoRaWAN solution to collect and display sensor data.

Static End-Nodes are placed at a meaningful distance from the Gateway. Mobile End-Nodes are attached to a vehicle of some sort that demonstrates the robustness of the protocol to a quickly changing RF environment. Both types of End-Nodes are battery powered.

The Gateway antenna is located to maximize radio signal quality, which ideally means locating the Gateway antenna on a tower, building rooftop or balcony with unobstructed sight lines to all of the End Nodes. The Gateway is connected to a power source and a network connection for backhaul (Ethernet is preferable). Our antenna is a 30 cm tall weatherproof whip with a magnetic base. The same antenna is used for both the Gateway and the End-Nodes.

A computer running instances of Network, Application, and End-User Servers is connected to the Gateway. A display connected to this computer presents sensor dashboards and relevant information pages.

5 A Power Systems Use Case for LPWAN Based Sensor Network

Although at first sight it may seem that wireless sensor networks used to monitor the electrical power system are rarely energy constrained, wireless sensors are in fact ubiquitous throughout the power system, with networks ranging from high speed WLANs used within distribution substations to satellite based wide-area monitoring platforms. Over the last thirty years, significant advances in monitoring and control practices used for power systems have resulted in several mature sensor network technologies optimized for the traditional power system.

The power system, though, is rapidly evolving to adapt to decentralized power generation and greater consumer interaction with energy markets. This demonstration is intended to highlight two specific use cases where an LPWAN may be used in the power system of the future.

5.1   Local Demand Models

The first use case considers the trend towards more local/ decentralized models for load behavior allowing an electrical distribution system to better dispatch decentralized generation.

It is known that air temperature and humidity directly affect energy demand [16, 17]. Existing methods to derive these correlations aggregate vast amounts of data from diverse climates and load portfolios to build ensemble forecasts. It is anticipated that distribution system operators of the future may want to update 'weather vs. load' forecasts for cities and/or feeders based on local environmental conditions. These local forecasts will have to meet the same statistical standards as existing forecasts while using local measurements that may be prone to increased variability over shorter time scales. An important step in ensuring the statistical confidence in forecasts is the 'selection' and 'combination' of measurement time series. As discussed in [17], correlation models typically use a single virtual time series of environmental data to generate forecasts. This virtual time series is generated by optimally selecting certain measurement sites and combining them to maximize forecast robustness.

For the example of a local forecast, this process would require a sufficiently large set of measurement sites so that the forecast algorithm could initialize several populations of physical measurement series with randomly assigned weights. Individual measurements drawn across populations represent a spectrum that may be scored for bias against the validation measurement. At this point, only populations with low bias are combined to produce a forecast. Subsequent iterations update the weights to improve the goodness of fit. If this approach were to be used to forecast the load changes for a single neighborhood or city, a sufficiently large set of weather stations near the validation site would be required. Ideally, the spatial distribution of these weather stations will have to be updated several times to maximize populations meeting the selection criteria. These stations would have to operate in the field long enough to compute robust forecast weights.

These constraints justify the use of an LPWAN to collect local weather measurements. A LoRaWAN system comprised of several battery-operated weather stations would enable easy reconfiguration of measurement sites within a range of several kilometers while maximizing battery life. The entire system could be rapidly deployed; not being dependent on any other networking infrastructure. The static End-Node used for this demonstration is intended to illustrate such a battery powered weather station with environmental sensors like Temperature, Humidity, Barometric Pressure, and Irradiance.

5.2   Intra-hour Forecasts of Solar Power Production

The second power systems use case is premised on recent developments in the real-time optimization of distribution grids. Real-time optimization presents several computational and implementation challenges. One of the frequently cited implementation challenges is the tight coupling between convexity of the optimization problem and the determinism in real-time updates to the system state. Traditional power systems treat variations in measurement timing as independently distributed sensor noise, but as optimization time scales are reduced and decentralized algorithms are used to solve optimization problems, temporal variations are known to induce instabilities in the solution.

A specific case where temporal determinism is required of measurements obtained over a 50 km × 50 km area is in forecasting the short time scale output of photovoltaic systems in urban environments. Consider the methodology proposed in [18] where a sensor network is proposed to monitor changes in surface irradiance over a 2500 km^2 area. The sensor grid is comprised of sensors placed approximately 3 km apart reporting irradiance measurements every 15 min. The authors also propose an approach to optimize sensor placement in order to improve the quality of the forecast. This optimized sensor placement may not coincide with existing network communication infrastructure but can be shown to minimize the root mean square error of the forecasts. The need for determinism is highlighted in the observation that velocimetry-based forecasting methods are inherently dependent on the spatio-temporal correlation of irradiance ramp-rates (caused by clouds moving relative to the sun) in a given geographical area. Most existing algorithms estimate velocity by analyzing the pairwise covariance in ramp-rates for irradiance sensors. Forecast errors are directly affected by uncertainty in the covariance computed for all possible pairwise combinations of sensors in the network.

One can see how this use case would be well served by an LPWAN. First, the operational area required is within the specification for LoRa. Second, the poll rate of 15 min for a sensor network of a few hundred sensors is within the bandwidth limits for LoRaWAN. Third, the low-power/ portable nature of sensor End-Nodes allows them to be placed conveniently and therefore more closely reflecting the ideal placement for minimum error. Lastly, the need for determinism in the data collection process is critical to accurate velocimetry. By adopting a LoRaWAN system, the end user is not subject to the varying network latencies of a cellular connection. Also, the system designers have ownership of software in the Gateway and Network Server allowing direct control over the logical scheduling used to obtain each sensor measurement. This control allows much more precise time alignment of measurements and also allows the network schedule to be updated to match the pairwise correlations being computed by the forecasting algorithm further improving the forecast accuracy.

For our demonstration, we use a battery powered mobile End-Node that transmits location periodically while affixed to a moving vehicle, as a proxy for this application. The mobile End-Node has to meet all the performance requirements described in the previous section while also reporting measurements in a deterministic fashion in order to accurately report the real-time position of the vehicle being tracked. Variations in the reporting rate are clearly illustrated as gaps in the tracks presented in the visualization.

6   Discussion

This paper presents a demonstration of Low Power Wide Area Networking for city-scale monitoring applications illustrated using a power systems use case. However, this is only one of many use case scenarios with requirements such as a broad coverage area, massive deployment of inexpensive sensors, or restricted power consumption that could take advantage of LPWAN features. LPWAN extends IoT beyond the capabilities provided by regular telecommunications technologies such as Wi-Fi, Bluetooth, V-Sat, 4G, etc. The use of LPWAN in traditional disciplines such as Agriculture [19], Wildlife protection [20, 21], and Environmental Monitoring [22]—among others—makes it possible to obtain more and better information for decision making.

Disclaimer

Certain commercial equipment, instruments, or materials are identified in this paper in order to specify the experimental procedure adequately. Such identification is not intended to imply recommendation or endorsement by the National Institute of Standards and Technology, nor is it intended to imply that the materials or equipment identified are necessarily the best available for the purpose.

Acknowledgement. Many thanks to Monsieur Erwan Rohou, for his generous willingness to provide LuxTram vehicles to make this demonstration possible. Special thanks to all the colleagues of the NIST Smart Grid Program for invaluable collaboration to make this happen. Many thanks to Dr. Raghu Kacker and Gustavo Escudero, for their infinite trust and support. Many Thanks to Héctor Laiz and Osvaldo H. Jalon, for trusting my professionalism to represent INTI with world-class excellence abroad. Infinite thanks to Maria Betania Antico, for incommensurable help, support, and patience to empower my professional career.

References

1. Farrell, S.: Low-Power Wide Area Network (LPWAN) Overview. IEEE (2018). https://buildbot.tools.ietf.org/html/rfc8376
2. Blenn, N., Kuipers, F.: LoRaWAN in the Wild: Measurements from the Things Network (2017)
3. Semtech Corporate: What is LoRa. LoRa-Alliance. https://www.semtech.com/lora/what-is-lora
4. LoRa Alliance Technical Committee Regional Parameters Workgroup: LoRaWANTM 1.1 Regional Parameters, January 2018. https://lora-alliance.org/sites/default/files/2018-04/lorawantm_regional_parameters_v1.1rb_-_final.pdf
5. Adelantado, F., et al.: Understanding the limits of LoRaWAN. IEEE Commun. Mag. **55**(9), 34–40 (2017)
6. LoRa Alliance Technical Committee: LoRaWANTM 1.1 Specification, October 2017. https://lora-alliance.org/sites/default/files/2018-04/lorawantm_specification_-v1.1.pdf
7. LoRa Alliance: About LoRa Alliance. LoRa Alliance. https://lora-alliance.org/about-lora-alliance
8. LoRa Alliance: LoRa Alliance Passes 100 LoRaWAN Network Operator Milestone with Coverage in 100 Countries. LoRa Alliance. https://lora-alliance.org/in-the-news/lora-alliance-passes-100-lorawantm-network-operator-milestone-coverage-100-countries
9. The Things Network: The Things Network Coverage Map. The Things Network. https://www.thethingsnetwork.org/map
10. Pycom.: Pycom Products documentation. Pycom. https://docs.pycom.io/products/
11. RisingHF: RisingHF RHF0M301 description. RisingHF. http://www.risinghf.com/#/product-details?product_id=6&lang=en
12. Brocaar, O.: About LoRaServer. LoRaServer. www.loraserver.io

13. myDevices: Cayenne Docs. myDevices.com. https://mydevices.com/cayenne/docs/lora/#lora-cayenne-low-power-payload
14. InfluxData Inc.: InfluxDB. Influx Data. https://www.influxdata.com
15. Grafana Labs: Grafana. Grafana. https://grafana.com
16. Guan, H., et al.: Incorporating residual temperature and specific humidity in predicting weather-dependent warm-season electricity consumption. Environ. Res. Lett. **12**(2), 024021 (2017)
17. Sobhani, M., et al.: Combining weather stations for electric load forecasting. Energies **12**(8), 1510 (2019)
18. Lonij, V.P.A., et al.: Intra-hour forecasts of solar power production using measurements from a network of irradiance sensors. Sol. Energy **97**, 58–66 (2013)
19. Talavera, J.M., et al.: Review of IoT applications in agro-industrial and environmental fields. Comput. Electron. Agric. **142**, 283–297 (2017)
20. Smart Parks: Smart Parks Work. Smart Parks. https://www.smartparks.org/work/
21. Semtech Corporate: Press Releases. Semtech (2017). https://www.semtech.com/company/press/Semtech-LoRa-Technology-Tracks-Location-of-Endangered-Black-Rhinos-in-Africa
22. Tzortzakis, K., Papafotis, K., Sotiriadis, P.P.: Wireless self powered environmental monitoring system for smart cities based on LoRa. In: 2017 Panhellenic Conference on Electronics and Telecommunications (PACET). IEEE (2017)

Floater: Post-disaster Communications via Floating Content

Flavien Bonvin[1], Gaetano Manzo[1,3], Christian Esposito[2], Torsten Braun[3], and Gianluca Rizzo[1(✉)]

[1] University of Applied Sciences and Arts Western Switzerland,
Delémont, Switzerland
gianluca.rizzo@hevs.ch
[2] University of Napoli "Federico II", Naples, Italy
[3] University of Bern, Bern, Switzerland

Abstract. In the immediate aftermath of nature-based disasters such as earthquakes, fires, or floods, have a clear vision of the situation and the population involved is of main priority for rescue operations—it is a matter of life and death. But these disaster events may cause malfunctions in communication services making the exchange information impossible—the experienced delay sending a message in an overcrowded area is a shred of evidence.

In this demo, we introduce Floater, a mobile awareness-based communication application for the immediate aftermath of a disaster, when ad hoc infrastructure support has not been deployed yet. Floater enables communications between peers in a common area without requiring the support of a cellular network. The application is developed for Android and it does not require an account or an Internet connection. Floater exploits local knowledge and constraints opportunistic replication (peer to peer) of information to build a global view of the involved area efficiently.

The app is the first to implement Floating Content, an infrastructureless communication paradigm based on opportunistic replication of a piece of content in a geographically constrained location and for a limited amount of time.

The demo illustrates the feasibility and the main functionalities of Floater and presents disaster assistance use cases for supporting rescue operations.

1 Introduction

In the immediate aftermath of nature-based disasters such as earthquakes, fires, or floods, have a clear vision of the situation and the population involved is of main priority for rescue operations [3]—it is a matter of life and death. But these disaster events may cause malfunctions in communication services making the exchange information impossible—the experienced delay sending a message in an overcrowded area is a shred of evidence.

© Springer Nature Switzerland AG 2019
M. R. Palattella et al. (Eds.): ADHOC-NOW 2019, LNCS 11803, pp. 619–626, 2019.
https://doi.org/10.1007/978-3-030-31831-4_45

In this demo, we introduce Floater, a mobile awareness-based communication application for the immediate aftermath of a disaster, when ad hoc infrastructure support has not been deployed yet. Floater enables communications between peers in a common area without requiring the support of a cellular network. The application is developed for Android and it does not require an account or an Internet connection. Communication is essential for rescue operations at the occurrence of a disaster. When a catastrophic event occurs such as a flood, an earthquake or a wildfire, the exchange of information between people enables the population involved to make decisions and potentially saving lives. But disaster events may disrupt communication networks due to power cuts to prevent further damages to the power lines, to avoid fires, and to reduce the risk of cascading effects on the power distribution network [1].

Portable radio access networks, as well as point-to-point radio communications, are a way to mitigate such problems providing communication when the cellular network is unavailable. However, their deployment naturally takes a few days lowering the likelihood of surviving in such disaster events. It is crucial to facilitate information exchange in the immediate aftermath of a disaster, empowering all people on-site and first respondents with potentially vital information.

Opportunistic communications have been proposed as a mode of communication that fits particularly well the absence of infrastructure support such as in a disaster scenario [2]. The ubiquity of smartphones makes them particularly suited for creating an ad-hoc network that allows content sharing and eventually connects to the Internet in a delay-tolerant mode [4]. Smartphones provide point-to-point communications and not necessarily require infrastructure availability in the form of WiFi Access Point or Cellular Access Networks.

Opportunistic communications connect peers in a delay-tolerant mode exchanging text, video, or real-time voice interactions. With no geographical and time constraints, such a mobile ad hoc network solution does not scale jeopardizing the opportunistic communication channels. Sharing information among groups is indeed a crucial aspect of post-disaster communications, and several existing solutions address this aspect [5,6]. However, in the majority of the proposed solutions, there is no control over the amount of information shared nor on its relevance. As a result, these approaches are unsuitable for real-disaster cases where resources (e.g., energy and bandwidth) are limited.

Floating Content (FC) is an opportunistic communications paradigm [7]. FC geographically constrains message replication implementing infrastructure-less spatial information storage within an area denoted as Anchor Zone.

In this demo, we present Floater, the prototype of a mobile application that applies the concept of Floating Content in order to implement in a distributed fashion a situation awareness service for post-disaster scenarios. Floater faces the communication difficulties of a disaster scenario enabling infrastructure-less communication between peers only equipped with smartphones. Through Floater, a tagged map of the disaster area is shared among participating peers, in order to exchange critical information. The demo shows how information is produced, categorized, and shared on the platform, and how a simple decentralized mechanism of trust allows users to evaluate the usefulness, relevance, and level of accuracy of a given piece of information.

2   Floating Content Basics

Floating Content [7] or Hovering information [8] is an infrastructure-less communication model that enables context-aware message exchange in an area denoted as Anchor Zone (AZ) and over a limited amount of time. A user interesting in sharing a piece of content, denoted as Seeder node, initializes an AZ based on the application requirement (see the blue node in Fig. 1a). Within the AZ, the opportunistic exchange takes place enabling probabilistic content storing. Every time a node with the content comes in contact with a node without it within the AZ, the content is exchanged as shown in Fig. 1b. The Floating Content paradigm assumes that the time taken to replicate the content is negligible with respect to contact time. Nodes entering the AZ do not possess a copy of the content, and those exiting the AZ discard their copy as shown in Fig. 1c. Hence, the typical behavior of a node consists in entering the AZ with no content, receiving the content from another node, distributing the content to nodes with no content met within the AZ, leaving the AZ and dropping the content. Based on the implementation, the AZ is either static or dynamically adapted to achieve the given application performance.

As a result of such opportunistic exchange, the content *floats* (i.e., it persists probabilistically in the AZ even after the seeder(s) left the AZ) if the critical conditions in [7] are satisfied. In this way, the content is made available to nodes traversing the AZ for the whole duration of its floating lifetime without infrastructure support.

3   Situation Awareness via Floater

Floater enables communications between peers in a common area without requiring the support of a cellular network. The application is developed for Android and it does not require an account or an Internet connection [9].

The Floater app enables a user to send, receive, and manage messages in the Anchor Zone—according to the Floating Content communication model. The user that sends a new message can label it as follows:

- Victims, a user requiring help such as in a car breakdown situation;
- Danger, a user spotting a particular danger such as a rough road surface;
- Resource, a user localizing a new resource such as a restaurant;
- Caretaker, a user localizing health-point such as an ambulance.

The above categories identify the main application use cases. For instance, a shop owner can advertise particular deals by floating a *Resource* message around the interested shop; a pedestrian can exchange a *Danger* message that spots a malfunction in the cross traffic light; or a skier can request help by sending a *Victim* message aftermath an avalanche.

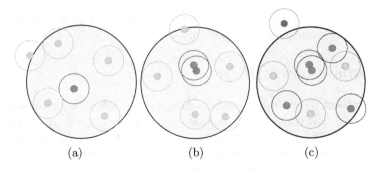

(a)   (b)   (c)

Fig. 1. Basic operation of Floating Content. (a) Seeder (blue) defines the AZ. (b) Opportunistic message exchange between nodes. (c) Nodes going out of the AZ (red) discard the content. (Color figure online)

After selecting the category as shown in Fig. 2a, the user can add title, description, and pictures to the message. Floater enables seamless nearby interactions using Bluetooth, WiFi, or ultrasound network interfaces. The transmission radius is based on the message category. User can select the receiver radius in the application setting—displayed on the app map page—discarding messages far away from the actual user position.

Every user in the AZ is allowed to validate a message (as shown in Fig. 2b), as a way to confirm the validity of the information carried by the message. In this way, the freshness and accuracy of the information spread via FC is checked. The app automatically eliminates a message once it has been confirmed as wrong multiple times or out of date.

The follow list summarizes the main actions enabled by the Floater App:

- send messages with a title, category, and position, plus possibly an image;
- receive every message in a configured zone; For instance, a driver can lunch Floater to receive traffic information in the local area avoiding congested roads.
- Ask about the validity of a message; The receiver can validate or not the message. The automatic mechanism implemented in Floater deletes rejected advertise messages avoiding spam and overhead.
- Filter the messages by categories, distance, date;
- see the messages on a map labeled with different markers;
- see deleted messages in the bin.

We implemented Floater using Google Nearby to establish direct communication channels with other devices without having to be connected to the Internet. Google Nearby increases the possibility of exchanging information between two nodes, as it is based on the use of Bluetooth, WiFi, and ultrasounds interfaces. In addition, whenever cellular communications are available, they are used. This allows to take advantage of the surviving infrastructure available in a post-disaster scenario. Of the four communication technologies, the choice of the one

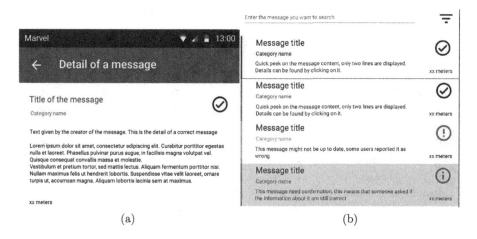

Fig. 2. Floater message category: (a) Mock-up message details. (b) Mock-up message list.

used for exchanging content between two nearby nodes is managed by the Nearby interface in a way which is transparent to the App, and based on considerations on the quality of the channel (and hence also on interference levels), and on the amount of information to be exchanged.

The choice of the communication technologies used for exchanging content between two nearby nodes is managed by the Google Nearby Interface in a way which is transparent to Floater, and based on considerations on the quality of the channel (and hence also on interference levels) and on the amount of information to be exchanged. Table 1 lists the fundamental differences between Floater (implemented with Google API) and the existing solutions on the market. We can see that Floater does not have special requirements, and supports the most message types.

Authors in [10] introduce a cooperative opportunistic alert diffusion scheme for trapped survivors during disaster scenarios to support rescue operations. But they do not implement any specific opportunistic communication model leaving open the network optimization. By implement Floating Content, Floater limits the opportunistic communication within the Anchor Zone, preventing network overhead. Drones and vehicles can support Floater increasing the number of peers within the communication area. Authors in [11,12] presents a vision for future unmanned aerial vehicles assisted disaster management that can be included in the Floating Content scheme.

Figure 3 shows Google Nearby connection procedure:

– Advertise and discovery procedures, respectively *StartAdvertising* and *StartDiscovery* methods, are called as soon as the application starts.
– *ConnectionLifecycle* method handles incoming connection.

Table 1. Floater vs. existing communication solutions

Feature		Floater	goTenna	FireChat	NearbyChat	Zello
Instant Message		✗	✓	✓	✓	✓
Require specific hardware		✗	✓	✗	✗	✗
Infrastructure-based		✗	✗	✗	✗	✓
Require the Internet		✗	✗	✗	✓	✗
Message supported	Text	✓	✓	✓	✓	✗
	Voice	✗	✗	✗	✗	✓
	Position	✓	✓	✗	✗	✗
	Images	✓	✗	✓	✓	✗
Require an account		✗	✓	✓	✓	✓
Routing type	Text	✗	✓	✓	✗	✓
	Voice	✗	✓	✓	✗	✓
	Position	✓	✓	✓	✓	✗

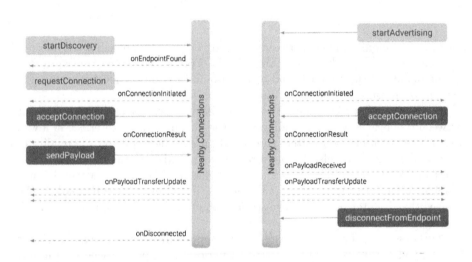

Fig. 3. Google Nearby connection procedure (Android Developers, 2017).

- As soon as an advertiser has been found, *"EndpointDiscovery"* method requires a connection by sending the name of the device and an identifier. Only applications with the same identifier can connect each other—no unwanted third-party peers.
- *Payload* method fires when a new payload is received.

4   Disaster Assistance Use Case

Let us consider an earthquake scenario. Many victims are injured, stuck under ruins, and requiring urgent support. Other such as fireman, police, and volunteer

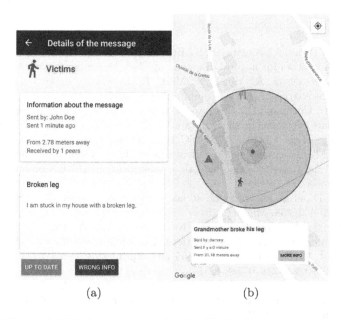

Fig. 4. (a) Mock-up message details. (b) Mock-up message list.

provide the first aid to save as many lives as possible. In such disaster event, we identify two main roles: victims, people requesting help; and, helpers, people assisting victims. We assume that victims and helpers are equipped with a smartphone and able to lunch Floater.

Victims send messages requiring support. Figure 4a shows the message reported by a person stuck in the house with a broken leg. Floater makes available the Victims messages to nearby devices—helpers—through ad hoc communication.

Helpers, in the local area, consult victims messages and take action to them (e.g., reply to the Victims messages or validate them). Helpers, validate messages ensuring the freshness of the information.

As described above, a message has a title, a description, a category, and the sender position. A message can also include images for content clarity. Floater app filters messages based on category, distance, and date. Both victims and helpers can see their position on the map, as shown in Fig. 4b, where each message has a different marker. Finally, the app automatically deletes past useless messages.

Acknowledgements. This article is based upon work from COST Action CA15127 ("Resilient communication services protecting end-user applications from disaster-based failures - RECODIS") supported by COST (European Cooperation in Science and Technology), and on RCSO MOVNET.

References

1. O'Reilly, G., Jrad, A., Nagarajan, R., Brown, T., Conrad, S.: Critical infrastructure analysis of telecom for natural disasters, pp. 1–6, December 2006
2. Martí, R., Crowcroft, A., Yoneki, J., Martí, E.: Evaluating opportunistic networks in disaster scenarios. J. Netw. Comput. Appl. (2012)
3. Cinque, M., Cotroneo, D., Esposito, C., Fiorentino, M., Russo, S.: A reliable crisis information system to share data after the event of a large-scale disaster. In: Proceedings of the CIT/IUCC/DASC/PICom Conference, pp. 941–946 (2015)
4. Schurgot, M.R., Comaniciu, C., Jaffres-Runser, K.: Beyond traditional DTN routing: social networks for opportunistic communication. IEEE Commun. Mag. **50** (2011)
5. Gutiérrez, D., et al.: A survey on ad hoc networks for disaster scenarios. In: IEEE INCoS, pp. 433–438, March 2015
6. Miaoudakis, A.I., Petroulakis, N.E., Kastanis, D., Askoxylakis, I.G.: Communications in emergency and crisis situations. In: Streitz, N., Markopoulos, P. (eds.) DAPI 2014. LNCS, vol. 8530, pp. 555–565. Springer, Cham (2014). https://doi.org/10.1007/978-3-319-07788-8_51
7. Hyytiä, E., Virtamo, J., Lassila, P., Kangasharju, J., Ott, J.: When does content float? Characterizing availability of anchored information in opportunistic content sharing. In: IEEE INFOCOM (2011)
8. Castro, A.A.V., Serugendo, G.D.M., Konstantas, D.: Hovering information-self-organizing information that finds its own storage. In: Vasilakos, A., Parashar, M., Karnouskos, S., Pedrycz, W. (eds.) Autonomic Communication, pp. 111–145. Springer, Boston (2009). https://doi.org/10.1007/978-0-387-09753-4_5
9. Bonvin, F.: Floater. https://play.google.com/store/apps/floater
10. Mezghani, F.: An android application for opportunistic alert diffusion in disaster scenario. In: IEEE PIMRC 2017 Demo Exhibits, October 2017
11. Erdelj, M., Natalizio, E., Chowdhury, K.R., Akyildiz, I.F.: Help from the sky: leveraging UAVs for disaster management. IEEE Pervasive Comput. **16**, 24–32 (2017)
12. Erdelj, M., Natalizio, E.: Drones, smartphones and sensors to face natural disasters. In: The 4th ACM Workshop (2018)

DMSS: Decision Management System for Safer Spacecrafts

Olivier Parisot[✉], Philippe Pinheiro, and Patrik Hitzelberger

Luxembourg Institute of Science and Technology (LIST),
5 avenue des Hauts-Fourneaux, 4362 Esch-sur-Alzette, Luxembourg
olivier.parisot@list.lu

Abstract. The fast growing number of low earth orbit exploitation and deep space missions results in enormous volumes of telemetry data. In order to operate efficiently satellites constellations as well as spacecrafts, DMSS offers a self-learning visual platform for anomaly detection in telemetry data coming from embedded sensors. As use-case, the data of two space missions operated by the European Space Agency were analyzed: Mars Express and GAIA.

Keywords: Spacecraft telemetry · Anomaly detection · Visualization

1   Introduction

Traditionally, mission control systems only monitor incoming telemetry measurements against pre-defined soft and hard limits. Spacecraft operator engineers (SOE) are warned in real-time and in out-of-limit logs when telemetry parameters go out of limit [12]. Then they have to check manually if it corresponds to a real anomaly.

Recently, the increase in downlink bandwidth and available processing power on space platforms has resulted in an increase in the number of telemetry measurements available to monitor the health and safety of spacecraft. With more and more on-board sensors (typically in the order of tens of thousands), it becomes impossible to check manually all potential anomalies on a daily basis. As a result, automatic checks and computer-assisted data analysis are needed to help SOE to detect anomalies in telemetry series at an early stage, improving the likelihood that measures can be taken to prolong the lifetime of the spacecraft.

The rest of this article is organized as follows. Firstly, related works about telemetry data analysis are mentioned. Then, the architecture of architecture of Decision Management System for Safer Spacecrafts (DMSS) is presented. Finally, two use-cases are shown through the developed user interface.

2   Related Works

Various approaches and tools were recently proposed to inspect spacecraft telemetry data, and especially for anomalies detection:

© Springer Nature Switzerland AG 2019
M. R. Palattella et al. (Eds.): ADHOC-NOW 2019, LNCS 11803, pp. 627–632, 2019.
https://doi.org/10.1007/978-3-030-31831-4_46

- Fine-grain visualization platform to inspect telemetry time series [11].
- Data-driven extraction of dependencies in mission parameters [10].
- System based on LSTM Neural Networks was deployed by NASA to control the Curiosity rover operated by NASA [6].
- Application of a fully automatized data processing workflow [1].
- Forecasting of telemetry parameters values [7].

Additionally, several tools have been developed by the European Space Agency to support their activity, and many of them are based on MUST, a framework to efficiently manage space missions telemetry data [9].

In this work, we propose with DMSS an interactive web application allowing SOE to investigate the results of automatic anomalies calculations and to perform data selections in order to visually detect correlations with anomalies. To avoid saturating the SOE with many false positives [6], DMSS focuses on guiding the SOE towards the *most relevant* potential anomalies of the day.

3   Approach and Software Architecture

DMSS is composed of three components (Fig. 1), each of them being developed upon the appropriated technology [3]:

- A Python batch analytical engine ingests the raw mission data coming from the spacecraft sensors and it pre-calculates daily anomaly scores for each telemetry parameter following a method developed by Katholieke Universiteit Leuven [12]. At the end, it stores the obtained results in a huge HDF5 database (HDF5 being an efficient format to manage telemetry data [5]).
- The Java-based Backend uses the previously generated HDF5 database and makes it available as *ready-to-visualize* data through a REST API by using SparkJava – a framework to build micro-services [13]. In order to optimize the data transmission, the Backend tries to minimize the bandwith usage by applying simple well-known techniques like data caching or time series reduction (Ramer-Douglas-Peucker algorithm [4]).
- The web-based rich Frontend application allows SOEs to search and analyse anomalies in spacecraft telemetry data. Based on the node.js framework for the network communication [14] and using D3.js for the visualization [2], the Frontend interacts with the Backend according to the end-user actions.

In the next sections, two use-cases are quickly described and the DMSS user interface is presented.

4   Use-Cases: Mars Express and GAIA

The telemetry data of two space missions operated by the European Space Agency were studied. The first one is Mars Express, a space scientific mission initially launched in 2003 to explore Mars. The second one is GAIA, an astrometry spacecraft operated since 2013. Its purpose is to build precise 3D space catalog.

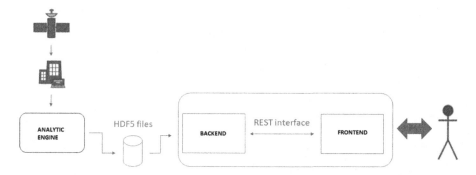

Fig. 1. The DMSS architecture: the analytical engine provides precomputed results to the Backend which pre-digests data for the interactive web-based Frontend.

In both cases, we have integrated in DMSS the telemetry parameters data of the missions for 2016 (5127 parameters i.e. 141 GB for Mars Express, 28209 parameters i.e. 1.46 TB of data for GAIA - including raw time series and statistical pre-calculations). For example, the number of points per time series is very variable, from a few samples up to 13 million samples.

5   User Interface

DMSS follows a Visual Analytics approach to help SOE to detect anomalies during mission control [8]. More precisely, DMSS provides visual representations of telemetry data and derived computational data under the form of interactive and connected diagrams (such as Poincaré plots, KDE schemas, Heatmap, and time series). The interactivity and the connectivity are both materialized by the fact that choosing data in one diagram highlights corresponding data in a related other diagram (Fig. 2). For instance, selecting data in the the Poincaré Plot automatically highlight the corresponding information in the KDE schema.

In order to facilitate the daily work of SOE, the main screen of DMSS presents an Heatmap displaying all telemetry anomaly scores for a specific day (Fig. 3). The goal is to quickly show which telemetry parameter potentially shows an uncommon behaviour.

More precisely, the Heatmap is a colored grid cell, each square represents a telemetry parameter anomaly score:

– Blue means that no anomaly score has been calculated for this date (due to missing or incomplete data).
– Grey means that the anomaly score is zero, the corresponding parameter has a standard behaviour for the selected date.

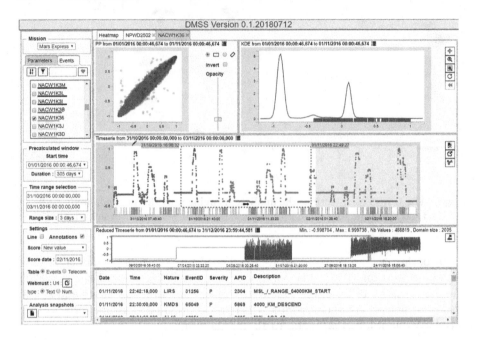

Fig. 2. The User Interface of DMSS: the user can select a time slot for a given telemetry parameter (green box) and visually see its status with the different plots. (Color figure online)

- Red means that the anomaly score is positive, this parameter has an uncommon behaviour, user should click on it to see more details and investigate more to see if it's due to an anomaly.
- Green means that the anomaly score is negative, negative scores may occur for some score type when during the one or more days the anomaly score was positive and now the scoring system detects that the parameter behaviour is coming back to normal.

With this view, end-users can see if a group of telemetry parameters has a high anomaly score and also see if one specific telemetry parameter has an high score compared to other similar telemetry parameters.

If the case seems interesting for the SOE (i.e. synonym for potential existing or upcoming problem), then the current User Interface configuration can be stored in a *Snapshot* for further investigation.

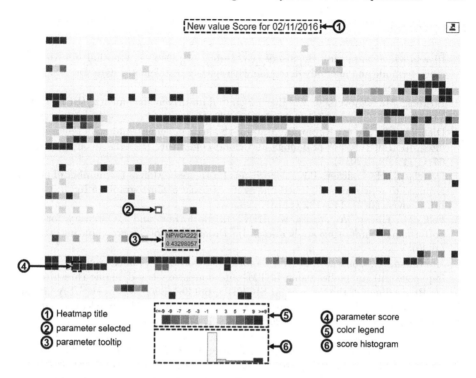

Fig. 3. The Heatmap for the Mars Express mission for 2/11/2016. This view is used to visually display all parameter anomalies in a single view for a specific day.

6   Conclusion

DMSS helps to analyse large volumes of time series data coming from spacecraft sensors - which is a typical scenario for IoT applications. In this use case, operational risks are high, and efficient support of spacecraft operator engineers is of paramount importance. These requirements in terms of efficient software architecture and semi-automatic data analytics support are high. We reckon that the approach could be applied to a large extend in other IoT scenarios.

In further works, we plan to adapt the architecture of DMSS – and especially the data analytics engine and the Backend – to apply recent data stream mining algorithms to detect anomalies.

Acknowledgments. We would like to thank the Institute of Astronomy of KU Leuven, and especially Bart Vandenbussche, Pierre Royer and Joris De Ridder for the excellent and fruitful collaboration. We also wish to thank David Evans and Jose Martinez-Heras from the European Space Agency.

References

1. Biswas, G., Khorasgani, H., Stanje, G., Dubey, A., Deb, S., Ghoshal, S.: An approach to mode and anomaly detection with spacecraft telemetry data. Int. J. Progn. Health Manag. **7** (2016)
2. Bostock, M., Ogievetsky, V., Heer, J.: D^3 data-driven documents. IEEE Trans. Vis. Comput. Graph. **17**(12), 2301–2309 (2011)
3. Díaz, M., Martín, C., Rubio, B.: State-of-the-art, challenges, and open issues in the integration of Internet of Things and cloud computing. J. Netw. Comput. Appl. **67**(C), 99–117 (2016)
4. Douglas, D.H., Peucker, T.K.: Algorithms for the reduction of the number of points required to represent a digitized line or its caricature. Cartographica Int. J. Geogr. Inf. Geovis. **10**(2), 112–122 (1973)
5. Folk, M., Cheng, A., Yates, K.: HDF5: a file format and I/O library for high performance computing applications. In: Proceedings of Supercomputing, vol. 99 (1999)
6. Hundman, K., Constantinou, V., Laporte, C., Colwell, I., Soderstrom, T.: Detecting spacecraft anomalies using LSTMs and nonparametric dynamic thresholding. In: Proceedings of the 24th ACM SIGKDD, pp. 387–395, New York, USA (2018)
7. Ibrahim, S.K., Ahmed, A., Eldin Zeidan, M.A., Ziedan, I.: Machine learning methods for spacecraft telemetry mining. IEEE Trans. Aerosp. Electr. **55**, 1816–1827 (2018)
8. Keim, D., Andrienko, G., Fekete, J.-D., Görg, C., Kohlhammer, J., Melançon, G.: Visual analytics: definition, process, and challenges. In: Kerren, A., Stasko, J.T., Fekete, J.-D., North, C. (eds.) Information Visualization. LNCS, vol. 4950, pp. 154–175. Springer, Heidelberg (2008). https://doi.org/10.1007/978-3-540-70956-5_7
9. Martińez-Heras, J., Baumgartner, A., Donati, A.: MUST: mission utility & support tools. In: DASIA 2005-Data Systems in Aerospace, vol. 602 (2005)
10. Martinez, J., Lucas, L., Donati, A.: Dependency finder: surprising relationships in telemetry. In: 2018 SpaceOps Conference, p. 2696 (2018)
11. Oliveira, H., Lais, A., Francisco, T., Donati, A.: Enabling visualization of large telemetry datasets. In: SpaceOps 2012, Stockholm, pp. 11–15 (2012)
12. Royer, P., et al.: Data mining spacecraft telemetry: towards generic solutions to automatic health monitoring and status characterisation. In: Observatory Operations: Strategies, Processes, and Systems VI (2016)
13. SparkJava: Spark: A micro framework for creating web applications in Kotlin and Java 8 with minimal effort (2019). http://sparkjava.com. Accessed 6 June 2019
14. Tilkov, S., Vinoski, S.: Node. js: using JavaScript to build high-performance network programs. IEEE Internet Comput. **14**(6), 80–83 (2010)

Sensor Network Schedule Adaptation for Varying Operating Temperature

Krzysztof Trojanowski$^{(\boxtimes)}$ ⓘ and Artur Mikitiuk ⓘ

Cardinal Stefan Wyszyński University, Warsaw, Poland
{k.trojanowski,a.mikitiuk}@uksw.edu.pl

Abstract. A problem of the sensor network lifetime maximization is typically solved for a fixed temperature, which means that the sensor battery performance is constant over the network time. However, networks usually have to operate in the varying temperature conditions, for example, outdoors, or in unheated rooms. The operating temperature variations influence network lifetime. Notably, sensors may discharge faster in temperatures below the one determined at the planning stage. Thus, the network cannot guarantee the required level of coverage over its entire lifetime. In this paper, we test network lifetime for the systems operating in conditions typical for the moderate climate zone in February and March. We also propose a method of the sensor schedule adaptation to the varying temperature conditions. The results show that appropriate rearrangement of slots in a schedule may significantly decrease the schedule corruption caused by the premature discharge of the sensors.

Keywords: Maximum lifetime coverage problem ·
Schedule optimization · Adaptation to varying temperature

1 Introduction

In the problem of sensor network schedule optimization, the aim is the maximization of the network lifetime. The network consists of a set of sensors deployed over an area to monitor N_P points of interest (POI). Each sensor has a sensing range and a limited battery capacity. In the beginning, its battery is fully loaded. Optimization methods take advantage of overlapping sensing regions and try to save energy by turning off the redundant sensors. This problem has many versions which differ in the constraints concerning sensor mobility, monitoring range, sensor battery capacity, communication between sensors, power consumption for communication, mobility of POIs, coverage rules, for example, whether a redundant coverage for each of POIs is necessary or not, and what coverage level is regarded as satisfying. In this research, we assume that both POIs and sensors are immobile, all sensors have the same sensing range r_{sens} and the same fully charged batteries at the beginning of the monitoring [4–6].

Because of the chemical reactions within the cells, battery capacity depends on various factors [1], such as the operating temperature of the device, and can

© Springer Nature Switzerland AG 2019
M. R. Palattella et al. (Eds.): ADHOC-NOW 2019, LNCS 11803, pp. 633–642, 2019.
https://doi.org/10.1007/978-3-030-31831-4_47

be hard to predict. Therefore, optimization algorithms work typically on a model where the temperature is constant and known, which allows calculating energy consumption per time unit. In [4–6] we use a discrete-time model where schedules of sensor activity consist of slots which represent the same time units. During every time slot, a sensor is either active or asleep. Every sensor consumes one unit of energy per time unit for its activity while in a sleeping state, the energy consumption is negligible.

A regular time structure in the proposed model allows incorporating temperature dependencies. In the most straightforward approach, every slot has assigned its temperature, which influences sensor energy consumption. This way varying temperature also varies lifetime of sensors, which is particularly crucial in low-temperature conditions when the battery performance drops. Unfortunately, the temperature forecast is still far from perfect, and there is no chance for precise prediction of the temperature minute by minute in the given place for several days ahead. Thus, schedule optimization of network lifetime taking into account future temperature conditions is still out of our range, and no publications related to this problem can be found. However, we can validate already found schedules for a recorded series of temperature measurements, and this way verify their suitability in real-world circumstances. Moreover, we can try to adjust the schedules to particular temperature conditions, and this way test their flexibility and robustness. These two goals are the subject of the research presented in the paper.

The paper consists of five sections. Application of the model of sensor network control is presented in Sect. 2. Section 3 discusses the process of schedule adaptation to the varying temperature conditions in the proposed model. Section 4 describes the experimental part of the research. Section 5 concludes the paper.

2   Temperature in the Model of a Sensor Network

It is well known that in cold weather, battery performance drops significantly. Different battery capacity is a severe problem, for example in regions situated in a moderate climate zone where the weather changes together with four seasons of a year. Scheduling of battery-powered outdoor devices working in such region should be adjusted to the current season and its temperature characteristic. Moreover, in addition to the annual cycle, one can also observe daily cycles of temperature. Figure 1 depicts two series of measurements performed by a dedicated measurement system every five minutes in a backyard of a house in a town near Warsaw for the weather typical for February and March. Series A in Fig. 1(a) represents colder weather and Series B in Fig. 1(b)—warmer weather. The temperature is higher in a day with a peak in the early afternoon and decreases at night. Such amplitude can be particularly important for small devices where the entire lifetime of a device with a given battery equals just a few days. Influence of low temperatures on Li-ion batteries performance was described, e.g., in [7].

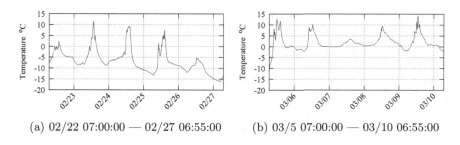

(a) 02/22 07:00:00 — 02/27 06:55:00   (b) 03/5 07:00:00 — 03/10 06:55:00

Fig. 1. Two series of outdoor temperatures measured every 5 min

2.1   A Battery Discharge Model

In Fig. 4 [7] Wang shows 0.5 C-rate discharge curves of Li-ion battery at nine different temperatures: 25, 10, 0, −5, −10, −15, −20, −25, and −30 °C. Based on these characteristics, we proposed a simplified model of battery discharge at different temperatures. In the model, for a given temperature, the battery discharges linearly from its initial voltage to a threshold value of 3 V. When the voltage is below 3 V, we assume that the battery is out of order.

In the first step, we defined the energy consumption in a unit of time by a device running in 25 °C as the nominal *amount of discharge* of size 1. This way, for a given device (e.g., sensor), we can measure the battery capacity in time units rather than in milliamps × hours. So, for different temperatures given in Fig. 4 [7] we can estimate respective battery lifetimes in operating time units. When we take the battery lifetime in 25 °C as the reference value, the number of units shrinks as the temperature falls. For example, in the case of the battery lifetime equal 10 time units, we observe 9.19 units for 10 °C, 8.57 for 0 °C, 7.76 for −10 °C, 6.95 for −20 °C, and 4.04 for −30 °C. Moreover, for each of the temperatures, a percentage amount of discharge in a unit of operating time equals one divided by the actual battery lifetime (given in time units).

Then, we assumed that there is a functional dependency between the percentage amount of discharge and the temperature. For five selected values of the battery lifetime T_{batt}: 10, 15, 20, 25, and 30, we estimated polynomials based on nine values of percentage amount of discharge calculated respectively for the temperatures given in Fig. 4 [7]. The polynomials are as follows:

10 : $0.00000018t^4 - 0.00000094t^3 - 0.00008656t^2 - 0.00094198t + 0.12244781,$

15 : $0.00000012t^4 - 0.00000062t^3 - 0.00005771t^2 - 0.00062798t + 0.08163187,$

20 : $0.00000009t^4 - 0.00000047t^3 - 0.00004328t^2 - 0.00047099t + 0.06122391,$

25 : $0.00000007t^4 - 0.00000037t^3 - 0.00003462t^2 - 0.00037679t + 0.04897912,$

30 : $0.00000006t^4 - 0.00000031t^3 - 0.00002885t^2 - 0.00031399t + 0.04081594,$

where the value in bold represents T_{batt} and t represents the operating temperature of the device.

This model does not represent real processes occurring in the battery under the influence of temperature changes. However, it allows approximating the battery discharge based on actual weather conditions. Proposed polynomials approximate respective nine points just with some precision.

The proposed model of the battery discharge process simulates dependencies between the sensor lifetime and the operating temperature. Its purpose is to provide battery behavior in our experiments aimed at the evaluation of schedule adaptability to the outdoor weather. It must be stressed that it refers neither to any particular battery nor the sensor device real discharge curves. It takes into account neither costs of a transition from low power mode to high power mode nor the side effects of drawing current at a rate higher or lower than the discharge rate.

2.2   Schedule Representation

A schedule is a matrix H of 0s and 1s. The i-th row of this matrix defines the activity of the i-th sensor over time. The j-th column of H denoted H^j defines the state of all sensors during the j-th time unit. $H^j[i] = 1$ means that the i-th sensor is active at time j while $H^j[i] = 0$ means that the i-th sensor is at time j in a sleeping state. Each of the columns (called slots) guarantees the required level of coverage, that is, for every slot all its active sensors cover the appropriate percentage of POIs. The number of slots is identical with the lifetime of the network because every slot takes precisely one unit of time. The number of 1s in a row of a schedule represents the working time of the corresponding sensor. It should not be higher than T_{batt}.

Schedules which are a subject of experiments are suboptimal. Therefore, we assume, that turning off even a single sensor in a slot can make this slot incorrect. The schedules have been generated under the assumption that the amount of sensor battery discharge in every slot is the same and equals one operating time unit, that is, the network works at a constant temperature of 25 °C all the time. All schedules come from our earlier research (for more details, the reader is referred to [3–6]).

2.3   Varying Temperature During the Schedule Execution

In the proposed model, every slot has its temperature, which is constant and can be different than in the neighboring slots. In the real world, the temperature may also differ slightly depending on the location of the sensor because, for example, objects in the monitored terrain may cast a shadow on some sensors. However, we consider a simplified model where the temperature is always precisely the same for all sensors.

Figure 2 shows an example schedule for the network consisting of 5 sensors. The network lifetime equals 6. Two versions of the same schedule for two different operating temperatures contain the battery discharge values in the table cells. Zero means that the sensor is in the sleeping state, and non-zero—in an active state. All sensors are the same and have the same batteries. In the case of $t = 25\,°C$, the battery discharge during a time unit equals 1. In the case of

$t = -20\,^\circ$C the battery discharge is higher and equals 1.43 (as for $T_{batt} = 10$). The last column contains sums of values in every row.

1	2	3	4	5	6	sum	1	2	3	4	5	6	sum
1.0	1.0	1.0	1.0	0	0	4.0	1.43	1.43	1.43	1.43	0	0	5.72
1.0	0	1.0	0	1.0	0	3.0	1.43	0	1.43	0	1.43	0	4.29
0	0	1.0	1.0	1.0	1.0	4.0	0	0	1.43	1.43	1.43	1.43	5.72
1.0	1.0	0	0	1.0	1.0	4.0	1.43	1.43	0	0	1.43	1.43	5.72
0	1.0	0	1.0	0	1.0	3.0	0	1.43	0	1.43	0	1.43	4.29

     (a) operating temperature: 25°C   (b) operating temperature: −20°C

Fig. 2. Example schedule for 5 sensors; the network lifetime equals 6. The table contains battery discharge values of sensors for $t = 25\,^\circ$C (left), and for $t = -20\,^\circ$C (right)

In the case of a low temperature, execution of a schedule discharges sensor batteries more, than in the case of a high temperature. Particularly, if we assumed, that $T_{batt} = 5$, the schedule in Fig. 2(b) could not be executed for $-20\,^\circ$C, because sensors no. 1, 3, and 4 discharge their batteries above the level of $T_{batt} = 5$. In this case, slots no. 4 and 6 are incorrect, because of the lack of energy for full working time of three sensors: sensor no. 1 in slot no. 4, and sensors no. 3 and 4 in slot no. 6. Such schedule can be denoted as $[C_1, C_2, C_3, I_4, C_5, I_6]$ (where C means a correct slot and I—an incorrect one) and its lifetime deteriorates to 3 because the third slot is the last one in the uninterrupted sequence of correct slots. Typically, in the case of the schedule application in a low temperature, slots located on the left end of the schedule are still fine, but in the slots located on the right end, some sensors have to be off. We assumed the worst-case scenario, where none of the active sensors in a slot can be off. Otherwise, the slot becomes incorrect and has to be removed from the schedule. If this is the case, there appears extra energy in all the remaining active sensors which can be used by them in the slots standing in the schedule after the removed one. For example, when we remove slot no. 4, sensors no. 3 and 5 decrease their battery discharge.

Finally, we also assumed that we could not try to fix the coverage by changing the set of active sensors within a slot because we know neither the sensor nor POIs localization. The only option is to remove incorrect slots.

3   Method of the Schedule Adjustment

In our experiments, every schedule was adjusted to the given series of temperature measurements to assure the most extended lifetime of the network. This process consists of two phases: shifting and searching. Before the process starts, we identify *correct* and *incorrect* slots in a schedule. The slot is correct when the battery load is sufficient to guarantee work of all activated sensors throughout this slot. Otherwise, the slot is called incorrect. The correctness of slots depends on their position in a schedule, precisely, on the discharge level of sensor batteries caused by their activity in previous slots.

3.1 Shifting

The shifting phase consists of a loop where two steps are executed: slots shifting and slots revalidation. Typically, the beginning slots in a schedule are correct. They create a long sequence until the first incorrect slot. The length of this sequence also represents the lifetime of the schedule for the operating temperature. However, almost always some correct slots can be found after the first incorrect slot. In the step of slots shifting, we defragment the sequence of correct slots in the schedule. We can shift them to the left, and this way try to decrease the deterioration of the schedule lifetime. For example, for a schedule of size 14: $[C_1, C_2, C_3, C_4, C_5, I_6, I_7, C_8, I_9, C_{10}, I_{11}, I_{12}, I_{13}, I_{14}]$ (C—a correct slot; I—an incorrect one) the execution of slots shifting changes the order of slots as follows: $[C_1, C_2, C_3, C_4, C_5, C_8, C_{10}, I_6, I_7, I_9, I_{11}, I_{12}, I_{13}, I_{14}]$. The rearrangement is stable, that is the order of shifted correct slots is the same in the sorted schedule as it was in the original schedule. The relative order of incorrect slots is preserved as well.

After a single step of slots shifting the order of slots changes, so moved slots work in other temperature conditions and sensor energy consumption over time may be different than before. Therefore, all slots starting from the first shifted correct slot have to be revalidated, that is, we check again if the battery load is sufficient to guarantee work of all activated sensors in these slots. Slots revalidation is executed synchronously, that is, it starts when the single step of slots shifting is over. A correct slot can become incorrect in the new position when its new working temperature is lower than before shift. In the worst case, such incorrect slot may be the first of incorrect slots in the schedule. In the example above, this could be the case of the slot C_8. It took the position of the slot I_6 but became incorrect due to a low temperature at this time. Even so, this move has not deteriorated the schedule because its lifetime remains on the same level as before. The next execution of the slots shifting shall bring hopefully better rearrangement.

The steps of slots shifting and slots revalidation have to be repeated in the loop as long as changes in the order of the slots occur. Eventually, we obtain a defragmented sequence of correct slots S_C occupying the beginning of the schedule and a sequence of incorrect slots S_I on the right of them.

3.2 Searching/Freezing

When the shifting is over, we can start searching for a broader defragmented sequence of correct slots in a schedule. We decided to work just with the set of incorrect slots S_I. The sequence of correct slots S_C in the beginning part of a schedule does not require modification. S_C defines how the sensor batteries are discharged, so we use it only to calculate the level of remaining energy in the batteries of sensors after the execution of the last correct slot. After calculating the battery charge, we are not interested in S_C any longer.

Then we try to utilize slots in S_I because some of them can become correct when they change their positions. We build a sequence of correct slots selected from S_I. Then, we attach this sequence at the end of S_C, and this way extend the overall sequence of correct slots in a schedule.

For better efficiency, we decided to introduce a mechanism protecting correct slots already found in S_I. Once the first such slot is found, it is located in the leftmost position and *frozen*. Slot freezing means that the search method ceases moving it anywhere else in the newly build sequence until the end of the search process. Every next found correct slot becomes the right neighbor of the last frozen one and also becomes frozen instantly. This way frozen slots make up a new defragmented sequence which eventually can be attached directly at the right end of S_C.

3.3 The Random Search Procedure

For the maximization of a defragmented sequence of correct slots in a schedule, we apply a random search approach extended by the slot freezing procedure. The input data consist of four elements: a schedule, a series of temperature measurements, max battery capacity, and the polynomial defining battery discharge characteristic.

First, we apply shifting and then calculate the sensor battery discharge level from zeros and ones written in correct slots located in S_C. Then we take slots from S_I and try to rearrange them to get the most extended sequence of correct slots in its beginning part. The method shuffles these slots randomly and checks if the first slot on the left (just a single one or a sequence) is correct. If so, the slot is frozen. Then the step is repeated, that is, remaining unfrozen slots are reshuffled, and so on. Due to freezing, the number of slots in subsequent shuffles decreases. After the shuffle, there is no shifting, that is, the correct slots located alone at the right end are not shifted to the left. The shuffle can be repeated as many times as there exists a chance that correct slots can be found in S_I.

4 Experiments

4.1 Benchmark and Plan of Experiments

We used the two series of temperature measurements presented in Fig. 1. The measuring system made measurements every 5 min. For simplicity, we assumed that 5 min represents one unit of time, so the series represent temperature values in subsequent time units.

The maximum battery capacity represents the number of time units when the device can be in an active state running in 25 °C. Due to the fact, that the sensor lifetime depends on both the battery capacity and the device energy consumption, we can assume without loss of generality that the tested sensor battery capacities T_{batt} can be precisely the same as the ones used in earlier experiments: 10, 15, 20, 25, and 30 units [3–6], that is, 50, 75, 100, 125, and 150 min of the sensor activity, respectively.

The adoption of T_{batt} from previous experiments allows us to use schedules obtained in these experiments. Schedules have been generated for SCP1, which consists of 320 instances of problems (eight test cases, 40 instances each). In all test cases of SCP1, there are 2000 sensors with sensing range r_{sens} 1 unit. We require the coverage level $cov = 80\%$ with tolerance $\delta = 5\%$. The remaining parameters vary between test cases. There are two types of distribution of POIs – in nodes of a triangular grid or a rectangular grid. Coordinates of sensor localization can be obtained using either a random generator or a Halton generator [2]. The area under consideration is a square. Its side size can be 13, 16, 19, 22, 25, or 28 units. The number of POIs is the same for different area sizes. Thus, the distances between the POIs grow as the square side grows. We want to avoid full regularity in the POIs distribution. Therefore, 20% of nodes in the grid has no POIs. These nodes are selected randomly for every instance of the test case. The number of POIs in subsequent test cases varies from 199 to 240 for the triangular grid and from 166 to 221 for the rectangular grid. Sensors can control more than one POI, however, the number of such sensors decreases as the square side stretches. In the test case no. 8, almost 75% of sensors cover only one POI. The experiments were conducted for five values of sensor battery capacity T_{batt}, which eventually gave 1600 schedules in total.

The battery discharge characteristics have been generated as described in Subsect. 2.1.

The experiments consist of two groups, for the temperature measurement series A and B, respectively. In every group, the random search procedure searched for the most extended sequence of correct slots in each of 1600 schedules obtained from experiments with SCP1. In each of the groups, we get five mean lengths of final sequences because we defined five values of T_{batt}.

4.2   The Results

Figure 3 shows the results of experiments. For each of the five values of T_{batt}, we present three mean lengths: (1) of the input schedules, (2) of the intermediate schedules being an outcome of the shifting phase and (3) output schedules obtained from the searching procedure. In our tests, the searching procedure repeats the shuffle step 100 times. This number was set experimentally, that is, further increasing of the number of executions did not give further improvement.

Graphs in Fig. 3 show that for the colder weather, both intermediate and final schedules are shorter than for the warmer one. They also show that mean relative improvement of the intermediate sequences after application of random search with freezing is the largest for low battery capacity (T_{batt}) and decreases as the capacity grows. For Series A of temperature measurements, mean length of intermediate schedules represents 72.03% of mean length of output schedules for $T_{batt} = 10$, 78.55% for $T_{batt} = 15$, 81.95% for $T_{batt} = 20$, 83.35% for $T_{batt} = 25$, and 84.44% for $T_{batt} = 30$. For Series B of temperature measurements: 74.92% for

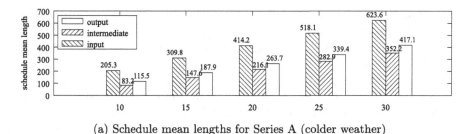

(a) Schedule mean lengths for Series A (colder weather)

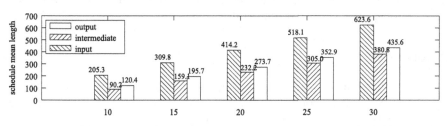

(b) Schedule mean lengths for Series B (warmer weather)

Fig. 3. Mean numbers of slots in the input schedules, intermediate schedules after shifting, and output schedules for $T_{batt} \in \{10, 15, 20, 25, 30\}$

$T_{batt} = 10$, 81.30% for $T_{batt} = 15$, 84.84% for $T_{batt} = 20$, 86.43% for $T_{batt} = 25$, and 87.42% for $T_{batt} = 30$.

5 Conclusions

Wireless sensor networks consist of many low-cost and low-powered sensor devices which can be sensitive to weather conditions they have to work in. Particularly, optimization of the network lifetime should take into consideration the influence of temperature on the effective battery capacity. Sensor schedules consist of a sequence of sessions called slots, where different network configurations are active to monitor a set of points of interest. The configurations define sets of active sensors guaranteeing monitoring level above the minimal quality. Thus, the lack of energy in any of the active sensors dumps the monitoring level, and the configuration becomes unacceptable. The interval of the proper network functionality ends with the first of such unacceptable sessions.

In our research, we verified the robustness of schedules generated for ideal weather conditions. We evaluated the network lifetime for varying temperature conditions typical for the moderate climate zone in February and March. The results show that the lifetime drops drastically, and some changes in the sensor activity schedule are necessary.

We also applied a two-stage procedure for schedule adaptation. In the first stage, we shift incorrect slots to the end to get the most extended sequence of correct slots at the beginning of a schedule. In the second stage, we search for the best arrangements of incorrect slots, which can turn some of them into correct ones. In this stage, a crucial role takes the slot freezing strategy, which guarantees that once found correct slots are never lost.

In future work, some new strategies concerning modifications in sensor control within slots should be considered, like for example swap of selected control activities in pairs of slots. Another direction concerns the prediction of the weather conditions. In the presented research, we study schedule adaptation when the operating temperature is already known. It would be interesting to identify regularities in temperature cycles and adjust sensor controls in slots taking into account predicted temperature changes.

References

1. Dargie, W., Poellabauer, C.: Fundamentals of Wireless Sensor Networks: Theory and Practice. Wiley Series on Wireless Communications and Mobile Computing. Wiley, Hoboken (2010). https://doi.org/10.1002/9780470666388
2. Halton, J.H.: Algorithm 247: radical-inverse quasi-random point sequence. Commun. ACM **7**(12), 701–702 (1964). https://doi.org/10.1145/355588.365104
3. Trojanowski, K., Mikitiuk, A.: Local search approaches with different problem-specific steps for sensor network coverage optimization. In: Le Thi, H.A., Le, H.M., Pham Dinh, T. (eds.) WCGO 2019. AISC, vol. 991, pp. 407–416. Springer, Cham (2020). https://doi.org/10.1007/978-3-030-21803-4_41
4. Trojanowski, K., Mikitiuk, A., Guinand, F., Wypych, M.: Heuristic optimization of a sensor network lifetime under coverage constraint. In: Nguyen, N.T., Papadopoulos, G.A., Jędrzejowicz, P., Trawiński, B., Vossen, G. (eds.) ICCCI 2017. LNCS, vol. 10448, pp. 422–432. Springer, Cham (2017). https://doi.org/10.1007/978-3-319-67074-4_41
5. Trojanowski, K., Mikitiuk, A., Kowalczyk, M.: Sensor network coverage problem: a hypergraph model approach. In: Nguyen, N.T., Papadopoulos, G.A., Jędrzejowicz, P., Trawiński, B., Vossen, G. (eds.) ICCCI 2017. LNCS, vol. 10448, pp. 411–421. Springer, Cham (2017). https://doi.org/10.1007/978-3-319-67074-4_40
6. Trojanowski, K., Mikitiuk, A., Napiorkowski, K.J.M.: Application of local search with perturbation inspired by cellular automata for heuristic optimization of sensor network coverage problem. In: Wyrzykowski, R., Dongarra, J., Deelman, E., Karczewski, K. (eds.) PPAM 2017. LNCS, vol. 10778, pp. 425–435. Springer, Cham (2018). https://doi.org/10.1007/978-3-319-78054-2_40
7. Wang, K.: Study on low temperature performance of Li ion battery. Open Access Libr. J. **4**(11) (2017). https://doi.org/10.4236/oalib.1104036

Retraction Note to: Mobility Aided Context-Aware Forwarding Approach for Destination-Less OppNets

Vishnupriya Kuppusamy⬤, Asanga Udugama⬤,
and Anna Förster⬤

Retraction Note to:
Chapter "Mobility Aided Context-Aware Forwarding Approach for Destination-Less OppNets"
in: M. R. Palattella et al. (Eds.): *Ad-Hoc, Mobile, and Wireless Networks*, LNCS 11803,
https://doi.org/10.1007/978-3-030-31831-4_11

The authors have retracted this conference paper [1]. After publication, the authors discovered a coding error in their simulations of RRS, impacting the results and conclusions of the article. A summary of the re-analyses of the data can be found below. All authors agree with this retraction.

In our paper, we present a new data dissemination approach for opportunistic networks, based on the general idea of combining two existing protocols, which are used in different scenarios. For our study we have taken two existing and well-known protocols: Epidemic and RRS (Randomized Rumor Spreading). Previous evaluations in simulation of these two protocols have shown that they perform very differently in different scenarios: while Epidemic has a very good delivery rate and delivery delay, its overhead is very high. For RRS, it seemed the opposite to be true: very low overhead with not very good delivery rate and delay. These preliminary results laid the basis for our work - we wanted to combine both to combine also their advantages. The results we obtained are described in the paper.

Unfortunately, when continuing our work after the publication of our paper, we discovered a minor error in our simulations of RRS - the statistics of the overhead of RRS was not computed correctly and represented only a fraction of the true one. After re-running all simulations, we realized the assumptions, which laid our research basis, are wrong. RRS had even higher network overhead than Epidemic. The difference between the new and old data is shown below in Fig. 1.

The retracted version of this chapter can be found at
https://doi.org/10.1007/978-3-030-31831-4_11

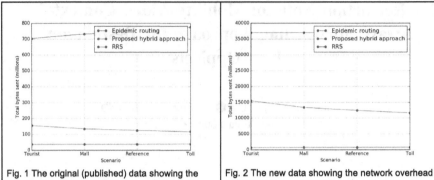

Fig. 1 The original (published) data showing the network overhead for RRS to be much lower than for Epidemic.

Fig. 2 The new data showing the network overhead for RRS to be much HIGHER than for Epidemic.

The described mistake had unfortunately an impact only on the network overhead, thus leaving the results for delivery delay and rate the same. Thus, our hybrid protocol does not perform any better than any of the two original protocols.

However, we would like to stress at this point, that we still believe our general approach of combining two protocols with different performance is a valuable direction. However, we would need to select two other protocols for this, since RRS and Epidemic are not a good match.

We apologize once again to you and to the scientific community for this mistake.

[1] Kuppusamy, V., Udugama, A., Förster, A.: Mobility aided context-aware forwarding approach for destination-less oppNets. In: Palattella, M.R., Scanzio, S., Coleri Ergen, S. (eds.) ADHOC-NOW 2019. LNCS, vol. 11803, pp. 153–166. Springer, Cham (2019). https://doi.org/10.1007/978-3-030-31831-4_11

Author Index

Printed in the United States
By Bookmasters